8TH EDITION

Invitation to Computer Science

G. Michael Schneider
Macalester College

Judith L. Gersting
Indiana University-Purdue University
at Indianapolis

CENGAGE

Australia • Brazil • Mexico • Singapore • United Kingdom • United States

CENGAGE

Invitation to Computer Science, 8th Edition

G. Michael Schneider & Judith L. Gersting

SVP, GM Skills & Global Product Management: Jonathan Lau

Product Director: Lauren Murphy

Product Team Manager: Kristin McNary

Product Manager: Kate Mason

Executive Director, Development: Marah Bellegarde

Senior Content Development Manager: Leigh Hefferon

Developmental Editor: Deb Kaufmann

Senior Content Developer, Media: Michelle Ruelos Cannistraci

Project Manager: Ann Loch

Product Assistant: Jake Toth

Vice President, Marketing Services: Jennifer Ann Baker

Marketing Manager: Stephanie Albracht

Senior Content Project Manager: Jennifer Feltri-George

Content Digitization Project Manager: Laura Ruschman

Senior Digital Project Manager: Noah Vincelette

Senior Art Director: Diana Graham

Cover Designer: Angela Sheehan

Cover image(s): sumkinn/Shutterstock.com; sumkinn/Shutterstock.com; Studiojumpee/Shutterstock.com

Production Service/Composition: SPi Global

For product information and technology assistance, contact us at **Cengage Customer & Sales Support, 1-800-354-9706**

For permission to use material from this text or product, submit all requests online at **www.cengage.com/permissions**. Further permissions questions can be e-mailed to **permissionrequest@cengage.com**

Library of Congress Control Number: 2017955994

Student Edition ISBN: 978-1-3375-6191-4
Loose Leaf ISBN: 978-1-337-68593-1

Cengage
20 Channel Center Street
Boston, MA 02210
USA

Cengage is a leading provider of customized learning solutions with employees residing in nearly 40 different countries and sales in more than 125 countries around the world. Find your local representative at **www.cengage.com.**

Cengage products are represented in Canada by Nelson Education, Ltd.

To learn more about Cengage platforms and services, register or access your online learning solution, or purchase materials for your course, visit **www.cengage.com.**

Notice to the Reader

Publisher does not warrant or guarantee any of the products described herein or perform any independent analysis in connection with any of the product information contained herein. Publisher does not assume, and expressly disclaims, any obligation to obtain and include information other than that provided to it by the manufacturer. The reader is expressly warned to consider and adopt all safety precautions that might be indicated by the activities described herein and to avoid all potential hazards. By following the instructions contained herein, the reader willingly assumes all risks in connection with such instructions. The publisher makes no representations or warranties of any kind, including but not limited to, the warranties of fitness for particular purpose or merchantability, nor are any such representations implied with respect to the material set forth herein, and the publisher takes no responsibility with respect to such material. The publisher shall not be liable for any special, consequential, or exemplary damages resulting, in whole or part, from the readers' use of, or reliance upon, this material.

Printed in Mexico
Print Number: 05   Print Year: 2018

To my wife, Ruthann, our children, Benjamin, Rebecca, and Trevor, grandson, Liam, and granddaughter, Sena.

G. M. S.

To my husband, John, and to: Adam and Francine; Jason, Cathryn, Sammie, and Johnny.

J. L. G.

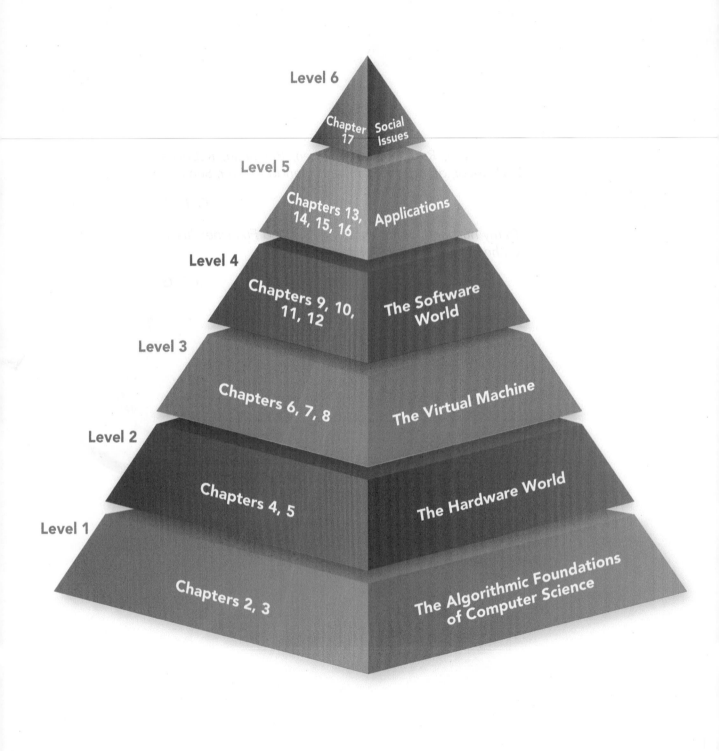

Level 6 — Chapter 17 — Social Issues

Level 5 — Chapters 13, 14, 15, 16 — Applications

Level 4 — Chapters 9, 10, 11, 12 — The Software World

Level 3 — Chapters 6, 7, 8 — The Virtual Machine

Level 2 — Chapters 4, 5 — The Hardware World

Level 1 — Chapters 2, 3 — The Algorithmic Foundations of Computer Science

Brief Contents

Online Chapters

This text includes five language-specific online-only downloadable chapters on Ada, C++, C#, Java, and Python, available on the companion site for this text (*www.cengage.com*) and in MindTap.

Contents

LEVEL 3   The Virtual Machine   278

Chapter 6   An Introduction to System Software and Virtual Machines   280

LEVEL 4   The Software World   432

Online Chapters

This text includes five language-specific online-only downloadable chapters on Ada, C++, C#, Java, and Python, available on the companion site for this text (*www.cengage.com*) and in MindTap.

LEVEL 6   Social Issues in Computing   790

Preface to the Eighth Edition

Overview

This text is intended for a one-semester introductory course in computer science. It presents a broad-based overview of the discipline that assumes no prior background in computer science, programming, or mathematics. It would be appropriate for a college or university service course for students not majoring in computer science, as well as for schools that implement their first course for majors using a breadth-first approach that surveys the fundamental aspects of computer science. It would be highly suitable for a high school computer science course, especially the AP Computer Science Principles course created by the College Board in cooperation with the National Science Foundation and colleges and universities around the United States.

The Non-Majors Service Course

The introductory computer science service course (often called CS 0) has undergone numerous changes. In the 1970s and early 1980s, it was usually a class in FORTRAN, BASIC, or Pascal programming. In the mid-to-late 1980s, a rapid increase in computer use caused the service course to evolve into something called "computer literacy," in which students learned about new applications of computing in fields such as business, medicine, law, and education. With the growth of personal computers and productivity software, a typical early to mid-1990s version of this course would teach students how to use word processors, databases, spreadsheets, and email. The most recent change was its evolution into a web-centric course in which students learned to design and implement webpages using HTML, XML, ASP, and Java applets.

In many institutions, the computer science service course is evolving once again. There are two reasons for this change. First, virtually all college and high school students are familiar with personal computers and productivity software. They have been using word processors and search engines since elementary school and are familiar with social media, online retailing, and email; many have designed webpages and even manage their own websites and blogs. In today's world, a course that focuses on computing applications would be of little or no interest.

But a more important reason for rethinking the structure of the CS 0 service course, and the primary reason why we authored this book, is the following observation:

> *Most computer science service courses do not teach students the foundations and fundamental concepts of computer science!*

We believe that students in a computer science service course should receive a solid grounding in the fundamental concepts of the discipline, just as introductory courses in biology, physics, and geology present the central concepts of their fields. Topics in a breadth-first computer science service course would not be limited to "fun" applications such as webpage creation, blogging, game design, and interactive graphics, but would also cover foundational issues such as algorithms, abstraction, hardware, computer organization, system software, language models, and the social and ethical issues of computing. An introduction to these core ideas exposes students to the overall richness and beauty of the field and allows them not only to use computers and software effectively, but also to understand and appreciate the basic ideas underlying the discipline of computer science and the creation of computational artifacts. As a side benefit, students who complete such a course will have a much better idea of what a major or a minor in computer science will entail.

This last point was the primary reason for the development of the AP Computer Science Principles high school course, which is quite similar to the breadth-first overview model just described. By learning about the field in its entirety, rather than seeing only the small slice of it called "programming," high school students will be in a better position to decide if computer science is a subject they wish to study when they begin college.

The First Course for Majors

Since the emergence of computer science as an academic discipline in the 1960s, the first course in the major (often called CS 1) has usually been an introduction to programming—from Fortran to BASIC to Pascal, and, later, C++, Java, and Python. But today there are numerous alternatives, including a breadth-first overview. A first course for computer science majors using the breadth-first model emphasizes early exposure to the field's sub-disciplines rather than placing exclusive emphasis on programming. This gives new majors a complete and well-rounded understanding of the field, including the concepts and ways of thinking that are part of computer science.

Our book—intended for either majors or non-majors—is organized around this breadth-first approach as it presents a wide range of subject matter drawn from diverse areas of computer science. However, to avoid drowning students in a sea of seemingly unrelated facts and details, a breadth-first presentation must be carefully woven into a coherent fabric, a theme, a "big picture" that ties together the individual topics and presents computer science as a unified and integrated discipline. To achieve this, our text divides the study of computer science into a hierarchy of six subareas, called layers, with each layer building upon concepts presented in earlier chapters.

A Hierarchy of Abstractions

The central theme of this book is that *computer science is the study of algorithms.* Our hierarchy utilizes this definition by initially looking at the algorithmic foundations of computer science and then moving upward from this central theme to higher-level issues such as hardware, systems, software, applications, and ethics.

The six levels in our computer science hierarchy are:

Level 1.   The Algorithmic Foundations of Computer Science
Level 2.   The Hardware World
Level 3.   The Virtual Machine
Level 4.   The Software World
Level 5.   Applications
Level 6.   Social Issues in Computing

Level 1

Following an introductory chapter, Level 1 (Chapters 2–3) introduces "The Algorithmic Foundations of Computer Science," the bedrock on which all other aspects of the discipline are built. It presents fundamental ideas such as the design of algorithms, algorithmic problem solving, abstraction, pseudocode, and iteration and illustrates these ideas using well-known examples. It also introduces the concepts of algorithm efficiency and asymptotic growth and demonstrates that not all algorithms are, at least in terms of running time, created equal.

The discussions in Level 1 assume that our algorithms are executed by something called a "computing agent," an abstract concept for any entity that can carry out the instructions in our solution.

Level 2

However, in Level 2 (Chapters 4–5), "The Hardware World," we want our algorithms to be executed by "real" computers to produce "real" results. Thus begins our discussion of hardware, logic design, and computer organization. The initial discussion introduces the basic building blocks of computer systems—binary numbers, Boolean logic, gates, and circuits. It then shows how these elementary concepts can be combined to construct a real computer using the Von Neumann architecture, composed of processors, memory, and input/output. This level presents a simple machine language instruction set and explains how the algorithmic primitives of Level 1, such as assignment and conditional, can be implemented in machine language and run on the Von Neumann hardware of Level 2, conceptually tying together these two areas. It ends with a discussion of important new directions in hardware design—multicore processors and massively parallel machines.

By the end of Level 2, students have been introduced to basic concepts in logic design and computer organization, and they can appreciate the complexity inherent in these ideas.

Level 3

This complexity is the motivation for the material contained in Level 3 (Chapters 6–8), "The Virtual Machine." This section describes how system software is used to create a user-friendly, user-oriented problem-solving environment that hides many of the ugly hardware details just described. Level 3 looks at the same problems discussed in Level 2, encoding and executing algorithms, but shows how this can be done easily in a virtual environment containing helpful tools like a graphical user interface, editors, language translators, file systems, and debuggers. This section discusses the services and responsibilities of the operating system and how it has evolved. It investigates one of the most important virtual environments in current use, computer networks, and shows how technologies such as Ethernet, the Internet, and the web link together independent systems via transmission media and communications software. This creates a virtual environment in which we seamlessly and transparently use not only the computer on our desk or in our hand, but also computing devices located around the world. This transparency has progressed to the point where we can now use systems located "in the cloud" without regard for where they are, how they provide their services, and even whether they exist as real physical entities. Level 3 concludes with a look at one of the most important services provided by a virtual machine, namely information security, and describes algorithms for protecting the user and the system from accidental or malicious damage.

Level 4

Once we have created this powerful user-oriented virtual environment, what do we want to do with it? Most likely we want to write programs to solve interesting problems. This is the motivation for Level 4 (Chapters 9–12), "The Software World." Although this book should not be viewed as a programming text, it contains an overview of the features found in modern procedural programming languages. This gives students an appreciation for the interesting and challenging task of the computer programmer and the power of the problem-solving environment created by a modern high-level language. (More detailed introductions to five important high-level programming languages are available via online, downloadable chapters accessible through

MindTap, as well as at *www.cengage.com*.) There are many different language models, so Level 4 also includes a discussion of other language types, including special-purpose languages such as SQL, HTML, JavaScript, and R, as well as the functional, logic, and parallel language paradigms. An introduction to the design and construction of a compiler shows how high-level languages can be translated into machine language for execution. This latter discussion ties together numerous ideas from earlier chapters, as we show how an algorithm (Level 1), expressed in a high-level language (Level 4), can be compiled and executed on a typical Von Neumann machine (Level 2) using system software tools (Level 3). These "recurring themes" and frequent references to earlier concepts help reinforce the idea of computer science as an integrated set of topics. At the conclusion of Level 4, we introduce the idea of computability and insolvability to show students that there are provable limits to what programs, computers, and computer science can achieve.

Level 5

We now have a high-level programming environment in which it is possible to write programs to solve important problems. In Level 5 (Chapters 13–16), "Applications," we take a look at some important uses of computers. There is no way to cover more than a fraction of the many applications of computers and information technology in a single section. We have included applications drawn from the sciences and engineering (simulation and modeling), business and finance (ecommerce, databases, data science), the social sciences (artificial intelligence), and everyday life (computer-generated imagery, video gaming, virtual communities). Our goal is to show students that these applications are not "magic boxes" whose inner workings are totally unfathomable. Rather, they are the direct result of building upon the core concepts of computer science presented in the previous chapters.

Level 6

Finally, we reach the highest level of study, Level 6 (Chapter 17), "Social Issues in Computing," which addresses the social, ethical, moral, and legal issues raised by pervasive computer technology. This section, based on contributions by Professor Bo Brinkman of Miami University, examines issues such as the theft of intellectual property, national security concerns, the erosion of personal privacy, and the political impact of the proliferation of fake news distributed using social media. This chapter does not attempt to provide easy solutions to these many-faceted problems. Instead, it focuses on techniques that students can use to think about ethical issues and reach their own conclusions. Our goal in this final section is to make students aware of the enormous impact that information technology is having on our society and to give them tools for making informed decisions.

This, then, is the hierarchical structure of our text. It begins with the algorithmic foundations of the discipline and works its way from lower-level hardware concepts through virtual machine environments, high-level languages, software, and applications, to the social issues raised by computer technology. This organizational structure, along with the use of recurring themes, enables students to view computer science as a unified and coherent field of study. The material in Chapters 1–12 is intended to be covered sequentially, but the applications discussed in Chapters 13–16 can be covered in any order and the social issues in Chapter 17 can be presented at any time.

What's New in This Edition

This eighth edition of *Invitation to Computer Science* addresses a number of emerging issues in computer science. We have added new material on ransomware, code repositories, electronic payment systems, new programming languages such as R and Milk, data science, artificial intelligence, and drones. There is an entirely new section on fake news, politics, and social media.

New and updated Special Interest Boxes highlight interesting historical vignettes, new developments in computing, biographies of important people in the field, and news items showing how computing affects our everyday lives.

An Interactive Experience— MindTap

This edition offers significantly enhanced supplementary material and additional resources available online through MindTap. MindTap, an online teaching and learning solution, helps students be more successful and confident in the course and in their real life. MindTap guides students through the course by combining the complete textbook with interactive multimedia activities, assessments, and learning tools. Readings and activities engage students in learning core concepts, practicing needed skills, and applying what they learn. Instructors can rearrange and add content to personalize their MindTap course, and easily track students' progress with real-time analytics. MindTap integrates seamlessly with any learning management system.

An Experimental Science— Laboratory Software and Manual

Another important aspect of computer science education is the realization that, like such scientific fields as physics, chemistry, and biology, computer science is an empirical, laboratory-based discipline in which learning comes not only from watching and listening but also from doing and trying. Many ideas in computer science cannot be fully understood and appreciated until they are visualized, manipulated, and tested. Today, most computer science faculty see structured laboratories as an essential part of an introductory course, and this view is fully reflected in our approach to the material.

Associated with this text is a laboratory manual and custom-designed laboratory software that enables students to experiment with the concepts we present. The manual contains 20 laboratory experiences, closely coordinated with the main text, that cover all levels except Level 6. These labs give students the chance to observe, study, analyze, and modify an important concept. For example, associated with Level 1 (the algorithmic foundations of computer science) are experiments that animate the algorithms in Chapters 2 and 3 and ask students to observe and discuss what is happening in these animations. There are also labs that allow students to measure the running time of these algorithms for different-sized data sets and discuss their behavior, thus providing concrete observations of an abstract concept like algorithmic efficiency. There are similar labs available for Levels 2, 3, 4, and 5 that highlight and clarify the material presented in the text.

Each lab experiment includes an explanation of how to use the software, a description of how to conduct the experiment, and problems for students to complete. For these lab projects, students can either work on their own or in teams, and the course may utilize either a closed-lab (formal, scheduled) or open-lab (informal, unscheduled) setting. The manual and software work well with all these laboratory models. The text contains "Laboratory Exercise" boxes that describe each lab and identify the point in the text where it would be most appropriate.

In this new eighth edition, the Laboratory Manual has been integrated into the MindTap for this text.

Programming and Online Language Modules

Programming concepts are presented in the text in the form of a survey of the features each high-level language provides and how they differ based on the computing tasks for which they were intended. Code examples are shown only to illustrate how algorithms can be embedded into the varying syntax of different languages. For instructors who want their students to have additional programming experience, online language modules for Ada, C++, C#, Java, and Python are available. Students may download any or all of these for free by going to *www.cengage.com*. These PDF documents can be read online, downloaded to the student's computer, or printed. Each chapter includes language-specific practice problems and exercises. The exercises are also included in our educational Integrated Development Environment (IDE) within MindTap. This exposes your students to an important developer tool.

Computer science is a young and exciting discipline, and we hope that the new material in this edition, along with the laboratory projects and online modules, will convey this feeling of excitement to students.

Instructor Resources

The following supplemental teaching tools are available when this book is used in a classroom setting. All supplements are available to instructors for download at *www.cengage.com*.

Instructor's Manual

The Instructor's Manual follows the text chapter by chapter and includes material to assist in planning and organizing an effective, engaging course. The Instructor's Manual includes Overviews, Learning Objectives, Teaching Tips, Quick Quizzes, Class Discussion Topics, Additional Projects, Additional Resources, and Key Terms. A sample syllabus is also available.

Solutions

Complete solutions to chapter exercises are provided online for instructors.

Test Bank

Cengage Learning Testing, powered by Cognero, is a flexible, online system that allows instructors to:

- Author, edit, and manage test bank content from multiple Cengage Learning solutions
- Create multiple test versions in an instant
- Deliver tests from your Learning Management System (LMS), your classroom, or anywhere you want

PowerPoint Presentations

Microsoft PowerPoint slides to accompany each chapter are available. Slides may be used to guide classroom presentation or to print as classroom hand-outs, or they may be made available to students for chapter review. Instructors may customize the slides to best suit their course.

Acknowledgments

The authors would like to thank Bo Brinkman, Ph.D., Miami University, for his contributions to the Social Issues in Computing content. The authors would also like to thank Deb Kaufmann and Emma Newsom for their invaluable assistance in developing this new edition, as well as the reviewers for this edition, whose comments were very helpful.

- Travis Dalton, Columbia College

- Debbie Collins, Black Hawk College

- Barry Poulson, University of Colorado, Boulder

- Akira Kawaguchi, The City College of New York

- H. Paul Haiduk, West Texas A&M University

- Melissa Stange, Lord Fairfax Community College

- Tom Schendl, Benedictine University

Any errors, of course, are the fault solely of the authors.

–G. Michael Schneider
Macalester College
schneider@macalester.edu

–Judith L. Gersting
Indiana University-Purdue University at Indianapolis
gersting@iupui.edu

An Introduction to Computer Science

AFTER STUDYING THIS CHAPTER, YOU WILL BE ABLE TO:

- Understand the definition of the term algorithm
- Understand the formal definition of computer science
- Write down everyday algorithms
- Determine if an algorithm is ambiguous or not effectively computable
- Understand the roots of modern computer science in mathematics and mechanical machines
- Summarize the key points in the historical development of modern electronic computers

1.1 Introduction

This text is an invitation to learn about one of the youngest and most exciting scientific disciplines—*computer science*. Almost every day our newspapers, televisions, and electronic media carry reports of significant advances in computing, such as high-speed supercomputers that perform more than 90 quadrillion (10^{15}) mathematical operations per second; wireless networks that stream high-definition video and audio to the remotest corners of the globe in fractions of a second; minute computer chips that can be embedded into appliances, clothing, and even our bodies; and artificial intelligence systems that understand and respond to English language questions faster and more accurately than humans. The next few years will see technological breakthroughs that, until a few years ago, existed only in the minds of dreamers and science fiction writers. These are exciting times in computing, and our goal in this text is to provide you with an understanding of computer science and an appreciation for the diverse areas of research and study within this important field.

Although the average person can produce a reasonably accurate description of most scientific fields, even if he or she did not study the subject in school, many people do not have an intuitive understanding of the types of problems studied by computer science professionals. For example, you probably know that biology is the study of living organisms and that chemistry deals with the structure and composition of matter. However, you might not have the same fundamental understanding of the work that goes on in computer science. In fact, many people harbor one or more of the following common misconceptions about this field.

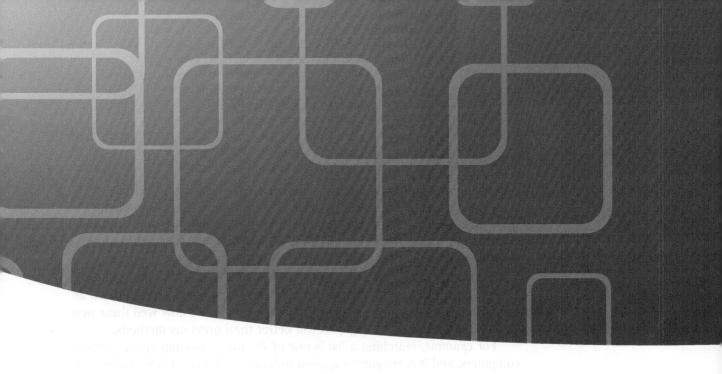

MISCONCEPTION 1: *Computer science is the study of computers.*

This apparently obvious definition is actually incorrect or, to put it more precisely, incomplete. For example, some of the earliest and most fundamental theoretical work in computer science took place from 1920 to 1940, many years before the development of the first computer system. (This pioneering work was initially considered a branch of logic and applied mathematics. Computer science did not come to be recognized as a separate and independent field of scientific study until the late 1950s and early 1960s.) Even today, there are branches of computer science quite distinct from the study of "real" machines. In *theoretical computer science*, for example, researchers study the logical and mathematical properties of problems and their solutions. Frequently, these researchers investigate problems not with actual computers but rather with *formal models* of computation, which are easier to study and analyze mathematically. Their work involves pencil and paper, not circuit boards and disks.

This distinction between computers and computer science was beautifully expressed by computer scientists Michael R. Fellows and Ian Parberry in an article in the journal *Computing Research News:*

> Computer science is no more about computers than astronomy is about telescopes, biology is about microscopes, or chemistry is about beakers and test tubes. Science is not about tools. It is about how we use them and what we find out when we do.[1]

MISCONCEPTION 2: *Computer science is the study of how to write computer programs.*

Many people are introduced to computer science when learning to write programs in a language such as C++, Python, or Java. This almost universal

---

[1]Fellows, M. R., and Parberry, I. "Getting Children Excited About Computer Science," *Computing Research News,* vol. 5, no. 1 (January 1993).

use of programming as the entry to the discipline can create the misunderstanding that computer science is equivalent to computer programming.

Programming is extremely important to the discipline—researchers use it to study new ideas and build and test new solutions—but, like the computer itself, programming is a tool. When computer scientists design and analyze a new approach to solving a problem or create new ways to represent information, they often implement their ideas as programs to test them on an actual computer system. This enables researchers to see how well these new ideas work and whether they perform better than previous methods.

For example, searching a list is one of the most common applications of computers, and it is frequently applied to huge problems, such as finding one specific account among the approximately 63,000,000 active listings in the Social Security Administration database. A more efficient lookup method could significantly reduce the time that telephone-based customers must wait before receiving answers to questions regarding their accounts. Assume that we have designed what we believe to be a "new and improved" search technique. After analyzing it theoretically, we would study it empirically by writing a program to implement our new method, executing it on our computer, and measuring its performance. These tests would demonstrate under what conditions our new method is or is not faster than the search procedures currently in use.

In computer science, it is not simply the construction of a high-quality program that is important but also the methods it embodies, the services it provides, and the results it produces. It is possible to become so enmeshed in writing code and getting it to run that we forget that a program is only a means to an end, not an end in itself.

MISCONCEPTION 3: *Computer science is the study of the uses and applications of computers and software.*

If one's introduction to computer science is not programming, then it might be a course on the application of computers and software. Such a course typically teaches the use of a number of popular packages, such as word processors, search engines, database systems, spreadsheets, presentation software, smartphone apps, and web browsers.

These packages are widely used by professionals in all fields. However, learning to use a software package is no more a part of computer science than driver's education is a branch of automotive engineering. A wide range of people *use* computer software, but it is the computer scientist who is responsible for *specifying*, *designing*, *building*, and *testing* these software packages as well as the computer systems on which they run.

These three misconceptions about computer science are not entirely wrong; they are just woefully incomplete. Computers, programming languages, software, and applications *are* part of the discipline of computer science, but neither individually nor combined do they capture the richness and diversity of this field.

We have spent a good deal of time saying what computer science is *not*. What, then, is it? What are its basic concepts? What are the fundamental questions studied by professionals in this field? Is it possible to capture the breadth and scope of the discipline in a single definition? We answer these fundamental questions in the next section and, indeed, in the remainder of the text.

In the Beginning …

There is no single date that marks the beginning of computer science. Indeed, there are many "firsts" that could be used to mark this event. For example, some of the earliest theoretical work on the logical foundations of computer science occurred in the 1930s. The first general-purpose, electronic computers appeared during the period 1940–1946. (We will discuss the history of these early machines in Section 1.4.) These first computers were one-of-a-kind experimental systems that never moved outside the research laboratory. The first commercial machine, the UNIVAC I, did not make its appearance until March 1951, a date that marks the real beginning of the computer industry. The first high-level (i.e., based on natural language) programming language was FORTRAN. Some people mark its debut in 1957 as the beginning of the "software" industry. The appearance of these new machines and languages created new occupations, such as programmer, numerical analyst, and computer engineer. To address the intellectual needs of these workers, the first professional society for people in the field of computing, the Association for Computing Machinery (ACM), was established in 1947. (The ACM has more than 100,000 members and is the largest professional computer science society in the world. Its home page is *www.acm.org*.) To help meet the rapidly growing need for computer professionals, the first Department of Computer Science was established at Purdue University in October 1962. It awarded its first M.Sc. degree in 1964 and its first Ph.D. in computer science in 1966. An undergraduate program was established in 1967.

Thus, depending on what you consider the most important "first," the field of computer science is somewhere between 50 and 80 years old. Compared with such classic scientific disciplines as mathematics, physics, chemistry, and biology, computer science is the new kid on the block.

1.2 The Definition of Computer Science

There are many definitions of computer science, but the one that best captures the richness and breadth of ideas embodied in this branch of science was first proposed by professors Norman Gibbs and Allen Tucker.[2] According to their definition, the central concept in computer science is the algorithm. It is not possible to understand the field without a thorough understanding of this critically important idea.

The Gibbs and Tucker definition says that it is the task of the computer scientist to design and develop algorithms to solve a range of important problems. This design process includes the following operations:

- Studying the behavior of algorithms to determine if they are correct and efficient (their formal and mathematical properties)

- Designing and building computer systems that are able to execute algorithms (their hardware realizations)

- Designing programming languages and translating algorithms into these languages so that they can be executed by the hardware (their linguistic realizations)

- Identifying important problems and designing correct and efficient software packages to solve these problems (their applications)

Because it is impossible to appreciate this definition fully without knowing what an algorithm is, let's look more closely at this term. The Merriam-Webster dictionary (*www.merriam-webster.com/dictionary/*) defines the word *algorithm* as follows:

> *al • go • rithm n. A procedure for solving a mathematical problem in a finite number of steps that frequently involves repetition of an operation; broadly: a step-by-step method for accomplishing some task.*

Informally, an algorithm is an ordered sequence of instructions that is guaranteed to solve a specific problem. It is a list that looks something like this:

STEP 1:   Do something

STEP 2:   Do something

STEP 3:   Do something

.   .

.   .

.   .

STEP N: Stop, you are finished

---

[2]Gibbs, N. E., and Tucker, A. B. "A Model Curriculum for a Liberal Arts Degree in Computer Science," *Comm. of the ACM*, vol. 29, no. 3 (March 1986).

If you are handed this list and carefully follow its instructions in the order specified, when you reach the end you will have solved the task at hand.

All the operations used to construct algorithms belong to one of only three categories:

1. Sequential operations. A sequential instruction carries out a single well-defined task. When that task is finished, the algorithm moves on to the next operation. Sequential operations are usually expressed as simple declarative sentences.
   - Add 1 cup of butter to the mixture in the bowl.
   - Subtract the amount of the check from the current account balance.
   - Set the value of x to 1.

2. Conditional operations. These are the "question-asking" instructions of an algorithm. They ask a question, and the next operation is then selected on the basis of the answer to that question.
   - If the mixture is too dry, then add one-half cup of water to the bowl.
   - If the amount of the check is less than or equal to the current account balance, then cash the check; otherwise, tell the person there are insufficient funds.
   - If x is not equal to 0, then set y equal to $1/x$; otherwise, print an error message that says you cannot perform division by 0.

3. Iterative operations. These are the "looping" instructions of an algorithm. They tell us not to go on to the next instruction but, instead, to go back and repeat the execution of a previous block of instructions.
   - Repeat the previous two operations until the mixture has thickened.
   - While there are still more checks to be processed, do the following five steps.
   - Repeat Steps 1, 2, and 3 until the value of y is equal to $+1$.

We use algorithms (although we don't call them that) all the time—whenever we follow a set of instructions to assemble a child's toy, bake a cake, balance a checkbook, or go through the college registration process. A good example of an algorithm used in everyday life is the set of instructions shown in Figure 1.1 for programming a DVR to record a collection of television shows. Note the three types of instructions in this algorithm: sequential (Steps 3, 4, 5, and 7), conditional (Steps 1 and 6), and iterative (Step 2).

Mathematicians use algorithms all the time, and much of the work done by early Greek, Roman, Persian, and Indian mathematicians involved the discovery of algorithms for important problems in geometry and arithmetic; an example is *Euclid's algorithm* for finding the greatest common divisor of two positive integers. (Exercise 10 at the end of the chapter presents this 2,300-year-old algorithm.) We also studied algorithms in elementary school, even if we didn't know it. For example, in the first grade we learned an algorithm for adding two numbers such as

```
  47
+ 25
----
  72
```

[handwritten margin notes: Sequential, conditional, iterative]

FIGURE 1.1

Step 1	If the clock and the calendar are not correctly set, then go to page 9 of the instruction manual and follow the instructions there before proceeding to Step 2
Step 2	Repeat Steps 3 through 6 for each program that you want to record
Step 3	Enter the channel number that you want to record and press the button labeled CHAN
Step 4	Enter the time that you want recording to start and press the button labeled TIME-START
Step 5	Enter the time that you want recording to stop and press the button labeled TIME-FINISH. This completes the programming of one show
Step 6	If you do not want to record anything else, press the button labeled END-PROG
Step 7	Turn off your DVR. Your DVR is now in TIMER mode, ready to record

Programming your DVR: An example of an algorithm

The instructions our teachers gave were as follows: First add the rightmost column of numbers $(7 + 5)$, getting the value 12. Write down the 2 under the line and carry the 1 to the next column. Now move left to the next column, adding $(4 + 2)$ and the previous carry value of 1 to get 7. Write this value under the line, producing the correct answer 72.

Although as children we learned this algorithm informally, it can, like the DVR instructions in Figure 1.1, be written formally as an explicit sequence of instructions. Figure 1.2 shows an algorithm for adding two positive m-digit numbers. It expresses formally the operations informally described previously. Again, note the three types of instructions used to construct the algorithm: sequential (Steps 1, 2, 4, 6, 7, 8, and 9), conditional (Step 5), and iterative (Step 3).

Even though it might not appear so, this is the same "decimal addition algorithm" that you learned in grade school; if you follow it rigorously, it is guaranteed to produce the correct result. Let's watch it work.

Add $(47 + 25)$

$m = 2$

$a_1 = 4$ $a_0 = 7$ The input

$b_1 = 2$ $b_0 = 5$

STEP 1: $carry = 0$

STEP 2: $i = 0$

STEP 3:   We now repeat Steps 4 through 6 while i is less than or equal to 1

First repetition of the loop (i has the value 0)

STEP 4:   Add $(a_0 + b_0 + carry)$, which is $7 + 5 + 0$, so $c_0 = 12$

STEP 5:   Because $c_0 \geq 10$, we reset **c_0 to 2** and reset *carry* to 1

FIGURE 1.2

Given: $m \geq 1$ and two positive numbers each containing m digits, $a_{m-1} \, a_{m-2} \cdots a_0$ and $b_{m-1} \, b_{m-2} \cdots b_0$

Wanted: $c_m \, c_{m-1} \, c_{m-2} \cdots c_0$, where $c_m \, c_{m-1} \, c_{m-2} \cdots c_0 = (a_{m-1} \, a_{m-2} \cdots a_0) + (b_{m-1} \, b_{m-2} \cdots b_0)$

Algorithm:

Step 1   Set the value of *carry* to 0

Step 2   Set the value of *i* to 0

Step 3   While the value of *i* is less than or equal to $m - 1$, repeat the instructions in Steps 4 through 6

Step 4   Add the two digits a_i and b_i to the current value of *carry* to get c_i

Step 5   If $c_i \geq 10$, then reset c_i to $(c_i - 10)$ and reset the value of *carry* to 1; otherwise, set the new value of *carry* to 0

Step 6   Add 1 to *i*, effectively moving one column to the left

Step 7   Set c_m to the value of *carry*

Step 8   Print out the final answer, $c_m \, c_{m-1} \, c_{m-2} \cdots c_0$

Step 9   Stop

Algorithm for adding two *m*-digit numbers

STEP 6:   Reset *i* to $(0 + 1) = 1$. Because *i* is less than or equal to 1, go back to Step 4

Second repetition of the loop (i has the value 1)

STEP 4:   Add $(a_1 + b_1 + carry)$, which is $4 + 2 + 1$, so $\mathbf{c_1 = 7}$

STEP 5:   Because $c_1 < 10$, we reset *carry* to 0

STEP 6:   Reset *i* to $(1 + 1) = 2$. Because *i* is greater than 1, we do not repeat the loop but instead go to Step 7

STEP 7:   Set $\mathbf{c_2 = 0}$

STEP 8:   Print out the answer $c_2 \, c_1 \, c_0 = 072$ (see the **boldface** values)

STEP 9:   Stop

We have reached the end of the algorithm, and it has correctly produced the sum of the two numbers 47 and 25, the three-digit result 072. (A more clever algorithm would omit the unnecessary leading zero at the beginning of the number if the last carry value is a zero. That modification is an exercise—Exercise 6—at the end of the chapter.) Try working through the algorithm shown in Figure 1.2 with another pair of numbers to be sure that you understand exactly how it functions.

The addition algorithm shown in Figure 1.2 is a highly formalized representation of a technique that most people learned in the first or second grade and that virtually everyone knows how to do informally. Why would we take such a simple task as adding two numbers and express it in so

Abu Ja'far Muhammad ibn Musa Al-Khwarizmi (AD 780–850?)

The word *algorithm* is derived from the last name of Muhammad ibn Musa Al-Khwarizmi, a famous Persian mathematician and author from the eighth and ninth centuries. Al-Khwarizmi was a teacher at the House of Wisdom in Baghdad and the author of the book *Kitab al jabr w'al muqabala*, which in English means "The Concise Book of Calculation by Reduction." Written in AD 820, it is one of the earliest mathematical textbooks, and its title gives us the word *algebra* (the Arabic word *al jabr* means "reduction").

In AD 825, Al-Khwarizmi wrote another book about the base-10 positional numbering system that had recently been developed in India. In this book, he described formalized, step-by-step procedures for doing arithmetic operations, such as addition, subtraction, and multiplication, on numbers represented in this new decimal system, much like the addition algorithm diagrammed in Figure 1.2. In the twelfth century, this book was translated into Latin, introducing the base-10 Hindu–Arabic numbering system to Europe, and Al-Khwarizmi's name became closely associated with these formal numerical techniques. His last name was rendered as Algoritmi in Latin characters, and eventually the formalized procedures that he pioneered and developed became known as *algorithms* in his honor.

complicated a fashion? Why are formal algorithms so important in computer science? Because of the following fundamental idea:

If we can specify an algorithm to solve a problem, then we can automate its solution.

Once we have formally specified an algorithm, we can build a machine (or write a program or hire a person) to carry out the steps contained in the algorithm. The machine (or program or person) need not understand the concepts or ideas underlying the solution. It merely has to do Step 1, Step 2, Step 3, … exactly as written. In computer science terminology, the machine, robot, person, or thing carrying out the steps of the algorithm is called a computing agent.

Thus, computer science can also be viewed as the *science of algorithmic problem solving.* Much of the research and development work in computer science involves discovering correct and efficient algorithms for a wide range of interesting problems, studying their properties, designing programming languages into which those algorithms can be encoded, and designing and building computer systems that can automatically execute these algorithms in an efficient manner.

At first glance, it might seem that every problem can be solved algorithmically. However, you will learn in Chapter 12 the startling fact (first proved by the German logician Kurt Gödel in the early 1930s) that there are problems for which no generalized algorithmic solution can possibly exist. These problems are, in a sense, *unsolvable*. No matter how much time and effort is put into obtaining a solution, none will ever be found. Gödel's discovery, which staggered the mathematical world, effectively places a limit on the ultimate capabilities of computers and computer scientists.

There are also problems for which it is theoretically possible to specify an algorithm but a computing agent would take so long to execute it that the solution is essentially useless. For example, to get a computer to play winning chess, we could adopt a *brute force* approach. Given a board position as input, the computer would examine every legal move it could possibly make, then every legal response an opponent could make to each initial move, then every response it could select to that move, and so on. This analysis would continue until the game reached a win, lose, or draw position. With that information, the computer would be able to optimally choose its next move. If, for simplicity's sake, we assume that there are 40 legal moves from any given position on a chessboard, and it takes about 30 moves to reach a final conclusion, then the total number of board positions that our brute force program would need to evaluate in deciding its first move is

$$\underbrace{40 \times 40 \times 40 \times \ldots \times 40}_{\text{30 times}} = 40^{30}, \text{ which is roughly } 10^{48}$$

If we use a supercomputer that evaluates 1 quadrillion (10^{15}) board positions per second, it would take about 30,000,000,000,000,000,000,000,000 years for the computer to make its first move! Obviously, a computer could not use a brute force technique to play a real chess game.

There also exist problems that we do not yet know *how* to solve algorithmically. Many of these involve tasks that require a degree of what we term "intelligence." For example, after only a few days a baby recognizes the face of his or her mother from among the many faces he or she sees. In a few months, the baby begins to develop coordinated sensory and motor control skills and can efficiently plan how to use them—how to get from the playpen to the toy on the floor without bumping into either the chair or the desk that is in the way. After a few years, the child begins to develop powerful language skills and abstract reasoning capabilities.

We take these abilities for granted, but, even though artificial intelligence research and implementation has made enormous strides in the past few years, with regard to the operations just mentioned—high-level problem solving, abstract reasoning, sophisticated natural-language understanding—the computer and software systems currently available in the marketplace have not yet achieved the intelligence level of an adult human being. The primary reason is that researchers do not yet know how to specify these operations algorithmically. That is, they do not yet know how to specify a solution formally in a detailed step-by-step fashion. As humans, we are able to do them simply by using the "algorithms" in our heads. To appreciate this problem, imagine trying to describe algorithmically exactly what steps you follow when you are painting a picture, composing a love poem, or formulating a business plan.

Thus, algorithmic problem solving has many variations. Sometimes solutions do not exist; sometimes a solution is too inefficient to be of any use; sometimes a solution is not yet known. However, discovering an algorithmic solution has enormously important consequences. As we noted earlier, if we can create a correct and efficient algorithm to solve a problem, and if we encode it into a programming language, then we can take advantage of the speed and power of a computer system to automate the solution and produce the desired result. This is what computer science is all about.

1.3 Algorithms

1.3.1 The Formal Definition of an Algorithm

The formal definition of an algorithm is rather imposing and contains a number of important ideas. Let's take it apart, piece by piece, and analyze each of its separate points.

> *…a well-ordered collection…*

An algorithm is a collection of operations, and there must be a clear and unambiguous *ordering* to these operations. Ordering means that we know which operation to do first and precisely which operation to do next as each step is successfully completed. After all, we cannot expect a computing agent to carry out our instructions correctly if it is confused about which instruction it should be doing next.

Consider the following "algorithm" that was taken from the back of a shampoo bottle and is intended to be instructions on how to use the product.

STEP 1:   Wet hair

STEP 2:   Lather

STEP 3:   Rinse

STEP 4:   Repeat

At Step 4, what operations should be repeated? If we go back to Step 1, we will be unnecessarily wetting our hair. (It is presumably still wet from the previous operations.) If we go back to Step 3 instead, we will not be getting our hair any cleaner because we have not reused the shampoo. The Repeat instruction in Step 4 is ambiguous in that it does not clearly specify what to

---

DEFINITION

Algorithm: a well-ordered collection of unambiguous and effectively computable operations that, when executed, produces a result and halts in a finite amount of time.

do next. Therefore, it violates the well-ordered requirement of an algorithm. (It also has a second and even more serious problem—it never stops! We will have more to say about this second problem shortly.) Statements such as

- Go back and do it again. (Do *what* again?)
- Start over. (From *where?*)
- If you understand this material, you may skip ahead. (How *far?*)
- Do either Part 1 or Part 2. (How do I decide *which* one to do?)

are ambiguous and can leave us confused and unsure about what operation to do next. We must be extremely precise in specifying the order in which operations are to be carried out. One possible way is to number the steps of the algorithm and use these numbers to specify the proper order of execution. For example, the ambiguous operations just shown could be made more precise as follows:

- Go back to Step 3 and continue execution from that point.
- Start over from Step 1.
- If you understand this material, skip ahead to Line 21.
- If you are 18 years of age or older, do Part 1 beginning with Step 9; otherwise, do Part 2 beginning with Step 40.

...of unambiguous and effectively computable operations...

Algorithms are composed of things called "operations," but what do those operations look like? What types of building blocks can be used to construct an algorithm? The answer to these questions is that the operations used in an algorithm must meet two criteria—they must be *unambiguous*, and they must be *effectively computable*.

Here is a possible "algorithm" for making a cherry pie:

STEP 1:   Make the crust

STEP 2:   Make the cherry filling

STEP 3:   Pour the filling into the crust

STEP 4:   Bake at 350°F for 45 minutes

For a professional baker, this algorithm would be fine. He or she would understand how to carry out each of the operations listed. Novice cooks, like most of us, would probably understand the meaning of Steps 3 and 4. However, we would probably look at Steps 1 and 2, throw up our hands in confusion, and ask for clarification. We might then be given more detailed instructions.

STEP 1:   Make the crust
       1.1   Take one and one-third cups flour
       1.2   Sift the flour

1.3   Mix the sifted flour with one-half cup butter and one-fourth cup water

1.4   Roll into two 9-inch pie crusts

STEP 2:   Make the cherry filling

2.1   Open a 16-ounce can of cherry pie filling and pour into bowl

2.2   Add a dash of cinnamon and nutmeg, and stir

With this additional information, most people—even inexperienced cooks—would understand what to do and could successfully carry out this baking algorithm. However, there might be some people, perhaps young children, who still do not fully understand each and every line. For those people, we must go through the simplification process again and describe the ambiguous steps in even more elementary terms.

For example, the computing agent executing the algorithm might not know the meaning of the instruction "Sift the flour" in Step 1.2, and we would have to explain it further.

1.2   Sift the flour

1.2.1   Get out the sifter, which is the device shown on page A-9 of your cookbook, and place it directly on top of a 2-quart bowl

1.2.2   Pour the flour into the top of the sifter and turn the crank in a counterclockwise direction

1.2.3   Let all the flour fall through the sifter into the bowl

Now, even a child should be able to carry out these operations. But if that were not the case, then we would go through the simplification process yet one more time, until every operation, every sentence, every word was clearly understood.

An unambiguous operation is one that can be understood and carried out directly by the computing agent without further simplification or explanation. When an operation is unambiguous, we call it a *primitive operation,* or simply a primitive of the computing agent carrying out the algorithm. An algorithm must be composed entirely of primitives. Naturally, the primitive operations of different individuals (or machines) vary depending on their sophistication, experience, and intelligence, as is the case with the cherry pie recipe, which varies with the baking experience of the person following the instructions. Hence, an algorithm for one computing agent might not be an algorithm for another.

One of the most important questions we will answer in this text is, *What are the primitive operations of a typical modern computer system?* Which operations can a hardware processor "understand" in the sense of being able to carry out directly, and which operations must be further refined and simplified?

However, it is not enough for an operation to be understandable. It must also be *doable* by the computing agent. If an algorithm tells me to flap my arms really quickly and fly, I understand perfectly well what it is asking me to do. However, I am incapable of doing it. "Doable" means there exists a computational process that allows the computing agent to complete that operation successfully. The formal term for "doable" is effectively computable.

For example, the following is an incorrect technique for finding and printing the 100th prime number. (A prime number is a whole number not evenly divisible by any numbers other than 1 and itself, such as 2, 3, 5, 7, 11, 13, ...)

STEP 1:   Generate a list L of all the prime numbers: $L_1, L_2, L_3, ...$

STEP 2:   Sort the list L into ascending order

STEP 3:   Print out the 100th element in the list, L_{100}

STEP 4:   Stop

The problem with these instructions is in Step 1, "Generate a list L of *all* the prime numbers...." That operation cannot be completed. There are an infinite number of prime numbers, and it is not possible in a finite amount of time to generate the desired list L. No such computational process exists, and the operation described in Step 1 is not effectively computable. Here are some other examples of operations that, under certain circumstances, may not be effectively computable:

> Set *number* to 0.
> Set *average* to *(sum ÷ number)*. (Division by 0 is not permitted.)

> Set N to −1.
> Set the value of *result* to $\sqrt{N}$. (You cannot take the square root of negative values using real numbers.)

> Add 1 to the current value of *x*. (What if *x* currently has no value?)

This last example explains why we had to initialize the value of the variable called *carry* to 0 in Step 1 of Figure 1.2. In Step 4, the algorithm says, "Add the two digits a_i and b_i to the current value of *carry* to get c_i." If *carry* has no current value, then when the computing agent tries to perform the instruction in Step 4, it will not know what to do, and this operation is not effectively computable.

...that produces a result...

Algorithms solve problems. To know whether a solution is correct, an algorithm must produce a result that is observable to a user, such as a numerical answer, a new object, or a change to its environment. Without some observable result, we would not be able to say whether the algorithm is right or wrong or even if it has completed its computations. In the case of the DVR algorithm (Figure 1.1), the result will be a set of recorded TV programs. The addition algorithm (Figure 1.2) produces an *m*-digit sum.

Note that we use the word *result* rather than *answer*. Sometimes it is not possible for an algorithm to produce the correct answer because for a given set of input, a correct answer does not exist. In those cases, the algorithm may produce something else, such as an error message, a red warning light, or an approximation to the correct answer. Error messages, lights, and approximations, although not necessarily what we wanted, are all observable results.

...and halts in a finite amount of time.

Another important characteristic of algorithms is that the result must be produced after the execution of a finite number of operations, and we must guarantee that the algorithm eventually reaches a statement that says, "Stop, you are done" or something equivalent. We have already pointed out that the shampooing algorithm was not well ordered because we did not know which statements to repeat in Step 4. However, even if we knew which block of statements to repeat, the algorithm would still be incorrect because it makes no provision to terminate. It will essentially run forever, or until we run out of hot water, soap, or patience. This is called an infinite loop, and it is a common error in the design of algorithms.

Figure 1.3 shows an algorithmic solution to the shampooing problem that meets all the criteria discussed in this section if we assume that you want to wash your hair twice. The algorithm of Figure 1.3 is well ordered. Each step is numbered, and the execution of the algorithm unfolds sequentially, beginning at Step 1 and proceeding from instruction i to instruction $i + 1$, unless the operation specifies otherwise. (For example, the iterative instruction in Step 3 says that after completing Step 6, you should go back and start again at Step 4 until the value of *WashCount* equals 2.) The intent of each operation is (we assume) clear, unambiguous, and doable by the person washing his or her hair. Finally, the algorithm will halt. This is confirmed by observing that *WashCount* is initially set to 0 in Step 2. Step 6 says to add 1 to *WashCount* each time we lather and rinse our hair, so it will take on the values 0, 1, 2, ... However, the iterative statement in Step 3 says stop lathering and rinsing when the value of *WashCount* reaches 2. At that point, the algorithm goes to Step 7 and terminates execution with the desired result: clean hair. (Although it is correct, do not expect to see this algorithm on the back of a shampoo bottle in the near future.)

As is true for any recipe or set of instructions, there is always more than a single way to write a correct solution. For example, the algorithm of Figure 1.3 could also be written as shown in Figure 1.4. Both of these are correct solutions to the shampooing problem. (Although they are both

---

FIGURE 1.3

Step	Operation
1	Wet your hair
2	Set the value of *WashCount* to 0
3	Repeat Steps 4 through 6 until the value of *WashCount* equals 2
4	Lather your hair
5	Rinse your hair
6	Add 1 to the value of *WashCount*
7	Stop, you have finished shampooing your hair

A correct solution to the shampooing problem

FIGURE 1.4

Step	Operation
1	Wet your hair
2	Lather your hair
3	Rinse your hair
4	Lather your hair
5	Rinse your hair
6	Stop, you have finished shampooing your hair

Another correct solution to the shampooing problem

correct, they are not necessarily equally elegant. This point is addressed in Exercise 9 at the end of the chapter.)

1.3.2 The Importance of Algorithmic Problem Solving

The instruction sequences in Figures 1.1–1.4 are examples of the types of algorithmic solutions designed, analyzed, implemented, and tested by computer scientists, although they are much shorter and simpler. The operations shown in these figures could be encoded into some appropriate language and given to a computing agent (such as a personal computer or a robot) to execute. The device would mechanically follow these instructions and successfully complete the task. The device could do this without having to understand the creative processes that went into the discovery of the solution and without knowing the principles and concepts that underlie the problem. The robot simply follows the steps in the specified order (a required characteristic of algorithms), successfully completing each operation (another required characteristic), and ultimately producing the desired result after a finite amount of time (also required).

Just as the Industrial Revolution of the nineteenth century allowed machines to take over the drudgery of repetitive physical tasks, the "computer revolution" of the twentieth and twenty-first centuries has enabled us to implement algorithms that mechanize and automate the drudgery of repetitive mental tasks, such as adding long columns of numbers, finding one specific name or account number within a massive database, sorting student records by course number, and retrieving hotel or airline reservations from a file containing millions of pieces of data. This mechanization process offers the prospect of enormous increases in productivity. It also frees people to do those things that humans do much better than computers, such as creating new ideas, setting policy, doing high-level planning, and determining the significance of the results produced by a computer. Certainly, these operations are a much more effective use of that unique computing agent called the human brain.

Practice Problems

Get a copy of the instructions that describe how to do the following:

1. Register for classes at the beginning of the semester.

2. Use the online catalog to see what is available in the college library on a given subject.

3. Place an order for a product on Amazon.

4. Do an "Advanced Search" using Google.

5. Add someone as a friend to your Facebook account.

Look over the instructions and decide whether they meet the definition of an algorithm given in this section. If not, explain why, and rewrite each set of instructions so that it constitutes a valid algorithm. Also state whether each instruction is a sequential, a conditional, or an iterative operation.

1.4 A Brief History of Computing

Although computer science is not simply a study of computers, there is no doubt that the field was formed and grew in popularity as a direct response to their creation and widespread use. This section takes a brief look at the historical development of computer systems.

The appearance of some technologies, such as the telephone, the light bulb, and the first heavier-than-air flight, can be traced directly to a single place, a specific individual, and an exact instant in time. Examples include the flight of Orville and Wilbur Wright on December 17, 1903, in Kitty Hawk, North Carolina, and the famous phrase "Mr. Watson—come here—I want to see you." uttered by Alexander Graham Bell over the first telephone on March 10, 1876.

Computers were not like that. They did not appear in a specific room on a given day as the creation of some individual genius. The ideas that led to the design of the first computers evolved over hundreds of years, with contributions coming from many people, each building on and extending the work of earlier discoverers.

1.4.1 The Early Period: Up to 1940

If this were a discussion of the history of mathematics and arithmetic instead of computer science, it would begin 3,000 years ago with the early work of the Greeks, Egyptians, Babylonians, Indians, Chinese, and Persians. All these cultures were interested in and made important contributions to the fields of mathematics, logic, and numerical computation. For example, the Greeks developed the fields of geometry and logic; the Babylonians and Egyptians developed numerical methods for generating square roots, multiplication tables, and trigonometric tables used by early sailors; Indian mathematicians developed both the base-10 decimal numbering system and the concept of zero; and in the ninth century, the Persians developed algorithmic problem solving (as you learned in the Abu Ja'far Muhammad ibn Musa Al-Khwarizmi Special Interest Box earlier in the chapter).

The first half of the seventeenth century saw a number of important developments related to automating and simplifying the drudgery of arithmetic computation. (The motivation for this work appears to be the sudden increase in scientific research during the sixteenth and seventeenth centuries in the areas of astronomy, chemistry, and medicine. This work required the solution of larger and more complex mathematical problems.) In 1614, the Scotsman John Napier invented *logarithms* as a way to simplify difficult mathematical computations. The early seventeenth century also witnessed the development of new and quite powerful mechanical devices designed to help reduce the burden of arithmetic. The first *slide rule* appeared around 1622. In 1642, the French philosopher and mathematician Blaise Pascal designed and built one of the first *mechanical calculators* (named the *Pascaline*) that could do addition and subtraction. A model of this early calculating device is shown in Figure 1.5.

The famous German mathematician Gottfried Leibnitz (who, along with Isaac Newton, was one of the inventors of calculus) was also excited by the idea of automatic computation. He studied the work of Pascal and others, and in 1673, he constructed a mechanical calculator called *Leibnitz's Wheel* that could do not only addition and subtraction but multiplication and division as well. Both Pascal's and Leibnitz's machines used interlocking

FIGURE 1.5

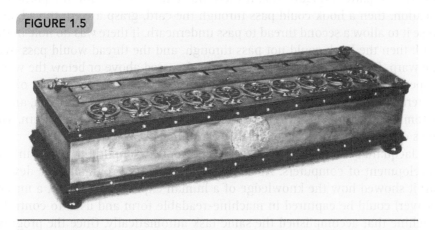

The Pascaline, one of the earliest mechanical calculators

Source: INTERFOTO / Alamy Stock Photo

mechanical cogs and gears to store numbers and perform basic arithmetic operations. Considering the state of technology available to Pascal, Leibnitz, and others in the seventeenth century, these first calculating machines truly were mechanical wonders.

These early developments in mathematics and arithmetic were important milestones because they demonstrated how mechanization could simplify and speed up numerical computation. For example, Leibnitz's Wheel enabled seventeenth-century mathematicians to generate tables of mathematical functions many times faster than was possible by hand. (It is hard to believe in our modern high-tech society, but in the seventeenth century the generation of a table of logarithms could represent a *lifetime's* effort of one person!) However, the slide rule and mechanical calculators of Pascal and Leibnitz, although certainly impressive devices, were not computers. Specifically, they lacked two fundamental characteristics:

- They did not have a *memory* where information could be stored in machine-readable form.

- They were not *programmable*. A person could not provide *in advance* a sequence of instructions that could be executed by the device without manual intervention.

Surprisingly, the first actual "computing device" to include both these features was not created for the purposes of mathematical computations. Rather, it was a loom used for the manufacture of rugs and clothing. It was developed in 1801 by the Frenchman Joseph Jacquard. Jacquard wanted to automate the weaving process, at the time a painfully slow and cumbersome task in which each separate row of the pattern had to be set up by the weaver and an apprentice. Because of this, anything but the most basic style of clothing was beyond the means of most people.

Jacquard designed an automated loom that used *punched cards* to create the desired pattern (Figure 1.6). If there was a hole in the card in a particular location, then a hook could pass through the card, grasp a warp thread, and raise it to allow a second thread to pass underneath. If there was no hole in the card, then the hook could not pass through, and the thread would pass over the warp. Depending on whether the thread passed above or below the warp, a specific design was created. Each punched card described one row of the pattern. Jacquard connected the cards and fed them through his loom, and it automatically sequenced from card to card, weaving the desired pattern. The rows of connected punched cards can be seen at the top of the device.

Jacquard's loom represented an enormously important stage in the development of computers. Not only was it the first programmable device, but it showed how the knowledge of a human expert (in this case, a master weaver) could be captured in machine-readable form and used to control a machine that accomplished the same task automatically. Once the program was created, the expert was no longer needed. The lowliest apprentice could load the cards into the loom, turn it on, and produce a finished, high-quality product over and over again.

FIGURE 1.6

Drawing of the Jacquard loom
Source: Bettmann/Getty Images

These pioneers had enormous influence on the designers and inventors who came after them, among them a mathematics professor at Cambridge University named Charles Babbage. Babbage was interested in automatic computation. In 1823, he extended the ideas of Pascal and Leibnitz and constructed a working model of the largest and most sophisticated mechanical calculator of its time. This machine, called the *Difference Engine,* could do addition, subtraction, multiplication, and division to six significant digits, and it could solve polynomial equations and other complex mathematical problems as well. Babbage tried to construct a larger model of the Difference Engine that would be capable of working to an accuracy of 20 significant

The Original "Technophobia"

The development of the automated Jacquard loom and other technological advances in the weaving industry was so frightening to the craft guilds of the early nineteenth century that in 1811 it led to the formation of a group called the Luddites. The Luddites, named after their leader Ned Ludd of Nottingham, England, were violently opposed to this new manufacturing technology, and they burned down factories that attempted to use it. The movement lasted only a few years and its leaders were all jailed, but their name lives on today as a pejorative term for any group that is frightened and angered by the latest developments in any branch of science and technology, including computers.

digits, but after 12 years of work he had to give up his quest. The technology available in the 1820s and 1830s was not sufficiently advanced to manufacture cogs and gears to the precise tolerances his design required. Like Leonardo da Vinci's helicopter or Jules Verne's atomic submarine, Babbage's ideas were fundamentally sound but years ahead of their time. (In 1991, the London Museum of Science, using Babbage's original plans, built an actual working model of the Difference Engine. It was 7 feet high and 11 feet wide, weighed 5 tons, and had 4,000 moving parts. It worked exactly as Babbage had planned.)

Babbage did not stop his investigations with the Difference Engine. In the 1830s, he designed a more powerful and general-purpose computational machine that could be configured to solve a much wider range of numerical problems. His machine had four basic components: a *mill* to perform the arithmetic manipulation of data, a *store* to hold the data, an *operator* to process the instructions contained on punched cards, and an *output unit* to put the results onto separate punched cards. Although it would be about 110 years before a "real" computer would be built, Babbage's proposed machine, called the Analytical Engine, is amazingly similar in design to a modern computer. The four components of the Analytical Engine are virtually identical in function to the four major components of today's computer systems:

Babbage's Term	Modern Terminology
mill	arithmetic/logic unit
store	memory
operator	processor
output unit	input/output

Babbage died before a working steam-powered model of his Analytical Engine could be completed, but his ideas lived on to influence others, and many computer scientists consider the Analytical Engine the first "true" computer system, even if it existed only on paper and in Babbage's dreams.

Another person influenced by the work of Pascal, Jacquard, and Babbage was a young statistician at the U.S. Census Bureau named Herman Hollerith. Because of the rapid increase in immigration to America at the end of the nineteenth century, officials estimated that doing the 1890 enumeration manually would take from 10 to 12 years. The 1900 census would begin before the previous one was finished. Something had to be done.

Hollerith designed and built programmable card-processing machines that could automatically read, tally, and sort data entered on punched cards. Census data were coded onto cards using a machine called a *keypunch*. The cards were taken either to a *tabulator* for counting and tallying or to a *sorter* for ordering alphabetically or numerically. Both of these machines were programmable (via wires and plugs) so that the user could specify such things as which card columns should be tallied and in what order the cards should be sorted. In addition, the machines had a small amount of memory to store results. Thus, they had all four components of Babbage's Analytical Engine.

Hollerith's machines were enormously successful, and they were one of the first examples of the use of automated information processing to solve large-scale, real-world problems. Whereas the 1880 census required 8 years to be completed, the 1890 census was finished in about 1 year, even though there was a 26% increase in the U.S. population during that decade.

These machines were not really general-purpose computers because each machine could do only a single task such as tabulate or sort. Nevertheless, Hollerith's card machines were a very clear and very successful demonstration of the enormous advantages of automated information processing. This fact was not lost on Hollerith, who left the Census Bureau in 1902 to run his own Tabulating Machine Company to build and sell these machines. He planned to market his new product to a country that was just entering the Industrial Revolution and that, like the Census Bureau, would be generating and processing enormous volumes of inventory, production, accounting, and sales data. His punched-card machines became the dominant form of data-processing equipment during the first half of the twentieth century, well into the 1950s and 1960s. During this period, virtually every major U.S. corporation had data-processing rooms filled with keypunches, sorters, and tabulators, as well as drawer upon drawer of punched cards. In 1924, Hollerith's company changed its name to IBM, and it eventually evolved into the largest computing company in the world.

We have come a long way from the 1640s and the Pascaline, the early adding machine constructed by Pascal. We have seen the development of more powerful mechanical calculators (Leibnitz), automated programmable manufacturing devices (Jacquard), a design for the first computing device (Babbage), and the initial applications of information processing on a massive scale (Hollerith). However, we still have not yet entered the "computer age." That did not happen until around 1940, and it was motivated by an

Charles Babbage (1791–1871)
Ada Augusta Byron, Countess of Lovelace (1815–1852)

Charles Babbage, the son of a banker, was born into a life of wealth and comfort in eighteenth-century England. He attended Cambridge University and displayed an aptitude for mathematics and science. He was also an inventor and "tinkerer" who loved to build all sorts of devices. Among the devices he constructed were unpickable locks, skeleton keys, speedometers, and even the first cow catcher for trains. His first and greatest love, though, was mathematics, and he spent much of his life creating machines to do automatic computation. Babbage was enormously impressed by the work of Jacquard in France. (In fact, Babbage had on the wall of his home a woven portrait of Jacquard that was created using 24,000 punched cards.) He spent the last 30–40 years of his life trying to build a computing device, the Analytical Engine, based on Jacquard's ideas.

In that quest, he was helped by Countess Ada Augusta Byron, daughter of the famous English poet, Lord Byron. The countess was introduced to Babbage and was enormously impressed by his ideas about the Analytical Engine. As she put it, "We may say most aptly that the Analytical Engine weaves algebraic patterns just as the Jacquard Loom weaves flowers and leaves." Lady Lovelace worked closely with Babbage to specify how to organize instructions for the Analytical Engine to solve a particular mathematical problem. Because of that pioneering work, she is generally regarded as history's first computer programmer.

Babbage died in 1871 without realizing his dream. His work was generally forgotten until the twentieth century, when it became instrumental in moving the world into the computer age.

event that, unfortunately, has fueled many of the important technological advances in human history—the outbreak of war.

1.4.2 The Birth of Computers: 1940–1950

World War II created another, quite different set of information-based problems. Instead of inventory, sales, and payroll, the concerns became ballistics tables, troop deployment data, and secret codes. A number of research projects were started, funded largely by the military, to build automatic computing machines to perform these tasks and assist the Allies in the war effort.

Beginning in 1937, the U.S. Navy and IBM jointly funded a project under the direction of Professor Howard Aiken at Harvard University to build a computing device called Mark I. This was a general-purpose, electromechanical programmable computer that used a mix of relays, magnets, and gears to process and store data. The Mark I was the first computing device to use the base-2 binary numbering system, which we will discuss in Chapter 4. It used electromechanical switches and electric current to represent the two binary values, off for 0, on for 1. Until then, computing machines had used decimal representation, typically using a 10-toothed gear, each tooth representing one of the digits from 0 to 9. The Mark I was completed in 1944, about 110 years after Babbage's dream of the Analytical Engine, and is generally considered one of the first working general-purpose computers. The Mark I had a memory capacity of 72 numbers, and it could be programmed to perform a 23-digit multiplication in the lightning-like time of 4 seconds. Although laughably slow by modern standards, the Mark I was operational for almost 15 years, and it carried out a good deal of important mathematical work for the U.S. during the war.

At about the same time, a much more powerful machine was taking shape at the University of Pennsylvania in conjunction with the U.S. Army. During the early days of World War II, the Army was producing many new artillery pieces, but it found that it could not produce the firing tables equally as fast. These tables told the gunner how to aim the gun on the basis of such input as distance to the target and current temperature, wind, and elevation. Because of the enormous number of variables and the complexity of the computations (which use both trigonometry and calculus), these firing tables were taking more time to construct than the gun itself—a skilled person with a desk calculator required about 20 hours to analyze a single 60-second trajectory.

To help solve this problem, in 1943 the Army initiated a research project with J. Presper Eckert and John Mauchly of the University of Pennsylvania to build a completely electronic computing device. The machine, dubbed the ENIAC (Electronic Numerical Integrator and Calculator), was completed in 1946 (too late to assist in the war effort) and was the first fully electronic general-purpose programmable computer. This pioneering machine is shown in Figure 1.7.

ENIAC contained 18,000 vacuum tubes and nearly filled a building; it was 100 feet long and 10 feet high and weighed 30 tons. Because it was fully electronic, it did not contain any of the slow mechanical components found in Mark I, and it executed instructions much more rapidly. The ENIAC could add two 10-digit numbers in about 1/5,000 of a second and could multiply two numbers in 1/300 of a second, 1,000 times faster than the Mark I.

The Mark I and ENIAC are two well-known examples of early computers, but they are by no means the only ones of that era. For example, the ABC system (Atanasoff–Berry Computer), designed and built by Professor John Atanasoff and his graduate student Clifford Berry at Iowa State University, was actually the first electronic computer, constructed during the period 1939–1942. However, it never received equal recognition because it was useful for only one task, solving systems of simultaneous linear equations.

FIGURE 1.7

Photograph of the ENIAC computer

Source: U.S. Army, from the Collections of the University of Pennsylvania Archives

In England, a computer called Colossus was built in 1943 under the direction of Alan Turing, a famous mathematician and computer scientist whom we will meet again in Chapter 12. This machine, one of the first computers built outside the United States, was used to crack the famous German Enigma code that the Nazis believed to be unbreakable. Colossus has also not received as much recognition as ENIAC because of the secrecy that shrouded the Enigma project. Its very existence was not widely known until the late 1970s, more than 30 years after the end of World War II.

At about the same time that Colossus was taking form in England, a German engineer named Konrad Zuse was working on a computing device for the German army. The machine, code named Z1, was similar in design to the ENIAC—a programmable, general-purpose, fully electronic computing device. Fortunately for the Allied forces, the Z1 project was not completed before the end of World War II.

Although the machines just described—ABC, Mark I, ENIAC, Colossus, and Z1—were computers in the fullest sense of the word (they had memory and were programmable), they did not yet look like modern computer systems. One more step was necessary, and that step was taken in 1946 by the one individual who was most instrumental in creating the computer as we know it today, John Von Neumann.

Von Neumann was not only one of the most brilliant mathematicians who ever lived, he was also a genius in many other areas as well, including experimental physics, chemistry, economics, and computer science. Von Neumann, who taught at Princeton University, had worked with Eckert and Mauchly on the ENIAC project at the University of Pennsylvania. Even though that project was successful, he recognized a number of fundamental shortcomings in ENIAC. In 1946, he proposed a radically different computer design based on a model called the stored program computer. Until then, all computers were programmed *externally* using wires, connectors, and plugboards. The memory unit stored only data, not instructions. For each different problem, users had to rewire virtually the entire computer. For example, the plugboards on the ENIAC contained 6,000 separate switches, and reprogramming the ENIAC involved specifying the new settings for all these switches—not a trivial task.

Von Neumann proposed that the instructions that control the operation of the computer be encoded as binary values and stored internally in the memory unit along with the data. To solve a new problem, instead of rewiring the machine, you would rewrite the sequence of instructions—that is, create a new program. Von Neumann invented programming as it is known today.

The model of computing proposed by Von Neumann included many other important features found on all modern computing systems, and to honor him this model of computation has come to be known as the Von Neumann architecture. We will study this architecture in great detail in Chapters 4 and 5.

Von Neumann's research group at the University of Pennsylvania implemented his ideas, and they built one of the first stored program computers, called EDVAC, in 1949. At about the same time, a stored program computer called EDSAC was built at Cambridge University in England under the direction of Professor Maurice Wilkes. The appearance of these machines and others like them ushered in the modern computer age. Even though they were much slower, bulkier, and less powerful than our current machines, EDVAC and EDSAC executed programs in a fashion surprisingly similar to the miniaturized and immensely more powerful computers of the twenty-first century. A commercial model of the EDVAC, called UNIVAC I—the first computer actually sold—was built by Eckert and Mauchly and delivered to the U.S. Bureau of the Census on March 31, 1951. (It ran for 12 years before it was retired, shut off for the last time, and moved to the Smithsonian Institution.) This date marks the true beginning of the "computer age."

The importance of Von Neumann's contributions to computer systems development cannot be overstated. Although his original proposals are about 70 years old, virtually every computer built today is a Von Neumann machine in its basic design. A lot has changed in computing, and a sleek new iPad and the bulky EDVAC would appear to have little in common. However, the basic principles on which these two very disparate machines are constructed are virtually identical, and the same theoretical model underlies their operation. There is an old saying in computer science: "There is nothing new since Von Neumann!" This saying is certainly not true (much *has* happened), but it demonstrates the importance and amazing staying power of Von Neumann's original design.

John Von Neumann
(1903–1957)

John Von Neumann was born in Budapest, Hungary. He was a child prodigy who could divide 8-digit numbers in his head by the age of 6. He was a genius in virtually every field that he studied, including physics, economics, engineering, and mathematics. At 18, he received an award as the best mathematician in Hungary, a country known for excellence in the field, and he received his Ph.D., summa cum laude, at 21. He came to the United States in 1930 to be a guest lecturer at Princeton University and taught there for 3 years. Then, in 1933 he became one of the founding members (along with Albert Einstein) of the Institute for Advanced Studies, where he worked for 20 years.

Source: Los
Alamos National
Laboratory

He was one of the most brilliant minds of the twentieth century, a true genius in every sense, both good and bad. He could do prodigious mental feats in his head, and his thought processes usually raced far ahead of "ordinary" mortals, who found him quite difficult to work with. One of his colleagues described him as possessing the most fearsome technical intellect of the century. Another joked that "Johnny wasn't really human, but after living among them for so long, he learned to do a remarkably good imitation of one."

Von Neumann was a brilliant theoretician who did pioneering work in pure mathematics, operations research, game theory, and theoretical physics. He was also an engineer, concerned about practicalities and real-world problems, and it was this interest in applied issues that led Von Neumann to design and construct the first stored program computer. One of the early computers built by the RAND Corp. in 1953 was affectionately called "Johnniac" in his honor, although Von Neumann detested that name. Following its shutdown, it was moved to the Computer History Museum in Mountain View, California.

1.4.3 The Modern Era: 1950 to the Present

The last 65 or so years of computer development have involved taking the Von Neumann architecture and improving it in terms of hardware and software. Since 1950, computer systems development has been primarily an *evolutionary* process, not a revolutionary one. The enormous number of changes in computers in recent decades has made them faster, smaller, cheaper, more reliable, and easier to use but has not drastically altered their basic underlying structure.

The period 1950–1957 (these dates are very rough approximations) is often called the *first generation* of computing. This era saw the appearance of UNIVAC I, the first computer built for sale, and the IBM 701, the first computer

And the Verdict Is …

Our discussion of what was happening in computing from 1939 to 1946 showed that many groups were involved in designing and building the first computers. Therefore, it would seem that no single individual can be credited with the title "Inventor of the Electronic Digital Computer."

Surprisingly, that is not true. In February 1964, the Sperry Rand Corp. (now UNISYS) was granted a U.S. patent on the ENIAC computer as the first fully electronic computing device, with J. Presper Eckert and John Mauchly listed as its designers and builders. However, in 1967 a suit was filed in U.S. District Court in Minneapolis, Minnesota, to overturn that patent. The suit, *Honeywell v. Sperry Rand*, was heard before U.S. Federal Judge Earl Larson, and on October 19, 1973, Judge Larson handed down his verdict. (This enormously important verdict was never given the media coverage it deserved because it happened in the middle of the Watergate hearings and on the very day that Vice President Spiro Agnew resigned in disgrace for tax fraud.) Judge Larson overturned the ENIAC patent on the basis that Eckert and Mauchly had been significantly influenced in their 1943–1944 work on ENIAC by earlier research and development work by John Atanasoff at Iowa State University. During the period 1939–1943, Mauchly had communicated extensively with Atanasoff and had even traveled to Iowa to see the ABC machine in person. In a sense, the verdict declared that Professor Atanasoff was the inventor of the electronic digital computer. This decision was never appealed. Therefore, the official honor of having designed and built the first computer, at least in U.S. District Court, goes to Professor John Vincent Atanasoff.

On November 13, 1990, in a formal ceremony at the White House, President George H.W. Bush awarded Professor Atanasoff the National Medal of Technology for his pioneering contributions to the development of the computer.

built by the company that would soon become a leader in this new field. These early systems were similar in design to EDVAC, and they were bulky, expensive, slow, and unreliable. They used vacuum tubes for processing and storage, and they were extremely difficult to maintain. The simple act of turning on the machine could blow out a dozen tubes! For this reason, first-generation machines were used only by trained personnel and only in specialized locations such as large corporations, government and university research labs, and military installations, which could provide this expensive support environment.

The *second generation* of computing, roughly 1957–1965, heralded a major change in the size and complexity of computers. In the late 1950s, the bulky vacuum tube was replaced by a single transistor only a few millimeters in size, and memory was now constructed using tiny magnetic cores only 1/50th of an inch in diameter. (We will introduce and describe both devices in Chapter 4.) These technologies not only dramatically reduced the size of computers but also increased their reliability and reduced costs. Suddenly, buying and using a computer became a real possibility for some small and medium-sized businesses, colleges, and government agencies. This was also the era of the appearance of FORTRAN and COBOL, the first high-level (English-like) programming languages. (We will study this type of programming language in Chapters 9 and 10.) Now it was no longer necessary to be an electrical engineer to solve a problem on a computer. One simply needed to learn how to write commands in a high-level language. The occupation called *programmer* was born.

This miniaturization process continued into the *third generation* of computing, which lasted from about 1965 to 1975. This was the era of the *integrated circuit.* Rather than using discrete electronic components, integrated circuits with transistors, resistors, and capacitors were photographically etched onto a piece of silicon, which further reduced the size and cost of computers. From building-sized to room-sized, computers now became desk-sized, and this period saw the birth of the first minicomputer—the PDP-1 manufactured by the Digital Equipment Corp. It also saw the birth of the *software industry,* as companies sprang up to provide programs such as accounting packages and statistical programs to the ever-increasing numbers of computer users. By the mid-1970s, computers were no longer a rarity. They were being widely used throughout industry, government, the military, and education.

The *fourth generation,* roughly 1975–1985, saw the appearance of the first microcomputer. Integrated circuit technology had advanced to the point that a complete computer system could be contained on a single circuit board that you could hold in your hand. The desk-sized machine of the early 1970s now became a desktop machine, shrinking to the size of a typewriter. The Altair 8800, the world's first microcomputer, appeared in January 1975 (see the Special Interest Box on the next page).

It soon became unusual *not* to see a computer on someone's desk. The software industry poured forth all types of new packages—spreadsheets, databases, word processors, and presentation graphics—to meet the needs of the burgeoning user population. This era saw the appearance of the first *computer networks*, as users realized that much of the power of computers lies in their facilitation of communication with other users. (We will look at networking in great detail in Chapter 7.) *Electronic mail* became an important application. Because so many users were computer novices, the concept of *user-friendly systems* emerged. This included new *graphical user interfaces* with pull-down menus, icons, and other visual aids to make computing easier and more fun. *Embedded systems*—devices that contain a computer to control their internal operation— first appeared during this generation. Computers were becoming small enough to be placed inside cars, thermostats, microwave ovens, and wristwatches.

The World's First Microcomputer

The Altair 8800, shown below, was the first microcomputer and made its debut on the cover of *Popular Electronics* in January 1975. Its developer, Ed Roberts, owned a tiny electronics store in Albuquerque, New Mexico. His company was in desperate financial shape when he read about a new microprocessor from Intel, the Intel 8080. Roberts reasoned that this new chip could be used to sell a complete personal computer in kit form. He bought these new chips from Intel at the bargain basement price of $75 each and packaged them in a kit called the Altair 8800 (named after a location in the TV series Star Trek), which he offered to hobbyists for $397. Roberts figured he might sell a few hundred kits a year, enough to keep his company afloat temporarily. He ended up selling hundreds of them per day! The Altair microcomputer kits were so popular that he could not keep them in stock, and legend has it that people even drove to New Mexico and camped out in the parking lot to buy their computers.

This is particularly amazing in view of the fact that the original Altair was difficult to assemble and had only 256 memory cells, no I/O devices, and no software support. To program it, the user had to enter binary machine language instructions directly from the console switches. But even though it could do very little, people loved it because it was a real computer, and it was theirs.

The Intel 8080 chip did have the capability of running programs written in the language called BASIC that had been developed at Dartmouth in the early 1960s. A small software company located in Washington state wrote Ed Roberts a letter telling him that it had a BASIC compiler that could run on his Altair, making it much easier to use. That company was called Microsoft—and, as they say, the rest is history.

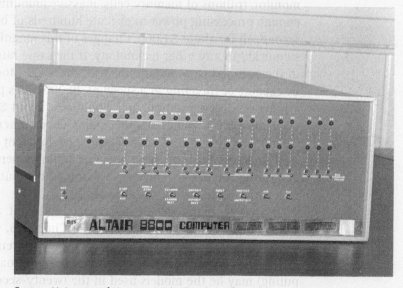

Source: University of Hawai'i at Hilo Graphics Services

The *fifth generation*, 1985–?, is where we are today. However, so much is changing so fast that the concept of distinct generations of computer development has outlived its usefulness. In computer science, change is now a constant companion. Some of the recent developments in computer systems include the following:

- Massively parallel processors containing millions of processors and capable of quadrillions (10^{15}) of computations per second

- Ultra-high-resolution graphics for 3D imaging, animation, movie making, video games, and virtual reality

- Powerful multimedia user interfaces incorporating sound, voice recognition, touch, photography, video, television, and body measurement data such as fingerprints, heartbeat, and retinal scans

- Integrated digital devices incorporating data, television, telephone, camera, fax, the Internet, and medical monitoring

- Self-driving, computer-controlled cars and automated computerized robotics

- Massive cloud storage devices capable of holding 100 exabytes (10^{20}) of data; that is equivalent to 100 billion gigabytes

- Ubiquitous computing, in which miniature computers are embedded into cars, cameras, kitchen appliances, home heating systems, clothing, and even our bodies

In only a few decades, computers have progressed from the UNIVAC I, which cost millions of dollars, had a few thousand memory locations, and was capable of only a few thousand operations per second, to today's top-of-the-line graphics design workstations with a high-definition, flat panel monitor, trillions of memory cells, massive amounts of external storage, and enough processing power to execute hundreds of billions of instructions per second, all for about $1,000. Changes of this magnitude have never occurred so quickly in any other technology. If the same rate of change had occurred in the auto industry, beginning with the 1909 Model-T, today's cars would be capable of traveling at a speed of 20,000 miles per hour, would get about 1 million miles per gallon, and would cost about $1.00!

Figure 1.8 summarizes the major developments that occurred during each of the generations of computer development discussed in this section. And underlying all of these amazing improvements, the theoretical model describing the design and construction of computers has not changed significantly in the last 70 years.

However, many people feel that significant and important structural changes are on the way. At the end of Chapter 5, we will introduce models of computing that are fundamentally quite different from the Von Neumann architecture in use today. These totally new approaches (e.g., quantum computing) may be the models used in the twenty-second century and beyond.

FIGURE 1.8

Generation	Approximate Dates	Major Advances
First	1950–1957	First commercial computers
		First symbolic programming languages
		Use of binary arithmetic, vacuum tubes for storage
		Punched card input/output
Second	1957–1965	Transistors and core memories
		First disks for mass storage
		Size reduction, increased reliability, lower costs
		First high-level programming languages
		First operating systems
Third	1965–1975	Integrated circuits
		Further reduction in size and cost, increased reliability
		First minicomputers
		Time-shared operating systems
		Appearance of the software industry
		First set of computing standards for compatibility between systems
Fourth	1975–1985	Large-scale and very-large-scale integrated circuits
		Further reduction in size and cost, increased reliability
		First microcomputers
		Growth of new types of software and of the software industry
		Computer networks
		Graphical user interfaces
Fifth	1985–?	Ultra-large-scale integrated circuits
		Supercomputers and parallel processors
		Laptops, tablets, smartphones, and handheld wireless devices
		Mobile computing
		Massive external data storage devices
		Ubiquitous computing
		High-resolution graphics, visualization, virtual reality
		Worldwide networks and cloud computing
		Multimedia user interfaces
		Widespread use of digitized sound, images, and movies

Some of the major advancements in computing

DEFINITION
Computer science: the study of algorithms, including

1. Their formal and mathematical properties
2. Their hardware realizations
3. Their linguistic realizations
4. Their applications

1.5 Organization of the Text

This book is divided into six separate sections, called levels, each of which addresses one aspect of the definition of computer science that appears at the beginning of this chapter. Let's repeat the definition and see how it maps into the sequence of topics to be presented.

Computer science is the study of algorithms, including

1. *Their formal and mathematical properties.* Level 1 of the text (Chapters 2 and 3) is titled "The Algorithmic Foundations of Computer Science." It continues the discussion of algorithmic problem solving begun in Sections 1.2 and 1.3 by introducing important mathematical and logical properties of algorithms. Chapter 2 presents the development of several algorithms that solve important technical problems—certainly more "technical" than shampooing your hair. It also looks at concepts related to the problem-solving process, such as how we discover and create good algorithms, what notation we can use to express our solutions, and how we can check to see whether our proposed algorithm correctly solves the desired problem.

   Our brute force chess example illustrates that it is not enough simply to develop a correct algorithm; we also want a solution that is efficient and that produces the desired result in a reasonable amount of time. (Would you want to market a chess-playing program that takes 10^{25} years to make its first move?) Chapter 3 describes ways to compare the efficiency of different algorithms and select the best one to solve a given problem. The material in Level 1 provides the necessary foundation for a study of the discipline of computer science.

2. *Their hardware realizations.* Although our initial look at computer science investigated how an algorithm behaved when executed by some abstract "computing agent," we ultimately want to execute our algorithms on "real" machines to get "real" answers. Level 2 of the text (Chapters 4 and 5) is titled "The Hardware World," and it looks at how to design and construct computer systems. It approaches this topic from two quite different viewpoints.

   Chapter 4 presents a detailed discussion of the underlying hardware. It introduces the basic building blocks of computers—binary numbers, transistors, logic gates, and circuits—and shows how these elementary electronic devices can be used to construct components to perform arithmetic and logic functions such as addition, subtraction, comparison, and sequencing. Although it is both interesting and important, this perspective produces a rather low-level view of a computer system. It is difficult to understand how a computer works by studying only these elementary components, just as it would be difficult to understand human behavior by investigating the behavior of individual cells. Therefore, Chapter 5 takes a higher-level view of computer hardware. It looks at computers not as a bunch of wires and circuits but as an integrated collection of subsystems called memory, processor, storage, input/output, and communications. It will explain in great detail the principles of the Von Neumann architecture introduced in Section 1.4.

A study of computer systems can be done at an even higher level. To understand how a computer works, we do not need to examine the functioning of every one of the thousands of components inside a machine. Instead, we need only be aware of a few critical pieces that are essential to our work. From the user's perspective, everything else is superfluous. This "user-oriented" view of a computer system and its resources is called a virtual machine or a virtual environment. A virtual machine is composed only of the resources that the user perceives rather than of all the hardware resources that actually exist.

This viewpoint is analogous to our level of understanding of what happens under the hood of a car. There may be thousands of mechanical components inside an automobile engine, but most of us concern ourselves only with the items reported on the dashboard—for example, oil pressure, fuel level, engine temperature. This is our "virtual engine," and that is all we need or want to know. We are all too happy to leave the remaining details about engine design to our friendly neighborhood mechanic.

Level 3 (Chapters 6, 7, and 8), titled "The Virtual Machine," describes how a virtual environment is created using a component called *system software*. Chapter 6 takes a look at the most important and widely used piece of system software on a modern computer system, the *operating system*, which controls the overall operation of a computer and makes it easier for users to access. Chapter 7 then goes on to describe how this virtual environment can extend beyond the boundaries of a single system as it examines how to interconnect individual machines into *computer networks* and *distributed systems* that provide users with access to a huge collection of computer systems and information as well as an enormous number of other users. It is the system software, and the virtual machine it creates, that makes computer hardware manageable and usable. Finally, Chapter 8 discusses a critically important component of a virtual machine—the *security system* that validates who you are and ensures that you are not attempting to carry out an improper, illegal, or unsafe operation. As computers become central to the management of such sensitive data as medical records, military information, and financial data, this aspect of system software is taking on even greater importance.

3. *Their linguistic realizations.* After studying hardware design, computer organization, and virtual machines, you will have a good idea of the techniques used to design and build computers. In the next section of the text, we ask the question, how can this hardware be used to solve important and interesting problems? Level 4, titled "The Software World" (Chapters 9–12), takes a look at what is involved in designing and implementing computer software. It investigates the programs and instruction sequences executed by the hardware, rather than the hardware itself.

Chapter 9 compares several high-level programming languages and introduces fundamental concepts related to the topic of computer programming regardless of the particular language being studied. This single chapter is certainly not intended to make you a proficient programmer, and this book is not meant to be a programming text. Instead, its purpose is to illustrate some basic features of modern programming languages and give you an appreciation for the interesting and challenging task of the computer programmer. Rather than print a separate version of this text for each programming language, the textual material specific to each language can be found on the website for this text, and you can download the pages for the language specified by your instructor and used in your class. See the Preface of this text for instructions on accessing these webpages.

There are many programming languages, such as C++, Python, Java, and Perl, that can be used to encode algorithms. Chapter 10 provides an overview of a number of different languages and language models in current use, including the functional and parallel models. Chapter 11 describes how a program written in a high-level programming language can be translated into the low-level machine language codes first described in Chapter 5. Finally, Chapter 12 shows that, even when we marshal all the powerful hardware and software ideas described in the first 11 chapters, problems exist that cannot be solved algorithmically. Chapter 12 demonstrates that there are, indeed, limits to computing.

4. *Their applications*. Most people are concerned not with creating programs but with using programs, just as there are few automotive engineers but many, many drivers. Level 5, titled "Applications" (Chapters 13–16), moves from *how* to write a program to *what* these programs can do.

Chapters 13 through 16 explore just a few of the many important and rapidly growing applications of computers, such as simulation, visualization, ecommerce, databases, artificial intelligence, computer graphics, and entertainment. Amazing as these applications seem, underneath their "shiny covers" they rely on the computer concepts of earlier chapters. Of course, we cannot possibly survey all the ways in which computers are being used today or will be used in the future. Indeed, there is hardly an area in our modern, complex society that has not been affected in some important way by information technology. (An excellent demonstration of this is that there are now 2.8 million apps available to Android users and 2.2 million available for downloading from the Apple App Store.) Readers interested in applications not discussed here should seek readings specific to their own areas of interest.

Some computer science professionals are not concerned with building computers, creating programs, or using any of the applications just described. Instead, they are interested in the social and cultural impact—both positive and negative—of this ever-changing technology. The sixth level of this text addresses this important perspective on computer science. This is not part of the original definition of computer science but has become an important area of study. In Level 6, titled "Social Issues" (Chapter 17), we move to the highest level of abstraction—the view furthest removed from the computer itself—to discuss social, ethical, legal, and professional issues related to computer and information technology. These issues are critically important because even individuals not directly involved in developing or using computers are deeply affected by them, just as society has been drastically and permanently altered by such technological developments as telephones, televisions, automobiles, and nuclear power. This last chapter takes a look at such thorny and difficult topics as computer crime, information privacy, and intellectual property. It also looks at one of the most important phenomena supported by this new technology, the creation of social networks such as Facebook, Twitter, LinkedIn, and Pinterest. Because it is impossible to resolve all the complex questions that arise in these areas, our intent is simply to raise your awareness and provide some decision-making tools to help you reach your own conclusions.

The overall six-layer hierarchy of this text is summarized in Figure 1.9. The organizational structure diagrammed in Figure 1.9 is one of the most

FIGURE 1.9

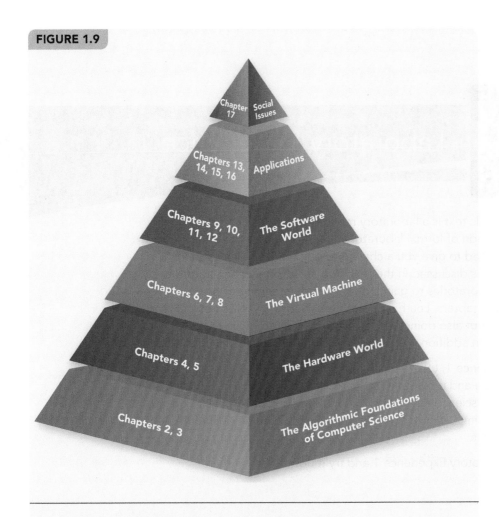

Organization of the text into a six-layer hierarchy

important aspects of this text. To describe a field of study, it is not enough to present a mass of facts and explanations. For learners to absorb, understand, and integrate this information, there must be a theme, a relationship, a thread that ties together the various parts of the narrative—in essence, a "big picture." Our big picture is Figure 1.9.

We first lay out the basic foundations of computer science (Level 1). We then proceed upward through five distinct layers of abstraction, from extremely low-level machine details such as electronic circuits and computer hardware (Level 2), through intermediate levels that address virtual machines (Level 3) and programming languages and software development (Level 4), to higher levels that investigate computer applications (Level 5), and address the use and misuse of information technology (Level 6). The material in each level provides a foundation to reveal the beauty and complexity of a higher and more abstract view of the discipline of computer science.

Laboratory Experience 1

Associated with this text is a laboratory manual that includes software packages and a collection of formal laboratory exercises. These Laboratory Experiences are designed to give you a chance to build on, modify, and experiment with the ideas discussed in the text. You are strongly encouraged to carry out these laboratories to gain a deeper understanding of the concepts presented in the chapters. Learning computer science involves not just reading and listening but also doing and trying. Our laboratory exercises will give you that chance. (In addition, we hope that you will find them fun.)

Laboratory Experience 1, titled "Building A Glossary," introduces you to this laboratory package and provides a useful tool that you may use during your study of computer science and in other courses as well. You will learn how to build a glossary of important technical terms along with their definitions and locations in the text.

Please open Laboratory Experience 1 and try it now.

EXERCISES

1. Identify some algorithms, apart from DVR instructions and cooking recipes, that you encounter in your everyday life. Write them out in any convenient notation, and explain how they meet all of the criteria for algorithms presented in this chapter.

2. A concept related, but not identical, to an algorithm is the idea of a *heuristic*. Read about heuristics and identify differences between the two. Describe a heuristic for obtaining an approximate answer to the sum of two three-digit numbers and show how this "addition heuristic" differs from the addition algorithm of Figure 1.2.

3. In the DVR instructions in Figure 1.1, Step 3 says, "Enter the channel number that you want to record and press the button labeled CHAN." Is that an unambiguous and well-defined operation? Explain why or why not.

4. Identify which type of algorithmic operation each one of the following steps belongs to:

    a. Get a value for x from the user.

    b. Test to determine if x is positive. If not, tell the user that he or she has made a mistake.

    c. Take the cube root of x.

    d. Do Steps 1.1, 1.2, and 1.3 x times.

5. Trace through the decimal addition algorithm of Figure 1.2 using the following input values:

$$m = 3 \quad a_2 = 1 \quad a_1 = 4 \quad a_0 = 9$$
$$b_2 = 0 \quad b_1 = 2 \quad b_0 = 9$$

    At each step, show the values for c_3, c_2, c_1, c_0, and *carry*.

6. Modify the decimal addition algorithm of Figure 1.2 so that it does not print out nonsignificant leading zeroes; that is, the answer to Exercise 5 would appear as 178 rather than 0178.

7. Modify the decimal addition algorithm of Figure 1.2 so that the two numbers being added need not have the same number of digits. That is, the algorithm should be able to add a value *a* containing *m* digits to a value *b* containing *n* digits, where *m* may or may not be equal to *n*.

8. Under what conditions would the well-known quadratic formula

$$Roots = \frac{-b \pm \sqrt{b^2 - 4ac}}{2a}$$

    not be effectively computable? (Assume that you are working with real numbers.)

9. Compare the two solutions to the shampooing algorithm shown in Figures 1.3 and 1.4. Which do you think is a better general-purpose solution? Why? (*Hint:* What if you wanted to wash your hair 1,000 times?)

10. The following is Euclid's 2,300-year-old algorithm for finding the greatest common divisor of two positive integers *I* and *J*.

Step	Operation
1	Get two positive integers as input; call the larger value *I* and the smaller value *J*
2	Divide *I* by *J*, and call the remainder *R*
3	If *R* is *not* 0, then reset *I* to the value of *J*, reset *J* to the value of *R*, and go back to Step 2
4	Print out the answer, which is the value of *J*
5	Stop

    a. Go through this algorithm using the input values 20 and 32. After each step of the algorithm is completed, give the values of *I*, *J*, and *R*. Determine the final output of the algorithm.

    b. Does the algorithm work correctly when the two inputs are 0 and 32? Describe exactly what happens, and modify the algorithm so that it gives an appropriate error message.

11. A salesperson wants to visit 25 cities while minimizing the total number of miles she must drive. Because she has studied computer science, she decides to design an algorithm to determine the optimal order in which to visit the cities to (1) keep her driving distance to a minimum, and (2) visit each city exactly once. The algorithm that she has devised is the following:

> The computer first lists *all* possible ways to visit the 25 cities and then, for each one, determines the total mileage associated with that particular ordering. (Assume that the computer has access to data that gives the distances between all cities.) After determining the total mileage for each possible trip, the computer searches for the ordering with the minimum mileage and prints out the list of cities on that optimal route, that is, the order in which the salesperson should visit her destinations.

If a computer could analyze 10,000,000 separate paths per second, how long would it take to determine the optimal route for visiting these 25 cities? On the basis of your answer, do you think this is a feasible algorithm? If it is not, can you think of a way to obtain a reasonable solution to this problem?

12. One way to do multiplication is by repeated addition. For example, 47 × 25 can be evaluated as 47 + 47 + 47 + ... + 47 (25 times). Sketch out an algorithm for multiplying two positive numbers a and b using this technique.

13. A student was asked to develop an algorithm to find and output the largest of three numerical values x, y, and z that are provided as input. Here is what was produced:

Input: x, y, z

Algorithm: Check if $(x > y)$ and $(x > z)$. If it is, then output the value of x and stop. Otherwise, continue to the next line.
Check if $(y > x)$ and $(y > z)$. If it is, then output the value of y and stop. Otherwise, continue to the next line.
Check if $(z > x)$ and $(z > y)$. If it is, then output the value of z and stop.

Is this a correct solution to the problem? Explain why or why not. If it is incorrect, fix the algorithm so that it is a correct solution.

14. Read about one of the early pioneers mentioned in this chapter—Pascal, Liebnitz, Jacquard, Babbage, Lovelace, Hollerith, Eckert, Mauchly, Aiken, Zuse, Atanasoff, Turing, or Von Neumann. Write a paper describing in detail that person's contribution to computing and computer science.

15. Get the technical specifications of the computer on which you are working (either from a technical manual or from your computer center staff). Determine its cost, its processing speed (in GIPS, billions of instructions per second), its computational speed (in GFlops, billions of floating point operations per second), and the size of its primary memory.

Compare those values with what was typically available on first-, second-, and third-generation computer systems, and calculate the percentage improvement between your computer and the first commercial machines of the early 1950s.

16. A rapidly growing area of computer science is *ubiquitous computing*, in which computers automatically provide services for a user without that user's knowledge or awareness. For example, a computer located in your car contacts the garage door opener and tells it to open the garage door when the car is close to home. Read about this new model of computing and write a paper describing some of its applications. What are some of the possible problems that could result?

17. Another important new area of computer science is *cloud computing*, which relies on a computer network, along with networking software, to provide transparent access to remote data and applications. Read about

this new model of data and software access and write a paper describing some of the important uses, as well as potential risks, of this new information structure.

18. A standard computer DVD holds approximately 5 billion characters. Estimate how many linear feet of shelf space would be required to house 5 billion characters encoded as printed bound books rather than as electronic media. Assume there are 5 characters per word, 300 words per page, and 300 pages per inch of shelf.

CHALLENGE WORK

1. Assume we have a "computing agent" that knows how to do one-digit subtraction where the first digit is at least as large as the second (i.e., we do not end up with a negative number). Thus, our computing agent can do such operations as $7 - 3 = 4$, $9 - 1 = 8$, and $5 - 5 = 0$. It can also subtract a one-digit value from a two-digit value in the range 10–18 as long as the final result has only a single digit. This capability enables it to do such operations as $13 - 7 = 6$, $10 - 2 = 8$, and $18 - 9 = 9$.

   Using these primitive capabilities, design an algorithm to do *decimal subtraction* on two *m*-digit numbers, where $m \geq 1$. You will be given two unsigned whole numbers (a_{m-1}, $a_{m-2} \ldots a_0$) and b_{m-1}, $b_{m-2} \ldots b_0$. Your algorithm must compute the value $c_{m-1} c_{m-2} \ldots c_0$, the difference of these two values.

   $$\begin{array}{r} a_{m-1}a_{m-2}\ldots a_0 \\ - b_{m-1}b_{m-2}\ldots b_0 \\ \hline c_{m-1}c_{m-2}\ldots c_0 \end{array}$$

   You may assume that the top number ($a_{m-1} \, a_{m-2} \ldots a_0$) is greater than or equal to the bottom number ($b_{m-1} \, b_{m-2} \ldots b_0$) so that the result is not a negative value. However, do not assume that each individual digit a_i is greater than or equal to b_i. If the digit on the bottom is larger than the digit on the top, then you must implement a *borrowing scheme* to allow the subtraction to continue. (*Caution:* It may have been easy to learn subtraction as a first grader, but it is devilishly difficult to tell a computer how to do it!)

2. Our definition of the field of computer science is only one of many that have been proposed. Because it is so young, people working in the field are still debating how best to define exactly what they do. Review the literature of computer science (see the companion site for this text and chapter for some ideas) and browse the web to locate other definitions of computer science. Compare these definitions with the one presented in this chapter and discuss the differences among them. Discuss how different definitions may give you a vastly different perspective on the field and what people in this field do. [*Note:* A very well-known and widely used definition of computer science was presented in "Report of the ACM Task Force on the Core of Computer Science," reprinted in the journal *Communications of the ACM*, vol. 32, no. 1 (January 1989).]

3. Our focus on the history of computing looked primarily at the U.S. and the U.K.—devices like the Mark I, ENIAC, EDVAC, Colossus, ABC, and UNIVAC I. However, in a recent article by Herbert Bruderer in the *Communications of the ACM* entitled "Computing History Beyond the UK and the US: Selected Landmarks From Continental Europe" (Vol. 60, No 2, pp. 76-84), the author takes a closer look at the contributions to computer science by engineers, scientists, and mathematicians from France, Germany, Switzerland, Spain, and other European centers of learning. Take a look at that article and write a report on the fundamental contributions to computing from one specific scholar or from one specific country.

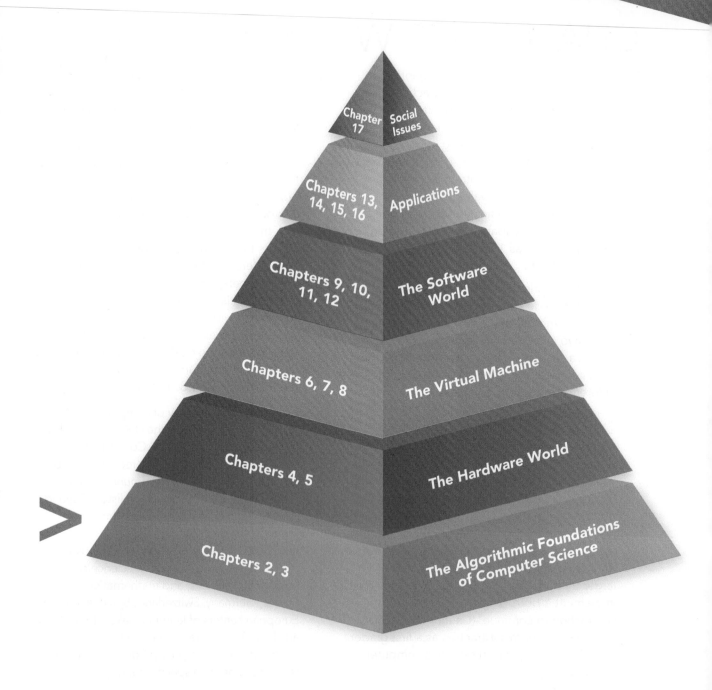

Level 1 of the text continues our exploration of algorithms and algorithmic problem solving—essential material for studying any branch of computer science. It first introduces methods for designing and representing algorithms. It then uses these ideas to develop solutions to some real-world problems, including an important application in medicine and biology.

When judging the quality of an essay or book report, we do not look only at sentence structure, spelling, and punctuation. Although grammatical issues are important, we also must evaluate the work's style, for it is a combination of correctness and expressiveness that produces a written document of high quality. So, too, for algorithms: Correctness is not the only measure of excellence. This section will present criteria for evaluating the quality and elegance of the algorithmic solutions that you develop.

2 Algorithm Discovery and Design

AFTER STUDYING THIS CHAPTER, YOU WILL BE ABLE TO:

- Explain the benefits of pseudocode over natural language or a programming language
- Represent algorithms using pseudocode
- Identify algorithm statements as sequential, conditional, or iterative
- Define abstraction and top-down design, and explain their use in breaking down complex problems
- Illustrate the operation of algorithms for:
    - Multiplication by repeated addition
    - Sequential search of a collection of values
    - Finding the maximum element in a collection
    - Finding a pattern string in a larger piece of text

2.1 Introduction

Chapter 1 introduced algorithms and algorithmic problem solving, two of the most fundamental concepts in computer science. Our introduction used examples drawn from everyday life, such as programming a DVR (Figure 1.1) and washing your hair (Figures 1.3 and 1.4). Although these are perfectly valid examples of algorithms, they are not of much interest to computer scientists. This chapter develops more fully the notions of algorithms and algorithmic problem solving and applies these ideas to problems that *are* of interest to computer scientists: searching lists, finding maxima and minima, and matching patterns.

2.2 Representing Algorithms

2.2.1 Pseudocode

Before presenting any algorithms, we must first make an important decision. How should we represent them? What notation should we use to express our algorithms so that they are clear, precise, and unambiguous?

One possibility is *natural language*, the language we speak and write in our everyday lives. (This could be English, Spanish, Arabic, Japanese, Swahili,

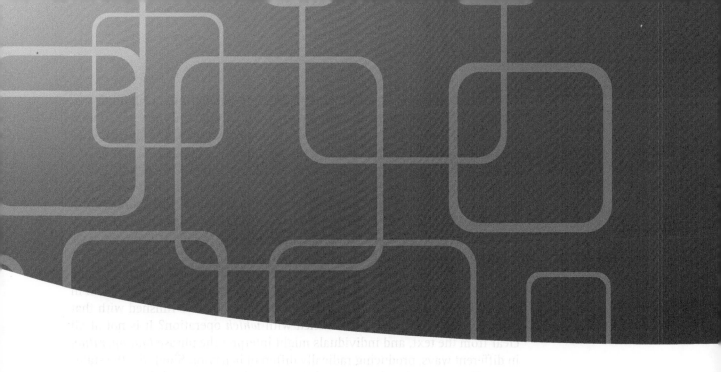

or any language.) This is an obvious choice because it is the language with which we are most familiar. If we use natural language, then our algorithms would read much the same as a term paper or an essay. For example, when expressed in natural language, the addition algorithm in Figure 1.2 might look something like the paragraph shown in Figure 2.1.

Comparing Figure 1.2 with Figure 2.1 illustrates the problems of using natural language to represent algorithms. Natural language can be extremely verbose, causing the resulting algorithms to be rambling, unstructured, and hard to follow. (Imagine reading 5, 10, or even 100 pages of text like Figure 2.1.) An unstructured, "free-flowing" writing style might be wonderful for novels and essays, but it is horrible for algorithms. The lack of structure makes it difficult for the reader to locate specific sections of the algorithm because they are buried deep within the text. For example, about two-thirds of the way through Figure 2.1 is the phrase, "… and begin the loop all over again." To what part of the algorithm does this refer? Without

---

FIGURE 2.1

Initially, set the value of the variable *carry* to 0 and the value of the variable i to 0. When these initializations have been completed, begin looping as long as the value of the variable i is less than or equal to $(m - 1)$. First, add together the values of the two digits a_i and b_i and the current value of the carry digit to get the result called c_i. Now check the value of c_i to see whether it is greater than or equal to 10. If c_i is greater than or equal to 10, then reset the value of *carry* to 1 and reduce the value of c_i by 10; otherwise, set the value of *carry* to 0. When you are finished with that operation, add 1 to i and begin the loop all over again. When the loop has completed execution, set the leftmost digit of the result c_m to the value of *carry* and print out the final result, which consists of the digits $c_m \, c_{m-1} \cdots c_0$. After printing the result, the algorithm is finished, and it terminates.

The addition algorithm of Figure 1.2 expressed in natural language any clues to guide us, such as indentation, line numbering, or highlighting, locating the beginning of that loop can be a daunting and time-consuming task. (For the record, the beginning of the loop corresponds to the sentence that starts, "When these initializations have been completed ... ." It is certainly not easy to determine this from a casual reading of the text.)

A second problem is that natural language is too "rich" in interpretation and meaning. Natural language frequently relies on either context or a reader's experiences to give precise meaning to a word or phrase. This permits different readers to interpret the same sentence in totally different ways. This may be acceptable, even desirable, when writing poetry or fiction, but it is disastrous when creating algorithms that must always execute in the same way and produce identical results. We can see an example of this problem in the sentence of Figure 2.1 that starts with "When you are finished with that operation ... ." When we are finished with *which* operation? It is not at all clear from the text, and individuals might interpret the phrase *that operation* in different ways, producing radically different behavior. Similarly, the statement "Determine the shortest path between the source and destination" is ambiguous until we know the precise meaning of the phrase "shortest path." Does it mean shortest in terms of travel time, distance, or something else?

Because natural languages are not sufficiently precise to represent algorithms, we might be tempted to go to the other extreme. If we are ultimately going to execute our algorithm on a computer, why not immediately write it out as a computer program using a *high-level programming language* such as C++ or Java? If we adopt that approach, the addition algorithm of Figure 1.2 might start out looking like the program fragment shown in Figure 2.2.

As an algorithmic design language, this notation is also seriously flawed. During the initial phases of design, we should be thinking at a highly abstract level. However, using a formal programming language to express our design forces us to deal immediately with highly detailed language issues, such as punctuation, grammar, and syntax. For example, the algorithm in Figure 1.2 contains an operation that says, "Set the value of *carry* to 0." This is an easy statement to understand. However, when translated into a language like C++ or Java, that statement becomes

    carry = 0;

Is this operation setting *carry* to 0 or asking if *carry* is equal to 0? Why does a semicolon appear at the end of the line? Would the statement

    Carry = 0;

mean the same thing? Similarly, what is meant by the utterly cryptic statement on Line 4 of Figure 2.2: int [] a = new int [100];? These technical details clutter our thoughts and at this point in the solution process are totally out of place. When creating algorithms, a programmer should no more worry about semicolons and capitalization than a novelist should worry about typography and cover design when writing the first draft!

If the two extremes of natural languages and high-level programming languages are both less than ideal, what notation should we use? What is the best way to represent the solutions shown in this chapter and the rest of the book?

FIGURE 2.2

```
{
    Scanner inp = new Scanner(System.in);
    int i, m, carry;
    int[] a = new int[100];
    int[] b = new int[100];
    int[] c = new int[100];
    m = inp.nextInt();
    for (int j = 0;j <= m-1;j++) {
        a[j] = inp.nextInt();
        b[j] = inp.nextInt();
    }
    carry = 0;
    i = 0;
    while (i < m) {
        c[i] = a[i] + b[i] + carry;
        if (c[i] >= 10)
                     .
                     .
                     .
```

The beginning of the addition algorithm of Figure 1.2 expressed in a high-level programming language

Most computer scientists use a notation called pseudocode to design and represent algorithms. This is a set of English-language constructs designed to more or less resemble statements in a programming language but that do not actually run on a computer. Pseudocode represents a compromise between the two extremes of natural and formal languages. It is simple, highly readable, and has virtually no grammatical rules. (In fact, pseudocode is sometimes jokingly referred to as "a programming language without the details.") However, because it contains only statements that have a well-defined structure, it is easier to visualize the organization of a pseudocode algorithm than one represented as long, rambling natural-language paragraphs. In addition, because pseudocode closely resembles many popular programming languages, the subsequent translation of the algorithm into a computer program is relatively simple. The algorithms shown in Figures 1.1–1.4, and Exercise 10 of Chapter 1 are all written in pseudocode.

In the following sections, we will introduce a set of popular and easy-to-understand constructs for the three types of algorithmic operations introduced in Chapter 1: sequential, conditional, and iterative. Keep in mind, however, that pseudocode is *not* a formal language with rigidly standardized syntactic and semantic rules and regulations. On the contrary, it is an informal design notation used solely to express algorithms. If you do not like the constructs presented in the next two sections, feel free to modify them or select others that are more helpful to you. One of the nice features of pseudocode is that you can adapt it to your own personal way of thinking and problem solving.

2.2.2 Sequential Operations

Our pseudocode must include instructions to carry out the three basic *sequential operations* called computation, input, and output.

The instruction for performing a computation and saving the result looks like the following. (Words and phrases inside quotation marks represent specific elements that you must insert when writing an algorithm.)

Set the value of "variable" to "arithmetic expression"

This operation evaluates the "arithmetic expression," gets a result, and stores that result in the "variable." A variable is simply a named storage location that can hold a data value. A variable is often compared with a mailbox into which you can place a value and from which you can retrieve a value. Let's look at an example.

Set the value of *carry* to 0

First, evaluate the arithmetic expression, which in this case is the constant value 0. Then store that result in the variable called *carry*. If *carry* had a previous value, say 1, that value will be discarded and replaced by 0. If *carry* did not yet have a value, it now does—the value 0. You can visualize the result of this operation as follows:

carry | 0 |

Here is another example:

Set the value of *Area* to (πr^2)

Assuming that the variable r has been given a value by a previous instruction in the algorithm, this statement evaluates the arithmetic expression πr^2 to produce a numerical result. This result is then stored in the variable called *Area*. If r does not have a value, an error condition occurs because this instruction is not effectively computable, and it cannot be completed.

We can see additional examples of computational operations in Steps 4, 6, and 7 of the addition algorithm of Figure 1.2:

Step 4:   Add the two digits a_i and b_i to the current value of *carry* to get c_i

Step 6:   Add 1 to i, effectively moving one column to the left

Step 7:   Set c_m to the value of *carry*

Note that these three steps are not written in exactly the format just described. If we had used that notation, they would have looked like this:

Step 4:   Set the value of c_i to ($a_i + b_i + carry$)

Step 6:   Set the value of i to ($i + 1$)

Step 7:   Set the value of c_m to *carry*

However, in pseudocode, it doesn't matter exactly how you choose to write your instructions as long as the intent is clear, effectively computable, and unambiguous. At this point in the design of a solution, we do not care about the minor linguistic differences between

> Add *a* and *b* to get *c*

and

> Set the value of *c* to (*a* + *b*)

Remember that pseudocode is not a precise set of notational rules to be memorized and rigidly followed. It is a flexible notation that can be adjusted to fit your own view about how best to express ideas and algorithms.

When writing arithmetic expressions, you may assume that the computing agent executing your algorithm has all the capabilities of a typical multifunction calculator. Therefore, it "knows" how to do all basic arithmetic operations such as $+$, $-$, $\times$, $\div$, $\sqrt{\ }$, absolute value, sine, cosine, and tangent. It also knows the value of important constants such as π.

The remaining two sequential operations enable our computing agent to communicate with "the outside world," which means everything other than the computing agent itself:

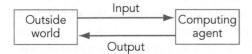

Input operations provide the computing agent with data values from the outside world that it may then use in later instructions. **Output** operations send results from the computing agent to the outside world. When the computing agent is a computer, communications with the outside world are done via the input/output equipment available on a typical computer, tablet, or smartphone, such as a physical keyboard, virtual keypad, screen, mouse, printer, hard drive, camera, or touch screen. However, when designing algorithms, we generally do not concern ourselves with the technical specifications of a particular device. At this point in the design process, we care only that data is provided to us when we request it, and that results are issued for presentation.

Our pseudocode instructions for input and output are expressed as follows:

> *Input:*   Get values for "variable", "variable", …
>
> *Output:*   Print the values of "variable", "variable", …

For example,

> Get a value for *r*, the radius of the circle

When the algorithm reaches this input operation, it waits until someone or something provides it with a value for the variable *r*. (In a computer, this may be done by entering a value at the keyboard.) When the algorithm has received and stored a value for *r*, it continues on to the next instruction.

Here is an example of an output operation:

Print the value of *Area*

Assuming that the algorithm has already computed the area of the circle, this instruction says to display that value to the outside world. This display may be viewed on a screen (computer, tablet, smartphone) or printed on paper by a printer.

Sometimes we use an output instruction to display a message in place of the desired results. If, for example, the computing agent cannot complete a computation because of an error condition, we might have it execute something like the following operation. (We will use 'single quotation marks' to enclose messages so as to distinguish them from such pseudocode constructs as "variable" and "arithmetic expression," which are enclosed in double quotation marks.)

Print the message 'Sorry, no answers could be computed.'

Using these three sequential operations—computation, input, and output—we can now write some simple but useful algorithms. Figure 2.3 presents an algorithm to compute the average miles per gallon on a trip, when given as input the number of gallons used and the starting and ending mileage readings on the odometer.

2.2.3 Conditional and Iterative Operations

The average miles per gallon algorithm in Figure 2.3 performs a set of operations once and then stops. It cannot select among alternative operations or perform a block of instructions more than once. A purely sequential algorithm of the type shown in Figure 2.3 is sometimes termed a *straight-line algorithm* because it executes its instructions in a straight line from top to bottom and then stops. Unfortunately, virtually all real-world problems are not straight-line in nature. They involve nonsequential operations such as branching and repetition.

To allow us to address these more interesting problems, our pseudocode needs two additional statements to implement conditional and iterative operations. Together, these two types of operations are called control operations; they allow us to alter the normal sequential flow of control in an algorithm. As we saw in Chapter 1, control operations are an essential part of all but the very simplest of algorithms.

FIGURE 2.3

Step	Operation
1	Get values for *gallons used, starting mileage, ending mileage*
2	Set value of *distance driven* to (*ending mileage – starting mileage*)
3	Set value of *average miles per gallon* to (*distance driven ÷ gallons used*)
4	Print the value of *average miles per gallon*
5	Stop

Algorithm for computing average miles per gallon (version 1)

Practice Problems

Write pseudocode versions of the following:

1. An algorithm that gets three data values x, y, and z as input and outputs the average of those three values.

2. An algorithm that gets the radius r of a circle as input. Its output is both the circumference and the area of a circle of radius r.

3. An algorithm that gets the amount of electricity used in kilowatt-hours and the cost of electricity per kilowatt-hour. Its output is the total amount of the electric bill, including an 8% sales tax.

4. An algorithm that inputs your current credit card balance, the total dollar amount of new purchases, and the total dollar amount of all payments. The algorithm computes the new balance, which includes a 12% interest charge on any unpaid balance.

5. An algorithm that is given the length and width, in feet, of a rectangular carpet and determines its total cost given that the material cost is $23 per square yard.

6. An algorithm that is given three numbers corresponding to the number of times a race car driver has finished first, second, and third. The algorithm computes and displays how many points that driver has earned given 5 points for a first, 3 points for a second, and 1 point for a third place finish.

Conditional statements are the "question-asking" operations of an algorithm. They allow an algorithm to ask a yes/no question and select the next operation to perform on the basis of the answer to that question. There are a number of ways to phrase a question, but the most common conditional statement is the *if/then/else* statement, which has the following format:

> If "a true/false condition" is true then
>   first set of algorithmic operations
> Else (or otherwise)
>   second set of algorithmic operations

The meaning of this statement is as follows:

1. Evaluate the true/false condition on the first line to determine whether it is true or false.

2. If the condition is true, then do the first set of algorithmic operations and skip the second set entirely.

3. If the condition is false, then skip the first set of operations and do the second set.

4. Once the appropriate set of operations has been completed, continue executing the algorithm with the operation that follows the if/then/else instruction.

Figure 2.4 is a visual model of the execution of the if/then/else statement. We evaluate the condition shown in the diamond. If the condition is true, we execute the sequence of operations labeled T1, T2, T3, ... If the condition is false, we execute the sequence labeled F1, F2, F3, ... In either case, however, execution continues with statement S, which is the one that immediately follows the if/then/else statement.

FIGURE 2.4

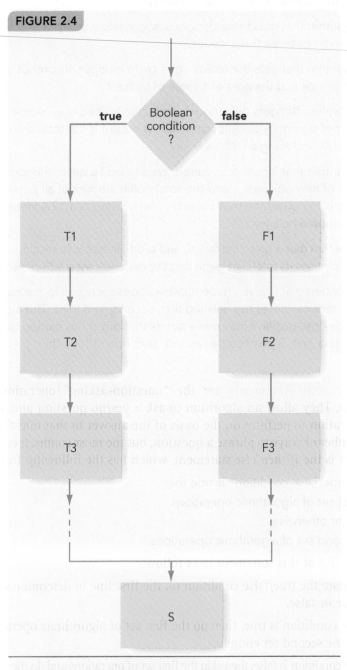

The if/then/else pseudocode statement

Basically, the if/then/else statement allows you to select exactly one of two alternatives—either/or, this or that. We saw an example of this statement in Step 5 of the addition algorithm shown in Figure 1.2. (The statement has been reformatted slightly to highlight the two alternatives clearly, but it has not been changed.)

If $(c_i \geq 10)$ then

   Set the value of c_i to $(c_i - 10)$

   Set the value of *carry* to 1

Else

   Set the value of *carry* to 0

The condition $(c_i \geq 10)$ can be only true or false. If it is true, then there is a carry into the next column, and we must do the first set of instructions—subtracting 10 from c_i and setting *carry* to 1. If the condition is false, then there is no carry—we skip over these two operations and perform the second block of operations, which simply sets the value of *carry* to 0.

Figure 2.5 shows another example of the if/then/else statement. It extends the miles per gallon algorithm of Figure 2.3 to include a second line of output stating whether you are getting good gas mileage. Good gas mileage is defined as a value for average miles per gallon strictly greater than 25.0 miles per gallon.

The last algorithmic statement to be introduced allows us to implement a *loop*—the repetition of a block of instructions. The real power of a computer comes not from doing a calculation once but from doing it many, many times. If, for example, we need to compute a single value of average miles per gallon, it would be foolish to convert an algorithm like Figure 2.5 into a computer program and execute it on a computer—it would be far faster to use a calculator, which could complete the job in a few seconds. However, if we need to do the same computation 1 million times, the power

FIGURE 2.5

Step	Operation
1	Get values for *gallons used, starting mileage, ending mileage*
2	Set value of *distance driven* to (*ending mileage – starting mileage*)
3	Set value of *average miles per gallon* to (*distance driven ÷ gallons used*)
4	Print the value of *average miles per gallon*
5	If *average miles per gallon* is >25.0 then
6	Print the message 'You are getting good gas mileage'
	Else
7	Print the message 'You are NOT getting good gas mileage'
8	Stop

Second version of the average miles per gallon algorithm

of a computer to repetitively execute a block of statements becomes quite apparent. If each computation of average miles per gallon takes 5 seconds on a hand calculator, then 1 million of them would require about 2 months, not allowing for such luxuries as sleeping and eating. Once the algorithm is developed and the program written, a computer could carry out that same task in a fraction of a second!

The first algorithmic statement that we will use to express the idea of iteration, also called *looping*, is the *while* statement:

While ("a true/false condition") do Step i to Step j

> Step i: operation
>
> Step $i + 1$:   operation
>
> .
>
> .
>
> .
>
> Step j: operation

This instruction initially evaluates the "true/false condition"—called the continuation condition—to determine if it is true or false. If the condition is true, all operations from Step i to Step j, inclusive, are executed. This block of operations is called the loop body. (Operations within the loop body should be indented so that it is clear to the reader of the algorithm which operations belong inside the loop.) When the entire loop body has finished executing, the algorithm again evaluates the continuation condition. If it is still true, then the algorithm executes the entire loop body, statements i through j, again. This looping process continues until the continuation condition evaluates to false, at which point execution of the loop body terminates and the algorithm proceeds to the statement immediately following the loop—Step $j + 1$ in the above pseudocode. If for some reason the continuation condition never becomes false, then we have violated one of the fundamental properties of an algorithm, and we have the error, first mentioned in Chapter 1, called an *infinite loop*.

Figure 2.6 is a visual model of the execution of a while loop. The algorithm first evaluates the continuation condition inside the diamond-shaped symbol. If it is true, then it executes the sequence of operations labeled S1, S2, S3, ... , which are the operations of the loop body. Then the algorithm returns to the top of the loop and reevaluates the condition. If the condition is false, then the loop has ended, and the algorithm continues executing with the statement after the loop, the one labeled S_n in Figure 2.6.

Here is a simple example of a loop:

Step	Operation
1	Set the value of *count* to 1
2	While (*count* ≤ 100) do Step 3 through Step 5
3	Set *square* to (*count* × *count*)
4	Print the values of *count* and *square*
5	Add 1 to *count*

FIGURE 2.6

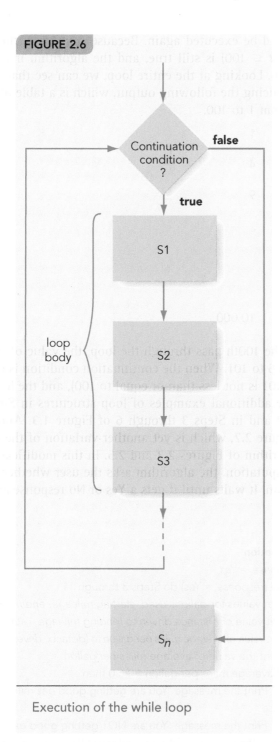

Execution of the while loop

Step 1 initializes *count* to 1, the next operation determines that (*count* ≤ 100), and then the loop body is executed, which in this case includes the three statements in Steps 3–5. Those statements compute the value of *count* squared (Step 3) and print the value of both *count* and *square* (Step 4). The last operation inside the loop body (Step 5) adds 1 to *count* so that it now has the value 2. At the end of the loop, the algorithm must determine whether it should be executed again. Because *count* is 2, the continuation condition (*count* ≤ 100) is still true, and the algorithm must perform the loop body again. Looking at the entire loop, we can see that it will execute 100 times, producing the following output, which is a table of numbers and their squares from 1 to 100.

1	1
2	4
3	9
.	.
.	.
.	.
100	10,000

At the end of the 100th pass through the loop, the value of *count* is incremented in Step 5 to 101. When the continuation condition is evaluated, it is false (because 101 is not less than or equal to 100), and the loop terminates.

We can see additional examples of loop structures in Steps 3 through 6 of Figure 1.2 and in Steps 3 through 6 of Figure 1.3. Another example is shown in Figure 2.7, which is yet another variation of the average miles per gallon algorithm of Figures 2.3 and 2.5. In this modification, after finishing one computation, the algorithm asks the user whether to repeat this calculation again. It waits until it gets a Yes or No response and repeats the

FIGURE 2.7

Step	Operation
1	*response* = Yes
2	While (*response* = Yes) do Steps 3 through 11
3	Get values for *gallons used, starting mileage, ending mileage*
4	Set value of *distance driven* to (*ending mileage – starting mileage*)
5	Set value of *average miles per gallon* to (*distance driven* ÷ *gallons used*)
6	Print the value of *average miles per gallon*
7	If average miles per gallon > 25.0 then
8	Print the message 'You are getting good gas mileage'
	Else
9	Print the message 'You are NOT getting good gas mileage'
10	Print the message 'Do you want to do this again? Enter Yes or No'
11	Get a new value for *response* from the user
12	Stop

Third version of the average miles per gallon algorithm

entire loop body until the response provided by the user is No. (Note that the algorithm must initialize the value of *response* to Yes because the very first thing that the loop does is test the value of this quantity.)

There are many variations of this particular looping construct in addition to the while statement just described. For example, it is common to omit the line numbers from algorithms and simply execute them in order, from top to bottom. In that case, we could use an "End of the loop" construct (or something similar) to mark the end of the loop rather than explicitly stating which steps are contained in the loop body. Using this approach, our loops would be written something like this:

While ("a true/false condition") do

    operation

      .

      .

      .

    operation

End of the loop

In this case, the loop body is delimited not by explicit step numbers but by the two lines that read, "While ..." and "End of the loop".

The type of loop just described is called a *pretest loop* because the continuation condition is tested at the *beginning* of each pass through the loop, and therefore it is possible for the loop body never to be executed. (This would happen if the continuation condition were *initially* false.) Sometimes this can be inconvenient, as we see in Figure 2.7. In that algorithm, the value of the variable called *response* is tested for the first time long before we ask the user if he or she wants to solve the problem again. Therefore, we had to give *response* a "dummy" value of Yes so that the test would be meaningful when the loop was initially entered.

A useful variation of the looping structure is called a *posttest loop*, which also uses a true/false continuation condition to control execution of the loop. However, now the test is done at the *end* of the loop body, not the beginning. The loop is typically expressed using the *do/while* statement, which is usually written as follows:

Do

    operation

    operation

     .

     .

     .

    operation

While ("a true/false condition")

This type of iteration performs all the algorithmic operations contained in the loop body before it evaluates the true/false condition specified at the end of the loop. If this condition is false, the loop is terminated and execution continues with the operation following the loop. If the condition is true, then the entire loop body is executed again. Note that in the do/while variation, the loop body is always executed at least once, whereas the while loop can execute 0, 1, or more times. Figure 2.8 diagrams the execution of the posttest do/while looping structure.

FIGURE 2.8

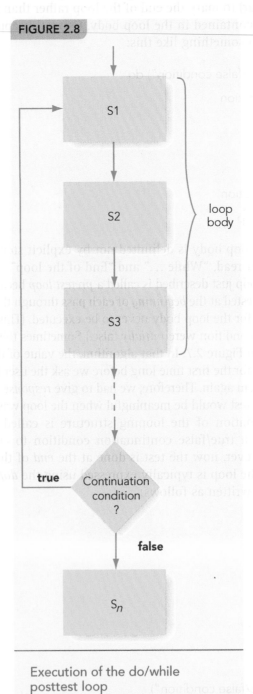

Execution of the do/while posttest loop

Figure 2.9 summarizes the algorithmic operations introduced in this section. These represent the primitive operations of our computing agent. These are the instructions that we assume our computing agent understands and is capable of executing without further explanation or simplification. In the next section, we will use these operations to design algorithms that solve some interesting and important problems.

FIGURE 2.9

Computation:
     Set the value of "variable" to "arithmetic expression"
Input/Output:
     Get a value for "variable", "variable"...
     Print the value of "variable", "variable", ...
     Print the message 'message'
Conditional:
     If "a true/false condition" is true then
        first set of algorithmic operations
     Else
        second set of algorithmic operations
Iterative:
     While ("a true/false condition") do Step i through Step j
        Step i: operation

          .

          .

          .

        Step j: operation

     While ("a true/false condition") do
        operation

          .

          .

          .

        operation
     End of the loop

     Do
        operation
        operation

          .

          .

        operation
     While ("a true/false condition")

Summary of pseudocode language instructions

From Little Primitives Mighty Algorithms Grow

Although the set of algorithmic primitives shown in Figure 2.9 might seem quite puny, it is anything but! In fact, an important theorem in theoretical computer science proves that the operations shown in Figure 2.9 are sufficient to represent *any* valid algorithm. No matter how complicated it might be, if a problem can be solved algorithmically, it can be expressed using only the sequential, conditional, and iterative operations just discussed. This includes not only the simple addition algorithm of Figure 1.2 but also the exceedingly complex algorithms needed to operate the International Space Station, manage billions of Facebook accounts, and implement all the Internal Revenue Service's tax rules and regulations.

In many ways, building algorithms is akin to constructing essays or novels using only the 26 letters of the English alphabet, plus a few punctuation symbols. Expressive power does not always come from having a huge set of primitives. It can also arise from a small number of simple building blocks combined in interesting and complex ways. This is the real secret of building algorithms.

2.3 Examples of Algorithmic Problem Solving

2.3.1 Example 1: Go Forth and Multiply

Our first example of algorithmic problem solving addresses a problem originally posed in Chapter 1 (Exercise 12). That problem asked you to implement an algorithm to multiply two numbers using repeated addition. This problem can be formally expressed as follows:

Given two nonnegative integer values, $a \geq 0$, $b \geq 0$, compute and output the product $(a \times b)$ using the technique of repeated addition. That is, determine the value of the sum $a + a + a + \ldots + a$ (b times).

Obviously, we need to create a loop that executes exactly b times, with each execution of the loop adding the value of a to a running total. These operations will not make any sense (that is, they will not be effectively computable) until we have explicit values for a and b. So one of the first operations in our algorithm must be to input these two values.

Get values for a and b

Practice Problems

1. Write an if/then/else statement that sets the variable y to the value 1 if $x \geq 0$. If $x < 0$, then the statement should set y to the value 2. (Assume x already has a value.)

2. Write an algorithm that gets as input three data values x, y, and z and outputs the average of these values if the value of x is positive. If the value of x is either 0 or negative, your algorithm should not compute the average but should print the error message 'Bad Data' instead.

3. Write an algorithm that gets as input your current credit card balance, the total dollar amount of new purchases, and the total dollar amount of all payments. The algorithm computes the new balance, which this time includes an 8% interest charge on any unpaid balance below $100, 12% interest on any unpaid balance between $100 and $500, inclusive, and 16% on any unpaid balance above $500.

4. Write an algorithm that gets as input a single nonzero data value x and outputs the three values x^2, sin x, and $1/x$. This process is repeated until the input value for x is equal to 999, at which time the algorithm terminates.

5. Write an algorithm that inputs the length and width, in feet, of a rectangular carpet and the price of the carpet in dollars per square yard. It then determines if you can afford to purchase this carpet, given that your total budget for carpeting is $500.

6. Add the following feature to the algorithm created in the previous Practice Problem: If the cost of the carpet is less than or equal to $250, output a message that this is a particularly good deal.

7. Add the following feature to the algorithm created in Practice Problem 4 above. Assume the input for the data value x can be any value, including 0. Since the value $1/x$ cannot be computed if $x = 0$, you will have to check for this condition and output an error message saying that you are unable to compute the value $1/x$.

To create a loop that executes exactly b times, we create a counter, let's call it *count*, initialized to 0 and incremented by (increased by) 1 after each pass through the loop. This means that when we have completed the loop once, the value of *count* is 1; when we have completed the loop twice, the value of *count* is 2; and so forth. Because we want to stop when we have completed the loop b times, we want to stop when (*count* = *b*). Therefore, the condition for continuing execution of the loop is (*count* < *b*). Putting all these pieces together produces the following algorithmic structure, which is a loop that executes exactly *b* times as the variable *count* ranges from 0 up to (*b* − 1).

> Get values for *a* and *b*
>
> Set the value of *count* to 0
>
> While (*count* < *b*) do
>
> > ... the rest of the loop body will go here ...
> >
> > Set the value of *count* to (*count* + 1)
>
> End of the loop

The purpose of the loop body is to add the value of *a* to a running total, which we will call *product*. We express that operation in the following manner:

> Set the value of *product* to (*product* + *a*)

This statement says the new value of *product* is to be reset to the current value of *product* plus *a*.

What is the current value of *product* the first time this operation is encountered? Unless we initialize it, it has no value, and this operation is not effectively computable. Before starting the loop, we must be sure to include the following step:

> Set the value of *product* to 0

Now our solution is starting to take shape. Here is what we have developed so far:

> Get values for *a* and *b*
>
> Set the value of *count* to 0
>
> Set the value of *product* to 0
>
> While (*count* < *b*) do
>
> > Set the value of *product* to (*product* + *a*)
> >
> > Set the value of *count* to (*count* + 1)
>
> End of the loop

There are only a few minor "tweaks" left to make this a correct solution to our problem.

When the while loop completes, we have computed the desired result, namely (*a* × *b*), and it is stored in *product*. However, we have not displayed that result, and as it stands, this algorithm produces no output. Remember from Chapter 1 that one of the fundamental characteristics of an algorithm is that it produces an observable result. In this case, the desired result is the final value of *product*, which we can display using our output primitive:

Print the value of *product*

The original statement of the problem said that the two inputs a and b must satisfy the following conditions: $a \geq 0$ and $b \geq 0$. The previous algorithm works for positive values of a and b, but what happens when either $a = 0$ or $b = 0$? Does it still function correctly?

If $b = 0$, there is no problem. If you look at the while loop, you see that it continues executing so long as ($count < b$). The variable $count$ is initialized to 0. If the input variable b also has the value 0, then the test ($0 < 0$) is initially false, and the loop is *never* executed. The variable *product* keeps its initial value of 0, and that is the output that is displayed, which is the correct answer.

Now let's look at what happens when $a = 0$ and b is any nonzero value, say 5,386. Of course we know immediately that the correct answer to $0 \times 5{,}386$ is 0, but our algorithm does not. Instead, the loop will execute 5,386 times, the value of b, each time adding the value of a, which is 0, to *product*. Because adding 0 to anything has no effect, *product* remains at 0, and that is the output that will be displayed. In this case, we do get the right answer, and our algorithm does work correctly. However, it gets that correct answer only after doing 5,386 unnecessary and time-wasting repetitions of the loop.

In Chapter 1, we stated that it is not only algorithmic correctness we are after but efficiency and elegance as well. The algorithms designed and implemented by computer scientists are intended to solve important real-world problems, and they must accomplish that task in a correct and reasonably efficient manner. Otherwise they are not of much use to their intended audience.

In this case, we can eliminate all of those needless repetitions of the loop by using our if/then/else conditional primitive. Right at the start of the algorithm, we ask if either a or b is equal to 0. If the answer is yes, we can immediately set the final result to 0 without requiring any further computations:

If (either $a = 0$ or $b = 0$) then

       Set the value of *product* to 0

Else

       … solve the problem as described above …

We will have much more to say about the critically important concepts of algorithmic efficiency and elegance in Chapter 3.

This completes the development of our multiplication algorithm, and the finished solution is shown in Figure 2.10.

FIGURE 2.10

```
Get values for a and b
If (either a = 0 or b = 0) then
    Set the value of product to 0
Else
    Set the value of count to 0
    Set the value of product to 0
    While (count < b) do
        Set the value of product to (product + a)
        Set the value of count to (count + 1)
    End of loop
Print the value of product
Stop
```

Algorithm for multiplication of nonnegative values via repeated addition

Practice Problems

1. Manually work through the algorithm in Figure 2.10 using the input values $a = 2$, $b = 4$. After each completed pass through the loop, write down the current value of the four variables a, b, $count$, and $product$.

2. Trace the execution of the algorithm in Figure 2.10 using the "special" input values $a = 0$ and $b = 0$. Does the algorithm produce the result you expect?

3. Describe exactly what would be output by the algorithm in Figure 2.10 for each of the following two cases, and state whether that output is or is not correct. (*Note*: Because one of the two inputs is negative, these values violate the basic conditions of the problem.)

    case 1: $a = -2$, $b = 4$ case 2: $a = 2$, $b = -4$

4. If the algorithm of Figure 2.10 produced the wrong answer for either case 1 or case 2 of Practice Problem 3, explain exactly how you could fix the algorithm so it works correctly and produces the correct answer.

5. Explain why the multiplication algorithm shown in Figure 2.10 is or is not an efficient way to do multiplication. Justify and explain your answer.

6. Modify the algorithm in Figure 2.10 so it examines the two inputs a and b and if either one is greater than 10,000, it displays a message saying that for large numbers like this we should use a different, and more efficient, multiplication algorithm. It then terminates without computing a result.

This first example needed only two integer values, a and b, as input. That is a bit unrealistic, as most interesting computational problems deal not with a few numbers but with huge collections of data, such as long lists of names or large sets of experimental data. In the following sections, we will show examples of the types of processing—searching, reordering, comparing—often done on huge collections of information.

2.3.2 Example 2: Looking, Looking, Looking

Finding a solution to a given problem is called algorithm discovery, and it is the most challenging and creative part of the problem-solving process. We developed an algorithm for a fairly simple problem (multiplication by repeated addition) in Example 1. Discovering a correct and efficient algorithm to solve a complicated problem can be difficult and can involve equal parts of intelligence, hard work, past experience, technical skill, and plain good luck. In the remaining examples, we will develop solutions to a range of problems to give you more experience in working with algorithms. Studying these examples, together with lots of practice, is by far the best way to learn creative problem solving, just as experience and practice are the best ways to learn how to write essays, hit a golf ball, or repair cars.

The next problem we address involves finding a person's name given his or her telephone number, an application often referred to as *reverse telephone lookup*. This is the type of important but rather menial repetitive task so well suited to computerization. (Apple has a half-dozen reverse telephone lookup apps in its App Store.)

This algorithm could be used, for example, to implement *Caller ID*, in which the caller's name (if it is found) is shown on a screen so you can decide whether or not to answer the phone. It can also be used with missed calls to determine whether the caller is someone with whom you actually wish to speak. Since there are more than 350 million listed phone numbers in the United States, reverse telephone lookup can only be implemented using computer-based search techniques.

Assume that we have a list of 10,000 telephone numbers (rather than hundreds of millions) that we represent symbolically as $T_1, T_2, T_3, \ldots, T_{10,000}$, along with the 10,000 names of the individuals associated with each specific phone number, denoted as $N_1, N_2, N_3, \ldots, N_{10,000}$. That is, N_1 is the name of the person who "owns" the telephone with the number T_1, and so forth. On this first attempt to build an algorithm, let's assume that the 10,000 telephone numbers are not necessarily in numerical order. (In Chapter 3, we will modify the problem to search a list of phone numbers sorted into ascending order.)

Essentially what we have described is randomly ordered pairs of number/ name lists with the following structure:

Telephone Number	Name
T_1	N_1
T_2	N_2
T_3	N_3
.	.
.	.
.	.
$T_{10,000}$	$N_{10,000}$

10,000 (phone number, name) pairs

Our algorithm should allow us to input a specific telephone number, which we will symbolically denote as *NUMBER*. The algorithm will then search to see if *NUMBER* matches any of the 10,000 numbers contained in our reverse directory. If *NUMBER* matches T_j, where j is some value between 1 and 10,000, then the output of our algorithm will be the name of the person associated with that number: the value N_j. If *NUMBER* is not in our reverse directory, then the output of our algorithm will be the message 'I am sorry but this number is not in our directory.' This type of lookup algorithm has many additional uses. For example, it could be used to locate the zip code of a particular city, the seat number of a specific airline passenger, or the room number of a hotel guest.

Because the numbers in our directory are not in numerical order, there is no clever way to speed up the search. With a randomly ordered collection, there is no method more efficient than starting at the beginning and looking at each number in the list, one at a time, until we either find the one we are looking for or we come to the end of the list. This rather simple and straightforward technique is called *sequential search*, and it is the standard algorithm for searching an *unordered* list of values. For example, this is how we would search a bookshelf for a book with a particular title if the books were sorted by the author's name instead of by title. It is also the way that we would search a shuffled deck of cards trying to locate one particular card. A first attempt at designing a sequential search algorithm to solve our search problem might look something like Figure 2.11.

The solution shown in Figure 2.11 is extremely long. At 66 lines per page, it would require about 150 pages to write out the 10,002 steps in the completed solution. It would also be unnecessarily slow. If we are lucky enough to find *NUMBER* in the very first position of the list, T_1, then we get the answer N_1 almost immediately. However, the algorithm does not stop at that point. Even though it has already found the correct answer, it foolishly asks 9,999 more questions looking for *NUMBER* in positions T_2, ..., $T_{10,000}$. Of course, humans have enough common sense to know that when they find the answer they are searching for, they can stop. However, we cannot assume common sense in a computer system. On the contrary, a computer will mechanically execute the entire algorithm from the first step to the last.

FIGURE 2.11

Step	Operation
1	Get values for NUMBER, T_1, ... , $T_{10,000}$, and N_1, ... , $N_{10,000}$
2	If NUMBER = T_1 then print the value of N_1
3	If NUMBER = T_2 then print the value of N_2
4	If NUMBER = T_3 then print the value of N_3
.	.
.	.
.	.
10,000	If NUMBER = $T_{9,999}$ then print the value of $N_{9,999}$
10,001	If NUMBER = $T_{10,000}$ then print the value of $N_{10,000}$
10,002	Stop

First attempt at designing a sequential search algorithm

Not only is the algorithm excessively long and highly inefficient, it is also wrong. If the desired *NUMBER* is not in the list, this algorithm simply stops (at Step 10,002) rather than providing the desired result, a message that the number you requested could not be found. An algorithm is deemed correct only when it produces the correct result for *all* possible cases.

The problem with this first attempt is that it does not use the powerful algorithmic concept of *iteration*. Instead of writing an instruction 10,000 separate times, it is far better to write it only once and indicate that it is to be repetitively *executed* 10,000 times, or however many times it takes to obtain the answer. As you learned in the previous section, much of the power of a computer comes from being able to perform a *loop*—the repetitive execution of a block of statements a large number of times. Virtually every algorithm developed in this text contains at least one loop and most contain many. (This is the difference between the two shampooing algorithms shown in Figures 1.3 and 1.4. The algorithm in the former contains a loop; that in the latter does not.)

The algorithm in Figure 2.12 shows how we might write a loop to implement the sequential search technique. It uses a variable called *i* as an *index*, or *pointer*, into the list of all numbers. That is, T_i refers to the *i*th number in the list. The algorithm then repeatedly executes a group of statements using different values of *i*. The variable *i* can be thought of as a "moving finger" scanning the list of telephone numbers and pointing to the one on which the algorithm is currently working.

The first time through the loop, the value of the index *i* is 1, so the algorithm checks (in Step 4) to see whether *NUMBER* is equal to T_1, the first one on the list. If it is, then the algorithm writes out the result and sets the variable *Found* to YES, which causes the loop in Steps 4 through 7 to terminate. If T_1 is not the desired *NUMBER*, then *i* is incremented by 1 (in Step 7) so that it now has the value 2, and the loop is executed again. The algorithm

FIGURE 2.12

Step	Operation
1	Get values for $NUMBER$, $T_1, \ldots, T_{10,000}$, and $N_1, \ldots, N_{10,000}$
2	Set the value of i to 1 and set the value of $Found$ to NO
3	While ($Found$ = NO) do Steps 4 through 7
4	If $NUMBER$ is equal to the ith number on the list, T_i, then
5	Print the name of the corresponding person, N_i
6	Set the value of $Found$ to YES
	Else ($NUMBER$ is not equal to T_i)
7	Add 1 to the value of i
8	Stop

Second attempt at designing a sequential search algorithm

now checks to see whether $NUMBER$ is equal to T_2, the second number on the list. In this way, the algorithm uses the single conditional statement "If $NUMBER$ is equal to the ith number on the list …" to check up to 10,000 different values. It executes that one line over and over, each time with a different value of i. This is the advantage of using iteration.

However, the attempt shown in Figure 2.12 is not yet a complete and correct algorithm because it still does not work correctly when the desired $NUMBER$ does not appear anywhere in our reverse directory. This final problem can be solved by terminating the loop either when the desired phone number is found or when we reach the end of the list. The algorithm can determine exactly what happened by checking the value of $Found$ when the loop terminates. If the value of $Found$ is NO, then the loop terminated because the index i exceeded 10,000, and we searched the entire list without finding the desired $NUMBER$. The algorithm should then produce an appropriate message.

An iterative solution to the sequential search algorithm that incorporates this feature is shown in Figure 2.13. The sequential search algorithm shown in Figure 2.13 is a correct solution to our reverse telephone lookup problem. It meets all the requirements listed in Section 1.3.1: It is well ordered, each of the operations is clearly defined and effectively computable, and it is certain to halt with the desired result after a finite number of operations. (In Exercise 12 at the end of this chapter, you will develop a formal argument that proves that this algorithm will always halt.) Furthermore, this algorithm requires only 10 steps to write out fully, rather than the 10,002 steps of the first attempt in Figure 2.11. As you can see, not all algorithms are created equal.

Looking at the algorithm in Figure 2.13, our first thought might be that this is not at all how people would manually search a list of telephone numbers looking for one specific value. Humans would never turn to page 1, column 1, and start scanning all numbers beginning with (000) 000-0001

FIGURE 2.13

Step	Operation
1	Get values for *NUMBER*, T_1, ... , $T_{10,000}$, and N_1, ... , $N_{10,000}$
2	Set the value of *i* to 1 and set the value of *Found* to NO
3	While both (*Found* = NO) and ($i \leq 10,000$) do Steps 4 through 7
4	If NUMBER is equal to the ith number on the list, T_i, then
5	Print the name of the corresponding person, N_i
6	Set the value of *Found* to YES
	Else (*NUMBER* is not equal to T_i)
7	Add 1 to the value of *i*
8	If (*Found* = NO) then
9	Print the message 'Sorry, this number is not in the directory'
10	Stop

The sequential search algorithm

(which is not actually a valid telephone number according to the North American Numbering Plan that covers the United States, Canada, and many Caribbean islands). In all likelihood, a communications company located in New York City would not be satisfied with the performance of the sequential search algorithm of Figure 2.13 when applied to the 20 million or so phones in its city.

But because our reverse directory was not sorted into numerical order, we really had no choice in the design of our search algorithm. However, in real life we can do much better than sequential search, because these types of directories *are* sorted numerically, and we can exploit this fact during the search process. For example, we know that the digit 5 is about halfway through the set of decimal digits 0–9. So when looking for the owner of phone number (555) 123-4567 in a sorted reverse directory, we could start our search somewhere in the middle rather than on the first page. We then see exactly where we are by looking at the first digit of the phone numbers on the current page and then move forward or backward toward numbers beginning with 5. This approach allows us to find the desired telephone number much more quickly than searching the numbers sequentially from the beginning of the list.

This use of different search techniques points out a very important concept in the design of algorithms:

> *The selection of an algorithm to solve a problem is greatly influenced by the way the input data for that problem is organized.*

An algorithm is a method for processing some data to produce a result, and the way the data is organized has an enormous influence both on the algorithm we select and on how speedily that algorithm can produce the desired result.

Laboratory Experience 2

Computer science is an empirical discipline as well as a theoretical one. Learning comes not just from reading about concepts like algorithms but also from manipulating and observing them. The laboratory manual for this text includes laboratory exercises that enable you to engage the ideas and concepts presented on these pages. Laboratory Experience 2 introduces the concept of *algorithm animation*, in which you can observe an algorithm being executed and watch as data values are dynamically transformed into final results.

Bringing an algorithm to life in this way can help you understand what the algorithm does and how it works. The first animation that you will work with is the sequential search algorithm shown in Figure 2.13. The laboratory software allows you to create a list of data values and to watch as the algorithm searches this list to determine whether a special target value occurs.

We strongly encourage you to work through these Laboratory Experiences to deepen your understanding of the ideas presented in this and the following chapters.

In Chapter 3, we will expand on the concept of the efficiency and quality of algorithms, and we will present an algorithm for searching *sorted* reverse directories that is far superior to the one shown in Figure 2.13.

2.3.3 Example 3: Big, Bigger, Biggest

The third algorithm we will develop is similar to the sequential search in Figure 2.13 in that it also searches a list of values. However, this time the algorithm will search not for a particular value supplied by the user but for the numerically largest value in a list of numbers. This type of "find largest" algorithm could be used to answer a number of important questions. (With only a single trivial change, the same algorithm also finds the smallest value, so a better name for it might be "find extreme values.") For example, given a list of examinations, which student received the highest (or lowest) score? Given a list of annual salaries, which employee earns the most (or least) money? Given a list of grocery prices from different stores, where should I shop to find the lowest price? All these questions could be answered by executing this type of algorithm.

In addition to being important in its own right, such an algorithm can also be used as a "building block" for the construction of solutions to other problems. For example, the Find Largest algorithm that we will develop could be used to implement a *sorting algorithm* that puts an unordered list of numbers into ascending order. (Find and remove the largest item in list A and move it to the last position of list B. Now repeat these operations, each time moving the largest remaining number in list A to the last unfilled slot of list B. We will develop and write this algorithm in Chapter 3.)

The use of a "building-block" component is a very important concept in computer science. The examples in this chapter might lead you to believe that every algorithm you write must be built from only the most elementary and basic of primitives—the sequential, conditional, and iterative operations shown in Figure 2.9. However, once an algorithm has been developed, it may itself be used in the construction of other, more complex algorithms, just as we will use Find Largest in the design of a sorting algorithm. This is similar to what a builder does when constructing a home from prefabricated units rather than bricks and boards. Our problem-solving task need not always begin at the beginning but can instead build on ideas and results that have come before. Every algorithm that we create becomes, in a sense, a primitive operation of our computing agent and can be used as part of the solution to other problems. That is why a collection of useful, prewritten algorithms, called a library, is such an important tool in the design and development of algorithms.

Formally, the problem we will be solving in this section is defined as follows:

> Given a value $n \geq 1$ and a list containing exactly n unique numbers called $A_1, A_2, \ldots, A_n$, find and print both the largest value in the list and the position in the list where that largest value occurred.

For example, if our list contained the five values

    19, 41, 12, 63, 22   ($n = 5$)

then our algorithm should locate the largest value, 63, and print that value together with the fact that it occurred in the fourth position of the list. (*Note*: Our definition of the problem states that all numbers in the list are unique, so there can be only a single occurrence of the largest number. Exercise 15 at the end of the chapter asks how our algorithm would behave if the numbers in the list were not unique and the largest number could occur two or more times.)

When faced with a problem statement like the one just given, how do we go about creating a solution? What strategies can we employ to discover a correct and efficient answer to the problem? One way to begin is to ask ourselves how the same problem might be solved by hand. If we can understand and explain how we would approach the problem manually, we might be able to express that manual solution as a formal algorithm.

For example, suppose we were given a pile of papers, each of which contains a single number, and were asked to locate the largest number in the pile. (The following diagrams assume the papers contain the five values 19, 41, 12, 63, and 22.)

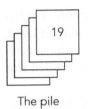

The pile

We might start off by saying that the first number in the pile (the top one) is the largest one that we have seen so far, and then putting it to the side where we are keeping the largest value.

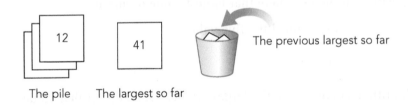

The pile   The largest so far

Now we compare the top number in the pile with the one that we have called the largest one so far. In this case, the top number in the pile, 41, is larger than our current largest, 19, so we make it the new largest. To do this, we throw the value 19 into the wastebasket (or, better, into the recycle bin) and put the number 41 to the side because it is the largest value encountered so far.

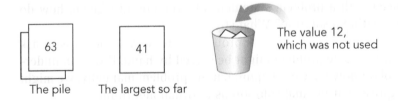

The pile   The largest so far   The previous largest so far

We now repeat this comparison operation, asking whether the number on top of the pile is larger than the largest value seen so far, now 41. This time the value on top of the pile, 12, is not larger, so we do not want to save it. We simply throw it away and move on to the next number in the pile.

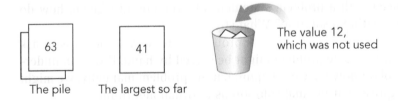

The pile   The largest so far   The value 12, which was not used

This compare-and-save-or-discard process continues until our original pile of numbers is empty, at which time the largest so far is the largest value in the entire list.

Let's see how we can convert this informal, pictorial solution into a formal algorithm that is built from the primitive operations shown in Figure 2.9.

We certainly cannot begin to search a list for a largest value until we have a list to search. Therefore, our first operation must be to get a value for n, the size of the list, followed by values for the n-element list $A_1, A_2, \ldots, A_n$. This can be done using our input primitive:

Get a value for n, the size of the list

Get values for $A_1, A_2, \ldots, A_n$, the list to be searched

Now that we have the data, we can begin to implement a solution.

Our informal description of the algorithm stated that we should begin by calling the first item in the list, A_1, the largest value so far. (We know that this operation is meaningful because we stated that the list must always have at least one element.) We can express this formally as

Set the value of *largest so far* to A_1

Our solution must also determine where that largest value occurs. To remember this value, let's create a variable called *location* to keep track of the position in the list where the largest value occurs. Because we have initialized *largest so far* to the first element in the list, we should initialize *location* to 1.

Set the value of *location* to 1

We are now ready to begin looking through the remaining items in list A to find the largest one. However, if we write something like the following instruction:

If the second item in the list is greater than *largest so far* then ...

we will have made exactly the same mistake that occurred in the initial version of the sequential search algorithm shown in Figure 2.11. This instruction explicitly checks only the second item of the list. We would need to rewrite that statement to check the third item, the fourth item, and so on. Again, we are failing to use the idea of *iteration*, where we repetitively execute a loop as many times as it takes to produce the desired result.

To solve this problem, let's use the same technique used in the sequential search algorithm. Let's not talk about the second, third, fourth, ... item in the list but about the *i*th item in the list, where *i* is a variable that takes on different values during the execution of the algorithm. Using this idea, a statement such as

If A_i > *largest so far* then ...

can be executed with different values for i. This allows us to check all n values in the list with a single statement. Initially, i should be given the value 2 because the first item in the list was automatically set to the largest value. Therefore, we want to begin our search with the second item in the list.

.
.
.

Set the value of *i* to 2

.
.
.

If A_i > *largest so far* then …

What operations should appear after the word *then*? A check of our earlier discussion shows that the algorithm must reset the values of both *largest so far* and *location*.

If A_i > *largest so far* then
    Set *largest so far* to A_i
    Set *location* to *i*

If A_i is not larger than *largest so far*, then we do not want the algorithm to do anything. To indicate this, the if/then instruction can include an else clause that looks something like

Else
    Don't do anything at all to *largest so far* and *location*

This is certainly correct, but instructions that tell us not to do anything are usually omitted from an algorithm because they do not carry any meaningful information.

Regardless of whether the algorithm resets the values of *largest so far* and *location*, it needs to move on to the next item in the list. Our algorithm refers to A_i, the *i*th item in the list, so it can move to the next item by simply adding 1 to the value of *i* and repeating the if/then statement. The outline of this iteration can be sketched as follows:

   → If A_i > *largest so far* then
       Set *largest so far* to A_i
       Set *location* to *i*
     Add 1 to the value of *i*
      .

.
.

However, we do not want the loop to repeat forever. (Remember that one of the properties of an algorithm is that it must eventually halt.) What stops this iterative process? When does the algorithm display an answer and terminate execution?

The conditional operation "If $A_i > $ *largest so far* then ..." is meaningful only if A_i represents an actual element of list A. Because A contains n elements numbered 1 to n, the value of i must be in the range 1 to n. If $i > n$, then the loop has searched the entire list, and it is finished. Therefore, our continuation condition should be expressed as $(i \leq n)$. When this condition becomes false, the algorithm can stop looping and print the values of both *largest so far* and *location*. Using our looping primitive, we can describe this iteration as follows:

While $(i \leq n)$ do

    If $A_i > $ *largest so far* then

        Set *largest so far* to A_i

        Set *location* to i

    Add 1 to the value of i

End of the loop

We have now developed all the pieces of the algorithm and can finally put them together. Figure 2.14 shows the completed Find Largest algorithm. Note that the steps are not numbered. This omission is quite common, especially as algorithms get larger and more complex.

FIGURE 2.14

Get a value for n, the size of the list
Get values for $A_1, A_2, \ldots, A_n$, the list to be searched
Set the value of *largest so far* to A_1
Set the value of *location* to 1
Set the value of i to 2

While $(i \leq n)$ do
    If $A_i > $ *largest so far* then
        Set *largest so far* to A_i
        Set *location* to i
    Add 1 to the value of i
End of the loop
Print out the values of *largest so far* and *location*
Stop

Algorithm to find the largest value in a list

Practice Problems

1. What part(s) of the sequential search algorithm of Figure 2.13 would need to be changed if our phone book contained 1 million numbers rather than 10,000?

2. Rewrite the sequential search algorithm to use the do/while looping structure shown in Figure 2.9 in place of the while structure.

3. Modify the algorithm of Figure 2.14 so that it finds the smallest value in a list rather than the largest. Describe exactly what changes were necessary.

4. Describe exactly what would happen to the algorithm in Figure 2.14 if you tried to apply it to an empty list of length $n = 0$. Describe exactly how you could fix this problem.

5. Describe exactly what happens to the algorithm in Figure 2.14 when it is presented with a list with exactly one item, that is, $n = 1$. Determine whether this algorithm will or will not work correctly on this one-item list.

6. Would the Find Largest algorithm of Figure 2.14 still work correctly if the test on Line 7 were written as ($A_i \geq$ *largest so far*)? Explain why or why not.

Laboratory Experience 3

Like Laboratory Experience 2, this laboratory also uses animation to help you better understand the concept of algorithm design and execution. It presents an animation of the Find Largest algorithm discussed in the text and shown in Figure 2.14.

This Laboratory Experience allows you to create a list of data and watch as the algorithm attempts to determine the largest numerical value contained in that list. You will be able to observe dynamic changes to the variables *index*, *location*, and *maximum*, and will be able to see how values are set and discarded as the algorithm executes. Like the previous Laboratory Experience, it is intended to give you a deeper understanding of how this algorithm works by allowing you to observe its behavior.

2.3.4 Example 4: Meeting Your Match

The last algorithm we develop in this chapter solves a common problem in computer science called *pattern matching*. For example, imagine that you have a large collection of Civil War data files that you want to use as resource material for an article on Abraham Lincoln. Your first step would probably be to search these files to locate every occurrence of the text patterns "Abraham Lincoln," "A. Lincoln," and "Lincoln." The process of searching for a special pattern of symbols within a larger collection of information is called *pattern matching*. Most good word processors provide this service as a menu item called *Find* or something similar. Furthermore, most web search engines try to match your search terms to the keywords that appear on a webpage.

Pattern matching can be applied to almost any kind of information, including graphics, sound, and photographs. For example, an important medical application of pattern matching is to input an X-ray or CT scan image into a computer and then have the computer search for special patterns, such as dark spots, which represent conditions that should be brought to the attention of a physician. This can help speed up the interpretation of X-rays and avoid the problem of human error caused by fatigue or oversight. (Computers do not get tired or bored!)

One of the most interesting and exciting applications of pattern matching is to assist microbiologists and geneticists studying and analyzing the *human genome,* the basis for all human life. The Human Genome Project was started in 1990 with the goal of determining the sequence of chemical base pairs that comprise the human genome. The mammoth project was completed in April 2003, and today this genetic information is available via online databases to biological and medical researchers worldwide.

The human genome is composed of approximately 3.5 billion *nucleotides*, each of which can be one of only four different chemical compounds. These compounds (adenine, cytosine, thymine, and guanine) are usually referred to by the first letter of their chemical names: A, C, T, and G. Thus, the basis for our existence can be conceptually viewed as a very large "text file" written in a four-letter alphabet.

...T C G G A C T A A C A T C G G G A T C G A G A T G ...

(If you were to write out the entire sequence of nucleotides, at 12 characters per inch, it would stretch from New York City to Moscow.) Sequences of these nucleotides are called *genes*. There are about 25,000 genes in the human genome, and they determine virtually all of our physical characteristics—sex, race, eye color, hair color, and height, to name just a few. Genes are also an important factor in the occurrence of certain diseases. A missing or flawed nucleotide can result in one of a number of serious genetic disorders, such as Down syndrome or Tay–Sachs disease. To help find a cure for these diseases, researchers attempt to locate individual genes that, when exhibiting a certain defect, cause a specific malady. The process of locating the starting and ending boundaries of an individual gene within the 3+ billion nucleotides is called *genome annotation*, and because of the scale of the problem it is done using automated algorithms that search DNA sequences in genomic databases—not unlike the algorithm we will develop in this section.

A gene is typically composed of thousands of nucleotides, and researchers generally do not know the entire sequence. However, they may know what a small portion of the gene—say, a few hundred nucleotides—looks like. Therefore, to search for one particular gene, they must match the sequence of nucleotides that they do know, called a *probe*, against the entire 3.5 billion-element genome to locate every occurrence of that probe. From this matching information, researchers hope to locate and isolate specific genes. For example,

Genome: ... *T C A G G C* | *T A A T C* | *G T A G G* ...

Probe: | *T A A T C* | a match

When a match is found, researchers examine the nucleotides located before and after the probe to see whether they have located the desired gene and, if so, whether the gene is defective. Physicians hope someday to be able to "clip out" a bad sequence and insert in its place a correct sequence. (This goal took a giant step forward in 2016 with the development of CRISPR, a powerful genome-editing tool that makes cutting-and-pasting of DNA sequences far more precise and efficient.)

This application of pattern matching dispels any notion that the algorithms discussed here—sequential search (Figure 2.13), Find Largest (Figure 2.14), and pattern matching—are nothing more than academic exercises that serve as examples for introductory classes but have absolutely no role in solving real-world problems. The algorithms that we have presented (or will present) *are* important, either in their own right or as building blocks for algorithms used by physical scientists, mathematicians, engineers, biologists, and social scientists.

Let's formally define the pattern-matching problem as follows:

You will be given some *text* composed of n characters that will be referred to as $T_1 \, T_2 \, ... \, T_n$. (*Note*: n may be very, very large.) You will also be given a *pattern* of m characters, $m \leq n$, that will be represented as $P_1 \, P_2 \, ... \, P_m$. (*Note*: m will usually be much, much smaller than n.) The algorithm must locate every occurrence of the given pattern within the text. The output of the algorithm is the location in the text where each match occurred. For this problem, the location of a match is defined to be the index position in the text where the match begins.

For example, if our text is the phrase "to be or not to be, that is the question" and the pattern for which we are searching is the word *to*, then our algorithm produces the following output:

Text: **to** *be or not to be, that is the question*

Pattern: **to**

Output: *Match starting at position 1.*

Text: *to be or not* **to** *be, that is the question*

Pattern: **to**

Output: *Match starting at position 14. (The t is in position 14, including blanks.)*

The pattern-matching algorithm that we will implement is composed of two parts. In the first part, the pattern is aligned under a specific position of the text, and the algorithm determines whether there is a match at that given position. The second part of the algorithm "slides" the entire pattern ahead one character position. Assuming that we have not gone beyond the end of the text, the algorithm returns to the first part to check for a match at this new position. Pictorially, this algorithm can be represented as follows:

Repeat the following two steps.

    Step 1: The matching process: $T_1\ T_2\ T_3\ T_4\ T_5\ \ldots$

                                    $P_1\ P_2\ P_3$

    Step 2: The slide forward: $T_1\ T_2\ T_3\ T_4\ T_5\ \ldots$

          one-character slide $\rightarrow$ $P_1\ P_2\ P_3$

The algorithm involves repetition of these two steps beginning at position 1 of the text and continuing until the pattern has slid off the right-hand end of the text.

A first draft of an algorithm that implements these ideas is shown in Figure 2.15, in which not all of the operations are expressed in terms of the basic algorithmic primitives of Figure 2.9. Although statements like "Set *k*, the starting location for the attempted match, to 1" and "Print the value of *k*, the starting location of the match" are just fine, the instructions "Attempt to match every character in the pattern beginning at position *k* of the text" and "Keep going until we have fallen off the end of the text" are certainly not primitives. On the contrary, they are high-level operations that, if written out using only the operations in Figure 2.9, would expand into many instructions.

FIGURE 2.15

Get values for *n* and *m*, the size of the text and the pattern, respectively
Get values for both the text $T_1 T_2 \ldots T_n$ and the pattern $P_1 P_2 \ldots P_m$
Set *k*, the starting location for the attempted match, to 1
Keep going until we have fallen off the end of the text
    Attempt to match every character in the pattern beginning at
       position *k* of the text (this is Step 1 from the previous page)
    If there was a match then
       Print the value of *k*, the starting location of the match
    Add 1 to *k*, which slides the pattern forward one position (this is Step 2)
End of the loop
Stop

First draft of the pattern-matching algorithm

Is it okay to use high-level statements like this in our algorithm? Wouldn't their use violate the requirement stated in Chapter 1 that algorithms be constructed only from unambiguous operations that can be directly executed by our computing agent?

In fact, it is perfectly acceptable, and quite useful, to use high-level statements like this during the *initial phase* of the algorithm design process. When starting to design an algorithm, we might not want to think only in terms of elementary operations such as input, computation, output, conditional, and iteration. Instead, we might want to express our proposed solution in terms of high-level and broadly defined operations that represent dozens or even hundreds of primitive instructions. Here are some examples of these higher-level constructs:

- Sort the entire list into ascending order.

- Attempt to match the entire pattern against the text.

- Find a root of the equation.

Using instructions like these in an algorithm allows us to postpone worrying about how to implement that operation and lets us focus instead on other aspects of the problem. This is equivalent to inserting the phrase "put a brief historical introduction right here" into a story that you are writing. It functions as a reminder of something that you must add but that can be postponed until a later time. With our algorithm, we will come back to these high-level constructs and either express them in terms of our available primitives or use existing building-block algorithms taken from a program library. However, we can do this at our convenience.

The use of high-level instructions during the design process is an example of one of the most important intellectual tools in computer science—abstraction.

Abstraction refers to the separation of the high-level view of an entity or an operation from the low-level details of its implementation. It is abstraction that allows us to understand and intellectually manage any large, complex system, whether it is a mammoth corporation, a complex piece of machinery, or an intricate and very detailed algorithm. For example, the president of General Motors views the company in terms of its major corporate divisions and high-level policy issues, not in terms of every worker, every supplier, every car, or every bolt. Attempting to manage the company at that level of detail would drown the president in a sea of detail.

In computer science, we frequently use abstraction because of the complexity of hardware and software. For example, abstraction allows us to view the hardware component called "memory" as a single, indivisible high-level entity without paying heed to the billions of electronic devices that go into constructing a memory unit. (Chapter 4 examines how computer memories are built, and it makes extensive use of abstraction.) In algorithm design and software development, we use abstraction whenever we think of an operation at a high level and temporarily ignore how we might actually implement that operation. This allows us to decide which details to address now and which to postpone until later. Viewing an operation at a high level of abstraction and fleshing out the details of its implementation at a later time constitute an important computer science problem-solving strategy called top-down design.

Ultimately, however, we do have to describe how each of these high-level abstractions can be represented using the available algorithmic primitives. The fifth line of the first draft of the pattern-matching algorithm shown in Figure 2.15 reads:

Attempt to match every character in the pattern beginning at position k of the text

When this statement is reached, the pattern is aligned under the text beginning with the kth character. Pictorially, we are in the following situation:

Text: $T_1 T_2 T_3 \ldots$ $T_k T_{k+1} T_{k+2} \ldots T_{k+(m-1)} \ldots$

Pattern: $P_1 P_2 P_3 \ldots P_m$

The algorithm must now perform the following comparisons:

Compare P_1 to T_k

Compare P_2 to T_{k+1}

Compare P_3 to T_{k+2}

.

.

.

Compare P_m to $T_{k+(m-1)}$

If every single one of these pairs is equal, then there is a match starting at position k. However, if even one pair is not equal, then there is no match, and the algorithm can immediately cease making comparisons at this location. Thus, we must construct a loop that executes until one of two things happens—it has either completed m successful comparisons (i.e., we have matched the entire pattern) or detected a mismatch. When either of these conditions occurs, the loop stops; however, if neither condition has occurred, the loop must keep going. Algorithmically, this iteration can be expressed in the following way. (Remember that k is the starting location in the text.)

> Set the value of i to 1
>
> Set the value of *Mismatch* to NO
>
> While both ($i \leq m$) and (*Mismatch* = NO)
>
>> If $P_i \neq T_{k+(i-1)}$ then
>>
>>> Set *Mismatch* to YES
>>
>> Else
>>
>>> Increment i by 1 (to move to the next character)
>
> End of the loop

When the loop has finished, we can determine whether there was a match by examining the current value of the variable *Mismatch*. If *Mismatch* is YES, then there was not a match because at least one of the characters was out of place. If *Mismatch* is NO, then every character in the pattern matched its corresponding character in the text, and there is a match starting at position k.

> If *Mismatch* = NO then
>
>> Print the message 'There is a match at position '
>>
>> Print the value of k

Regardless of whether there was a match at position k, we now must add 1 to k to begin searching for a match at the next position. This is the "sliding forward" step diagrammed earlier.

The final high-level statement in Figure 2.15 that needs to be expanded is the loop on Line 4.

> Keep going until we have fallen off the end of the text

What does it mean to "fall off the end of the text"? Where is the last possible place that a match can occur? To answer these questions, let's draw a diagram in which the last character of the pattern, P_m, lines up directly under T_n, the last character of the text.

Text: $T_1\ T_2\ T_3\ \dots\quad T_{n-m+1}\ \dots\quad T_{n-2}\qquad T_{n-1}\qquad T_n$

Pattern: $P_1\ \dots\qquad P_{m-2}\qquad P_{m-1}\qquad P_m$

This diagram illustrates that the last possible place a match could occur is when the first character of the pattern is aligned under the character at position T_{n-m+1} of the text because P_m is aligned under T_n, P_{m-1} is under T_{n-1}, P_{m-2} is aligned under T_{n-2}, and so on. Thus, P_1, which can be written as $P_{m-(m-1)}$, is aligned under $T_{n-(m-1)}$, which is T_{n-m+1}. If we tried to slide the pattern forward any further, we would truly "fall off" the right-hand end of the text. Therefore, our loop must terminate when k, the starting point for the match, strictly exceeds the value of $n - m + 1$. We can express this as follows:

While $(k \le (n - m + 1))$ do

Now we have all the pieces of our algorithm in place. We have expressed every statement in Figure 2.15 in terms of our basic algorithmic primitives and are ready to put it all together. The final draft of the pattern-matching algorithm is shown in Figure 2.16.

FIGURE 2.16

Get values for n and m, the size of the text and the pattern, respectively
Get values for both the text $T_1\ T_2 \dots T_n$ and the pattern $P_1\ P_2 \dots P_m$
Set k, the starting location for the attempted match, to 1
While $(k \le (n - m + 1))$ do
    Set the value of i to 1
    Set the value of *Mismatch* to NO
    While both $(i \le m)$ and $(Mismatch = NO)$ do
        If $P_i \ne T_{k+(i-1)}$ then
            Set *Mismatch* to YES
        Else
            Increment i by 1 (to move to the next character)
    End of the loop
    If *Mismatch* = NO then
        Print the message 'There is a match at position'
        Print the value of k
    Increment k by 1
End of the loop
Stop

Final draft of the pattern-matching algorithm

Hidden Figures

When it comes to telling the history of computer science, Hollywood often focuses on the contributions of white men to the exclusion of both women and people of color—Alan Turing (*The Imitation Game*, 2014), Bill Gates (*Pirates of Silicon Valley*, 1999), Steven Jobs (*Jobs*, 2013; *Steve Jobs*, 2015), Mark Zuckerberg (*The Social Network*, 2010). That all changed in January, 2017 with the release of the movie *Hidden Figures*, the true story of three African-American women who worked as mathematicians and computer specialists at the NASA Space Research Center in Langley, Virginia in the early 1960s. (The movie received three Oscar nominations, including one for Best Picture.) These women, Katherine Johnson, Dorothy Vaughn, and Mary Jackson, were charged with carrying out the complex orbital calculations needed to send John Glenn into orbit and bring him back safely. Katherine Johnson went on to work on the launch of Apollo 11 to the moon and Apollo 13. She received the Presidential Medal of Freedom in 2015, and in 2016 the Langley Space Research Center was renamed the Katherine G. Johnson Computational Research Facility.

2.4 Conclusion

You have now had a chance to see the step-by-step design and development of some interesting, nontrivial algorithms. You have also been introduced to a number of fundamental concepts related to problem solving, including algorithm design and discovery, pseudocode, control statements, iteration, libraries, abstraction, and top-down design. However, this by no means marks the end of our discussion of algorithms. The development of a correct solution to a problem is only the first step in creating a useful piece of software.

Designing a technically correct algorithm to solve a given problem is only part of what computer scientists do. They must also ensure that they have created an *efficient* algorithm that generates results quickly enough for its intended users. Chapter 1 described a brute force chess algorithm that would, at least theoretically, play perfect chess but that would be unusable because it would take millions of centuries to make its first move. Similarly, a reverse directory lookup program that takes 30 minutes to locate a person's name would be of little or no use. The caller would surely have hung up long before we learned who it was. This practical concern for efficiency and usefulness, in addition to correctness, is one of the hallmarks of computer science.

Therefore, after developing a correct algorithm, we must analyze it thoroughly and study its efficiency properties and operating characteristics. We must ask ourselves how quickly it will give us the desired results and whether it is better than other algorithms that solve the same problem. This analysis, which is the central topic of Chapter 3, enables us to create algorithms that are not only correct but elegant, efficient, and useful as well.

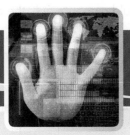

Practice Problems

1. Consider the following "reverse telephone directory."

Number	Name
(648) 555-1285	Smith
(247) 834-6543	Jones
(771) 921-5281	Adams
(356) 327-8900	Doe

   Trace the sequential search algorithm of Figure 2.13 using each of the following *NUMBERs* and show the output produced.

   a. (771) 921-5281

   b. (488) 351-1673

2. Consider the following list of seven data values.

   22, 18, 23, 17, 25, 30, 2

   Trace the Find Largest algorithm of Figure 2.14 and show the output produced.

3. Consider the following text.

   Text: A man and a woman

   Trace the pattern-matching algorithm of Figure 2.16 using the two-character pattern *an* and show the output produced.

4. Explain exactly what would happen to the algorithm of Figure 2.16 if m, the length of the pattern, were greater than n, the length of the text.

5. Explain exactly what would happen to the algorithm of Figure 2.16 if Line 5 had been incorrectly written as "set the value of i to 0".

6. Determine whether the pattern-matching algorithm of Figure 2.16 will work if n, the length of the text, is exactly the same size as m, the length of the pattern.

EXERCISES

1. Write pseudocode instructions to carry out each of the following computational operations:

   a. Determine the area of a triangle given values for the base b and the height h.

   b. Compute the interest earned in 1 year given the starting account balance B and the annual interest rate I and assuming simple interest, that is, no compounding. Also determine the final balance at the end of the year.

   c. Determine the flying time between two cities given the mileage M between them and the average speed of the airplane.

2. Using only the sequential operations described in Section 2.2.2, write an algorithm that gets values for the starting account balance B, annual interest rate I, and annual service charge S. Your algorithm should output the amount of interest earned during the year and the final account balance at the end of the year. Assume that interest is compounded monthly and the service charge is deducted once, at the end of the year.

3. Using only the sequential operations described in Section 2.2.2, write an algorithm that gets four numbers corresponding to scores received on three semester tests and a final examination. Your algorithm should compute and display the average of all four tests, weighting the final exam twice as heavily as a regular test.

4. Write an algorithm that gets the price for item A plus the quantity purchased. The algorithm prints the total cost, including a 6% sales tax.

5. Write an if/then/else primitive to do each of the following operations:

   a. Compute and display the value $x \div y$ if the value of y is not 0. If y does have the value 0, then display the message 'Unable to perform the division'.

   b. Compute the area and circumference of a circle given the radius r if the radius is greater than or equal to 1.0; otherwise, you should compute only the circumference.

6. Modify the algorithm of Exercise 2 to include the annual service charge only if the starting account balance at the beginning of the year is less than $1,000. If it is greater than or equal to $1,000, then there is no annual service charge.

7. Write an algorithm that uses a loop (1) to input 10 pairs of numbers, where each pair represents the score of a football game with the Computer State University (CSU) score listed first, and (2) for each pair of numbers, to determine whether CSU won or lost. After reading in these 10 pairs of values, print the won/lost/tie record of CSU. In addition, if this record is a perfect 10-0, then print the message 'Congratulations on your undefeated season'.

8. Modify the test-averaging algorithm of Exercise 3 so that it reads in 15 test scores rather than 4. There are 14 regular tests and a final examination, which counts twice as much as a regular test. Use a loop to input and sum the scores.

9. Modify the sales computation algorithm of Exercise 4 so that after finishing the computation for one item, it starts on the computation for the next. This iterative process is repeated until the total cost exceeds $1,000.

10. Write an algorithm that is given your electric meter readings (in kilowatt-hours) at the beginning and end of each month of the year. The algorithm determines your annual cost of electricity on the basis of a charge of 6 cents per kilowatt-hour for the first 1,000 kilowatt-hours of each month and 8 cents per kilowatt-hour

beyond 1,000. After printing out your total annual charge, the algorithm also determines whether you used less than 500 kilowatt-hours for the entire year and, if so, prints out a message thanking you for conserving electricity.

11. Develop an algorithm to compute gross pay. The inputs to your algorithm are the hours worked per week and the hourly pay rate. The rule for determining gross pay is to pay the regular pay rate for all hours worked up to 40, time-and-a-half for all hours over 40 up to 54, and double time for all hours over 54. Compute and display the value for gross pay using this rule. After displaying one value, ask the user whether he or she wants to do another computation. Repeat the entire set of operations until the user says no.

12. Develop a formal argument that "proves" that the sequential search algorithm shown in Figure 2.13 cannot have an infinite loop; that is, prove that it will always stop after a finite number of operations.

13. Modify the sequential search algorithm of Figure 2.13 so that it works correctly even if the numbers in the reverse directory are not unique, that is, if the desired number occurs more than once. (For example, a single number may be listed separately under the husband's name and the wife's name.) Your modified algorithm should find *every* occurrence of *NUMBER* in the directory and print the name corresponding to every match. In addition, after all the names have been displayed, your algorithm should print how many occurrences were located. For example, if *NUMBER* occurred twice, the output of the algorithm might look something like this:

    Susan Doe

    John Doe

    A total of two occurrences were located.

14. Use the Find Largest algorithm of Figure 2.14 to help you develop an algorithm to find the median value in a list containing *N* unique

numbers. The median of *N* numbers is defined as the value in the list in which approximately half the values are larger than it and half the values are smaller than it. For example, consider the following list of seven numbers.

    26, 50, 83, 44, 91, 20, 55

The median value is 50 because three values (20, 26, and 44) are smaller and three values (55, 83, and 91) are larger. If *N* is an even value, then the number of values larger than the median will be one greater than the number of values smaller than the median.

15. With regard to the Find Largest algorithm of Figure 2.14, if the numbers in our list were not unique and therefore the largest number could occur more than once, would the algorithm find the first occurrence? The last occurrence? Every occurrence? Explain precisely how this algorithm would behave when presented with this new condition.

16. On the sixth line of the Find Largest algorithm of Figure 2.14, there is an instruction that reads,

    While ($i \leq n$) do

Explain exactly what would happen if we changed that instruction to read as follows:

a. While ($i \geq n$) do

b. While ($i < n$) do

c. While ($i = n$) do

17. On the seventh line of the Find Largest algorithm of Figure 2.14, there is an instruction that reads,

    If $A_i >$ largest so far then ...

Explain exactly what would happen if we changed that instruction to read as follows:

a. If $A_i \geq$ largest so far then ...

b. If $A_i <$ largest so far then ...

Looking back at your answers in Exercises 16 and 17, what do they say about the importance of using the correct *relational operation* ($<, =, >, \geq, \leq, \neq$) when writing out either an iterative or conditional algorithmic primitive?

18. Refer to the pattern-matching algorithm in Figure 2.16.

    a. What is the output of the algorithm as it currently stands if our text is

    > *Text:* We must band together and handle adversity

    and we search for the pattern "and"?

    b. How could we modify the algorithm so that it finds only the complete word *and* rather than the occurrence of the character sequence a, n, and d that is contained within another word, such as *band*?

19. Refer to the pattern-matching algorithm in Figure 2.16. Explain how the algorithm would behave if we accidentally omitted the statement on Line 16 that says,

    > Increment k by 1

20. Design an algorithm that is given a positive integer N and determines whether N is a prime number, that is, not evenly divisible by any value other than 1 and itself. The output of your algorithm is either the message 'not prime', along with a factor of N, or the message 'prime'.

21. Write an algorithm that generates a Caesar cipher—a secret message in which each letter is replaced by the one that is k letters ahead of it in the alphabet, in a circular fashion. For example, if k = 5, then the letter a would be replaced by the letter f, and the letter x would be replaced by the letter c. (We'll talk more about the Caesar cipher and other encryption algorithms in Chapter 8.) The input to your algorithm is the text to be encoded, ending with the special symbol "$", and the value k. (You may assume that, except for the special ending character, the text contains only the 26 letters a ... z.) The output of your algorithm is the encoded text.

22. Design and implement an algorithm that is given as input an integer value $k \geq 0$ and a list of k numbers $N_1, N_2, \ldots, N_k$. Your algorithm should reverse the order of the numbers in the list. That is, if the original list contained:

    $$N_1 = 5, N_2 = 13, N_3 = 8, N_4 = 27, N_5 = 10$$
    $$(k = 5)$$

    then when your algorithm has completed, the values stored in the list will be:

    $$N_1 = 10, N_2 = 27, N_3 = 8, N_4 = 13, N_5 = 5$$

23. Design and implement an algorithm that gets as input a list of k integer values $N_1, N_2, \ldots, N_k$ as well as a special value SUM. Your algorithm must locate a pair of values in the list N that sum to the value SUM. For example, if your list of values is 3, 8, 13, 2, 17, 18, 10, and the value of SUM is 20, then your algorithm would output either of the two values (2, 18) or (3, 17). If your algorithm cannot find any pair of values that sum to the value SUM, then it should print the message 'Sorry, there is no such pair of values'.

24. Instead of reading in an entire list $N_1, N_2, \ldots$ all at once, some algorithms (depending on the task to be done) read in only one element at a time and process that single element completely before inputting the next one. This can be a useful technique when the list is very big (e.g., billions of elements) and there might not be enough memory in the computer to store it in its entirety. Write an algorithm that reads in a sequence of values $V \geq 0$, one at a time, and computes the average of all the numbers. You should stop the computation when you input a value of V = −1. Do *not* include this negative value in your computations; it is not a piece of data but only a marker to identify the end of the list.

25. Write an algorithm to read in a sequence of values $V \geq 0$, one at a time, and determine if the list contains at least one adjacent pair of values that are identical. The end of the entire

list is marked by the special value $V = -1$. For example, if you were given the following input:

14, 3, 7, 7, 9, 1, 804, 22, −1

the output of your algorithm should be a 'Yes' because there is at least one pair of adjacent numbers that are equal (the 7s). However, given the following input:

14, 3, 7, 77, 9, 1, 804, 22, −1

the output of your algorithm should be a 'No' because there are no adjacent pairs that are equal. You may assume in your solution that there are at least two numbers in the list.

26. Modify the algorithm that you developed in Exercise 25 so that if there is a pair of identical adjacent values, your algorithm also outputs, in addition to the phrase 'Yes', the value of the identical numbers. So, given the first list of numbers shown in Exercise 25, the output of your algorithm would be something like 'Yes, the numbers 7 and 7 are adjacent to each other in the list'.

CHALLENGE WORK

1. Design an algorithm to find the *root* of a function $f(x)$, where the root is defined as a point x such that $f(x) = 0$. Pictorially, the root of a function is the point where the graph of that function crosses the x-axis.

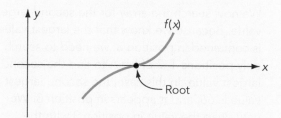

Your algorithm should operate as follows. Initially it will be given three values:

   1. A starting point for the search

   2. A step size

   3. The accuracy desired

Your algorithm should begin at the specified starting point and begin to "walk up" the x-axis in units of step size. After taking a step, it should ask the question "Have I passed a root?" It can determine the answer to this question by seeing whether the sign of the function has changed from the previous point to the current point. (Note that below the axis, the sign of $f(x)$ is negative; above the axis, it is positive. If it crosses the x-axis, it must change its sign.) If the algorithm has not passed a root, it should keep walking up the x-axis until it does. This is expressed pictorially as:

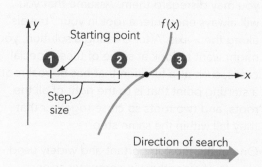

When the algorithm passes a root, it must do two things. First, it changes the sign of step size so that it starts walking in the reverse direction because it is now past the root. Second, it multiplies step size by 0.1, so our steps are 1/10 as big as they were before. We now repeat the operation described previously, walking down the x-axis until we pass the root.

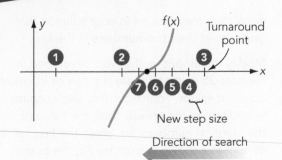

Again, the algorithm changes the sign of step size to reverse direction and reduces it to 1/10 its previous size. As the diagrams show, we are slowly zeroing in on the root—going past it, turning around, going past it, turning around, and so forth. This iterative process stops when the algorithm passes a root and the step size is smaller than the desired accuracy. It has now bracketed the root within an interval that is smaller than the accuracy we want. At this point, it should print the midpoint of the interval and terminate.

There are many special cases that this algorithm must deal with, but in your solution you may disregard them. Assume that you will always encounter a root in your "travels" along the x-axis. After creating a solution, you might want to look at some of these special cases, such as a function that has no real roots, a starting point that is to the right of all the roots, and two roots so close together that they fall within the same step.

2. One of the most important and widely used classes of algorithms in computer science is *sorting*, the process of putting a list of elements into a predefined order, usually numeric or alphabetic. There are many different sorting algorithms, and we will look at some of them in Chapter 3. One of the simplest sorting algorithms is called *selection sort*, and it can be implemented using the tools that you have learned in this chapter. It is also one of the easiest to understand as it mimics how we often sort collections of values when we must do so by hand.

Assume that we are given a list named A, containing eight values that we want to sort into ascending order, from smallest to largest:

A:	23	18	66	9	21	90	32	4
Position:	1	2	3	4	5	6	7	8

We first look for the largest value contained in positions 1–8 of list A. We can do this using something like the Find Largest algorithm that appears in Figure 2.14. In this case, the largest value is 90, and it appears in position 6. Because this is the largest value in list A, we swap it with the value in position 8 so that it is in its correct place at the back of the list. The list is now partially sorted from position 8 to position 8:

A:	23	18	66	9	21	4	32	90
Position:	1	2	3	4	5	6	7	8

We now search the array for the second largest value. Because we know that the largest value is contained in position 8, we need to search only positions 1–7 of list A to find the second largest value. In this case, the second largest value is 66, and it appears in position 3. We now swap the value in position 3 with the value in position 7 to get the second largest value into its correct location. This produces the following:

A:	23	18	32	9	21	4	66	90
Position:	1	2	3	4	5	6	7	8

The list is now partially sorted from position 7 to position 8, with those two locations holding the two largest values. The next search goes from position 1 to position 6 of list A, this time trying to locate the third largest value, and we swap that value with the number in position 6. After repeating this process seven times, the list is completely sorted. (That is because if the last seven items are in their correct place, the item in position 1 must also be in its correct place.)

Using the Find Largest algorithm shown in Figure 2.14 (which may have to be slightly modified) and the primitive pseudocode operations listed in Figure 2.9, implement the selection sort algorithm that we have just described. Assume that *n*, the size of the list, and the *n*-element list A are input to your algorithm. The output of your algorithm should be the sorted list.

3. Most people are familiar with the work of the great mathematicians of ancient Greece and Rome, such as Archimedes, Euclid, Pythagoras, and Plato. However, a great deal of important work in arithmetic, geometry, algebra, number theory, and logic was carried out by scholars working in Egypt, Persia, India, and China. For example, the concept of zero was first developed in India, and positional numbering systems (like our own decimal system) were developed and used in China, India, and the Middle East long before they made their way to Europe. Read about the work of some mathematician (such as Al-Khwarizmi) from one of these places or another place, and write a paper describing his or her contributions to mathematics, logic, and (ultimately) computer science.

The Efficiency of Algorithms

AFTER STUDYING THIS CHAPTER, YOU WILL BE ABLE TO:

- Describe algorithm attributes and why they are important
- Explain the purpose of efficiency analysis and apply it to new algorithms to determine the order of magnitude of their time efficiencies
- Describe, illustrate, and use the algorithms from the chapter, including: sequential and binary search, selection sort, data cleanup algorithms, pattern-matching
- Explain which orders of magnitude grow faster or slower than others
- Describe what a "suspected intractable" problem is, giving one or more examples, and the purpose of approximation algorithms that partially solve them

3.1 Introduction

Finding algorithms to solve problems of interest is an important part of computer science. Any algorithm that is developed to solve a specific problem has, by definition, certain required characteristics (see the formal definition in Chapter 1, Section 1.3.1), but are some algorithms better than others? That is, are there other desirable but nonessential characteristics of algorithms?

Consider the automobile: There are certain features that are part of the "definition" of a car, such as four wheels and an engine. These are the basics. However, when purchasing a car, we almost certainly take into account other things, such as ease of handling, style, and fuel efficiency. This analogy is not as superficial as it seems—the properties that make better algorithms are in fact very similar.

3.2 Attributes of Algorithms

First and foremost, we expect *correctness* from our algorithms. An algorithm intended to solve a problem must, again by formal definition, give a result and then halt. But this is not enough; we also want the result to be a correct solution to the problem. You could consider this an inherent property of the definition of an algorithm (like a car being capable of transporting us where we want to go), but it bears emphasizing. An elegant and efficient algorithm that gives wrong results for the problem at hand is worse than useless. It can lead to mistakes that are enormously expensive or even fatal.

Determining that an algorithm gives correct results might not be as straight-forward as it seems. For one thing, our algorithm might indeed be providing correct results—but to the wrong problem. This can happen when we design an algorithm without a thorough understanding of the real problem we are trying to solve, and it is one of the most common causes of "incorrect" algorithms. Also, once we understand the problem, the algorithm must provide correct results for all possible input values, not just for those values that are the most likely to occur. Do we know what all those correct results are? Probably not, or we would not be writing an algorithm to solve this problem. But there may be a certain standard against which we can check the result for reasonableness, thus giving us a way to determine when a result is obviously incorrect. In some cases, as noted in Chapter 1, the correct result may be an error message say-ing that there is no correct answer. There may also be an issue of the accuracy of the result we are willing to accept as correct. If the "real" answer is π, for example, then we can only approximate its decimal value. Is 3.14159 close enough to "correct"? Is 3.1416 close enough? What about 3.14? Computer scientists often summarize these two views of correctness by asking, "Are we solving the right problem? Are we solving the problem right?"

If an algorithm to solve a problem exists and we determine, after taking into account all the considerations of the previous paragraph, that it gives correct results, what more can we ask? To many mathematicians, this would be the end of the matter. After all, once a solution has been obtained and shown to be correct, it is no longer of interest (except possibly for use in obtaining solutions to other problems). This is where computer science dif-fers significantly from theoretical disciplines such as pure mathematics and begins to take on an "applied" character more closely related to engineering or applied mathematics. The algorithms developed by computer scientists are not merely of academic interest. They are also intended to be *used*.

Suppose, for example, that a road to the top of a mountain is to be built. An algorithmic solution exists that gives a correct answer for this problem in the sense that a road is produced: Just build the road straight up the mountain. Problem solved. But the highway engineer knows that the road must be usable by real traffic and that this constraint limits the grade of the road. The existence and correctness of the algorithm is not enough; there are practical considerations as well.

The practical considerations for computer science arise because the algorithms developed are executed in the form of computer programs running on real computers to solve problems of interest to real people. Let's consider the "people aspect" first. A computer program is seldom written to be used only once to solve a single instance of a problem. It is written to solve many instances of that problem with many different input values, just as the sequential search algorithm of Chapter 2 would be used many times with different lists of telephone numbers and associated names, and different target *NUMBER* values. Furthermore, the problem itself does not usually "stand still." If the program is successful, people will want to use it for slightly different versions of the problem, which means they will want the program slightly enhanced to do more things. Therefore, after a program is written, it needs to be maintained, both to fix any errors that are uncovered through repeated usage with different input values and to extend the program to meet new requirements. A great deal of time and money are devoted to *program maintenance*. The person who has to modify a program, either to correct errors or to expand its functionality, often is not the person who wrote the original program. To make program maintenance as easy as possible, the algorithm the program uses should be easy to understand. *Ease of understanding,* clarity, "ease of handling"—whatever you want to call it—is a highly desirable characteristic of an algorithm.

On the other hand, there is a certain satisfaction in having an "elegant" solution to a problem. *Elegance* is the algorithmic equivalent of style. The classic example, in mathematical folklore, is the story of the German mathematician Karl Frederick Gauss (1777–1855), who was asked as a schoolchild to add up the numbers from 1 to 100. The straightforward algorithm of adding $1 + 2 + 3 + 4 + \ldots + 100$ by adding one number at a time can be expressed in pseudocode as follows:

1. Set the value of *sum* to 0

2. Set the value of *x* to 1

3. While *x* is less than or equal to 100, do Steps 4 and 5

4.   Add *x* to *sum*

5.   Add 1 to the value of *x*

6. Print the value of *sum*

7. Stop

This algorithm can be executed to find that the sum has the value 5,050. It is fairly easy to read this pseudocode and understand how the algorithm works. It is also fairly clear that if we want to change this algorithm to one that adds the numbers from 1 to 1,000, we only have to change the loop condition to

3. While *x* is less than or equal to 1,000, do Steps 4 and 5

However, Gauss noticed that the numbers from 1 to 100 could be grouped into 50 pairs of the form

$$1 + 100 = 101$$
$$2 + 99 = 101$$

.

.

.

$$50 + 51 = 101$$

so that the sum equals $50 \times 101 = 5{,}050$. This is certainly an elegant and clever solution, but is it easy to understand? If a computer program just said to multiply

$$\left(\frac{100}{2}\right)101$$

with no further explanation, we might guess how to modify the program to add up the first 1,000 numbers, but would we really grasp what was happening enough to be sure the modification would work? (The Practice Problems at the end of this section discuss this.) Sometimes elegance and ease of understanding work at cross-purposes; the more elegant the solution, the more difficult it may be to understand. Do we win or lose if we have to trade ease of understanding for elegance? Of course, if an algorithm has both characteristics—ease of understanding and elegance—that's a plus.

Now let's consider the real computers on which programs run. Although these computers can execute instructions very rapidly and have some memory in which to store information, time and space are not unlimited resources. The computer scientist must be conscious of the resources consumed by a given algorithm, and if there is a choice between two (correct) algorithms that perform the same task, the one that uses fewer resources is preferable. The term used to describe an algorithm's careful use of resources is efficiency. Efficiency, in addition to *correctness, ease of understanding,* and *elegance,* is an extremely desirable attribute of an algorithm.

Because of the rapid advances in computer technology, today's computers have much more memory capacity and execute instructions much more quickly than computers of just a few years ago. Efficiency in algorithms might seem to be a moot point; we can just wait for the next generation of technology and it won't matter how much time or space is required. There is some truth to this, but as computer memory capacity and processing speed increase, people find more complex problems to be solved, so the boundaries of the computer's resources continue to be pushed. Furthermore, we will see in this chapter that there are algorithms that consume so many resources that they will never be practical, no matter what advances in computer technology occur.

How should we measure the time and space consumed by an algorithm to determine whether it is efficient? Space efficiency can be judged by the amount of information the algorithm must store in the computer's memory to do its job, in addition to the initial data on which the algorithm is operating. If it uses only a few extra memory locations while processing the input data, the algorithm is relatively space efficient. If the algorithm requires almost as much additional storage as the input data itself takes up, or even more, then it is relatively space inefficient.

How can we measure the time efficiency of an algorithm? Consider the sequential search algorithm shown in Figure 2.13, which finds a person's name given his or her telephone number in a reverse telephone directory in which the telephone numbers are not arranged in numerical order. How about running the algorithm on a real computer and timing it to see how many seconds (or maybe what small fraction of a second) it takes to find a name or announce that the phone number is not present? The difficulty with this approach is that there are three factors involved, each of which can affect the answer to such a degree as to make whatever number of seconds we come up with rather meaningless.

1. On which computer will we run the algorithm? Should we use a smart-phone, a modest laptop, or a supercomputer capable of doing many trillions of calculations per second?

2. Which reverse telephone book (list of numbers) will we use: one limited to a relatively small geographic area or one that covers all listed numbers in the North American Numbering Plan?

3. Which number will we search for? What if we pick a number that happens to be first in the list? What if it happens to be last in the list?

Simply timing the running of an algorithm is more likely to reflect machine speed or variations in input data than the efficiency (or lack thereof) of the algorithm itself.

This is not to say that you can't obtain meaningful information by timing an algorithm. Using the same input data (for example, searching for the same number in the same reverse directory) and timing the algorithm on different machines gives a comparison of machine speeds because the task is identical. Using the same machine and the same reverse directory, but searching for different numbers, gives an indication of how the choice of *NUMBER* affects the algorithm's running time on that particular machine. This type of comparative timing is called benchmarking. Benchmarks are useful for rating one machine against another and for rating how sensitive a particular algorithm is with respect to variations in input on one particular machine.

However, what we mean by an algorithm's time efficiency is an indication of the amount of "work" required by the algorithm itself. It is a measure of the inherent efficiency of the method, independent of the speed of the machine on which it executes or the specific input data being processed. Is the amount of work an algorithm does the same as the number of instructions it executes? Not all instructions do the same things, so perhaps they should not all be "counted" equally. Some instructions are carrying out work that is fundamental to the way the algorithm operates, whereas other instructions are carrying out peripheral tasks that must be done in support of the fundamental work. To measure time efficiency, we identify the fundamental unit (or units) of work of an algorithm and count how many times the work unit is executed. Later in this chapter, we will see why we can ignore peripheral tasks.

Practice Problems

1. Use Gauss's approach to find a formula for the sum of the numbers from 1 to n,

   $1 + 2 + 3 + ... + n$

   where n is an even number. Your formula will be an expression involving n.

2. Test your formula from Practice Problem 1 for the following sums:

   a. $1 + 2$

   b. $1 + 2 + ... + 6$

   c. $1 + 2 + ... + 10$

   d. $1 + 2 + ... + 100$

   e. $1 + 2 + ... + 1000$

3. Now see if the same formula from Practice Problem 1 works when n is odd; try it on the following sums:

   a. $1 + 2 + 3$

   b. $1 + 2 + ... + 5$

   c. $1 + 2 + ... + 9$

3.3 Measuring Efficiency

The study of the efficiency of algorithms is called the analysis of algorithms, and it is an important part of computer science. As a first example of the analysis of an algorithm, we'll look at the sequential search algorithm that we created to solve the reverse telephone lookup problem.

3.3.1 Sequential Search

The pseudocode description of the sequential search algorithm from Chapter 2 appears in Figure 3.1, where we have assumed that the list contains n entries instead of 10,000 entries.

The central unit of work is the comparison of the *NUMBER* being searched for against a single phone number in the list. The essence of the algorithm is the repetition of this task against successive numbers in the list until *NUMBER* is found or the list is exhausted. The comparison takes place at Step 4, within the loop body composed of Steps 4 through 7. Peripheral tasks include setting the initial value of the index i and the initial value of

FIGURE 3.1

1. Get values for *NUMBER*, *n*, T_1, ... , T_n and N_1, ... , N_n
2. Set the value of *i* to 1 and set the value of *Found* to NO
3. While (*Found* = NO) and (*i* ≤ *n*) do Steps 4 through 7
4.   If *NUMBER* is equal to the *i*th number on the list, T_i, then
5.   Print the name of the corresponding person, N_i
6.   Set the value of *Found* to YES
         Else (*NUMBER* is not equal to T_i)
7.   Add 1 to the value of *i*
8. If (*Found* = NO) then
9.   Print the message 'Sorry, this number is not in our directory'
10. Stop

Sequential search algorithm

Found, writing the output, adjusting *Found*, and moving the index forward in the list of numbers. Why are these considered peripheral tasks?

Setting the initial value of the index and the initial value of *Found* requires executing a single instruction, done at Step 2. Writing output requires executing a single instruction, either at Step 5 if *NUMBER* is in the list or at Step 9 if *NUMBER* is not in the list. Note that instruction 5, although it is part of the loop, writes output at most once (if *NUMBER* equals T_i). Similarly, setting *Found* to YES occurs at most once (if *NUMBER* equals T_i) at Step 6. We can ignore the small contribution of these single-instruction executions to the total work done by the algorithm.

Moving the index forward is done once for each comparison, at Step 7. We can get a good idea of the total amount of work the algorithm does by simply counting the number of comparisons and then multiplying by some constant factor to account for the index-moving task. The constant factor could be 2 because we do one index move for each comparison, so we would double the work. It could be less because it is less work to add 1 to *i* than it is to compare *NUMBER* digit by digit against T_i. As we will see later, the precise value of this constant factor is not very important.

So again, the basic unit of work in this algorithm is the comparison of *NUMBER* against a list element. One comparison is done at each pass through the loop in Steps 4 through 7, so we must ask how many times the loop is executed. Of course, this depends on when, or if, we find *NUMBER* in the list.

The minimum amount of work is done if *NUMBER* is the very first number in the list. This requires only one comparison because *NUMBER* has then been found and the algorithm exits the loop after only one pass. This is the *best case*, requiring the least work. The *worst case*, requiring the maximum amount of work, occurs if *NUMBER* is the very last number in the list or is absent. In either of these situations, *NUMBER* must be compared against all *n* numbers in the list before the loop terminates because *FOUND* gets set to

YES (if *NUMBER* is the last number in the list) or because the value of the index i exceeds n (if *NUMBER* is not in the list).

When *NUMBER* occurs somewhere in the middle of the list, it requires somewhere between 1 (the best case) and n (the worst case) comparisons. If we were to run the sequential search algorithm many times with random *NUMBERs* occurring at various places in the list and count the number of comparisons done each time, we would find that the average number of comparisons done is about $n/2$. (The exact average is actually slightly higher than $n/2$; see Exercise 5 at the end of the chapter.) It is not hard to explain why an average of approximately $n/2$ comparisons are done (or the loop is executed approximately $n/2$ times) when *NUMBER* is in the list. If *NUMBER* occurs halfway down the list, then roughly $n/2$ comparisons are required; random *NUMBERs* in the list occur before the halfway point about half the time and after the halfway point about half the time, and these cases of less work and more work balance out.

This means that the average number of comparisons needed to find a *NUMBER* that occurs in a 10-element list is about 5, in a 100-element list about 50, and in a 1,000-element list about 500. With small values of n—say, a few hundred or a few thousand numbers—the values of $n/2$ (the average case) or n (the worst case) are small enough that a computer could execute the algorithm quickly and get the desired answer in a fraction of a second. However, computers are generally used to solve not tiny problems but very large ones. Therefore, we are usually interested in the behavior of an algorithm as the size of a problem (n) gets very, very large. In our reverse directory example, the total number of publicly listed telephone numbers exceeds 350,000,000. (Cell phone numbers are usually unlisted.) If the sequential search algorithm were executed on a computer that could do 50,000 comparisons per second, it would require on the average about

$$\frac{350,000,000}{2} \text{ comparisons} \times \frac{1}{50,000} \text{ seconds/comparison} = 3,500 \text{ seconds}$$

or nearly an hour just to do the comparisons necessary to locate a specific number. Including the constant factor for advancing the index, the actual time needed would be even greater. It would require almost 2 hours to do the comparisons required to determine that a number is not in the reverse directory! Sequential search is not sufficiently time efficient for large values of n to be useful as a reverse directory lookup algorithm.

Information about the number of comparisons required to perform the sequential search algorithm on a list of n numbers is summarized in Figure 3.2. Note that the values for both the worst case and the average case depend on n, the number of numbers in the list. The bigger the list, the more work must be done to search it. Few algorithms do the same amount of work on large inputs as on small inputs, simply because most algorithms process the input data, and more data to process means more work. The work an algorithm does can usually be expressed in terms of a formula that depends on the size of the problem input. In the case of searching a list of numbers, the input size is the length of the list.

Let's say a word about the space efficiency of sequential search. The algorithm stores the list of numbers/names and the target *NUMBER* as part of the

FIGURE 3.2

Best Case	Worst Case	Average Case
1	n	n/2

Number of comparisons to find NUMBER in a list of n numbers using sequential search

input. The only additional memory required is storage for the index value i and the *Found* indicator. Two single additional memory locations are insignificant compared with the size of the list, just as executing a single instruction to initialize the value of i and *Found* is insignificant beside the repetitive comparison task. Therefore, sequential search uses essentially no more memory storage than the original input requires, so it is very space efficient.

While we have presented sequential search in the context of searching for a particular telephone number from an unsorted list of numbers, the algorithm applies to searching any unordered list of items for one particular "target" item. And again, although it does not seem to be a time-efficient algorithm for a large value of n, it is the best approach available to search an unsorted list.

3.3.2 Order of Magnitude—Order n

When we analyzed the time efficiency of the sequential search algorithm, we glossed over the contribution of the constant factor for the peripheral work. To see why this constant factor doesn't particularly matter, we need to understand a concept called *order of magnitude*.

The worst-case behavior of the sequential search algorithm on a list of n items requires n comparisons, and if c is a constant factor representing the peripheral work, it requires cn total work. Suppose that c has the value 2. Then the values of n and $2n$ are

n	$2n$
1	2
2	4
3	6

and so on

These values are shown in Figure 3.3, which illustrates how the value of $2n$, which is the total work, changes as n changes. We can add to this graph to show how the value of cn changes as n changes, where $c = 1$ or $c = 1/2$ as well as $c = 2$ (see Figure 3.4; these values of c are completely arbitrary). Figure 3.5 presents a different view of the growth rate of cn as n changes for these three values of c.

Both Figures 3.4 and 3.5 show that the amount of work cn increases as n increases, but at different rates. The work grows at the same rate as n when $c = 1$, at twice the rate of n when $c = 2$, and at half the rate of n when

FIGURE 3.3

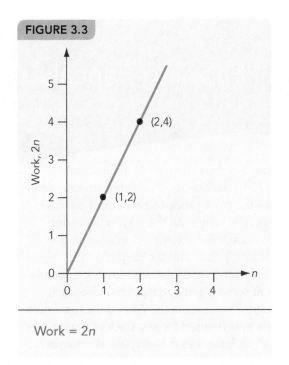

Work = 2n

FIGURE 3.4

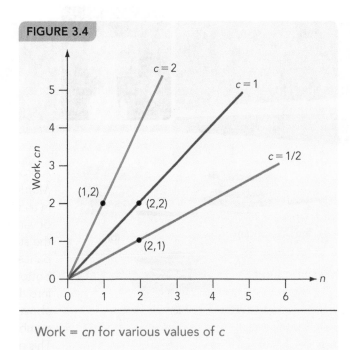

Work = cn for various values of c

$c = 1/2$. However, Figure 3.4 also shows that all of these graphs follow the same basic straight-line shape of n. Anything that varies as a constant times n (and whose graph follows the basic shape of n) is said to be of order of magnitude n, written $\Theta(n)$ and pronounced "order n." We will classify algorithms according to the order of magnitude of their time efficiency. Sequential search is therefore an $\Theta(n)$ algorithm (an order-n algorithm) in both the worst case and the average case.

FIGURE 3.5

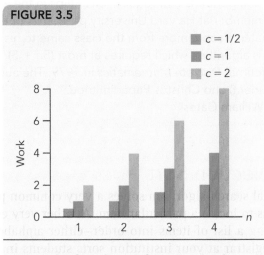

Growth of work = cn for various values of c

Flipping Pancakes

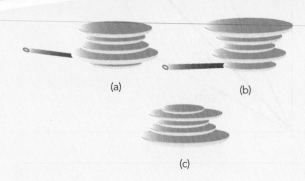

(a)

(b)

(c)

A problem posed in the *American Mathematical Monthly* in 1975 by Jacob Goodman concerned a waiter in a café where the cook produced a stack of pancakes of varying sizes. The waiter, on the way to delivering the stack to the customer, attempted to arrange the pancakes in order by size, with the largest on the bottom. The only action available was to stick a spatula into the stack at some point and flip the entire stack above that point. The question is: What is the maximum number of flips ever needed for any stack of n pancakes? This number, P_n, is known as the *nth pancake number*.

Here's a fairly simple algorithm to arrange the pancakes. Put the spatula under the largest pancake, as shown in (a) in the figure, and flip. This puts the largest pancake on top [(b) in the figure]. Put the spatula at the bottom of the unordered section (in this case at the bottom) and flip. This puts the largest pancake on the bottom [(c) in the figure], where it belongs. Repeat with the rest of the pancakes. Each pancake therefore requires two flips, which would give a total of $2n$ flips required. But the last two pancakes require at most one flip; if they are already in order, no flips are needed, and if they are out of order, only one flip is needed. So this algorithm requires at most $2(n-2) + 1 = 2n - 3$ flips in the worst case, which means that $P_n \leq 2n - 3$. Are there other algorithms that require fewer flips in the worst case?

A faculty member at Harvard University posed this question to his class; several days later, a sophomore from the class came to his office with a better algorithm. This algorithm, which requires at most $(5n + 5)/3$ flips, was published in the journal *Discrete Mathematics* in 1979. The authors were William Gates (the student) and Christos Papadimitriou.

Yes, *that* William Gates!

3.3.3 Selection Sort

The sequential search algorithm solves a very common problem: searching a list of items to locate a particular item. Another very common problem is that of sorting a list of items into order—either alphabetical or numerical order. The registrar at your institution sorts students in a class by name, a mail-order business sorts its customer list by name, and the IRS sorts tax records by Social Security number. In this section, we'll examine a sorting algorithm and analyze its efficiency.

Practice Problem

Using the information in Figure 3.2, fill in the following table for the number of comparisons required in the sequential search algorithm.

n	Best Case	Worst Case	Average Case
10			
50			
100			
1,000			
10,000			
100,000			

Suppose we have a list of numbers to sort into ascending order—for example, 5, 7, 2, 8, 3. The result of sorting this list is the new list 2, 3, 5, 7, 8. The selection sort algorithm performs this task. The selection sort "grows" a sorted subsection of the list from the back to the front. We can look at "snapshots" of the progress of the algorithm on our sample list, using a vertical line as the marker between the unsorted section at the front of the list and the sorted section at the back of the list in each case. At first the sorted subsection is empty; that is, the entire list is unsorted. This is how the list looks when the algorithm begins.

5, 7, 2, 8, 3 |

Unsorted subsection (entire list)   Sorted subsection (empty)

Later, the sorted subsection of the list has grown from the back so that some of the list members are in the right place.

5, 3, 2, | 7, 8

Unsorted subsection   Sorted subsection

Finally, the sorted subsection of the list contains the entire list; there are no unsorted numbers, and the algorithm stops.

| 2, 3, 5, 7, 8

Unsorted subsection (empty)   Sorted subsection (entire list)

At any point, then, there is both a sorted and an unsorted section of the list. A pseudocode version of the algorithm is shown in Figure 3.6.

Before we illustrate this algorithm at work, take a look at Step 4, which finds the largest number in some list of numbers. We developed an algorithm

FIGURE 3.6

1. Get values for *n* and the *n* list items
2. Set the marker for the unsorted section at the end of the list
3. While the unsorted section of the list is not empty, do Steps 4 through 6
4.   Select the largest number in the unsorted section of the list
5.   Exchange this number with the last number in the unsorted section of the list
6.   Move the marker for the unsorted section left one position
7. Stop

Selection sort algorithm

for this task in Chapter 2 (Figure 2.14). A detailed version of the selection sort algorithm would replace Step 4 with the instructions from this existing algorithm. New algorithms can be built up from "parts" consisting of previous algorithms, just as a recipe for pumpkin pie might begin with the instruction, "Prepare crust for a one-crust pie." The recipe for pie crust is a previous algorithm that is now being used as one of the steps in the pumpkin pie algorithm.

Let's follow the selection sort algorithm. Initially, the unsorted section is the entire list, so Step 2 sets the marker at the end of the list.

5, 7, 2, 8, 3 |

Step 4 says to select the largest number in the unsorted section—that is, in the entire list. This number is 8. Step 5 says to exchange 8 with the last number in the unsorted section (the whole list). To accomplish this exchange, the algorithm must determine not only that 8 is the largest value but also the location in the list where 8 occurs. The Find Largest algorithm from Chapter 2 provides both these pieces of information. The exchange to be done is

5, 7, 2, 8, 3 |

After this exchange and after the marker is moved left as instructed in Step 6, the list looks like

5, 7, 2, 3 | 8

The number 8 is now in its correct position at the end of the list. It becomes the sorted section of the list, and the first four numbers are the unsorted section.

The unsorted section is not empty, so the algorithm repeats Step 4 (find the largest number in the unsorted section); it is 7. Step 5 exchanges 7 with the last number in the unsorted section, which is 3.

5, 7, 2, 3 | 8

After the marker is moved, the result is

5, 3, 2 | 7, 8

The sorted section is now 7, 8 and the unsorted section is 5, 3, 2.

Repeating the loop of Steps 4 through 6 again, the algorithm determines that the largest number in the unsorted section is 5, and exchanges it with 2, the last number in the unsorted section.

5, 3, 2 | 7, 8

After the marker is moved, we get

2, 3 | 5, 7, 8

Now the unsorted section (as far as the algorithm knows) is 2, 3. The largest number here is 3. Exchanging 3 with the last number of the unsorted section (that is, with itself) produces no change in the list ordering. The marker is moved, giving

2 | 3, 5, 7, 8

When the only part of the list that is unsorted is the single number 2, there is also no change in the list ordering produced by carrying out the exchange. The marker is moved, giving

| 2, 3, 5, 7, 8

The unsorted section of the list is empty, and the algorithm terminates.

To analyze the amount of work the selection sort algorithm does, we must first decide on the unit of work to count. When we analyzed sequential search, the unit of work that we measured was the comparison between the item being searched for and the items in the list. At first glance, there seem to be no comparisons of any kind going on in the selection sort. Remember, however, that there is a subtask within the selection sort: the task of finding the largest number in a list. The algorithm from Chapter 2 for finding the largest value in a list begins by taking the first number in the list as the largest so far. The largest-so-far value is compared against successive numbers in the list; if a larger value is found, it becomes the largest so far.

When the selection sort algorithm begins, the largest-so-far value, initially the first number, must be compared with all the other numbers in the list. If there are n numbers in the list, $n - 1$ comparisons must be done. The next time through the loop, the last number is already in its proper place, so it is never again involved in a comparison. The largest-so-far value, again initially the first number, must be compared with all the other numbers in the unsorted part of the list, which will require $n - 2$ comparisons. The number of comparisons keeps decreasing as the length of the unsorted section of the list gets smaller, until finally only one comparison is needed. The total number of comparisons is

$$(n - 1) + (n - 2) + (n - 3) + \ldots + 3 + 2 + 1$$

Reviewing our sample problem, we can see that the following comparisons are done:

- To put 8 in place in the list 5, 7, 2, 8, 3 |
  Compare 5 (largest so far) to 7
     7 becomes largest so far
  Compare 7 (largest so far) to 2
  Compare 7 (largest so far) to 8
     8 becomes largest so far
  Compare 8 to 3
  8 is the largest
  Total number of comparisons: 4 (which is 5 – 1)

- To put 7 in place in the list 5, 7, 2, 3 | 8
  Compare 5 (largest so far) to 7
     7 becomes largest so far
  Compare 7 to 2
  Compare 7 to 3
  7 is the largest
  Total number of comparisons: 3 (which is 5 – 2)

- To put 5 in place in the list 5, 3, 2 | 7, 8
  Compare 5 (largest so far) to 3
  Compare 5 to 2
  5 is the largest
  Total number of comparisons: 2 (which is 5 – 3)

- To put 3 in place in the list 2, 3 | 5, 7, 8
  Compare 2 (largest so far) to 3
  3 is the largest
  Total number of comparisons: 1 (which is 5 – 4)

To put 2 in place requires no comparisons; there is only one number in the unsorted section of the list, so it is of course the largest number. It gets exchanged with itself, which produces no effect. The total number of comparisons is $4 + 3 + 2 + 1 = 10$.

The sum

$$(n - 1) + (n - 2) + (n - 3) + \ldots + 3 + 2 + 1$$

turns out to be equal to

$$\left(\frac{n-1}{2}\right)n = \frac{1}{2}n^2 - \frac{1}{2}n$$

(Recall from earlier in this chapter how Gauss computed a similar sum.) For our example with five numbers, this formula says that the total number of comparisons is (using the first version of the formula):

$$\left(\frac{5-1}{2}\right)5 = \left(\frac{4}{2}\right)5 = (2)5 = 10$$

which is the number of comparisons we had counted.

Figure 3.7 uses this same formula

$$\frac{1}{2}n^2 - \frac{1}{2}n$$

to compute the comparisons required for larger values of n. Remember that n is the size of the list we are sorting. If the list becomes 10 times longer, the work increases by much more than a factor of 10; it increases by a factor closer to 100, which is 10^2.

The selection sort algorithm not only does comparisons, it also does exchanges. Even if the largest number in the unsorted section of the list is already at the end of the unsorted section, the algorithm exchanges this number with itself. Therefore, the algorithm does n exchanges, one for each position in the list to put the correct value in that position. With every exchange, the marker gets moved. However, the work contributed by exchanges and marker moving is so much less than the amount contributed by comparisons that it can be ignored.

We haven't talked here about a best case, a worst case, or an average case for the selection sort. This algorithm does the same amount of work no matter how the numbers are initially arranged. It has no way to recognize, for example, that the list might already be sorted at the outset.

A word about the space efficiency of the selection sort: The original list occupies n memory locations, and this is the major space requirement. Some storage is needed for the marker between the unsorted and sorted sections and for keeping track of the largest-so-far value and its location in the list, used in Step 4. Surprisingly, the process of exchanging two values at Step 5 also requires an extra storage location. Here's why. If the two numbers to be

FIGURE 3.7

Length n of List to Sort	n^2	Number of Comparisons Required
10	100	45
100	10,000	4,950
1,000	1,000,000	499,500

Comparisons required by selection sort

exchanged are at position X and position Y in the list, we might think the following two steps will exchange these values:

1. Copy the current value at position Y into position X
2. Copy the current value at position X into position Y

The problem is that after Step 1, the value at position X is the same as that at position Y. Step 2 does not put the original value of X into position Y. In fact, we don't even have the original value of position X anymore. In Figure 3.8(a), we see the original X and Y values. At Figure 3.8(b), after execution of Step 1, the current value of position Y has been copied into position X, writing over what was there originally. At Figure 3.8(c), after execution of Step 2, the current value at position X (which is the original Y value) has been copied into position Y, but the picture looks the same as Figure 3.8(b).

Here's the correct algorithm, which makes use of one extra temporary storage location that we'll call T.

1. Copy the current value at position X into location T
2. Copy the current value at position Y into position X
3. Copy the current value at location T into position Y

Figure 3.9 illustrates that this algorithm does the job. In Figure 3.9(a), the temporary location contains an unknown value. After execution of Step 1 (Figure 3.9(b)), it holds the current value of X. When Y's current value is put into X at Step 2 (Figure 3.9(c)), T still holds the original X value. After Step 3 (Figure 3.9(d)), the current value of T goes into position Y, and the original values of X and Y have been exchanged. (Step 5 of the selection sort algorithm is thus performed by another algorithm, just as Step 4 is.)

All in all, the extra storage required for the selection sort, over and above that required to store the original list, is slight. Selection sort is space efficient.

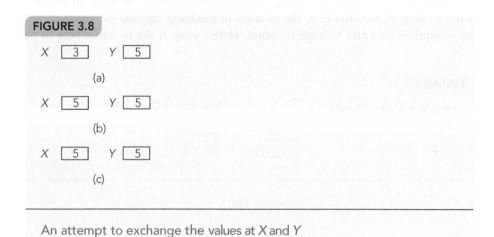

FIGURE 3.8

X [3]   Y [5]

(a)

X [5]   Y [5]

(b)

X [5]   Y [5]

(c)

An attempt to exchange the values at X and Y

FIGURE 3.9

X ⬚3⬚ Y ⬚5⬚ T ⬚⬚

(a)

X ⬚3⬚ Y ⬚5⬚ T ⬚3⬚

(b)

X ⬚5⬚ Y ⬚5⬚ T ⬚3⬚

(c)

X ⬚5⬚ Y ⬚3⬚ T ⬚3⬚

(d)

Exchanging the values at X and Y

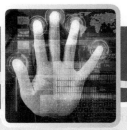

Practice Problems

1. For each of the following lists, perform a selection sort and show the list after each exchange that has an effect on the list ordering:

    a. 4, 8, 2, 6

    b. 12, 3, 6, 8, 2, 5, 7

    c. D, B, G, F, A, C, E, H

    d. 3, 7, 12, 16, 21

2. How many comparisons are required to sort each of the four lists shown in Practice Problem 1? How many exchanges?

3.3.4 Order of Magnitude—Order n^2

We saw that the number of comparisons done by the selection sort algorithm does not grow at the same rate as the problem size n; it grows at approximately the *square* of that rate. An algorithm that does cn^2 work for any constant c is order of magnitude n^2, or $\Theta(n^2)$. Figure 3.10 shows how cn^2 changes as n changes, where $c = 1$, 2, and 1/2. The work grows at the same rate as n^2 when $c = 1$, at twice that rate when $c = 2$, and at half that rate when $c = 1/2$. But all three graphs in Figure 3.10 follow the basic shape of n^2, which is different from all of the straight-line graphs that are of $\Theta(n)$. Thus,

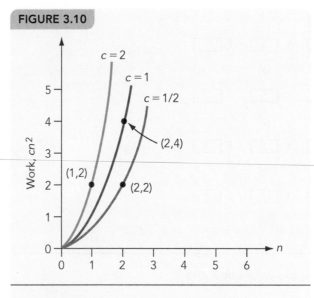

FIGURE 3.10

Work = cn^2 for various values of c

we have come up with two different "shape classifications": one including all graphs that are $\Theta(n)$ and the other including all graphs that are $\Theta(n^2)$.

If it is not important to distinguish among the various graphs that make up a given order of magnitude, why is it important to distinguish between the two different orders of magnitude n and n^2? We can find the answer by comparing the two basic shapes n and n^2, as is done in Figure 3.11.

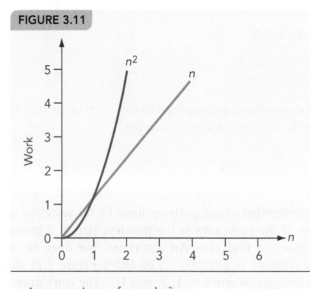

FIGURE 3.11

A comparison of n and n^2

Figure 3.11 illustrates that n^2 grows at a much faster rate than n. The two curves cross at the point (1,1), and for any value of n larger than 1, n^2 has a value increasingly greater than n. Furthermore, anything that is order of magnitude n^2 eventually has larger values than anything that is of order n, no matter what the constant factors are. For example, Figure 3.12 shows that if we choose a graph that is $\Theta(n^2)$ but has a small constant factor (to keep the values low), say $0.25n^2$, and a graph that is $\Theta(n)$ but has a larger constant factor (to pump the values up), say $10n$, it is still true that the $\Theta(n^2)$ graph eventually has larger values. (Note that the vertical scale and the horizontal scale are different.)

Selection sort is an $\Theta(n^2)$ algorithm (in all cases) and sequential search is an $\Theta(n)$ algorithm (in the worst case), so these two algorithms are different orders of magnitude. Because these algorithms solve two different problems, this is somewhat like comparing apples and oranges—what does it mean? But suppose we have two different algorithms that solve the same problem and count the same units of work but have different orders of magnitude. Suppose that algorithm A does $0.0001n^2$ units of work to solve a problem with input size n and that algorithm B does $100n$ of the same units of work to solve the same problem. Here algorithm B's factor of 100 is *1 million times larger* than algorithm A's factor of 0.0001. Nonetheless, when the problem gets large enough, the inherent inefficiency of algorithm A causes it to do more work than algorithm B. Figure 3.13 shows that the "crossover" point occurs at a value of 1,000,000 for n. At this point, the two algorithms do the same amount of work and therefore take the same

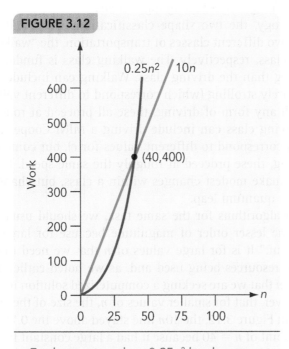

FIGURE 3.12

For large enough n, $0.25n^2$ has larger values than $10n$

FIGURE 3.13

| | Number of Work Units Required | |
| | Algorithm A | Algorithm B |
n	$0.0001n^2$	$100n$
1,000	100	100,000
10,000	10,000	1,000,000
100,000	1,000,000	10,000,000
1,000,000	100,000,000	100,000,000
10,000,000	10,000,000,000	1,000,000,000

A comparison of two extreme $\Theta(n^2)$ and $\Theta(n)$ algorithms

amount of time to run. For larger values of n, the order-n^2 algorithm A runs increasingly slower than the order-n algorithm B. (Input sizes in the millions are not that uncommon; as of April 2017, Facebook had 1.97 billion monthly active users.)

As we have seen, if an $\Theta(n^2)$ algorithm and an $\Theta(n)$ algorithm exist for the same task, then for large enough n, the $\Theta(n^2)$ algorithm does more work and takes longer to execute, regardless of the constant factors for peripheral work. *This is the rationale for ignoring constant factors and concentrating on the basic order of magnitude of algorithms.*

As an analogy, the two shape classifications $\Theta(n^2)$ and $\Theta(n)$ may be thought of as two different classes of transportation, the "walking" class and the "driving" class, respectively. The walking class is fundamentally more time consuming than the driving class. Walking can include jogging, running, and leisurely strolling (which correspond to different values for c), but compared with any form of driving, these all proceed at roughly the same speed. The driving class can include driving a MINI Cooper and driving a Ferrari (which correspond to different values for c), but compared with any form of walking, these proceed at roughly the same speed. In other words, varying c can make modest changes within a class, but changing to a different class is a quantum leap.

Given two algorithms for the same task, we should usually choose the algorithm of the lesser order of magnitude because for large enough n, it always "wins out." It is for large values of n that we need to be concerned about the time resources being used and, as we noted earlier, it is often for large values of n that we are seeking a computerized solution in the first place.

Note, however, that for smaller values of n, the size of the constant factor is significant. In Figure 3.12, the $10n$ line stayed above the $0.25n^2$ curve up to the crossover point of $n = 40$ because it had a large constant factor relative to the factor for n^2. Varying the factors changes the crossover point. If $10n$ and $0.25n^2$ represented the work of two different algorithms for the same task, and if we are sure that the size of the input is never going to exceed 40, then

The Tortoise and the Hare

One way to compare performance among different makes of computers is to give the number of arithmetic operations, such as additions or subtractions of real numbers, that each one can do in 1 second. These operations are called *floating-point operations*, and computers are often compared in terms of the number of **flops** (floating-point operations per second) they can crank out.

In March 2016, AMD (Advanced Micro Devices) announced a new graphics card with dual processors and an overall speed of 16 *teraflops* (16 trillion floating-point operations per second; that's 16,000,000,000,000). Such a card would be useful for a PC targeted toward video-game playing, although such a machine could perform general-purpose computing as well. In November 2016, the Sunway TaihuLight at the National SuperComputing Center in Wuxi, China, was declared the world's top-speed supercomputer. It is a parallel processor system with 10,649,600 core processors. It performs at the rate of 93 *petaflops* (93 quadrillion floating-point operations per second; that's 93,000,000,000,000,000). The supercomputer is almost 6,000 times faster than the gaming computer. In some sense this is a meaningless comparison because the two machines are optimized for entirely different purposes. Nonetheless, in terms of raw speed, the stage is set for the race between the tortoise and the hare.

Not fair, you say? We'll see. Let's suppose the gaming machine is assigned to run an $\Theta(n)$ algorithm, whereas the supercomputer gets an $\Theta(n^2)$ algorithm for the same task. The work units are floating-point operations, and for simplicity, we'll take the constant factor to be 1 in each case. Here are the timing results:

n	Desktop	Supercomputer
1,000	0.0000000000625 sec	0.0000000000108 sec
100,000,000	0.00000625 sec	0.108 sec
10,000,000,000,000	0.625 sec	1,075,268,817 sec = 34 years

Out of the gate—that is, for relatively small values of *n* such as 1,000—the supercomputer has the advantage and takes slightly less time. When *n* reaches 100,000,000, however, the supercomputer is falling behind. And for the largest value of *n*, the desktop leaves the supercomputer in the dust. The difference in order of magnitude between the algorithms was enough to slow down the mighty supercomputer and let the desktop pull ahead, chugging along doing its more efficient $\Theta(n)$ algorithm. Where would one need to perform 10,000,000,000,000 operations? Complex problems involving weather simulations, biomedical research, and economic modeling might utilize such number-crunching applications. Both China and the United States are

(Continued)

pursuing development of *exaflop* supercomputers capable of a billion billion calculations per second.

The point of this little tale is not to say that supercomputers will be readily replaced by desktop gaming computers! It is to demonstrate that the order of magnitude of the algorithm being executed can play a more important role than the raw speed of the computer.

the $0.25n^2$ algorithm is preferable in terms of time resources used. (To continue the transportation analogy, for traveling short distances—say, to the end of the driveway—walking is faster than driving because of the overhead of getting the car started, and so on. But for longer distances, driving is faster.)

However, making assumptions about the size of the input on which an algorithm will run can be dangerous. A program that runs quickly on small input size may at some point be selected, perhaps because it seems efficient, to solve instances of the problem with large input size, at which point the efficiency may go down the drain! (Software that served Facebook well when it was a startup company with 1,000 active users may not translate satisfactorily to managing 1.97 billion active users.) Part of the job of program documentation is to make clear any assumptions or restrictions about the input size the program was designed to handle.

Comparing algorithm efficiency only makes sense if there is a choice of algorithms for the task at hand. Are there any tasks for which a choice of algorithms exists? Yes; because sorting a list is such a common task, a lot of research has gone into finding good sorting algorithms. Selection sort is one sorting algorithm, but there are many others, including the bubble sort, described in Exercises 11–14 at the end of this chapter. You might wonder why people don't simply use the one "best" sorting algorithm. It's not that

Laboratory Experience 4

This Laboratory Experience allows you to step through animations of various sorting algorithms to understand how they work. The sorting algorithms available in the laboratory software include selection sort and bubble sort—which are described in this text—as well as insertion sort and quicksort, which are described in the laboratory manual. You'll be able to see values being switched around according to the various algorithms and see how lists eventually settle into sorted order.

You'll also do some experiments to measure the amount of work the various algorithms perform.

Practice Problem

An algorithm does $14n^2 + 5n + 1$ units of work on input of size n. Explain why this is considered an $\Theta(n^2)$ algorithm even though there is a term that involves just n.

simple. Some algorithms (unlike the selection sort) are sensitive to what the original input looks like. One algorithm might work well if the input is already close to being sorted, whereas another algorithm might work better if the input is random. An algorithm such as selection sort has the advantage of being relatively easy to understand. If the size of the list, n, is fairly small, then an easy-to-understand algorithm might be preferable to one that is more efficient but more obscure.

3.4 Analysis of Algorithms

3.4.1 Data Cleanup Algorithms

In this section, we'll look at three different algorithms that solve the same problem—the *data cleanup problem*—and then do an analysis of each. Suppose a survey includes a question about the age of the person filling out the survey, and that some people choose not to answer this question. When data from the survey are entered into the computer, an entry of 0 is used to denote "no response" because a legitimate value for age would have to be a positive number. For example, assume that the age data from 10 people who completed the survey are stored in the computer as the following 10-entry list, where the positions in the list range from 1 (far left) to 10 (far right).

0	24	16	0	36	42	23	21	0	27
1	2	3	4	5	6	7	8	9	10

Eventually, the average age of the survey respondents is to be computed. Because the 0 values are not legitimate data—including them in the average would produce too low a value—we want to perform a "data cleanup" and remove them from the list before the average is computed. In our example, the cleaned data could consist of a 10-element list, where the seven legitimate elements are the first seven entries of the list, and some quantity—let's call it *legit*—has the value 7 to indicate that only the first seven entries are legitimate. An alternative acceptable result would be a seven-element list consisting of the seven legitimate data items, in which case there is no need for a *legit* quantity.

The Shuffle-Left Algorithm. Algorithm 1 to solve the data cleanup problem works in the way we might solve this problem using a pencil and paper (and an eraser) to modify the list. We proceed through the list from left to right, pointing with a finger on the left hand to keep our place, and passing over nonzero values. Every time we encounter a 0 value, we squeeze it out of the list by copying each remaining data item in the list one cell to the left. We could use a finger on the right hand to move along the list and point at what to copy next. The value of *legit*, originally set to the length of the list, is reduced by 1 every time a 0 is encountered. (Sounds complicated, but you'll see that it is easy.)

The original configuration is

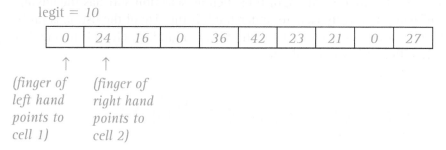

Because the first cell on the left contains a 0, the value of *legit* is reduced by 1, and all of the items to the right of the 0 must be copied one cell left. After the first such copy (of the 24), the scenario looks like

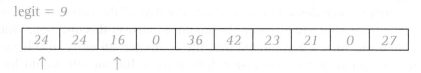

After the second copy (of the 16), we get

And after the third copy (of the 0), we get

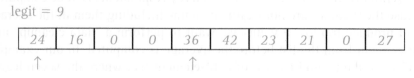

Proceeding in this fashion, we find that after we copy the last item (the 27), the result is

legit = 9

| 24 | 16 | 0 | 36 | 42 | 23 | 21 | 0 | 27 | 27 |

Because the right-hand finger has moved past the end of the list, one entire shuffle-left process has been completed. It required copying nine items. We reset the right-hand finger to start again.

legit = 9

| 24 | 16 | 0 | 36 | 42 | 23 | 21 | 0 | 27 | 27 |

We must again examine position 1 for a 0 value because if the original list contained 0 in position 2, it would have been copied into position 1. If the value is not 0, as is the case here, both the left-hand finger and the right-hand finger move forward.

legit = 9

| 24 | 16 | 0 | 36 | 42 | 23 | 21 | 0 | 27 | 27 |

Moving along, we pass over the 16.

legit = 9

| 24 | 16 | 0 | 36 | 42 | 23 | 21 | 0 | 27 | 27 |

Another cycle of seven copies takes place to squeeze out the 0; the result is

legit = 8

| 24 | 16 | 36 | 42 | 23 | 21 | 0 | 27 | 27 | 27 |

The 36, 42, 23, and 21 are passed over, which results in

legit = 8

| 24 | 16 | 36 | 42 | 23 | 21 | 0 | 27 | 27 | 27 |

and then copying three items to squeeze out the final 0 gives

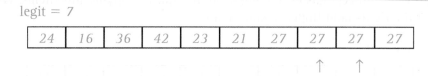

legit = 7

| 24 | 16 | 36 | 42 | 23 | 21 | 27 | 27 | 27 | 27 |

The left-hand finger is pointing at a nonzero element, so another advance of both fingers gives

legit = 7

| 24 | 16 | 36 | 42 | 23 | 21 | 27 | 27 | 27 | 27 |

At this point, we can stop because the left-hand finger is past the number of legitimate data items (*legit* = 7). In total, this algorithm (on this list) examined all 10 data items, to see which ones were 0, and copied $9 + 7 + 3 = 19$ items.

A pseudocode version of the shuffle-left algorithm to act on a list of n items appears in Figure 3.14. The quantities *left* and *right* correspond to the positions where the left-hand and right-hand fingers point, respectively. You should trace through this algorithm for the preceding example to see that it does what we described.

To analyze the time efficiency of an algorithm, you begin by identifying the fundamental units of work the algorithm performs. For the data cleanup

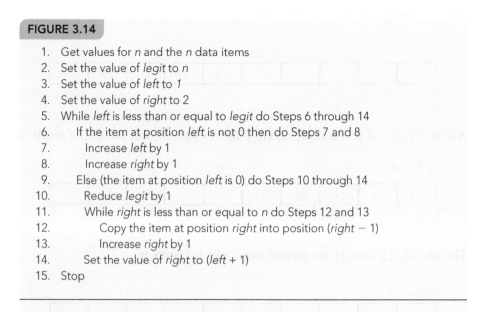

FIGURE 3.14

1. Get values for *n* and the *n* data items
2. Set the value of *legit* to *n*
3. Set the value of *left* to *1*
4. Set the value of *right* to *2*
5. While *left* is less than or equal to *legit* do Steps 6 through 14
6.   If the item at position *left* is not 0 then do Steps 7 and 8
7.   Increase *left* by 1
8.   Increase *right* by 1
9.   Else (the item at position *left* is 0) do Steps 10 through 14
10.   Reduce *legit* by 1
11.   While *right* is less than or equal to *n* do Steps 12 and 13
12.   Copy the item at position *right* into position (*right* − 1)
13.   Increase *right* by 1
14.   Set the value of *right* to (*left* + 1)
15. Stop

The shuffle-left algorithm for data cleanup

problem, any algorithm must examine each of the n elements in the list to see whether they are 0. This gives a base of at least $\Theta(n)$ work units.

The other unit of work in the shuffle-left algorithm is copying numbers. The best case occurs when the list has no 0 values because no copying is required. The worst case occurs when the list has all 0 values. Because the first element is 0, the remaining $n - 1$ elements are copied one cell left and *legit* is reduced from n to $n - 1$. After the 0 in position 2 gets copied into position 1, the first element is again 0, which again requires $n - 1$ copies and reduces *legit* from $n - 1$ to $n - 2$. This repeats until *legit* is reduced to 0, a total of n times. Thus there are n passes, during each of which $n - 1$ copies are done. The algorithm does

$$n(n - 1) = n^2 - n$$

copies. If we were to draw a graph of $n^2 - n$, we would see that for large n, the curve follows the shape of n^2. The second term can be disregarded because as n increases, the n^2 term grows much larger than the n term; the n^2 term dominates and determines the shape of the curve. The shuffle-left algorithm is thus an $\Theta(n^2)$ algorithm in the worst case.

The shuffle-left algorithm is space efficient because it only requires four memory locations to store the quantities n, *legit*, *left*, and *right* in addition to the memory required to store the list itself.

The Copy-Over Algorithm. The second algorithm for solving the data cleanup problem also works as we might if we decided to write a new list using a pencil and paper. It scans the list from left to right, copying every legitimate (nonzero) value into a new list that it creates. After this algorithm is finished, the original list still exists, but so does a new list that contains only nonzero values.

For our example, the result would be

0	24	16	0	36	42	23	21	0	27

24	16	36	42	23	21	27

Every list entry is examined to see whether it is 0 (as in the shuffle-left algorithm), and every nonzero list entry is copied once (into the new list), so altogether seven copies are done for this example. This is fewer copies than the shuffle-left algorithm requires, but a lot of extra memory space is required because an almost complete second copy of the list is stored. Figure 3.15 shows the pseudocode for this copy-over algorithm.

The best case for this algorithm occurs if all elements are 0; no copies are done so the work is just the $\Theta(n)$ work to examine each list element and see that it is 0. No extra space is used. The worst case occurs if there are no 0 values in the list. The algorithm copies all n nonzero elements into the new list and doubles the space required. Combining the two types of work units, we find that the copy-over algorithm is only $\Theta(n)$ in time efficiency even in the worst case because $\Theta(n)$ examinations and $\Theta(n)$ copies still equal $\Theta(n)$ steps.

FIGURE 3.15

1. Get values for *n* and the *n* data items
2. Set the value of *left* to 1
3. Set the value of *newposition* to 1
4. While *left* is less than or equal to *n* do Steps 5 through 8
5.   If the item at position *left* is not 0 then do Steps 6 and 7
6.   Copy the item at position *left* into position *newposition* in new list
7.   Increase *newposition* by 1
8.   Increase *left* by 1
9. Stop

The copy-over algorithm for data cleanup

Comparing the shuffle-left algorithm and the copy-over algorithm, we see that no 0 elements is the best case of the first algorithm and the worst case of the second, whereas all 0 elements is the worst case of the first and the best case of the second. The second algorithm is more time efficient and less space efficient. This choice is called the *time/space tradeoff*—you gain something by giving up something else. Seldom is it possible to improve both dimensions at once, but our next algorithm accomplishes just that.

The Converging-Pointers Algorithm. For the third algorithm, imagine that we move one finger along the list from left to right and another finger from right to left. The left finger slides to the right over nonzero values. Whenever the left finger encounters a 0 item, we reduce the value of *legit* by 1, copy whatever item is at the right finger into the left-finger position, and slide the right finger one cell left. Initially in our example

legit = *10*

0	24	16	0	36	42	23	21	0	27
↑									↑

And because a 0 is encountered at position *left*, the item at position *right* is copied into its place, and both *legit* and *right* are reduced by 1. This results in

legit = *9*

27	24	16	0	36	42	23	21	0	27
↑								↑	

The value of *left* increases until the next 0 is reached.

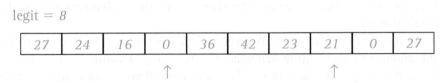

legit = 9

| 27 | 24 | 16 | 0 | 36 | 42 | 23 | 21 | 0 | 27 |

Again, the item at position *right* is copied into position *left*, and *legit* and *right* are reduced by 1.

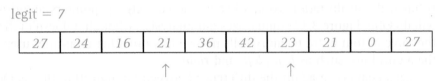

legit = 8

| 27 | 24 | 16 | 0 | 36 | 42 | 23 | 21 | 0 | 27 |

The item at position left is still 0, so another copy takes place.

legit = 7

| 27 | 24 | 16 | 21 | 36 | 42 | 23 | 21 | 0 | 27 |

From this point, the left finger advances until it meets the right finger, which is pointing to a nonzero element, and the algorithm stops. Once again, each element is examined to see whether it equals 0. For this example, only three copies are needed—fewer even than for algorithm 2, but this algorithm requires no more memory space than algorithm 1. The pseudocode version of the converging-pointers algorithm is given in Figure 3.16.

FIGURE 3.16

1. Get values for *n* and the *n* data items
2. Set the value of *legit* to *n*
3. Set the value of *left* to 1
4. Set the value of *right* to *n*
5. While *left* is less than *right* do Steps 6 through 10
6.   If the item at position *left* is not 0 then increase *left* by 1
7.   Else (the item at position *left* is 0) do Steps 8 through 10
8.   Reduce *legit* by 1
9.   Copy the item at position *right* into position *left*
10.   Reduce *right* by 1
11. If the item at position *left* is 0, then reduce *legit* by 1
12. Stop

The converging-pointers algorithm for data cleanup

The best case for this algorithm, as for the shuffle-left algorithm, is a list containing no 0 elements. The worst case, as for the shuffle-left algorithm, is a list of all 0 entries. With such a list, the converging-pointers algorithm repeatedly copies the element at position *right* into the first position, each time reducing the value of *right*. *Right* goes from n to 1, with one copy done at each step, resulting in $n - 1$ copies. This algorithm is $\Theta(n)$ in the worst case. Like the shuffle-left algorithm, it is space efficient. It is possible in this case to beat the time/space trade-off, in part because the data cleanup problem requires no particular ordering of the nonzero elements in the "clean" list; the converging-pointers algorithm moves these elements out of their original order.

It is hard to define what an "average" case is for any of these algorithms; the amount of work done depends on how many 0 values there are in the list and perhaps on where in the list they occur. If we assume, however, that the number of 0 values is some percentage of n and that these values are scattered throughout the list, then it can be shown that the shuffle-left algorithm will still do $\Theta(n^2)$ work, whereas the converging-pointers algorithm will do $\Theta(n)$. Figure 3.17 summarizes our analysis, although it doesn't reflect the three or four extra memory cells needed to store other quantities used in the algorithms, such as *legit*, *left*, and *right*.

Let's emphasize again the difference between an algorithm that is $\Theta(n)$ in the amount of work it does and one that is $\Theta(n^2)$. In an $\Theta(n)$ algorithm, the work is proportional to n. Hence if you double n, you double the amount of work; if you multiply n by 10, you multiply the work by 10. But in an $\Theta(n^2)$ algorithm, the work is proportional to the *square* of n. Hence if you double n, you multiply the amount of work by 4; if you multiply n by 10, you multiply the work by 100.

This is probably a good place to explain why the distinction between n and $2n$ is important when we are talking about space, but we simply classify n and $8000n$ as $\Theta(n)$ when we are talking about units of work. Units of work translate into time when the algorithm is executed, and time is a much more elastic resource than space. Whereas we want an algorithm to run in the shortest possible time, in many cases there is no fixed limit to the amount of

FIGURE 3.17

	1. Shuffle-left		2. Copy-over		3. Converging-pointers	
	Time	Space	Time	Space	Time	Space
Best case	$\Theta(n)$	n	$\Theta(n)$	n	$\Theta(n)$	n
Worst case	$\Theta(n^2)$	n	$\Theta(n)$	$2n$	$\Theta(n)$	n
Average case	$\Theta(n^2)$	n	$\Theta(n)$	$n \leq x \leq 2n$	$\Theta(n)$	n

Analysis of three data cleanup algorithms

time that can be expended. There is, however, always a fixed upper bound on the amount of memory that the computer has available to use while executing an algorithm, so we track space consumption more closely.

3.4.2 Binary Search

The sequential search algorithm searches a list of n items for a particular item; it is an $\Theta(n)$ algorithm. Another algorithm, the binary search algorithm, is more efficient but it works only when the search list is already sorted.

To understand how binary search operates, let us go back to the problem of searching for *NUMBER* in a reverse telephone directory, but now we assume that the directory is sorted in increasing numerical order by phone number. As we noted in Chapter 2, you would not search for (555) 123-4567 in such a directory by starting with the first number and proceeding sequentially through the list. Instead you would look for this number near the middle of the list, and if you didn't find it immediately, you would continue your search on the front half or the back half of the list.

This is exactly how the binary search algorithm works on a sorted list. It first looks for *NUMBER* at roughly the halfway point in the list. If the number there equals *NUMBER,* the search is over. If *NUMBER* comes numerically before the number at the halfway point, then the search is narrowed to the front half of the list, and the process begins again on this smaller list. If *NUMBER* comes numerically after the number at the halfway point, then the search is narrowed to the back half of the list, and the process begins again on *this* smaller list. The algorithm halts when *NUMBER* is found or when the sublist becomes empty.

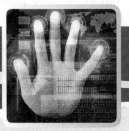

Practice Problems

In the data cleanup problem, suppose the original data list is

2	0	4		1	

1. Write the data list after completion of algorithm 1, the shuffle-left algorithm.

2. Write the two data lists after completion of algorithm 2, the copy-over algorithm.

3. Write the data list after completion of algorithm 3, the converging-pointers algorithm.

4. Make up a data list such that Step 11 of the converging-pointers algorithm (Figure 3.16) is needed.

FIGURE 3.18

1. Get values for NUMBER, n, $T_1, \ldots, T_n$ and $N_1, \ldots, N_n$
2. Set the value of *beginning* to 1 and set the value of *Found* to NO
3. Set the value of *end* to n
4. While *Found* = NO and *beginning* is less than or equal to *end* do Steps 5 through 10
5. Set the value of *m* to the middle value between *beginning* and *end*
6. If NUMBER = T_m, the number found at the midpoint between *beginning* and *end*, then do Steps 7 and 8
7.   Print the name of the corresponding person, N_m
8.   Set the value of *Found* to YES
9. Else if NUMBER < T_m, then set *end* = m − 1
10. Else (NUMBER > T_m) set *beginning* = m + 1
11. If (*Found* = NO) then print the message 'Sorry, this number is not in our directory'
12. Stop

Binary search algorithm (list must be sorted)

Figure 3.18 gives a pseudocode version of the binary search algorithm on a sorted *n*-element list. Here *beginning* and *end* mark the beginning and end of the section of the list under consideration. Initially the whole list is considered, so at first *beginning* is 1 and *end* is *n*. If NUMBER is not found at the midpoint *m* of the current section of the list, then setting *end* equal to one less than the midpoint (Step 9) means that at the next pass through the loop, the front half of the current section is searched. Setting *beginning* equal to one more than the midpoint (Step 10) means that at the next pass through the loop, the back half of the current section is searched. Thus, as the algorithm proceeds, the *beginning* marker can move toward the back of the list, and the *end* marker can move toward the front of the list. If the *beginning* marker and the *end* marker cross over—that is, *end* becomes less than *beginning*—then the current section of the list is empty and the search terminates. Of course it also terminates if NUMBER is found.

Let's do an example, using seven telephone numbers sorted in increasing order. The following list shows not only the numbers in the list but also their locations in the list. For clarity, we have removed the punctuation from the numbers and written them simply as 10-digit numerals.

2478346543	3563278900	3597211488	5656170224	6485551285	7719215281	8796562127
1	2	3	4	5	6	7

Suppose we search this list for the number 3597211488. We set *beginning* to 1 and *end* to 7; the midpoint between 1 and 7 is 4. We compare 3597211488 with the position 4 number, 5656170224. The number 3597211488 is less than 5656170224, so the algorithm sets *end* to 4 − 1 = 3 (Step 9) to continue the search on the front half of the list,

2478346543   3563278900   3597211488

    1   2   3

The midpoint between *beginning* = 1 and *end* = 3 is 2, so we compare 3597211488 with the position 2 number, 3563278900. The number 3597211488 is greater than 3563278900, so the algorithm sets *beginning* to 2 + 1 = 3 (Step 10) in order to continue the search on the back half of this list, namely

3597211488

   3

At the next pass through the loop, the midpoint between *beginning* = 3 and *end* = 3 is 3, so we compare 3597211488 with the position 3 number, 3597211488. We have found the target number; the corresponding name can be printed and *Found* changed to YES. The loop terminates, and then the algorithm terminates.

Now suppose we search this same list for the number 7213350096. As before, the first midpoint is 4, so 7213350096 is compared with 5656170224. Because 7213350096 > 5656170224, the search continues with *beginning* = 5, *end* = 7 on the back half:

6485551285   7719215281   8796562127

    5   6   7

The midpoint is 6, so 7213350096 is compared with 7719215281. Because 7213350096 < 7719215281, the search continues with *beginning* = 5, *end* = 5 on the front half:

6485551285

   5

The midpoint is 5, so 7213350096 is compared with 6485551285. Because 7213350096 > 6485551285, *beginning* is set to 6 to continue the search on the "back half" of this list. The algorithm checks the condition at Step 4 to see whether to repeat the loop again and finds that *end* is less than *beginning* (*end* = 5, *beginning* = 6). The loop is abandoned, and the algorithm moves on to Step 11 and indicates that our target number is not in the list.

It is easier to see how the binary search algorithm operates if we list the locations of the numbers checked in a treelike structure. The tree in Figure 3.19 shows the possible search locations in a seven-element list. The search starts at the top of the tree, at location 4, the middle of the original list. If the number at location 4 is *NUMBER*, the search halts. If *NUMBER* comes after the number at location 4, the right branch is taken and the next location searched is location 6. If *NUMBER* comes before the number at location 4, the left branch is taken and the next location searched is location 2. If *NUMBER* is not found at location 2, the next location searched is either

1 or 3. Similarly, if *NUMBER* is not found at location 6, the next location searched is either 5 or 7.

In Figure 3.18, the binary search algorithm, we assume in Step 5 that there is a middle position between *beginning* and *end*. This happens only when there is an odd number of elements in the list. Let us agree to define the "middle" of an even number of entries as the end of the first half of the list. With eight elements, for example, the midpoint position is location 4.

1 2 3 4̲ 5 6 7 8

With this understanding, the binary search algorithm can be used on sorted lists of any size. And of course, the list items need not be numbers; they could also be text items that are sorted alphabetically.

Like the sequential search algorithm, the binary search algorithm relies on comparisons, so to analyze the algorithm, we count the number of comparisons as an indication of the work done. The best case, as in sequential search, requires only one comparison—the target is located on the first try. The worst case, as in sequential search, occurs when the target is not in the list. However, we learn this much sooner in binary search than in sequential search. In our list of seven telephone numbers, only three comparisons are needed to determine that 7213350096 is not in the list. The number of comparisons needed is the number of circles in some branch from the top to the bottom of the tree in Figure 3.19. These circles represent searches at the midpoints of the whole list, half the list, one quarter of the list, and so on. This process continues as long as the sublists can be cut in half.

FIGURE 3.19

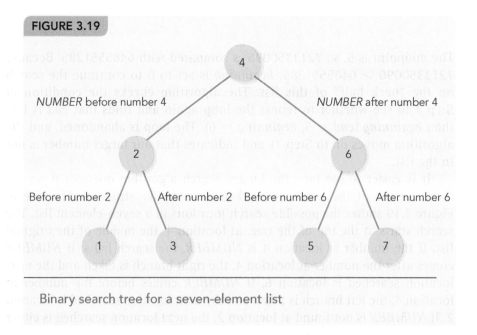

NUMBER before number 4   NUMBER after number 4

Before number 2   After number 2   Before number 6   After number 6

Binary search tree for a seven-element list

Let's do a minor mathematical digression here. The number of times a number n can be cut in half and not go below 1 is called the *logarithm of n to the base 2*, which is abbreviated lg n (also written in some texts as $\log_2 n$). For example, if n is 16, then we can do four such divisions by 2:

16 / 2 = 8
8 / 2 = 4
4 / 2 = 2
2 / 2 = 1

so lg 16 = 4. This is another way of saying that $2^4 = 16$. In general,

lg $n = m$ is equivalent to $2^m = n$

Figure 3.20 shows a few values of n and lg n. From these, we can see that as n doubles, lg n increases by only 1, so lg n grows much more slowly than n. Figure 3.21 shows the two basic shapes of n and lg n and again conveys that lg n grows much more slowly than n.

Remember the analogy we suggested earlier about the difference in time consumed between $\Theta(n^2)$ algorithms, equivalent to various modes of walking, and $\Theta(n)$ algorithms, equivalent to various modes of driving? We carry that analogy further by saying that algorithms of order of magnitude lg n, $\Theta(\lg n)$, are like various modes of flying. Changing the coefficients of lg n can mean that we go from a Cessna 172 Skyhawk (top speed about 185 miles per hour) to an F-35 Lightning II fighter plane (top speed about 1200 miles per hour) but flying, in any form, is still a fundamentally different—and much faster—mode of travel than walking or driving.

Suppose we are doing a binary search on n items. In the worst case, as we have seen, the number of comparisons is related to the number of times the list of length n can be halved. Binary search does $\Theta(\lg n)$ comparisons in

FIGURE 3.21

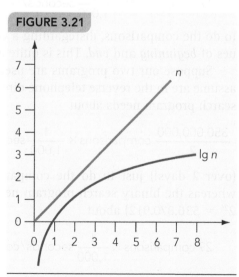

FIGURE 3.20

n	lg n
8	3
16	4
32	5
64	6
128	7

Values for n and lg n

A comparison of n and lg n

the worst case (see Exercise 31 at the end of the chapter for an exact formula for the worst case). As a matter of fact, it also does $\Theta(\lg n)$ comparisons in the average case (although the exact value is a smaller number than in the worst case). This is because most of the items in the list occur at or near the bottom of the tree, where the maximum amount of work must be done. As Figure 3.19 shows, relatively few locations, where the target might be found and the algorithm terminate sooner, are higher in the tree.

The two search algorithms, binary search and sequential search, differ in the order of magnitude of the work they do. Binary search is an $\Theta(\lg n)$ algorithm, whereas sequential search is an $\Theta(n)$ algorithm, in both the worst case and the average case. To compare the binary search algorithm with the sequential search algorithm, suppose there are 100 elements in the list. In the worst case, sequential search requires 100 comparisons, and binary search requires 7 ($2^7 = 128$). In the average case, sequential search requires about 50 comparisons, and binary search 6 or 7 (still much less work). The improvement in binary search becomes even more apparent as the search list gets longer. For example, if $n = 100,000$, then in the worst case, sequential search requires 100,000 comparisons, whereas binary search requires 17 (because $2^{16} = 65,536$ and $2^{17} = 131,072$). If we wrote two programs, one using sequential search and one using binary search, and ran them on a computer that can do 1,000 comparisons per second, then to determine that an item is not in the list (the worst case) the sequential search program would use

$$100,000 \text{ comparisons} \times \frac{1}{1,000} \text{ seconds/comparison} = 100 \text{ seconds}$$

or 1.67 minutes, just to do the necessary comparisons, disregarding the constant factor for advancing the index. The binary search program would use

$$17 \text{ comparisons} \times \frac{1}{1,000} \text{ seconds/comparison} = 0.017 \text{ seconds}$$

to do the comparisons, disregarding a constant factor for updating the values of *beginning* and *end*. This is quite a difference.

Suppose our two programs are used with the 350,000,000 numbers we assume are in the reverse telephone directory. On the average, the sequential search program needs about

$$\frac{350,000,000}{2} \text{ comparisons} \times \frac{1}{1,000} \text{ seconds/comparison} = 175,000 \text{ seconds}$$

(over 2 days!) just to do the comparisons to find a number in the list, whereas the binary search program needs (because $2^{28} = 268,435,456$ and $2^{29} = 536,870,912$) about

$$29 \text{ comparisons} \times \frac{1}{1,000} \text{ seconds/comparison} = 0.029 \text{ seconds}$$

This is an even more impressive difference. Furthermore, it's a difference due to the inherent inefficiency of an $\Theta(n)$ algorithm compared with an $\Theta(\lg n)$ algorithm; the difference can be mitigated but not eliminated by using a faster computer. If our computer does 50,000 comparisons per second, then the average times become about

$$\frac{350,000,000}{2} \text{ comparisons} \times \frac{1}{50,000} \text{ seconds/comparison} = 3,500 \text{ seconds}$$

or nearly an hour for sequential search and about

$$29 \text{ comparisons} \times \frac{1}{50,000} \text{ seconds/comparison} = 0.00058 \text{ seconds}$$

for binary search. The sequential search alternative is simply not acceptable. That is why analyzing algorithms and choosing the best one can be so important. We also see, as we noted in Chapter 2, that the way the problem data are organized can greatly affect the best choice of algorithm.

The binary search algorithm works only on a list that has already been sorted. An unsorted list could be sorted before using a binary search, but sorting also takes a lot of work, as we have seen. If a list is to be searched only a few times for a few particular items, then it is more efficient to do sequential search on the unsorted list (a few $\Theta(n)$ tasks). But if the list is to be searched repeatedly, it is more efficient to sort it and then use binary search: one $\Theta(n^2)$ task and many $\Theta(\lg n)$ tasks, as opposed to many $\Theta(n)$ tasks.

As to space efficiency, binary search, like sequential search, requires only a small amount of additional storage to keep track of beginning, end, and midpoint positions in the list. Thus, it is space efficient; in this case, we did not have to sacrifice space efficiency to gain time efficiency. But we did have to sacrifice generality—binary search works only on a sorted list whereas sequential search works on any list.

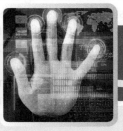

Practice Problems

1. Suppose that, using the list of seven numbers from this section, we try binary search to decide whether 6485551285 is in the list. What numbers would be compared with 6485551285?

2. Suppose that, using the list of seven numbers from this section, we try binary search to decide whether 9342426855 is in the list. What numbers would be compared with 9342426855?

3. In the worst case, how many comparisons will be required to find a single Social Security number (SSN) from among the approximately 453,700,000 numbers issued since Social Security began if the data file is sorted numerically by SSN? How many will be required in the worst case if the data file is sorted alphabetically by the individual's last name?

Laboratory Experience 5

In this Laboratory Experience, you will be able to run animations of the shuffle-left algorithm and the converging-pointers algorithm for the data cleanup problem. You'll be able to see the left and right pointers take on different values, which represent changing positions in the data list. As the algorithms run on various lists, you can count the number of copies of data elements that are required and see how they relate to the original positions of any 0 items in the list.

You will also work with an animation of the binary search algorithm and see how the work done compares with the theoretical results we discovered in this section.

3.4.3 Pattern Matching

The pattern-matching algorithm in Chapter 2 involves finding all occurrences of a pattern of the form $P_1 P_2 \ldots P_m$ within text of the form $T_1 T_2 \ldots T_n$. Recall that the algorithm simply does a "forward march" through the text, at each position attempting to match each pattern character against the text characters. The process stops only after text position $n - m + 1$, when the remaining text is not as long as the pattern so that there could not possibly be a match. This algorithm is interesting to analyze because it involves two measures of input size: n, the length of the text string, and m, the length of the pattern string. The unit of work is comparison of a pattern character with a text character.

Surprisingly, both the best case and the worst case of this algorithm can occur when the pattern is not in the text at all. The difference hinges on exactly *how* the pattern fails to be in the text. The best case occurs if the first character of the pattern is nowhere in the text, as in

Text: *KLMNPQRSTX*
Pattern: *ABC*

In this case, $n - m + 1$ comparisons are required, trying (unsuccessfully) to match P_1 with $T_1, T_2, \ldots, T_{n-m+1}$ in turn. Each comparison fails, and the algorithm slides the pattern forward to try again at the next position in the text.

The maximum amount of work is done if the pattern *almost* occurs everywhere in the text. Consider, for example, the following case:

Text: *AAAAAAAAA*
Pattern: *AAAB*

Starting with T_1, the first text character, the match with the first pattern character is successful. The match with the second text character and the second pattern character is also successful. Indeed $m - 1$ characters of the pattern match with the text before the mth comparison proves a failure. The process starts over from the second text character, T_2. Once again, m comparisons are required to find a mismatch. Altogether, m comparisons are required for each of the $n - m + 1$ starting positions in the text.

Another version of the worst case occurs when the pattern is found at each location in the text, as in

Text: *AAAAAAAAA*
Pattern: *AAAA*

This results in the same comparisons as are done for the other worst case, the only difference being that the comparison of the last pattern character is successful.

Unlike our simple examples, pattern matching usually involves a pattern length that is short compared with the text length, that is, when m is much less than n. In such cases, $n - m + 1$ is essentially n. The pattern-matching algorithm is therefore $\Theta(n)$ in the best case and $\Theta(m \times n)$ in the worst case.

It requires somewhat improbable situations to create the worst cases we have described. In general, the forward-march algorithm performs quite well on text and patterns consisting of ordinary words. Other pattern-matching algorithms are conceptually more complex but require less work in the worst case.

3.4.4 Summary

Figure 3.22 shows an order-of-magnitude summary of the time efficiency for the algorithms we have analyzed.

FIGURE 3.22

Problem	Unit of Work	Algorithm	Best Case	Worst Case	Average Case
Searching	Comparisons	Sequential search	1	$\Theta(n)$	$\Theta(n)$
		Binary search	1	$\Theta(\lg n)$	$\Theta(\lg n)$
Sorting	Comparisons and exchanges	Selection sort	$\Theta(n^2)$	$\Theta(n^2)$	$\Theta(n^2)$
Data cleanup	Examinations and copies	Shuffle-left	$\Theta(n)$	$\Theta(n^2)$	$\Theta(n^2)$
		Copy-over	$\Theta(n)$	$\Theta(n)$	$\Theta(n)$
		Converging-pointers	$\Theta(n)$	$\Theta(n)$	$\Theta(n)$
Pattern matching	Character comparisons	Forward march	$\Theta(n)$	$\Theta(m \times n)$	

Order-of-magnitude time efficiency summary

Practice Problem

Use the first sample pattern and text given in Section 3.4.3 for the worst case of the pattern-matching algorithm. What is m? What is n? What is $m \times n$? This algorithm is $\Theta(m \times n)$ in the worst case, but what is the exact number of comparisons done?

3.5 When Things Get Out of Hand

We have so far found examples of algorithms that are $\Theta(\lg n)$, $\Theta(n)$, and $\Theta(n^2)$ in time efficiency. Order of magnitude determines how quickly the values grow as n increases. An algorithm of order $\lg n$ does less work as n increases than does an algorithm of order n, which in turn does less work than one of order n^2. The work done by any of these algorithms is no worse than a constant multiple of n^2, which is a polynomial in n. Therefore, these algorithms are polynomially bounded in the amount of work they do as n increases.

Some algorithms must do work that is not polynomially bounded. Consider four cities, A, B, C, and D, that are connected as shown in Figure 3.23, and ask the following question: Is it possible to start at city A, go through every other city exactly once, and end up back at A? Of course, we as humans can immediately see in this small problem that the answer is "yes" and that there are two such paths: A-B-D-C-A and A-C-D-B-A. However, an algorithm doesn't get to "see" the entire picture at once, as we can; it has available to it only isolated facts such as "A is connected to B and to C," "B is connected to A and to D," and so on. If the number of *nodes* and

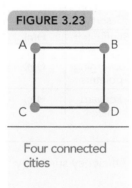

FIGURE 3.23

Four connected cities

connecting *edges* is large, humans also might not "see" the solution immediately. A collection of nodes and connecting edges is called a *graph*. A path
through a graph that begins and ends at the same node and goes through all
other nodes exactly once is called a *Hamiltonian circuit*, named for the Irish
mathematician William Rowan Hamilton (1805–1865). If there are n nodes
in the graph, then a Hamiltonian circuit, if it exists, must have exactly n
links. In the case of the four cities, for instance, if the path must go through
exactly A, B, C, D, and A (in some order), then there are five nodes on the
path (counting A twice) and four links.

Our problem is to determine whether an arbitrary graph has a
Hamiltonian circuit. An algorithm to solve this problem examines all possible paths through the graph that are the appropriate length to see whether
any of them are Hamiltonian circuits. The algorithm can trace all paths
by beginning at the starting node and choosing at each node where to go
next. Without going into the details of such an algorithm, let's represent the
possible paths with four links in the graph of Figure 3.23. Again, we use a
tree structure. In Figure 3.24, A is the tree "root," and at each node in the
tree, the nodes directly below it are the choices for the next node. Thus, any
time B appears in the tree, it has the two nodes A and D below it because
edges exist from B to A and from B to D. The "branches" of the tree are all
the possible paths from A with four links. Once the tree has been built, an
examination of the paths shows that only the two dark paths in the figure
represent Hamiltonian circuits.

FIGURE 3.24

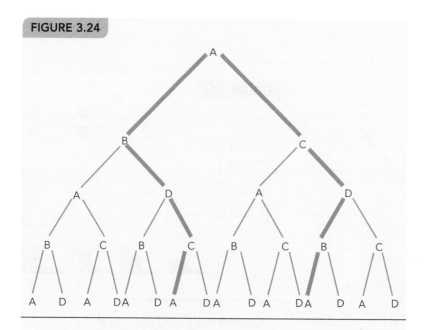

Hamiltonian circuits among all paths from A in Figure 3.23
with four links

The number of paths that must be examined is the number of nodes at the bottom level of the tree. There is one node at the top of the tree; we'll call the top of the tree level 0. The number of nodes is multiplied by 2 for each level down in the tree. At level 1, there are 2 nodes; at level 2, there are $2^2 = 4$ nodes; at level 3, there are $2^3 = 8$ nodes; and at level 4, the bottom of the tree, there are $2^4 = 16$ nodes.

Suppose we are looking for a Hamiltonian circuit in a graph with n nodes and two choices at each node. The bottom of the corresponding tree is at level n, and there are 2^n paths to examine. If we take the examination of a single path as a unit of work, then this algorithm must do 2^n units of work. This is more work than any polynomial in n. An $\Theta(2^n)$ algorithm is called an exponential algorithm. Hence the trial-and-error approach to solving this Hamiltonian circuit problem is an exponential algorithm. (We could improve on this algorithm by letting it stop tracing a path whenever a repeated node different from the starting node is encountered, but it is still exponential. If there are more than two choices at a node, the amount of work is even greater.)

Figure 3.25 shows the four curves $\lg n$, n, n^2, and 2^n. The rapid growth of 2^n is not really apparent here, however, because that curve is off the scale for values of n above 5. Figure 3.26 compares these four curves for values of n that are still small, but even so, 2^n is already far outdistancing the other values.

To appreciate fully why the order of magnitude of an algorithm is important, let's again imagine that we are running various algorithms as

FIGURE 3.25

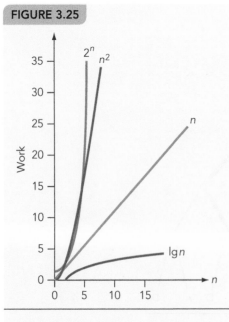

Comparison of $\lg n$, n, n^2, and 2^n

FIGURE 3.26

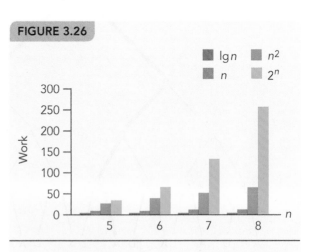

Comparisons of $\lg n$, n, n^2, and 2^n for larger values of n

FIGURE 3.27

Order	10	50	n 100	1,000
lg n	0.0003 sec	0.0006 sec	0.0007 sec	0.001 sec
n	0.001 sec	0.005 sec	0.01 sec	0.1 sec
n^2	0.01 sec	0.25 sec	1 sec	1.67 min
2^n	0.1024 sec	3,570 years	4×10^{16} centuries	*Too big to compute!!*

A comparison of four orders of magnitude

programs on a computer that can perform a single operation (unit of work) in 0.0001 second. Figure 3.27 shows the amount of time it takes for algorithms of $\Theta(\lg n)$, $\Theta(n)$, $\Theta(n^2)$, and $\Theta(2^n)$ to complete their work for various values of n.

The expression 2^n grows unbelievably fast. An algorithm of $\Theta(2^n)$ can take so long to solve even a small problem that it is of no practical value. Even if we greatly increase the speed of the computer, the results are much the same. We now see more than ever why we added *efficiency* as a desirable feature for an algorithm and why future advances in computer technology won't change this. No matter how fast computers get, they will not be able to solve a problem of size $n = 100$ using an algorithm of $\Theta(2^n)$ in any reasonable period of time.

The algorithm we have described here for testing an arbitrary graph for Hamiltonian circuits is an example of a *brute force algorithm*—one that beats the problem into submission by trying all possibilities. In Chapter 1, we described a brute force algorithm for winning a chess game; it consisted of looking at all possible game scenarios from any given point on and then picking a winning one. This is also an exponential algorithm. Some very practical problems have exponential solution algorithms. For example, an email message that you send over the Internet is routed along the shortest possible path through intermediate computers from your mail server computer to the destination mail server computer. An exponential algorithm to solve this problem would examine all possible paths to the destination and then use the shortest one. As you can imagine, the Internet uses a better (more efficient) algorithm than this one!

Are there problems for which no polynomially bounded algorithm exists? Such problems are called intractable; they are solvable, but the solution algorithms all require so much work as to be virtually useless. The Hamiltonian circuit problem is suspected to be such a problem, but we don't really know for sure! No one has yet found a solution algorithm that works in polynomial time, but neither has anyone proved that such an algorithm does not exist. This is a problem of great interest in computer science. A surprising number of problems fall into this "suspected intractable" category. Here's another one, called the *bin-packing problem*: Given an unlimited number of bins of volume X units and given n objects, all of volume between 0 and X, find the minimum number of bins needed to store the n objects. A brute force algorithm would try all possibilities, which again is not a polynomial algorithm. Any manufacturer who ships sets of various items in standard-sized cartons or anyone who wants to store variable-length video clips on a set of DVDs in the most efficient way would be interested in a polynomial algorithm that solves this minimization problem.

Problems for which no known polynomial solution algorithm exists are sometimes approached via approximation algorithms. These algorithms don't give the exact answer to the problem, but they provide a close approximation to a solution (see Exercise 2 of Chapter 1). For example, an approximation algorithm to solve the bin-packing problem is to take the objects in order, put the first one into bin 1, and stuff each remaining object into the first bin that can hold it. This (reasonable) approach may not give the absolute minimum number of bins needed, but it gives a first cut at the answer. (Anyone who has watched passengers stowing carry-on baggage in an airplane has seen this approximation algorithm at work.)

For example, suppose a sequence of four objects with volumes of 0.3, 0.4, 0.5, and 0.6 are stored in bins of size 1.0 using the "first-fit" algorithm described previously. The result requires three bins, which would be packed as shown in Figure 3.28. However, this is not the optimal solution (see Exercise 39 at the end of the chapter).

In Chapter 12, we will learn that there are problems that cannot be solved algorithmically, even if we are willing to accept an extremely inefficient solution.

FIGURE 3.28

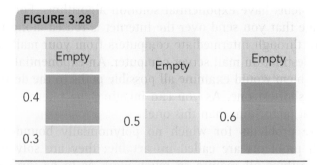

A first-fit solution to a bin-packing problem

Practice Problems

1. Consider the following graph:

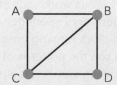

   Draw a tree similar to Figure 3.24 showing all paths from A and highlighting those that are Hamiltonian circuits (these are the same two circuits as before). How many paths must be examined?

2. The following tree shows all paths with two links that begin at node A in some graph. Draw the graph.

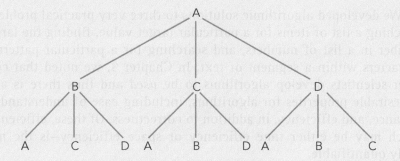

3. If an algorithm were determined to have an order of magnitude of n^n, do you think it would be classified as polynomial or exponential? Explain.

3.6 Summary of Level 1

We defined computer science as the study of algorithms, so it is appropriate that Level 1 was devoted to exploring algorithms in more detail. In Chapter 2, we discussed how to represent algorithms using pseudocode. Pseudocode provides us with a flexible language for expressing the building blocks from which algorithms can be constructed. These building blocks include assigning a particular value to a quantity, choosing one of two next steps on the basis of some condition, or repeating steps in a loop.

Laboratory Experience 6

The various sorting algorithms examined in Laboratory Experience 4 (selection sort, quicksort, etc.) do different amounts of work on the same data sets. But how do these various workloads affect the actual running time of the algorithms? In this Laboratory Experience, you can run these sorting algorithms and find their wall-clock running time on different sizes of input. In addition, because you can see the patterns of values falling into place in a large list while an algorithm runs, you will get a much better understanding of how each sorting algorithm moves values around to accomplish its task.

We developed algorithmic solutions to three very practical problems: searching a list of items for a particular target value, finding the largest number in a list of numbers, and searching for a particular pattern of characters within a segment of text. In Chapter 3, we noted that computer scientists develop algorithms to be *used* and thus there is a set of desirable properties for algorithms, including ease of understanding, elegance, and efficiency, in addition to correctness. Of these, efficiency—which may be either time efficiency or space efficiency—is the most easily quantifiable.

A convenient way to classify the time efficiency of algorithms is by examining the order of magnitude of the work they do. Algorithms that are of differing orders of magnitude do fundamentally different amounts of work. Regardless of the constant factor that reflects peripheral work or how fast the computer on which these algorithms execute, for problems with sufficiently large input, the algorithm of the lowest order of magnitude requires the least time.

We analyzed the time efficiency of the sequential search algorithm and discovered that it is an $\Theta(n)$ algorithm in both the worst case and the average case. We found a selection sort algorithm that is $\Theta(n^2)$, we found a binary search algorithm that is $\Theta(\lg n)$, and we analyzed the pattern-matching algorithm from Chapter 2. By examining the data cleanup problem, we learned that algorithms that solve the same task can indeed differ in the order of magnitude of the work they do, sometimes by employing a time/space trade-off. We also learned that there are algorithms that require more than polynomially bounded time to complete their work and that such algorithms may take so long to execute, regardless of the speed of the computer on which they are run, that they provide no practical solution. Some important problems may be intractable—that is, have no polynomially bounded solution algorithms.

Some computer scientists work on trying to decide whether a particular problem is intractable. Some work on finding more efficient algorithms for problems—such as searching and sorting—that are so common that a more efficient algorithm would greatly improve productivity. Still others seek to discover algorithms for new problems. Thus, as we said, the study of algorithms underlies much of computer science. But everything we have done so far has been a pencil-and-paper exercise. In terms of the definition of computer science that we gave in Chapter 1, we have been looking at the formal and mathematical properties of algorithms. It is time to move on to the next part of that definition: the hardware realizations of algorithms. When we execute real algorithms on real computers, those computers are electronic devices. How does an electronic device "understand" an algorithm and carry out its instructions? We begin to explore these questions in Chapter 4.

EXERCISES

1. a. Use Gauss's approach to find the following sum:

    $$2 + 4 + 6 + ... + 100$$

    b. Use Gauss's approach to find a formula for the sum of the even numbers from 2 to $2n$:

    $$2 + 4 + 6 + ... + 2n$$

    Your formula will be an expression involving n.

2. An English Christmas carol, "The Twelve Days of Christmas," dates from the late 1700s. The 12 verses in the song are cumulative, each verse adding an additional gift given by "my true love." The twelfth verse says "On the twelfth day of Christmas, my true love gave to me ..."

    12 Drummers Drumming

    11 Pipers Piping

    10 Lords-a-Leaping

    ... and so forth down to ...

    3 French Hens

    2 Turtle Doves

    And a Partridge in a Pear Tree.

    a. Use Gauss's formula to find the total number of gifts given on Day 12.

    b. How many total gifts are given over all 12 days? *Hint*:

    $$1(2) + 2(3) + 3(4) + ... + n(n+1) = \frac{n(n+1)(n+2)}{3}$$

3. The *Fibonacci sequence* of numbers is defined as follows: The first and second numbers are both 1. After that, each number in the sequence is the sum of the two preceding numbers. Thus, the Fibonacci sequence is as follows:

   1, 1, 2, 3, 5, 8, 13, 21, ...

   If $F(n)$ stands for the nth value in the sequence, then this definition can be expressed as

   $$F(1) = 1$$

   $$F(2) = 1$$

   $$F(n) = F(n-1) + F(n-2) \text{ for } n > 2$$

   a. The value of F at position n is defined using the value of F at two smaller positions. Something that is defined in terms of "smaller versions" of itself is said to be *recursive*, so the Fibonacci sequence is recursive. Using the definition of the Fibonacci sequence, compute the value of $F(20)$.

   b. A formula for $F(n)$ is

   $$F(n) = \frac{\sqrt{5}}{5}\left(\frac{1+\sqrt{5}}{2}\right)^n - \frac{\sqrt{5}}{5}\left(\frac{1-\sqrt{5}}{2}\right)^n$$

   Using the formula (and a calculator), compute the value of $F(20)$.

   c. What is your opinion on the relative clarity, elegance, and efficiency of the two algorithms (using the definition and using the formula) to compute $F(20)$? Would your answer change if you considered $F(100)$?

   d. If you have access to a spreadsheet, program it to compute successive values of the Fibonacci sequence. (*Hint:* Enter 1 in cells A1 and B1, and enter = A1 + B1 in cell C1. Continue along row 1 with a similar formula.) Use this method to compute $F(20)$.

   e. Elsewhere on the same spreadsheet, use one cell to enter the value of n, and another cell to enter the formula from part (b) above. (*Hint:* you will need the squareroot function and the power function.) Use this method to compute $F(20)$.

   f. On your spreadsheet, use both methods to compute $F(50)$. Which appears to be more efficient?

4. A tennis tournament has 342 players. A single match involves 2 players. The winner of a match will play the winner of a match in the next round, whereas losers are eliminated from the tournament. The 2 players who have won all previous rounds play in the final game, and the winner wins the tournament. What is the total number of matches needed to determine the winner?

   a. Here is one algorithm to answer this question. Compute 342/2 = 171 to get the number of pairs (matches) in the first round, which results in 171 winners to go on to the second round. Compute 171/2 = 85 with 1 left over, which results in 85 matches in the second round and 85 winners, plus the 1 left over, to go on to the third round. For the third round compute 86/2 = 43, so the third round has 43 matches, and so on. The total number of matches is 171 + 85 + 43 + ... Finish this process to find the total number of matches.

   b. Here is another algorithm to solve this problem. Each match results in exactly one loser, so there must be the same number of matches as losers in the tournament. Compute the total number of losers in the entire tournament. (*Hint:* This isn't really a computation; it is a one-sentence argument.)

   c. What is your opinion on the relative clarity, elegance, and efficiency of the two algorithms?

5. We have said that the average number of comparisons needed to find a target value in an n-element list using sequential search is slightly higher than $n/2$. In this problem, we find an exact expression for this average.

   a. Suppose the list has an odd number of items, say 15. At what position is the middle item? Using sequential search, how many comparisons are required to find the middle item? Repeat this exercise with a few more odd numbers until you can do the following: If there are n items in the list and n is an odd number, write an expression for the number of comparisons required to find the middle item.

b. Suppose the list has an even number of items, say 16. At what positions are the two "middle" items? Using sequential search, how many comparisons are required to find each of these? What is the average of these two numbers? Repeat this exercise with a few more even numbers until you can do the following: If there are n items in the list and n is an even number, write an expression for the average number of comparisons required to find the two middle items.

c. Noting that half the items in a list fall before the midpoint and half after the midpoint, use your answer to parts a and b to write an exact expression for the average number of comparisons done using sequential search to find a target value that occurs in an n-element list.

6. Here is a list of seven names:

   Sherman, Jane, Ted, Elise, Raul, Maki, John

   Search this list for each name in turn, using sequential search and counting the number of comparisons for each name. Now take the seven comparison counts and find their average. Did you get a number that you expected? Why?

7. The American Museum of Natural History in New York City contains more than 32 million specimens and artifacts in its various collections, including the world's largest collection of dinosaur fossils. Many of these are in storage away from public view, but all must be carefully inventoried.

   a. Suppose the inventory is unordered (!) and a sequential search is done to locate a specific artifact. Given that the search is executed on a computer that can do 12,000 comparisons per second, about how much time on the average would the search require?

   b. Assuming the inventory is sorted, about how much time would a binary search require?

8. In the Flipping Pancakes box, the original algorithm given requires at most $2n - 3$ flips in the worst case. The claim is made that the new algorithm, which requires at most $(5n + 5)/3$ flips, is a better algorithm. How many pancakes do you need to have before the second algorithm is indeed faster? (Use a calculator or spreadsheet.)

9. Perform a selection sort on the list 7, 4, 2, 9, 6. Show the list after each exchange that has an effect on the list ordering.

10. The selection sort algorithm could be modified to stop when the unsorted section of the list contains only one number, because that one number must be in the correct position. Show that this modification would have no effect on the number of comparisons required to sort an n-element list.

Exercises 11–14 refer to another algorithm, called **bubble sort**, which sorts an n-element list. Bubble sort makes multiple passes through the list from front to back, each time exchanging pairs of entries that are out of order. Here is a pseudocode version:

1. Get values for n and the n list items

2. Set the marker U for the unsorted section at the end of the list

3. While the unsorted section has more than one element, do Steps 4 through 8

4.   Set the current element marker C at the second element of the list

5.   While C has not passed U, do Steps 6 and 7

6.   If the item at position C is less than the item to its left, then exchange these two items

7.   Move C to the right one position

8. Move U left one position

9. Stop

11. For each of the following lists, perform a bubble sort, and show the list after each exchange. Compare the number of exchanges done here and in the Practice Problem at the end of Section 3.3.3.

    a. 4, 8, 2, 6

    b. 12, 3, 6, 8, 2, 5, 7

    c. D, B, G, F, A, C, E, H

12. Explain why the bubble sort algorithm does $\Theta(n^2)$ comparisons on an n-element list.

13. Suppose selection sort and bubble sort are both performed on a list that is already sorted. Does bubble sort do fewer exchanges than selection sort? Explain.

14. Bubble sort can be improved. **Smart bubble sort** keeps track of how many exchanges are done within any single pass through the unsorted section of the list. If no exchanges occur, then the list is sorted and the algorithm should stop.

    a. Write a pseudocode version of the smart bubble sort algorithm.

    b. Perform a smart bubble sort on the following list. How many comparisons are required?

       7, 4, 12, 9, 11

    c. Describe the best-case scenario for smart bubble sort on an n-element list. How many comparisons are required? How many exchanges are required?

    d. Under what circumstances does smart bubble sort do the same number of comparisons as regular bubble sort?

Exercises 15–17 refer to still another sorting algorithm, called **mergesort**. Mergesort breaks the list to be sorted into smaller and smaller lists until there is just a bunch of one-element (and thus obviously sorted) lists, then assembles the smaller sorted lists back together into larger and larger sorted lists. Here is a pseudocode version:

1. Get values for n and the n list items

2. While the current list has more than 1 item, do Steps 3 through 6

3. Split the list into two halves

4. Sort the first half of the list using mergesort

5. Sort the second half of the list using mergesort

6. Merge the two sorted halves A and B into a new sorted list C by comparing the next two items from A and B and always choosing the smaller value to go into C

7. Stop

Mergesort works by using the result of mergesort on two smaller lists, so mergesort, like the Fibonacci sequence in Exercise 3, is a recursive algorithm.

Step 6 in this algorithm deserves an example. Suppose that at one point in running mergesort we have two sorted lists A and B, as follows:

$$A = 2, 9 \quad B = 6, 7$$

To create C, we compare 2 from A and 6 from B. Because 2 is smaller, it is removed from A and goes into C.

$$A = 9 \quad B = 6, 7 \quad C = 2$$

Now compare 9 from A and 6 from B. Because 6 is smaller, it is removed from B and goes into C.

$$A = 9 \quad B = 7 \quad C = 2, 6$$

Comparing 9 and 7 results in

$$A = 9 \quad B = \quad C = 2, 6, 7$$

Finally, let us agree to count comparing 9 to nothing as a legitimate, if trivial, comparison resulting in 9, which is added to C, the final sorted list.

$$A = \quad B = \quad C = 2, 6, 7, 9$$

15. Show the steps in merging A and B into C where

    $$A = 8, 12, 19, 34 \quad B = 3, 5, 15, 21$$

16. Use mergesort to sort the list 6, 3, 1, 9. Count the total number of comparisons, including trivial comparisons.

17. The work in this algorithm occurs in Step 6 where sorted lists are merged together. The "work unit" is the comparison of two items. If A and B are each of size $k/2$, then k comparisons are needed to merge them into a sorted list C of size k. If the original list has 8 elements, then we can picture mergesort as shown on the next page:

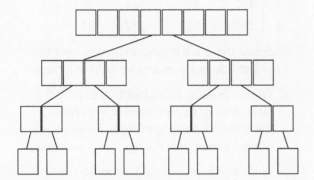

Starting from the bottom of the tree, merges occur at three levels (1-element lists merge to 2-element lists, lists of size 2 merge to lists of size 4, and lists of size 4 merge to the final list of size 8) and, looking across the entire tree, at each level there are 8 comparisons done to create the level above it. Therefore the total amount of work done is $3 \times 8 = 24$ comparisons.

a. If the original list has n items, how many levels will the tree have at which merges occur? (*Hint*: How many times can the number n be cut in half?)

b. If the original list has n items, how many comparisons occur at each merge level?

c. What is the order of magnitude of mergesort?

d. Does your answer to part c agree with your answer to Exercise 16? Explain.

18. This exercise discusses a new algorithm to sort an n-element list.

a. A permutation of a list is any arrangement of the list items. For example, 2, 4 and 4, 2 are the two permutations of the list 2, 4. Find all permutations of the list 4, 3, 7.

b. Given an n-element list, the number of permutations can be counted as follows. There are n positions in the list. Any of the n items can occupy position 1:

$\underline{n}, \underline{}, \underline{}, \underline{}, \ldots, \underline{}, \underline{}, \underline{}$

Once the item for position 1 has been chosen, any of the remaining $n - 1$ items can occupy position 2:

$\underline{n}, \underline{n-1}, \underline{}, \underline{}, \ldots, \underline{}, \underline{}, \underline{}$

There are then $n - 2$ choices for position 3, etc., until there is only one choice left for the last position:

$\underline{n}, \underline{n-1}, \underline{n-2}, \underline{n-3}, \ldots, 3, \underline{2}, \underline{1}$

The total number of permutations is the product

$n(n - 1)(n - 2)(n - 3) \ldots (3)(2)(1)$

This value is called n *factorial* and is denoted by $n!$. Compute the value of $3!$. How many permutations did you find in part a?

c. Here is a pseudocode description of the new sorting algorithm. It first generates all possible permutations of the list elements and then looks for which of these is the sorted-order permutation.

1. Get values for n and the n list items

2. Set the value of permutation counter i to 1

3. While ($i \leq n!$), do Steps 4 through 6

4.   Create a new empty list of size n

5.   Write the next permutation in this list

6.   Increase the value of i by 1

7. Set the value of list counter j to 1

8. Set the value of Sorted to NO

9. While ($j \leq n!$) and (Sorted = NO), do Steps 10 through 13

10.   Check whether list j is sorted

11.   If list j is sorted then

12.   Set the value of Sorted to YES

13.   Increase the value of j by 1

14. Print list ($j − 1$)

15. Stop

To write this algorithm in complete detail, we would need to explain Step 5:

Write the next permutation in this list

and Step 10:

Check whether list j is sorted

in terms of more primitive operations. For simplicity, assume that each execution of Step 5 is one work unit and that each execution of Step 10 is also one work unit. Explain the best case for this algorithm and give an expression for the total number of work units required. Explain the worst case and give an expression for the total number of work units required.

d. Selection sort is $\Theta(n^2)$ and the new sorting algorithm is $\Theta(n!)$. Fill in the following table, assuming a work rate of 0.0001 seconds per unit of work.

Order	n			
	3	5	10	20
n^2				
$n!$				

e. Comment on the space efficiency of the new algorithm.

19. Algorithms A and B perform the same task. On input of size n, algorithm A executes $0.003n^2$ instructions, and algorithm B executes $243n$ instructions. Find the approximate value of n above which algorithm B is more efficient. (You may use a calculator or spreadsheet.)

20. Suppose a metropolitan area is divided into four school districts: 1, 2, 3, 4. The State Board of Education keeps track of the number of student transfers from one district to another and the student transfers within a district. This information is recorded each year in a 4×4 table as shown here. The entry in row 1, column 3 (314), for example, shows the number of student transfers from district 1 to district 3 for the year. The entry in row 1,

column 1 (243) shows the number of student transfers within district 1.

	1	2	3	4
1	243	187	314	244
2	215	420	345	172
3	197	352	385	261
4	340	135	217	344

Suppose there are n school districts, and the Board of Education maintains an $n \times n$ table.

a. Write a pseudocode algorithm to print the table, that is, to print each of the entries in the table. Write an expression for the number of print statements the algorithm executes.

b. Write a pseudocode algorithm to print n copies of the table, one to give to each of the n school district supervisors. Write an expression for the number of print statements the algorithm executes.

c. What is the order of magnitude of the work done by the algorithm in part b if the unit of work is printing a table element?

21. Write the data list that results from running the shuffle-left algorithm to clean up the following data. Find the exact number of copies done.

3	0	0	2	6	7	0	0	5	1

22. Write the resulting data list and find the exact number of copies done by the converging-pointers algorithm when it is executed on the data in Exercise 21.

23. Explain in words how to modify the shuffle-left data cleanup algorithm to slightly reduce the number of copies it makes. (*Hint:* Must item n always be copied?) If this modified algorithm is run on the data list of Exercise 21, exactly how many copies are done?

24. The shuffle-left algorithm for data cleanup is supposed to perform $n(n − 1)$ copies on a list consisting of n 0s (zeros). Confirm this result for the following list:

0 0 0 0 0 0

25. Consider the following sorted list of names.

    Arturo, Elsa, JoAnn, John, José, Lee, Snyder, Tracy

    a. Use binary search to decide whether Elsa is in this list. What names will be compared with Elsa?

    b. Use binary search to decide whether Tracy is in this list. What names will be compared with Tracy?

    c. Use binary search to decide whether Emile is in this list. What names will be compared with Emile?

26. Use the binary search algorithm to decide whether 35 is in the following list:

    3, 6, 7, 9, 12, 14, 18, 21, 22, 31, 43

    What numbers will be compared with 35?

27. If a list is already sorted in ascending order, a modified sequential search algorithm can be used that compares against each element in turn, stopping if a list element exceeds the target value. Write a pseudocode version of this **short sequential search** algorithm.

28. This exercise refers to short sequential search (see Exercise 27).

    a. What is the worst-case number of comparisons of short sequential search on a sorted n-element list?

    b. What is the approximate average number of comparisons to find an element that is in a sorted list using short sequential search?

    c. Is short sequential search ever more efficient than regular sequential search? Explain.

29. Draw the tree structure that describes binary search on the eight-element list in Exercise 25. What is the number of comparisons in the worst case? Give an example of a name to search for that requires that many comparisons.

30. Draw the tree structure that describes binary search on a list with 16 elements. What is the number of comparisons in the worst case?

31. We want to find an exact formula for the number of comparisons that binary search requires in the worst case on an n-element list. (We already know the formula is $\Theta(\lg n)$.)

    a. If x is a number that is not an integer, then $\lfloor x \rfloor$, called the *floor function* of x, is defined to be the largest integer less than or equal to x. For example, $\lfloor 3.7 \rfloor = 3$ and $\lfloor 5 \rfloor = 5$. Find the following values: $\lfloor 1.2 \rfloor, \lfloor 2.3 \rfloor, \lfloor 8.9 \rfloor, \lfloor -4.6 \rfloor$.

    b. If n is not a power of 2, then $\lg n$ is not an integer. If n is between 8 and 16, for example, then $\lg n$ is between 3 and 4 (because $\lg 8 = 3$ and $\lg 16 = 4$). Complete the following table of values:

n	$\lfloor \lg n \rfloor$
2	1
3	
4	2
5	
6	
7	
8	3

    c. For $n = 2, 3, 4, 5, 6, 7, 8$, draw a tree structure similar to Figure 3.19 to describe the positions searched by binary search. For each value of n, use the tree structure to find the number of comparisons in the worst case, and complete the following table:

n	Number of Compares, Worst Case
2	
3	
4	3
5	
6	
7	3
8	

d. Comparing the tables of parts b and c, find a formula involving $\lfloor \lg n \rfloor$ for the number of comparisons binary search requires in the worst case on an *n*-element list. Test your formula by drawing trees for other values of *n*.

32. Using the tree in Figure 3.19, find the number of comparisons to find each of items 1–7 in a seven-element list using binary search. Then find the average. Compare this with the worst case.

33. At the end of Section 3.4.2, we talked about the trade-off between using sequential search on an unsorted list as opposed to sorting the list and then using binary search. If the list size is $n = 100,000$, about how many worst-case searches must be done before the second alternative is better in terms of number of comparisons? (*Hint*: Let *p* represent the number of searches done.)

34. Suppose the pattern-matching problem is changed to require locating only the first instance, if any, of the pattern within the text.

    a. Describe the worst case, give an example, and give the exact number of comparisons (of a pattern character with a text character) required.

    b. Describe the best case, give an example, and give the exact number of comparisons required.

35. Suppose you use the brute force (unimproved) algorithm to search for a Hamiltonian circuit in the graph shown here.

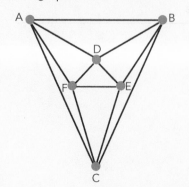

a. How many links would such a circuit have?

b. How many different paths would this algorithm examine?

c. If this algorithm is run on a computer where it takes 0.0001 seconds to examine a single path, what is the total time required to examine all paths?

d. On the same computer, what is the approximate total time required to examine all paths in a graph with 12 nodes, each of which has four choices for the next node?

36. An *Euler path* in a graph (named for the Swiss mathematician Leonhard Euler, 1707–1783) is a path that uses each edge of the graph exactly once. For example, this graph clearly has an Euler path A-B-D-C-A.

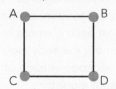

a. Decide which of the graphs below have Euler paths, and write out such a path if one exists. (Unlike Hamiltonian circuits, an Euler path need not end at the same node from which it starts, and can go through a given node more than once.)

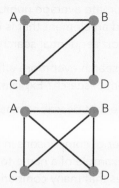

b. Like the Hamiltonian circuit problem, there is a brute force algorithm to determine whether a graph has an Euler path, again by testing all possibilities. You probably used a variation

(i)   (ii)   (iii)

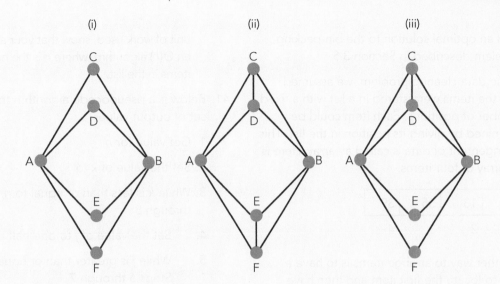

of this algorithm to solve part a. But the Euler path problem has another solution. The *degree* of a node is the number of edges at that node. A node with odd degree is an *odd node* and a node with even degree is an *even node*. In the first graph of part a, nodes A and D are even (degree 2) and nodes B and C are odd (degree 3). An Euler path exists in any graph with exactly 0 or 2 odd nodes. Which of the graphs at the top of the next page have Euler paths and why? Write out such a path if one exists.

c. Here is a pseudocode version of this algorithm for a graph with n nodes labeled 1 to n:

1. Get values for n and all edges of the graph

2. Set the value of *Odds* to 0

3. Set the value of node counter i to 1

4. While ($i \leq n$), do Steps 5 through 13

5.   Set the value of node counter j to 1

6.   Set the value of *Degree* to 0

7.   While ($j \leq n$), do Steps 8 through 10

8.   If an edge i-j exists then

9.   Increase *Degree* by 1

10.   Increase j by 1

11.   If *Degree* is an odd number then

12.   Increase *Odds* by 1

13.   Increase i by 1

14.   If *Odds* > 2 then

15.   Print the message 'No Euler path'

       Else

16.   Print the message 'Euler path exists'

17. Stop

What is the order of magnitude of this algorithm where the "work unit" is checking whether an edge exists (Step 8)?

d. Is the Euler path problem intractable?

37. At about what value of n does an algorithm that does $100n^2$ instructions become more efficient than one that does $0.01(2^n)$ instructions? (Use a calculator or spreadsheet.)

38. a. An algorithm that is $\Theta(n)$ takes 10 seconds to execute on a particular computer when $n = 100$. How long would you expect it to take when $n = 500$?

b. An algorithm that is $\Theta(n^2)$ takes 10 seconds to execute on a particular computer when $n = 100$. How long would you expect it to take when $n = 500$?

39. Find an optimal solution to the bin-packing problem described in Section 3.5.

40. In the data cleanup problem, we assumed that the items were stored in a list with a fixed number of positions. Each item could be examined by giving its position in the list. This arrangement of data is called an array. Here is an array of four items:

43	13	55	39
1	2	3	4

Another way to arrange items is to have a way to locate the first item and then have each item "point to" the next item. This arrangement of data is called a *linked list*. Here are the same four items in a linked list arrangement:

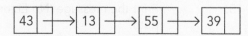

To examine any item in a linked list, one must start with the first item and follow the pointers to the desired item.

Unlike arrays, which are fixed in size, linked lists can shrink and grow. An item can be eliminated from a linked list by changing the pointer to that item so that it points to the next item instead.

a. Draw the linked list that results when item 13 is eliminated from the foregoing linked list.

b. Draw the linked list that results when data cleanup is performed on the following linked list.

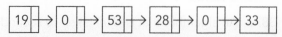

c. Describe (informally) an algorithm to do data cleanup on a linked list. You may assume that neither the first item nor the last item has a value of 0, and you may assume the existence of operations such as "follow pointer" and "change pointer." If these operations are the unit of work used, show that your algorithm is an $\Theta(n)$ algorithm, where n is the number of items in the list.

41. Below is a pseudocode algorithm that prints a set of output values:

1. Get value for n

2. Set the value of k to 1

3. While k is less than or equal to n, do Steps 4 through 8

4.   Set the value of j to one-half n

5.   While j is greater than or equal to 1, do Steps 6 through 7

6.   Print the value of j

7.   Set the value of j to one-half its former value

8.   Increase k by 1

9. Stop

a. Let n have the value 4. Write the values printed by this algorithm.

b. Let n have the value 8. Write the values printed by this algorithm.

c. Which of the following best describes the efficiency of this algorithm, where the "work unit" is printing a value?

$\Theta(n^2)$ $\Theta(n \lg n)$ $\Theta(n)$ $\Theta(\lg n)$

d. How many work units would you expect this algorithm to do if $n = 16$?

42. Chapter 2 contains an algorithm that finds the largest value in a list of n values.

a. What is the order of magnitude of the largest-value algorithm, where the "work unit" is comparisons of values from the list?

b. Suppose that you want to find the second-largest value in the list. Find the order of magnitude of the work done if you use the following algorithm: Sort the list, using selection sort, then directly get the second-largest value.

c. Suppose that you want to find the second-largest value in the list. Find the order of magnitude of the work done if you use the following algorithm: Run the largest-value algorithm twice, first to find (and eliminate from the list) the largest value, then to find the second-largest value.

CHALLENGE WORK

1. You are probably familiar with the children's song "Old MacDonald Had a Farm." The first verse is

    Old MacDonald had a farm, E-I-E-I-O.

    And on that farm he had a cow, E-I-E-I-O.

    With a moo-moo here and a moo-moo there,

    Here a moo, there a moo,

    Everywhere a moo-moo,

    Old MacDonald had a farm, E-I-E-I-O.

   In successive verses, more animals are added, and the middle refrain gets longer and longer. For example, the second verse is

    Old MacDonald had a farm, E-I-E-I-O.

    And on that farm he had a pig, E-I-E-I-O.

    With an oink-oink here and an oink-oink there,

    Here an oink, there an oink,

    Everywhere an oink-oink,

    With a moo-moo here and a moo-moo there,

    Here a moo, there a moo,

    Everywhere a moo-moo,

    Old MacDonald had a farm, E-I-E-I-O.

   a. Show that after *n* verses of this song have been sung, the total number of syllables sung would be given by the expression $22n(n + 1)/2 + 37n$. (You may assume that all animal names and all animal sounds consist of one syllable, as in cow, pig, moo, oink, and so on.)

   b. If singing this song is the algorithm, and the "work unit" is singing one syllable, what is the order of magnitude of the algorithm?[1]

2. *Linear programming* involves selecting values for a large number of quantities so that they satisfy a set of inequalities (such as $x + y + z \leq 100$) while at the same time maximizing (or minimizing) some particular function of these variables. Linear programming has many applications in communications and manufacturing. A trial-and-error approach to a linear programming problem would involve guessing at values for these variables until all of the inequalities are satisfied, but this might not produce the desired maximum (or minimum) value. In addition, real-world problems may involve hundreds or thousands of variables. A common algorithm to solve linear programming problems is called the *simplex method*. Although the simplex method works well for many common applications, including those that involve thousands of variables, its worst-case order of magnitude is exponential. Find information on the work of N. Karmarkar of Bell Labs, who discovered another algorithm for linear programming that is of polynomial order in the worst case and is faster than the simplex method in average cases.

----

[1]This exercise is based on work found in Chavey, D., "Songs and the Analysis of Algorithms," *Proceedings of the Twenty-Seventh SIGCSE Technical Symposium* (1996), pp. 4–8.

The Hardware World

- Chapter 17 — Social Issues
- Chapters 13, 14, 15, 16 — Applications
- Chapters 9, 10, 11, 12 — The Software World
- Chapters 6, 7, 8 — The Virtual Machine
- Chapters 4, 5 — The Hardware World
- Chapters 2, 3 — The Algorithmic Foundations of Computer Science

Some computer scientists are interested only in the logical and mathematical properties of algorithms—the material presented in Level 1. Others are interested in discovering and studying a solution and *using* that solution to produce results more efficiently than was previously possible. They want to execute algorithms on *real* computers.

Level 2 of the text takes us into a fascinating region of computer science, the world of hardware. Chapter 4 examines the fundamental building blocks used to construct computers. It discusses how to represent and store information inside a computer, how to use the principles of symbolic logic to design *gates*, and how to use gates to construct *circuits* that perform operations such as adding numbers, comparing numbers, and fetching instructions. These ideas are part of the branch of computer science known as *hardware design*, also called *logic design*. The second part of Level 2, Chapter 5, investigates computer hardware from a higher-level perspective called *computer organization*. This chapter introduces the four major subsystems of a modern computer (memory, input/output, arithmetic/logic unit, and control unit), demonstrates how they are built from the elementary building blocks described in Chapter 4, and shows how these subsystems can be organized into a complete, functioning computer system.

4 The Building Blocks: Binary Numbers, Boolean Logic, and Gates

AFTER STUDYING THIS CHAPTER, YOU WILL BE ABLE TO:

- Translate between base-ten and base-two numbers, and represent negative numbers using both sign-magnitude and two's complement representations

- Explain how fractional numbers, characters, sounds, and images are represented inside the computer

- Build truth tables for Boolean expressions and determine when they are true or false

- Describe the relationship between Boolean logic and electronic gates

- Construct circuits using the sum-of-products circuit design algorithm, and analyze simple circuits to determine their truth tables

- Explain how large, complex circuits, like 32-bit adder or compare-for-equality circuits, are constructed from simpler, 1-bit components

- Describe the purpose and workings of multiplexer and decoder control circuits

4.1 Introduction

Level 1 of this text investigated the algorithmic foundations of computer science. It developed algorithms for searching lists, finding largest and smallest values, locating patterns, sorting lists, and cleaning up bad data. It also showed how to analyze and evaluate algorithms to demonstrate that they are not only correct but efficient and useful as well.

Our discussion assumed that these algorithms would be executed by something called a *computing agent*, an abstract concept representing any entity capable of understanding and executing our instructions. At the time we didn't care what that computing agent was—person, mathematical model, computer, or robot. However, in this section of the text we *do* care what our computing agent looks like and how it is able to execute instructions and produce results.

In this chapter, we introduce the fundamental building blocks of all computer systems—binary representation, Boolean logic, gates, and circuits.

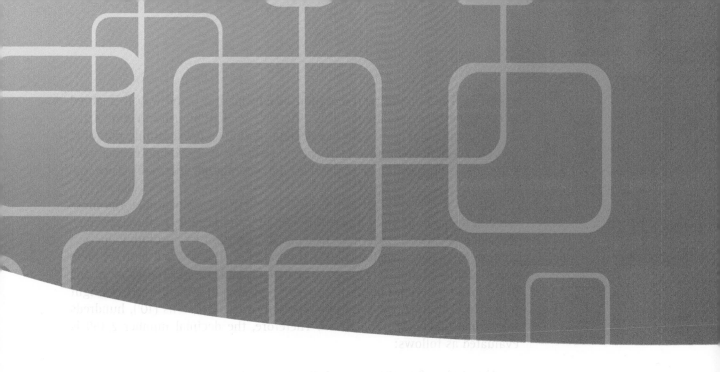

4.2 The Binary Numbering System

Our first concern with learning how to build computers is understanding how computers represent information. Their internal storage techniques are quite different from the way you and I represent information when we write a note or do a quick calculation on paper.

4.2.1 Binary Representation of Numeric and Textual Information

People generally represent numeric and textual information (language differences aside) by using the following notational conventions:

a. The 10 decimal digits 0, 1, 2, 3, 4, 5, 6, 7, 8, 9 for numeric values such as 459

b. *Sign/magnitude notation* for signed numbers—that is, a + or − sign placed immediately to the left of the digits; +31 and −789 are examples

c. *Decimal notation* for real numbers, with a decimal point separating the whole number part from the fractional part; an example is 12.34

d. The 26 letters A, B, C, ... , Z for textual information (as well as lowercase letters and a few special symbols for punctuation)

You might suppose that these well-known schemes are the same conventions that computers use to store information in memory. Surprisingly, this is not true.

There are two types of information representation: The *external* representation of information is the way information is represented by humans and the way it is entered at a keyboard or virtual keypad or displayed on a printer or screen. The *internal* representation of information is the way it is stored in the memory of a computer. This difference is diagrammed in Figure 4.1.

Externally, computers do use decimal digits, sign/magnitude notation, and the 26-character alphabet. However, virtually every computer ever built stores data—numbers, letters, graphics, images, sound—internally using the binary numbering system.

Binary is a base-2 positional numbering system not unlike the more familiar decimal, or base-10, system used in everyday life. In these systems, the value or "worth" of a digit depends not only on its absolute value but also on its specific position within a number. In the decimal system, there are 10 unique digits (0, 1, 2, 3, 4, 5, 6, 7, 8, and 9), and the value of the positions in a decimal number is based on powers of 10. Moving from right to left in a number, the positions represent ones (10^0), tens (10^1), hundreds (10^2), thousands (10^3), and so on. Therefore, the decimal number 2,359 is evaluated as follows:

$$(2 \times 10^3) + (3 \times 10^2) + (5 \times 10^1) + (9 \times 10^0)$$
$$= 2,000 + 300 + 50 + 9$$
$$= 2,359$$

The same concepts apply to binary numbers except that there are only two digits, 0 and 1, and the value of the positions in a binary number is based on powers of 2. Moving from right to left, the positions represent ones (2^0), twos (2^1), fours (2^2), eights (2^3), sixteens (2^4), and so on. The two digits,

FIGURE 4.1

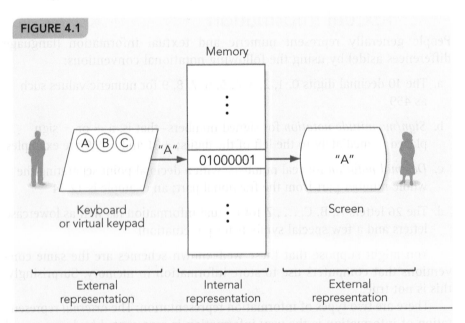

Distinction between external and internal representation of information

0 and 1, are frequently referred to as bits, a contraction of the two words *binary digits*.

For example, the six-digit binary number 111001 is evaluated as follows:

$$111001 = (1 \times 2^5) + (1 \times 2^4) + (1 \times 2^3) + (0 \times 2^2) + (0 \times 2^1) + (1 \times 2^0)$$
$$= 32 + 16 + 8 + 0 + 0 + 1$$
$$= 57$$

The five-digit binary quantity 10111 is evaluated in the following manner:

$$10111 = (1 \times 2^4) + (0 \times 2^3) + (1 \times 2^2) + (1 \times 2^1) + (1 \times 2^0)$$
$$= 16 + 0 + 4 + 2 + 1$$
$$= 23$$

Evaluating a binary number is quite easy, because 1 times any value is simply that value, and 0 times any value is always 0. Thus, when evaluating a binary number, use the following *binary-to-decimal algorithm*: Whenever there is a 1 in a column, add the positional value of that column to a running sum, and whenever there is a 0 in a column, add nothing. The final sum is the decimal value of this binary number. This is the procedure we followed in the previous two examples.

A binary-to-decimal conversion table for the values 0–31 is shown in Figure 4.2. You might want to evaluate a few of the binary values using this algorithm to confirm their decimal equivalents.

FIGURE 4.2

Binary	Decimal	Binary	Decimal
0	0	10000	16
1	1	10001	17
10	2	10010	18
11	3	10011	19
100	4	10100	20
101	5	10101	21
110	6	10110	22
111	7	10111	23
1000	8	11000	24
1001	9	11001	25
1010	10	11010	26
1011	11	11011	27
1100	12	11100	28
1101	13	11101	29
1110	14	11110	30
1111	15	11111	31

Binary-to-decimal conversion table for the decimal digits 0–31

Any whole number that can be represented in base 10 can also be represented in base 2, although it may take more digits because a single decimal digit contains more information than a single binary digit. Note that in the first example shown on the previous page it takes only two decimal digits (5 and 7) to represent the quantity 57 in base 10, but it takes six binary digits (1, 1, 1, 0, 0, and 1) to express the same value in base 2.

To go in the reverse direction—that is, to convert a decimal value into its binary equivalent—we use the *decimal-to-binary algorithm*, which is based on successive divisions by 2. Dividing the original decimal value by 2 produces a quotient and a remainder, which must be either a 0 or a 1. Record the remainder digit and then divide the quotient by 2, getting a new quotient and a second remainder digit. The process of dividing by 2, saving the quotient, and writing down the remainder is repeated until the quotient equals 0. The sequence of remainder digits, when written left to right from the last remainder digit to the first, is the binary representation of the original decimal value. For example, here is the conversion of the decimal value 19 into binary:

Convert the value 19 to binary:

19 ÷ 2	quotient = 9	remainder = 1
9 ÷ 2	quotient = 4	remainder = 1
4 ÷ 2	quotient = 2	remainder = 0
2 ÷ 2	quotient = 1	remainder = 0
1 ÷ 2	quotient = 0	remainder = 1

↑ order for reading the remainder digits

Stop, because the quotient is now 0.

In this example, the remainder digits, when written left to right from the last one to the first, are 10011. This is the binary form of the decimal value 19. To confirm this, we can convert this value back to decimal form using the binary-to-decimal algorithm.

$$10011 = (1 \times 2^4) + (0 \times 2^3) + (0 \times 2^2) + (1 \times 2^1) + (1 \times 2^0)$$
$$= 16 + 0 + 0 + 2 + 1$$
$$= 19$$

In every computer, there is a maximum number of binary digits that can be used to store an integer. Typically, this value is 16, 32, or 64 bits. Once we have fixed this maximum number of bits (as part of the design of the computer), we also have fixed the largest unsigned whole number that can be represented in this computer. For example, Figure 4.2 used at most 5 bits to represent binary numbers. The largest value that could be represented is 11111, not unlike the number 99999, which is the maximum mileage value that can be represented on a five-digit decimal odometer. 11111 is the binary representation for the decimal integer 31. If there were 16 bits available on a given computer, rather than 5, then the largest integer that could be represented is

1 1 1 1 1 1 1 1 1 1 1 1 1 1 1 1

This quantity is $2^{15} + 2^{14} + \ldots + 2^2 + 2^1 + 2^0 = 65,535$. Unsigned integers larger than this cannot be represented with 16 binary digits. Any operation on this computer that produces an unsigned value greater than 65,535 results in the error condition called arithmetic overflow. This is an attempt to represent an integer that exceeds the maximum allowable value. The computer could be designed to use more than 16 bits to represent integers, but no matter how many bits are ultimately used, there is always a maximum value beyond which the computer cannot correctly represent any integer. This characteristic is one of the major differences between the disciplines of mathematics and computer science. In mathematics, a quantity may usually take on any value, no matter how large. Computer science must deal with a finite—and sometimes quite limited—set of possible representations, and it must handle the errors that occur when those limits are exceeded.

Arithmetic in binary is quite easy because we have only 2 digits to deal with rather than 10. Therefore, the rules that define arithmetic operations such as addition and subtraction have only $2 \times 2 = 4$ entries, rather than the $10 \times 10 = 100$ entries for decimal digits. For example, here are the four rules that define binary addition:

```
  0      0      1      1
+ 0    + 1    + 0    + 1
---    ---    ---    ---
  0      1      1     10  (that is, 0 with a carry of 1)
```

The last rule says that $1 + 1 = 10$, which has the decimal value 2.

To add two binary numbers, you use the same technique first learned in grade school. Add each column one at a time from right to left, using the binary addition rules shown above. In the column being added, you write the sum digit under the line and any carry digit produced is written above the next column to the left. For example, addition of the two binary values 7 (00111) and 14 (01110) proceeds as follows:

```
   00111   (the binary value 7)
 + 01110   (the binary value 14)
 -------
```

Start by adding the two digits in the rightmost column—the 1 and 0. This produces a sum of 1 and a carry digit of 0; the carry digit gets "carried" to the second column.

```
     0      ← carry digit
   00111
 + 01110
 -------
       1
```

Now add the carry digit from the previous column to the two digits in the second column, which gives $0 + 1 + 1$. From the rules above, we see that the $(0 + 1)$ produces a 1. When this is added to the value 1, it produces a sum of 0 and a new carry digit of 1.

```
     1      ← carry digit
   00111
 + 01110
 -------
      01
```

A Not So Basic Base

The decimal system has been in use for so long that most people cannot imagine using a number system other than base 10. Tradition says it was chosen because we have 10 fingers and 10 toes. However, the discussion of the past few pages should convince you that there is nothing unique or special about decimal numbering, and the basic operations of arithmetic (addition, subtraction, multiplication, and division) work just fine in other bases, such as base 2. In addition to binary, computer science makes frequent use of *octal* (base 8) and *hexadecimal* (base 16). Furthermore, it is not only computers that utilize nondecimal bases. For example, the Native American Yuki tribe of northern California reportedly used base 4, or *quaternary* numbers, counting using the spaces between fingers rather than on the fingers themselves. The pre-Columbian Mayans of Mexico and Central America used a *vigesimal* system, or base 20, whereas ancient Babylonians employed *sexagesimal*, or base 60 (and we are quite sure that members of both cultures had the same number of fingers and toes as 21st-century human beings!).

Adding the two digits in the third column plus the carry digit from the second column produces $1 + 1 + 1$, which is 11, or a sum of 1 and a new carry digit of 1.

```
    1          ← carry digit
  00111
+ 01110
    101
```

Continuing in this right-to-left manner until we reach the leftmost column produces the final result, 10101 in binary, or 21 in decimal.

```
  00111
+ 01110
  10101   (the value 21 = 16 + 4 + 1)
```

Signed Numbers. Binary digits can represent not only whole numbers but also other forms of data, including signed integers, decimal numbers, and characters. For example, to represent signed integers, we can use the leftmost bit of a number to represent the sign, with 0 meaning positive (+) and 1 meaning negative (–). The remaining bits are used to represent the magnitude of the value. This form of signed integer representation is termed sign/magnitude notation, and it is one of a number of different techniques for representing positive and negative whole numbers. For example, to represent the quantity −49 in sign/magnitude, we could use seven binary digits with 1 bit for the sign and 6 bits for the magnitude:

$$\underbrace{1}_{-}\ \underbrace{1\,1\,0\,0\,0\,1}_{49} \qquad (2^5 + 2^4 + 2^0 = 32 + 16 + 1 = 49)$$

The value + 3 would be stored like this:

$$\underbrace{0}_{+}\ \underbrace{0\,0\,0\,0\,1\,1}_{3} \qquad (2^1 + 2^0 = 2 + 1 = 3)$$

You might wonder how a computer knows that the seven-digit binary number 1110001 in the first example above represents the signed integer value −49 rather than the unsigned whole number 113.

$$1110001 = (1 \times 2^6) + (1 \times 2^5) + (1 \times 2^4) + (1 \times 2^0)$$
$$= 64 + 32 + 16 + 1$$
$$= 113$$

The answer to this question is that a computer does *not* know. A sequence of binary digits can have many different interpretations, and there is no fixed, predetermined interpretation given to any binary value. A binary number stored in the memory of a computer takes on meaning only because it is used in a certain way. If we use the value 1110001 as though it were a signed integer, then it will be interpreted that way and will take on the value −49. If it is used, instead, as an unsigned whole number, then that is what it will become, and it will be interpreted as the value 113. The meaning of a binary number stored in memory is based solely on the context in which it is used.

Initially, this might seem strange, but we deal with this type of ambiguity all the time in natural languages. For example, in the Hebrew language, letters of the alphabet are also used as numbers. Thus the Hebrew character aleph (א) can stand for either the letter A or the number 1. The only way to tell which meaning is appropriate is to consider the context in which the character is used. Similarly, in English, the word *ball* can mean either a round object used to play games or an elegant formal party. Which interpretation is correct? We cannot say without knowing the context in which the word is used. The same is true for values stored in the memory of a computer system. It is the context that determines the meaning of a binary string.

Sign/magnitude notation is quite easy for people to work with and understand, but, surprisingly, it is used rather infrequently in real computer systems. The reason is the existence of the very "messy" and unwanted signed number: 10000 … 0000. Because the leftmost bit is a 1, this value is treated as negative. The magnitude is 0000 … 0000. Thus this bit pattern represents the numerical quantity "negative zero," a value that has no real mathematical meaning and should not be distinguished from the other representation for zero, 00000 … 0000. The existence of two distinct bit patterns for a single numerical quantity causes some significant problems for computer designers.

For example, assume we are executing the following algorithmic operation on two signed numbers a and b:

```
if (a = b)
    do operation 1
else
    do operation 2
```

when a has the value 0000 ... 0 and b has the value 1000 ... 0. Should they be considered equal to each other? Numerically, the value -0 does equal $+0$, so maybe we should do operation 1. However, the two bit patterns are not identical, so maybe these two values are not equal, and we should do operation 2. This situation can result in programs that execute in different ways on different machines.

Therefore, computer designers tend to favor signed integer representations that do not suffer from the problem of two zeros. One of the most widely used is called two's complement representation. To understand how this method works, you need to write down, in circular form, all binary patterns from 000 ... 0 to 111 ... 1 in increasing order. Here is what that circle might look like using three-digit numbers:

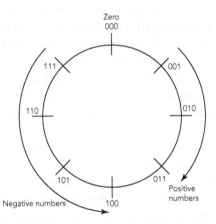

In this diagram, the positive numbers begin at 000 and proceed in order around the circle to the right. Negative numbers begin at 111 and proceed in order around the circle to the left. The leftmost digit specifies whether the number is to be given a positive interpretation (leftmost bit = 0) or a negative interpretation (leftmost bit = 1).

Bit Pattern	Decimal Value
000	0
001	+1
010	+2
011	+3
100	−4
101	−3
110	−2
111	−1

In this representation, if we add, for example, $3 + (-3)$, we get 0, as expected:

```
11    ← carry digits
011
101
000   (Note: The 1 that carries into column 4 can be discarded.)
```

Note that in the two's complement representation, there is only a single zero, the binary number $000 \ldots 0$. However, the existence of a single pattern for zero leads to another unusual situation. The total number of values that can be represented with n bits is 2^n, which is always an even number. In the previous example, $n = 3$, so there were $2^3 = 8$ possible values. One of these is used for 0, leaving seven remaining values, which is an odd number. It is impossible to divide these seven patterns equally between the positive and negative numbers, and in this example we ended up with four negative values but only three positive ones. The pattern that was previously "negative zero" (100) now represents the value -4, but there is no equivalent number on the positive side, that is, there is no binary pattern that represents $+4$. In the two's complement representation of signed integers, you can always represent one more negative number than positive. This is not as severe a problem as having two zeros, though, and two's complement is widely used for representing signed numbers inside a computer.

This has been only a brief introduction to the two's complement representation. A Challenge Work problem at the end of this chapter invites you to investigate further the underlying mathematical foundations of this interesting representational technique.

Fractional Numbers. Fractional numbers, such as 12.34 and -0.001275, can also be represented in binary by using the signed-integer techniques we have just described. To do that, however, we must first convert the number to scientific notation:

$$\pm M \times B^{\pm E}$$

where M is the *mantissa*, B is the *exponent base* (usually 2), and E is the *exponent*. For example, assume we want to represent the decimal quantity $+5.75$. In addition, assume that we will use 16 bits to represent the number, with 10 bits allocated for representing the mantissa and 6 bits for the exponent. (The exponent base B is assumed to be 2 and is not explicitly stored.) Both the mantissa and the exponent are signed integer numbers, so we can use either the sign/magnitude or two's complement notations that we just learned to represent each of these two fields. (In all the following examples, we have chosen to use sign/magnitude notation.)

In binary, the value 5 is 101. To represent the fractional quantity 0.75, we need to remember that the bits to the right of the decimal point (or binary point in our case) have the positional values r^{-1}, r^{-2}, r^{-3}, and so on, where r is the base of the numbering system used to represent the number. When using decimal notation, these position values are the tenths (10^{-1}), hundredths (10^{-2}), thousandths (10^{-3}), and so on. Because r is 2 in our case, the positional values of the digits to the right of the binary point are halves (2^{-1}), quarters (2^{-2}), eighths (2^{-3}), sixteenths (2^{-4}), and so on. Thus,

$$0.75 = 1/2 + 1/4 = 2^{-1} + 2^{-2} \text{ (which in binary is 0.11)}$$

Therefore, in binary 5.75 = 101.11. Using scientific notation, and an exponent base $B = 2$, we can write this value as

$$5.75 = 101.11 \times 2^0$$

Next, we must *normalize* the number so that its first significant digit is immediately to the right of the binary point. As we move the binary point, we adjust the value of the exponent so that the overall value of the number remains unchanged. If we move the binary point to the left one place (which makes the value smaller by a factor of 2), then we add 1 to the exponent (which makes it larger by a factor of 2). We do the reverse when we move the binary point to the right.

$$
\begin{aligned}
5.75 &= 101.11 \times 2^0 \\
&= 10.111 \times 2^1 \\
&= 1.0111 \times 2^2 \\
&= .10111 \times 2^3
\end{aligned}
$$
(which is $(1/2 + 1/8 + 1/16 + 1/32) \times 8 = 5.75$)

We now have the number in the desired format and can put all the pieces together. We separately store the mantissa (excluding the binary point, which is assumed to be to the left of the first significant digit) and the exponent, both of which are signed integers and can be represented in sign/magnitude notation. The mantissa is stored with its sign—namely, 0, because it is a positive quantity—followed by the assumed binary point, followed by the magnitude of the mantissa, which in this case is 10111. Next we store the exponent, which is +3, or 000011 in sign/magnitude. The overall representation, using 16 bits, is

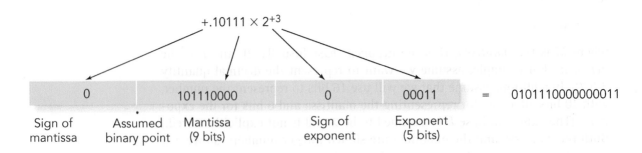

For another example, let's determine the internal representation of the fraction −5/16.

$$
\begin{aligned}
-5/16 &= -(1/4 + 1/16) \\
&= -.0101 \times 2^0 \quad \text{(this is the value } -5/16 \text{ in scientific notation)} \\
&= -.101 \times 2^{-1} \quad \text{(after normalization)}
\end{aligned}
$$

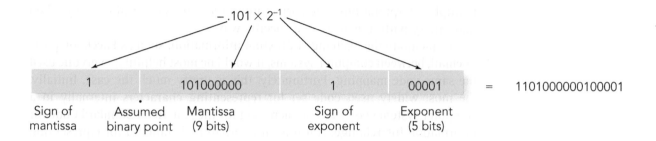

Textual Information. To represent textual material in binary, the system assigns to each printable letter or symbol in our alphabet a unique number (this assignment is called a *code mapping*), and then it stores that symbol internally using the binary equivalent of that number. For example, here is one possible mapping of characters to numbers, which uses 8 bits to represent each character.

Symbol	Decimal Value	Binary (Using 8 Binary Digits)
A	1	00000001
B	2	00000010
C	3	00000011
D	4	00000100
⋮	⋮	⋮
Z	26	00011010
⋮	⋮	⋮
@	128	10000000
!	129	10000001
⋮	⋮	⋮

To store the four-character string "BAD!" in memory, the computer would store the binary representation of each individual character using the above 8-bit code.

$$\text{BAD!} = \underbrace{00000010}_{B} \quad \underbrace{00000001}_{A} \quad \underbrace{00000100}_{D} \quad \underbrace{10000001}_{!}$$

We have indicated above that the 8-bit numeric quantity 10000001 is interpreted as the character "!". However, as we mentioned earlier, the only way a computer knows that the 8-bit value 10000001 represents the symbol "!" and not the unsigned integer value 129 (128 + 1) or the signed integer value –1 (sign bit = negative, magnitude is 1) is by the context in which it is used. If these 8 bits are sent to a display device that expects to be given characters, then this value will be interpreted as an "!". If, on the other hand, this 8-bit value is sent to an arithmetic unit that adds unsigned numbers, then it will be interpreted as 129 in order to make the addition operation meaningful. It is critical to remember that every pattern of binary digits has multiple interpretations. The correct interpretation is determined only when that binary pattern is used in a specific way.

To facilitate the exchange of textual information, such as Facebook posts or email, between computer systems, it would be most helpful if everyone used the same code mapping. Fortunately, this is pretty much the case. Initially, the most widely used code set for representing characters internally in a computer system was ASCII, an acronym for the American Standard Code for Information Interchange. ASCII is an international standard for representing textual information that uses 8 bits per character, so it is able to encode a total of $2^8 = 256$ different symbols. These are assigned the integer values 0 to 255. However, only the numbers 32 to 126 have been assigned to printable characters. The remainder either are unassigned or are used for representing nonprinting control characters such as tab, form feed, and return. Figure 4.3 shows the ASCII conversion table for the numerical values 32–126.

However, the code set called Unicode, developed in the early 1990s, has gained in popularity because it uses, at a minimum, a 16-bit representation for characters rather than the 8-bit format of ASCII. This means that it is able to represent at least $2^{16} = 65,536$ unique characters instead of the $2^8 = 256$ of ASCII. (*Note:* Unicode is a superset of ASCII. The decimal values 0–127 represent exactly the same characters in both ASCII and Unicode.) It might seem as though 256 characters should be more than enough to represent all the textual symbols that we would ever need—for example, 26 uppercase letters, 26 lowercase letters, 10 digits, and a few dozen special symbols, such as + = − { }] [\: " ? > < . , ; % $ # @. Add that all together and it still totals only about 100 symbols, far less than the 256 that can be represented in ASCII. However, that is true only if we limit our text to Arabic numerals and the Roman alphabet. The world is growing more connected all the time—helped along by computers, networks, and the web—and it is critically important that computers are able to represent and exchange textual information using the widest possible range of alphabets. When we start assigning codes to symbols drawn from alphabets such as Russian, Arabic, Chinese, Hebrew, Greek, Thai, Bengali, Sanskrit, Cherokee, Inuit, and Braille, as well as mathematical symbols, linguistic marks such as the tilde, umlaut, and accent grave, and numerous graphical symbols, it quickly becomes clear that ASCII does not have enough room to represent them all. Unicode, with its 16 bits and space for over 65,000 symbols, was initially considered large enough to accommodate this enormous range of text. However, it turned out that even 16 bits proved insufficient to handle the exploding range of textual information being produced around the world, and Unicode now includes a 32-bit variant in which each separate character is represented using 32 binary digits, allowing for the possibility of 2^{32} distinct textual symbols, or about 4 billion! Currently Unicode has assigned formal mappings to more than 128,000 characters drawn from over 135 modern and historical alphabets, including such rarities as Egyptian hieroglyphics. The Unicode home page, which gives all the current standard mappings, is located at *www.unicode.org*.

FIGURE 4.3

Keyboard Character	Binary ASCII Code	Integer Equivalent	Keyboard Character	Binary ASCII Code	Integer Equivalent
(blank)	00100000	32	P	01010000	80
!	00100001	33	Q	01010001	81
"	00100010	34	R	01010010	82
#	00100011	35	S	01010011	83
$	00100100	36	T	01010100	84
%	00100101	37	U	01010101	85
&	00100110	38	V	01010110	86
'	00100111	39	W	01010111	87
(	00101000	40	X	01011000	88
)	00101001	41	Y	01011001	89
*	00101010	42	Z	01011010	90
+	00101011	43	[	01011011	91
'	00101100	44	\	01011100	92
–	00101101	45	]	01011101	93
.	00101110	46	^	01011110	94
/	00101111	47	_	01011111	95
0	00110000	48	_	01100000	96
1	00110001	49	a	01100001	97
2	00110010	50	b	01100010	98
3	00110011	51	c	01100011	99
4	00110100	52	d	01100100	100
5	00110101	53	e	01100101	101
6	00110110	54	f	01100110	102
7	00110111	55	g	01100111	103
8	00111000	56	h	01101000	104
9	00111001	57	i	01101001	105
:	00111010	58	j	01101010	106
;	00111011	59	k	01101011	107
<	00111100	60	l	01101100	108
=	00111101	61	m	01101101	109
>	00111110	62	n	01101110	110
?	00111111	63	o	01101111	111
@	01000000	64	p	01110000	112
A	01000001	65	q	01110001	113
B	01000010	66	r	01110010	114
C	01000011	67	s	01110011	115
D	01000100	68	t	01110100	116
E	01000101	69	u	01110101	117
F	01000110	70	v	01110110	118
G	01000111	71	w	01110111	119
H	01001000	72	x	01111000	120
I	01001001	73	y	01111001	121
J	01001010	74	z	01111010	122
K	01001011	75	{	01111011	123
L	01001100	76	:	01111100	124
M	01001101	77	]	01111101	125
N	01001110	78	~	01111110	126
O	01001111	79			

ASCII conversion table

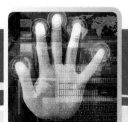

Practice Problems

1. What is the value of the 8-bit binary quantity 10101000 if it is interpreted (a) as an unsigned integer and (b) as a signed integer represented in sign/magnitude notation?

2. What does the unsigned decimal value 99 look like in binary using 8 bits?

3. What do the signed integers −300 and +254 look like in binary using 10 bits and sign/magnitude integer representation?

4. What is the value of the 8-bit binary quantity 10010111 when it is interpreted as a sign/magnitude integer?

5. Using 4 bits and two's complement representation, what is the binary representation of the following signed decimal values:

   a. +6
   b. −3

6. Perform the following 5-bit binary addition showing the carry bit that propagates to each column. Assume that the numbers are unsigned binary quantities:

   ```
     01110
   + 01011
   ```

7. What does the three-character string "X+Y" look like internally using the 8-bit ASCII code given in Figure 4.3? What does it look like in 16-bit Unicode? (Go to *www.unicode.org* to find the specific code mappings for these three characters.)

8. Using 10 bits to represent the mantissa (sign/magnitude) and 6 bits for the exponent (also sign/magnitude), show the internal representation of the following two values:

   a. +0.25
   b. − 32 1/16

9. Explain exactly what happens when you add a 1 to the following 5-bit, two's complement value: 01111

10. Explain exactly what happens when you perform addition on the following two sign/magnitude integer values:

   ```
      00111 (+7)
   + 01110 (+14)
   ```

4.2.2 Binary Representation of Sound and Images

During the first 30 to 40 years of computing, the overwhelming majority of applications, such as word processing and spreadsheets, were text based and limited to the manipulation of characters, words, and numbers. However, sound and images are now as important a form of representation as text and numbers because of the popularity of digitally encoded music, the rapid emergence of digital photography, the popularity of streaming videos, and the almost universal availability of online digital movies. Most of us, whether computer specialists or not, have had the experience of playing MP3 sound files, emailing vacation pictures to friends and family, or enjoying a YouTube video clip. In this section, we take a brief look at how sounds and images are represented in computers, using the same binary numbering system that we have been discussing.

Sound is analog information, unlike the digital format used to represent text and numbers discussed in the previous section. In a digital representation, the allowable values for a given object are drawn from a finite set, such as letters {A, B, C, ... , Z} or a subset of integers {0, 1, 2, 3, ... , MAX}.

In an analog representation, objects can take on any value. For example, in the case of sound, a tone is a continuous sinusoidal waveform that varies in a regular periodic fashion over time, as shown in Figure 4.4. (*Note*: This diagram shows only a single tone. Complex sounds, such as symphonic music, are composed of multiple overlapping waveforms. However, the basic ideas are the same.)

The amplitude (height) of the wave is a measure of its loudness—the greater the amplitude, the louder the sound. The period of the wave, designated as T, is the time it takes for the wave to make one complete cycle. The frequency f is the total number of cycles per unit time measured in cycles/second, also called *hertz*, and defined as $f = 1/T$. The frequency is a measure of the *pitch*, the highness or lowness of a sound. The higher the frequency, the higher the perceived tone. A healthy, young human ear can generally detect sounds in the range of 20 to 20,000 hertz.

FIGURE 4.4

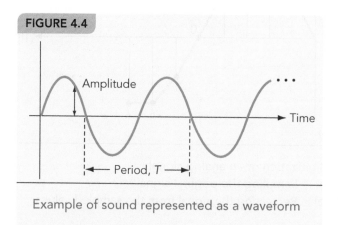

Example of sound represented as a waveform

To store a waveform (such as the one in Figure 4.4) in the computer, the analog signal first must be digitized, that is, converted to a digital representation. This can be done using a technique known as sampling. At fixed time intervals, the amplitude of the signal is measured and stored as an integer value. The wave is thus represented in the computer in digital form as a sequence of sampled numerical amplitudes. For example, Figure 4.5(a) shows the sampling of the waveform of Figure 4.4.

This signal can now be stored inside the computer as the series of signed integer values 3, 7, 7, 5, 0, –3, –6, –6, ..., where each numerical value is encoded in binary using the techniques described in the previous section. From these stored digitized values, the computer can recreate an approximation to the original analog wave. It would first generate an amplitude level of 3, then an amplitude level of 7, then an amplitude level of 7, and so on, as shown in Figure 4.5(b). These values would be sent to a sound-generating device, such as stereo speakers, which would produce the actual sounds based on the numerical values received.

FIGURE 4.5

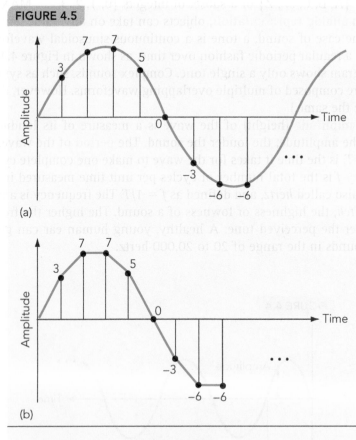

Digitization of an analog signal
(a)   Sampling the original signal
(b)   Recreating the signal from the sampled values

The accuracy with which the original sound can be reproduced is dependent on two key parameters—the sampling rate and the bit depth. The sampling rate measures how many times per second we sample the amplitude of the sound wave. Obviously, the more often we sample, the more accurate the reproduction. Note, for example, that the sampling shown in Figure 4.5(a) appears to have missed the peak value of the wave because the peak occurred between two sampling intervals. Furthermore, the more often we sample, the greater the range of frequencies that can be captured; if the frequency of a wave is greater than or equal to the sampling rate, we might not sample any points whatsoever on an entire waveform. For example, Figure 4.6 shows the sampling interval t, which is exactly equal to the period T of the wave being measured.

This rate of sampling produces a constant amplitude value, totally distorting the original sound. In general, a sampling rate of R samples/second allows you to reproduce all frequencies up to about $R/2$ hertz. Because the human ear can normally detect sound up to about 20,000 hertz, a sampling rate of at least 40,000 samples per second is necessary to capture all audible frequencies.

The bit depth is the number of bits used to encode each sample. In the previous section, you learned that ASCII is an 8-bit character code, allowing for 256 unique symbols. Unicode uses a minimum of 16 bits, allowing for more than 65,000 symbols and greatly increasing the number of symbols that can be represented. The same trend can be seen in sound reproduction. Initially, 8 bits per sample was the standard, but the 256 levels of amplitude that could be represented turned out to be insufficient for the sophisticated high-end sound systems produced and marketed today. Most audio encoding schemes today use either 16 or 24 bits per sample level, allowing for either 65,000 or 16,000,000 distinct amplitude levels.

There are many audio-encoding formats in use today, including AAC (Advanced Audio Coding), which is the standard audio format for Apple's iPhone and iPad, WMA (Windows Media Audio), WAV (Waveform Audio File Format), and MIDI (Musical Instrument Digital Interface). Another popular and

FIGURE 4.6

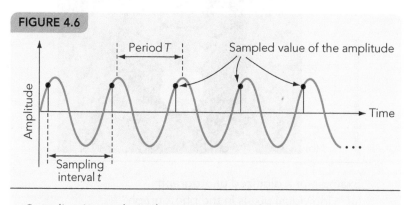

Sampling interval t is the same as period T

widely used digital audio format is *MP3*, an acronym for MPEG-1 (later updated to MPEG-2), Audio Level 3 Encoding. This is a digital audio encoding standard established by the Motion Picture Experts Group (MPEG), a committee of the International Organization for Standardization (ISO) of the United Nations. MP3 samples sound signals at the rate of 44,100 samples/second, using 16 bits per sample. This produces high-quality sound reproduction, which is why MP3 is the most widely used format for rock, opera, and classical music.

An image, such as a photograph, is also analog data but can also be stored using binary representation. An image is a continuous set of intensity and color values that can be digitized by sampling the analog information, just as is done for sound. The sampling process, often called *scanning,* consists of measuring the intensity values of distinct points located at regular intervals across the image's surface. These points are called *pixels,* short for picture elements, and the more pixels used, the more accurate the encoding of the image. The average human eye cannot accurately discern components closer together than about 0.05–0.1 mm, so if the pixels, or dots, are sufficiently dense, they appear to the human eye as a single, contiguous image. For example, a high-quality digital camera stores about 10–15 million pixels per photograph. For a 3 in. × 5 in. image, this is about 800,000 pixels/in.^{2}, or 900 pixels per linear inch. This means the individual pixels are separated by about 1/900th of an inch, or roughly 0.02 mm—much too close together to be individually visualized. (By comparison, an iPhone 7 camera contains two 12-million-pixel cameras.) Figure 4.7 enlarges a small section of a digitized photograph to better show how it is stored internally as a set of discrete picture elements.

FIGURE 4.7

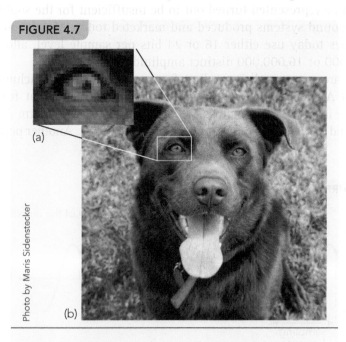

Photo by Maris Sidenstecker

(a)

(b)

Example of a digitized photograph
(a)   Individual pixels in the photograph
(b)   Photograph

One of the key questions we need to answer is how much information is stored for each pixel. Suppose we want to store a representation of a black-and-white image. The easiest and most space-efficient approach is to mark each pixel as either white, stored as a binary 0, or black, stored as a binary 1. The only problem is that this produces a stark *black-and-white image*, with a highly sharp and unpleasant visual contrast. A much better way, although it takes more storage, is to represent black-and-white images using a *gray scale* of varying intensity. For example, if we use 3 bits per pixel, we can represent $2^3 = 8$ shades of intensity from level 0, pure white, to level 7, pure black. An example of this eight-level gray scale is shown in Figure 4.8. If we wanted more detail than is shown there, we could use 8 bits per pixel, giving us $2^8 = 256$ distinct shades of gray.

We now can encode our image as a sequence of numerical pixel values, storing each row of pixels completely, from left to right, before moving down to store the next row. Each pixel is encoded as an unsigned binary value representing its gray scale intensity. This form of image representation is called raster graphics, and it is used by such well-known graphics standards as JPEG (Joint Photographer Experts Group), GIF (Graphics Interchange Format), and BMP (bitmap).

Today, most images are not black and white, but are in color. To digitize color images, we still measure the intensity value of the image at a discrete set of points, but we need to store more information about each pixel. The most common format for storing color images is the RGB encoding scheme, RGB being an acronym for red-green-blue. This technique describes a specific color by capturing the individual contribution to a pixel's color of each of the three colors, red, green, and blue. It uses one byte, or 8 bits, for each color, allowing us to represent an intensity range of 0 to 255 for each color. The value 0 means that there is no contribution from this color, whereas the value 255 means a full contribution of this color.

For example, the color magenta is an equal mix of pure red and blue, which would be RGB encoded as (255, 0, 255):

Red	Green	Blue
255	0	255

FIGURE 4.8

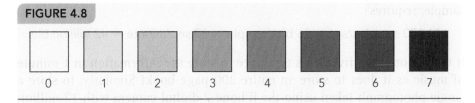

An eight-level gray scale

The color hot pink is produced by setting the three RGB values to

Red	Green	Blue
255	105	180

and harvest gold is rendered as

Red	Green	Blue
218	165	32

Using 3 bytes of information per pixel—24 bits—allows us to represent 2^{24} distinct colors, about 16.7 million. This 24-bit color-encoding scheme is often referred to as *True Color*, and it provides an enormous range of shades and an extremely accurate color image reproduction. That is why it is the encoding scheme used in the JPEG color imaging format. Newer high-resolution video standards are increasing the theoretical number of colors that can be represented on a screen. For example, the HDMI (High-Definition Multimedia Interface) 1.4 standard allows pixel bit depths of up to 48 bits, allowing for 2^{48} distinct colors, over 280 trillion!

However, representing 280 trillion, or even 16 million, colors requires a huge amount of memory space, and some image representation techniques reduce that value by using what is called a *color palette*. While theoretically supporting 16+ million different colors, they only allow you to use 256 (or some other small number) at any one time, just as a painter may have a lot of colors in his or her studio but puts only a few on the palette at a time. With a palette size of 256, we can encode each pixel using only 8 bits rather than 24, because $2^8 = 256$, thus reducing storage space demands by almost 67%. Each of these 256 values does not represent an explicit RGB color value but rather an index into a palette, or a color table. This index specifies which color on the palette is to be used to draw this pixel. This is the technique used, for example, in GIF, which uses a palette that can hold as few as 2 colors or as many as 256.

Sound and image data typically require huge amounts of storage, far more than is required for the numbers and text discussed in Section 4.2.1. For example, a 300-page novel contains about 100,000 words. Each word has on average about five characters and, as discussed in the previous section, each individual character can be encoded into Unicode using 16 bits. Thus, the total number of bits needed to represent this book is roughly

100,000 words $\times$ 5 char/word $\times$ 16 bits/char = *8 million bits*

By comparison, 1 minute of sound recording encoded using the MP3 standard, which samples 44,100 times per second using a bit depth of 16 bits per sample, requires

44,100 samples/sec $\times$ 16 bits/sample $\times$ 60 sec/minute = *42 million bits*

It takes more than five times the space to store the information in 1 minute of music as it does to store an entire 300-page book! Similarly, to store a single photograph taken using the iPhone 7 digital camera with 12 million pixels using 24-bit True-Color raster graphics requires:

12,000,000 pixels/photograph $\times$ 24 bits/pixel = *288 million bits*

A single iPhone color photograph could require 36 times more storage than an entire novel.

As these examples clearly show, the storage of analog information, such as sound, images, voice, and video, is enormously space intensive, and an important area of computer science research—data compression—is directed at addressing just this issue. Data compression algorithms attempt to represent information in ways that preserve accuracy while using significantly less space.

For example, a simple compression technique that can be used on almost any form of data is *run-length encoding*. This method replaces a sequence of identical values $v_1, v_2, \ldots, v_n$ by a pair of values (v, n), which indicates that the value v is replicated n times. If both v and n require 1 byte of storage, then we have reduced the total number of bytes required to store this sequence from n down to 2. Using this method, we could encode the following 5×3 image of the letter E, where $0 = $ white, and $255 = $ black:

255	255	255
255	0	0
255	255	255
255	0	0
255	255	255

like this:

(255, 4) (0, 2) (255, 4) (0, 2) (255, 3)

Run-length encoding reduces the number of bytes needed to store this image from 15, using the raster graphics representation, to the 10 bytes shown above. Compression schemes are usually evaluated by their compression ratio, which measures how much they reduce the storage requirements of the data:

$$\text{Compression ratio} = \frac{\text{size of the uncompressed data}}{\text{size of the compressed data}}$$

For the example shown above, this ratio is

Ratio = 15/10 = 1.5

meaning the scheme reduces the amount of space needed to store the image by 33%. Applied to a larger image, this might mean that a 4-million-bit representation could be reduced to about 2.7 million bits, a significant savings.

Another popular compression technique is the use of *variable-length code sets*, which are often used to compress text but can also be used with other forms of data. In Section 4.2.1, we showed that textual symbols, such as A, z, and $\#$, are represented internally by a code mapping that uses exactly the same number of bits for every symbol, either 8 (ASCII) or 16 (Unicode). That is a wasteful approach because some symbols occur much more frequently than others. (For example, in English, the letters E and A are much more common than J, Q, X, and Z.) If the codes representing commonly used symbols were shorter than the codes representing the less-common symbols, this could result in a significant saving of space.

Assume that we want to encode the Hawaiian alphabet, which only contains the five vowels A, E, I, O, and U, and the seven consonants H, K, L, M, N, P, and W. If we were to store these characters using a fixed-length code set, we would need at least 4 bits/symbol, because $2^4 = 16$. Figure 4.9(a) shows one possible encoding of these 12 letters using a fixed-length, 4-bit encoding. However, if we know that A and I are the most commonly used letters in the Hawaiian alphabet, with H and W next, we could represent A and I using 2 bits, H and W using 3 bits, and the remaining letters using either 4, 5, 6, or 7 bits, depending on their frequency. However, we must be sure that if the 2-bit sequence $s_1 s_2$ is used to represent an A, for example, then no other symbol representation can start with the same 2-bit sequence. Otherwise, if we saw the sequence $s_1 s_2$, we would not know if it was an A or the beginning of another character. One possible variable-length encoding for the Hawaiian alphabet is shown in Figure 4.9(b).

Representing the six-character word HAWAII using the fixed-length 4-bit encoding scheme of Figure 4.9(a) requires $6 \times 4 = 24$ bits. Representing it with the variable-length encoding shown in Figure 4.9(b) produces the following:

H	A	W	A	I	I
010	00	110	00	10	10

This is a total of 14 bits, producing a compression ratio of $24/14 = 1.71$, a reduction in storage demands of about 42%.

These two techniques are examples of what are called lossless compression schemes. This means that no information is lost in the compression, and it is possible to exactly reproduce the original data. Lossy compression schemes

FIGURE 4.9

Letter	4-Bit Encoding	Variable-Length Encoding
A	0000	00
I	0001	10
H	0010	010
W	0011	110
E	0100	0110
O	0101	0111
M	0110	11100
K	0111	11101
U	1000	11110
N	1001	111110
P	1010	1111110
L	1011	1111111
	(a)	(b)

Using variable-length code sets

(a)   Fixed length
(b)   Variable length

compress data in a way that does not guarantee that all of the information in the original data can be fully and completely recreated. They trade a possible loss of accuracy for a higher compression ratio because the small inaccuracies in sounds or images are often undetectable to the human ear or eye. Many of the compression schemes in widespread use today, including MP3 and JPEG, use lossy techniques, which permit significantly greater compression ratios than would otherwise be possible. Using lossy JPEG, for example, it is possible to achieve compression ratios of 10:1, 20:1, or more, depending on how much loss of detail we are willing to tolerate. This compares with the values of 1.5 and 1.7 in the earlier described lossless schemes. Using these lossy compression schemes, that 288-million bit, high-resolution image mentioned earlier could be reduced to only 15 or 30 million bits, certainly a much more manageable value. Data compression schemes are an essential component in allowing us to represent multimedia information in a concise and manageable way.

Practice Problems

1. Using MP3, how many bits are required to store a 3-minute song in uncompressed format? If the information is compressed with a ratio of 4:1, how many bits are required?

2. If we instead use a sampling rate of 66,000 samples per second and a bit depth of 24, how many bits are required to store that same 3-minute song?

3. How many bits are needed to store a single uncompressed RGB image from a 2.1 megapixel (millions of pixels) digital camera? How many bytes of memory is this?

4. If we want the image in Problem 3 to fit into 1 megabyte of memory, what compression ratio is needed? If we want it to fit into 256 kilobytes (thousands of bytes) of memory, what compression ratio is needed?

5. If we were able to reduce the storage space of an image to 3 megabits from its original size of 9.6 megabits, what would the compression ratio be?

6. How much space is saved by representing the Hawaiian word ALOHA in the variable-length code of Figure 4.9(b) as compared with the fixed-length representation of Figure 4.9(a)? What is the compression ratio?

7. Assume your smartphone has 16 GB available for music storage. If the average song is 3 minutes long, and it has been recorded using a sampling rate of 44,100 samples per second, a bit depth of 16 bits, and a compression ratio of 10:1, approximately how many songs can be stored on your phone?

4.2.3 The Reliability of Binary Representation

At this point, you might be wondering: Why are we bothering to use binary? Because we use a decimal numerical system for everyday tasks, wouldn't it be more convenient to use a base-10 representation for both the external and the internal representation of information? Then there would be no need to go through the time-consuming conversions diagrammed in Figure 4.1 or to learn the binary representation techniques discussed in the previous two sections.

As we stated in the Special Interest Box, "A Not So Basic Base," there is absolutely no theoretical reason why one could not build a "decimal" computer or, indeed, a computer that stored numbers using base 3 (ternary), base 8 (octal), or base 16 (hexadecimal). The techniques described in the previous two sections apply to information represented in *any* base of a positional numbering system, including base 10.

Computers use binary representation not for any theoretical reasons but for reasons of *reliability*. As we will see shortly, computers store information using electronic devices, and the internal representation of information must be implemented in terms of electronic quantities such as currents and voltage levels.

Building a base-10 "decimal computer" requires finding a device with 10 distinct and stable energy states that can be used to represent the 10 unique digits (0, 1, ... , 9) of the decimal system. For example, assume there exists a device that can store electrical charges in the range 0 to +45 volts. We could use it to build a decimal computer by letting certain voltage levels correspond to specific decimal digits:

Voltage Level	Corresponds to This Decimal Digit
+0	0
+5	1
+10	2
+15	3
+20	4
+25	5
+30	6
+35	7
+40	8
+45	9

Storing the two-digit decimal number 28 requires two of these devices, one for each of the digits in the number. The first device would be set to +10 volts to represent the digit 2, and the second would be set to +40 volts to represent the digit 8.

Although this is theoretically feasible, it is certainly not recommended. As electrical devices age, they become unreliable, and they may *drift*, or change their energy state, over time. What if the device representing the value 8 (the one set to +40 volts) lost 6% of its voltage (not a huge amount for an old, well-used piece of equipment)? The voltage would drop from

+40 volts to about +37.5 volts. The question is whether the value +37.5 represents the digit 7 (+35) or the digit 8 (+40). It is impossible to say. If that same device lost another 6% of its voltage, it would drop from +37.5 volts to about +35 volts. Our 8 has now become a 7, and the original value of 28 has unexpectedly changed to 27. Building a reliable decimal machine would be an engineering nightmare.

The problem with a base-10 representation is that it needs to store 10 unique symbols, and, therefore, it needs devices that have 10 stable states. Such devices are extremely rare. Electrical systems tend to operate best in a *bistable environment*, in which there are only two (rather than 10) stable states separated by a huge energy barrier. Examples of these bistable states include the following:

- Full on/full off
- Fully charged/fully discharged
- Charged positively/charged negatively
- Magnetized/nonmagnetized
- Magnetized clockwise/magnetized counterclockwise

In the binary numbering system, there are only two symbols (0 and 1), so we can let one of the two stable states of our bistable device represent a 0 and the other a 1. This is a much more reliable way to represent information inside a computer.

For example, if we use binary rather than decimal to store data in our hypothetical electronic device that stores voltages in the range from 0 to +45 volts, the representational scheme becomes much simpler:

    0 volts   = 0 (full off)
    +45 volts   = 1 (full on)

Now a 6% or even a 12% drift doesn't affect the interpretation of the value being represented. In fact, it takes an almost 50% change in voltage level to create a problem in interpreting a stored value. The use of binary for the internal representation of data significantly increases the inherent reliability of a computer. This single advantage is worth all the time it takes to convert from decimal to binary for internal storage and from binary to decimal for the external display of results.

4.2.4 Binary Storage Devices

As you learned in the previous section, binary computers can be built out of any bistable device. This idea can be expressed more formally by saying that it is possible to construct a binary computer and its internal components using any hardware device that meets the following four criteria:

1. The device has two stable energy states (one for a 0, one for a 1).

2. These two states are separated by a large energy barrier (so that a 0 does not accidentally become a 1, or vice versa).

3. It is possible to sense which state the device is in (to see whether it is storing a 0 or a 1) without permanently destroying the stored value.

4. It is possible to switch the state from a 0 to a 1, or vice versa, by applying a sufficient amount of energy.

There are many devices that meet these conditions, including some surprising ones such as a light switch. A typical light switch has two stable states (ON and OFF). These two states are separated by a large energy barrier so that a switch that is in one state will not accidentally change to the other. We can determine what state the switch is in by looking to see whether the label says ON or OFF (or just by looking at the light), and we can change the state of the switch by applying a sufficient amount of energy via our fingertips. Thus it would be possible to build a reliable (albeit very slow and bulky) binary computing device out of ordinary light switches and fingertips!

As you might imagine, computer systems are not built from light switches, but they have been built using a wide range of devices. This section describes two of these devices.

Magnetic cores were used to construct computer memories for about 20 years. From roughly 1955 to 1975, this was by far the most popular storage technology—even today, the memory unit of a computer is sometimes referred to as *core memory* even though it has been decades since magnetic cores have been used.

A *core* is a small, magnetizable, iron oxide-coated "doughnut," about 1/50 of an inch in inner diameter, with wires strung through its center hole. The two states used to represent the binary values 0 and 1 are based on the *direction* of the magnetic field of the core. When electrical current is sent through the wire in one specific direction, say left to right, the core is magnetized in a counterclockwise direction.[1] This state could represent the binary value 0. Current sent in the opposite direction produces a clockwise magnetic field that could represent the binary value 1. These scenarios are diagrammed in Figure 4.10. Because magnetic fields do not change much over time, these two states are highly stable, and they form the basis for the construction of memory devices that store binary numbers.

In the early 1970s, core memories began to be replaced by smaller, cheaper technologies that required less power and were easier to manufacture. One-fiftieth of an inch in diameter and a few grams of weight might not seem like much, but it can produce a bulky and unworkable structure when memory units must contain millions or billions of bits. For example, a typical core memory from the 1950s or 1960s had a density of about 500 cores/in^2. The memory in a modern computer typically has at least 16 GB (1 gigabyte = 1 billion 8-bit bytes), which is more than 128 billion bits. If we had to construct a modern memory unit using cores, it would require 260 million in^2 of space, which is a square about 416,000 inches, or 1,330 feet, on a side. Built from cores, our memory unit would stand more than 100 stories high!

---

[1]The *righthand rule* of physics says that if the thumb of your right hand is pointing in the direction of the electric current, then the fingers will be curled in the direction of the magnetic field.

FIGURE 4.10

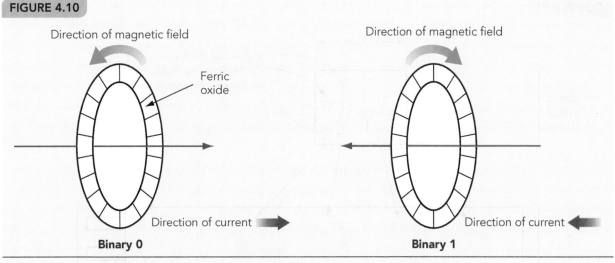

Using magnetic cores to represent binary values

Today, the elementary building block for all modern computer systems is no longer the core but the transistor. A transistor is much like the light switch mentioned earlier. It can be in an OFF state, which does not allow electricity to flow, or in an ON state, in which electricity can pass unimpeded. However, unlike the light switch, a transistor is a solid-state device that has no mechanical or moving parts. The switching of a transistor from the OFF to the ON state, and vice versa, is done electronically rather than mechanically. This allows the transistor to be fast as well as extremely small. A typical transistor can switch states in a billionth of a second, and at current technology levels about 1–2 billion transistors can fit into a space only 1 cm^2. Furthermore, hardware technology is changing so rapidly that both these numbers might be out of date by the time you read these words.

Transistors are constructed from special materials called *semiconductors*, such as silicon and gallium arsenide. A large number of transistors, as well as the electrical conducting paths that connect them, can be printed photographically on a wafer of silicon to produce a device known as an *integrated circuit* or, more commonly, a *chip*. The chip is mounted on a *circuit board*, which interconnects all the different chips (e.g., memory, processor, and communications) needed to run a computer system. This circuit board is then plugged into the computer using a set of connectors located on the end of the board. The relationships among transistors, chips, and circuit boards are diagrammed in Figure 4.11. The use of photographic rather than mechanical production techniques has numerous advantages. Because light can be focused very sharply, these integrated circuits can be manufactured in very high densities—high numbers of transistors per square centimeter—and with a very high degree of accuracy. The more transistors that can be packed into a fixed amount of space, the greater the processing power of the computer and the greater the amount of information that can be stored in memory.

FIGURE 4.11

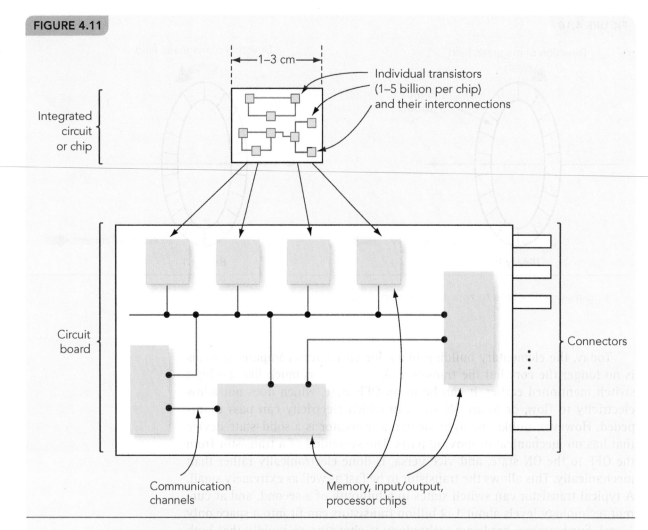

Relationships among transistors, chips, and circuit boards

Another advantage of photographic production techniques is that it is possible to make a standard template, called a *mask*, which describes the circuit. This mask can be used to produce a virtually unlimited number of copies of that chip, much as a photographic negative can be used to produce an unlimited number of prints.

Together, these characteristics can result in very small and very inexpensive high-speed circuits. Whereas the first computers of the early 1940s (as seen in Chapter 1, Figure 1.6) filled huge rooms and cost millions of dollars, the processor inside a modern workstation contains billions of transistors on a tiny chip just a few centimeters square, is thousands of times more powerful than those early machines, and can cost less than a few hundred dollars.

The theoretical concepts underlying the physical behavior of semiconductors and transistors, as well as the details of chip manufacture, are well beyond the scope of this book. They are usually discussed in courses in physics or electrical engineering. Instead, we will examine a transistor in terms of the simplified model shown in Figure 4.12 and then use this model to explain its behavior. (Here is another example of the importance of abstraction in computer science.)

In the model shown in Figure 4.12, each transistor contains three lines—two input lines (control and collector) and one output line (emitter), with each line either in the 1-state, with a high positive voltage, or in the 0-state, with a voltage close to 0. The first input line, called the *control* or the *base*, is used to open or close the switch inside the transistor. If we set the control line to a 1 by applying a sufficiently high positive voltage, the switch closes and the transistor enters the ON state. In this state, current from the input line called the *collector* can flow directly to the single output line called the *emitter*, and the associated voltage can be detected by a measuring device. This ON state could be used to represent the binary value 1. If instead we set the control line to a 0 by applying a voltage close to zero, the switch opens, and the transistor enters the OFF state. In this state, the flow of current through the transistor is blocked and no voltage is detected on the emitter line. The OFF state could be used to represent the binary value 0. This is diagrammed in Figure 4.13.

This type of solid-state switching device forms the basis for the construction of virtually all computers built today, and it is the fundamental building block for all high-level components described in the upcoming chapters. Remember, however, that there is no theoretical reason why we must use transistors as our "elementary particles" when designing computer systems. Just as cores were replaced by transistors, transistors may ultimately be replaced by some newer, perhaps molecular or biological, technology that is faster, smaller, and cheaper. (Researchers are beginning to investigate the possibility of using DNA molecules as the basic building blocks for computer systems, just as they are the basic building blocks for human "systems.") The only requirements for our building blocks are those given in the beginning of this section—that they be able to represent reliably the two binary values 0 and 1.

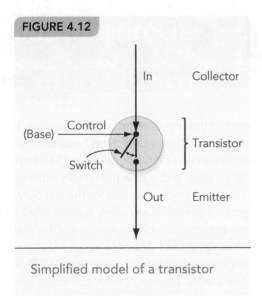

FIGURE 4.12

Simplified model of a transistor

FIGURE 4.13

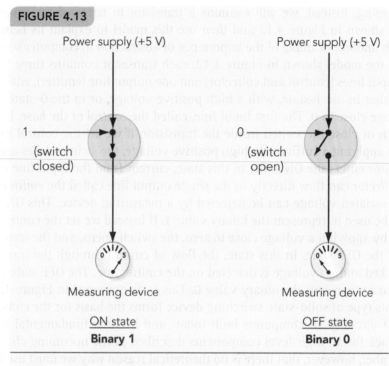

Binary ON and OFF states

Moore's Law and the Limits of Chip Design

Since the development of the first integrated circuits in the 1950s, the number of transistors on a circuit board has been doubling roughly every 24 months. This observation was first reported in a 1965 paper by Gordon E. Moore, the cofounder of Intel, and is now universally referred to as "Moore's law." This doubling has continued unabated for the last 50 years and represents a rate of improvement unequaled in any other technical field. More transistors on a chip means more speed and more power and is the reason for the enormous increase in performance (and decrease in size) of computers in the last 50 years. The following table details this growth from 1971, when chips held just a few thousand transistors, to today's microprocessors that hold billions.

Processor	Transistor Count	Date
Intel 404	2,300	1971
Intel 8080	4,500	1974
Intel 8088	29,000	1979
Intel 80286	134,000	1982
Intel 80386	275,000	1985
Intel 80486	1,200,000	1989
Pentium	3,100,000	1993
Pentium II	7,500,000	1997
Pentium 4	42,000,000	2000
Itanium 2	220,000,000	2003
Dual-Core Itanium 2	1,400,000,000	2006
Quad-Core Itanium Tukwila	2,000,000,000	2008
nVidiaGeForce 6800 Ultra	3,000,000,000	2011
62-core Xeon Phi	5,000,000,000	2015

It is impossible to maintain this type of exponential growth for an indefinitely extended period of time, and industry analysts have been predicting the demise of Moore's law for the last 10–15 years. However, the ongoing development of new materials and new manufacturing technologies has allowed the industry to continue this phenomenal rate of improvement. But there is a physical limit looming on the horizon that will be the most difficult hurdle yet. As more and more transistors are packed onto a single chip, distances between them get smaller and smaller, and experts estimate that in about 10–20 years intertransistor distances will approach the space between individual atoms. For example, transistors on today's chips are separated by about 25–50 nanometers (1 nanometer = 10^{-9} meter), only about 250–500 times greater than the diameter of a single atom of silicon, which is about 10^{-10} meters. In a few generations, these atomic distances will be reached, and a totally new approach to computer design will be required, perhaps one based on the emerging fields of nanotechnology and quantum computing.

4.3 Boolean Logic and Gates

4.3.1 Boolean Logic

The construction of computer circuits is based on the branch of mathematics and symbolic logic called Boolean logic. This area of mathematics deals with rules for manipulating the two logical values *true* and *false*, and it is used to construct circuits that perform operations such as adding numbers, comparing numbers, and fetching instructions. These ideas are part of the branch of computer science known as hardware design, also called logic design.

It is easy to see the relationship between Boolean logic and computer design: The truth value *true* could represent the binary value 1, and the truth value *false* could represent the binary value 0. Thus anything stored internally as a sequence of binary digits (which, as we saw in earlier sections, is everything stored inside a computer) can also be viewed as a sequence of the logical values true and false, and these values can be manipulated by the operations of Boolean logic.

Let us define a Boolean expression as any expression that evaluates to either true or false. For example, the expression $(x = 1)$ is a Boolean expression because it is true if x is 1, and it is false if x has any other value. Similarly, both $(a \neq b)$ and $(c > 5.23)$ are Boolean expressions.

In "traditional" mathematics (the mathematics of real numbers), the operations used to construct arithmetic expressions are $+$, $-$, $\times$, $\div$, and a^b, which map real numbers into real numbers. In Boolean logic, the three basic operations used to construct Boolean expressions are AND, OR, and NOT, and they map a set of (true, false) values into a single (true, false) result. (*Note*: There are other Boolean operations, such as XOR, NOR, and NAND, that we mention later in this chapter.)

The rule for performing the AND operation is as follows: If a and b are Boolean expressions, then the value of the expression (a AND b), also written as ($a \cdot b$), is *true* if and only if both a and b have the value *true*; otherwise, the expression (a AND b) has the value *false*. Informally, this rule says that the AND operation produces the value *true* if and only if both of its components are true. This idea can be expressed using a structure called a truth table, shown in Figure 4.14.

The two columns labeled Inputs in the truth table of Figure 4.14 list the four possible combinations of true/false values of a and b. The column labeled Output specifies the value of the expression (a AND b) for the corresponding values of a and b.

FIGURE 4.14

Inputs		Output a AND b
a	b	(also written a · b)
False	False	False
False	True	False
True	False	False
True	True	True

Truth table for the AND operation

To illustrate the AND operation, imagine that we want to check whether a test score S is in the range 90–100 inclusive. We want to develop a Boolean expression that is true if the score is in the desired range and false otherwise. We cannot do this with a single comparison. If we test only that $(S \geq 90)$, then a score of 105, which is greater than or equal to 90, will produce the result *true*, even though it is out of range. Similarly, if we test only that $(S \leq 100)$, then a score of 85, which is less than or equal to 100, will also produce a *true*, even though it too is not in the range 90–100.

Instead, we need to determine whether the score S is greater than or equal to 90 *and* whether it is less than or equal to 100. Only if both conditions are true can we say that S is in the desired range. We can express this idea using the following Boolean expression:

$$(S \geq 90) \ \text{AND} \ (S \leq 100)$$

Each of the two expressions in parentheses can be either true or false depending on the value of S. However, only if both conditions are true does the expression evaluate to *true*. For example, a score of $S = 70$ causes the first expression to be false (70 is not greater than or equal to 90), whereas the second expression is true (70 is less than or equal to 100). The truth table in Figure 4.14 shows that the result of evaluating (*false* AND *true*) is *false*. Thus, the overall expression is false, indicating (as expected) that 70 is not in the range 90–100.

The second Boolean operation is OR. The rule for performing the OR operation is as follows: If a and b are Boolean expressions, then the value of the Boolean expression $(a \ \text{OR} \ b)$, also written as $(a + b)$, is *true* if a is *true*, if b is *true*, or if both are *true*. Otherwise, $(a \ \text{OR} \ b)$ has the value *false*. The truth table for OR is shown in Figure 4.15.

To see the OR operation at work, imagine that a variable called *major* specifies a student's college major. If we want to know whether a student is majoring in either math or computer science, we cannot accomplish this with a single comparison. The test $(major = \text{math})$ omits computer science majors, whereas the test $(major = \text{computer science})$ leaves out the

FIGURE 4.15

Inputs		Output *a* OR *b*
a	*b*	(also written *a* + *b*)
False	False	False
False	True	True
True	False	True
True	True	True

Truth table for the OR operation

mathematicians. Instead, we need to determine whether the student is majoring in *either* math or computer science (or perhaps in both). This can be expressed as follows:

(*major* = math) OR (*major* = computer science)

If the student is majoring in either one or both of the two disciplines, then one or both of the two terms in the expression are true. Referring to the truth table in Figure 4.15, we see that (*true* OR *false*), (*false* OR *true*), and (*true* OR *true*) all produce the value *true*, which indicates that the student is majoring in at least one of these two fields. However, if the student is majoring in English, both conditions are false. As Figure 4.15 illustrates, the value of the expression (*false* OR *false*) is *false*, meaning that the student is not majoring in either math or computer science.

The final Boolean operator that we examine here is NOT. Unlike AND and OR, which require two operands and are, therefore, called *binary operators*, NOT requires only one operand and is called a *unary operator*, like the square root operation in arithmetic. The rule for evaluating the NOT operation is as follows: If *a* is a Boolean expression, then the value of the expression (NOT *a*), also written as $\bar{a}$, is *true* if *a* has the value *false*, and it is *false* if *a* has the value *true*. The truth table for NOT is shown in Figure 4.16.

Informally, we say that the NOT operation reverses, or *complements*, the value of a Boolean expression, making it true if currently false, and vice versa. For example, the expression (GPA > 3.5) is true if your grade point average is greater than 3.5, and the expression NOT (GPA > 3.5) is true only under the reverse conditions, that is when your grade point average is less than or equal to 3.5.

AND, OR, and NOT are the three operations of Boolean logic that we use in this chapter. Why have we introduced these Boolean operations in the first place? The previous section discussed hardware concepts such as energy states, electrical currents, transistors, and integrated circuits. Now it appears that we have changed direction and are discussing highly abstract ideas drawn from the discipline of symbolic logic. However, as we hinted earlier and will see in detail in the next section, there is a very close relationship between the hardware concepts of Section 4.2.4 and the operations of Boolean logic. In fact, the fundamental building blocks of a modern

FIGURE 4.16

Input	Output NOT *a*
a	(also written $\bar{a}$)
False	True
True	False

Truth table for the NOT operation

Practice Problems

1. Assuming that $x = 1$ and $y = 2$, determine the value of each of the following Boolean expressions:

   a. $(x = 1)$ AND $(y = 3)$

   b. $(x < y)$ OR $(x > 1)$

   c. NOT $[(x = 1)$ AND $(y = 2)]$

2. Assume that A, B, and C are Boolean variables that can take on the values true and false. Create a truth table to show all the possible values for the Boolean expression:

   ((NOT A) AND B) OR C

   (*Hint:* Your table will have eight rows.)

3. What is the value of the following Boolean expression:

   $(x = 5)$ AND $(y = 11)$ OR $([x + y] = z)$

   if $x = 5$, $y = 10$, and $z = 15$? Did you have to make some assumptions when you evaluated this expression?

4. Write a Boolean expression that is true if and only if x and y are both in the range 0–100 but x is not equal to y.

5. Write a Boolean expression that is true if and only if the variable *score* is *not* in the range 200–800, inclusive.

6. For what values of A and B will the value of the following Boolean expression be false?

   (A OR B) OR (NOT A)

7. Write a Boolean expression that is true if and only if a student is a senior who is majoring in either physics or chemistry. Assume that the student's year in school is stored in the variable *year* and the student's major is stored in the variable *major*. Use parentheses to indicate clearly the order in which the operations should be evaluated.

computer system (the objects with which engineers actually design) are not the transistors introduced in Section 4.2.4 but the gates that implement the Boolean operations AND, OR, and NOT. Surprisingly, it is the rules of logic—a discipline developed by the Greeks 2,300 years ago and expanded by George Boole (see the Special Interest Box on page 192) 160 years ago—that provide the theoretical foundation for constructing modern computer hardware.

4.3.2 Gates

A gate is an electronic device that operates on a collection of binary inputs to produce a binary output. That is, it transforms a set of (0,1) input values into a single (0,1) output value according to a specific transformation rule. Although gates can implement a wide range of different transformation rules, the ones we are concerned with in this section are those that implement the Boolean operations AND, OR, and NOT introduced in the previous section. As shown in Figure 4.17, these gates can be represented symbolically, along with the truth tables that define their transformation rules.

Comparing Figures 4.14 through 4.16 with Figure 4.17 shows that if the value 1 is equivalent to *true* and the value 0 is equivalent to *false*, then these three electronic gates directly implement the corresponding Boolean operation. For example, an AND gate has its output line set to 1 (set to some level of voltage that represents a binary 1) if and only if both of its inputs are 1. Otherwise, the output line is set to 0 (set to some level of voltage that represents a binary 0). This is functionally identical to the rule that says the result of (*a* AND *b*) is *true* if and only if both *a* and *b* are *true*; otherwise, (*a* AND *b*) is *false*. Similar arguments hold for OR and NOT.

A NOT gate can be constructed from a single transistor, as shown in Figure 4.18, in which the collector is connected to the power supply (Logical-1) and the emitter is connected to the ground (Logical-0). If the control line of the transistor (labeled Input) is set to 1, then the transistor is in the ON state, and it passes current through to the ground. In this case, the voltage on the line labeled Output is 0. However, if Input is set to 0, the transistor is in the OFF state, and it blocks passage of current to the ground. Instead, the current is transmitted to the Output line, producing a value of 1.

FIGURE 4.17

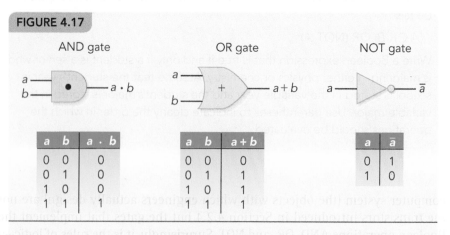

The three basic gates and their symbols

FIGURE 4.18

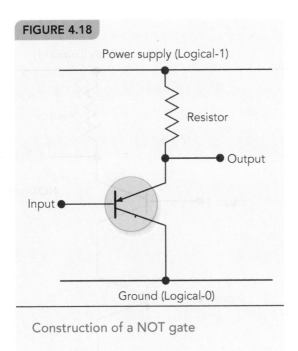

Power supply (Logical-1)

Resistor

Output

Input

Ground (Logical-0)

Construction of a NOT gate

Thus, the value appearing on the output line of Figure 4.18 is the complement—the NOT—of the value appearing on the input line.

To construct an AND gate, we begin by connecting two transistors *in series*, as shown in Figure 4.19(a), with the collector line of transistor 1 connected to the power supply (Logical-1) and the emitter line of transistor 2 connected to ground (Logical-0). If both control lines, called Input-1 and Input-2 in Figure 4.19(a), are set to 1, then both transistors are in the ON state, and the current will be connected to ground, resulting in a value of 0 on the output line. If either (or both) Input-1 or Input-2 is 0, then the corresponding transistor is in the OFF state and does not allow current to pass, resulting in a 1 on the output line. Thus, the output of the gate in Figure 4.19(a) is a 0 if and only if both inputs are a 1; otherwise, it is a 1. This is the exact *opposite* of the definition of AND, and Figure 4.19(a) represents a gate called NAND, an acronym for *NOT AND*. It produces the complement of the AND operation, and it is an important and widely used gate in hardware design.

If, however, we want to build an AND gate, then all we have to do is add a NOT gate (of the type shown in Figure 4.18) to the output line. This complements the NAND output and produces the AND truth table of Figure 4.14. This gate is shown in Figure 4.19(b). Note that the NAND of Figure 4.19(a) requires two transistors, whereas the AND of Figure 4.19(b) requires three. This is one reason why NAND gates are widely used to build computer circuits.

FIGURE 4.19

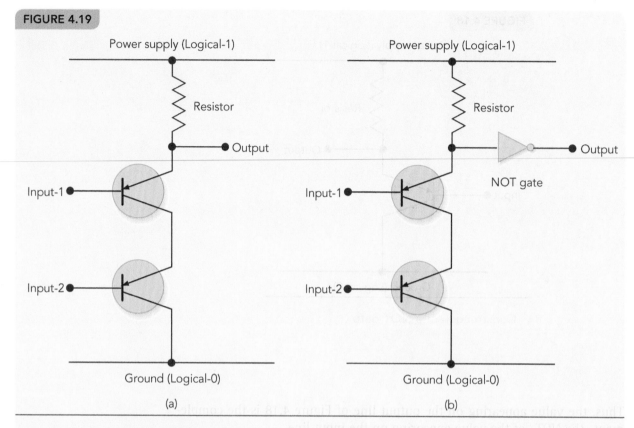

Construction of NAND and AND gates
(a)   A two-transistor NAND gate
(b)   A three-transistor AND gate

To construct an OR gate, we again start with two transistors. However, this time they are connected *in parallel* rather than in series, as shown in Figure 4.20(a).

In Figure 4.20(a) if either, or both, of the lines Input-1 and Input-2 are set to 1, then the corresponding transistor is in the ON state, and the current is connected to the ground, producing an output line value of 0. Only if both input lines are 0, effectively shutting off both transistors, will the output line contain a 1. Again, this is the exact opposite to the definition of OR given in Figure 4.15. Figure 4.20(a) is an implementation of a NOR gate, an acronym for NOT *OR*. To convert this to an OR gate, we do the same thing we did earlier—add a NOT gate to the output line. This gate is diagrammed in Figure 4.20(b).

Gates of the type shown in Figures 4.18 through 4.20 are not abstract entities that exist only in textbooks and classroom discussions. They are actual electronic devices that serve as the building blocks in the design and construction of modern computer systems. The reason for using gates rather than transistors is that a transistor is too elementary a device to act as the

FIGURE 4.20

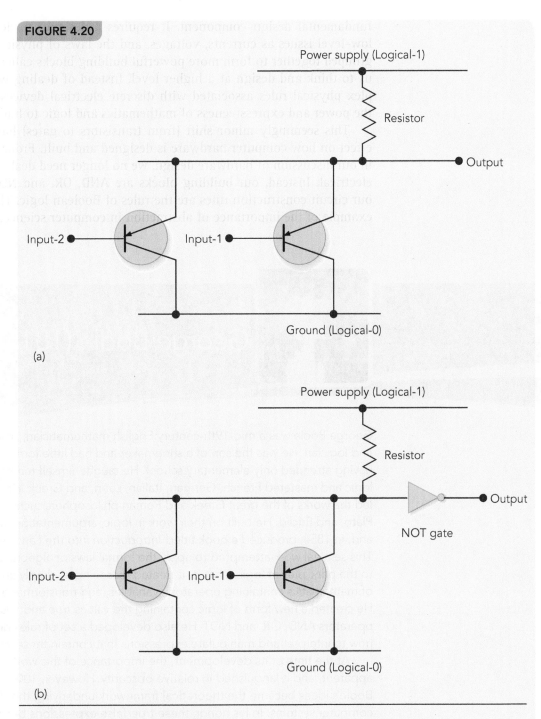

Construction of NOR and OR gates
(a) A two-transistor NOR gate
(b) A three-transistor OR gate

fundamental design component. It requires a designer to deal with such low-level issues as currents, voltages, and the laws of physics. Transistors, grouped together to form more powerful building blocks called gates, allow us to think and design at a higher level. Instead of dealing with the complex physical rules associated with discrete electrical devices, we can use the power and expressiveness of mathematics and logic to build computers.

This seemingly minor shift (from transistors to gates) has a profound effect on how computer hardware is designed and built. From this point on in our discussion of hardware design, we no longer need deal with anything electrical. Instead, our building blocks are AND, OR, and NOT gates, and our circuit construction rules are the rules of Boolean logic. This is another example of the importance of abstraction in computer science.

George Boole (1815–1864)

George Boole was a mid-19th-century English mathematician, philosopher, and logician. He was the son of a shoemaker and had little formal education, having attended only elementary school. He taught himself mathematics and logic and mastered French, German, Italian, Latin, and Greek. He avidly studied the works of the great Greek and Roman philosophers such as Aristotle, Plato, and Euclid. He built on their work in logic, argumentation, and reasoning and, in 1854, produced a book titled *Introduction into the Laws of Thought*. This seminal work attempted to apply the formal laws of algebra and arithmetic to the principles of logic. That is, it treated reasoning as simply another branch of mathematics containing operators, variables, and transformation rules. He created a new form of logic containing the values *true* and *false* and the operators AND, OR, and NOT. He also developed a set of rules describing how to interpret and manipulate expressions that contain these values.

At the time of its development, the importance of this work was not apparent, and it languished in relative obscurity. However, 100 years later, Boole's ideas became the theoretical framework underlying the design of all computer systems. In his honor, these true/false expressions became known as *Boolean expressions*, and this branch of mathematics is called *Boolean logic* or *Boolean algebra*.

Even though he had very little formal schooling, Boole was eventually appointed professor of mathematics at Queens College in Cork, Ireland. He received a gold medal from the Royal Mathematical Society and in 1857 was awarded an honorary doctoral degree from Oxford University. He is now universally recognized as one of the greatest mathematicians of the 19th century.

4.4 Building Computer Circuits

4.4.1 Introduction

A circuit is a collection of logic gates that transforms a set of binary inputs into a set of binary outputs and in which the values of the outputs depend only on the current values of the inputs. (Actually, this type of circuit is more properly called a *combinational circuit*. We use the simpler term *circuit* in this discussion.) A circuit C with m binary inputs and n binary outputs is represented as shown in Figure 4.21.

Internally, the circuit shown in Figure 4.21 is constructed from the AND, OR, and NOT gates introduced in the previous section. (*Note*: We do not use the NAND and NOR gates diagrammed in Figure 4.19(a) and Figure 4.20(a), respectively.) These gates can be interconnected in any way so long as the connections do not violate the constraints on the proper number of inputs and outputs for each gate. Each AND and OR gate must have exactly two inputs and one output. (Multiple-input AND and OR gates do exist, but we do not use them in our examples.) Each NOT gate must have exactly one input and one output. For example, Figure 4.22 diagrams a circuit with two inputs labeled a and b and two outputs labeled c and d. It contains one AND gate, one OR gate, and two NOT gates.

There is a direct relationship between Boolean expressions and *circuit diagrams* of this type. Every Boolean expression can be represented pictorially as a circuit diagram, and every output value in a circuit diagram can be written as a Boolean expression. For example, in the diagram shown, the two output values labeled c and d are equivalent to the following two Boolean expressions:

c = (a OR b)
d = NOT ((a OR b) AND (NOT b))

The choice of which representation to use, a circuit diagram or a Boolean expression, depends on what we want to do. The pictorial view better allows us to visualize the overall structure of the circuit, and is often used during

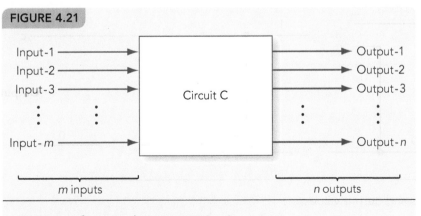

FIGURE 4.21

Diagram of a typical computer circuit

FIGURE 4.22

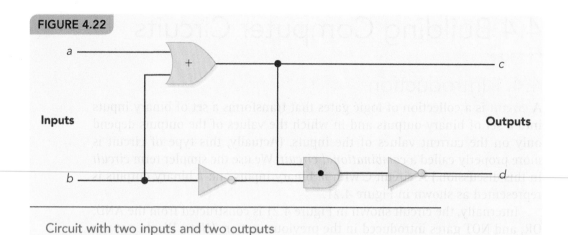

Circuit with two inputs and two outputs

the design stage. A Boolean expression may be better for performing math-ematical or logical operations, such as verification and optimization, on the circuit. We use both representations in the following sections.

The value appearing on any output line of a circuit can be determined if we know the current input values and the transformations produced by each logic gate. (*Note:* There are circuits, called sequential circuits, which contain feedback loops in which the output of a gate is fed back as input to an earlier gate. The output of these circuits depends not only on the current input values but also on *previous* inputs. These circuits are typically used to build memory units because, in a sense, they can "remember" inputs. We do not discuss sequential circuits here.)

In the previous example, if $a = 1$ and $b = 0$, then the value on the c output line is 1, and the value on the d output line is 0. These values can be determined as shown in Figure 4.23.

FIGURE 4.23

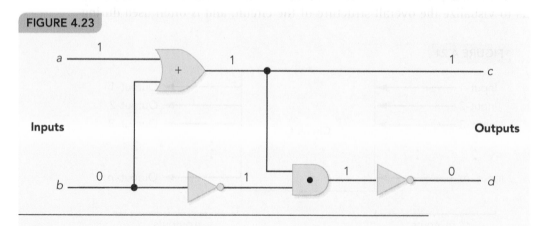

Input values and output values

Note that it is perfectly permissible to "split" or "tap" a line and send its value to two different gates. Here the input value b was split and sent to two separate gates.

The next section presents an algorithm for designing and building circuits from the three fundamental gate types AND, OR, and NOT. This enables us to move to yet a higher level of abstraction. Instead of thinking in terms of transistors and electrical voltages (as in Section 4.2.4) or in terms of logic gates and truth values (as in Section 4.3.2), we can think and design in terms of circuits for high-level operations such as addition and comparison. This makes understanding computer hardware much more manageable.

4.4.2 A Circuit Construction Algorithm

The circuit shown at the end of the previous section is simply an example and is not meant to carry out any meaningful operation. To create circuits that perform useful arithmetic and logical functions, we need a way to convert a description of a circuit's desired behavior into a circuit diagram, composed of AND, OR, and NOT gates, that does exactly what we want it to do.

There are a number of circuit construction algorithms to accomplish this task, and the remainder of this section describes one such technique, called the *sum-of-products algorithm*, that allows us to design circuits. Section 4.4.3 demonstrates how this algorithm works by constructing actual circuits that all computer systems need.

Step 1: Truth Table Construction. First, determine how the circuit should behave under all possible circumstances. That is, determine the binary value that should appear on each output line of the circuit for every possible combination of inputs. This information can be organized as a truth table. If a circuit has N input lines, and if each input line can be either a 0 or a 1, then there are 2^N combinations of input values, and the truth table has 2^N rows. For each output of the circuit, we must specify the desired output value for every row in the truth table.

For example, if a circuit has three inputs and two outputs, then a truth table for that circuit has $2^3 = 8$ input combinations and might look something like the following. (In this example, the output values are completely arbitrary.)

Inputs			Outputs	
a	b	c	Output-1	Output-2
0	0	0	0	1
0	0	1	0	0
0	1	0	1	1
0	1	1	0	1
1	0	0	0	0
1	0	1	0	0
1	1	0	1	1
1	1	1	0	0

$2^3 = 8$ input combinations

This circuit has two outputs labeled Output-1 and Output-2. The truth table specifies the value of each of these two output lines for every one of the eight possible combinations of inputs. We will use this example to illustrate the subsequent steps in the algorithm.

Step 2: Subexpression Construction Using AND and NOT Gates. Choose any one output column of the truth table built in Step 1 and scan down that column. Every place that you find a 1 in that output column, you build a Boolean *subexpression* that produces the value 1 (i.e., is true) for exactly that combination of input values and no other. To build this subexpression, you examine the value of each input for this specific case. If the input is a 1, use that input value directly in your subexpression. If the input is a 0, first take the NOT of that input, changing it from a 0 to a 1, and then use that *complemented* input value in your subexpression. You now have an input sequence of all 1s, and if all of these modified inputs are ANDed together (two at a time, of course), then the output value is a 1. For example, let's look at the output column labeled Output-1 in the truth table below.

	Inputs			
a	b	c	Output-1	
0	0	0	0	
0	0	1	0	
0	1	0	1	← case 1
0	1	1	0	
1	0	0	0	
1	0	1	0	
1	1	0	1	← case 2
1	1	1	0	

There are two 1s in the column labeled Output-1; they are referred to as case 1 and case 2. We thus need to construct two subexpressions, one for each of these two cases.

In case 1, the inputs a and c have the value 0 and the input b has the value 1. Thus we apply the NOT operator to both a and c, changing them from 0 to 1. Because the value of b is 1, we can use b directly. We now have three modified input values, all of which have the value 1. ANDing these three values together yields the Boolean expression $(\bar{a} \cdot b \cdot \bar{c})$ This expression produces a 1 only when the input is exactly $a = 0$, $b = 1$, $c = 0$. In any other case, at least one of the three factors in the expression is 0, and when the AND operation is carried out, it produces a 0. (Check this yourself by trying some other input values and seeing what is produced.) Thus the desired subexpression for case 1 is

$$(\bar{a} \cdot b \cdot \bar{c})$$

The subexpression for case 2 is developed in an identical manner, and it results in

$$(a \cdot b \cdot \overline{c})$$

This subexpression produces a 1 only when the input is exactly $a = 1$, $b = 1$, $c = 0$.

Step 3: Subexpression Combination Using OR Gates. Take each of the subexpressions produced in Step 2 and combine them, two at a time, using OR gates. Each of the individual subexpressions produces a 1 for exactly one particular case where the truth table output is a 1, so the OR of the output of all of them produces a 1 in each case where the truth table has a 1 and in no other case. Consequently, the Boolean expression produced in Step 3 implements exactly the function described in the output column of the truth table on which we are working. In the current example, the final Boolean expression produced during Step 3 is

$$(\overline{a} \cdot b \cdot \overline{c}) + (a \cdot b \cdot \overline{c})$$

Step 4: Circuit Diagram Production. Construct the final circuit diagram. To do this, convert the Boolean expression produced at the end of Step 3 into a circuit diagram, using AND, OR, and NOT gates to implement the AND, OR, and NOT operators appearing in the Boolean expression. This circuit diagram produces the output described in the corresponding column of the truth table created in Step 1. The circuit diagram for the Boolean expression developed in Step 3 is shown in Figure 4.24.

We have successfully built the part of the circuit that produces the output for the column labeled Output-1 in the truth table shown in Step 1. We now repeat Steps 2, 3, and 4 for any additional output columns contained in

FIGURE 4.24

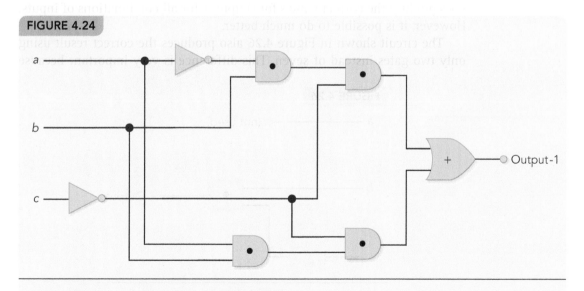

Circuit diagram for the output labeled Output-1

FIGURE 4.25

1. Construct the truth table describing the behavior of the desired circuit
2. While there is still an output column in the truth table, do Steps 3 through 6
3.   Select an output column
4.   Subexpression construction using AND and NOT gates
5.   Subexpression combination using OR gates
6.   Circuit diagram production
7. Done

The sum-of-products circuit construction algorithm

the truth table. (In this example, there is a second column labeled Output-2. We leave the construction of that circuit as a practice exercise.) When we have constructed a circuit diagram for every output of the circuit, we are finished. The sum-of-products algorithm is summarized in Figure 4.25.

This has been a formal introduction to one particular circuit construction algorithm. The algorithm is not easy to comprehend in an abstract sense. The next section clarifies this technique by using it to design two circuits that perform the operations of comparison and addition, respectively. Seeing it used to design actual circuits will make the steps of the algorithm easier to understand and follow.

We end this section by noting that the circuit construction algorithm just described does not always produce an optimal circuit, where *optimal* means that the circuit accomplishes its desired function using the smallest number of logic gates. For example, using the truth table shown on page 196, our sum-of-products algorithm produced the seven-gate circuit shown in Figure 4.24. This is a correct answer in the sense that the circuit does produce the correct values for Output-1 for all combinations of inputs. However, it is possible to do much better.

The circuit shown in Figure 4.26 also produces the correct result using only two gates instead of seven. This difference is very important because

FIGURE 4.26

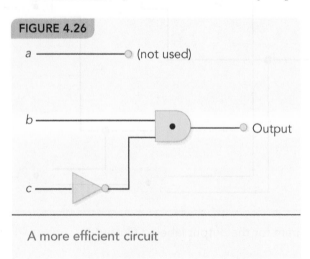

A more efficient circuit

each AND, OR, and NOT gate is a physical entity that costs real money, takes up space on the chip, requires power to operate, and generates heat that must be dissipated.

Eliminating five unnecessary gates produces a real savings. The fewer gates we use, the cheaper, more efficient, and more compact are our circuits and hence the resulting computer. Algorithms for circuit optimization—that is, for reducing the number of gates needed to implement a circuit—are an important part of hardware design. Challenge Work problem 1 at the end of the chapter invites you to investigate this interesting topic in more detail.

Practice Problems

1. Design the circuit to implement the output described in the column labeled Output-2 in the truth table on page 195.

2. Design a circuit using AND, OR, and NOT gates to implement the following truth table.

a	b	Output
0	0	0
0	1	1
1	0	1
1	1	0

This is the *exclusive-OR* operation, *XOR*. It is true if and only if *a* is 1 or *b* is 1, but not both.

3. Build a circuit using AND, OR, and NOT gates to implement the following truth table.

a	b	c	Output
0	0	0	1
0	0	1	0
0	1	0	0
0	1	1	0
1	0	0	0
1	0	1	0
1	1	0	0
1	1	1	1

This is called a *full-ON/full-OFF* circuit. It is true if and only if all three of its inputs are OFF (0) or all three are ON (1).

(Continued)

4. Design a circuit to implement the following truth table.

a	b	Output
0	0	1
0	1	1
1	0	0
1	1	0

After completing the design, count how many AND, OR, and NOT gates were required to build this circuit. Now take a careful look at the truth table above and see if you can come up with a more efficient way to build the same circuit, where efficient means using fewer gates. How many gates did your efficient circuit require?

5. Assume that you are going to construct a circuit called C that has 4 inputs, a, b, c, and d, and 3 outputs, *output-1*, *output-2*, and *output-3*. Describe the dimensions of the truth table for circuit C.

4.4.3 Examples of Circuit Design and Construction

Let's use the algorithm described in Section 4.4.2 to construct two circuits important to the operation of any real-world computer: a compare-for-equality circuit and an addition circuit.

A Compare-for-Equality Circuit. The first circuit we will construct is a *compare-for-equality circuit*, or CE circuit, which tests two unsigned binary numbers for exact equality. The circuit produces the value 1 (*true*) if the two numbers are equal and the value 0 (*false*) if they are not. Such a circuit could be used in many situations. For example, in the shampooing algorithm in Chapter 1, Figure 1.3(a), there is an instruction that says,

Repeat Steps 4 through 6 until the value of *WashCount* equals 2

Laboratory Experience 7

To give you hands-on experience working with logic circuits, the first Laboratory Experience in this chapter introduces you to a software package called a *circuit simulator*. This is a program that enables you to construct logic circuits from the AND, OR, and NOT gates just described, and then test them by observing the outputs of the circuits using any desired inputs.

The output of each gate will be displayed on the screen, which allows you to determine if your circuit is or is not behaving correctly as the signals propagate from input lines to output lines.

Our CE circuit could accomplish the comparison between the number currently stored in *WashCount* and the value 2 and return true or false, depending on whether these two values were equal or not equal.

Let's start by using the sum-of-products algorithm in Figure 4.25 to construct a simpler circuit called 1-CE, short for 1-bit compare for equality. A 1-CE circuit compares two 1-bit values *a* and *b* for equality. That is, the circuit 1-CE produces a 1 as output if both its inputs are 0 or both its inputs are 1. Otherwise, 1-CE produces a 0. After designing 1-CE, we will use it to create a full-blown comparison circuit that can handle numbers of any size.

Step 1 of the algorithm says to construct the truth table that describes the behavior of the desired circuit. The truth table for the 1-CE circuit is

a	b	Output
0	0	1 ← case 1 (both numbers equal to 0)
0	1	0
1	0	0
1	1	1 ← case 2 (both numbers equal to 1)

In the output column of the truth table, there are two 1 values, labeled case 1 and case 2, so Step 2 of the algorithm is to construct two subexpressions, one for each of these two cases. The subexpression for case 1 is $(\bar{a} \cdot \bar{b})$ because this produces the value 1 only when $a = 0$ and $b = 0$. The subexpression for case 2 is $(a \cdot b)$, which produces a 1 only when $a = 1$ and $b = 1$.

We now combine the outputs of these two subexpressions with an OR gate, as described in Step 3, to produce the Boolean expression

$$(\bar{a} \cdot \bar{b}) + (a \cdot b)$$

Finally, in Step 4, we convert this expression to a circuit diagram, which is shown in Figure 4.27. The circuit shown in Figure 4.27 correctly compares

FIGURE 4.27

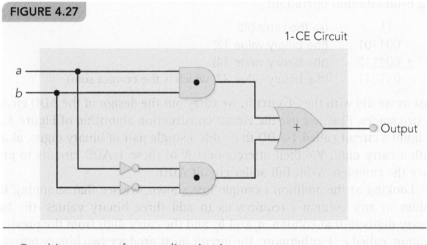

One-bit compare-for-equality circuit

two 1-bit quantities and determines if they are equal. If they are equal, it outputs a 1. If they are unequal, it outputs a 0.

However, the numbers compared for equality by a computer are usually much larger than a single binary digit. We want a circuit that correctly compares two numbers that contain N binary digits. To build this "N-bit compare-for-equality" circuit, we use N of the 1-CE circuits shown in Figure 4.27, one for each bit position in the numbers to be compared. Each 1-CE circuit produces a 1 if the two binary digits in its specific location are identical and produces a 0 if they are not. If every circuit produces a 1, then the two numbers are identical in every bit position, and they are equal. To check whether all our 1-CE circuits produce a 1, we simply AND together (two at a time) the outputs of all N 1-CE circuits. Remember that an AND gate produces a 1 if and only if both of its inputs are a 1. Thus the final output of the N-bit compare circuit is a 1 if and only if every pair of bits in the corresponding location of the two numbers is identical—that is, the two numbers are equal.

Figure 4.28 shows the design of a complete *N-bit compare-for-equality circuit* called CE. Each of the two numbers being compared, a and b, contains N bits, and they are labeled $a_{N-1} a_{N-2} \ldots a_0$ and $b_{N-1} b_{N-2} \ldots b_0$. The box labeled 1-CE in Figure 4.28 is the 1-bit compare-for-equality circuit shown in Figure 4.27. Looking at these figures, you can see that we have designed a very complex electrical circuit without the specification of a single electrical device. The only "devices" in those diagrams are gates to implement the logical operations AND, OR, and NOT, and the only "rules" we need to know to understand the diagrams are the transformation rules of Boolean logic. George Boole's work in algebraic logic from the 1850s is now the starting point for the design of every circuit found inside a modern 21st-century computer.

An Addition Circuit. Our second example of circuit construction is an addition circuit called ADD that performs binary addition on two unsigned N-bit integers. Typically, this type of circuit is called a *full adder*. For example, assuming $N = 6$, our ADD circuit would be able to perform the following 6-bit addition operation:

11	(← the carry bit)
001101	(the binary value 13)
+ 001110	(the binary value 14)
011011	(the binary value 27, which is the correct sum)

Just as we did with the CE circuit, we carry out the design of the ADD circuit in two stages. First, we use the circuit construction algorithm of Figure 4.25 to build a circuit called 1-ADD that adds a single pair of binary digits, along with a carry digit. We then interconnect N of these 1-ADD circuits to produce the complete N-bit full adder circuit ADD.

Looking at the addition example just shown, we see that summing the values in any column i requires us to add three binary values—the two binary digits in that column, a_i and b_i, and the carry digit from the previous column, called c_i. Furthermore, the circuit must produce two binary outputs: a sum digit s_i and a new carry digit c_{i+1} that propagates to the next column.

FIGURE 4.28

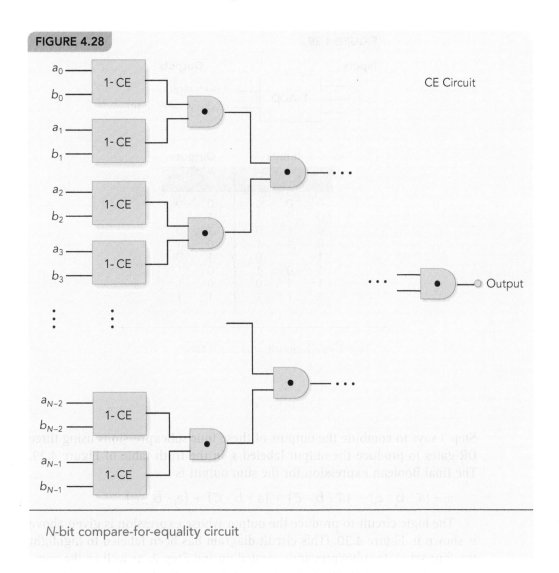

N-bit compare-for-equality circuit

The pictorial representation of the 1-bit adder circuit 1–ADD and its accompanying truth table are shown in Figure 4.29.

Because the 1–ADD circuit being constructed has two outputs, s_i and c_{i+1}, we must use Steps 2, 3, and 4 of the circuit construction algorithm twice, once for each output. Let's work on the sum output s_i first.

The s_i output column of Figure 4.29 contains four 1s, so we need to construct four subexpressions. In accordance with the guidelines given in Step 2 of the construction algorithm, these four subexpressions are

Case 1: $\bar{a}_i \cdot \bar{b}_i \cdot c_i$
Case 2: $\bar{a}_i \cdot b_i \cdot \bar{c}_i$
Case 3: $a_i \cdot \bar{b}_i \cdot \bar{c}_i$
Case 4: $a_i \cdot b_i \cdot c_i$

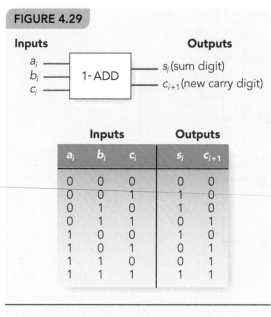

FIGURE 4.29

Inputs			Outputs	
a_i	b_i	c_i	s_i	c_{i+1}
0	0	0	0	0
0	0	1	1	0
0	1	0	1	0
0	1	1	0	1
1	0	0	1	0
1	0	1	0	1
1	1	0	0	1
1	1	1	1	1

The 1-ADD circuit and truth table

Step 3 says to combine the outputs of these four subexpressions using three OR gates to produce the output labeled s_i in the truth table of Figure 4.29. The final Boolean expression for the sum output is

$$s_i = (\bar{a}_i \cdot \bar{b}_i \cdot c_i) + (\bar{a}_i \cdot b_i \cdot \bar{c}_i) + (a_i \cdot \bar{b}_i \cdot \bar{c}_i) + (a_i \cdot b_i \cdot c_i)$$

The logic circuit to produce the output whose expression is given above is shown in Figure 4.30. (This circuit diagram has been labeled to highlight the four separate subexpressions created during Step 2, as well as the combining of the subexpressions in Step 3 of the construction algorithm.)

We are not yet finished, because the 1–ADD circuit in Figure 4.29 has a second output—the carry into the next column. That means the circuit construction algorithm must be repeated for the second output column, labeled c_{i+1}.

The c_{i+1} column also contains four 1s, so we again need to build four separate subcircuits, just as for the sum output, and combine them using OR gates. The construction proceeds in a fashion similar to the first part, so we leave the details as an exercise for the reader. The Boolean expression describing the carry output $c_{i\,+1}$ of the 1–ADD circuit is

$$c_{i+1} = (\bar{a}_i \cdot b_i \cdot c_i) + (a_i \cdot \bar{b}_i \cdot c_i) + (a_i \cdot b_i \cdot \bar{c}_i) + (a_i \cdot b_i \cdot c_i)$$

We have now built the two parts of the 1–ADD circuit that produce the sum and the carry outputs. The complete 1–ADD circuit is constructed by simply putting these two pieces together. Figure 4.31 shows the complete (and admittedly quite complex) 1–ADD circuit to implement 1-bit addition.

FIGURE 4.30

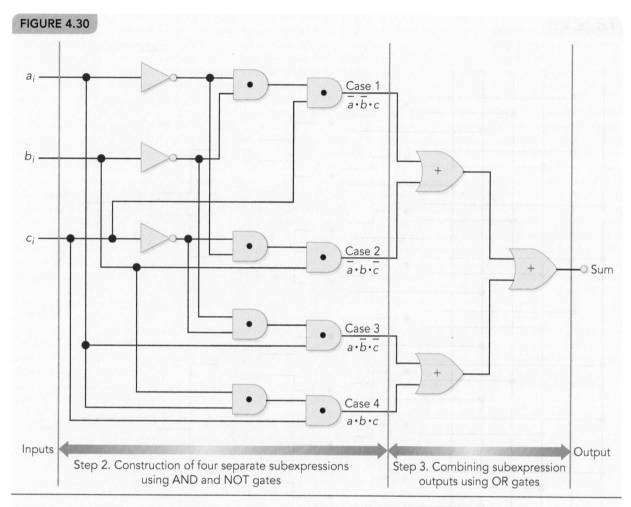

Inputs

Step 2. Construction of four separate subexpressions
using AND and NOT gates

Step 3. Combining subexpression
outputs using OR gates

Output

Sum output for the 1-ADD circuit

To keep the diagram from becoming an incomprehensible tangle of lines, we
have drawn it in a slightly different orientation from Figures 4.27 and 4.30.
Everything else is exactly the same.

When looking at this rather imposing diagram, do not become overly
concerned with the details of every gate, every connection, and every operation. Figure 4.31 more importantly illustrates the *process* by which we
design such a complex and intricate circuit: by transforming the idea of
1-bit binary addition into an electrical circuit using the tools of algorithmic
problem solving and symbolic logic.

How is the 1-ADD circuit shown in Figure 4.31 used to add numbers
that contain N binary digits rather than just one? The answer is simple if we
think about the way numbers are added by hand. (We discussed exactly this
topic when developing the addition algorithm of Figure 1.2 in Chapter 1.)
We add numbers one column at a time, moving from right to left, generating

FIGURE 4.31

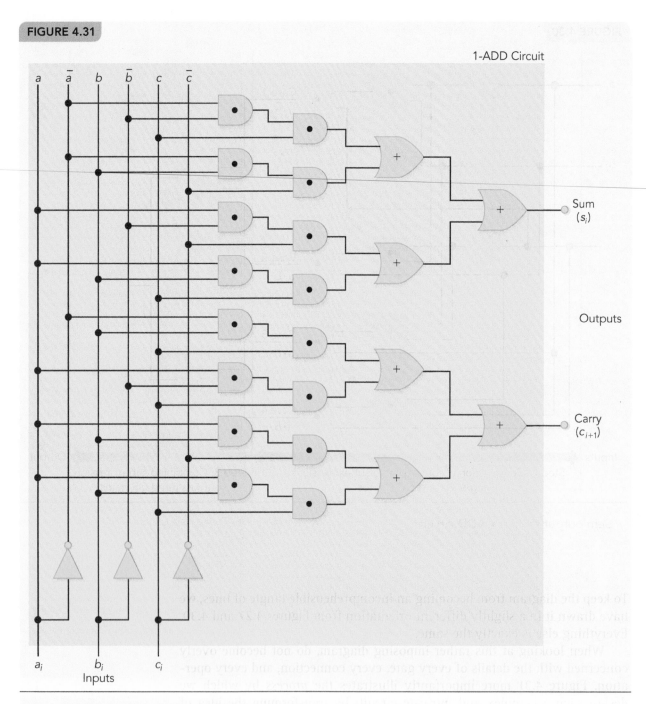

Complete 1-ADD circuit for 1-bit binary addition

the sum digit, writing it down, and sending any carry to the next column. The same thing can be done in hardware. We use N of the 1-ADD circuits shown in Figure 4.31, one for each column. Starting with the rightmost circuit, each 1-ADD circuit adds a single column of digits, generates a sum digit that is part of the final answer, and sends its carry digit to the 1-ADD circuit on its left, which replicates this process. After N repetitions of this process, all sum digits have been generated, and the N circuits have correctly added the two numbers.

The complete full adder circuit called ADD is shown in Figure 4.32. It adds the two N-bit numbers $a_{N-1} a_{N-2}, \ldots a_0$ and $b_{N-1} b_{N-2} \ldots b_0$ to produce the $(N+1)$-bit sum $s_N s_{N-1} s_{N-2} \ldots s_0$. Because addition is one of the most common arithmetic operations, the circuit shown in Figure 4.32 (or something equivalent) is one of the most important and most frequently used arithmetic components. Addition circuits are found in every computer, tablet, smartphone, and handheld calculator in the marketplace. They are even found in computer-controlled thermostats, clocks, and microwave ovens, where they enable us, for example, to add 30 minutes to the cooking time.

Figure 4.32 is, in a sense, the direct hardware implementation of the addition algorithm shown in Figure 1.2. Although Figure 1.2 and Figure 4.32 are quite

FIGURE 4.32

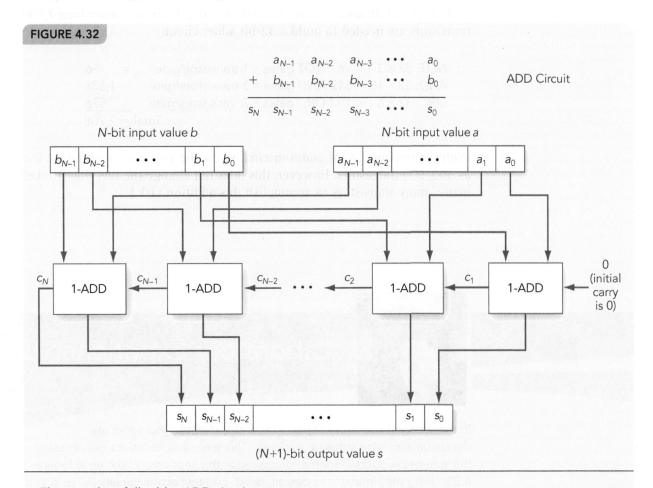

The complete full adder ADD circuit

different, both represent essentially the same algorithm: the column-by-column addition of two N-bit numerical values. This demonstrates quite clearly that there are many different ways to express the same algorithm—in this case, pseudocode (Figure 1.2) and hardware circuits (Figure 4.32). Later chapters show additional ways to represent algorithms, such as machine language programs and high-level language programs. However, regardless of whether we use English, pseudocode, mathematics, or transistors to describe an algorithm, its fundamental properties are the same, and the central purpose of computer science—algorithmic problem solving—remains the same.

It may also be instructive to study the size and complexity of the ADD circuit just designed. Figure 4.32 shows that the addition of two N-bit integer values requires N separate 1-ADD circuits. Let's assume that $N = 32$, a typical value for modern computers. Referring to Figure 4.31, we see that each 1-ADD circuit uses 3 NOT gates, 16 AND gates, and 6 OR gates, a total of 25 logic gates. Thus the total number of logic gates used to implement 32-bit binary addition is $32 \times 25 = 800$ gates. Figure 4.18 shows that each NOT gate requires one transistor, and Figures 4.19(b) and 4.20(b) show that each AND and OR gate requires three transistors. Therefore, more than 2,200 transistors are needed to build a 32-bit adder circuit:

$$
\begin{aligned}
NOT: 32 \times 3 &= 96 \quad NOT \text{ gates} \times 1 \text{ transistor/gate} &= 96 \\
AND: 32 \times 16 &= 512 \; AND \text{ gates} \times 3 \text{ transistors/gate} &= 1{,}536 \\
OR: 32 \times 6 &= 192 \; OR \text{ gates} \times 3 \text{ transistors/gate} &= \underline{576} \\
& & \text{Total} = 2{,}208
\end{aligned}
$$

(*Note*: Optimized 32-bit addition circuits can be constructed using as few as 500–600 transistors. However, this does not change the fact that it takes many, many transistors to accomplish this addition task.)

Laboratory Experience 8

In the second Laboratory Experience of this chapter, you again use the circuit simulator software package. This time, you construct circuits using the sum-of-products algorithm discussed in this section and shown in Figure 4.25. Using the simulator to design, build, and test actual circuits will give you a deeper understanding of how to use the sum-of-products algorithm to create circuits that solve specific problems.

Practice Problems

1. Determine how many transistors are required to build the *N*-bit compare-for-equality circuit of Figure 4.28. Assume *N* = 32.

2. Design a circuit that implements a 1-bit compare-for-greater-than (1-GT) operation. This circuit is given two 1-bit values, *a* and *b*. It outputs a 1 if *a* > *b*, and outputs a 0 otherwise.

3. Use the circuit construction algorithm just described to implement the NOR operation shown in Figure 4.20(a). Remember that the truth table for the NOR operation is:

a	b	(a NOR b)
0	0	1
0	1	0
1	0	0
1	1	0

4. Use the circuit construction algorithm to implement the NXOR, the Not of the Exclusive OR operation, whose truth table is the following:

a	b	(a NXOR b)
0	0	1
0	1	0
1	0	0
1	1	1

Dr. William Shockley
(1910–1989)

Dr. William Shockley was the inventor (along with John Bardeen and Walter Brattain) of the transistor. His discovery has probably done as much to shape our modern world as any scientific advancement of the 20th century. He received the 1956 Nobel Prize in Physics and, at his death, was a distinguished professor at Stanford University.

(Continued)

Shockley and his team developed the transistor in 1947 while working at Bell Laboratories. He left there in 1954 to set up the Shockley Semiconductor Laboratory in California—a company that was instrumental in the birth of the high-technology region called Silicon Valley. The employees of this company eventually went on to develop other fundamental advances in computing, such as the integrated circuit and the microprocessor and started a number of important high-technology companies, including Fairchild Semiconductor, Advanced Micro Devices (AMD), and Intel.

Although Shockley's work has been compared with that of Pasteur, Salk, and Einstein in importance, his reputation and place in history have been forever tarnished by his outrageous and controversial racial theories. His education and training were in physics and electrical engineering, but Shockley spent the last years of his life trying to convince people of the genetic inferiority of black people, even though he was ridiculed and shunned by colleagues who abandoned all contact with him. By the time of his death in 1989 he had become estranged from virtually all his friends and family. It is said that his children learned about his death only through stories in the newspaper. His intense racial bigotry prevented him from receiving the recognition that would otherwise have been his for monumental contributions in physics, engineering, and computer science.

This computation emphasizes the importance of the continuing research into the miniaturization of electrical components. (See the Special Interest Box on Moore's Law earlier in this chapter.) If vacuum tubes were used instead of transistors, as was done in computers from about 1940 to 1955, the adder circuit shown in Figure 4.32 would be extraordinarily bulky; 2,208 vacuum tubes would occupy a space about the size of a large refrigerator. It would also generate huge amounts of heat, necessitating sophisticated cooling systems, and it would be very difficult to maintain. (Imagine the time it would take to locate a single burned-out vacuum tube from a cluster of 2,000.) Using something on the scale of the magnetic core technology described in Section 4.2.4 and shown in Figure 4.9, the adder circuit would fit into an area a few inches square. However, modern circuit technology can now achieve transistor densities greater than 1 billion transistors/cm^2. At this level, the entire ADD circuit of Figure 4.32 would easily fit in an area much, much smaller than the size of the period at the end of this sentence. That is why it is now possible to put powerful computer-processing facilities not only in a room or on a desk but also inside a watch, a thermostat, or even inside the human body.

4.5 Control Circuits

The previous section described the design of circuits for implementing arithmetic and logical operations. However, there are other, quite different, types of circuits that are also essential to the proper functioning of a computer system. This section briefly describes one of these important circuit types, control circuits, which are used not to implement arithmetic operations but to determine the order in which operations are carried out and to select the correct data values to be processed. In a sense, they are the sequencing and decision-making circuits inside a computer. These circuits are essential to the proper function of a computer because, as we noted in Chapter 1, algorithms and programs must be well ordered and must always know which operation to do next. The two major types of control circuits are called *multiplexers* and *decoders*, and, like everything else described in this chapter, they can be completely described in terms of gates and the rules of logic.

A multiplexer is a circuit that has 2^N *input lines* and 1 *output line*. Its function is to select exactly one of its 2^N input lines and copy the binary value on that input line onto its single output line. A multiplexer chooses one specific input by using an additional set of N lines called *selector lines*. (Thus the total number of inputs to the multiplexer circuit is $2^N + N$.) The 2^N input lines of a multiplexer are numbered 0, 1, 2, 3, ... , $2^N - 1$. Each of the N selector lines can be set to either a 0 or a 1, so we can use the N selector lines to represent all binary values from 000 ... 0 (N zeros) to 111 ... 1 (N ones), which represent all integer values from 0 to $2^N - 1$. These numbers correspond exactly to the numbers of the input lines. Thus the binary number that appears on the selector lines can be interpreted as the identification number of the input line that is to be selected. Pictorially, a multiplexer looks like the diagram in Figure 4.33.

FIGURE 4.33

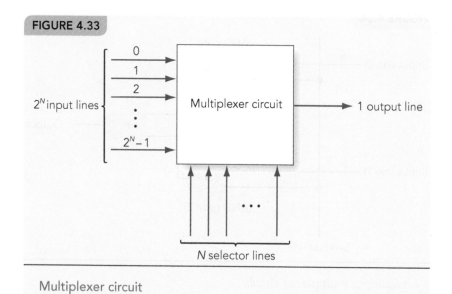

Multiplexer circuit

For example, if we had four (2^2) input lines (i.e., $N = 2$) coming into our multiplexer, numbered 0, 1, 2, and 3, then we would need two selector lines. The four binary combinations that can appear on this pair of selector lines are 00, 01, 10, and 11, which correspond to the decimal values 0, 1, 2, and 3, respectively (refer to Figure 4.2). The multiplexer selects the one input line whose identification number corresponds to the value appearing on the selector lines and copies the value on that input line to the output line. If, for example, the two selector lines were set to 1 and 0, then a multiplexer circuit would pick input line 2 because 10 in binary is 2 in decimal notation.

Implementing a multiplexer using logic gates is not difficult. Figure 4.34 shows a simple multiplexer circuit with $N = 1$. This is a multiplexer with two (2^1) input lines and a single selector line.

In Figure 4.34 if the value on the selector line is 0, then the bottom input line to AND gate 2 is always 0, so its output is always 0. Looking at AND gate 1, we see that the NOT gate changes its bottom input value to a 1. Because (1 AND a) is always a, the output of the top AND gate is equal to the value of a, which is the value of the input from line 0. Thus the two inputs to the OR gate are 0 and a. Because the value of the expression (0 OR a) is identical to a, by setting the selector line to 0 we have, in effect, selected as our output the value that appears on line 0. You should confirm that if the selector line has the value 1, then the output of the circuit in Figure 4.34 is b, the value appearing on line 1. We can design multiplexers with more than two inputs in a similar fashion, although they rapidly become more complex.

The second type of control circuit is called a decoder (Figure 4.35) and it operates in the opposite way from a multiplexer. A decoder has N input lines numbered 0, 1, 2, ... , $N - 1$ and 2^N output lines numbered 0, 1, 2, 3, ... , $2^N - 1$.

FIGURE 4.34

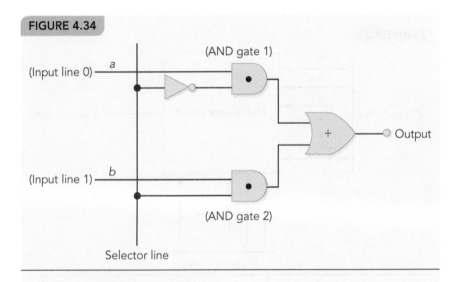

A two-input multiplexer circuit

FIGURE 4.35

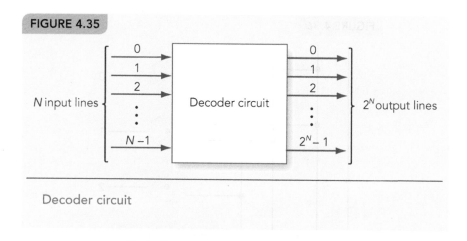

Decoder circuit

Each of the *N* input lines of the decoder can be set to either a 0 or a 1, and when these *N* values are interpreted as a single binary number, they can represent all integer values from 0 to $2^N - 1$. It is the job of the decoder to determine the value represented on its *N* input lines and then send a signal (i.e., a 1) on the single output line that has that identification number. All other output lines are set to 0.

For example, if our decoder has three input lines, it has eight (2^3) output lines numbered 0 to 7. These three input lines can represent all binary values from 000 to 111, which is from 0 to 7 in decimal notation. If, for example, the binary values on the three input lines are 101, which is a 5, then a signal (a binary 1) would be sent out by the decoder on output line 5. All other output lines would contain a 0.

Figure 4.36 shows the design of a 2-to-4 decoder circuit with two input lines and four (2^2) output lines. These four output lines are labeled 0, 1, 2, and 3, and the only output line that carries a signal value of 1 is the line whose identification number is identical to the value appearing on the two input lines. For example, if the two inputs are 11, then line 3 should be set to a 1 (11 in binary is 3 in decimal). This is, in fact, what happens because the AND gate connected to line 3 is the only one whose two inputs are equal to a 1. You should confirm that this circuit behaves properly when it receives the inputs 00, 01, and 10 as well.

Together, decoder and multiplexer circuits enable us to build computer systems that execute the correct instructions using the correct data values. For example, assume we have a computer that can carry out four different types of arithmetic operations—add, subtract, multiply, and divide. Furthermore, assume that these four instructions have code numbers 0, 1, 2, and 3, respectively. We could use a decoder circuit to ensure that the computer performs the correct instruction. We need a decoder circuit with two input lines. It receives as input the two-digit code number (in binary) of the instruction that we want to perform: 00 (add), 01 (subtract), 10 (multiply), or 11 (divide). The decoder interprets this value and sends out a signal on the correct output line. This signal is used to select the proper arithmetic circuit and cause it to perform the desired operation. This behavior is diagrammed in Figure 4.37.

FIGURE 4.36

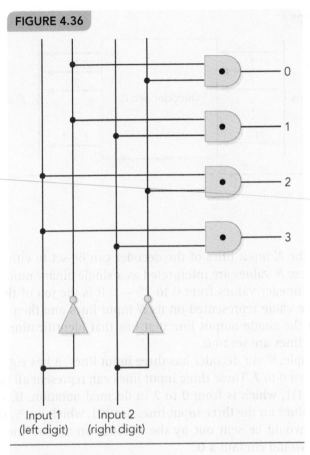

Input 1   Input 2
(left digit) (right digit)

A 2-to-4 decoder circuit

FIGURE 4.37

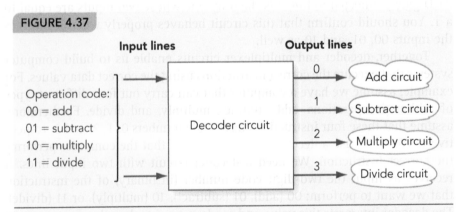

Example of the use of a decoder circuit

FIGURE 4.38

Registers

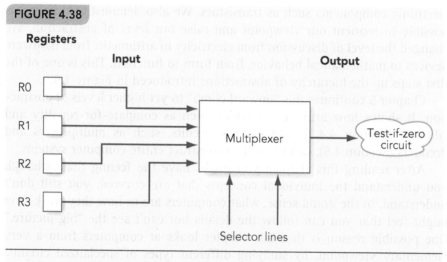

Example of the use of a multiplexer circuit

Whereas a decoder circuit can be used to select the correct instruction, a multiplexer can help ensure that the computer executes this instruction using the correct data. For example, suppose our computer has four special registers called R0, R1, R2, and R3. (For now, just consider a register to be a place to store a data value. We describe registers in more detail in the next chapter.) Assume that we have built a circuit called *test-if-zero* that can test whether any of these four registers contains the value 0. (This is actually quite similar to the CE circuit of Figure 4.28.) We can use a multiplexer circuit to select the register that we want to send to the test-if-zero circuit. This is shown in Figure 4.38. If we want to test if register R2 in Figure 4.38 is 0, we simply put the binary value 10 (2 in decimal notation) on the two selector lines. This selects register R2, and only its value passes through the multiplexer and is sent to the test circuit.

There are many more examples of the use of control circuits in Chapter 5, which examines the execution of programs and the overall organization of a computer system.

4.6 Conclusion

We began our discussion on the representation of information and the design of computer circuits with the most elementary component, bistable electronic devices such as transistors. We showed how they can be used to construct logic gates that in turn can be used to implement circuits to carry out useful functions. Our purpose here was not to make you an expert in specifying and designing computer circuits but to demonstrate how it is possible to implement high-level arithmetic operations using only low-level electronic components such as transistors. We also demonstrated how it is possible to reorient our viewpoint and raise our level of abstraction. We changed the level of discussion from electricity to arithmetic, from hardware devices to mathematical behavior, from form to function. This is one of the first steps up the hierarchy of abstractions introduced in Figure 1.9.

Chapter 5 continues this "upward climb" to yet higher levels of abstraction. It shows how arithmetic circuits, such as compare-for-equality and addition (Section 4.4.3), and control circuits, such as multiplexers and decoders (Section 4.5), can be used to construct entire computer systems.

After reading this chapter, you might have the feeling that although you understand the individual concepts that are covered, you still don't understand, in the grand sense, what computers are or how they work. You might feel that you can follow the details but can't see the "big picture." One possible reason is that this chapter looks at computers from a very elementary viewpoint, by studying different types of specialized circuits. This is analogous to studying the human body as a collection of millions of cells of different types—blood cells, brain cells, skin cells, and so on. Cytology (the study of cells) is certainly an important part of the field of biology, but understanding only the cellular structure of the human body provides no intuitive understanding of what people are and how we do such characteristic things as walk, eat, and breathe. Understanding these complex actions derives not from a study of molecules, genes, or cells but from a study of higher-level organs and their interactions, such as the lungs, heart, and muscles.

That is exactly what happens in Chapter 5, in which we examine higher-level computer components such as processors, memory, and instructions, and begin our study of the topic of computer organization.

EXERCISES

1. Given our discussion of positional numbering systems in Section 4.2.1, see whether you can determine the decimal value of the following numbers:

   a. 133 (base 4)

   b. 367 (base 8, also called octal)

   c. 1BA (base 16, also called hexadecimal. B is the digit that represents 11; A is the digit that represents 10.)

2. In Exercise 1c, we use the letters A and B as digits of the base-16 number. Explain why that is necessary.

3. Determine the decimal value of the following unsigned binary numbers:

   a. 11000

   b. 110001

   c. 1111111

   d. 1000000000

4. Using 8 bits, what is the unsigned binary representation of each of the following values:

   a. 23

   b. 55

   c. 275

   Did anything unusual happen when determining the correct answer to Part c?

5. Assume that the following 10-bit numbers represent signed integers using sign/magnitude notation. The sign is the leftmost bit and the remaining 9 bits represent the magnitude. What is the decimal value of each?

   a. 1000110001

   b. 0110011000

   c. 1000000001

   d. 1000000000

6. Give the 8-bit sign/magnitude representation of each of the following decimal values:

   a. +71

   b. − 1

   c. − 81

7. Assume that you tried to store the signed integer value −200 using an 8-bit sign/magnitude representation. What happened? What type of error does this represent?

8. Assume that we use 10 bits to represent signed integers, using sign/magnitude notation. What are the largest (in absolute value) positive and negative numbers that can be represented on our system?

9. Show the step-by-step addition of the following two 10-bit unsigned binary values, including showing the carry bit to each successive column:

$$\begin{array}{r} 0011100011 \\ + \ 0001101110 \\ \hline \end{array}$$

10. Assume that our computer stores decimal numbers using 16 bits—10 bits for a sign/magnitude mantissa and 6 bits for a sign/magnitude base-2 exponent. (This is exactly the same representation shown on page 162) Show the internal representation of the following decimal quantities.

    a. +7.5

    b. −20.25

    c. −1/64

11. Using the same decimal representation scheme described in Exercise 10, give the decimal value of each of the following 16-bit binary strings:

    a. 0111000000000111

    b. 1010001000100001 (*Note*: Is there something unusual about this representation? If so, what is it?)

12. In Exercises 10 and 11, we used 16 bits to represent decimal numbers, allocating 10 bits for the mantissa and 6 bits for the exponent. What would be the impact on our representation if we still used 16 bits for each number but instead allocated 12 bits for the mantissa and 4 bits for the exponent?

13. Using the ASCII code set given in Figure 4.3, show the internal binary representation for the following character strings:

   a. AbC

   b. Mike

   c. $25.00

   d. (a + b)

14. How many binary digits would it take to represent the following phrase in ASCII code? In 16-bit Unicode? (Do not include the " " marks.)

   "Invitation to Computer Science"

15. a. How many bits does it take to store a 3-minute song using an audio encoding method that samples at the rate of 40,000 samples/second, has a bit depth of 16, and does not use compression? What if it uses a compression scheme with a compression ratio of 5:1?

   b. How many bits does it take to store an uncompressed 1,200 × 800 RGB color image? If we found out that the image actually takes only 2.4 Mbits, what is the compression ratio?

16. Show how run-length encoding can be used to compress the following text stream:

   xxxyyyyyyyzzzzAAxxxx

   What is the compression ratio? (Assume each digit and letter requires 8 bits.)

17. Using the variable-length code shown in Figure 4.9, give the internal coding of the following Hawaiian words along with the amount of savings over the standard fixed-length 4-bit representation:

   a. KAI

   b. MAUI

   c. MOLOKAI

   Explain the problem that occurred with Part c.

18. The primary advantage of using the binary numbering system rather than the decimal system to represent data is reliability, as noted in Section 4.2.3. Describe two disadvantages of using binary rather than decimal notation for the internal representation of information.

19. Assume that $a = 1$, $b = 2$, and $c = 2$. What is the value of each of the following Boolean expressions?

   a. $(a > 1)$ OR $(b = c)$

   b. $[(a + b) > c]$ AND $(b < c)$

   c. NOT $(a = 1)$

   d. NOT $[(a = b)$ OR $(b = c)]$

   e. $(a = 1)$ AND $(b = 1)$ AND $(c = 2)$

20. Assume that $a = 5$, $b = 2$, and $c = 3$. What problem do you encounter when attempting to evaluate the following Boolean expression?

   $(a = 1)$ AND $(b = 2)$ OR $(c = 3)$

   How can this problem be solved?

21. The truth table for a Boolean expression with two variables has four rows. The truth table for a Boolean expression with three variables has eight rows. How many rows would there be in a truth table with five variables?

22. Using the circuit construction algorithm of Section 4.4.2, design a circuit using only AND, OR, and NOT gates to implement the following truth table:

a	b	Output
0	0	1
0	1	1
1	0	1
1	1	0

This operation is termed *NAND*, for Not AND, and it can be constructed as a single gate, as shown in Figure 4.19(a). Assume that you do not have access to a NAND gate and must construct it from AND, OR, and NOT.

23. Using the circuit construction algorithm of Section 4.4.2, design a circuit using only AND, OR, and NOT gates to implement the following truth table.

a	b	Output
0	0	1
0	1	1
1	0	0
1	1	1

This operation is termed *logical implication*, and it is an important operator in symbolic logic.

24. Build a *majority-rules circuit*. This is a circuit that has three inputs and one output. The value of its output is 1 if and only if two or more of its inputs are 1; otherwise, the output of the circuit is 0. For example, if the three inputs are 0, 1, 1, your circuit should output a 1. If its three inputs are 0, 1, 0, it should output a 0. This circuit is frequently used in **fault-tolerant computing**—environments where a computer must keep working correctly no

matter what, for example as on a deep-space vehicle where making repairs is impossible. In these conditions, we might choose to put three computers on board and have all three do every computation; if two or more of the systems produce the same answer, we accept it. Thus, one of the machines could fail and the system would still work properly.

25. Design an *odd-parity circuit*. This is a circuit that has three inputs and one output. The circuit outputs a 1 if and only if an even number (0 or 2) of its inputs are a 1. Otherwise, the circuit outputs a 0. Thus, the sum of the number of 1 bits in the input and the output is always an odd number. (This circuit is used in error checking. By adding up the number of 1 bits, we can determine whether any single input bit was accidentally changed. If it was, the total number of 1s is an even number when we know it should be an odd value.)

26. Design a *1-bit subtraction circuit*. This circuit takes three inputs—two binary digits a and b and a borrow digit from the previous column. The circuit has two outputs—the difference (a − b), including the borrow, and a new borrow digit that propagates to the next column. Create the truth table and build the circuit. This circuit can be used to build *N*-bit subtraction circuits.

27. How many selector lines would be needed on a four-input multiplexer? On an eight-input multiplexer?

28. Design a *four-input multiplexer circuit*. Use the design of the two-input multiplexer shown in Figure 4.34 as a guide.

29. Design a *3-to-8 decoder circuit*. Use the design of the 2-to-4 decoder circuit shown in Figure 4.36 as a guide.

CHALLENGE WORK

1. Circuit optimization is a very important area of hardware design. As we mentioned earlier in the chapter, each gate in the circuit represents a real hardware device that takes up space on the chip, generates heat that must be dissipated, and increases costs. Therefore, the elimination of unneeded gates can represent a real savings. Circuit optimization investigates techniques to construct a new circuit that behaves identically to the original one but with fewer gates. The basis for circuit optimization is the transformation rules of symbolic logic. These rules allow you to transform one Boolean expression into an equivalent one that entails fewer operations. For example, the *distributive law* of logic says that $(a \cdot b) + (a \cdot c) = a \cdot (b + c)$. The expressions on either side of the = sign are functionally identical, but the one on the right determines its value using one less gate (one AND gate and one OR gate instead of two AND gates and one OR gate).

   Read about the transformation rules of binary logic and techniques of circuit optimization. Using these rules, improve the full adder circuit of Figure 4.32 so that it requires fewer than 2,208 transistors. Explain your improvements and determine exactly how many fewer transistors are required for your "new-and-improved" full adder circuit.

2. This chapter briefly described an alternative signed integer representation technique called two's complement representation. This popular method is based on the concepts of *modular arithmetic*, and it does not suffer from the problem of two different representations for the quantity 0. Read more about two's complement and write a report describing how this method works, as well as algorithms for adding and subtracting numbers represented in two's complement notation. In your report, give the 16-bit, two's complement representation for the signed integer values +45, −68, −1, and 0. Then show how to carry out the arithmetic operations 45 + 45, 45 + (−68), and 45 − (−1).

3. In Section 4.2.2, we describe lossless compression schemes, such as run-length encoding and variable-length codes. However, most compression schemes in use today are lossy and only achieve extremely high rates of compression at the expense of losing some of the detail contained in the sound or image. Often they base their compression techniques on specific knowledge of the characteristics of the human ear or eye. For example, it is well known that the eye is much more sensitive to changes in brightness (luminance) than to changes in color (chrominance). The JPEG compression algorithm exploits this fact when it is compressing a photographic image.

   Read about the JPEG image compression algorithm to learn how it is able to achieve compression ratios of 10:1 or even 20:1. A good place to start would be the JPEG home page, located at *www.jpeg.org*.

Computer Systems Organization

AFTER STUDYING THIS CHAPTER, YOU WILL BE ABLE TO:

- Enumerate the characteristics of the Von Neumann architecture
- Describe the components of a random access memory system, including how fetch and store operations work, and the use of cache memory to speed up access time
- Diagram the components of a typical arithmetic/logic unit (ALU) and illustrate how the ALU data path operates
- Describe the operation of the control unit and explain how it implements the stored program characteristic of the Von Neumann architecture
- List and explain the types of instructions in a typical instruction set, and how instructions are commonly encoded
- Diagram the organization of a typical Von Neumann machine
- Show the sequence of steps, using the book's notation, in the fetch, decode, and execute cycle to perform a typical instruction

5.1 Introduction

Chapter 4 introduced the elementary building blocks of computer systems—transistors, gates, and logic circuits. Although this information is essential to understanding computer hardware—just as knowledge of atoms and molecules is necessary for any serious study of chemistry—it produces a very low-level view of computer systems. Even students who have mastered the material may still ask, "OK, but how do computers *really* work?" Gates and circuits operate on the most elemental of data items, binary 0s and 1s, whereas people reason and work with more complex units of information, such as decimal numbers, character strings, variables, and instructions. To understand how computers process this kind of information, we must look at higher-level components than gates and circuits. We must study computers as collections of functional units or subsystems that perform tasks such as instruction processing, information storage, computation, and data transfer. The branch of computer science that studies computers in terms of their major functional units is computer organization, and that is the subject of this chapter. This higher-level viewpoint will give us a much better understanding of how a computer really works.

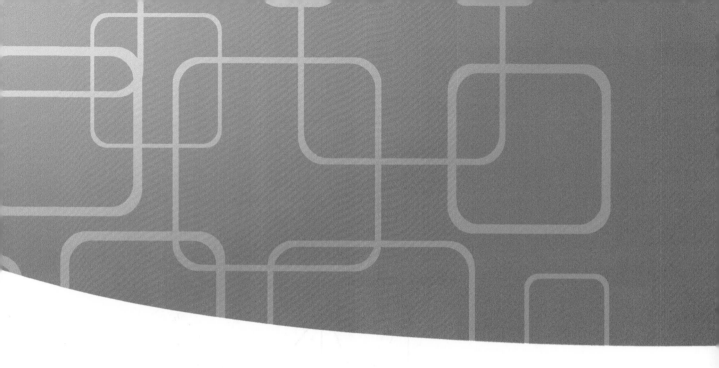

All of the functional units introduced in this chapter are built from the gates and circuits of Chapter 4. However, those elementary components will no longer be visible because we will adopt a different viewpoint, a different perspective, a different level of abstraction. This is an extremely important point; as we have said, the concept of abstraction is used throughout computer science. Without it, it would be virtually impossible to study computer design or any other large, complex system.

For example, suppose that system S is composed of a large number of elementary components a_1, a_2, a_3,... interconnected in very intricate ways, as shown in Figure 5.1(a). This is equivalent to viewing a computer system as millions or billions of individual gates. For some purposes, it might be necessary to view system S at this level of detail, but for other applications, the amount of complexity could become overwhelming. To deal with this problem, we can redefine the primitives of system S by grouping the elementary components a_1, a_2, a_3, ..., as shown in Figure 5.1(b), and calling these larger units (A, B, C) the basic building blocks of system S. The three units A, B, and C are then treated as nondecomposable elements whose internal construction is hidden from view. We care only about what functions these components perform and how they interact. This leads to the higher-level system view shown in Figure 5.1(c), which is certainly a great deal simpler than the one shown in Figure 5.1(a), and this is how this chapter approaches the topic of computer hardware. Our primitives are much larger components, similar to A, B, and C, but internally they are still made up of the gates and circuits of Chapter 4.

This "abstracting away" of unnecessary detail can be done more than once. For example, at a later point in the study of system S, we might no longer care about the behavior of individual components A, B, and C. Instead, we might want to treat the entire system as a single primitive, nondecomposable entity whose inner workings are no longer important. This leads to the extremely simple system view shown in Figure 5.1(d), a view that we will adopt in later chapters.

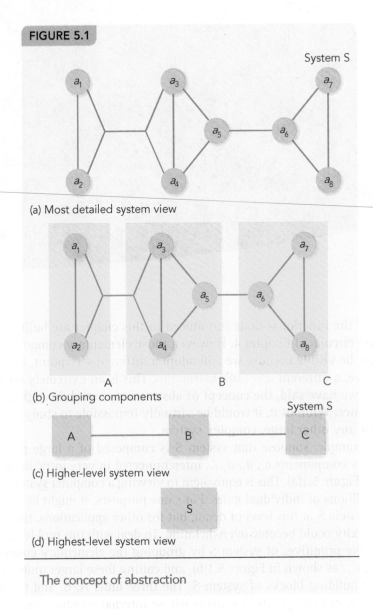

FIGURE 5.1

(a) Most detailed system view

(b) Grouping components

(c) Higher-level system view

(d) Highest-level system view

The concept of abstraction

Figures 5.1(a), (c), and (d) form what is called a hierarchy of abstractions. A hierarchy of abstractions of computer science forms the central theme of this text, and it was initially diagrammed in Figure 1.9. We have already seen this idea in action in Chapter 4, where transistors are grouped into gates and gates into circuits (see Figure 5.2).

This process continues into Chapter 5, where we use the addition and comparison circuits of Section 4.4.3 to build an arithmetic unit and use the multiplexer and decoder circuits of Section 4.5 to construct a processor. These higher-level components become our building blocks in all future discussions.

FIGURE 5.2

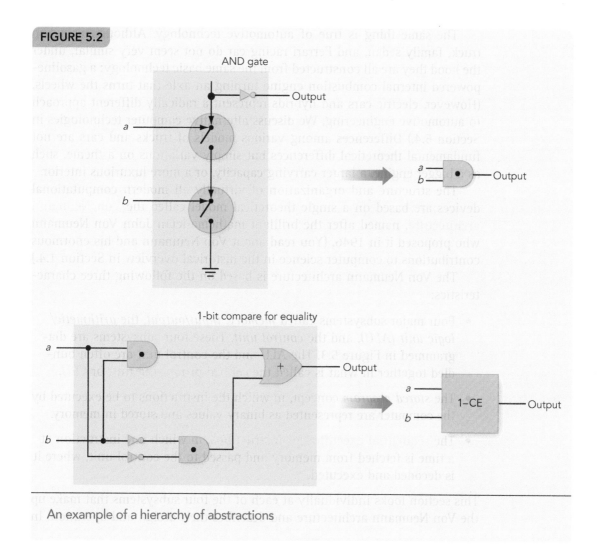

An example of a hierarchy of abstractions

5.2 The Components of a Computer System

There are a huge number of computer systems on the market, manufactured by dozens of different vendors. There are $50 million supercomputers, $1 million mainframes, and $1,000 laptops, as well as tablets and smartphones that may cost less than $100. In addition to size and cost, computers also differ in speed, memory capacity, input/output capabilities, and available software. The hardware marketplace is diverse, multifaceted, and ever changing.

However, in spite of all these differences, virtually every computer in use today is based on a single design. Although a $1 million mainframe, a $1,000 laptop, and a $100 smartphone might not seem to have much in common, they are all based on the same fundamental principles.

The same thing is true of automotive technology. Although a pickup truck, family sedan, and Ferrari racing car do not seem very similar, under the hood they are all constructed from the same basic technology: a gasoline-powered internal combustion engine turning an axle that turns the wheels. (However, electric cars and hybrids represent a radically different approach to automotive engineering. We discuss alternative computer technologies in Section 5.4.) Differences among various models of trucks and cars are not fundamental theoretical differences but simply variations on a theme, such as a bigger engine, a larger carrying capacity, or a more luxurious interior.

The structure and organization of virtually all modern computational devices are based on a single theoretical model called the Von Neumann architecture, named after the brilliant mathematician John Von Neumann who proposed it in 1946. (You read about Von Neumann and his enormous contributions to computer science in the historical overview in Section 1.4.)

The Von Neumann architecture is based on the following three characteristics:

- Four major subsystems called *memory, input/output*, the *arithmetic/logic unit (ALU)*, and the *control unit*. These four subsystems are diagrammed in Figure 5.3. The ALU and the control unit are often bundled together in what is called the central processing unit or CPU.

- The *stored program* concept, in which the instructions to be executed by the computer are represented as binary values and stored in memory.

- The sequential execution of instructions, in which one instruction at a time is fetched from memory and passed to the control unit, where it is decoded and executed.

This section looks individually at each of the four subsystems that make up the Von Neumann architecture and describes their design and operation. In

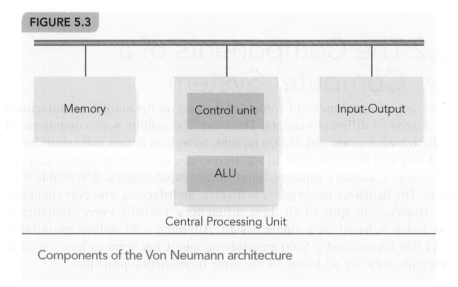

FIGURE 5.3

Memory   Control unit   Input-Output

ALU

Central Processing Unit

Components of the Von Neumann architecture

the following section, we put all these pieces together to show the operation of the overall Von Neumann model.

5.2.1 Memory and Cache

Memory is the functional unit of a computer that stores and retrieves instructions and data. All information stored in memory is represented internally using the binary numbering system described in Section 4.2.

Computer memory uses an access technique called *random access,* and the memory unit is frequently referred to as random access memory (RAM). RAM has the following three characteristics:

- Memory is divided into fixed-size units called cells, and each cell is associated with a unique identifier called an address. These addresses are the unsigned integers 0, 1, 2, ..., MAX.

- All accesses to memory are to a specified address, and we must always fetch or store a complete cell—that is, all the bits in that cell. The cell is the minimum unit of access.

- The time it takes to fetch or store the contents of a single cell is the same for all cells in memory.

A model of a random access memory unit is shown in Figure 5.4. (*Note:* Read-only memory (ROM) is a special type of random access memory into which information has been prerecorded during manufacture. This information cannot be modified or removed, only fetched. ROM is used to hold

FIGURE 5.4

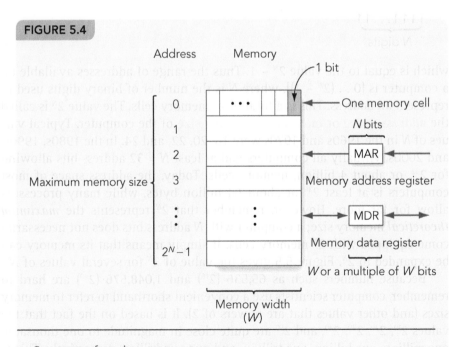

Structure of random access memory

important system instructions and data in a place where a user cannot accidentally or intentionally overwrite them.)

As shown in Figure 5.4, the memory unit is made up of cells that contain a fixed number of binary digits. The number of bits per cell is called the cell size or the memory width, and it is usually denoted as W.

Earlier generations of computers had no standardized value for cell size, and computers were built with values of $W = 6, 8, 12, 16, 24, 30, 32, 36, 48,$ and 60 bits. However, computer manufacturers now use a standard cell size of 8 bits, and this 8-bit unit is universally called a *byte*. Thus, the generic term *cell* has become relatively obsolete, and it is more common now to refer to memory bytes as the basic unit. However, keep in mind that this is not a generic term but rather refers to a memory cell that contains exactly 8 binary digits.

With a cell size of 8 bits, the largest unsigned integer value that can be stored in a single cell is 11111111, which equals 255—not a very large number. Therefore, computers with a cell size of $W = 8$ often use multiple memory cells to store a single data value. For example, many computers use 2 or 4 bytes (16 or 32 bits) to store one integer, and either 4 or 8 bytes (32 or 64 bits) to store a single real number. This gives the range needed, but at a price. It may take several trips to memory, rather than one, to fetch a single data item. (To solve this problem, all memory units today allow you to fetch and/or store 2, 4, or 8 adjacent memory bytes with a single access. We will have more to say about this feature later in the chapter.)

Each memory cell in RAM is identified by a unique unsigned integer address 0, 1, 2, 3, ... If there are N bits available to represent the address of a cell, then the smallest address is 0 and the largest address is a string of N 1s:

$$\underbrace{1111\ldots11}_{N \text{ digits}}$$

which is equal to the value $2^N - 1$. Thus the range of addresses available on a computer is $[0 \ldots (2^N - 1)]$, where N is the number of binary digits used to represent an address. This is a total of 2^N memory cells. The value 2^N is called the address space or maximum memory size of the computer. Typical values of N in the 1960s and 1970s were 16, 20, 22, and 24. In the 1980s, 1990s, and 2000s, virtually all computers had at least $N = 32$ address bits allowing for 2^{32}, or about 4 billion, memory cells. Today, the address space of most computers is at least 2^{36} or about 64 billion bytes, while many processors allow for far more. However, remember that 2^N represents the *maximum theoretical* memory size; a computer with N address bits does not necessarily come equipped with 2^N memory cells. It simply means that its memory can be expanded to 2^N. Figure 5.5 gives the value of 2^N for several values of N.

Because numbers such as 65,536 (2^{16}) and 1,048,576 (2^{20}) are hard to remember, computer scientists use a convenient shorthand to refer to memory sizes (and other values that are powers of 2). It is based on the fact that the values $2^{10}, 2^{20}, 2^{30}, 2^{40},$ and 2^{50} are quite close in magnitude to one thousand, one million, one billion, one trillion, and one quadrillion, respectively. Therefore, the letters K (*kilo*, or thousand), M (*mega*, or million), G (*giga*, or billion), T (*tera*, or trillion), and P (*peta*, or quadrillion) are used to refer to these units.

FIGURE 5.5

N	Maximum Memory Size (2^N)
16	65,536
20	1,048,576
22	4,194,304
24	16,777,216
32	4,294,967,296
40	1,099,511,627,776
50	1,125,899,906,842,624

Maximum memory sizes

2^{10} = 1K (= 1,024)   1 KB = 1 *kilobyte* = one thousand bytes

2^{20} = 1M (= 1,048,576)   1 MB = 1 *megabyte* = one million bytes

2^{30} = 1G (= 1,073,741,824)   1 GB = 1 *gigabyte* = one billion bytes

2^{40} = 1T (= 1,099,511,627,776)   1 TB = 1 *terabyte* = one trillion bytes

2^{50} = 1P (= 1,125,899,906,842,624) 1 PB = 1 *petabyte* = one quadrillion bytes

Thus, a computer with a 16-bit address and 2^{16} = 65,536 bytes of storage would have 64 KB of memory, because 2^{16} = $2^6 \times 2^{10}$ = 64 × 2^{10} = 64 KB. A 64-bit memory address would allow, at least theoretically, an address space of 2^{64} bytes = $2^{14} \times 2^{50}$, which is approximately 16,000 petabytes!

When dealing with memory, it is important to keep in mind the distinction between an *address* and the *contents* of that address.

Address   **Contents**

42 | 1 |

The address of this memory cell is 42. The content of cell 42 is the integer value 1. As you will soon see, some instructions operate on addresses, whereas others operate on the contents of an address. A failure to distinguish between these two values can cause confusion about how some instructions behave.

The two basic memory operations are *fetching* and *storing*, and they can be described formally as follows:

- *value = Fetch(address)*

   Meaning: Fetch a copy of the contents of the memory cell with the specified *address* and return those contents as the result of the operation. The original contents of the memory cell that was accessed are unchanged. This is termed a nondestructive fetch. Given the preceding diagram, the operation Fetch(42) returns the number 1. The value 1 remains in address 42.

- *Store(address, value)*

  Meaning: Store the specified *value* into the memory cell specified by *address*. The previous contents of the cell are lost. This is termed a destructive store. The operation Store(42, 2) stores the value 2 into cell 42, overwriting the previous value 1.

Powers of 10

When we talk about volumes of information such as megabytes, gigabytes, and terabytes, it is hard to fathom exactly what those massive numbers mean. Here are some rough approximations (say, to within an order of magnitude) of how much textual information corresponds to each of the storage quantities just introduced, as well as the next few on the scale.

Quantity in Bytes	Base-10 Value	Amount of Textual Information
1 byte	10^0	One character
1 kilobyte	10^3	One typed page
1 megabyte	10^6	Two or three novels
1 gigabyte	10^9	A departmental library or a large personal library
1 terabyte	10^{12}	The library of a major academic research university
1 petabyte	10^{15}	All printed material in all libraries in North America
1 exabyte	10^{18}	All words ever printed throughout human history
1 zettabyte	10^{21}	As of 2014, the total amount of information stored globally on the World Wide Web was about 4–5 zettabytes
1 yottabyte	10^{24}	According to an article in Gizmodo,[1] a design and technology blog, storing 1 yottabyte of data on hard drives would require 1 million data centers that would fill the states of Rhode Island and Delaware

[1] www.gizmodo.com.au/2010/06/the-one-hundred-trillion-dollars-hard-drive/

One of the characteristics of random access memory is that the time to carry out either a fetch or a store operation is the same for all 2^N addresses. At current levels of technology, this time, called the memory access time, is typically about 5–10 nanoseconds (nanosecond = 1 nsec = 10^{-9} seconds = 1 billionth of a second). Also note that fetching and storing are allowed only to an entire cell. If we want, for example, to modify a single bit of memory, we first need to fetch the entire cell containing that bit, change the one bit, and then store the entire cell. The cell is the minimum accessible unit of memory.

There is one component of the memory unit shown in Figure 5.4 that we have not yet discussed, the *memory registers*. These two registers are used to implement the fetch and store operations. Both operations require two operands: the address of the cell being accessed and the value, either the value stored by the store operation or the value returned by the fetch operation.

The memory unit contains two special registers whose purpose is to hold these two operands. The memory address register (MAR) holds the address of the cell to be accessed. Because the MAR must be capable of holding any address, it must be at least N bits wide, where 2^N is the address space of the computer.

The memory data register (MDR) contains the data value being fetched or stored. We might be tempted to say that the MDR should be W bits wide, where W is the cell size. However, as mentioned earlier, on most computers the cell size is only 8 bits, and most data values occupy multiple cells. Thus the size of the MDR is usually a multiple of 8. Typical values of MDR width are 32 and 64 bits, which would allow us to fetch, in a single step, either an integer or a real value, respectively.

Given these two registers, we can describe a little more formally what happens during the fetch and store operations in a random access memory.

- Fetch(address)
    1. Load the address into the MAR.
    2. Decode the address in the MAR.
    3. Copy the contents of that memory location into the MDR.
- Store(address, value)
    1. Load the address into the MAR.
    2. Load the value into the MDR.
    3. Decode the address in the MAR.
    4. Store the contents of the MDR into that memory location.

For example, to retrieve the contents of cell 123, we would load the value 123 (in binary, of course) into the MAR and perform a fetch operation. When the operation is done, a copy of the contents of cell 123 would be in the MDR. (We may, for some operations, also automatically fetch the contents of memory cells immediately adjacent to cell 123, e.g., cells 124, 125, ...) To store the value 98 into cell 4, we load a 4 into the MAR and a 98 into the MDR and perform a store. When the operation is completed, the contents of cell 4 will have been set to 98, discarding whatever was there previously.

The operation "Decode the address in the MAR" means that the memory unit must translate the N-bit binary address stored in the MAR into the set of signals needed to access that one specific memory cell (or sequence of contiguous memory cells if that feature is allowed). That is, the memory unit must be able to convert the integer value 7, for example, in the MAR into the electronic signals needed to access *only* address 7 from all 2^N addresses in the memory unit. This might seem like magic, but it is actually a relatively easy task that applies ideas presented in the previous chapter. We can decode the address in the MAR using a decoder circuit of the type described in Section 4.5 and shown in Figure 4.36. (Remember that a decoder circuit has N inputs and 2^N outputs numbered 0, 1, 2, ... , $2^N - 1$. The circuit puts the signal 1 on the output line whose number equals the numeric value on the N input lines.) We simply copy the N bits in the MAR to the N input lines of a decoder circuit. Exactly one of its 2^N output lines is ON, and this line's identification number corresponds to the address value in the MAR.

For example, if $N = 4$ (the MAR contains 4 bits), then we have 16 addressable cells in our memory, numbered 0000 to 1111 (that is, 0 to 15). We could use a 4-to-16 decoder whose inputs are the 4 bits of the MAR. Each of the 16 output lines is associated with the one memory cell whose address is in the MAR and enables us to fetch or store its contents. This situation is shown in Figure 5.6.

If the MAR contains the 4-bit address 0010 (decimal 2), then only the output line labeled 0010 in Figure 5.6 is ON (that is, carries a value of 1). All others are OFF. The output line 0010 is associated with the unique memory cell that has memory address 2, and the appearance of an ON signal on this line causes the memory hardware to copy the contents of location 2 to the

FIGURE 5.6

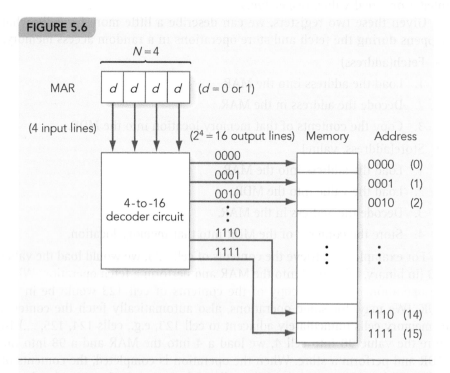

Organization of memory and the decoding logic

MDR if it is doing a fetch, or to load the contents of the MDR into location 2 if it is doing a store.

The only problem with the memory organization shown in Figure 5.6 is that it does not scale very well. That is, it cannot be used to build a large memory unit. For example, if the number of bits used to represent an address on our computer is 32, a decoder circuit with 32 input lines would have 2^{32}, or more than 4 billion, output lines. That is not a feasible design.

To solve this problem, memories are physically organized into a two-dimensional rather than a one-dimensional organization. In this structure, the 16-byte memory of Figure 5.6 would be organized into a two-dimensional 4×4 structure, rather than the one-dimensional 16×1 organization shown earlier. This two-dimensional layout is shown in Figure 5.7.

The memory locations are stored in *row major* order, with bytes 0–3 in row 0, bytes 4–7 in row 1 (01 in binary), bytes 8–11 in row 2 (10 in binary), and bytes 12–15 in row 3 (11 in binary). Each memory cell is connected to two selection lines, one called the *row selection line* and the other called the *column selection line*. When we send a signal down a single row selection line and a single column selection line, only the memory cell located at the *intersection* of these two selection lines carries out a memory fetch or a memory store operation.

How do we choose the correct row and column selection lines to access the proper memory cell? Instead of using one decoder circuit, we use two.

FIGURE 5.7

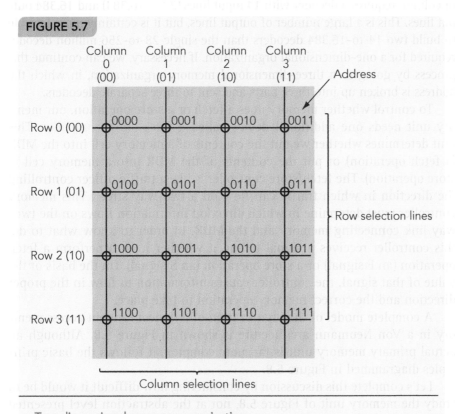

Two-dimensional memory organization

The first two binary digits of the addresses in Figure 5.7 are identical to the row number. Similarly, the last two binary digits of the addresses are identical to the column number. Thus, we should no longer view the MAR as being composed of a single 4-bit address, but as a 4-bit address made up of two distinct parts—the leftmost 2 bits, which specify the number of the row containing this cell, and the rightmost 2 bits, which specify the number of the column containing this cell. Each of these 2-bit fields is input to a separate decoder circuit that pulses, respectively, the correct row and column lines to access the desired memory cell.

For example, if the MAR contains the 4-bit value 1101 (a decimal 13), then the two high-order (leftmost) bits 11 are sent to the row decoder, whereas the two low-order (rightmost) bits 01 are sent to the column decoder. The row decoder sends a signal on the line labeled 11 (row 3), and the column decoder sends a signal on the line labeled 01 (column 1). Only the single memory cell in row 3, column 1 becomes active and performs the fetch or store operation. Figure 5.7 shows that the memory cell in row 3, column 1 is the correct one—the cell with memory address 1101.

The two-dimensional organization of Figure 5.7 is far superior to the one-dimensional structure in Figure 5.6 because it can accommodate a much larger number of cells. For example, a memory unit containing 256 MB (2^{28} bytes) is organized into a $16,384 \times 16,384$ two-dimensional array. To select any one row or column requires a decoder with 14 input lines ($2^{14} = 16,384$) and 16,384 output lines. This is a large number of output lines, but it is certainly more feasible to build two 14-to-16,384 decoders than the single 28-to-256 million decoder required for a one-dimensional organization. If necessary, we can continue this process by going to a three-dimensional memory organization, in which the address is broken up into three parts and sent to three separate decoders.

To control whether memory does a fetch or a store operation, our memory unit needs one additional device called a fetch/store controller. This unit determines whether we put the contents of a memory cell into the MDR (a fetch operation) or put the contents of the MDR into a memory cell (a store operation). The fetch/store controller is like a traffic officer controlling the direction in which traffic can flow on a two-way street. This memory controller must determine in which direction information flows on the two-way link connecting memory and the MDR. In order to know what to do, this controller receives a signal telling it whether it is to perform a fetch operation (an F signal) or a store operation (an S signal). On the basis of the value of that signal, the controller causes information to flow in the proper direction and the correct memory operation to take place.

A complete model of the organization of a typical random access memory in a Von Neumann architecture is shown in Figure 5.8. Although an actual primary memory unit is far more complex, it follows the basic principles diagrammed in Figure 5.8.

Let's complete this discussion by considering how difficult it would be to study the memory unit of Figure 5.8, not at the abstraction level presented in that diagram, but at the gate and circuit level presented in Chapter 4. Let's assume that our memory unit contains 2^{32} cells (4 GB), each byte

FIGURE 5.8

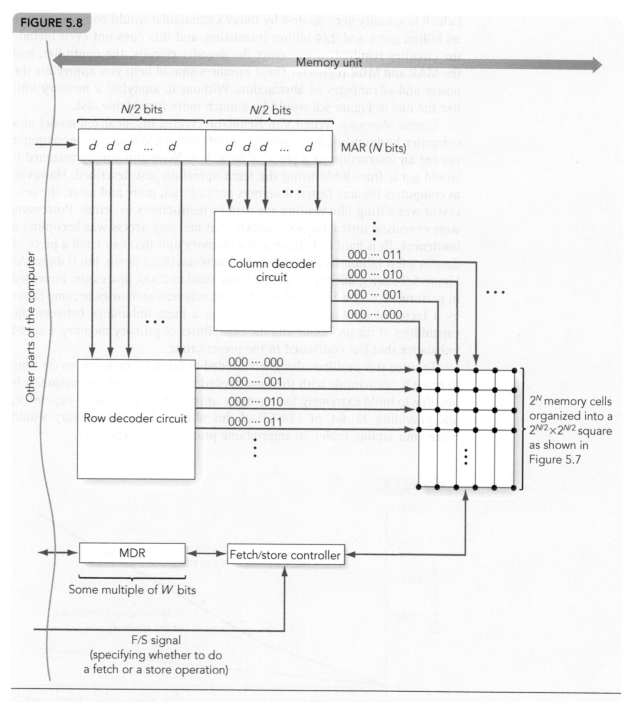

Overall RAM organization

containing 8 bits. There is a total of about 32 billion bits of storage in this memory unit. A typical memory circuit used to store a single bit generally requires about three gates (1 AND, 1 OR, and 1 NOT) containing seven transistors (3 per AND, 3 per OR, and 1 per NOT). Thus, our 4 GB memory unit (which is actually very modest by today's standards) would contain roughly 96 billion gates and 224 billion transistors, and this does not even include the circuitry required to construct the decoder circuits, the controller, and the MAR and MDR registers! These numbers should help you appreciate the power and advantages of abstraction. Without it, studying a memory unit like the one in Figure 5.8 would be a much more formidable task.

Cache Memory. When Von Neumann created his idealized model of a computer, he described only a single type of memory. Whenever the computer needed an instruction or a piece of data, Von Neumann simply assumed it would get it from RAM using the fetch operation just described. However, as computers became faster, designers noticed that, more and more, the processor was sitting idle waiting for data or instructions to arrive. Processors were executing instructions so quickly that memory access was becoming a bottleneck. (It is hard to believe that a memory unit that can fetch a piece of data in a few billionths of a second can slow anything down, but it does.) As Figure 5.9 shows, during the period from 1980 to 2000, processors increased in performance by a factor of about 3,000, whereas memories became faster by a factor of only about 10.[2] This led to a huge imbalance between the capabilities of the processor and the capabilities of primary memory, a speed imbalance that has continued to the present time.

To solve this problem, designers needed to decrease memory access time to make it comparable with the time needed to carry out an instruction. It is possible to build extremely fast memory units, but they are quite expensive, and providing 32, 64, or 128 GB of this ultra-high-speed memory would make your laptop, tablet, or smartphone prohibitively expensive.

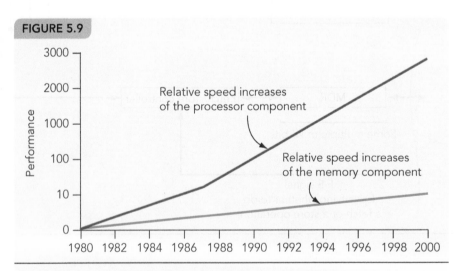

FIGURE 5.9

Changes in memory speed vs. processor speed over time

---

[2]From Hennessy, J., and Patterson, D. (2006). *Computer architecture: A quantitative approach* (4th ed.). Burlington, MA: Morgan Kaufmann.

However, computer designers discovered that in order to obtain a significant increase in speed it is not necessary to construct *all* of the memory from expensive, high-speed cells. They observed that when a program fetches a piece of data or an instruction, there is a high likelihood that

1. It will access that same instruction or piece of data in the very near future.

2. It will soon access the instructions or data that are located near that piece of data, where "near" means an address whose numerical value is close to this one.

Simply stated, this observation, called the principle of locality, says that when the computer uses something, it will probably use it again very soon, and it will probably use the "neighbors" of this item very soon. (Think about a loop in an algorithm that keeps repeating the same instruction sequence over and over.) To exploit this observation, the first time that the computer references a piece of data, it should copy that data from regular RAM memory to a special, high-speed memory unit called cache memory (pronounced "cash," from the French word *cacher*, meaning "to hide"). It should also copy the contents of memory cells located near this item into the cache. A cache is typically 5–10 times faster than RAM but much smaller—on the order of a few megabytes rather than a few dozen gigabytes. This limited size is not a problem because the computer does not keep all of the data there, just those items that were accessed most recently and that, presumably, will be needed again immediately. The organization of the "two-level memory hierarchy" is shown in Figure 5.10.

When the computer needs a piece of information, it does not immediately do the memory fetch operation described earlier. Instead, it carries out the following three steps:

1. Look first in cache memory to see whether the information is there. If it is, then the computer can access it at the higher speed of the cache.

2. If the desired information is not in the cache, then access it from RAM at the slower speed, using the fetch operation described earlier.

FIGURE 5.10

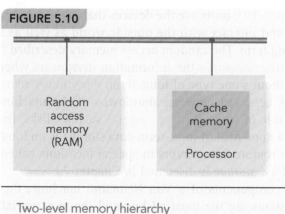

Two-level memory hierarchy

3. Copy the data just fetched into the cache along with the k immediately following memory locations. If the cache is full, then copy the new data into the cache so as to overwrite some of the older items that have not recently been accessed. (The assumption is that we will not need them again for a while.)

This algorithm significantly reduces the average time to access information. For example, assume that the average access time of our RAM is 10 nsec, whereas the average access time of the cache is 2 nsec. Furthermore, assume that the information we need is in the cache 70% of the time, a value called the cache hit rate. In this situation, 70% of the time we get what we need in 2 nsec, and 30% of the time we have wasted that 2 nsec because the information is not in the cache and must be obtained from RAM, which will take 10 nsec. Our overall average access time will now be

Average access time = $(0.70 \times 2) + 0.30 \times (2 + 10) = 5.0$ nsec

which is a 50% reduction in access time from the original value of 10 nsec. A higher cache hit rate can lead to even greater savings.

A good analogy to cache memory is a home refrigerator. Without one we would have to go to the grocery store every time we needed an item; this corresponds to slow, regular memory access. Instead, when we go to the store we buy not only what we need now but also what we think we will need in the near future, and we put those items into our refrigerator. Now, when we need something, we first check the refrigerator. If it is there, we can get it at a much higher rate of speed. We only need to go to the store when the food item we want is not there.

Caches are found on every modern computer system, and they are a significant contributor to the higher computational speeds achieved by new machines. (In fact, most modern processors have not just a single cache but two, three, or even four levels of cache memory, each serving a different purpose.) Even though the formal Von Neumann model contained only a single memory unit, most computers built today have a multilevel hierarchy of random access memory.

5.2.2 Input/Output and Mass Storage

The input/output (I/O) units are the devices that allow a computer system to communicate and interact with the outside world as well as store information for the long term. The random access memory described in the previous section is volatile memory—the information disappears when the power is turned off. Without some type of long-term, nonvolatile memory, information could not be saved between shutdowns of the machine. Nonvolatile storage is the role of mass storage systems such as disks, flash drives, and tapes. (Today, a good deal of long-term data storage is no longer on local I/O devices but on remote data servers in special locations called data centers. This type of *cloud storage* is discussed in Chapter 7.)

Of all the components of a Von Neumann machine, the I/O and mass storage subsystems are the most ad hoc and the most variable. Unlike the memory unit, I/O does not adhere to a single well-defined theoretical model. On the contrary, there are dozens of different I/O and mass storage devices

Practice Problems

Assume that our memory unit is organized as a 1,024 × 1,024 two-dimensional array of 8-bit bytes.

1. How big does the MAR register have to be?

2. How many bits of the MAR must be sent to the row decoder? To the column decoder?

3. Why is it unlikely that the size of the MDR register would be 8 bits?

4. If the average access time of this memory is 25 nsec and the average access time for cache memory is 10 nsec, what is the overall average access time if our cache hit rate is 80%?

5. What would happen to the overall average access time from Practice Problem 4 if we could somehow increase the cache hit rate to 90%?

6. In the previous problem, what would the cache hit rate have to be to reduce the average access time to 12.0 nsec?

7. If our memory stores signed integers using a two's complement representation and 8 bytes, what is the largest positive value that can be represented? The largest negative value?

8. Do you think that human memory is or is not a random access memory? Give an argument why or why not.

manufactured by dozens of different companies and exhibiting many alternative organizations, making generalizations difficult. However, two important principles transcend the device-specific characteristics of particular vendors—*I/O access methods* and *I/O controllers*.

Input/output devices come in two basic types: those that represent information in *human-readable* form for human consumption and those that store information in *machine-readable* form for access by a computer system. The former includes such well-known I/O devices as keyboards, both physical and virtual, screens, and printers. The latter group of devices includes flash memory, hard drives, DVDs, and streaming tapes. Mass storage devices themselves come in two distinct forms: direct access storage devices (DASDs) and sequential access storage devices (SASDs).

Our discussion on random access memory in Section 5.2.1 described the fundamental characteristics of *random* access:

1. Every memory cell has a unique address.

2. It takes the same amount of time to access every cell.

A *direct access storage device (DASD)* is one in which requirement number 2, equal access time, has been eliminated. That is, in a direct access storage device, every unit of information still has a unique address, but the time needed to access that information depends on its physical location and the current state of the device.

The best examples of DASDs are the types of disks listed earlier: hard drives, DVDs, and so on. A magnetic disk stores information in units called sectors, each of which contains an address and a data block containing a fixed number of bytes, illustrated in Figure 5.11. (*Note*: Flash memory devices and solid-state drives do not have rotating disks or the moveable read/write arms described in this section. They operate more like nonvolatile primary storage and should be considered as random access mass storage devices rather than direct access storage.)

A fixed number of these sectors are placed in a concentric circle on the surface of the disk, called a track, shown in Figure 5.12.

Finally, the surface of the disk contains many tracks, and there is a single *read/write head* that can be moved in or out to be positioned over any track on the disk surface. The entire disk rotates at high speed under the read/write head. The overall organization of a typical rotating disk is shown in Figure 5.13.

The access time to any individual sector of the disk is made up of three components: seek time, latency, and transfer time. Seek time is the time needed to position the read/write head over the correct track; latency is the time for the beginning of the desired sector to rotate under the read/write head; and transfer time is the time for the entire sector to pass under the read/write head and have its contents read into or written from memory. These values depend on the specific sector being accessed and the current position of the read/write head. Let's assume a disk drive with the following physical characteristics (msec = milliseconds):

> Rotation speed = 7,200 rev/min = 120 rev/sec = 8.33 msec/rev
>
>   (1 msec = 0.001 sec)
>
> Arm movement time = 0.02 msec to move to an adjacent track
>
>   (i.e., moving from track *i* to either track *i* + 1 or *i* − 1)
>
> Number of tracks/surface = 1,000 (numbered 0 to 999)
>
> Number of sectors/track = 64
>
> Number of bytes/sector = 1,024

FIGURE 5.11

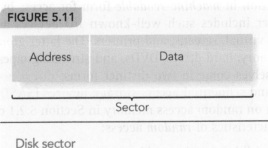

Disk sector

FIGURE 5.12

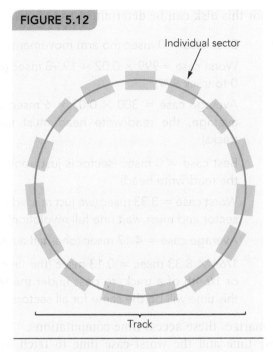

Individual sector

Track

A single disk track

FIGURE 5.13

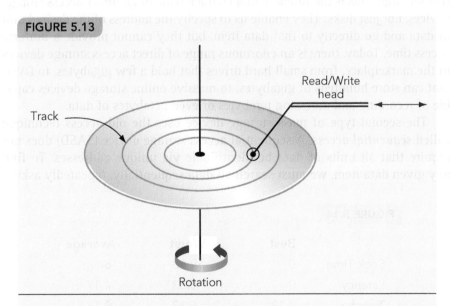

Read/Write head

Track

Rotation

Overall organization of a typical rotating disk

The access time for this disk can be determined as follows.

1. Seek Time   Best case = 0 msec (no arm movement)

Worst case = 999 × 0.02 = 19.98 msec (move from track 0 to track 999)

Average case = 300 × 0.02 = 6 msec (assume that on average, the read/write head must move about 300 tracks)

2. Latency   Best case = 0 msec (sector is just about to come under the read/write head)

Worst case = 8.33 msec (we just missed the first bit of the sector and must wait one full revolution)

Average case = 4.17 msec (one-half a revolution)

3. Transfer   1/64 × 8.33 msec = 0.13 msec (the time for one sector, or 1/64th of a track, to pass under the read/write head; this time will be the same for all sectors)

Figure 5.14 summarizes these access time computations.

The best-case time and the worst-case time to fetch or store a sector on the disk differ by a factor of more than 200, that is, 0.13 msec versus 28.44 msec. The average access time is about 10 msec, a typical value for current hard drive technology. However, even as direct access storage devices get faster and faster, this difference in best case versus worst case access times will remain large. This is the fundamental characteristic of all direct access storage devices, not just disks: They enable us to specify the address of the desired unit of data and go directly to that data item, but they cannot provide a uniform access time. Today, there is an enormous range of direct access storage devices in the marketplace, from small hard drives that hold a few gigabytes, to DVDs that can store hundreds of gigabytes, to massive online storage devices capable of recording and accessing terabytes or even petabytes of data.

The second type of mass storage device uses the old access technique called *sequential access*. A sequential access storage device (SASD) does not require that all units of data be identifiable via unique addresses. To find any given data item, we must search all data sequentially, repeatedly asking

FIGURE 5.14

	Best	Worst	Average
Seek Time	0	19.98	6
Latency	0	8.33	4.17
Transfer	0.13	0.13	0.13
Total	0.13	28.44	10.3

Example disk access times in milliseconds

the question, "Is this what I'm looking for?" If not, we move on to the next unit of data and ask the question again. Eventually we find what we are looking for or come to the end of the data.

A sequential access storage device behaves just like the old audio cassette tapes of the 1980s and 1990s. To locate a specific song, we run the tape for a while and then stop and listen. This process is repeated until we find the desired song or come to the end of the tape. In contrast, a direct access storage device behaves like a music DVD that numbers the songs and allows you to select any one. (The song number is the address.) Direct access storage devices are generally much faster at accessing individual pieces of information, and that is why they are much more widely used for mass storage. However, sequential access storage devices can be useful in specific situations, such as sequentially copying the entire contents of memory or of a disk drive. This backup operation fits the SASD model well, and *streaming tape backup units* are common storage devices on computer systems.

One of the fundamental characteristics of many (although not all) I/O devices is that they are very, very *slow* when compared with other components of a computer. For example, a typical memory access time is about 10 nsec. The time to complete the I/O operation "locate and read one disk sector" was shown in the previous example to be about 10 msec.

Units such as nsec (billionths of a second), μsec (millionths of a second), and msec (thousandths of a second) are so small compared with human time scales that it is sometimes difficult to appreciate the immense difference between values like 10 nsec and 10 msec. The difference between these two quantities is a factor of 1,000,000, that is, 6 orders of magnitude. Consider that this is the same order of magnitude difference as between 1 mile and 40 complete revolutions of the Earth's equator, or between 1 day and 30 centuries!

It is not uncommon for I/O operations such as displaying an image on a screen or printing a page on a printer to be 3, 4, 5, or even 6 orders of magnitude slower than any other aspect of computer operation. If there isn't something in the design of a computer to account for this difference, components that operate on totally incompatible time scales will be trying to talk to each other, which will produce enormous inefficiencies. The high-speed components will sit idle for long stretches of time while they wait for the slow I/O unit to accept or deliver the desired character. It would be like talking at the normal human rate of 240 words per minute (4 words per second) to someone who could respond only at the rate of 1 word every 8 hours—a difference of 5 orders of magnitude. You wouldn't get much useful work done!

One solution to this problem is to use a device called an I/O controller. An I/O controller is like a special-purpose computer whose responsibility is to handle the details of input/output and to compensate for any speed differences between I/O devices and other parts of the computer. It has a small amount of memory, called an *I/O buffer*, and enough *I/O control and logic* processing capability to handle the mechanical functions of the I/O device, such as the read/write head, paper feed mechanism, and screen display. It is also able to transmit to the processor a special hardware signal, called an interrupt signal, when an I/O operation is done. The organization of a typical I/O controller is shown in Figure 5.15.

FIGURE 5.15

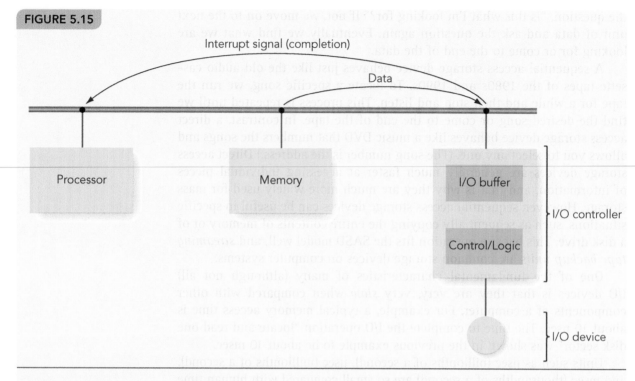

Organization of an I/O controller

Practice Problems

Assume a disk with the following characteristics:

Number of sectors per track = 20
Number of tracks per surface = 50
Number of surfaces = 2 (called a *double-sided* disk)
Number of characters per sector = 1,024
Arm movement time = 0.4 msec to move 1 track in any direction
Rotation speed = 2,400 rev/min

1. How many characters can be stored on this disk?

2. What are the best-case, worst-case, and average-case access times for this disk? (Assume that the average seek operation must move 20 tracks.)

3. What would be the average-case access time if we could increase the rotation speed from 2,400 rev/min to 7,200 rev/min?

4. What would be the average-case access time of the disk of the previous problem if we could reduce the arm movement time to 0.2 msec to move 1 track in any direction? (Again, assume that the average seek operation must move 20 tracks.)

5. *Defragmenting* a disk means to reorganize files on the disk so that as many pieces of the file as possible are stored in sectors on the same track, regardless of the surface it is on. Explain why defragmentation can be beneficial.

6. What would be the best-case, worst-case, and average-case access time of the disk in Problem 2 if we could reduce the seek time to 0.0? We could do this by having a separate read/write head for every track so there would be no arm motion. This type of "head per track" storage unit is often called a *drum*.

Let's assume that we want to display a 12-megapixel photograph on our tablet screen. First, the 12 million bits (assuming 1 bit per pixel; there may be more) representing the photograph are transferred from their current location in primary memory to the I/O buffer storage within the I/O controller. This operation takes place at the high-speed data transfer rates of most computer components—billions or tens of billions of bits per second. Once this information is in the I/O buffer, the processor can instruct the I/O controller to begin the output operation. The control logic of the I/O controller handles the actual transfer and display of these 12 million pixels to the screen. This transfer may be at a much slower rate—perhaps only hundreds or thousands or a few million bits per second. However, the processor does not have to sit idle for the one or two seconds it may take to display the image. It is free to do something else, perhaps work on another program. The potential slowness of the I/O operation now affects *only* the I/O controller. When all pixels have been displayed, the I/O controller sends an interrupt signal to the processor. The appearance of this special signal indicates to the processor that the I/O operation is finished.

5.2.3 The Arithmetic/Logic Unit

The arithmetic/logic unit (ALU) is the subsystem that performs such mathematical and logical operations as addition, subtraction, and comparison for equality. Although they can be conceptually viewed as separate components, in all modern machines the ALU and the control unit (discussed in the next section) have become fully integrated into a single component called the processor (the CPU). (Today, virtually all computers contain multiple processing elements called multicore CPUs. We will talk about this type of architecture in Section 5.4.) However, for reasons of clarity and convenience, we will describe the functions of the ALU and the control unit separately.

The ALU is made up of three parts: the registers, the interconnections between components, and the ALU circuitry. Together these components are called the data path.

A register is a special high-speed storage cell that holds the operands of an arithmetic operation and that, when the operation is complete, holds its result. Registers are quite similar to the random access memory cells described in the previous section, with the following minor differences:

- They do not have a numeric memory address but are accessed by a special *register designator* such as A, X, or R0.

- They can be accessed much more quickly than regular memory cells. Because there are only a few registers (typically, a few dozen up to a few hundred), it is reasonable to utilize the expensive circuitry needed to make the fetch and store operations 5–10 times faster than regular memory cells, of which there will be billions.

- They are not used for general-purpose storage but for specific purposes such as holding operands for an upcoming arithmetic computation.

For example, an ALU might have three special registers called A, B, and C. Registers A and B hold the two input operands, and register C holds the result. This organization is diagrammed in Figure 5.16.

In most cases, however, three registers are not nearly enough to hold all the values that we might need. A typical ALU will have somewhere between 16 and 128 registers. To see why this many ALU registers are needed, let's take a look at what happens during the evaluation of the expression $(a \,/\, b) \times (c - d)$. After we compute the expression $(a \,/\, b)$, it would be nice to keep this result temporarily in a high-speed ALU register while evaluating the second

FIGURE 5.16

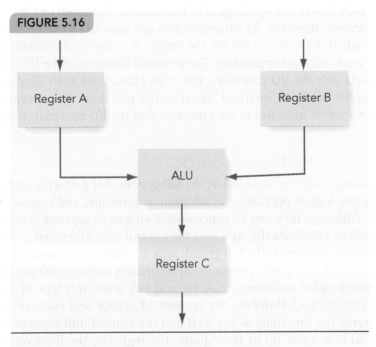

Three-register ALU organization

expression $(c - d)$. Of course, we could always store the result of (a / b) in a memory cell, but keeping it in a register allows the computer to fetch it more quickly when it is ready to complete the computation. In general, the more registers available in the ALU, the faster programs will run.

A more typical ALU organization is illustrated in Figure 5.17, which shows an ALU data path containing 16 registers designated R0–R15. Any of the 16 ALU registers in Figure 5.17 could be used to hold the operands of the computation, and any register could be used to store the result.

To perform an arithmetic operation with the ALU of Figure 5.17, we first move the operands from memory to the ALU registers. Then we specify which register holds the left operand by connecting that register to the communication path called "Left." In computer science terminology, a path for electrical

FIGURE 5.17

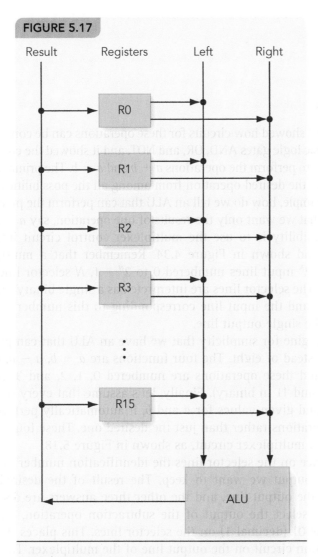

Multiregister ALU organization

signals is termed a bus. We then specify which register to use for the right operand by connecting it to the bus labeled "Right." (Like RAM, registers also use nondestructive fetch so that when it is needed, the value is only copied to the ALU. It is still in the register.) The ALU is enabled to perform the desired operation, and the answer is sent to any of the 16 registers along the bus labeled "Result." (The destructive store principle says that the previous contents of the destination register will be lost.) If desired, the result can be moved from an ALU register back into memory for longer-term storage.

The final component of the ALU is the ALU circuitry itself. These are the circuits that carry out such operations as

$a + b$ (Figure 4.32)
$a = b$ (Figure 4.28)
$a - b$
$a \times b$
a / b
$a < b$
$a > b$
a AND b

Chapter 4 showed how circuits for these operations can be constructed from the three basic logic gates AND, OR, and NOT, and it showed the construction of logic circuits to perform the operations $a + b$ and $a = b$. The primary concern is how to select the desired operation from among all the possibilities for a given ALU. For example, how do we tell an ALU that can perform the preceding eight operations that we want only the results of one operation, say $a - b$?

One possibility is to use the multiplexer control circuit introduced in Chapter 4 and shown in Figure 4.34. Remember that a multiplexer is a circuit with 2^N input lines numbered 0 to $2^N - 1$, N selector lines, and one output line. The selector lines are interpreted as a single binary number from 0 to $2^N - 1$, and the input line corresponding to this number has its value placed on the single output line.

Let's imagine for simplicity that we have an ALU that can perform four functions instead of eight. The four functions are $a + b$, $a - b$, $a = b$, and a AND b, and these operations are numbered 0, 1, 2, and 3, respectively (00, 01, 10, and 11 in binary). Finally, let's assume that every time the ALU is enabled and given values for a and b, it automatically performs all four possible operations rather than just the desired one. These four outputs can be input to a multiplexer circuit, as shown in Figure 5.18.

Now place on the selector lines the identification number of the operation whose output we want to keep. The result of the desired operation appears on the output line, and the other three answers are discarded. For example, to select the output of the subtraction operation, we input the binary value 01 (decimal 1) on the selector lines. This places the output of the subtraction circuit on the output line of the multiplexer. The outputs of the addition, comparison, and AND circuits are discarded.

FIGURE 5.18

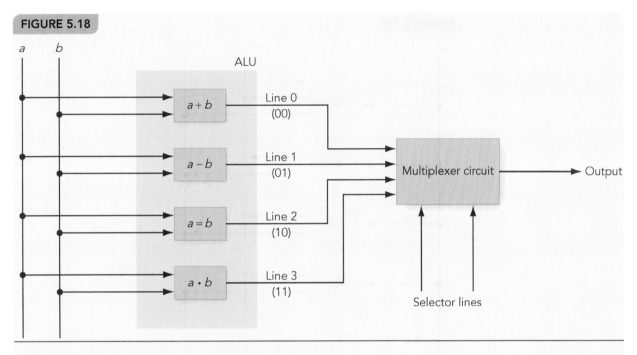

Using a multiplexer circuit to select the proper ALU result

Thus, one possible design philosophy for building an ALU is not to have it perform only the correct operation. Instead, it is to have *every* ALU circuit "do its thing" but then keep only the one desired answer.

Putting Figures 5.17 and 5.18 together produces the overall organization of the ALU of the Von Neumann architecture. This model is shown in Figure 5.19.

5.2.4 The Control Unit

The most fundamental characteristic of the Von Neumann architecture is the stored program—a sequence of machine language instructions stored as binary values in memory. It is the task of the control unit to (1) *fetch* from memory the next instruction to be executed, (2) *decode* it—that is, determine what is to be done, and (3) *execute* it by issuing the appropriate command to the ALU, memory, or I/O controllers. These three steps are repeated over and over until we reach the last instruction in the program, typically something called HALT, STOP, or QUIT.

To understand the behavior of the control unit, we must first investigate the characteristics of machine language instructions.

Machine Language Instructions. The instructions that can be decoded and executed by the control unit of a computer are represented in machine language. Instructions in this language are expressed in binary, and a typical format is shown in Figure 5.20.

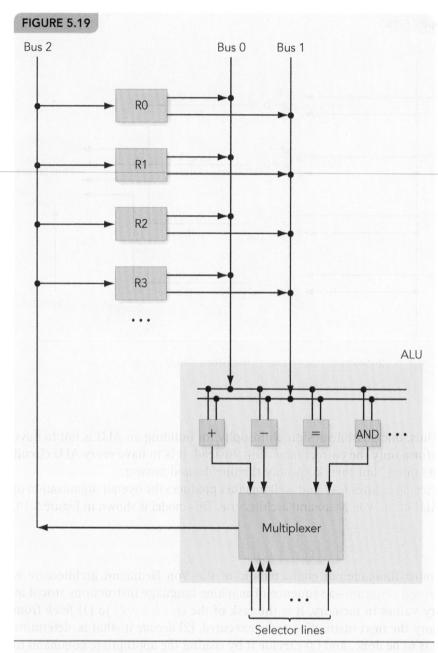

FIGURE 5.19

Bus 2   Bus 0   Bus 1

RO

R1

R2

R3

• • •

ALU

+   −   =   AND • • •

Multiplexer

• • •

Selector lines

Overall ALU organization

The *operation code* field (referred to by the shorthand phrase *op code*) is a unique unsigned integer value assigned to each machine language operation recognized by the hardware. For example, 0 could be an ADD, 1 could be a COMPARE, and so on. If the operation code field contains k bits, then the maximum number of unique machine language operation codes is 2^k.

The *address field(s)* are the memory addresses of the values on which this operation will work. If our computer has a maximum of 2^N memory cells,

FIGURE 5.20

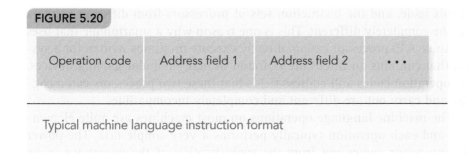

Typical machine language instruction format

then each address field must be *N* bits wide to enable us to address every cell because it takes *N* binary digits to represent all addresses in the range 0 to $2^N - 1$. The number of address fields in an instruction typically ranges from 0 to about 3, depending on what the operation is and how many operands it needs to do its work. For example, an instruction to add the contents of memory cell X to memory cell Y requires at least two addresses, X and Y. It could require three if the result were stored in a location different from either operand. In contrast, an instruction that tests the contents of memory cell X to see whether it is negative needs only a single address field, the location of cell X.

To see what this might produce in terms of machine language instructions, let's see what the following hypothetical instruction would actually look like when stored in memory.

Operation   Meaning

ADD X, Y   Add contents of memory addresses X and Y
and put the sum back into memory address Y.

Let's assume that the op code for ADD is a decimal 9, X and Y correspond to memory addresses 99 and 100 (decimal), and the format of instructions is

op code	address 1	address 2
8	16	16

bits →

A decimal 9, in 8-bit binary, is 00001001. Address 99, when converted to an unsigned 16-bit binary value, is 0000000001100011. Address 100 is 1 greater: 0000000001100100. Putting these values together produces the instruction ADD X, Y as it would appear in memory:

00001001   0000000001100011   0000000001100100
op code   *address 1*   *address 2*

This is somewhat cryptic to a person, but is easily understood by a control unit.

The set of all operations that can be executed by a processor is called its instruction set, and the choice of exactly which operations to include or exclude from the instruction set is one of the most important and difficult decisions in the design of a new computer. There is no universal agreement on this issue, and the instruction sets of processors from different vendors may be completely different. This is one reason why a smartphone that uses the Apple A10 processor cannot directly execute programs written for a system that contains an Intel Core i7 found in many popular gaming devices. The operation codes and address fields that these two processors can recognize and carry out are different and completely incompatible.

The machine language operations on most machines are quite elementary, and each operation typically performs a very simple task. The power of a processor comes not from the sophistication of the operations in its instruction set but from the fact that it can execute each instruction very quickly, typically in a few billionths of a second.

One approach to designing instruction sets is to make them as small and as simple as possible, with perhaps as few as 30–50 instructions. Machines with this sort of instruction set are called *reduced instruction set computers* or RISC machines. This approach minimizes the amount of hardware circuitry (gates and transistors) needed to build a processor. The extra space on the chip can be used to optimize the speed of the instructions and allow them to execute very quickly. A RISC processor may require more instructions to solve a problem (because the instructions are so simple), but this is compensated for by the fact that each instruction executes much faster so the overall running time is less. The opposite philosophy is to include a much larger number, say 300–500, of very powerful instructions in the instruction set. These types of processors are called *complex instruction set computers*, or CISC machines, and they are designed to directly provide a wide range of powerful features so that finished programs for these processors are shorter. Of course, CISC machines are more complex, more expensive, and more difficult to build. As is often the case in life, it turns out that compromise is the best path—most modern processors use a mix of the two design philosophies.

A little later in this chapter, we will present an instruction set for a hypothetical computer to examine how machine language instructions are executed by a control unit. For clarity, we will not show these instructions in binary, as we did earlier. Instead, we will write out the operation code in English (for example, ADD, COMPARE, MOVE) rather than binary; use the capital letters X, Y, and Z to symbolically represent binary memory addresses; and use the letter R to represent an ALU register. Remember, however, that this notation is just for convenience. All machine language instructions are stored internally using binary representation.

Machine language instructions can be grouped into four basic classes called data transfer, arithmetic, compare, and branch.

1. *Data transfer.* These operations move information between or within the different components of the computer—for example:

> Memory cell → ALU register
>
> ALU register → memory cell
>
> One memory cell → another memory cell
>
> One ALU register → another ALU register

All data transfer instructions follow the nondestructive fetch/destructive store principle described earlier. That is, the contents of the *source cell* (where it is now) are never destroyed, only copied. The contents of the *destination cell* (where it is going) are overwritten, and its previous contents are lost.

Examples of data transfer operations include the following:

Operation	Meaning
LOAD X	Load register R with the contents of memory cell X.
STORE X	Store the contents of register R into memory cell X.
MOVE X,Y	Copy the contents of memory cell X into memory cell Y.

2. *Arithmetic*. These operations cause the arithmetic/logic unit to perform a computation. Typically, they include arithmetic operations like +, −, ×, and /, as well as logical operations such as AND, OR, and NOT. Depending on the instruction set, the operands may reside in memory or they may be in an ALU register.

Possible formats for arithmetic operations include the following examples. (*Note*: The notation CON(X) means the contents of memory address X.)

Operation	Meaning
ADD X,Y, Z	Add the contents of memory cell X to the contents of memory cell Y and put the result into memory cell Z. This is called a *three-address instruction*, and it performs the operation CON(Z) = CON(X) + CON(Y).
ADD X,Y	Add the contents of memory cell X to the contents of memory cell Y. Put the result back into memory cell Y. This is called a *two-address instruction*, and it performs the operation CON(Y) = CON(X) + CON(Y).
ADD X	Add the contents of memory cell X to the contents of register R. Put the result back into register R. This is called a *one-address instruction*, and it performs the operation R = CON(X) + R. (Of course, R must be loaded with the proper value before executing the instruction.)

Other arithmetic operations such as SUBTRACT, MULTIPLY, DIVIDE, AND, and OR would be structured in a similar fashion.

3. *Compare*. These operations compare two values and set an indicator on the basis of the results of the compare. Most Von Neumann machines have a special set of bits inside the processor called *condition codes* (or a special register called a *status register* or *condition register*); these bits are set by the compare operations. For example, assume there are three 1-bit condition codes called GT, EQ, and LT that stand for greater than, equal to, and less than, respectively. The operation

Operation	Meaning
COMPARE X,Y	Compare the contents of memory cell X to the contents of memory cell Y and set the condition codes accordingly. Assume memory cells X and Y hold signed integer values.

would set these three condition codes in the following way:

Condition	How the Condition Codes Are Set
CON (X) > CON (Y)	GT = 1 EQ = 0 LT = 0
CON (X) = CON (Y)	GT = 0 EQ = 1 LT = 0
CON (X) < CON (Y)	GT = 0 EQ = 0 LT = 1

4. *Branch.* These operations alter the normal sequential flow of control. The normal mode of operation of a Von Neumann machine is *sequential.* After completing the instruction in address i, the control unit executes the instruction in address $i + 1$. (*Note*: If each instruction occupies k memory cells rather than 1, then after finishing the instruction starting in address i, the control unit executes the instruction starting in address $i + k$. In the following discussions, we assume for simplicity that each instruction occupies one memory cell.) The *branch instructions* can alter this sequential mode.

Typically, determining whether to branch is based on the current settings of the condition codes. Thus, a branch instruction is almost always preceded by either a compare instruction or some other instruction that sets the condition codes. Typical branch instructions include the following:

Operation	Meaning
JUMP X	Take the next instruction unconditionally from memory cell X.
JUMPGT X	If the GT indicator is a 1, take the next instruction from memory cell X. Otherwise, take the next instruction from the next sequential location.

(JUMPEQ and JUMPLT would work similarly on the other two condition codes.)

JUMPGE X	If *either* the GT or the EQ indicator is a 1, take the next instruction from memory location X. Otherwise, take the next instruction from the next sequential location.

(JUMPLE and JUMPNEQ would work in a similar fashion.)

HALT	Stop program execution. Don't go on to the next instruction.

These are some of the typical instructions that a Von Neumann computer can decode and execute. Problem 2 in the Challenge Work at the end of this chapter asks you to investigate the instruction set of a real processor found inside a modern computer and compare it with what we have described here.

The instructions presented here are quite simple and easy to understand. The power of a Von Neumann computer comes not from having thousands of built-in, high-level instructions but from the ability to combine a great number of these rather simple instructions into large, complex programs that can be executed extremely quickly. Figure 5.21 shows examples of how these simple machine language instructions can be combined to carry out some of the high-level algorithmic operations first introduced in Level 1 and shown in Figure 2.9. (The examples assume that the variables a, b, and c are stored in memory locations 100, 101, and 102, respectively, and that the instructions occupy one cell each and are located in memory locations 50, 51, 52, ...)

FIGURE 5.21

Address	Contents
100	Value of *a*
101	Value of *b*
102	Value of *c*

Algorithmic notation	Machine language instruction sequences		
	Address	Contents	(commentary)
		⋮	
1. Set *a* to the value *b*+*c*	50	LOAD 101	Put the value of *b* into register R.
	51	ADD 102	Add *c* to register R. It now holds *b* + *c*.
	52	STORE 100	Store the contents of register R into *a*.
2. If *a*>*b* then	50	COMPARE 100, 101	Compare *a* and *b* and set condition codes.
set *c* to the value *a*	51	JUMPGT 54	Go to location 54 if *a*>*b*.
Else	52	MOVE 101, 102	Get here if *a* ≤ *b*, so move *b* into *c*
set *c* to the value *b*	53	JUMP 55	and skip the next instruction.
	54	MOVE 100, 102	Move *a* into *c*.
	55	• • •	Next statement begins here.

Examples of simple machine language instruction sequences

Don't worry if these "miniprograms" are a little confusing. We treat the topic of machine language programming in more detail in the next chapter. For now, we simply want you to know what machine language instructions look like so that we can see how to build a control unit to carry out their functions.

Control Unit Registers and Circuits. It is the task of the control unit to fetch and execute instructions of the type shown in Figures 5.20 and 5.21. To accomplish this task, the control unit relies on two special registers called the program counter (PC) and the instruction register (IR) and on an *instruction decoder circuit*. The organization of these three components is shown in Figure 5.22.

FIGURE 5.22

Bus

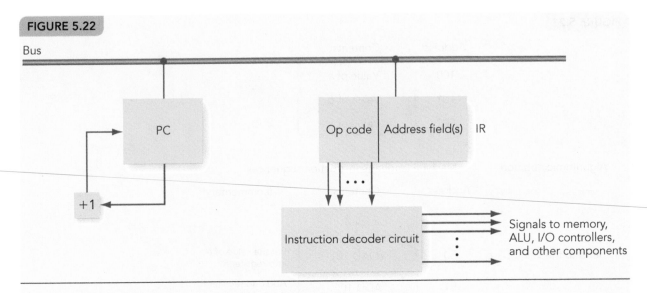

Organization of the control unit registers and circuits

Practice Problems

Assume that the variables a, b, c, and d are stored in memory locations 100, 101, 102, and 103, respectively, and that the constant value +1 is stored in memory location 104. Using any of the sample machine language instructions given in this section, translate the following pseudocode operations into machine language instruction sequences. Have your instruction sequences begin in memory location 50.

1. Set a to the value b + c + d

2. Set a to the value (b × d) − (c/d)

3. Set a to the value (a − 1)

4. If (a = b) then set c to the value of d

5. If (a ≤ b) then

    Set c to the value of d

  Else

    Set c to the value of 2d (that is, d + d)

6. Initialize a to the value d

  While a ≤ c

    Set a to the value (a + b)

  End of the loop

The program counter holds the address of the *next* instruction to be executed. It is like a "pointer" specifying which address in memory the control unit must go to in order to get the next instruction. To get that instruction, the control unit sends the contents of the PC to the MAR in memory and executes the Fetch(address) operation described in Section 5.2.1. For example, if the PC holds the value 73 (in binary, of course), then when the current instruction is finished, the control unit sends the value 73 to the MAR and fetches the instruction contained in cell 73. The PC gets incremented by 1 after each fetch because the normal mode of execution in a Von Neumann machine is sequential. (Again, we are assuming that each instruction occupies one cell. If an instruction occupied k cells, then the PC would be incremented by k.) Therefore, the PC frequently has its own incrementor $(+1)$ circuit to allow this operation to be done quickly and efficiently.

The instruction register (IR) holds a copy of the instruction just fetched from memory. The IR holds both the op code portion of the instruction, abbreviated IR_{op}, and the address(es), abbreviated IR_{addr}.

To determine what instruction is in the IR, the op code portion of the IR must be decoded using an *instruction decoder*. This is the same type of decoder circuit discussed in Section 4.5 and used in the construction of the memory unit (Figure 5.8). The k bits of the op code field of the IR are sent to the instruction decoder, which interprets them as a numerical value between 0 and $2^k - 1$. Exactly one of the 2^k output lines of the decoder is set to a 1—specifically, the output line whose identification number matches the operation code of this instruction.

Figure 5.23 shows a decoder that accepts a 3-bit op code field and has $2^3 = 8$ output lines, one for each of the eight possible machine language operations. The 3 bits of the IR_{op} are fed into the instruction decoder, and they are interpreted as a value from 000 (0) to 111 (7). If the bits are, for example, 000, then line 000 in Figure 5.23 is set to a 1. This line enables the ADD operation because the operation code for ADD is 000. When a 1 appears on this line, the ADD operation (1) fetches the two operands of the add and sends them to the ALU; (2) has the ALU perform all of its possible operations; (3) selects the output of the adder circuit, discarding all others; and (4) moves the result of the add to the correct location.

If the op code bits are 001 instead, then line 001 in Figure 5.23 is set to a 1. This time the LOAD operation is enabled because the operation code for LOAD is the binary value 001. Instead of performing the previous four steps, the hardware carries out the LOAD operation by: (1) sending the value of IR_{addr} to the MAR in the memory unit, (2) fetching the contents of that address and putting them in the MDR, and (3) copying the contents of the MDR into ALU register R.

For every one of the 2^k machine language operations in our instruction set, there exists the circuitry needed to carry out, step-by-step, function of that operation. The instruction decoder has 2^k output lines, and each output line enables the circuitry that performs the desired operation.

FIGURE 5.23

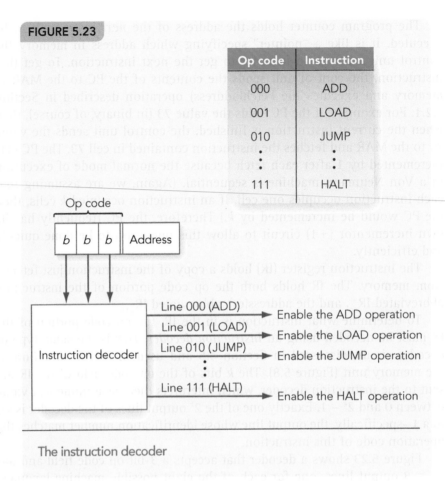

Op code	Instruction
000	ADD
001	LOAD
010	JUMP
⋮	⋮
111	HALT

The instruction decoder

5.3 Putting the Pieces Together— the Von Neumann Architecture

We have now described each of the four components that make up the Von Neumann architecture:

- Memory (Figure 5.8)

- Input/output (Figure 5.15)

- ALU (Figure 5.19)

- Control unit (Figures 5.22 and 5.23)

This section puts these pieces together and shows how the entire model functions. The overall organization of a Von Neumann computer is shown in Figure 5.24. Although highly idealized and simplified, the structure in this diagram is quite similar to virtually every computer, tablet, and smartphone ever built!

FIGURE 5.24

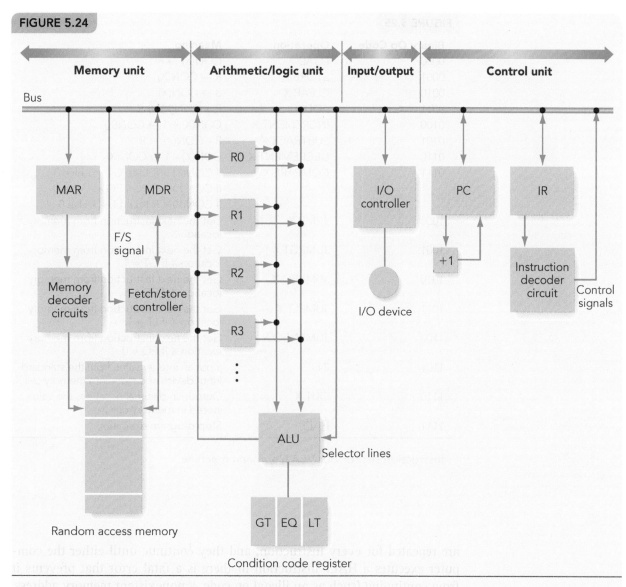

The organization of a Von Neumann computer

To see how the Von Neumann machine of Figure 5.24 executes instructions, let's pick a hypothetical instruction set for our system, as shown in Figure 5.25. We will use the same instruction set in the Laboratory Experience for this chapter and again in Chapter 6 when we introduce and study assembly languages. (*Reminder*: CON(X) means the contents of memory cell X; R stands for an ALU register; and GT, EQ, and LT are condition codes that have the value of 1 for ON and 0 for OFF.)

The execution of a program on the computer shown in Figure 5.24 proceeds in three distinct phases: *fetch*, *decode*, and *execute*. These three steps

FIGURE 5.25

Binary Op Code	Operation	Meaning
0000	LOAD X	CON(X) → R
0001	STORE X	R → CON(X)
0010	CLEAR X	0 → CON(X)
0011	ADD X	R + CON(X) → R
0100	INCREMENT X	CON(X) + 1 → CON(X)
0101	SUBTRACT X	R – CON(X) → R
0110	DECREMENT X	CON(X) – 1 → CON(X)
0111	COMPARE X	if CON(X) > R then GT = 1 else 0
		if CON(X) = R then EQ = 1 else 0
		if CON(X) < R then LT = 1 else 0
1000	JUMP X	Get the next instruction from memory location X.
1001	JUMPGT X	Get the next instruction from memory location X if GT = 1.
1010	JUMPEQ X	Get the next instruction from memory location X if EQ = 1.
1011	JUMPLT X	Get the next instruction from memory location X if LT = 1.
1100	JUMPNEQ X	Get the next instruction from memory location X if EQ = 0.
1101	IN X	Input an integer value from the standard input device and store into memory cell X.
1110	OUT X	Output, in decimal notation, the value stored in memory cell X.
1111	HALT	Stop program execution.

Instruction set for our Von Neumann machine

are repeated for every instruction, and they continue until either the computer executes a HALT instruction or there is a fatal error that prevents it from continuing (such as an illegal op code, a nonexistent memory address, or division by zero). Algorithmically, the process can be described as follows:

While we do not have a HALT instruction or a fatal error

Fetch phase

Decode phase

Execute phase

End of the loop

This repetition of the fetch/decode/execute phase is called the *Von Neumann cycle*. To describe the behavior of our computer during each of these three phases, we will use the following notational conventions:

CON(A)   The contents of memory cell A. We assume that an instruction occupies 1 cell.

A → B   Send the value stored in register A to register B. The following abbreviations refer to the special registers and functional units of the Von Neumann architecture introduced in this chapter:

PC	The program counter
MAR	The memory address register
MDR	The memory data register
IR	The instruction register, which is further divided into IR_{op} and IR_{addr}
ALU	The arithmetic/logic unit
R	Any ALU register
GT, EQ, LT	The condition codes of the ALU
+1	A special increment unit attached to the PC

FETCH   Initiate a memory fetch operation (that is, send an F signal on the F/S control line of Figure 5.24).

STORE   Initiate a memory store operation (that is, send an S signal on the F/S control line of Figure 5.24).

ADD   Instruct the ALU to select the output of the adder circuit (that is, place the code for ADD on the ALU selector lines shown in Figure 5.24).

SUBTRACT   Instruct the ALU to select the output of the subtract circuit (that is, place the code for SUBTRACT on the ALU selector lines shown in Figure 5.24).

A. *Fetch phase.* During the fetch phase, the control unit gets the next instruction from memory and moves it into the IR. The fetch phase is the same for every instruction and consists of the following four steps.

     1. PC → MAR   Send the address in the PC to the MAR register.

     2. FETCH   Initiate a fetch operation using the address in the MAR. The contents of that cell are placed in the MDR.

     3. MDR → IR   Move the instruction in the MDR to the instruction register so that we are ready to decode it during the next phase.

     4. PC + 1 → PC   Send the contents of the PC to the incrementor and put it back. This points the PC to the next instruction.

The control unit now has the current instruction in the IR and has updated the program counter so that it will correctly fetch the next instruction when the execution of this instruction is completed. It is ready to begin decoding and executing the current instruction.

B. *Decode phase.* Decoding the instruction is simple because all that needs to be done is to send the op code portion of the IR to the instruction decoder, which determines its type. The op code is the 4-bit binary value in the first column of Figure 5.25.

1. $IR_{op} \rightarrow$ instruction decoder

The instruction decoder generates the proper control signals to activate the circuitry to carry out the instruction.

C. *Execution phase.* The specific actions that occur during the execution phase are different for each instruction. Therefore, there will be a unique set of circuitry for each of the 2^k distinct instructions in the instruction set. The control unit circuitry generates the necessary sequence of control signals and data transfer signals to the other units (ALU, memory, and I/O) to carry out the intent of this instruction. The following examples show what signals and transfers take place during the execution phase of some of the instructions in Figure 5.25 using the Von Neumann model of Figure 5.24.

a) LOAD X   Meaning: Load register R with the current contents of memory cell X.

   1. $IR_{addr} \rightarrow$ MAR   Send address X (currently in IR_{addr}) to the MAR.

   2. FETCH   Fetch contents of cell X and place that value in the MDR.

   3. MDR $\rightarrow$ R   Copy the contents of the MDR into register R.

b) STORE X   Meaning: Store the current contents of register R into memory cell X.

   1. $IR_{addr} \rightarrow$ MAR   Send address X (currently in IR_{addr}) to the MAR.

   2. R $\rightarrow$ MDR   Send the contents of register R to the MDR.

   3. STORE   Store the value in the MDR into memory cell X.

c) ADD X   Meaning: Add the contents of cell X to the contents of register R and put the result back into register R.

   1. $IR_{addr} \rightarrow$ MAR   Send address X (currently in IR_{addr}) to the MAR.

   2. FETCH   Fetch the contents of cell X and place it in the MDR.

   3. MDR $\rightarrow$ ALU   Send the two operands of the ADD to the ALU.

   4. R $\rightarrow$ ALU

   5. ADD   Activate the ALU and select the output of the ADD circuit as the desired result.

   6. ALU $\rightarrow$ R   Copy the selected result into the R register.

d) JUMP X   Meaning: Jump to the instruction located in memory location X.

   1. $IR_{addr} \rightarrow$ PC   Send address X to the PC so the instruction stored there is fetched during the next fetch phase.

e) COMPARE X   Meaning: Determine whether CON(X) < R, CON(X) = R, or CON(X) > R, and set the condition codes GT, EQ, and LT to appropriate values. (Assume all codes are initially 0.)

1. $IR_{addr} \rightarrow MAR$ Send address X to the MAR.

2. FETCH   Fetch the contents of cell X and place it in the MDR.

3. $MDR \rightarrow ALU$ Send the contents of address X and register R to the ALU.

4. $R \rightarrow ALU$

5. SUBTRACT   Evaluate CON(X) − R. The result is not saved, and is used only to set the condition codes. If CON(X) − R > 0, then CON(X) > R and set GT to 1. If CON(X) − R = 0, then they are equal and set EQ to 1. If CON(X) − R < 0, then CON(X) < R and set LT to 1.

f) JUMPGT X   Meaning: If GT condition code is 1, jump to the instruction in location X. We do this by loading the address field of the IR, which is the address of location X, into the PC. Otherwise, continue to the next instruction.

1. IF GT = 1 THEN $IR_{addr} \rightarrow PC$

These are six examples of the sequence of signals and transfers that occur during the execution phase of the fetch/decode/execute cycle. There is a unique sequence of actions for each of the 16 instructions in the sample instruction set of Figure 5.25 and for the approximately 50–300 instructions in the instruction set of a typical Von Neumann computer. When the execution of one instruction is done, the control unit fetches the next instruction, starting the cycle all over again. That is the fundamental sequential behavior of the Von Neumann architecture.

These six examples clearly illustrate the concept of abstraction at work. In Chapter 4, we built complex arithmetic/logic circuits to do operations like addition and comparison. Using these circuits, this chapter describes a computer that can execute machine language instructions such as ADD X and COMPARE X,Y. A machine language instruction such as ADD X is a complicated concept, but it is quite a bit easier to understand than the enormously detailed full adder circuit shown in Figure 4.32, which contains 800 gates and more than 2,000 transistors.

Abstraction has allowed us to replace a complex sequence of gate-level manipulations with the single machine language command ADD, which does addition without our having to know how—the very essence of abstraction. Well, why should we stop here? Machine language commands, although better than hardware, are hardly user friendly. (Some might even call them "user intimidating.") Programming in binary and writing sequences of instructions such as

0101101000011110010100001

is cumbersome, confusing, and very error-prone. Why not take these machine language instructions and make them more user oriented and user friendly?

An Alphabet Soup of Speed Measures: MHz, GHz, MIPS, and GFLOPS

It is easy to identify the fastest car, plane, or train—just compare their top speeds in miles per hour (or kilometers per hour) and pick the greatest. However, in the computer arena things are not so simple, and there are many different measures of speed.

The unit you might be most familiar with is *clock speed*, measured in billions of cycles per second, called gigahertz (GHz). The actions of every computer are controlled by a central clock, and the "tick" rate of this clock is one possible speed measure. Processors today have clock rates of about 3–5 GHz, while the fastest processor on the market has a clock rate of 8.80 GHz. However, clock speed can be misleading because a machine's capability depends not only on the tick rate but also on how much work it can do during each tick. If machine A has a clock rate twice as fast as machine B, but each instruction on machine A takes twice as many clock cycles as machine B to complete, then there is no discernible speed difference.

Therefore, a more accurate measure of machine speed is *instruction rate*, measured in MIPS, an acronym for millions of instructions per second, or GIPS, billions of instructions per second. The instruction rate measures how many machine language instructions of the type listed in Figure 5.25 (e.g., LOAD, STORE, COMPARE, ADD) can be fetched, decoded, and executed in one second. If a computer completes one instruction for every clock cycle, then the instruction rate is identical to the clock rate. However, many instructions require multiple clock ticks, whereas parallel computers can often complete multiple instructions in a single tick. Thus, MIPS and GIPS are a better measure of performance because they can tell you how much work is actually being done, in terms of completed instructions, in a given amount of time.

Finally, some people are only interested in how fast a computer executes the subset of instructions most important to their applications. For example, scientific programs do an enormous amount of floating-point (i.e., decimal) arithmetic, so the computers that execute these programs must be able to execute arithmetic instructions as fast as possible. For these machines, a better measure of speed might be the *floating-point instruction rate*, measured in GFLOPS—billions of floating-point operations per second, TFLOPS, trillions of floating point operations per second, or PFLOPS, quadrillions of floating point operations per second. These are like MIPS and GIPS, except the instructions we focus most closely on are those for adding, subtracting, multiplying, and dividing real numbers.

So, as you can see, there is no universally agreed upon measure of computer speed, and that is what allows different computer vendors all to stand up and claim, "My machine is the fastest!"

Laboratory Experience 9

This Laboratory Experience introduces a software package that simulates the behavior of a Von Neumann computer. It will give you a chance to work with and observe the behavior of a Von Neumann machine quite similar to the one shown in Figure 5.24. Our simulated computer contains the same functional units introduced in this section, including memory, registers, arithmetic/logic unit, and control unit, and it uses the instruction set shown in Figure 5.25. The simulator allows you to observe the step-by-step execution of machine language instructions and watch the flow of information that occurs during the fetch, decode, and execute phases. It also allows you to write and execute your own machine language programs.

Why not give them features that allow us to write correct, reliable, and efficient programs more easily? Why not develop *user-oriented programming languages* designed for people, not machines? This is the next level of abstraction in our hierarchy, and we introduce that important concept in Level 3 of the text.

5.4 Non–Von Neumann Architectures

The Von Neumann architecture, which is the central theme of this chapter, has served the field well for over 60 years, but some computer scientists believe it may be reaching the end of its useful life.

The problems that computers are being asked to solve have grown significantly in size and complexity since the appearance of the first-generation machines in the late 1940s and early 1950s. Designers have been able to keep up with these larger and larger problems by building faster and faster Von Neumann machines. Through advances in hardware design, manufacturing methods, and circuit technology, computer designers have been able to take the basic sequential architecture described by Von Neumann in 1946 and improve its performance by four or five orders of magnitude. First-generation machines were able to execute about 10,000 machine language instructions per second. By the second generation, that had grown to about 1 million instructions per second. Today, even a small desktop PC can perform 1 billion instructions per second, whereas larger and more powerful workstations can execute instructions at the rate of 10–20 billion instructions per second. Figure 5.26 shows the changes in computer speeds from the mid-1940s to the present.

(*Note*: The graph shown in Figure 5.26 is logarithmic. Each unit on the vertical axis is 10 times the previous one.) The period from about 1945 to about 1970 is characterized by exponential increases in computation

FIGURE 5.26

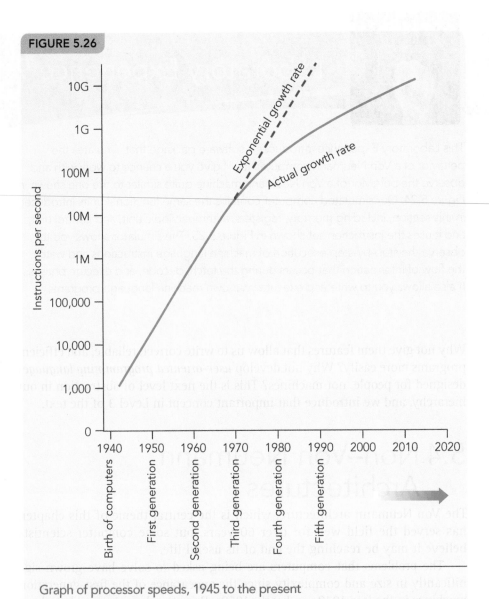

Graph of processor speeds, 1945 to the present

speed. However, as Figure 5.26 shows, even though computer speeds are still increasing, the rate of improvement appears to be slowing down.

This slowdown is due to many things. One important limit on increased processor speed is the inability to place gates any closer together on a chip. (See the Special Interest Box "Moore's Law and the Limits of Chip Design" in Chapter 4.) Today's high-density chips contain billions of transistors separated by distances of only 10–25 nanometers (10^{-9} meters), and it is becoming exceedingly difficult (not to mention expensive) to accurately place individual components closer together. However, the time it takes to send signals between two parts of a computer separated by a given distance is limited by the fact that electronic signals cannot travel faster than the speed of light—299,792,458 meters per second. That is, when we carry out an operation such as:

PC → MAR

the signals traveling between these two registers cannot exceed 300 million meters per second. If, for example, these two components were separated by 1 meter, it would take signals leaving the PC about 3 nanoseconds to reach the MAR, and nothing in this universe can reduce that value except a reduction of the distance separating them.

Even while the rate of increase in the performance of newer machines is slowing down, the problems that researchers are attempting to solve are growing ever larger and more complex. New applications in areas such as computational modeling and high-resolution real-time imaging are increasing the demands placed on new computer systems. (We will look at some of these applications in Level 5, Chapters 13–16.) For example, to have a computer generate and display animated images without flicker, it must generate 30 new frames each second. Each frame may contain as many as $4,000 \times 4,000$ separate picture elements (pixels) whose position, color, and intensity must be individually recomputed. This means that $30 \times 4,000 \times 4,000 = 480,000,000$ pixel computations need to be completed every second. Each of those computations may require the execution of many instructions. (Where does this point move to in the next frame? What color is it? How bright is it? Is it visible or hidden behind something else?) If we assume that it requires 2,000 instructions per pixel to answer these questions (a reasonable approximation), then real-time computer animation requires a computer capable of executing $480,000,000 \times 2,000 = 960$ billion instructions per second. This is well beyond the abilities of most current processors, which are limited to about 20–50 billion instructions per second. The inability of the sequential one-instruction-at-a-time Von Neumann model to handle today's large-scale problems is called the Von Neumann bottleneck, and it is a major problem in computer organization.

To solve this problem, computer engineers are rethinking many of the fundamental ideas presented in this chapter, and they are studying nontraditional approaches to computer organization called non–Von Neumann architectures. They are asking the question, "Is there a different way to design and build computers that can solve problems 10 or 100 or 1,000 times larger than what can be handled by today's computers?" Fortunately, the answer to this question is a resounding, Yes! (This is equivalent to today's automotive engineers who have stopped trying to improve the performance of the traditional gasoline-powered engine but are investigating totally new designs, such as electric cars and hybrids.)

One of the most important areas of research in these non–Von Neumann architectures is based on the following fairly obvious principle:

> *If you cannot build something to work twice as fast, build it to do two things at once. The results will be identical.*

From this truism comes the principle of parallel processing—building computers not with one processor, as shown in Figure 5.24, but with hundreds, thousands, or even tens of thousands. If we can keep each processor occupied with meaningful work, then it should be possible to speed up the solution to large problems by one, two, or three orders of magnitude and overcome the Von Neumann bottleneck. For example, in the graphical animation example discussed earlier, we determined that we needed a machine that could execute 960 billion instructions per second, but the processors currently available may only work at a speed of 20 billion instructions per second. However, let's say that we could have 48 (or more) processors all working together on this one problem; then we should (in theory) have a sufficiently powerful system to solve our problem because 20 billion operations per second per processor × 48 processors = 960 billion operations per second. This is the idea behind *dual-core* and *quad-core* processors that have two or four independent processors on a single chip. (Note: The A10 processor inside the Apple iPhone 7 is a quad-core system containing four separate processors.)

The approach of placing multiple processors on a single chip is fine for a small number of processors, say two, four, or eight. However, we need a completely different approach to build large-scale parallel systems that may contain thousands or tens of thousands of processors. (Amazingly, the Chinese Sunway TaihuLight computer mentioned in the Special Interest Box "Speed to Burn" contains almost 11 million core processors.)

Most large-scale parallel processors use an architecture called MIMD parallel processing (*m*ultiple *i*nstruction stream/*m*ultiple *d*ata stream), also called cluster computing. In MIMD parallelism, a computer system has multiple, independent processors each with its own primary memory unit, and every processor is capable of executing its own separate program in its own private memory at its own rate. This model of parallel processing is diagrammed in Figure 5.27. (Note that each processor in the diagram of Figure 5.27 may itself contain two, four, or eight independent processors.)

Each processor/memory pair in Figure 5.27 is a Von Neumann machine of the type described in this chapter. For example, it could be a processor board

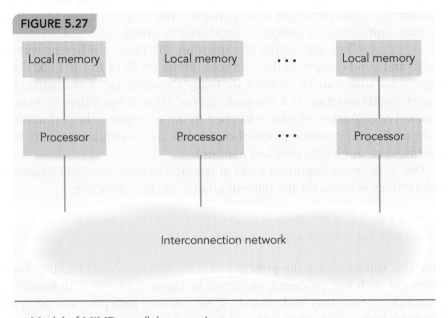

FIGURE 5.27

Model of MIMD parallel processing

Speed to Burn

The first computer to achieve a speed of 1 million floating-point operations per second, 1 *megaflop*, was the Control Data 6600 in the mid-1960s. The first machine to achieve 1 billion floating-point operations per second, 1 *gigaflop*, was the Cray X-MP in the early 1980s. Today almost all machines, even inexpensive laptops and tablets, can achieve gigaflop speeds. In 1996, the Intel Corporation announced that its ULTRA computer had successfully become the world's first *teraflop* machine. This $55 million computer contained 9,072 Pentium Pro processors, and on December 16, 1996, it achieved a sustained computational speed of 1 trillion operations per second.

On June 9, 2008, another major milestone in computer performance was reached. The Roadrunner massively parallel computer, constructed jointly by Los Alamos National Laboratories and IBM, achieved a sustained computational speed of 1,026 trillion floating-point operations per second, or 1 *petaflop*. To get an idea of how fast that is, consider that if all 6 billion people in the world worked together on a single problem, each person would have to perform 170,000 computations per second to equal the speed of this one machine. The system, which contained 18,000 processors and 98 terabytes of memory, cost about $100 million to design and build. It was used for basic research in astronomy, energy, and human genome science.

As of early 2017, the fastest computer in the world was the Sunway TaihuLight supercomputer at the National Supercomputing Center in Wuxi, Jiangsu, China. The system contains a total of 10,649,600 core processors, 1.31×2^{50} bytes of memory, and cost $US273 million to build. In 2016, it achieved a peak computational rate of 93 petaflops (see "The Tortoise and the Hare" Special Interest Box in Chapter 3). Estimates show that the system, when fully operational, should be able to achieve a peak speed of about 125 petaflops. By the time you are reading this, though, there will likely be an even faster computer. That's how fast the field of parallel computation is moving!

of the type shown in Figure 5.24. Alternately, it could be a complete computer system, such as a desktop machine in a computer lab or the laptop in your dorm room. Each system is executing its own program in its own local memory at its own rate. However, rather than each having to solve the entire problem by itself, the problem is solved in a parallel fashion by all processors simultaneously. Each of the processors tackles a small part of the overall problem and then communicates its result to the other processors via the *interconnection network*, a communications system that allows processors to exchange messages and data.

A massively parallel processor would be an excellent system to help us speed up the reverse telephone directory lookup problem initially discussed in Chapter 2. In the sequential approach that we described, the single processor doing the work must search all 350,000,000 entries from beginning to end (or until the desired telephone number is found). The analysis in Chapter 3 showed that using sequential search and a computer that can examine 50,000 numbers per second, it would take, on average, almost one hour to find a particular number—much too long for the typical person to wait.

However, if we were to use 1,000 processors instead of one, the problem is easily solved—just divide the 350,000,000 numbers into 1,000 equal-sized pieces and assign each piece to a different processor. Now each processor searches *in parallel* to see whether the desired telephone number is in its own section. If it finds the number, it broadcasts that information on the interconnection network to the other 999 processors so that they can stop searching. Each processor needs only to look through a list of 350,000 numbers, which is 1/1000th the amount of work it had to do previously. Instead of an average of 3,500 seconds, almost one hour, we now get our answer in 1/1000th the time—about 3.5 seconds. Parallel processing has elegantly solved our problem.

MIMD parallelism is also a scalable architecture. *Scalability* means that, at least theoretically, it is possible to match the number of processors to the size of the problem. For example, if 1,000 processors were insufficient to solve the reverse telephone lookup problem, then 2,000 or 5,000 can be used instead, assuming the interconnection network can provide the necessary level of communications. (Communications can become a serious bottleneck in a parallel system.) In short, the resources applied to a problem can be in direct proportion to the amount of work that needs to be done and the speed with which the answer is needed. Massively parallel MIMD machines containing hundreds of thousands or millions of independent processors have achieved solutions to large problems thousands of times faster than is possible using a single processor. (For an up-to-date listing of the fastest parallel computers, check the home page of *Top500*, a listing of the 500 most powerful computers in the world. Its web address is *www.top500.org*.)

The multiple processors within a MIMD cluster do not have to be identical or belong to a single administrative organization. Computer scientists realized that it is possible to address and solve massive problems by utilizing the resources of idle computers located around the world, regardless of whom they belong to. This realization led to an exciting new form of large-scale parallelism called grid computing. Grid computing acts much like popular sharing applications that allow homeowners to rent out their houses when they are not there or allow car owners to let someone use their vehicles when they would otherwise be sitting idle.

Grid computing enables researchers to easily and transparently access unused computer facilities without regard for their location. For example, one of the most well-known computer sharing projects is BOINC (Berkeley Open Infrastructure for Networked Computing) hosted by the University of California-Berkeley. BOINC allows users around the world to download BOINC software to their computer (Windows, Mac, Linux, or Android) and then donate idle computer time to assist with a range of scientific projects—curing diseases, studying global warming, analyzing pulsars—that are too massive to be attacked by a single machine. Currently, there are an average of over 672,000 computer systems connected to BOINC at any instant in time, providing a total of 18 petaflops of computing power to this "virtual supercomputer environment." You can read about the activities of BOINC (and learn how to become a contributing part of the system) at *http://boinc.berkeley.edu/*.

The real key to using massively parallel processors is to design solution methods that effectively utilize the large number of available processors. It does no good to have 1,000 processors available if only 1 or 2 are doing useful work while 998 or 999 are sitting idle. That would be like having a large construction crew at a building site, where the roofers, painters, and plumbers are sitting around waiting for one person to put up the walls. The field of parallel algorithms, the study of techniques that make efficient use of parallel architectures, is an important branch of research in computer science. Advances in this area will go a long way toward speeding the development and use of large-scale parallel systems of the type shown in Figure 5.27. (Problem 1 in this chapter's Challenge Work asks you to design a parallel addition algorithm.)

To solve the scientific problems of the 21st century, the computers of the 21st century are being organized much more like the massively parallel processing systems of Figure 5.27 than like the 70-year-old Von Neumann model of Figure 5.24.

5.5 Summary of Level 2

In Chapter 4, we looked at the basic building blocks of computers: binary codes, transistors, gates, and circuits. This chapter examined the standard model for computer design, called the Von Neumann architecture. It also discussed some of the shortcomings of this sequential model of computation and described briefly how these might be overcome by the use of parallel computers or a system of grid computers.

At this point in our hierarchy of abstractions, we have created a fully functional computer system capable of executing an algorithm encoded as sequences of machine language instructions. The only problem is that the machine we have created is enormously difficult to use and about as unfriendly and unforgiving as it could be. It has been designed and engineered from a machine's perspective, not a person's. Sequences of binary encoded machine language instructions such as

```
1011010000001011
1001101100010111
0000101101011001
```

give a computer no difficulty, but they cause people to throw up their hands in despair. We need to create a friendlier environment—to make the computer

Quantum Computing

One of the most fascinating (and complex) models of non-Von Neumann computing is called **quantum computing**. In a "regular" (i.e., Von Neumann) machine an individual bit of data is always in a well-defined state—either a 0 or a 1. However, quantum computers are built using the quantum mechanical principle called *superposition*, in which a single bit of data, now called a *qubit*, can be either a 0 or a 1 or *both* a 0 and a 1 simultaneously! In theory, this would allow a quantum computer to examine every possible combination of input values in a single step, greatly speeding up the solution to complex problems. For example, 2 qubits could, at the same time, represent all combinations of two binary values: 00, 01, 10, and 11.

In 2012, a company called D-Wave Systems, of British Columbia, Canada, built the first working model of a quantum computer, the D-Wave 1 with 128 qubits. A second prototype, the D-Wave 2 with 512 qubits, was launched in 2013. Soon after that, NASA, Google, the CIA, and a group of American and Canadian universities formed a research consortium to study how this radically new type of computer system could best be used, and with a goal of demonstrating a working quantum computer by 2020.

If you are a bit confused by the description of this strange new model of computation, don't worry—you have plenty of company. In a February 2014, *Time* magazine story about quantum computing, the following quote appeared on the cover: "It promises to solve some of humanity's most complex problems. It's backed by Jeff Bezos, NASA, and the CIA. Each one costs $10,000,000 and operates at 459° below zero. And nobody knows how it actually works."[3]

---

[3]Grossman, Lev, "The Infinity Machine," *Time*, February 14, 2014.

and its hardware resources more accessible. Such an environment would be more conducive to developing correct solutions to problems and satisfying a user's computational needs.

The component that creates this kind of friendly, problem-solving environment is called *system software*. It is an intermediary between the user and the hardware components of the Von Neumann machine. Without it, a Von Neumann machine would be virtually unusable by anyone but the most technically knowledgeable computer experts. We examine system software in the next level of our investigation of computer science.

EXERCISES

1. What are the advantages and disadvantages of using a very large memory cell size, say, $W = 64$ instead of the standard size $W = 8$? If each integer occupies *one* 64-bit memory cell and is stored using sign/magnitude notation, what are the largest (in terms of absolute value) positive and negative integers that can be stored? What if *two* cells are used to store integers?

2. At a minimum, how many bits are needed in the MAR with each of the following memory sizes?

    a. 1 million bytes

    b. 10 million bytes

    c. 100 million bytes

    d. 1 billion bytes

3. A memory unit that is said to be 640 KB would actually contain how many memory cells? What about a memory of 512 MB? What about a memory of 2 GB?

4. Explain what use read-only memory (ROM) serves in the design of a computer system. What type of information is kept in ROM, and how does that information originally get into the memory?

5. Assuming the square two-dimensional memory organization shown in Figure 5.7, what are the dimensions of a memory containing 1 MB (2^{20}) bytes of storage? How large would the MAR be? How many bits are sent to the row and column decoders? How many output lines would these decoders have?

6. Assume a 24-bit MAR that is organized as follows:

Row select lines	*Column select lines*
12 bits	12 bits

    What is the maximum size of the memory unit on this machine? What are the dimensions of the memory, assuming a square two-dimensional organization?

7. Assume that our MAR contains 20 bits, enabling us to access up to 2^{20} memory cells, which is 1 MB, but our computer has 4 MB of memory. Explain how it might be possible to address all 4 MB memory cells using a MAR that contains only 20 bits.

8. Assume that our MDR register is 16 bits wide while our machine language instructions are 32 bits wide. How might the fetch phase of the Von Neumann cycle have to be changed from what was described in the text?

9. Assume that a 1 gigaflop machine is connected to a printer that can print 780 characters per second. In the time it takes to print 1 page (65 lines of 60 characters per line), how many floating-point operations can the machine perform?

10. Assume that we have an arithmetic/logic unit that can carry out 20 distinct operations. Describe exactly what kind of multiplexer circuit would be needed to select exactly one of those 20 operations.

11. A CISC-style instruction set has a large number of high-level instructions that perform highly complex operations in a single step. What would be the major advantages of such a design? What would be some of the primary disadvantages?

12. Assume that a hard disk has the following characteristics:

>   Rotation speed = 7,200 rev/min
>
>   Arm movement time = 0.5 msec fixed startup time + 0.05 msec for each track crossed. (The startup time is a constant no matter how far the arm moves.) Assume on average the disk arm must move 150 tracks. Number of surfaces = 2 (This is a *double-sided* disk. A single read/write arm holds both read/write heads.)
>
>   Number of tracks per surface = 500
>
>   Number of sectors per track = 20
>
>   Number of characters per sector = 1,024

   a. How many characters can be stored on this disk?

   b. What are the best-case, worst-case, and average-case access times for this disk?

13. What are the best-case, worst-case, and average-case access times for the disk described in Exercise 12 if we increase the rotational speed to 9,600 rpm?

14. In general, information is stored on a disk not at random but in specific locations that help to minimize the time it takes to retrieve that information. Using the specifications given in Exercise 12, where would you store the information in a 50 KB file on the disk to speed up subsequent access to that information?

15. Assume that our disk unit has one read/write head per *track* instead of only one per surface.

Using the specifications given in Exercise 12, what are the best-case, worst-case, and average-case access times? How much have the additional read/write heads helped reduce access times?

16. Using the specifications given in Exercise 12, what is the worst-case time required to read the entire contents of the disk, that is, to read every single sector on the disk? Assume the read arm is initially positioned at the beginning of the first sector of the first track, and that every track must be read from the very beginning, that is, from the very first sector on that track. This is actually a quite common operation and is used for things like making copies and backing up a disk.

17. Discuss some situations in which a sequential access storage device such as a tape could be a useful form of mass storage.

18. Assume that we are receiving a message across a network using a modem with a rate of 56,000 bits/second. Furthermore, assume that we are working on a workstation with an instruction rate of 500 MIPS. How many instructions can the processor execute between the receipt of each individual bit of the message?

19. Consider the following structure of the instruction register.

Op code	Address-1	Address-2
6 bits	18 bits	18 bits

   a. What is the maximum number of distinct operation codes that can be recognized and executed by the processor on this machine?

   b. What is the maximum memory size on this machine?

   c. How many bytes are required for each operation?

20. If the size of the op code field in Exercise 19 were increased from 6 bits to 8 bits, what would now be the theoretical maximum size of the instruction set?

21. Assume that the variables v, w, x, y, and z are stored in memory locations 200, 201, 202, 203, and 204, respectively. Also assume that the code sequence you are writing begins in memory location 50. Using any of the machine language instructions shown in Section 5.2.4, translate the following algorithmic operations into their machine language equivalents.

    a. Set v to the value of $x - y + z$ (Assume the existence of the machine language command SUBTRACT X, Y, Z that computes CON(Z) = CON(X) − CON(Y).)

    b. Set v to the value $(w + x) - (y + z)$

    c. If $(v \geq w)$ then

    > Set x to y

    Else

    > Set x to z

    d. While $y < z$ do

    > Set y to the value $(y + w + z)$
    >
    > Set z to the value $(z + v)$

    End of the loop

22. Assume that the variables a and b are stored in memory locations 300 and 301, respectively. Also assume that the three integer values +1, −1, and 0 are stored in memory locations 400, 401, and 402, respectively. Finally, assume that the code sequence you are writing begins in memory location 50. Using any of the machine language instructions shown in Section 5.2.4, translate the following algorithmic operations into their machine language equivalents.

    a. Set a to the value of $a + b - 1$

    b. if $a > 0$

    > Set b to the value +1

23. A student was asked to translate the following algorithmic operation into machine language, where x and y were stored in locations 500 and 501, respectively:

    > Set x to the value of $y + 19$

    Here is what was produced:

    > LOAD 501
    >
    > ADD 19
    >
    > STORE 500

    Is this translation correct? If not, describe the error and explain how to correct it.

24. Describe the sequence of operations that might go on inside the computer during the execution phase of the following machine language instructions. Use the notation shown in Section 5.3. Assume that the IR is divided into three separate parts that contain the op code and the first and second address fields.

    a. MOVE X, Y   Move the contents of memory cell X to memory cell Y.

    b. ADD X, Y   Add the contents of memory cells X and Y. Put the result back into memory cell Y.

25. Describe the sequence of operations that might go on inside the computer during the execution phase of the following machine language instruction. Use the notation shown in Section 5.3. Assume that the IR is now divided into four separate parts (instead of three) that contain the op code, and the first, second, and third address fields.

    ADD X, v, Y   Add the contents of memory cell X and the integer value v. Put the result into memory cell Y.

    So, for example, the operation ADD X, 1, Y would compute $Y = X + 1$.

26. One of the major BOINC research projects is called SETI@home. SETI stands for "Search for ExtraTerrestrial Intelligence," and it involves analyzing observational data collected by the Arecibo Radio Telescope and its massive 1,000-foot diameter dish, looking for signal patterns that could be indications of intelligent life. The telescope collects massive amounts of data each day, chops this data into small chunks based on frequency and time, and sends these small chunks out to the computers that have volunteered to be part of this astronomical research project.

Explain why this project is an excellent candidate for a large-scale grid computing environment such as BOINC.

CHALLENGE WORK

1. It is easy to write a sequential algorithm that sums up a 100-element vector:

$$Sum = a_1 + a_2 + a_3 + ... + a_{100}$$

It would look something like

   Set i to 1

   Set Sum to 0

   While $i < 101$ do the following

      $Sum = Sum + a_i$

      $i = i + 1$

   End of the loop

   Write out the value of Sum

   Stop

It is pretty obvious that this algorithm will take about 100 units of time, where a unit of time is equivalent to the time needed to execute one iteration of the loop. However, it is less easy to see how we might exploit the existence of *multiple* processors to speed up the solution to this problem.

   Assume that instead of having only a single processor, you have 100. Design a parallel algorithm that utilizes these additional resources to speed up the solution to the previous computation. Exactly how much faster would your *parallel summation algorithm* execute than the sequential one? Did you need all 100 processors? Could you have used more than 100?

2. In this chapter, we described the Von Neumann architecture in broad, general terms. However, "real" Von Neumann processors, such as an Intel Quad-Core and the Apple A10, are much more complex than the simple model shown in Figure 5.24. Pick one of these processors (perhaps the processor inside the computer you are using for this class) and take an in-depth look at its design. Specifically, examine such issues as

   • Its instruction set and how it compares with the instruction set shown in Figure 5.25

   • The collection of available registers

   • The existence of cache memory

   • Its computing speed in MIPS and MFLOPS or GFLOPS

   • How much primary memory it has and how memory is addressed in the instructions

   • Memory access time

   • In what size "chunks" memory can be accessed

Write a report describing the real-world characteristics of the processor you selected.

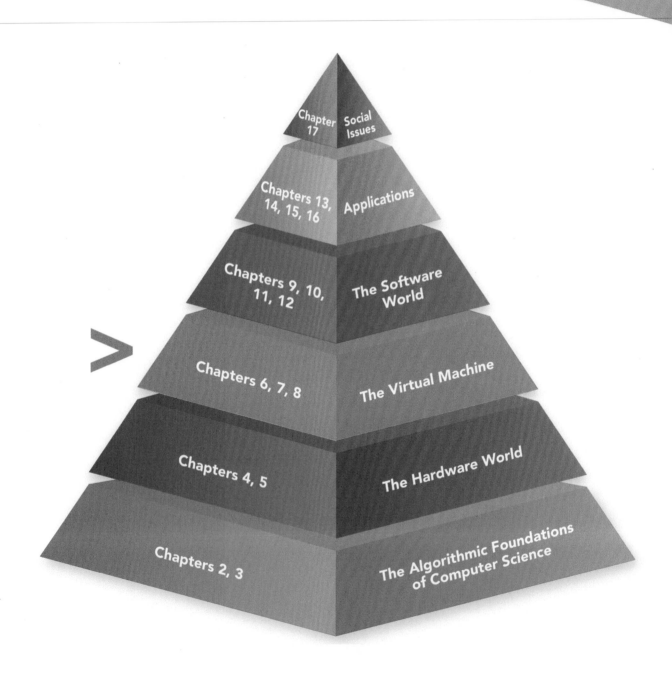

It has been said that computer science is "the science of building pretend worlds," meaning that the underlying hardware structure of a computer can be so difficult to work with that we must create more friendly and more usable "virtual worlds" in which to work and solve problems. Without that layer of abstraction between us and the machine, we would have to solve problems by applying only the ideas and capabilities presented in Level 2—binary numbers, digital circuits, absolute memory addresses, and machine language instructions.

In Level 3 (Chapters 6, 7, and 8), you will learn how these user-friendly "microworlds" are created to produce an environment in which efficient, safe, and productive problem solving is possible.

AFTER STUDYING THIS CHAPTER, YOU WILL BE ABLE TO:

- Compare the virtual machine created for the user by system software with the naked machine
- Describe the different types of system software
- Explain the benefits of writing programs in assembly language rather than machine language
- Describe how an assembler translates assembly language programs into machine instructions
- List five key tasks of an operating system, and explain what each is and why it is critical to modern systems
- Describe the different generations of operating systems, their features, and how each generation solved a drawback of the previous generation

6.1 Introduction

Chapters 4 and 5 described a computer model, the *Von Neumann architecture*, that is capable of executing programs written in machine language. This computer has all the hardware needed to solve important real-world problems, but it has no "support tools" to make that problem-solving task easy. The computer described in Chapter 5 is informally known as a naked machine: hardware bereft of any helpful user-oriented features.

Imagine what it would be like to work on a naked machine. To solve a problem, you would have to create hundreds or thousands of cryptic machine language instructions that look like this:

```
1011010011010001110011110001000
```

and you would have to do that without making a single mistake because, to execute properly, a program must be completely error free. Imagine the likelihood of writing a correct program containing thousands of instructions like the one shown above. Even worse, imagine trying to locate an error buried deep inside that incomprehensible mass of 0s and 1s!

On a naked machine, the data as well as the instructions must be represented in binary. For example, a program cannot refer to the decimal integer +9 directly but must express it as

0000000000001001   (the binary representation of +9 using 16 bits)

You cannot use the symbol *A* to refer to the first letter of the alphabet but must represent it using its 8-bit ASCII code value, which is decimal 65:

01000001   (the 8-bit ASCII code for A; see Figure 4.3)

As you can imagine, writing programs for a naked machine is very difficult.

Even if you write the program correctly, your work is still not done. A program for a Von Neumann computer must be stored in memory prior to execution. Therefore, you must now take the program and store its instructions into sequential cells in memory. On a naked machine, the programmer must perform this task, one instruction at a time. Assuming that each instruction occupies one memory cell, the programmer loads the first instruction into address 0, the second instruction into address 1, the third instruction into address 2, and so on, until all have been stored.

Finally, what starts the program running? A naked machine does not do this automatically. (As you are probably coming to realize, a naked machine does not do *anything* automatically, except fetch, decode, and execute machine language instructions.) The programmer must initiate execution by storing a 0, the address of the first instruction of the program, into the program counter (PC) and pressing the START button. This begins the fetch/decode/execute cycle described in Chapter 5. The control unit fetches from memory the contents of the address in the PC, currently 0, and executes that instruction. The program continues sequentially from that point while the user prays that everything works because he or she cannot bear to face a naked machine again!

As this portrayal demonstrates, working directly with the underlying hardware is practically impossible for a human being. The functional units described in Chapter 5 are built according to what is easy for hardware to do, not what is easy for people to do.

To make a Von Neumann computer usable, we must create an *interface* between the user and the hardware. This interface does the following things:

- Hides from the user the messy details of the underlying hardware

- Presents information about what is happening in a way that does not require in-depth knowledge of the internal structure of the system

- Allows easy user access to the resources available on this computer

- Prevents accidental or intentional damage to hardware, programs, and data

By way of analogy, let's look at how people use another common tool—an automobile. The internal combustion engine is a highly complex piece of technology. For most of us, the functions of fuel-injection systems, distributors, and camshafts are a total mystery. However, most people find driving a car quite easy. This is because the driver does not have to lift the hood and interact directly with the hardware; that is, he or she does not have to drive a "naked automobile." Instead, there is an interface, the *dashboard*, which simplifies things considerably. The dashboard hides the details of engine operation that a driver does not need to know. The important things—such as oil pressure, fuel level, and vehicle speed—are presented in a simple, "people-oriented" way: oil indicator warning light, fuel gauge, and speed in miles or kilometers per hour. Access to the engine and transmission is achieved via a few easy-to-understand devices: a key to start and stop, pedals to speed up or slow down, a shift lever to go forward or backward, and a steering wheel to direct movement.

We need a similar interface for our Von Neumann machine. This "computer dashboard" would eliminate most of the hassles of working on a naked machine and let us view the hardware resources of Chapter 5 in a much friendlier way. Such an interface does exist, and it is called system software.

6.2 System Software

6.2.1 The Virtual Machine

System software is a collection of computer programs that manage the resources of a computer and facilitates access to those resources. This contrasts with application software that allows a user to address some specialized task of interest to that user, for example, write a document, create an image, browse the web, or solve a system of equations. (Application software is addressed in Level 5 of this text.) It is important to remember that we are describing software, not hardware. There are no black boxes wired to a computer labeled "system software." Software consists of sequences of instructions—namely, programs—that solve a problem. But again, instead of solving *user* problems, system software solves the problem of making a computer and its resources easier to access and use.

System software acts as an *intermediary* between the users and the hardware, as shown in Figure 6.1. System software presents the user with a set of services and resources across the interface labeled A in Figure 6.1. These resources may actually exist, or they may be simulated by the software to give the user the illusion that they exist. The set of services and resources created by the software and seen by the user is called a virtual machine or a virtual environment. The system software, not the user, interacts with the actual hardware (that is, the naked machine) across the interface labeled B in Figure 6.1.

The system software has the following responsibilities, analogous to those of the automobile dashboard:

- Hides the complex and unimportant (to the user) details of the internal structure of the Von Neumann architecture

- Presents important information to the user in a way that is easy to understand

- Allows the user to access machine resources in a simple and efficient way

- Provides a secure and safe environment in which to operate

For example, to add two numbers, it is much easier to use notation such as $a = b + c$ than to worry about (1) loading ALU registers from memory cells b and c, (2) activating the ALU, (3) selecting the output of the addition circuit, and (4) sending the result to memory cell a. The programmer should not have to know about registers, addition circuits, and memory addresses but instead should see a virtual machine that "understands" the mathematical symbols + and =.

After a program has been written (or purchased), it should automatically be loaded into memory without the programmer having to specify where in memory it should be placed or having to set the program counter. Instead, he or she should be able to issue one simple command (or mouse

FIGURE 6.1

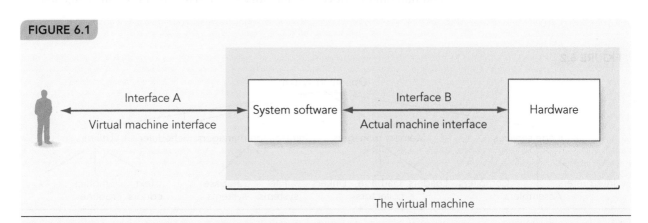

The role of system software

click or finger tap) to the virtual machine that says, "Run this application." Finally, when the program is running and generating results, the programmer should be able to instruct the virtual machine to send the program's output to the printer in Room 105, without reference to the details related to I/O controllers, interrupt signals, and code sets.

All the useful services just described are provided by the system software available on any modern computer system. The following sections show how this friendly, user-oriented environment is created.

6.2.2 Types of System Software

System software is not a single monolithic entity but a collection of many different programs. The types found on a typical computer are shown in Figure 6.2.

The program that controls the overall operation of the computer is the operating system, and it is the single most important piece of system software on a computer. It is the operating system that communicates with users, determines what they want, and activates other system programs, applications packages, or user programs to carry out their requests. The software packages that handle these requests include the following:

- *User interface*–All modern operating systems provide a powerful graphical user interface (GUI) that gives the user an intuitive visual overview as well as graphical control of the capabilities and services of the computer. Control of the GUI is typically done with keystrokes, mouse clicks, finger taps, voice activation, or biometric scans such as fingerprints.

- *Language services*–These programs, called *assemblers*, *compilers*, and *interpreters*, allow you to write programs in a high-level, user-oriented language rather than the machine language of Chapter 5 and to execute these programs easily and efficiently. They often include components such as text editors and debuggers.

- *Memory managers*–These programs allocate memory space for programs and data and retrieve this memory space when it is no longer needed.

FIGURE 6.2

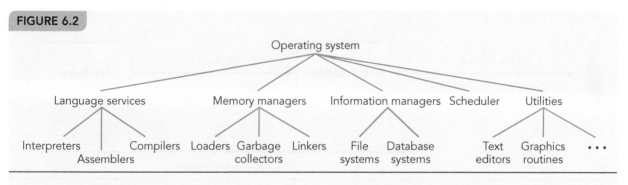

Types of system software

- *Information managers*—These programs handle the organization, storage, and retrieval of information on storage devices such as the hard drives, DVDs, flash drives, and tapes described in Section 5.2.2, as well as information stored remotely in data centers (*cloud storage*). They allow you to organize your information in an efficient hierarchical manner, using directories, folders, and files and to keep your personal data safe from accidental or intentional misuse.

- *I/O* systems—These software packages allow you to easily and efficiently use the many different types of input and output devices that exist on a modern computer system.

- *Scheduler*—This system program keeps a list of programs ready to run on the processor, and it selects the one that will execute next. The scheduler allows you to have several different programs active at a single time, for instance, surfing the web while you are waiting for a file to finish printing.

- *Utilities*—These collections of library routines provide a wide range of useful services either to a user or to other system routines. Text editors, online help routines, image and sound applications, and control panels are examples of utility routines. Sometimes these utilities are organized into collections called program libraries.

These system routines are used during every phase of problem solving on a computer, and it would be virtually impossible to get anything done without them. Let's go back to the problem described earlier—the job of writing a program, loading it into memory, running it, and printing the results. On a naked machine, this job would be formidable. On the virtual machine created by system software, it is much simpler:

Step	Task
1	Use a text editor to create program P written in a high-level, English-like notation rather than binary.
2	Use an information manager to store program P in a directory on your cloud storage account.
3	Use a language translator to translate program P from a high-level language into an equivalent machine language program M.
4	Use a scheduler to load, schedule, and run program M. The scheduler itself uses the memory manager to obtain memory space for program M.
5	Use the I/O system to display the output of your program on your screen.
6	If the program did not complete successfully, use a debugger to help you locate the error. Use a text editor to correct the program and the information manager to store the newly modified program.

Furthermore, most of these operations are easily invoked via mouse clicks or finger taps using the graphical interface provided by the operating system.

On a virtual machine, the low-level details of machine operation are no longer visible, and a user can concentrate on higher-level issues: writing the program, executing the program, and saving and analyzing results.

There are many types of system software, and it is impossible to cover them all in this section of the text. Instead, we will investigate two types of system software and use these as representatives of the entire group. Section 6.3 examines assemblers, and Section 6.4 looks at the design and construction of operating systems. These two packages create a friendly and usable virtual machine. In Chapter 7, we will extend that virtual environment from a single computer to a collection of computers by looking at the system software required to create one of the most important and widely used virtual environments—a computer network. Finally, in Chapter 8 we will investigate one of the most important services provided by the operating system—system security.

6.3 Assemblers and Assembly Language

6.3.1 Assembly Language

One of the first places where we need a friendlier virtual environment is in our choice of programming language. Machine language, which is designed from a machine's point of view, not a person's, is complicated and virtually impossible to understand. What specifically are the problems with machine language?

- It uses binary. There are no natural language words, mathematical symbols, or other convenient mnemonics to make the language more readable.

- It allows only numeric memory addresses (in binary). A programmer cannot name an instruction or a piece of data and refer to it by name.

- It is difficult to change. If we insert or delete an instruction, all memory addresses following that instruction will change. For example, if we place a new instruction into memory location 503, then the instruction previously in location 503 is now in 504. All references to address 503 must be updated to point to 504. There may be hundreds of such references.

- It is difficult to create data. If a user wants to store a piece of data in memory, he or she must compute the internal binary representation for that data item. These conversion algorithms are complicated and time consuming.

Programmers working on early first-generation computers quickly realized the shortcomings of machine language. They developed a new language, called assembly language, designed for people as well as computers. Assembly languages created a more productive, user-oriented environment, and assemblers were one of the first pieces of system software to be widely used. When assembly languages first appeared in the early 1950s, they were one of the most important new developments in programming—so important, in fact, that they were considered an entirely new generation of language, analogous to the new generations of hardware described in Section 1.4.3. Assembly languages were termed *second-generation languages* to distinguish them from machine languages, which were viewed as *first-generation languages.*

Today, assembly languages are more properly called low-level programming languages, which means they are closely related to the machine language of Chapter 5. Each symbolic assembly language instruction is translated into exactly *one* binary machine language instruction.

This contrasts with languages like C++, Java, and Python, which are high-level programming languages. High-level languages are more user oriented, they are not machine specific, and they use both natural language and mathematical notation in their design. A single high-level language instruction is typically translated into *many* machine language instructions, and the virtual environment created by a high-level language is far more powerful than the one produced by an assembly language. We discuss high-level programming languages in detail in Chapters 9 and 10.

Figure 6.3 shows a "continuum of languages," from the lowest level (closest to the hardware) to the highest level (most abstract, farthest from the hardware).

The machine language of Chapter 5 is the most primitive; it is the language of the hardware itself. Assembly language, the topic of this section, represents the first step along the continuum from machine language. High-level programming languages like C++, Java, and Python are closer in style and structure to natural languages and are quite distinct from assembly language. Natural languages, such as English, Spanish, and Japanese, are the highest level; they are totally unrelated to hardware design.

Although it is rare today to write a program in assembly language, it is important to understand the philosophy behind its design. It was the very first time that computer scientists asked the question, "What can I do to make these machines easier to use and easier to understand?" This same question is still being asked and answered today.

A program written in assembly language is called the source program; it uses the features and services provided by the language. However, the processor

FIGURE 6.3

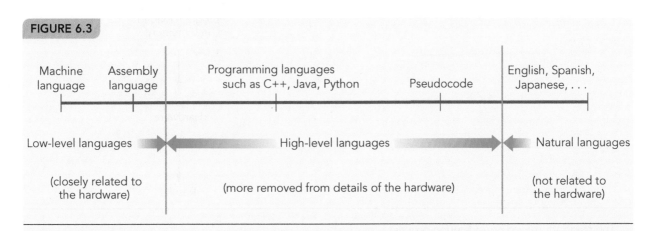

The continuum of programming languages

does not "understand" assembly language instructions, in the sense of being able to fetch, decode, and execute them as described in Chapter 5. The source program must be translated into a corresponding machine language program, called the object program. This translation is carried out by a piece of system software called an assembler. (Translators for high-level languages are called compilers. They are discussed in Chapter 11.) The assembler goes through the entire program, carrying out a translation of one instruction at a time. Once the complete object program has been produced, its instructions can be loaded into memory and executed by the processor exactly as described in Section 5.3. The complete translation/loading/execution process is diagrammed in Figure 6.4.

There are three major advantages to writing programs in assembly language rather than machine language:

- Use of symbolic operation codes rather than numeric (binary) ones
- Use of symbolic memory addresses rather than numeric (binary) ones
- Pseudo-operations that provide useful user-oriented services such as data generation

FIGURE 6.4

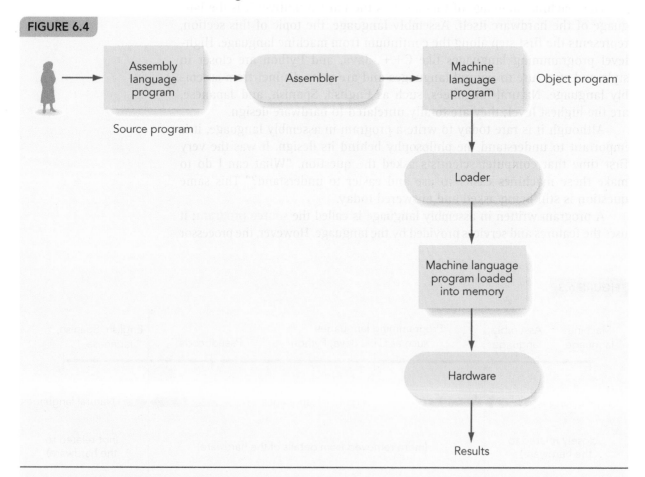

The translation/loading/execution process

This section describes a simple, but realistic, assembly language that demonstrates these three advantages.

Our hypothetical assembly language is composed of instructions in the following format:

label: op code mnemonic   address field   --comment

The *comment field*, preceded in our notation by a double dash (--), is not really part of the instruction. It is a helpful explanation added to the instruction by a programmer and intended for readers of the program. It is ignored by the machine during translation and execution.

Assembly languages allow the programmer to refer to op codes using a symbolic name, called the *op code mnemonic*, rather than by a number. We can write op codes using meaningful words like LOAD, ADD, and STORE rather than obscure binary codes like 0000, 0011, and 0001. Figure 6.5 shows an assembly language instruction set for a Von Neumann machine

FIGURE 6.5

Binary Op Code	Operation	Meaning
0000	LOAD X	$CON(X) \to R$
0001	STORE X	$R \to CON(X)$
0010	CLEAR X	$0 \to CON(X)$
0011	ADD X	$R + CON(X) \to R$
0100	INCREMENT X	$CON(X) + 1 \to CON(X)$
0101	SUBTRACT X	$R - CON(X) \to R$
0110	DECREMENT X	$CON(X) - 1 \to CON(X)$
0111	COMPARE X	if $CON(X) > R$ then GT = 1 else 0
		if $CON(X) = R$ then EQ = 1 else 0
		if $CON(X) < R$ then LT = 1 else 0
1000	JUMP X	Get the next instruction from memory location X.
1001	JUMPGT X	Get the next instruction from memory location X if GT = 1.
1010	JUMPEQ X	Get the next instruction from memory location X if EQ = 1.
1011	JUMPLT X	Get the next instruction from memory location X if LT = 1.
1100	JUMPNEQ X	Get the next instruction from memory location X if EQ = 0.
1101	IN X	Input an integer value from the standard input device and store into memory cell X.
1110	OUT X	Output, in decimal notation, the value stored in memory cell X.
1111	HALT	Stop program execution.

Typical assembly language instruction set

that has a single ALU register R and three condition codes GT, EQ, and LT. Each numeric op code, its assembly language mnemonic, and its meaning are listed. This table is identical to Figure 5.25, which summarizes the language used in Chapter 5 to introduce the Von Neumann architecture and explains how instructions are executed. (However, Chapter 5 describes binary machine language and uses symbolic names only for convenience. In this chapter, we are describing assembly language, where symbolic names such as LOAD and ADD are actually part of the language.)

Another advantage of assembly language is that it lets programmers use *symbolic addresses* instead of numeric addresses. In machine language, to jump to the instruction stored in memory location 17, you must refer directly to address 17; that is, you must write JUMP 17 (in binary, of course). This is cumbersome, because if a new instruction is inserted anywhere within the first 17 lines of the program, the jump location changes to 18. The old reference to 17 is incorrect, and the address field must be changed. This makes modifying programs very difficult, and even small changes become big efforts. It is not unlike identifying yourself in a waiting line by position—as, say, the 10th person in line. As soon as someone in front of you leaves (or someone cuts in line ahead of you), that number changes. It is far better to identify yourself using a characteristic that does not change as people enter or exit the line. For example, you are the person wearing the green jacket and the orange shirt. Those characteristics won't change (though maybe they should).

In assembly language, we can attach a *symbolic label* to any instruction or piece of data in the program. The label then becomes a permanent identification for this instruction or data, regardless of where it appears in the program or where it may be moved in memory. A label is a name (followed by a colon to identify it as a label) placed at the beginning of an instruction.

LOOPSTART: LOAD X

The label LOOPSTART has been attached to the instruction LOAD X. This means that the name LOOPSTART is *equivalent to* the address of the memory cell that holds the instruction LOAD X. If, for example, the LOAD X instruction is stored in memory cell 62, then the name LOOPSTART is equivalent to address 62. Any use of the name LOOPSTART in the address field of an instruction is treated as though the user had written the numeric address 62. For example, to jump to the load instruction shown above, we do not need to know that it is stored in location 62. Instead, we need only write the instruction

JUMP   LOOPSTART

Symbolic labels have two advantages over numeric addresses. The first is *program clarity*. As with the use of mnemonics for op codes, the use of meaningful symbolic names can make a program much more readable. Names like LOOPSTART, COUNT, and ERROR carry a good deal of meaning and help people to understand what the code is doing. Memory addresses such as 73, 147, and 2001 do not. A second advantage of symbolic labels is *maintainability*. When we refer to an instruction via a symbolic label rather than an address, we no longer need to modify the address field when instructions are added to or removed from the program. Consider the following example:

```
            JUMP     LOOP

             ⋮            ← point A

LOOP:       LOAD     X
```

Say a new instruction is added to the program at point A. When the modified program is translated by the assembler into machine language, all instructions following point A are placed in a memory cell whose address is 1 higher than it was before (assuming that each instruction occupies one memory cell). However, the JUMP refers to the LOAD instruction only by the name LOOP, not by the address where it is stored. Therefore, neither the JUMP nor the LOAD instruction needs to be changed. We need only retranslate the modified program. The assembler determines the new address of the LOAD X instruction, makes the label LOOP equivalent to this new address, and places this new address into the address field of the JUMP LOOP instruction. The assembler does the messy bookkeeping previously done by the machine language programmer.

The final advantage of assembly language programming is *data generation*. In Section 4.2.1 we showed how to represent data types such as unsigned and signed integers, floating-point values, and characters in binary. When writing in machine language, the programmer must do these conversions. In assembly language, however, the programmer can ask the assembler to do them by using a special type of assembly language op code called a pseudo-op.

A pseudo-op (preceded in our notation by a period to indicate its type) does not generate a machine language instruction like other operation codes. Instead, it invokes a useful service of the assembler. One of these useful services is generating data in the proper binary representation for this system. There are typically assembly language pseudo-ops to generate integer, character, and (if the hardware supports it) real data values. In our sample language, we will limit ourselves to one data generation pseudo-op called .DATA that builds signed integers. This pseudo-op converts the signed decimal integer in the address field to the proper binary representation. For example, the pseudo-op

```
FIVE:       .DATA      +5
```

tells the assembler to generate the binary representation for the signed integer +5, put it into memory, and make the label "FIVE" equivalent to the address of that cell. If a memory cell contains 16 bits, and the next available memory cell is address 53, then this pseudo-op produces

address	contents
53	0000000000000101

and the name FIVE is equivalent to memory address 53. Similarly, the pseudo-op

    NEGSEVEN: .DATA   −7

might produce the following 16-bit quantity, assuming sign/magnitude representation:

address	contents
54	1000000000000111

and the symbol NEGSEVEN is equivalent to memory address 54.

We can now refer to these data items by their attached label. For example, to load the value +5 into register R, we can say

    LOAD   FIVE

This is equivalent to writing LOAD 53, which loads register R with the contents of memory cell 53—that is, the integer +5. Note that if we had incorrectly said

    LOAD   5

the *contents* of memory cell 5 would be loaded into register R. This is not what we intended, and the program would be wrong. This is a good example of why it is so important to distinguish between the address of a cell and its contents.

To add the value −7 to the current contents of register R, we write

    ADD   NEGSEVEN

The contents of R (currently +5) and the contents of address NEGSEVEN (address 54, whose contents are −7) are added together, producing −2. This becomes the new contents of register R.

When generating and storing data values, we must be careful not to place them in memory locations where they can be misinterpreted as instructions. In Chapter 4, we said that the only way a computer can tell that the binary value 01000001 represents the letter *A* rather than the decimal value 65 is by the context in which it appears. The same is true for instructions and data. They are indistinguishable from each other, and the only way a Von Neumann machine can determine whether a sequence of 0s and 1s is an instruction or a piece of data is by how we use it. If we attempt to execute a value stored in memory, then that value *becomes* an instruction whether we meant it to be or not.

For example, if we incorrectly have the following sequence in our program:

    LOAD   X
    .DATA   +1

then, after completing the execution of the LOAD X command, the processor will come to the memory location where the .DATA pseudo-op has stored the value +1. The processor will fetch, decode, and attempt to execute the data value +1 as if it were an "instruction." This might sound meaningless, but to a processor, it is not. The representation of +1, using 16 bits, is

0000000000000001

Because this value is being used as an instruction, some of the bits will be interpreted as the op code and some as the address field. If we assume a 16-bit, one-address instruction format, with the first 4 bits being the op code and the last 12 bits being the address field, then these 16 bits will be interpreted as follows:

0000   000000000001
op code   address

The "op code" is 0, which is a LOAD on our hypothetical machine (see Figure 6.5), and the "address field" contains a 1. Thus, the data value +1 has accidentally turned into the following instruction:

LOAD   1   --Load the contents of memory cell 1 into register R

This is obviously incorrect, but how is the problem solved? The easiest way is to remember to place all data created by the program using the .DATA pseudo-op in memory locations where they cannot possibly be misinterpreted as instructions and accidently executed. One convenient place that meets this criterion is after a HALT instruction because the HALT prevents any further execution. The data values can be referenced, but they cannot be executed.

A second service provided by pseudo-ops is *program construction.* Pseudo-ops that mark the beginning (.BEGIN) and end (.END) of the assembly language program specify where to start and stop the translation process, and they do not generate any instructions or data. Remember that it is the HALT instruction, not the .END pseudo-op, that terminates execution of the program. The .END pseudo-op ends the translation process. Figure 6.6, which shows the organization of a typical assembly language program, helps explain this distinction.

FIGURE 6.6

```
.BEGIN     --This must be the first line of the program
   :       --Assembly language instructions like those in Figure 6.5
  HALT --This instruction terminates execution of the program
   :       --Data generation pseudo-ops such as
           --.DATA are placed here, after the HALT
.END       --This must be the last line of the program
```

Structure of a typical assembly language program

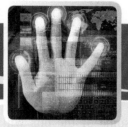

Practice Problems

1. Assume that register R and memory cells 80 and 81 contain the following values:

   R: 20   memory cell 80: 43   memory cell 81: 97

   Using the instruction set shown in Figure 6.5, determine what value ends up in register R and memory cells 80 and 81 after each of the following instructions is executed. Assume that each question begins with the values shown above.

   a. LOAD 80
   b. STORE 81
   c. COMPARE 80
   d. ADD 81
   e. IN 80
   f. OUT 81

2. Assume that memory cell 50 contains a 4 and label L is equivalent to memory location 50. What value does each of the following LOAD instructions load into register R?

   a. LOAD 50
   b. LOAD 4
   c. LOAD L
   d. LOAD L+1 (Assume that this is legal.)

3. Explain why both the HALT operation code described in Figure 6.5 and the .END pseudo-op mentioned at the end of this section are needed in an assembly language program and what might happen if one or both were omitted.

4. Explain exactly what would occur if a processor tried to execute the following pair of instructions:

   ```
        LOAD   L
   L:   .DATA  1
   ```

5. Assume machine language instructions occupy 16 bits, with the first four bits holding the op code (as given in Figure 6.5) and the final 12 bits holding the address of the operand. Also, assume that X corresponds to memory address 20 and Y corresponds to memory address 31. Show the internal binary representation of the following assembly language instructions:

   a. SUBTRACT X
   b. LOAD Y
   c. HALT

6.3.2 Examples of Assembly Language Code

This section describes how to use assembly language to translate algorithms into programs that can be executed on a Von Neumann computer. Today, software development is rarely performed in assembly language except for very special-purpose tasks; most programmers use higher-level languages such as those mentioned in Figure 6.3 and described in Chapters 9 and 10. Our purpose in offering these examples is to demonstrate how system software, in this case an assembler, can create a user-oriented virtual environment that supports effective and productive problem solving.

One of the most common operations in any algorithm is the evaluation of arithmetic expressions. For example, the sequential search algorithm of Figure 2.13 contains the following arithmetic operations:

Set the value of i to 1 (Line 2).

⋮

Add 1 to the value of i (Line 7).

These algorithmic operations can be translated quite easily into assembly language as follows:

```
        LOAD       ONE    --Put a 1 into register R
        STORE      I      --Store the constant 1 into I
        ⋮
        INCREMENT  I      --Add 1 to the contents of memory location  I
        ⋮
                          --The following .DATA statements should be
                            placed after the HALT instruction
I:      .DATA      0      --The memory location holding the variable I,
                            initially set to 0
ONE:    .DATA      1      --The integer constant 1
```

Note how readable this code is, compared with machine language, because of such op code mnemonics as LOAD and STORE and the use of descriptive labels such as I and ONE.

Another example is the following assembly language translation of the arithmetic expression $A = B + C - 7$. (Assume that B and C have already been assigned values.)

```
        LOAD       B      --Put the value B into register R
        ADD        C      --R now holds the sum (B + C)
        SUBTRACT   SEVEN  --R now holds (B + C - 7)
        STORE      A      --Store the result into A
        ⋮
                          --The following .DATA statements should
                            be placed after the HALT instruction
A:      .DATA      0
B:      .DATA      0
C:      .DATA      0
SEVEN:  .DATA      7      --The integer constant 7
```

Another important algorithmic operation involves testing and comparing values. The comparison of values and the subsequent use of the outcome to decide what to do next are termed a *conditional* operation, which we first saw in Section 2.2.3. Here is a conditional operation that outputs the larger of two values x and y. Algorithmically, it is expressed as follows:

Input the value of x

Input the value of y

If $x \geq y$ then

    Output the value of x

Else

    Output the value of y

In assembly language, this conditional operation can be translated as follows:

```
          IN        X         --Read the first data value
          IN        Y         --and now the second
          LOAD      X         --Load the value of X into register R
          COMPARE   Y         --Compare Y to X and set the condition codes
                                according to the outcome of the comparison
          JUMPGT    DONE      --If Y is greater than X, go to DONE
          OUT       X         --We get here only if X ≥ Y, so print X
          JUMP      NEXT      --Skip over the next instruction and continue
DONE:     OUT       Y         --We get here if Y > X, so print Y
          :

NEXT:     :                   --The program continues here

                              --The following .DATA statements go after
                                the HALT instruction
X:        .DATA     0         --Space for the two data values
Y:        .DATA     0
          :
```

Another important algorithmic primitive is *looping*, which was also introduced in Section 2.2.3. The following algorithmic example contains a while loop that executes 10,000 times.

Step	Operation	Explanation
1	Set i to 0	Start the loop counter at 0
2	While the value of $i < 10,000$ do	Lines 3 through 9
3–8	⋮	Here is the loop body that is to be done 10,000 times
9	Add 1 to the value of i	Increment the loop counter
10	End of the loop	
11	Stop	

This looping construct is easily translated into assembly language.

```
               LOAD        ZERO        --Initialize the loop counter to 0
               STORE       I           --This is Step 1 of the algorithm
    LOOP:      LOAD        MAXVALUE    --Put the integer value 10,000
                                          into register R

               COMPARE     I           --Compare I against 10,000
               JUMPEQ      DONE        --If I = 10,000 we are done (Step 2)
               :                       --Here is the loop body (Steps 3–8)
               INCREMENT   I           --Add 1 to I (Step 9)
               JUMP        LOOP        --End of the loop body (Step 10)
    DONE:      HALT                    --Stop execution (Step 11)
    ZERO:      .DATA       0           --This is the constant 0
    I:         .DATA       0           --The loop counter; it goes from
                                       --0 to 10,000
    MAXVALUE:  .DATA       10000       --Maximum number of executions
               :
```

As a final example, we will show a complete assembly language program (including all necessary pseudo-ops) to solve the following problem:

Read in a sequence of nonnegative numbers, one number at a time, and compute a running sum. When you encounter a negative number, print out the sum of the nonnegative values and stop.

Thus, if the input is

```
    8
   31
    7
    5
   −1
```

then the program should output the value 51, which is the sum (8 + 31 + 7 + 5). An algorithm to solve this problem is shown in Figure 6.7, using the pseudocode notation of Chapter 2.

Our next task is to convert the algorithmic primitives of Figure 6.7 into assembly language instructions. A program that does this is shown in Figure 6.8.

Of all the examples in this chapter, the program in Figure 6.8 demonstrates best what is meant by the phrase *user-oriented virtual environment*. Although it is not as clear as natural language or the pseudocode of Figure 6.7, this program can be read and understood by humans as well as computers. Tasks such as modifying the program and locating an error would be significantly easier using the assembly language code of Figure 6.8 than on its machine language equivalent.

FIGURE 6.7

Step	Operation
1	Set the value of *Sum* to 0
2	Input the first number *N*
3	While *N* is not negative do
4	Add the value of *N* to *Sum*
5	Input the next data value *N*
6	End of the loop
7	Print out *Sum*
8	Stop

Algorithm to compute the sum of nonnegative numbers

FIGURE 6.8

```
            .BEGIN                      --This marks the start of the program
            CLEAR        SUM            --Set the running sum to 0 (line 1)
            IN           N              --Input the first number N (line 2)
--The next three instructions test whether N is a negative number (line 3)
AGAIN:      LOAD         ZERO           --Put 0 into register R
            COMPARE      N              --Compare N and 0
            JUMPLT       NEG            --Go to NEG if N < 0
--We get here if N ≥ 0. We add N to the running sum (line 4)
            LOAD         SUM            --Put SUM into R
            ADD          N              --Add N. R now holds (N + SUM)
            STORE        SUM            --Put the result back into SUM
--Get the next input value (line 5)
            IN           N
--Now go back and repeat the loop (line 6)
            JUMP         AGAIN
--We get to this section of the program only when we encounter a negative
value
NEG:        OUT          SUM            --Print the sum (line 7)
            HALT                        --and stop (line 8)
--Here are the data generation pseudo-ops
SUM:        .DATA        0              --The running sum goes here
N:          .DATA        0              --The input data are placed here
ZERO:       .DATA        0              --The constant 0
--Now we mark the end of the entire program
            .END
```

Assembly language program to compute the sum of nonnegative numbers

The program in Figure 6.8 is an important milestone in our discussion of computer science in that it represents a culmination of the algorithmic problem-solving process. Earlier chapters introduced algorithms and problem solving (Chapters 1, 2, 3), discussed how to build computers to execute algorithms (Chapters 4, 5), and introduced system software that enables us to code algorithms into a language that computers can translate and execute (Chapter 6). The program in Figure 6.8 is the end product of this discussion: This program can be input to an assembler, translated into machine language, loaded into a Von Neumann computer, and executed to produce answers to our problem. This algorithmic problem-solving cycle is one of the central themes of computer science.

Practice Problems

1. Using the instruction set in Figure 6.5, translate the following algorithmic operations into assembly code. Show all necessary .DATA pseudo-ops.

   a. Add 1 to the value of x
   b. Add 50 to the value of x
   c. Set x to the value $y + z - 2$
   d. If $x > 50$ then output the value of x, otherwise input a new value of x
   e. sum = 0
      I = 0
      While $I < 50$ do
          sum = sum + I;
          I = I + 1;
      End of the loop

2. Using the instruction set in Figure 6.5, write a complete assembly language program (including all necessary pseudo-ops) that reads in numbers and counts how many nonnegative inputs it reads in until it encounters the first negative value. It then outputs that count and stops. For example, if the input data is 42, 108, 99, 60, 1, 42, 3, −27, then your program outputs the value 7 because there are seven nonnegative values before the appearance of the negative value −27.

3. Now modify your program from Practice Problem 2 so that if you have not encountered a negative value after 100 inputs, your program stops and outputs the value 100.

4. Discuss how the modifications you had to make in Practice Problem 3 were made easier by the use of assembly language in place of binary machine language.

Laboratory Experience 10

This section of Chapter 6 introduced assembly language instructions and programming techniques. However, as mentioned before, you do not learn programming and problem solving by reading and watching but rather by doing and trying. In this Laboratory Experience, you will program in an assembly language that is virtually identical to the one shown in Figure 6.5. You will be able to design and write programs like the one shown in Figure 6.8 and execute them on a simulated Von Neumann computer. You will observe the effect of individual instructions on the functional units of this machine and produce results.

This experience should give you a much deeper understanding of the concepts of assembly language programming and the Von Neumann architecture. It will also tie together the hardware concepts of Level 2 (Chapters 4 and 5) and the virtual machine system software concepts of Level 3. This lab shows how an assembly language program is written, translated, and loaded into a Von Neumann machine and executed by that machine using the ideas presented in the previous chapters.

6.3.3 Translation and Loading

What must happen in order for the assembly language program in Figure 6.8 to be executed on a processor? Figure 6.4 shows that before our source program can be run, we must invoke two system software packages—an *assembler* and a *loader*.

An assembler translates a symbolic assembly language program, such as the one in Figure 6.8, into machine language. We usually think of translation as an extremely difficult task. In fact, if two languages differ greatly in vocabulary, grammar, and syntax, it can be quite formidable. (This is why a translator for a high-level programming language is a very complex piece of software.) However, machine language and assembly language are very similar, and therefore an assembler is a relatively simple piece of system software. Understanding how an assembler works will give you a good appreciation for the tasks that system software must carry out in order to create a user-friendly virtual environment.

An assembler must perform the following four tasks, none of which is particularly difficult.

1. Convert symbolic op codes to binary.

2. Convert symbolic addresses to binary.

3. Perform the assembler services requested by the pseudo-ops.

4. Put the translated instructions into a file for future use.

Let's see how these operations are carried out using the hypothetical assembly language of Figure 6.5.

The conversion of symbolic op codes such as LOAD, ADD, and OUT to binary makes use of a structure called the *op code table*. This is an alphabetized list of all legal assembly language op codes and their binary equivalents. Part of an op code table for the instruction set of Figure 6.5 is shown in Figure 6.9. (The table assumes that the op code field is 4 bits wide.)

The assembler finds the operation code mnemonic in column 1 of the table and replaces the characters with the 4-bit binary value in column 2. (If the mnemonic is not found, then the user has written an illegal op code, which results in an error message.) Thus, for example, if we use the mnemonic OUT in our program, the assembler converts it to the binary value 1110.

To look up the code in the op code table, we could use the sequential search algorithm introduced in Chapter 2 and shown in Figure 2.13. However, using this algorithm could significantly slow down the translation of our program. The analysis of the sequential search algorithm in Chapter 3 showed that locating a single item in a list of N items takes, on the average, $N/2$ comparisons if the item is in the table and N comparisons if it is not. In Chapter 5, we stated that modern computers may have as many as 300 machine language instructions in their instruction set, so the size of the op code table of Figure 6.9 could be as large as $N = 300$. This means that using sequential search, we must perform an average of $N/2$, about 150, comparisons for every legal op code in our program. If our assembly language program contains 500,000 instructions (not an unreasonably large number for a complex piece of system software), the op code translation task requires a total of 500,000 instructions $\times$ 150 comparisons/instruction = 75 million comparisons. That is a lot of searching, even for a high-speed computer.

Because the op code table of Figure 6.9 is sorted alphabetically, we can instead use the more efficient binary search algorithm discussed in

FIGURE 6.9

Operation	Binary Value
ADD	0011
CLEAR	0010
COMPARE	0111
DECREMENT	0110
HALT	1111
OUT	1110
⋮	
STORE	0001
SUBTRACT	0101

Structure of the op code table

Section 3.4.2 and shown in Figure 3.18. On the average, the number of comparisons needed to find an element using binary search is not $N/2$ but lg N, the logarithm of N to the base 2. [*Note*: lg N is the value k such that $2^k = N$.] For a table of size $N = 300$, $N/2$ is 150, whereas (lg N) is approximately 8 ($2^8 = 256$). This says that on the average, we find an op code in the table, assuming it is there, in about 8 comparisons rather than 150. If our assembly language program contains 500,000 instructions, then the op code translation task now requires only about 500,000 × 8 = 4 million comparisons rather than 75 million, a reduction of 71 million lookups. By selecting a better search algorithm, we achieve an increase in speed of about 95%—quite a significant improvement!

This example demonstrates why algorithm analysis, introduced in Chapter 3, is such a critically important part of the design and implementation of software. Replacing a slow algorithm with a faster one can turn a practically-speaking unsolvable problem into a solvable one and a worthless solution into a highly worthwhile one. Remember that, in computer science, we are looking not just for correct solutions but for efficient ones as well.

After the op code has been converted into binary, the assembler must perform a similar task on the address field. It must convert the address from a symbolic value, such as X or LOOP, into the correct binary address. This task is a bit more difficult than converting the op code because the assembler itself must determine the correct numeric value of all symbols used in the label field. There is no "built-in" address conversion table equivalent to the op code table of Figure 6.9.

In assembly language, a symbol is defined when it appears in the label field of an instruction or data pseudo-op. Specifically, the symbol is given the value of the address of the instruction to which it is attached. Assemblers usually make two passes over the source code, where a pass is defined as the process of examining and processing every assembly language instruction in the program, one instruction at a time. During the *first pass* over the source code, the assembler looks at every instruction, keeping track of the memory address where this instruction will be stored when it is translated and loaded into memory. It does this by knowing where the program begins in memory and knowing how many memory cells are required to store each machine language instruction or piece of data. It also determines whether there is a symbol in the label field of the instruction. If there is, it enters the symbol and the address of this instruction into a special table that it is building called a symbol table.

We can see this process more clearly in Figure 6.10. The figure assumes that each instruction and data value occupies one memory cell and that the first instruction of the program will be placed into address 0.

The assembler looks at the first instruction in the program, IN X, and determines that when this instruction is loaded into memory, it will go into memory cell 0. Because the label LOOP is attached to that instruction, the name LOOP is made equivalent to address 0. The assembler enters the (name, value) pair (LOOP, 0) into the symbol table. This process of associating a

FIGURE 6.10

Label	Code		Location Counter	Symbol Table	
				Symbol	Address Value
LOOP:	IN	X	0	LOOP	0
	IN	Y	1	DONE	7
	LOAD	X	2	X	9
	COMPARE	Y	3	Y	10
	JUMPGT	DONE	4		
	OUT	X	5		
	JUMP	LOOP	6		
DONE:	OUT	Y	7		
	HALT		8		
X:	.DATA	0	9		
Y:	.DATA	0	10		

(a)   (b)

Generation of the symbol table

symbolic name with a physical memory address is called binding, and the two primary purposes of the first pass of an assembler are (1) to bind all symbolic names to address values and (2) to enter those bindings into the symbol table. Now, any time the programmer uses the name LOOP in the address field, the assembler can look up that symbol in column 1 of the symbol table and replace it with the address value in column 2, in this case address 0. (If it is not found, the programmer has used an undefined symbol, which produces an error message.)

The next six instructions of Figure 6.10(a), from IN Y to JUMP LOOP, do not contain labels, so they do not add new entries to the symbol table. However, the assembler must still update the counter it is using to determine the address where each instruction will ultimately be stored. The variable used to determine the address of a given instruction or piece of data is called the *location counter*. The location counter values are shown in the third column of Figure 6.10(a). Using the location counter, the assembler can determine that the address values of the labels DONE, X, and Y are 7, 9, and 10, respectively. It binds these symbolic names and addresses and enters them in the symbol table, as shown in Figure 6.10(b). When the first pass is done, the assembler has constructed a symbol table that it can use during pass 2. The algorithm for pass 1 of a typical assembler is shown (using an alternative form of algorithmic notation called a *flowchart*) in Figure 6.11.

During the *second pass*, the assembler translates the source program into machine language. It has the op code table to translate mnemonic op

FIGURE 6.11

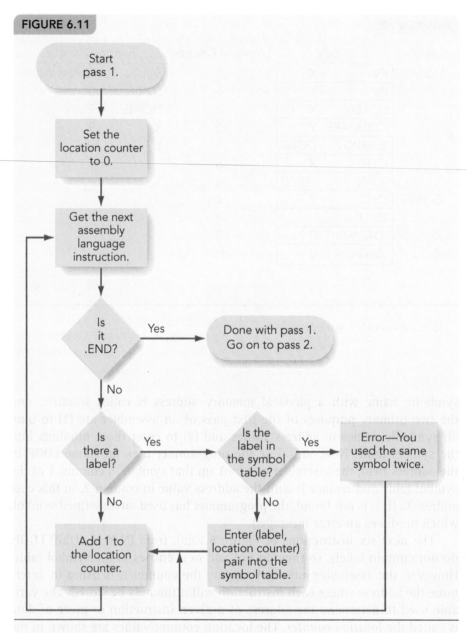

Outline of pass 1 of the assembler

codes to binary, and it has the symbol table to translate symbolic addresses to binary. Therefore, the second pass is relatively simple, involving two table lookups and the generation of two binary fields. For example, if we assume that our instruction format is a 4-bit op code followed by a single 12-bit address, then given the instruction

OUT   X

the assembler

1. looks up OUT in the op code table of Figure 6.9 and places the 4-bit binary value 1110 in the op code field

2. looks up the symbol X in the symbol table of Figure 6.10(b) and places the binary address value 0000 0000 1001 (decimal 9) into the address field

After these two steps, the assembler produces the 16-bit instruction

1110 0000 0000 1001

which is the correct machine language equivalent of the assembly language statement

OUT   X.

When it is done with one instruction, the assembler moves on to the next and translates it in the same fashion. This continues until it sees the pseudo-op .END, which terminates translation.

The other responsibilities of pass 2 are also relatively simple:

- Handling data generation pseudo-ops (only .DATA in our example)

- Producing the object file needed by the loader

The .DATA pseudo-op asks the assembler to build the proper binary representation for the signed decimal integer in the address field. To do this, the assembler must implement the sign/magnitude integer representation algorithms described in Section 4.2.

Finally, after all the fields of an instruction have been translated into binary, the newly built machine language instruction and the address of where it is to be loaded are written to a file called the object file. (On Windows machines, this is referred to as an .exe file, which stands for "executable program.") The algorithm for pass 2 of the assembler is shown in Figure 6.12.

After completion of pass 1 and pass 2, the object file contains the translated machine language object program, referred to in Figure 6.4. One possible object program for the assembly language program of Figure 6.10(a) is shown in Figure 6.13. (Note that a real object file contains only the address and instruction fields. The meaning field is included here for clarity only.)

The object program shown in Figure 6.13 becomes input to yet another piece of system software called a loader. It is the task of the loader to read instructions from the object file and store them into memory for execution. To do this, it reads an address value—column 1 of Figure 6.13—and a machine language instruction—column 2 of Figure 6.13—and stores that instruction into the specified memory address. This operation is repeated for every instruction in the object file. When loading is complete, the loader places the address of the first instruction (0 in this example) into the program counter (PC) to initiate execution. The hardware, as we learned in Chapter 5, then begins the fetch, decode, and execute cycle starting with the instruction whose address is located in the PC, namely, the beginning of this program.

FIGURE 6.12

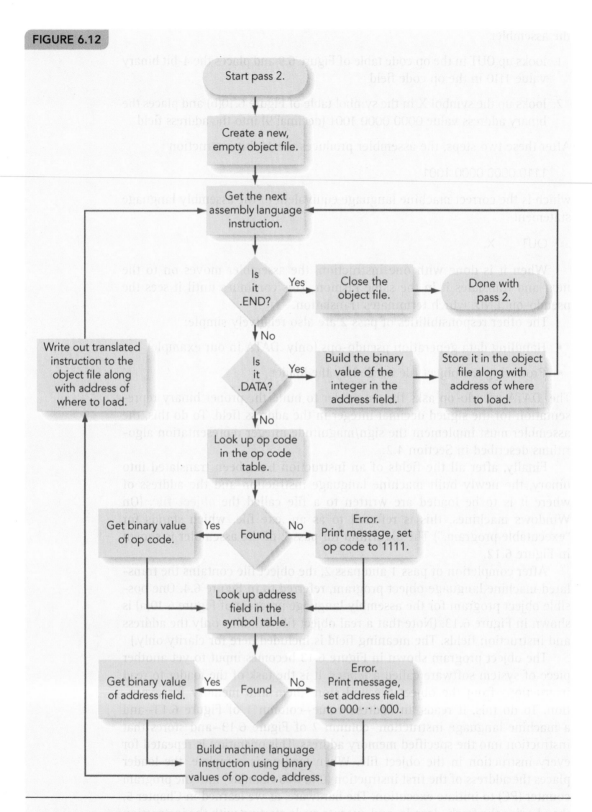

Outline of pass 2 of the assembler

FIGURE 6.13

Instruction Format:	Op Code	Address
	4 bits	12 bits

Object Program:

Address	Machine Language Instruction	Meaning
0000	1101 000000001001	IN X
0001	1101 000000001010	IN Y
0010	0000 000000001001	LOAD X
0011	0111 000000001010	COMPARE Y
0100	1001 000000000111	JUMPGT DONE
0101	1110 000000001001	OUT X
0110	1000 000000000000	JUMP LOOP
0111	1110 000000001010	OUT Y
1000	1111 000000000000	HALT
1001	0000 000000000000	The constant 0
1010	0000 000000000000	The constant 0

Example of an object program

Practice Problems

1. Translate the following algorithm into assembly language using the instructions in Figure 6.5.

Step	Operation
1	Set *Negative Count* to 0
2	Set *i* to 1
3	While *i* ≤ 50 do Lines 4 through 6
4	Input a number *N*
5	If *N* < 0 then increment *Negative Count* by 1
6	Increment *i* by 1
7	End of the loop
8	Output the value of *Negative Count*
9	Stop

2. What is the machine language representation of each of the following instructions? Assume the symbol table values are as shown in Figure 6.10(b) and the instruction format is that of Figure 6.13.

   a. COMPARE   Y
   b. JUMPNEQ   DONE
   c. DECREMENT   LOOP

(continued)

3. What is wrong or inconsistent with the instruction that is shown in Practice Problem 2c?

4. Take the assembly language program that you developed in Practice Problem 1 and determine the physical memory address associated with each label in the symbol table. (Assume the first instruction is loaded into address 0 and that each instruction occupies one cell.)

5. Is the following assembly language pseudo-op illegal? Explain why or why not.

        TWO: DATA   1

6.4 Operating Systems

To carry out the services just described (translate a program, load a program, run a program), a user must issue system commands, which are commands sent to the operating system to perform a service on the user's behalf. In earlier times these commands were lines of text typed at a terminal, such as

>assemble MyProg   (Invoke the assembler to translate a program
                      called MyProg.)

>run MyProg   (Load the translated MyProg and start execution.)

Today, however, these services are invoked using icons displayed on a screen and selected with a mouse, button, finger tap, or voice command.

Regardless of how the process is initiated, the important question is: Which program examines these commands? Which piece of system software waits for requests from a user and activates other system programs like a translator or information manager to service these requests? The answer is the operating system, and, as shown in Figure 6.2, it is the "top-level" system software component on a computer.

Some of the more well-known operating systems in widespread use today include Windows 10, macOS, and Linux for mainframes, desktops, and laptops, and Google Android and Apple iOS for mobile devices.

6.4.1 Functions of an Operating System

An operating system is an enormously large and complex piece of software that has many responsibilities within a computer system. This section examines five of the most important tasks that it performs.

The User Interface. The operating system is executing whenever no other piece of user or system software is using the processor. Its most important task is to wait for a user command delivered via a keypad, mouse, finger tap, voice command, or other input device. If the command is legal, the operating system activates and schedules the appropriate software package to process the request. In this sense, the operating system acts like the computer's *receptionist* and *dispatcher*.

Operating system commands usually request access to hardware resources (processor, output device, communication line, camera), software services (web browser, application program), or information (data files, contact lists). Examples of typical operating system commands are shown in Figure 6.14. Modern operating systems can typically recognize and execute hundreds of unique commands.

After a user enters a command, the operating system determines which software package needs to be loaded and put on the schedule for execution. When that package completes execution, control returns to the operating system, which waits for a user to enter the next command. This user interface algorithm is diagrammed in Figure 6.15.

The user interfaces on the operating systems of the 1950s, 1960s, and 1970s were text oriented. The system displayed a *prompt character* on the screen to indicate that it was waiting for input, and then it waited for something to happen. The user entered commands in a special, and sometimes quite cryptic, command language. For example, on the UNIX operating system, widely used on personal computers and workstations, the following command asks the system to list the names and access privileges of the files contained in the home directory of a user called mike:

> ls -al/usr/mike/home   (">" is the prompt character)

As you can see, commands were not always easy to understand, and learning the command language of the operating system was a major stumbling block for new users. Unfortunately, without first learning some basic commands, no useful work could be done.

Because users found text-oriented command languages very cumbersome, all modern operating systems utilize a graphical user interface, (GUI). To communicate with a user, a GUI supports visual aids and point-and-click or touchscreen operations, rather than textual commands. These interfaces use *icons, pull-down menus, scrolling, resizable windows,* and other visual

---

FIGURE 6.14

- Load a program into memory
- Run a program
- Save information in a file or a directory
- Retrieve a file previously stored on the local machine or in the cloud
- List all the files for this user
- Delete or rename a file
- Display a file on a specified device
- Copy a file from one device to another
- Establish a network connection
- Let the user set or change one of the current machine settings
- Tell how much memory or data storage is currently in use
- Put the device to sleep or turn it off

Some typical operating system commands

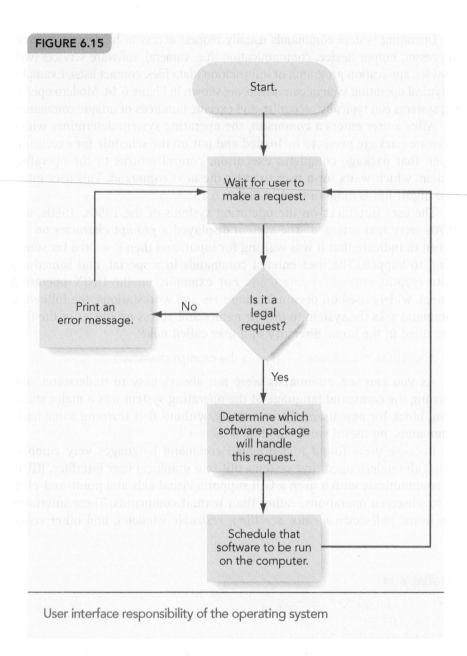

FIGURE 6.15

Start.

Wait for user to make a request.

Is it a legal request?

No → Print an error message.

Yes

Determine which software package will handle this request.

Schedule that software to be run on the computer.

User interface responsibility of the operating system

elements and graphical metaphors that make it much easier for a user to formulate requests. Operating systems for mobile devices such as tablets and smartphones allow users to employ finger taps and voice-activated commands to specify the operations they wish to perform.

Graphical, touchscreen, and voice-activated user interfaces are excellent examples of the high-level virtual machine created by the operating system. They hide the complexity of the underlying hardware and software and make your computer, tablet, or smartphone appear very easy to use. In reality, the processor inside is identical to the horribly complicated "naked" Von Neumann machine described in Chapters 4 and 5.

A Machine for the Rest of Us

In January 1984, Apple Computer launched its new line of Macintosh computers with a great deal of showmanship: a TV commercial at the 1984 NFL Super Bowl. The company described the Macintosh as a computer that anyone could understand and use—"a machine for the rest of us." People who saw and used it quickly agreed, and in the early days, its major selling point was that "a Macintosh is much easier to use than an IBM PC." However, the Macintosh and IBM PC were extremely similar in terms of hardware. Both systems used Von Neumann–type processors, and these processors executed similar sets of machine language instructions exactly as described in Chapter 5. (In fact, in 2006 Apple began using the same type of Intel processors as in the IBM PC and its clones.) It certainly was not the underlying hardware that created these huge differences in ease of use.

What made the Macintosh easier to use was its radically new graphical user interface that most users found much easier to understand than the text-oriented interface of MS-DOS, the most popular PC-based operating system at that time. IBM users quickly realized the importance of having a powerful visual interface, and in the early- and mid-1990s began to switch to Microsoft Windows, which provided a windowing environment similar to the Macintosh. Newer versions of these systems, such as macOS and Windows 10, represent attempts at creating an even more powerful and easy-to-use virtual environment.

We can see now that it was wrong for Apple to say that "a Macintosh is easier to use than a PC." What it should have said is that "the virtual machine environment created by the Macintosh operating system is easier to use than the virtual machine environment created by the MS-DOS operating system." However, maybe that was just a little too wordy!

System Security and Protection. In addition to being a receptionist, the operating system also has the responsibilities of a *security guard*—controlling access to the computer and its resources. It must prevent unauthorized users from accessing the system and prevent authorized users from doing unauthorized things.

At a minimum, the operating system must not allow people to access the computer if they have not been granted permission. In the "olden days" of computing (the 1950s and 1960s), security was implemented by physical means—walls and locked doors around the computer and security guards at the door to prevent unauthorized access. However, when telecommunications networks appeared on the scene in the late 1960s and 1970s (we will discuss them in detail in Chapter 7), access to computers over networks became possible from virtually anywhere in the world, and responsibility for access control migrated from the guard at the door to the operating system inside the machine.

In most operating systems, access control means requiring a user to enter a legal *username* and *password* before any other requests are accepted. If an incorrect username or password is entered, the operating system does not allow access to the computer.

It is also the operating system's responsibility to safeguard the *password file* that stores all valid username/password combinations. It must prevent this file from being accessed by any unauthorized users because that would compromise the security of the entire system. This is analogous to putting a lock on your door but also making sure that you don't lose the key. (Of course, some privileged users, called *superusers*—usually computer center employees or system administrators—must be able to access and maintain this file.) To provide this security, the operating system may choose to *encrypt* the password file using an encoding algorithm that is extremely difficult to crack. Operating systems use encryption algorithms whenever they must provide a high degree of security for sensitive information. We will learn more about these encryption algorithms in Chapter 8.

Even when valid users gain access to the system, there are operations they should not be allowed to do. For example, although users can delete any personal application programs on their smartphones, they are not allowed to delete system applications such as "Change Settings," "Notes," and "Calendar." On multiuser systems, users are allowed to access only their own personal information. They should not be able to look at the files of other users. Therefore, if the operating system gets a request such as

> open filename (Open a file and allow this user to access it.)

(Or click Open in the File menu.)

it must determine who is the owner of the file—that is, who created it. If the individual accessing the file is not the owner, then the operating system usually rejects the request.

Most modern operating systems not only determine whether you are allowed to access a file, they also check what operations you are permitted to perform on that file by keeping an *access control list*.

For example, the grade file GRADES of a student named Smith could have the access control list shown in Figure 6.16. This access control list says that Smith, the student whose grades are in the file, has the right to access his or her own file, but only to read the information. Jones, a clerk in the administration center, can read the file and can append new grades to the end of the file at the completion of the term. Adams, the school's registrar, can read and append information and also is allowed to change the student's grades if an error was made. Doe, the director of the computer center, can do all of these operations as well as delete the file and all its information.

Permission to look at information can be given to a number of people. However, changing information in a file is a sensitive operation (think about

FIGURE 6.16

File:　GRADES

Name	Permitted Operations
Smith	R (R = Read only)
Jones	RA (A = Append)
Adams	RAC (C = Change)
Doe	RACD (D = Delete)

Access control list for the file GRADES

changing a payroll file), and permission to make changes must be limited. Deleting information (such as smartphone system programs like "Settings") is the most powerful and potentially damaging operation of all, and its use must be restricted to people at the highest level. It is the operating system's responsibility to help ensure that individuals are authorized to carry out the operation they request.

Computers today play such a critical role in the storage and management of military, medical, economic, social, and personal data that this security responsibility of the operating system has taken on an increasingly important role. We will investigate this topic in more detail in Chapter 8.

Efficient Management of Resources. Section 5.2.2 described the enormous difference in speed between a processor and an I/O unit: up to 5 orders of magnitude. A hardware device called an I/O controller (Figure 5.15) frees the processor to do useful work while the I/O operation is being completed. What useful work can a processor do in this free time? What ensures that this valuable resource is used efficiently? Again, it is the operating system's responsibility to see that the resources of a computer system are used efficiently as well as correctly.

To ensure that a processor does not sit idle if there is useful work to do, the operating system keeps a *queue* (a waiting line) of programs that are ready to run. Whenever the processor is idle, the operating system picks one of these jobs and assigns it to the processor. This guarantees that the processor always has something to do.

To see how this algorithm might work, let's define the following three classes of programs:

Running	The one program currently executing on the processor (assume only a single processor on the computer)
Ready	Programs that are loaded in memory and ready to run but are not yet executing
Waiting	Programs that cannot run because they are waiting for an operation to complete or some special event, such as an incoming phone call, to occur

Here is how these three lists might look at some instant in time:

Waiting	Ready	Running
	B	A
	C	
	D	

There are four programs, called A, B, C, and D, in memory. Program A is executing on the processor; B, C, and D are ready to run and are in line waiting their turn. Assume that program A performs the I/O operation "read a sector from the disk." (Maybe it is a word processor, and it needs to get another piece of the document on which you are working.) We saw in Section 5.2.2 that, relative to processing speeds, this operation takes a long time, about 10 msec or so. While it is waiting for this disk I/O operation to finish, the processor has nothing to do, and system efficiency plummets.

To solve this problem, the operating system can do some shuffling. It first moves program A to the waiting list because it must wait for its I/O operation to finish before it can continue. It then selects one of the ready programs (say B) and assigns it to the processor, which starts executing it. This leads to the following situation:

Waiting	Ready	Running
A	C	B
	D	

Instead of sitting idle while A waits for I/O, the processor works on program B and gets something useful done. This is equivalent to working on another project while a large document is printing, instead of waiting and doing nothing.

Perhaps B also does an I/O operation, such as asking the user to input a piece of data. If so, then the operating system repeats the same steps. It moves B to the waiting list, picks any ready program (say C) and starts executing it, producing the following situation:

Waiting	Ready	Running
A	D	C
B		

As long as there is at least one program that is ready to run, the processor always has something useful to do.

At some point, the I/O operation that A started finishes, and the "I/O completed interrupt signal" described in Section 5.2.2 is generated. The appearance of that signal indicates that program A is now ready to run, but it cannot do so immediately because the processor is currently assigned to C. Instead, the operating system moves A to the ready list, producing the following situation:

Waiting	Ready	Running
B	D	C
	A	

Programs cycle from running to waiting to ready and back to running, each one using only a portion of the resources of the processor. (However, there are situations in which a program must be started immediately, ahead of other programs on the waiting list. For example, when a phone call arrives we immediately suspend whatever we are doing and execute the program that displays an "Incoming Call" message and allows us to accept the call. If we do not do that, the caller will most likely hang up.)

In Chapter 5, we stated that the execution of a program is an unbroken repetition of the fetch/decode/execute cycle from the first instruction of the program to the HALT. Now we see that this view may not be completely accurate. For reasons of efficiency or priority, the history of a program may be a sequence of starts and stops—a cycle of execution, waits for I/O operations, waits for the processor, followed again by execution. By having many programs loaded in memory and sharing the processor, the operating system can manage the processor to its fullest capability and run the overall system more efficiently.

The Safe Use of Resources. Not only must resources be used *efficiently,* they must also be used *safely.* That doesn't mean an operating system must prevent users from sticking their fingers in the power supply and getting electrocuted! The job of the operating system is to prevent programs or users from attempting operations that cause the computer system to enter a state in which it is incapable of doing any further work—a "frozen" state where all useful work comes to a grinding halt.

To see how this can happen, imagine a computer system that has one laser printer, one data file called D, and two programs A and B. Program A wants to load data file D and print it on the laser printer. Program B wants

Practice Problems

1. Assume that programs spend about 25% of their time waiting for I/O operations to complete. If there are two programs loaded into memory, what is the likelihood that both programs will be blocked waiting for I/O and there will be nothing for the processor to do? What percentage of time will the processor be busy? (This value is called *processor utilization.*) By how much does processor utilization improve if we have four programs in memory instead of two?

2. Why are passwords extremely vulnerable to security breaches? Suggest ways to improve their use and reduce the risk associated with them.

to do the same thing. Each of them makes the following requests to the operating system:

Program A	Program B
Get data file D.	Get the laser printer.
Get the laser printer.	Get data file D.
Print the file.	Print the file.

If the operating system satisfies the first request of each program, then A "owns" data file D, and B has the laser printer. When A requests ownership of the laser printer, it is told that the printer is being used by B. Similarly, B is told that it must wait for the data file until A is finished with it. Each program is waiting for a resource to become available that will never become free. This situation is called a deadlock. Programs A and B are in a permanent waiting state, and if there is no other program ready to run, all useful work on the system ceases.

More formally, deadlock means that there is a set of programs, each of which is waiting for an event to occur before it may proceed, but that event can be caused only by another waiting program in the set. Another example is a telecommunications system in which program A sends messages to program B, which acknowledges their correct receipt. Program A cannot send another message to B until it knows that the last one has been correctly received.

Program A	Program B
Message →	
	← Acknowledge
Message →	
	← Acknowledge
Message →	

Suppose B now sends an acknowledgment, but it gets lost. (Perhaps there was static on the line, or a lightning bolt jumbled the signal.) What happens? Program A stops and waits for receipt of an acknowledgment from B. Program B stops and waits for the next message from A. Deadlock! Neither side can proceed, and unless something is done, all communication between the two will cease.

How does an operating system handle deadlock conditions? There are two basic approaches, called *deadlock prevention* and *deadlock recovery*. In deadlock prevention, the operating system uses resource allocation algorithms that prevent deadlock from occurring in the first place. In the example of the two programs simultaneously requesting the laser printer and the data file, the problem is caused by the fact that each program has a portion of the resources needed to solve its problem, but neither has all that it requested. To prevent this, the operating system can use the following algorithm:

> If a program cannot get all the resources that it needs to solve a problem, it must give up all the resources it currently owns and issue a completely new request.

Essentially, this resource allocation algorithm says, "If you cannot get everything you need, then you get nothing." If we had used this algorithm, then after program A acquired the laser printer but not the data file, it would have had to relinquish ownership of the printer. Now B could get everything it needed to execute, and no deadlock would occur. (It could also work in the reverse direction, with B relinquishing ownership of the data file and A getting the needed resources. Which scenario unfolds depends on the exact order in which requests are made.)

In the telecommunications example, one deadlock prevention algorithm is to require that messages and acknowledgments never get garbled or lost. Unfortunately, that is impossible. Real-world communication systems (telephone, WiFi, satellite) do make errors, so we are powerless to guarantee that deadlock conditions can never occur. Instead we must detect them and recover from them when they do occur. This is typical of the class of methods called *deadlock recovery algorithms*.

For example, here is a possible algorithmic solution to our telecommunications problem:

Sender: Number your messages with the nonnegative integers 0, 1, 2, ... and send them in numerical order. If you send message number *i* and have not received an acknowledgment for 30 seconds, send message *i* again.

Receiver: When you send an acknowledgment, include the number of the message you received. If you get a duplicate copy of message *i*, send another acknowledgment and discard the duplicate.

Using this algorithm, here is what might happen:

Program A	**Program B**
Message (1) →	
	← Acknowledge (1)
Message (2) →	
	← Acknowledge (2)
	(Assume this acknowledgment is lost.)

At this point, we have exactly the same deadlock condition described earlier. However, this time we are able to recover in a relatively short period. For 30 seconds nothing happens. However, after 30 seconds A sends message (2) a second time. B acknowledges it and discards it (because it already has a copy), and communication continues:

Program A	**Program B**
(Wait 30 seconds.)	
Message (2) →	(Discard this duplicate copy but acknowledge it.)
	← Acknowledge (2)
Message (3) →	

We have successfully recovered from the error, and the system is again up and running.

Regardless of whether we prevent deadlocks from occurring or recover from those that do occur, it is the responsibility of the operating system to create a virtual machine in which the user never sees deadlocks and does not worry about them. The operating system should create the illusion of a smoothly functioning, highly efficient, error-free environment—even if, as we know from our glimpse behind the scenes, that is not always the case. (We all know how frustrating it can be when our computer or tablet freezes up, and we must restart the entire system. A well-designed operating system should make this an extremely rare event.)

Summary. In this section, we have highlighted some of the major responsibilities of the critically important software package called the operating system:

- User interface management (a receptionist)
- Control of access to the system and to data files (a security guard)
- Program scheduling and activation (a dispatcher)
- Efficient resource allocation (an efficiency expert)
- Deadlock detection and error detection (a traffic officer)

These are by no means the operating system's only responsibilities, which can also include such areas as input/output processing, allocating priorities to programs, swapping programs in and out of memory, recovering from power failures, managing the system clock, and dozens of other tasks, large and small, essential to keeping the computer system running smoothly.

As you can imagine, given all these responsibilities, an operating system is an extraordinarily complex piece of software. An operating system for a large network of computers can require millions of lines of code, take thousands of person-years to develop, and cost more to develop than the hardware on which it runs. Even operating systems for smartphones and tablets (such as Android and iOS) are huge programs developed over periods of years by teams of dozens of computer scientists. Designing and creating a high-level virtual environment is a difficult job, but without it, computers would not be so widely used nor anywhere near as important as they are today.

6.4.2 Historical Overview of Operating Systems Development

Like the hardware on which it runs, system software has gone through a number of changes since the earliest days of computing. The functions and capabilities of a modern operating system described in the previous section did not appear all at once but evolved over many years.

During the *first generation* of system software (roughly 1945–1955), there really were no operating systems and there was very little software support of any kind—typically just the assemblers and loaders described in Section 6.3. All machine operation was "hands-on." Programmers would sign up for a block of time and, at the appointed time, show up in the machine room carrying their programs on punched cards or tapes. They had the entire computer to themselves, and they were responsible for all machine operation. They loaded their assembly language programs into memory along with the assembler and, by punching some buttons on the console, started the translation process. Then they loaded their program into memory and started it running. Working with first-generation software was a lot like working on the naked machine described at the beginning of the chapter. It was attempted only by highly trained professionals intimately familiar with the computer and its operation.

System administrators quickly realized that this was a horribly inefficient way to use an expensive piece of equipment. (Remember that these early computers cost millions of dollars.) A programmer would sign up for an hour of computer time, but the majority of that time was spent analyzing results and trying to figure out what to do next. During this "thinking time," the system was idle and doing nothing of value. Eventually, the need to keep machines busy led to the development of a *second generation* of system software called batch operating systems (1955–1965).

In second-generation batch operating systems, rather than operate the machine directly, a programmer handed the program (typically entered on punched cards) to a trained computer operator, who grouped it into a "batch"—hence the name. After a few dozen programs were collected, the operator carried this batch of cards to a small I/O computer that put these programs on tape. This tape was carried into the machine room and loaded onto the "big" computer that actually ran the users' programs, one at a time, writing the results to yet another tape. During the last stage, this output tape was carried back to the I/O computer to be printed and handed to the programmer. The entire cycle is diagrammed in Figure 6.17.

This cycle might seem cumbersome and, from the programmer's point of view, it was. (Every programmer who worked in the late 1950s or early 1960s has horror stories about waiting many hours—even days—for a program to be returned, only to discover that there was a missing comma.) From the computer's point of view, however, this new batch system worked wonderfully, and system utilization increased dramatically. No longer were there delays while a programmer was setting up to perform an operation. There were no long periods of idleness while someone was mulling over what to do next. As soon as one job was either completed normally or halted because of an error, the computer went to the input tape, loaded the next job, and started execution. As long as there was work to be done, the computer was kept busy.

FIGURE 6.17

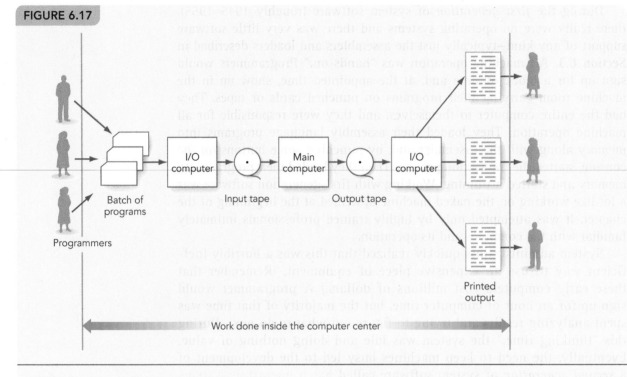

Operation of a batch computer system

Now That's Big!

The most widely used measure of program size is *source lines of code* (abbreviated SLOC). This is a count of the total number of nonblank, noncomment lines in a piece of software. According to Wikipedia (*www.wikipedia.org*), the estimated size of Mac OS X Tiger (10.4)—an older version but the latest for which there is reliable data—is 86 million SLOC. If you were to print out the entire program, at 60 lines per printed page, you would generate about 1,433,000 pages of output, or roughly the number of pages in 4,000 full-length novels. As an even more enormous example, the code required to run all of Google's popular applications—Gmail, Google Maps, Google Docs, Google+, and so on—contains *two billion* lines of code! If you were to store that output on a bookshelf, it would stretch for more than two miles.

It is estimated that the average programmer can produce about 40 lines of correct code per day. If that number is accurate, then the code for all Google apps represents about 50 million person-days, or (at 250 working days per year) about 200,000 person-years of effort.

Because programmers no longer operated the machine, they needed a way to communicate to the operating system what had to be done, and these early batch operating systems were the first to include a *command language*, also called a *job control language*. This was a special-purpose language in which users wrote commands specifying to the operating system (or the human operator) what operations to perform on their programs. These commands were interpreted by the operating system, which initiated the proper action. The "receptionist/dispatcher" responsibility of the operating system had been born. A typical batch job was a mix of programs, data, and commands, as shown in Figure 6.18.

By the mid-1960s, integrated circuits and other new technologies had boosted computational speeds enormously. The batch operating system just described kept only a single program in memory at any one time. If that job paused for a few milliseconds to complete an I/O operation (such as read a disk sector or print a file on the printer), the processor simply waited. As computers became faster, designers began to look for ways to use those idle milliseconds. The answer they came up with led to a *third generation* of operating systems called multiprogrammed operating systems (1965–1985).

FIGURE 6.18

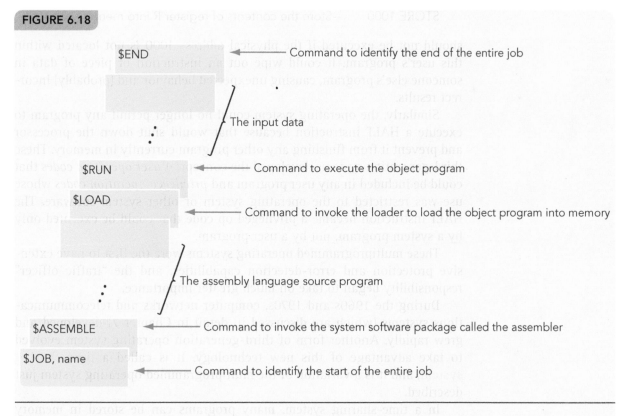

$END ———— Command to identify the end of the entire job

The input data

$RUN ———— Command to execute the object program

$LOAD ———— Command to invoke the loader to load the object program into memory

The assembly language source program

$ASSEMBLE ———— Command to invoke the system software package called the assembler

$JOB, name

———— Command to identify the start of the entire job

Structure of a typical batch job

In a multiprogrammed operating system, many user programs, rather than just one, are simultaneously loaded into memory:

Memory

Operating System
Program 1
Program 2
Program 3

If the currently executing program pauses for I/O, one of the other ready jobs is selected for execution so that no time is wasted. As we described earlier, this cycle of running/waiting/ready states led to significantly higher processor utilization.

To make this all work properly, the operating system had to protect user programs (and itself) from damage by other programs. When there was a single program in memory, the only user program that could be damaged was your own. Now, with many programs in memory, an erroneous instruction in one user's program could wreak havoc on any of the others. For example, the seemingly harmless instruction

STORE 1000   --Store the contents of register R into memory cell 1000

should not be executed if the physical address 1000 is not located within this user's program. It could wipe out an instruction or piece of data in someone else's program, causing unexpected behavior and (probably) incorrect results.

Similarly, the operating system could no longer permit any program to execute a HALT instruction because that would shut down the processor and prevent it from finishing any other program currently in memory. These third-generation systems developed the concept of *user operation codes* that could be included in any user program and *privileged operation codes* whose use was restricted to the operating system or other system software. The HALT instruction became a privileged op code that could be executed only by a system program, not by a user program.

These multiprogrammed operating systems were the first to have extensive protection and error-detection capabilities, and the "traffic officer" responsibility began to take on much greater importance.

During the 1960s and 1970s, computer networks and telecommunications systems (which are discussed in detail in Chapter 7) developed and grew rapidly. Another form of third-generation operating system evolved to take advantage of this new technology. It is called a time-sharing system, and it is a variation of the multiprogrammed operating system just described.

In a time-sharing system, many programs can be stored in memory rather than just one. However, instead of requiring the programmer to load all system commands, programs, and data in advance, a time-sharing

FIGURE 6.19

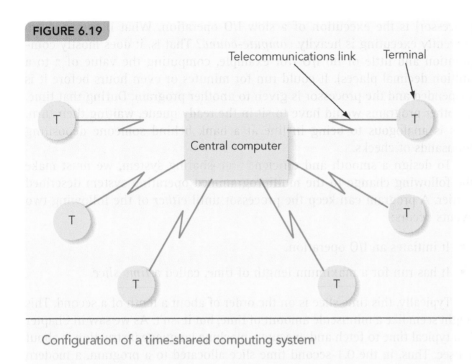

Telecommunications link   Terminal

Central computer

Configuration of a time-shared computing system

system allows them to be entered online—that is, entered dynamically by users sitting at terminals and communicating interactively with the operating system. This configuration is shown in Figure 6.19.

The terminals are connected to the central computer via communication links and can be located anywhere. This new system design freed users from the "tyranny of geography." No longer did they have to go to the computer to hand in their deck of cards; the services of the computer were delivered directly to them via their terminal. However, now that the walls and doors of the computer center no longer provided security and access control, the "security guard/watchman" responsibility became an extremely important part of operating system design. (We will discuss the topic of computer security at length in Chapter 8.)

In a time-sharing system, a user would sit down at a terminal, log in, and initiate a program or make a request by entering a command:

>run   MyJob

In this example, the program called MyJob would be loaded into memory and would compete for the processor with all other ready programs. When the program was finished running, the system would again display a prompt (">") and wait for the next command. The user could examine the results of the last program, think for a while, and decide what to do next, rather than having to determine the entire sequence of operations in advance.

However, one minor change was needed to make this new system work efficiently. In a "true" multiprogrammed environment, the only event, other than termination, that causes a program to be *suspended* (taken off the processor) is the execution of a slow I/O operation. What if the program currently executing is heavily *compute-bound*? That is, it does mostly computation and little or no I/O (for example, computing the value of π to a million decimal places). It could run for minutes or even hours before it is suspended and the processor is given to another program. During that time, all other programs would have to sit in the ready queue, waiting their turn. This is analogous to being in line at a bank behind someone depositing thousands of checks.

To design a smooth and efficient time-sharing system, we must make the following change to the multiprogrammed operating system described earlier. A program can keep the processor until *either* of the following two events occurs:

- It initiates an I/O operation.

- It has run for a maximum length of time, called a *time slice*.

Typically, this time slice is on the order of about a tenth of a second. This might seem like a minuscule amount of time, but it isn't. As we saw in Chapter 5, a typical time to fetch and execute a machine language instruction is about 1 nsec. Thus, in the 0.1-second time slice allocated to a program, a modern processor could execute roughly 100 million machine language instructions.

The basic idea in a time-sharing system is to service many users in a circular, round-robin fashion, giving each one a small amount of time and then moving on to the next. If there are not too many users on the system, the processor can get back to a user before he or she even notices any delay. Each one will believe that they have the entire system to themselves. Time-sharing was the dominant form of operating system during the 1970s and 1980s, and time-sharing terminals appeared throughout government offices, businesses, and campuses.

The early 1980s saw the appearance of the first personal computers (known as PCs or microcomputers), and in many business and academic environments the "dumb" terminal began to be replaced by these PCs. Initially, the PC was viewed as simply another type of terminal, and during its early days it was used primarily to access a central time-sharing system. However, as PCs became faster and more powerful, people soon realized that much of the computing being done on the centralized machine could be done much more conveniently and cheaply by the microcomputers sitting on their desktops.

During the late 1980s and the 1990s, computing rapidly changed from the centralized environment typical of batch, multiprogramming, and time-sharing systems to a *distributed environment* in which much of the computing was done remotely in the office, laboratory, classroom, and factory. Computing moved from the computer center out to where the real work was being done. The operating systems available for early personal computers were simple *single-user operating systems* that gave one user total access to the entire system. Because personal computers were so cheap, there was really no need for many users to share their resources, and the time-sharing and multiprogramming designs of the third generation became less important.

Although personal computers were relatively cheap (and were becoming cheaper all the time), many of the peripherals and supporting gear–laser printers, large disk drives, tape backup units, and specialized software packages– were not. In addition, email was growing in importance, and stand-alone PCs were unable to communicate easily with other users and partake in this important new application. The personal computer era required a new approach to operating system design. It needed a virtual environment that supported both *local computation* and *remote access* to other users and shared resources.

This led to the development of a *fourth-generation* operating system called a network operating system (1985–present). A network operating system manages not only the resources of a single computer but also the capabilities of a telecommunications system called a *local area network*, or *LAN* for short. (We will take a much closer look at these types of networks in Chapter 7.) A LAN is a network that is located in a geographically contiguous area such as a room, a building, or a campus. It is composed of personal computers (workstations), and special shared resources called *servers*, all interconnected via a high-speed link, either wireless or constructed from coaxial or fiber-optic cable. A typical LAN configuration is shown in Figure 6.20.

The users of the individual computers in Figure 6.20, called *clients*, can perform local computations without accessing the network. In this mode, the operating system provides exactly the same services described earlier: loading and executing programs and managing the resources of this one machine.

However, a user can also access any one of the shared network resources just as though it were local. These resources are provided by a computer called a *server* and can include a special high-quality laser printer, a shared file system, a large computational node, or access to an international network such as the Internet. The system software does all the work, hiding the complex details of communication and competition with other nodes for shared resources.

FIGURE 6.20

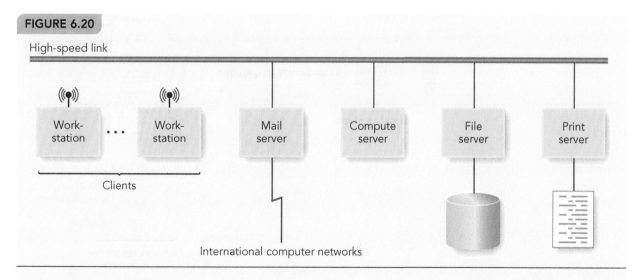

A local area network

Network operating systems create a virtual machine that extends beyond the boundaries of the local system on which the user is working. They let us access a huge pool of resources—computers, servers, and other users—exactly as though they were connected to our own computers. This fourth-generation virtual environment, exemplified by operating systems such as Windows 10, macOS, Linux, iOS, and Android, is diagrammed in Figure 6.21.

One important variation of the network operating system is called a real-time operating system. During the 1980s and 1990s, computers got smaller and smaller, and it became common to place them inside other pieces of equipment to control their operation. These types of computers are called embedded systems; examples include computers placed inside auto-mobile engines, microwave ovens, thermostats, assembly lines, airplanes, homes, and even the treadmill at your local fitness center.

For example, the Boeing 787 Dreamliner jet contains hundreds of embed-ded computer systems inside its engines, braking system, wings, landing gear, and cabin. The central computer controlling the overall operation of the airplane is connected to these embedded computers that monitor system functions and send status information.

In all the operating systems described thus far, we have implied that the system satisfies requests for services and resources in the order received. In some systems, however, certain requests are much more important than others, and when these important requests arrive, we must drop everything

FIGURE 6.21

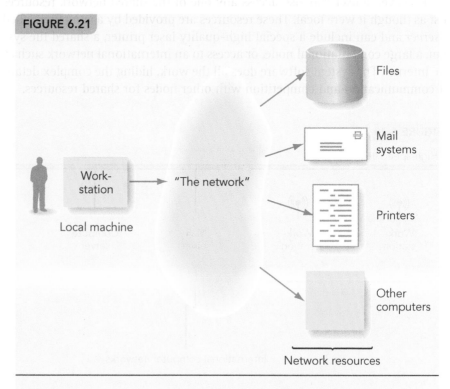

The virtual environment created by a network operating system

else to service them. Imagine that the central computer on our Boeing 787 receives two requests. The first request is from a cabin monitoring sensor that wants the central system to raise the cabin temperature a little for passenger comfort. The second message comes from the onboard collision-detection system and says that another plane is approaching on the same flight path, and there is about to be a midair collision. It would like the central computer to take evasive action. Which request should be serviced next? Of course, the collision-detection message, even though it arrived second.

A real-time operating system manages the resources of embedded computers that are controlling ongoing physical processes and that have requests that must be serviced within fixed time constraints. This type of operating system guarantees that it can service important requests within a fixed amount of time. For example, it may guarantee that, regardless of what else it is currently doing, if a collision-detection message arrives, the software implementing collision avoidance will be scheduled, activated, and executed within 50 milliseconds. Typically, the way that this guarantee is implemented is that all requests to a real-time operating system are *prioritized*. Instead of being handled in first-come, first-served order, they are handled in priority sequence, from most important to least important, where "importance" is defined in terms of the time-critical nature of the request. A real-time operating system lets passengers be uncomfortably cool for a few more seconds while it handles the problem of avoiding a midair collision.

6.4.3 The Future

The discussions in this chapter show that, just as there have been huge changes in hardware over the last 50 years, there have been equally huge changes in system software. We have progressed from a first-generation environment in which a user had to personally manage the computing hardware, to current fourth-generation systems in which users can request services from anywhere in the world using networking capabilities and powerful and easy-to-use graphical user interfaces.

And just as hardware capabilities continue to improve, there is a good deal of computer science research directed at further improving the high-level virtual environment created by a modern fourth-generation operating system. A fifth-generation operating system is certainly not far off.

Like Apple's personal assistant Siri and Google's Android Assistant, these next-generation operating systems will have powerful user interfaces that incorporate not only text, touch, and graphics but voice-activated commands, photography, facial and body gestures, video and TV, along with artificial intelligence capabilities that allow it to learn about your personal and professional characteristics. These *intelligent multimedia user interfaces* will interact with users and solicit requests in a variety of ways. Instead of point-and-click, a fully integrated fifth-generation system might allow you to speak the command, "What do I have planned for today?" The results may include a verbal reminder of an important meeting, a map of how to reach the meeting site, the agenda, articles that the system automatically determined you should read to prepare, and photographs of important people who will be attending. It may even make a comment on whether you are dressed appropriately! Just as text-only systems are now viewed as totally outmoded, today's GUIs will be viewed as far too limiting in terms of their user/system interaction.

A fifth-generation operating system will typically be running on a massively parallel processor, and it will need to efficiently manage a computer system containing hundreds or even thousands of processors (today's multicore machines typically contain only two, four, or six processors per chip). Such an operating system will need to recognize opportunities for parallel execution, send the separate tasks to the appropriate processor, and coordinate their concurrent execution, all in a way that is transparent to the user. On this virtual machine, a user will be unaware that multiple processors even exist except that programs now run 10, 100, or 1,000 times faster.

Finally, new fifth-generation operating systems will create a truly distributed computing environment in which users do not need to know the location of a given resource within the network. This is analogous to the way that the manager of a business gives instructions to an assistant: "Get this job done. I don't care how or where. Just do it, and when you are done, give me the results." The details of how and where to get the job done are left to the underling. The manager is concerned only with the final results.

In a truly distributed operating system, the user is the manager, the operating system is the assistant, and the user does not care where or how the system satisfies a request as long as it gets done correctly. The users of a distributed system do not see a network of distinct sites or "local" and "remote" nodes. Instead, they see a single logical system that provides resources and services. The individual nodes and the boundaries between them are no longer visible to the user, who thinks only in terms of *what* must be done, not *where* it will be done or *which* node will do it. This situation is diagrammed in Figure 6.22. The concept of a single large collection of accessible resources whose location is not known to the user is often referred to as *cloud computing* after the model of the computational cloud

FIGURE 6.22

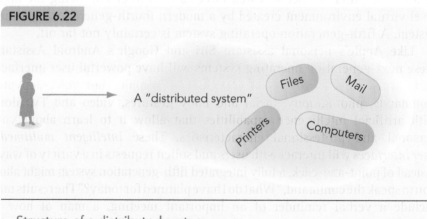

Structure of a distributed system

shown in Figure 6.22. Cloud computing will be discussed in much greater detail in the next chapter.

This is certainly the most powerful virtual environment we have yet described, and an operating system that creates such an environment would significantly enhance the productivity of all its users. These "fifth-generation dashboards" will make using the most powerful and most complex computer system as easy as driving a car—perhaps even easier. Surfing the web provides a good indicator of what it is like to work on a distributed system. When we click on a link, we have no idea where that webpage is located and, moreover, we don't care. We simply want it to appear on our screen. Similarly, when we back up our smartphone to the cloud, we have no idea where our data will be stored. We only know that we will be able to retrieve it whenever we need to. To us, both the web and the cloud behave like one giant logical system even though they may be spread out across hundreds of countries and millions of computers.

Figure 6.23 summarizes the historical evolution of operating systems, much as Figure 1.8 summarized the historical development of computer hardware.

FIGURE 6.23

Generation	Approximate Dates	Major Advances
First	1945–1955	No operating system available
		Programmers operated the machine themselves
Second	1955–1965	Batch operating systems
		Improved system utilization
		Development of the first command language
Third	1965–1985	Multiprogrammed operating systems
		Time-sharing operating systems
		Increasing concern for protecting programs from damage by other programs
		Creation of privileged instructions and user instructions
		Interactive use of computers
		Increasing concern for security and access control
		First personal computer operating systems
Fourth	1985–present	Network operating systems
		Client-server computing
		Remote access to resources
		Graphical user interfaces
		Real-time operating systems
		Embedded systems
Fifth	??	Multimedia user interfaces
		Massively parallel operating systems
		Distributed computing environments

Some of the major advances in operating systems development

Gesture-Based Computing

There have been enormous changes in the interface between humans and computers. From typed commands to mouse clicks to finger taps, the ability to select and activate operations has become ever more simple. Today, virtually everyone is familiar with the use of multitouch operations to rotate the screen, swipes to move from one image to the next, and shaking to randomize a playlist.

The use of body and facial motions to communicate computational requests is called gesture-based computing, and it is similar to what is being done today using game controllers such as Microsoft Kinect®. However, computer scientists want to develop algorithms that teach computers to understand human body language to broaden the possible applications of gesture-based computing. Think how convenient it would be to turn on a light by simulating the motion of flipping a switch; lower the volume of a sound system by moving your hand in a downward direction; select an option on the screen by pointing to it; or decline to answer the phone simply by moving your head left and right to indicate no. Researchers at the University of Minnesota have used Microsoft Kinect to evaluate a range of motion-related symptoms in children, including autism, attention-deficit disorder, and obsessive-compulsive disorder.

The operating system user interface of the future will involve even more intuitive and easy-to-learn movements. Many people have postulated that gesture-based computing will soon make "regular" input devices, such as the mouse and keypad, obsolete.

EXERCISES

1. Describe the user interface in other high-technology devices commonly found in the home or office, such as a smartphone, HD television, fitness watch, or microwave oven. Pick one specific device and discuss how well its interface is designed and how easy it is to use. Does the device use the same techniques as computer system interfaces, such as menus and icons?

2. Can you think of situations where you might *want* to see the underlying hardware of the computer system? That is, you want to interact with the actual machine, not the virtual machine. How could you accomplish this? (Essentially, how could you bypass the operating system?)

3. Assume that you write a letter in English and have a friend translate it into Spanish. In this scenario, what is equivalent to the source program of Figure 6.4? The object program? The assembler?

4. Assume that memory cells 60 and 61 and register R currently have the following values:

   Register R: 13
   60: 472
   61: −1

   Using the instruction set in Figure 6.5, what is in register R and memory cells 60 and 61 after completion of each of the following operations? Assume that each instruction starts from the above conditions.

   a. LOAD 60
   b. STORE 60
   c. ADD 60
   d. COMPARE 61
   e. IN 61 (Assume that the user enters 50.)
   f. OUT 61

5. Assume that memory cell 79 contains the value +6. In addition, the symbol Z is equivalent to memory location 79. What is placed in register R by each of the following load commands?

   a. LOAD 79
   b. LOAD 6
   c. LOAD Z
   d. LOAD Z + 1 (Assume that this is allowed.)

6. Say we accidentally execute the following piece of data:

   .DATA 16387

   Describe exactly what happens. Assume that the format of machine language instructions on this system is the same format shown in Figure 6.13.

7. What is the assembly language equivalent of each of the following binary machine language instructions? Assume the format described in Figure 6.13 and the numeric op code values shown in Figure 6.5.

   a. 0101001100001100
   b. 0011000000000111

8. Is the following data generation pseudo-op legal or illegal? Why?

   THREE: .DATA 2

9. Using the instruction set shown in Figure 6.5, translate the following algorithmic primitives into assembly language code. Show all necessary .DATA pseudo-ops.

   a. Add 3 to the value of K
   b. Set K to the value $(L + 1) − (M + N)$
   c. If $K > 10$ then output the value of K
   d. If $(K > L)$ then output the value of K and increment K by 1, otherwise output the value of L and increment L by 1
   e. Set K to 1
      Repeat the next two lines until $K > 100$
       Output the value of K
       Increment K by 1
      End of the loop

10. What, if anything, is the difference between the following two sequences of instructions for adding the value 2 to the variable X?

       LOAD X   INCREMENT X
       ADD TWO   INCREMENT X
       .
       .
       .
   TWO: .DATA 2

11. Look at the assembly language program in Figure 6.8. Is the statement CLEAR SUM on Line 2 necessary? Why or why not? Is the statement LOAD ZERO on Line 4 necessary? Why or why not?

12. Modify the program in Figure 6.8 so that it separately computes and prints the sum of all positive numbers and all negative numbers and stops when it sees the value 0. For example, given the input

   12, −2, 14, 1, −7, 0

your program should output the two values 27 (the sum of the three positive values 12, 14, and 1) and −9 (the sum of the two negative numbers −2 and −7) and then halt.

13. Write a complete assembly language program (including all necessary pseudo-ops) that reads in a series of integers, one at a time, and outputs the largest and smallest values. The input will consist of a list of integer values containing exactly 100 numbers.

14. Assume that we are using the 16 distinct op codes in Figure 6.5. If we write an assembly language program that contains 100 instructions and our processor can do about 50,000 comparisons per second, what is the maximum time spent doing operation code translation using:

a. Sequential search (Figure 2.9)

b. Binary search (Figure 3.19)

Which one of these two algorithms would you recommend using? Would your conclusions be significantly different if we were programming in an assembly language with 300 op codes rather than 16? If our program contained 50,000 instructions rather than 100?

15. What value is entered in the symbol table for the symbols AGAIN, ANS, X, and ONE in the following program? (Assume that the program is loaded beginning with memory location 0.)

```
          .BEGIN
          --Here is the program
          IN        X
          LOAD      X
AGAIN:    ADD       ANS
          SUBTRACT  ONE
          STORE     ANS
          OUT       ANS
          JUMP      AGAIN
          --Here are the data
ANS:      .DATA     0
X:        .DATA     0
ONE:      .DATA     1
          .END
```

16. Look at the assembly language program in Figure 6.8. Determine the physical memory address associated with every label in the symbol table. (Assume that the program is loaded beginning with memory location 0.)

17. Is the following pair of statements legal or illegal? Explain why.

```
LABEL:  .DATA   3
LABEL:  .DATA   4
```

If it is illegal, will the error be detected during pass 1 or pass 2 of the assembly process?

18. What are some drawbacks in using passwords to limit access to a computer system? Describe some other possible ways that an operating system could limit access. In what type of application might these alternative safeguards be appropriate?

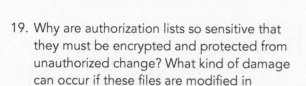

19. Why are authorization lists so sensitive that they must be encrypted and protected from unauthorized change? What kind of damage can occur if these files are modified in unexpected or unplanned ways?

20. Assume that any individual program spends about 50% of its time waiting for I/O operations to be completed. What percentage of time is the processor doing useful work (called *processor utilization*) if there are three programs loaded into memory? How many programs should we keep in memory if we want processor utilization to be at least 95%?

21. Here is an algorithm for calling a friend on the telephone:

    Step   Operation

    1.   Dial the phone and wait for either an answer or a busy signal
    2.   If the line is not busy then do Steps 3 and 4
    3.   Talk as long as you want
    4.   Hang up the phone, you are done
    5.   Otherwise (the line is busy)
    6.   Wait exactly 1 minute
    7.   Go back to Step 1 and try again

    During execution, this algorithm could get into a situation in which, as in the deadlock problem, no useful work can ever get done. Describe the problem, explain why it occurs, and suggest how it could be solved.

22. Explain why a batch operating system would be totally inadequate to handle such modern applications as airline reservations and automated teller machines.

23. In a time-sharing operating system, why is system performance so sensitive to the value that is selected for the time slice? Explain what type of system behavior would occur if the value selected for the time slice were too large. What if it were too small?

24. As hardware (processor/memory) costs became significantly cheaper during the 1980s and 1990s, time-sharing became a much less attractive design for operating systems. Explain why this is the case.

25. Determine whether the computer system on which you are working is part of a local area network. If it is, determine what servers are available and how they are used. Is there a significant difference between the ways you access local resources and remote resources?

26. The following four requests could come in to an operating system as it is running on a computer system:

    - The clock in the computer has just "ticked," and we need to update a seconds counter.

    - The program running on processor 2 is trying to perform an illegal operation code.

    - Someone pulled the plug on the power supply, and the system will run out of power in 50 msec.

    - The disk has just read the character that passed under the read/write head, and it wants to store it in memory before the next one arrives.

    In what order should the operating system handle these requests?

CHALLENGE WORK

1. In Chapter 2, we wrote a number of algorithms that worked on a list of values rather than a single value. That is, our algorithm contained statements such as

   Get values for A_1, A_2, ..., A_N, the list to be searched

   In statements like this, we are dealing with individual data items such as A_1 and A_2 but they are also part of a collection of items, the list called A. A collection of related data items is called a *data structure*. High-level programming languages like C++, Java, and Python provide users with a rich collection of data structures that go by such names as arrays, sets, and lists. We can program with these structures just as though they were an inherent part of the hardware of the computer. However, the discussions in the previous two chapters have shown that data structures such as lists of numbers do *not* exist directly in hardware. There are no machine language instructions that can carry out the type of algorithmic command shown in the pseudocode statement just given. When you write an instruction that uses a structure such as a list, the language translator (that is, the assembler or compiler) must map it into what is available on the hardware—the machine language instruction set shown in Figure 5.25

   and the sequential addresses in our memory. (This is another good example of the virtual environment created by a piece of system software.)

   Write an assembly language program to sum up a list of 50 numbers that are read in and stored in memory. Here is the algorithm you are to translate:

   Read in 50 numbers A_1, A_2,..., A_{50}
   Set *Sum* to 0
   Set *i* to 1
   While the value of *i* is less than or equal to 50
       Sum = *Sum* + A
       i = *i* + 1
   End of the loop
   Write out the value of *Sum*
   Stop

   To implement this algorithm, you must simulate the concept of a list of numbers using the assembly language resources that are available. (*Hint*: Remember that in the Von Neumann architecture there is no distinction between an instruction and a piece of data. Therefore, an assembly language instruction such as LOAD A can be treated as data and modified by other instructions.)

AFTER STUDYING THIS CHAPTER, YOU WILL BE ABLE TO:

- Describe and compare different network technologies, including dial-up, broadband, and wireless

- Explain how different kinds of networks (LAN, WLAN, WAN) are connected, and how communication works in each

- Explain the importance of standards and protocols for communication among computing devices

- Name the layers of the network protocol hierarchy, and describe the purpose of each layer

- Name four services that computer networks provide and explain their social impact

- Explain cloud computing and discuss its potential benefits

- Describe the highlights of the history of the internet and the web

7.1 Introduction

Every once in a while there occur a technological innovation of such importance that it forever changes society and the way people live, work, and communicate. The invention of the printing press by Johannes Gutenberg in the mid-15th century was one such development. The books and manuscripts it produced helped fuel the renewed interest in science, art, and literature that came to be called the Renaissance, an era that influenced Western civilization for more than 500 years. The Industrial Revolution of the 18th and early 19th centuries made consumer goods such as clothing, furniture, and cooking utensils affordable to the middle class and changed European and American societies from rural to urban and from agricultural to industrial. In the 20th century we are certainly aware of the massive social changes, both good and bad, wrought by inventions such as the telephone, automobile, airplane, television, computer, and smartphone.

We are no doubt witnessing yet another breakthrough, one with the potential to make as great a change in our lives as those just mentioned. This innovation is the computer network—computers connected together for the purpose of sharing personal communications, hardware and software resources, and information. During the early stages of network development, the only information exchanged was text such as email, database records, and technical papers. However, the material sent across a network

Computer Networks and Cloud Computing

AFTER STUDYING THIS CHAPTER, YOU WILL BE ABLE TO:

- Describe and compare different network technologies, including dial-up, broadband, and wireless

- Explain how different kinds of networks (LAN, WLAN, WAN) are connected, and how communication works in each

- Explain the importance of standards and protocols for communication among computing devices

- Name the layers of the network protocol hierarchy, and describe the purpose of each layer

- Name four services that computer networks provide and explain their social impact

- Explain cloud computing and discuss its potential benefits

- Describe the highlights of the history of the Internet and the web

7.1 Introduction

Every once in a while there occurs a technological innovation of such importance that it forever changes society and the way people live, work, and communicate. The invention of the printing press by Johannes Gutenberg in the mid-15th century was one such development. The books and manuscripts it produced helped fuel the renewed interest in science, art, and literature that came to be called the Renaissance, an era that influenced Western civilization for more than 500 years. The Industrial Revolution of the 18th and early 19th centuries made consumer goods such as clothing, furniture, and cooking utensils affordable to the middle class and changed European and American societies from rural to urban and from agricultural to industrial. In the 20th century we are certainly aware of the massive social changes, both good and bad, wrought by inventions such as the telephone, automobile, airplane, television, computer, and smartphone.

We are no doubt witnessing yet another breakthrough, one with the potential to make as great a change in our lives as those just mentioned. This innovation is the *computer network*–computers connected together for the purpose of sharing personal communications, hardware and software resources, and information. During the early stages of network development, the only information exchanged was text such as email, database records, and technical papers. However, the material sent across a network

today can be virtually anything—television and radio shows, videos, music, photographs, and movies, to name just a few. If information can be represented in binary, it can be transmitted across a network.

The possibilities created by this free flow of data are enormous. Networks equalize access to information and eliminate the concept of "information haves" and "information have-nots." Students in a poorly funded rural school are no longer handicapped by an out-of-date library collection. A physician practicing in an emerging economy is able to transmit patient records, test results, and medical images to specialists anywhere in the world and have immediate access to the databases and reference works of major medical centers. Small-business owners can locate suppliers and customers on an international scale. Researchers have the same ability to communicate with experts in their discipline whether they are in New York, New Delhi, or New Guinea.

Networking can also foster the growth of democracy and global understanding by providing unrestricted access to newspapers, magazines, radio, and television, as well as supporting the unfettered exchange of diverse and competing thoughts, ideas, and opinions. However, it can also be a vehicle for spreading rumors, falsehoods, and disinformation around the world in a fraction of a second. Because we live in an increasingly information-oriented society, network technology contains the seeds of massive social and economic change. It is no surprise that during civil uprisings, political leaders who want to prevent the dissemination of opposing ideas often move quickly to restrict access to the Internet, especially social media sites.

In Chapter 6, you saw how system software can create the appearance of a user-friendly "virtual machine" on top of the raw hardware of a single computer. In today's world, computers are seldom used as isolated, stand-alone devices, and the modern view of a virtual machine has expanded into a worldwide collection of interconnected systems and resources. In this chapter, we take a detailed look at the underlying technology of computer networks—what they are and how they work, with a focus on the most widely used network, the Internet, and its most important application, the World Wide Web (better known now as simply "the web"). We discuss the benefits networks can bring, including one of the most advanced and powerful forms of networking: cloud computing. We conclude with a survey of how the Internet and the web came to be.

7.2 Basic Networking Concepts

A computer network is a set of independent computer systems interconnected by telecommunication links for the purpose of sharing information and resources. The individual computers on a network are referred to as nodes or *hosts*, and they can range in size from smartphones, tablets, and tiny laptops to massively parallel supercomputers. In this section, we describe some of the basic technical characteristics of a computer network.

7.2.1 Communication Links

The communication links used to build a network vary widely in physical characteristics, error rate, and transmission speed. In the approximately 50 years that networks have existed, telecommunications facilities have undergone enormous changes.

In the early days of networking, the most common way to transmit data was via switched, dial-up telephone lines. The term *switched, dial-up* means that when you dial a telephone number, a circuit (i.e., a path) is temporarily established between the caller and the call recipient. This circuit lasts for the duration of the call, and when you hang up it is terminated.

The voice-oriented dial-up telephone network was originally an *analog* medium. As we first explained in Chapter 4, this means that the physical quantity used to represent information, usually voltage level, is continuous and can take on any value. An example of this is shown in Figure 7.1(a). Although analog is fine for transmitting the human voice, which varies continuously in pitch and volume, a computer produces *digital* information—specifically, a sequence of 0s and 1s, as shown in Figure 7.1(b).

For the binary signals of Figure 7.1(b) to be transmitted via a switched, dial-up telephone line, the signal must be restructured into the analog representation of Figure 7.1(a). The device that accomplishes this is a modem, which modulates, or alters, a standard analog signal called a *carrier wave* so that it encodes binary information. The modem modifies the physical characteristics of the carrier wave, such as amplitude or frequency, so that it is in one of two distinct states, one state representing 0 and the other state representing 1. Figure 7.2 shows how a modem can modulate the amplitude (height) of a carrier wave to encode the binary signal 1010.

FIGURE 7.1

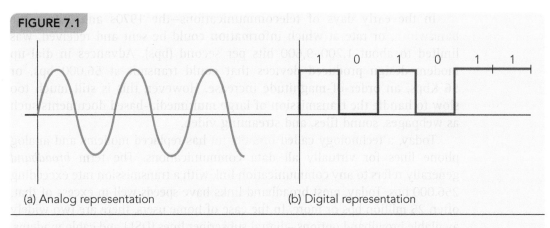

(a) Analog representation   (b) Digital representation

Two forms of information representation

FIGURE 7.2

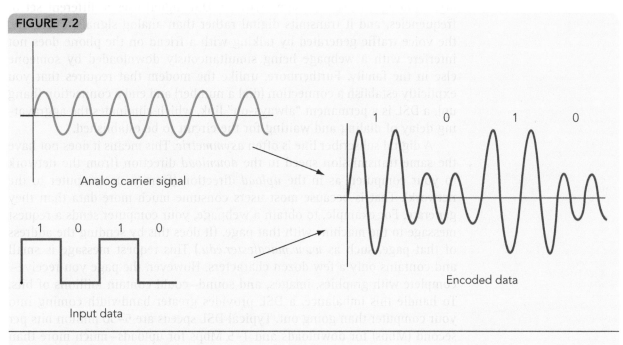

Analog carrier signal

Input data

Encoded data

Modulation of a carrier to encode binary information

At the other end of the transmission line, a modem performs the inverse operation, which is called *demodulation*. (Modem is a contraction of the two terms *mo*dulation and *dem*odulation.) It takes the received waveform, separates the carrier wave from the encoded digital signal, and passes on the digital data to the computer.

In the early days of telecommunications—the 1970s and 1980s—the bandwidth, or rate at which information could be sent and received, was limited to about 1,200–9,600 bits per second (bps). Advances in dial-up modem design produced devices that could transmit at 56,000 bps, or 56 Kbps, an order-of-magnitude increase. However, this is still much too slow to handle the transmission of large multimedia-based documents such as webpages, sound files, and streaming video.

Today, a technology called broadband has replaced modems and analog phone lines for virtually all data communications. The term *broadband* generally refers to any communication link with a transmission rate exceeding 256,000 bps. Today, most broadband links have speeds well in excess of that, often 25 million bps or more. In the case of home users, there are two widely available broadband options—digital subscriber lines (DSL) and cable modems.

A digital subscriber line (DSL) uses the same wires that carry regular telephone signals into your home and therefore is provided by either your local telephone company or someone certified to act as its intermediary. Although it uses the same wires, a DSL signal uses a different set of frequencies, and it transmits digital rather than analog signals. Therefore, the voice traffic generated by talking with a friend on the phone does not interfere with a webpage being simultaneously downloaded by someone else in the family. Furthermore, unlike the modem that requires that you explicitly establish a connection (dial a number) and end a connection (hang up), a DSL is a permanent "always-on" link, which eliminates the aggravating delay of dialing and waiting for the circuit to be established.

A digital subscriber line is often *asymmetric*. This means it does not have the same transmission speed in the *download* direction (from the network to your computer) as in the *upload* direction (from your computer to the network). That is because most users consume much more data than they generate. For example, to obtain a webpage, your computer sends a request message to the machine with that page. (It does this by sending the address of that page, such as *www.macalester.edu*.) This request message is small and contains only a few dozen characters. However, the page you receive—complete with graphics, images, and sound—could contain millions of bits. To handle this imbalance, a DSL provides greater bandwidth coming into your computer than going out. Typical DSL speeds are 5–50 million bits per second (Mbps) for downloads and 1–5 Mbps for uploads—much more than is available from a dial-up modem.

The second option for broadband communications is a cable modem. This technology makes use of the links that deliver cable TV signals into your home, so it is offered by cable TV providers. Some of the link capacity previously allocated for TV signals is now used for data communications. Like a DSL, a cable modem also provides an always-on link and offers speeds generally comparable to those provided by a DSL—10 to 100 Mbps for downloads and 1–5 Mbps for uploads.

In the commercial and office environment, the most widely used broadband technology is Ethernet. Ethernet was developed in the mid-1970s by computer scientists at the Xerox PARC research center in Palo Alto, California. It was originally designed to operate at 10 Mbps using coaxial cable. However, 10 Mbps proved too slow for many emerging applications, so in the early 1990s researchers developed a "new and improved" version, called Fast Ethernet, which transmits at 100 Mbps across coaxial cable, fiber-optic cable, or regular twisted-pair copper wire.

Because even 100 Mbps may not be fast enough for multimedia applications, computer science researchers began investigating the concept of gigabit networking—transmission lines that support speeds of 1 billion bits per second (Gbps). In 1998 the first international gigabit Ethernet standard was adopted by the IEEE (Institute of Electrical and Electronics Engineers), an international professional society responsible for, among other things, developing industrial standards in the area of telecommunications. The standard supports communication on an Ethernet cable at 1,000 Mbps (1 Gbps), 100 times faster than the original 10 Mbps standard. Most classrooms and office buildings today are wired to support Ethernet speeds of 1,000 Mbps—18,000 times faster than a 56K modem! In addition, virtually every desktop and laptop sold today comes with a built-in Ethernet interface, and new homes and dorm rooms are often equipped with Ethernet links.

However, not willing to rest on their laurels (and realizing that even faster networks will be needed to support future research and development), work immediately began on a new *10-gigabit Ethernet* standard, a version of Ethernet with a data rate of 10 billion bits per second. That standard was adopted by the IEEE in 2003. To get an idea of how fast that is, in a single second a 10 Gbps Ethernet network could transmit the contents of 1,700 books, each 300 pages long. In June 2010, the IEEE ratified the *100-gigabit Ethernet* standard defining a local area network that can transmit data at the almost unimaginable rate of 100 billion bits of information per second!

Do applications truly need to transmit information at billions of bits per second? To answer that question, let's determine how long it takes to transmit a high-resolution color image, such as a CAT scan, satellite image, or single movie frame, at different transmission speeds. As described in Section 4.2, a high-resolution color image contains at least 10 million picture elements (pixels), and each pixel is encoded using 8–24 bits. If we assume 16 bits per pixel, then a single uncompressed image would contain at least 160 million bits of data. If the image is compressed before it is sent, and the compression ratio is 20:1 (see Section 4.2 for a definition of compression ratio), then we must transmit a total of 8 million bits to send this single image. Figure 7.3 shows the time needed to send this amount of information at the speeds discussed in this chapter.

Figure 7.3 clearly demonstrates the need for high-speed communications to support applications such as video on demand and medical imaging. Receiving an 8 Mb image using a 56 Kbps modem takes 2.4 minutes, an agonizingly long time. That same 8 Mb image can be received in 4 seconds using a DSL or cable modem with a download speed

FIGURE 7.3

Line Type	Speed	Time to Transmit 8 Million Bits (One Compressed Image)	
Dial-up phone line	56 Kbps	2.4	minutes
DSL line, cable modem	2 Mbps	4	seconds
Ethernet	10 Mbps	0.8	second
Fast Ethernet	100 Mbps	0.08	second
Gigabit Ethernet	1 Gbps	0.008	second
10-gigabit Ethernet	10 Gbps	0.0008	second
100-gigabit Ethernet	100 Gbps	0.00008	second

Transmission time of an image at different transmission speeds

of 2 Mbps, 0.8 second using 10 Mbps Ethernet, and a blazing 0.08 second with 100 Mbps Ethernet.

However, even 0.08 second might not be fast enough if an application requires the rapid transmission of multiple images or a huge amount of data in a short period of time. For example, to watch a real-time video image without flicker or delay, you need to stream at least 24 frames per second. Any less and the human eye notices the time delay between frames. If each frame contains 8 Mb, you need a bandwidth of $8,000,000 \times 24 = 192$ Mbps. This is beyond the speed of modems, DSL, cable modems, and even 100 Mbps Ethernet, but it is achievable using gigabit networks.

An extremely important development in the field of telecommunications is the explosive growth in the use of wireless data communication using radio, microwave, and infrared signals. Although devices such as DSLs and cable modems provide high-speed network links, they require a user to be physically adjacent to the communication device and to have a plug and cable with the appropriate connector. This is often inconvenient or impossible.

However, in the wireless world, users' devices no longer need to be physically connected to a wired network to communicate across a network. Wireless data networks have liberated computer users just as mobile phones liberated telephone users. Using wireless, you can be sipping coffee in your favorite café, riding in a car, or working on the factory floor and still send and receive email, access online databases, post to a social networking account, and surf the web, provided you can connect (wirelessly, of course) to a wireless network. The ability to deliver data to users regardless of their physical location is called mobile computing.

There are three types of wireless networks, and they are classified by the distance that the wireless signal must travel—short, medium, and long distance. In a wireless local area network (WLAN), a short-distance form of wireless networking, a user transmits from his or her computer, tablet, or smartphone to a local *wireless base station*, often referred to as a *wireless router, access point,* or *hot spot,* that is no more than a few hundred feet away. This base station is then connected to a traditional wired network, such as a DSL or cable modem, to provide full Internet access. This is the type of short-distance wireless configuration typically found in a home, library, office, or coffee shop because it is cheap, simple, low powered, and easy to install. A typical local wireless configuration is shown in Figure 7.4.

One of the most widely used standards for wireless local access is Wi-Fi, also referred to by its official name, the IEEE 802.11 wireless network standard. Wi-Fi is used to connect a computer to the Internet when it is within range (typically 150–300 feet or 45–90 meters) of a wireless base station, often advertised as a Wi-Fi hot spot. Wi-Fi systems generally use the 2.4 GHz radio band for communications and support download transmission speeds of about 10–50 Mbps. Researchers are investigating the use of higher radio frequencies to support gigabit Wi-Fi communication speeds.

Another popular short-distance wireless standard is Bluetooth. It is a low-power wireless standard used to communicate between devices located very close to each other, typically no more than 20–30 feet (6–10 meters) apart. Bluetooth is often used to support communication from wireless peripherals such as mice, printers, earphones, or keyboards, to a laptop or desktop system located close by. It also supports exchanges between other digital devices including mobile phones, cameras, speakers, video game consoles, and your automobile's sound system. Bluetooth is a popular technique for implementing what is termed a personal area network (PAN), a collection of privately owned interconnected digital devices all located in close proximity.

A relatively new development in wireless networking is the medium-distance metropolitan area network (MAN). This is a wireless network whose scope is larger than the few hundred feet of a WLAN, typically a few blocks

FIGURE 7.4

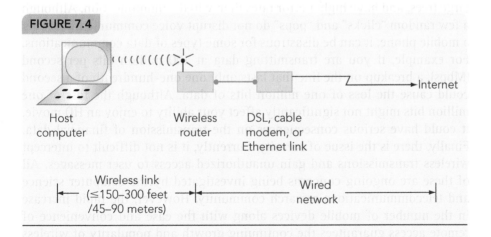

Typical WLAN configuration

up to an entire city. Its purpose is to provide full Internet connectivity to all computers within a neighborhood or metropolitan area. A number of cities in the United States, Europe, and Asia have installed public access Wi-Fi routers every few blocks, often on top of telephone poles or tall buildings. These routers provide convenient, low-cost wireless Internet access to all residents. The idea behind a MAN is to treat Internet services as a public utility, much like electricity, gas, and water, which is provided to individuals by a local or regional government agency.

The third wireless network category (after the short-distance LAN and the medium-distance MAN) is long-distance wireless service, called a wireless wide area network (WWAN). A wide area network or WAN connects devices that are not in close proximity but are across town, across the country, or across the ocean. In a WWAN, the computer (often a tablet or smartphone) transmits messages to a remote base station provided by a telecommunications company, which may be located many miles away. The base station is usually a large cellular antenna placed on top of a tower or building, providing both long-distance voice and data communication services to any system within sight of the tower. One of the most popular wide area wireless technologies is called 4G, for fourth generation technology. It offers voice services as well as data communication at rates of 50 to 500 Mbps, with peak speeds reaching 1 Gbps.

Although wireless data communication is an exciting development in computer networking, it is not without problems that must be studied and solved. For example, some forms of wireless, such as microwaves, are line of sight, traveling only in a straight line. Because of the curvature of the Earth, transmitters must be placed on top of hills or tall buildings, and they cannot be more than about 10–50 miles (15–80 kilometers) apart, depending on height. This can leave small geographical regions (often termed "dead zones") that do not have access to cellular data or voice services. Other types of wireless media suffer from environmental problems; they are strongly affected by rain and fog, cannot pass through obstacles such as buildings or large trees, and have higher error rates than wired communication. Although a few random "clicks" and "pops" do not disrupt voice communications over a mobile phone, it can be disastrous for some types of data communications. For example, if you are transmitting data at 100 million bits per second (Mbps), a breakup on the line that lasts only one one-hundredth of a second could cause the loss of one million bits of data. Although the loss of one million bits might not significantly affect your ability to enjoy an HD movie, it could have serious consequences on the transmission of financial data. Finally, there is the issue of security. Currently, it is not difficult to intercept wireless transmissions and gain unauthorized access to user messages. All of these are ongoing concerns being investigated by the computer science and telecommunications research community. However, the rapid increase in the number of mobile devices along with the ease and convenience of remote access guarantees the continuing growth and popularity of wireless data communications.

The Internet of Things

From all that we have said, you might get the idea that the Internet is solely a way for computer users, that is, people, to share computing resources or data in the form of text, images, or video. Although that was originally the case, it is no longer true. It is now possible to place uniquely identifiable network "tags" on objects as diverse as refrigerators, thermostats, automobiles, eyeglasses, TVs, pets, and machine tools. Today, any living object or mechanical entity with which we wish to communicate or to control is a candidate to be tagged.

This network tagging mechanism comes in many forms, one of the most popular being RFID, an acronym for a radio frequency identifier. An RFID is a communications device that has its own Internet address, the same type of network address that your laptop, tablet, or smartphone uses to communicate over the Internet. Once an RFID tag is placed on an object it can send and receive messages and is said to be *network ready*. This object can now be located and controlled by other devices on the Internet via the exchange of messages, such as the following exchange between a home thermostat and a control computer:

Thermostat → control computer: "The temperature has risen to 85°."

Control computer → thermostat: "Turn on air conditioning. Set to 76°."

The potential applications for Internet-ready devices are vast: In a business environment, inventory control becomes automatic as the company's computers can communicate directly with the stock on the shelf to determine if items need to be reordered. *Smart homes* include intelligent environmental controls that maximize comfort while minimizing cost and security systems that track what is happening inside the house to keep everyone safe—for example, turning off the oven or locking the front door if you forget. Urban planners can receive continuous streams of status information from transportation systems, utility plants, and safety offices to allow these publicly funded systems to be operated in the most cost-efficient manner.

The Internet is no longer a network of just computers and data, but also is becoming a true "Internet of Things."

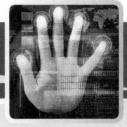

Practice Problems

1. Show how the 4-bit digital value 0110 is converted to an analog signal by a modem that modulates the *frequency* of a carrier wave, rather than its amplitude.

2. Consider an uncompressed 1,200 × 780 image, with each pixel stored using an 8-bit grayscale representation. If we want to transmit the entire image in under 1 second, what is the minimum acceptable transmission speed?

3. How long would it take to transmit that 1,200 × 780 image from Practice Problem 2 using a 1-gigabit Ethernet network?

7.2.2 Local Area Networks

A local area network (LAN) connects hardware devices such as computers, printers, and storage devices that are all in relatively close proximity (150–300 ft/45–90 m). (A diagram of a LAN was provided in Figure 6.20.) Examples of LANs include the interconnection of machines in one room or in the same office building. An important characteristic of a LAN is that the owner of the computers is also the owner of the means of communications. Because a LAN is located entirely on private property, the owner can install telecommunications facilities without having to purchase services from a third-party provider such as a phone or cable company, although a third-party provider is still needed to connect the LAN to the outside world.

The previous section described how a wireless local area network can be set up using Wi-Fi and a router connected to a wired network. Here we take a look at the properties of that wired network. Wired LANs can be constructed using a number of different topologies; some of the most common are shown in Figure 7.5. In the bus topology, Figure 7.5(a), all nodes are connected to a single, shared communication line. If two or more nodes use the link at the same time, the messages collide and are unreadable, and, therefore, nodes must take turns using the line. The cable modem technology described in Section 7.2.1 is based on a bus topology. A number of homes are all connected to the same shared coaxial cable. If two users want to download a webpage at the exact same time, then the effective transmission rate is lower than expected because one of them must wait.

The ring topology of Figure 7.5(b) connects the network nodes in a circular fashion, with messages circulating around the ring in either a clockwise or counterclockwise direction until they reach their destination. Finally, the star topology, Figure 7.5(c), has a single central node that is connected to all other sites. This central node can route information directly to any other node in the LAN. Messages are first sent to the central site, which then forwards them to the correct location.

Ethernet uses the bus topology of Figure 7.5(a). To send a message, a node places the message, including the destination address, on the cable. Because the line is shared, the message is received by every other node (assuming no one else sent at the exact same time and garbled the data). Each node looks at the destination address to see if it is the intended recipient. If so, it accepts the message; if not, it discards it.

There are two ways to construct an Ethernet LAN. In the first method, called the shared cable, a wire (such as twisted-pair copper wire, coaxial cable, or fiber-optic cable) is literally strung around and through a building. Users tap into the cable at its nearest point using a device called a *transceiver*, as shown in Figure 7.6(a). Because of technical constraints, an Ethernet cable has a maximum allowable length. For a large building or campus, it may be necessary to install two or more separate cables and connect them via hardware devices called repeaters or bridges.

A repeater is a device that simply amplifies and forwards a signal. In Figure 7.6(b), if the device connecting the two LANs is a repeater, then every message on LAN1 is forwarded to LAN2, and vice versa. Thus, when two Ethernet LANs are connected by a repeater, they function exactly as if they were a single network.

FIGURE 7.5

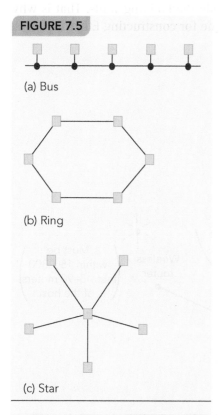

(a) Bus

(b) Ring

(c) Star

Some common LAN topologies

FIGURE 7.6

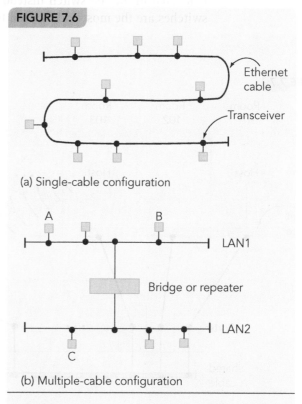

(a) Single-cable configuration

(b) Multiple-cable configuration

An Ethernet LAN implemented using shared cables

A bridge is a "smarter" device that has knowledge about the nodes located on each separate network. It examines every message to see if it should be forwarded from one network to another. For example, if node A is sending a message to node B, both of which are on LAN1, then the bridge does nothing with the message. However, if node A on LAN1 is sending a message to node C on LAN2, then the bridge copies the message from LAN1 onto LAN2 so node C is able to see it and read it.

In the second approach to constructing an Ethernet LAN, there is no shared cable strung throughout the building. Instead, there is a box called a switch located in a room called a *wiring closet*. The switch contains a number of *ports*, with a wire leading from each port to an Ethernet interface in the wall of a room in the building, or to a wireless router somewhere in the building. To connect to the network, you first activate the port located in your office, typically by flipping an on/off button, and then plug your machine into the wall socket. This approach is shown in Room 101 of Figure 7.7. Alternatively, you could use Wi-Fi to transmit from your computer to a wireless router located somewhere in the building. This router would then connect to one of the Ethernet ports in the switch. This approach is shown in Room 103 of Figure 7.7. In either case, it is no longer necessary to climb into the ceiling or crawl through ductwork looking for the cable because the shared cable is located inside the switch instead of inside the building walls. That is why switches are the most widely used technique for constructing Ethernet LANs.

FIGURE 7.7

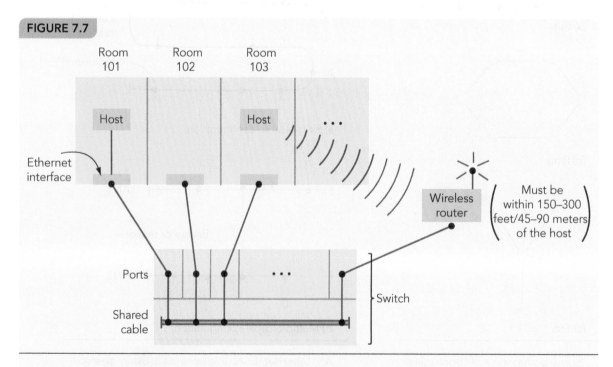

An Ethernet LAN implemented using a switch

Practice Problems

1. What changes, if any, must be made to our description of the Ethernet protocol to allow a message to be sent by node A on a local area network to *every other* node on that same LAN? This operation is called broadcasting.

2. Assume you are given the following configuration of three local area networks, called LAN1, LAN2, and LAN3, connected by bridges B1 and B2.

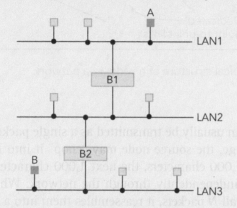

   Explain exactly how node A on LAN1 sends a message to node B on LAN3.

3. What security issues could arise from the use of an Ethernet-like bus topology to implement a local area network?

7.2.3 Wide Area Networks

As defined previously, a *wide area network* (*WAN*) connects devices that are not in close physical proximity. Because WANs cross public property, the WAN owner must purchase telecommunications services, like those described in Section 7.2.1, from an external provider. Typically, these are dedicated point-to-point lines or wireless links that directly connect two machines, not the shared channels found on a LAN such as Ethernet. The typical structure of a WAN is shown in Figure 7.8. This type of interconnection system in which a node is connected to other network nodes via direct links is called a mesh network.

Most WANs use a store-and-forward, packet-switched technology to deliver messages. Unlike a LAN, in which a message is broadcast on a shared channel and is received by all nodes, a WAN message must "hop" from one node to another to make its way from source to destination. The unit of transmission in a WAN is a packet—an information block with a fixed maximum size that is transmitted through the network as a single unit. If you send a short

FIGURE 7.8

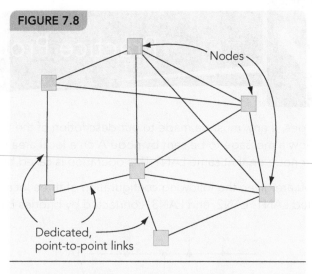

Nodes

Dedicated,
point-to-point links

Typical structure of a wide area network

message, then it can usually be transmitted as a single packet. However, if you send a long message, the source node may "chop" it into *N* separate packets (such as the first 1,000 characters, the next 1,000 characters, and so on) and send each packet independently through the network. When the destination node has received all *N* packets, it reassembles them into a single message.

For example, assume the six-node WAN shown in Figure 7.9. To send a message from source node A to destination node D, the message could go from A → B → C → D. Alternately, the message may travel from A → B → F → D or A → E → F → D. The exact route is determined by the network, not the user, based on which path can deliver the message most quickly. If the message has been broken up into multiple packets, each packet might take a different route.

FIGURE 7.9

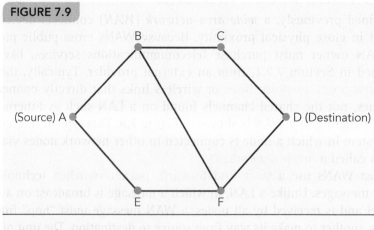

B   C

(Source) A   D (Destination)

E   F

Six-node WAN

One of the nicest features of a store-and-forward network is that the failure of a single line or a single node does not necessarily bring down the entire network. For example, assume the line connecting node B to node C in Figure 7.9 crashes. Nodes B and C can still communicate via the route B $\to$ F $\to$ D $\to$ C. Similarly, if node F fails completely, nodes E and D, located on either side of F, can still exchange messages. However, instead of talking via node F, they now use the route E $\to$ A $\to$ B $\to$ C $\to$ D.

Reliability and fault tolerance were the reasons that WANs were first studied in the late 1960s and early 1970s. The U.S. military was interested in communication systems that could survive and function even if some of their components were destroyed, as might happen in a time of war or civil unrest. Their research ultimately led to the creation of the Internet. (We will have much more to say about the history of networking and the Internet later in this chapter.)

7.2.4 Overall Structure of the Internet

We have defined three classes of networks, LANs, MANs, and WANs, but all real-world networks, including the Internet, are a complex mix of all three of these network types.

For example, a company or a college would typically have one or more LANs connecting its local computers—a computer science department LAN, a humanities division LAN, an administration building LAN, and so forth. These individual LANs might then be interconnected into a private company or campus network that allows users to send email to other employees in the company and access the resources of other departments. These individual networks are interconnected via a device called a router. Like the bridge in Figure 7.6(b), a router transmits messages between two distinct networks. However, unlike a bridge, which connects two identical types of networks, routers can transmit information between networks that use totally different communication techniques—much as an interpreter functions between two people who speak different languages. For example, a router, not a bridge, is used to send messages from a wireless Wi-Fi network to a wired Ethernet LAN or from an Ethernet LAN to a packet-switched, store-and-forward WAN. You can see this type of interconnection structure in Figure 7.10.

The configuration in Figure 7.10 allows the employees of a company or the students of a college to communicate with each other, or to access local resources. But how do these people reach users outside their institution or access remote resources such as webpages that are not part of their own network? Furthermore, how does an individual home user who is not part of any company or college network access the larger community? The answer is that a user's individual computer or a company's private network is connected to the rest of the world through an Internet service provider (ISP). An ISP is a business whose purpose is to provide access from a private network (such as a corporate or university network) to the Internet or from an individual's home computer to the Internet. This access occurs through a WAN owned by the ISP, as shown in Figure 7.11 or possibly through a MAN provided by a city or county. An ISP typically provides many ways for a user to connect to

FIGURE 7.10

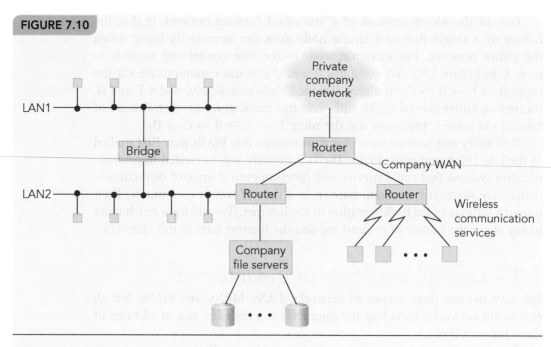

Structure of a typical company network

FIGURE 7.11

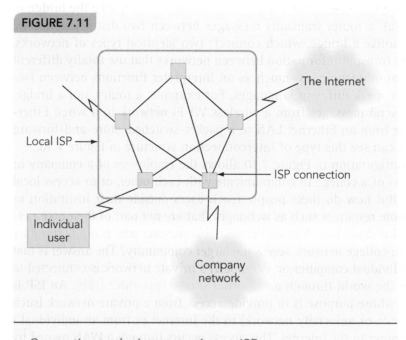

Connecting to the Internet using an ISP

this network, from 56 Kbps modems to dedicated broadband telecommunication links with speeds in excess of billions of bits per second.

The scope of networking worldwide is so vast that a single ISP cannot possibly hope to directly connect a single campus, company, or individual to every other computer in the world, just as a single airport cannot directly serve every possible destination. Therefore, ISPs (that is, ISP networks) are hierarchical, interconnecting to each other in multiple layers, or tiers, that provide ever-expanding geographic coverage. This hierarchical structure is diagrammed in Figure 7.12.

An individual or a company network connects to a *local ISP*, the first level in the hierarchy. This local ISP typically connects to a *regional* or *national ISP* that interconnects all local ISPs in a single geographic region or country. Finally, a regional or national ISP might connect to an *international ISP*, also called a *tier-1 network* or an *Internet backbone*, which provides global coverage. This hierarchy is similar to the standard telephone system. When you place a call to another country, your phone connects to a local switching center, which establishes a connection to a regional switching center, which establishes a connection to a national switching center. This

FIGURE 7.12

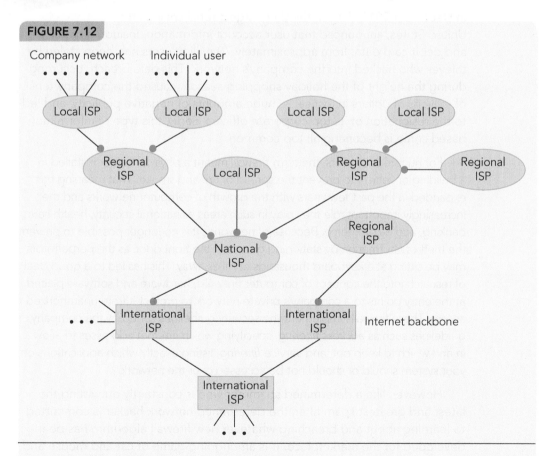

Hierarchy of Internet service providers

national center has high-speed connections to similar national switching centers in other countries, which are connected, in turn, to regional and then local switches to establish a connection to the phone you are calling.

The diagram in Figure 7.12 is a pictorial representation of that enormously complex telecommunications entity we call the Internet. The Internet is not a single computer network; instead, it is a huge interconnected "network of networks" that includes nodes, LANs, MANs, WANs, bridges, routers, and multiple levels of ISPs.

Firewalls

In December 2013, Target, the third largest retail chain in the United States, announced that user account information, including credit and debit card data, from approximately 70 million users had been stolen by thieves who hacked into the company's network. This data breach, occurring during the height of the holiday shopping season, caused the company tens of millions of dollars in lost sales, huge amounts of negative publicity, and led to the resignation of its top corporate officers. Sadly, this type of information-based crime is becoming all too common.

For hundreds of years, the term *firewall* meant a physical barrier installed in a building or vehicle to prevent the spread of fire and smoke. That meaning has expanded in the past few years with the growth of computer networks and the increasingly important role they play in such areas as national security, health care, banking, and e-commerce. Because of networks, it is no longer possible to prevent the theft of information by stationing guards at the front door, as the perpetrators may be sitting at a keyboard thousands of miles away. This has led to a good deal of research into the concept of computer firewalls, hardware and software placed at the entry points to a company's private network to protect it from unauthorized access. These firewalls implement the security guidelines set up by the company, guidelines such as *address filtering*, specifying which Internet addresses to allow in and which to keep out, and *service filtering*, listing exactly which applications on your system should or should not be accessed over the network.

However, like a determined spammer who is constantly outwitting the latest and greatest spam filter, the determined network hacker is committed to learning about and breaching whatever new firewall algorithm has been developed for the marketplace. It is an ongoing game of cat and mouse and, so far, it appears that the criminal community's mouse is keeping one step ahead of the IT developers' cat.

We'll have more to say about security issues in Chapter 8.

As of mid-2017, the Internet contained more than 1.06 billion nodes (hosts) and hundreds of thousands of networks located in more than 230 countries (data from *http://ftp.isc.org/www/survey/reports/current/*). A graph of the number of host computers on the Internet from 1994 is shown in Figure 7.13. (This figure is really an undercount because there are numerous computers located behind protective firewalls that will not respond to any external attempts to be counted.)

How does something as massive as the Internet actually work? How is it possible to get 1 billion machines around the world to function efficiently as a single system? We answer that important question in the next section.

FIGURE 7.13

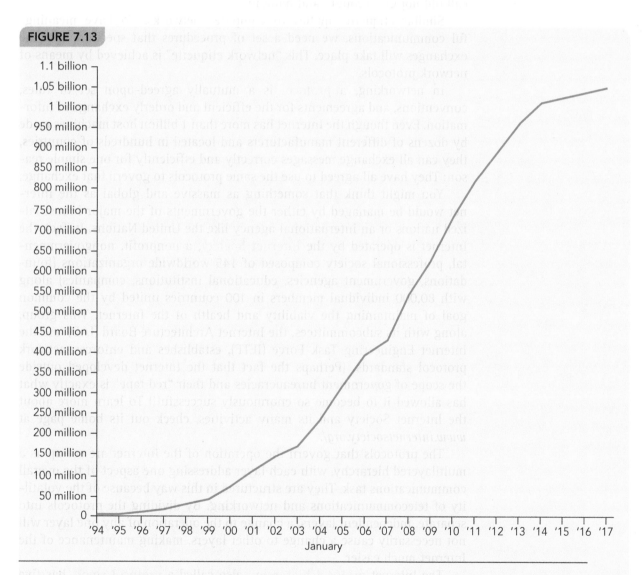

Internet domain survey host count graph

Source: Internet Systems Consortium (*www.isc.org/services/survey*)

7.3 Communication Protocols

When you talk on the telephone, there is an accepted set of procedures that you follow. For example, when you answer the phone, you say "Hello," and then wait for the individual on the other end to respond. The conversation continues until someone says "Goodbye," at which time both parties hang up. You might call this "telephone etiquette"—the conventions that allow orderly exchanges to take place. Imagine what would happen if someone were unaware of them. Such a person might pick up the phone but not say anything. Hearing silence, the caller would be totally confused, think the call did not get through, and hang up.

Similar etiquette applies to computer networks. To have meaningful communications, we need a set of procedures that specifies how the exchanges will take place. This "network etiquette" is achieved by means of network protocols.

In networking, a protocol is a mutually agreed-upon set of rules, conventions, and agreements for the efficient and orderly exchange of information. Even though the Internet has more than 1 billion host machines made by dozens of different manufacturers and located in hundreds of countries, they can all exchange messages correctly and efficiently for one simple reason: They have all agreed to use the same protocols to govern that exchange.

You might think that something as massive and global as the Internet would be managed by either the governments of the major industrialized nations or an international agency like the United Nations. In fact, the Internet is operated by the Internet Society, a nonprofit, nongovernmental, professional society composed of 145 worldwide organizations (foundations, government agencies, educational institutions, companies) along with 80,000 individual members in 100 countries united by the common goal of maintaining the viability and health of the Internet. This group, along with its subcommittees, the Internet Architecture Board (IAB) and the Internet Engineering Task Force (IETF), establishes and enforces network protocol standards. (Perhaps the fact that the Internet developed outside the scope of government bureaucracies and their "red tape" is exactly what has allowed it to become so enormously successful!) To learn more about the Internet Society and its many activities, check out its home page at *www.internetsociety.org/*.

The protocols that govern the operation of the Internet are set up as a multilayered hierarchy, with each layer addressing one aspect of the overall communications task. They are structured in this way because of the volatility of telecommunications and networking. By dividing the protocols into separate, independent layers, a change to the operation of any one layer will not necessarily cause a change to other layers, making maintenance of the Internet much easier.

The Internet protocol hierarchy, also called a protocol stack, has five layers, and their names and some examples are listed in Figure 7.14. This hierarchy is also referred to as TCP/IP, after the names of two of its most important protocols.

FIGURE 7.14

Layer	Name	Examples
5	Application	HTTP, SMTP, FTP
4	Transport	TCP, UDP
3	Network	IP
2b	Logical Link Control	PPP, Ethernet ⎫
2a	Medium Access Control	Ethernet ⎬ Data Link layer
1	Physical	Modem, DSL, Cable modem, Wi-Fi, 4G

The five-layer TCP/IP protocol hierarchy

In the following sections, we briefly describe the responsibilities of each of the five layers in the hierarchy shown in Figure 7.14.

7.3.1 Physical Layer

The Physical layer protocols govern the exchange of binary digits (bits) across a physical communication channel, such as a fiber-optic cable, copper wire, or wireless radio channel. These protocols specify such things as:

- How we know when a bit is present on the line

- How much time the bit will remain on the line

- Whether the bit is in the form of a digital or an analog signal

- The physical quantities used to represent a binary 0 and a binary 1

- The shape of the physical connector between the computer and transmission line

The goal of the Physical layer is to create a "bit pipe" between two computers, such that bits put into the pipe at one end can be read and understood by the computer located at the other end, as shown in Figure 7.15.

Once you select a standardized Physical layer protocol by purchasing a cable modem, getting a DSL, or using a mobile phone with Wi-Fi capabilities, you can transmit binary signals across a physical channel. From this point on in the protocol stack, you no longer need to be concerned about

FIGURE 7.15

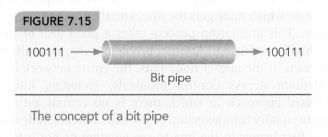

100111 ⟶ Bit pipe ⟶ 100111

The concept of a bit pipe

such engineering issues as voltage levels, wavelengths, or radio frequencies. These details are hidden inside the Physical layer, which provides all of the necessary bit transmission services. From now on, all you need to know about the communication channel is that when you ask the Physical layer to send a bit, it does so, and when you ask the Physical layer to get a bit, it retrieves a 0 or a 1.

7.3.2 Data Link Layer

The Physical layer protocols create a bit pipe between two machines connected by a communication link. However, this link is not an error-free channel, and due to interference or weather or any number of other factors, errors can be introduced into the transmitted bit stream. The bits that come out might not be an exact copy of the bits that went in. This creates what is called the error detection and correction problem—how do we detect when errors occur, and how do we correct them?

Also, because we want to receive complete messages, not just raw streams of bits, we need to know which bits in the incoming stream belong together; that is, we need to identify the start and the end of a message. This is called framing. It is the job of the Data Link protocols to address and solve these two issues—error handling and framing. This process is done in two stages called Layer 2a, *Medium Access Control*, and Layer 2b, *Logical Link Control*. Together these two services form the Layer 2 protocol called the Data Link layer.

In Section 7.2.1, we described how local area networks like Ethernet networks communicate by having multiple machines connected to a single, shared communication line (Figures 7.6 and 7.7). However, although shared by many machines, at any single point in time, this line is capable of sending and receiving only a single message. Attempting to send two or more messages at the same time results in all messages being garbled and none getting through. In this environment, a necessary first step in transmitting a message is determining how to allocate this shared line among the competing machines. The Medium Access Control protocols determine how to arbitrate ownership of a shared communication line when multiple nodes want to send messages at the same time.

This could be done in a *centralized* manner by creating a single master control node responsible for determining who gets ownership of the line at any instant in time. Although easy to do, centralized control is rarely used. One reason is that it can be slow. Each node sends its request to the master, who must decide which node gets the line, and then inform every other node of its decision. This arbitration process takes a good deal of time, making the network highly inefficient. Another problem is that centralized control is not fault tolerant. If the master node fails, the entire network is inoperable.

Most Medium Access Control protocols, including Ethernet, use a *contention-based* approach in which there is no central authority and all nodes compete equally for ownership of the line. When a node wants to send a message, it first listens to the line to see whether or not it is currently in use. If the line is idle, then the node transmits immediately. If the line is busy, the node wanting to send monitors the status of the line and, as soon as it becomes idle, it transmits. This situation is diagrammed in Figure 7.16(a), in which node B wants to send but notices that A is using the line. B listens and waits until A is finished, and as soon as that occurs, B is free to send.

FIGURE 7.16

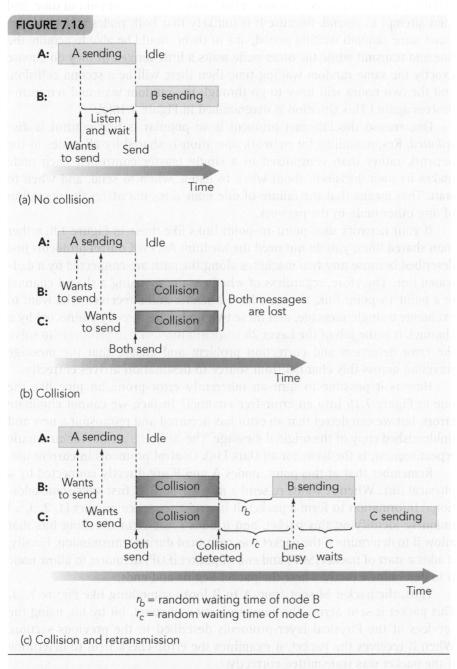

(a) No collision

(b) Collision

(c) Collision and retransmission

r_b = random waiting time of node B
r_c = random waiting time of node C

The Medium Access Control protocols in Ethernet

However, there is still a problem. If two or more users want to send a message while the line is in use, then both are monitoring its status. As soon as the line is idle, both transmit at exactly the same time. This is called a collision, and it is a common occurrence in contention-based networks like Ethernet. When a collision occurs, all information is lost. This scenario is shown in Figure 7.16(b). According to the Ethernet protocols, when a collision occurs, the colliding nodes immediately stop sending, wait a random amount of time, and then attempt to resend. Because it is unlikely that both nodes will select the exact same random waiting period, one of them should be able to acquire the line and transmit while the other node waits a little longer. (If they do choose exactly the same random waiting time then there will be a second collision, and the two nodes will have to go through the random wait and retransmit process again.) This situation is diagrammed in Figure 7.16(c).

One reason the Ethernet protocol is so popular is that control is *distributed*. Responsibility for network operation is shared by all nodes in the network rather than centralized in a single master controller. Each node makes its own decisions about when to listen, when to send, and when to wait. That means that the failure of one node does not affect the operation of any other node in the network.

If your network uses point-to-point links like those in Figure 7.8, rather than shared lines, you do not need the Medium Access Control protocols just described because any two machines along the path are connected by a dedicated line. Therefore, regardless of whether you are using a shared channel or a point-to-point link, you now have a sender and a receiver, who want to exchange a single message, and these two nodes are directly connected by a channel. It is the job of the Layer 2b Logical Link Control protocols to solve the error detection and correction problem and ensure that the message traveling across this channel from source to destination arrives correctly.

How is it possible to turn an inherently error-prone bit pipe like the one in Figure 7.15 into an error-free channel? In fact, we cannot eliminate errors, but we can detect that an error has occurred and retransmit a new and unblemished copy of the original message. The ARQ algorithm, for *automatic repeat request*, is the basis for all Data Link Control protocols in current use.

Remember that at this point, nodes A and B are directly connected by a physical link. When A wants to send a message to B, it first adds some additional information to form a packet. It inserts a sequence number (1, 2, 3, ...) uniquely identifying this packet, and it adds some error-checking bits that allow B to determine if the packet was corrupted during transmission. Finally, it adds a start of packet (SOP) and end of packet (EOP) delimiter to allow node B to determine exactly where the packet begins and ends.

Thus, the packet M sent from A to B looks something like Figure 7.17. This packet is sent across the communication channel, bit by bit, using the services of the Physical layer protocols described in the previous section. When B receives the packet, it examines the error-check field to determine if the packet was transmitted correctly.

What makes the ARQ algorithm work is that the sender, node A, maintains a *copy* of the packet after it has been sent. If B correctly receives the

FIGURE 7.17

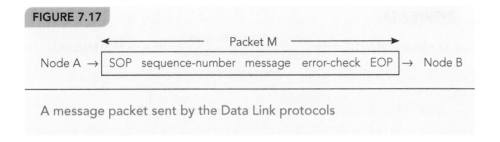

A message packet sent by the Data Link protocols

packet, it returns to A a special acknowledgment message, abbreviated ACK, containing the sequence number of the correctly received packet. Node A now knows that this packet was correctly received and can discard its local copy. It is free to send the next message:

A	B	
M(1) →		Send the first packet from A to B
	← ACK(1)	B says to A, "I got it," A can discard it
M(2) →		Send the second packet from A to B
	← ACK(2)	B says to A, "I got it," A can discard it
⋮		

If B does not correctly receive the packet (or the packet is lost entirely), then A will not receive the ACK message from B. After waiting a reasonable amount of time (typically two or three times the average round trip delivery time), A resends the message to B using the copy stored in its memory:

A	B	
M(1) →		Send the first packet from A to B
	← ACK(1)	B says to A, "I got it," A can discard it
M(2) →		Send the second packet from A to B
		No response from B; wait for a while and resend
M(2) →		the second packet from A to B
	← ACK(2)	B says to A, "I got it," A can discard it
⋮		

The ACK for a correctly received packet is itself a message and can be lost or damaged during transmission. If an ACK is lost, then A incorrectly assumes that the original packet was lost and retransmits it. However, B knows this is a duplicate because it has the same sequence number as the packet received earlier. It simply acknowledges the duplicate and discards it. This ARQ algorithm guarantees that every message sent (eventually) arrives at the destination.

Thus, we can think of the Data Link layer protocols as creating an error-free "message pipe," in which messages go in one end and always come out the other end correctly and in the proper sequence, as shown in Figure 7.18.

FIGURE 7.18

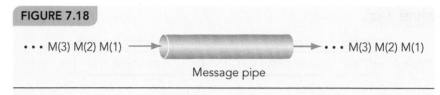

··· M(3) M(2) M(1) ——————▶ [   ] ▶ ··· M(3) M(2) M(1)

Message pipe

Data Link protocols create an error-free "message pipe"

Practice Problems

Node A and node B are exchanging messages using the ARQ algorithm described in this section. State what action node B should take in each of the following situations:

Node A	Node B
1. M(3) →	
	← ACK(3)
M(3) →	
	?
2. M(3) →	
	← ACK(3)
M(4) →	
	?
3. M(3) →	
	← ACK(3)
M(5) →	
	?

4. State why the following statement is true or false: Using a contention protocol like the Ethernet you can be guaranteed that a message will eventually arrive correctly at its intended destination.

5. Explain why message collisions would or would not occur on local area networks that used the ring topology of Figure 7.5(b) or the star topology of Figure 7.5(c).

6. Given a 100 Mbps Ethernet network supporting approximately 20 users sending messages that average 100 characters in length, do you think that collisions would or would not be a significant problem? Explain your reasoning.

7.3.3 Network Layer

The first two layers of the protocol stack enable us to transmit messages from node A to node B, but only if these two nodes are directly connected by a physical link. If we look back at the model of a wide area network shown in Figure 7.8, we see that the great majority of nodes are *not* directly connected. It is the job of the end-to-end Network layer protocols to deliver a message from the site where it was created to its ultimate destination. To accomplish this delivery task, every node must agree to use the same addressing scheme so that everyone is able to identify that ultimate destination. Thus, the two critical responsibilities of the Network layer are as follows:

- Creating a universal addressing scheme for all network nodes; and

- Delivering messages between any two nodes in the network.

Every node in the network must run the identical Network layer protocol, and it is one of the most important parts of the protocol stack. It is often said that the Network layer is the "glue" that holds the entire network together. The Network layer in the Internet is called IP, for Internet Protocol.

You have almost certainly been exposed to the host naming scheme used by the Internet, as you use it in all your email and web applications. For example, the machines of the two authors of this book have the following names:

macalester.edu

iupui.edu

However, these symbolic host names are not the actual names that nodes use to identify each other in IP. Instead, nodes identify each other using a 32-bit IP address, often written as four 8-bit numeric quantities in the range 0–255, each grouping separated by a dot. For example, the machine referred to as *macalester.edu* has the 32-bit IP address 141.140.1.5. In binary, it appears as follows:

10001101	10001100	00000001	00000101
141	140	1	5

and this is the actual destination address placed inside a message as it makes its way through the Internet. Looking at the numeric address shown above, it is easy to understand why people prefer symbolic names. Whereas it is easy for humans to remember mnemonic character strings, imagine having to remember a sequence of 32 binary digits. (This is reminiscent of the benefits of assembly language over machine language.)

It is the task of a special Internet application called the Domain Name System (DNS) to convert from a symbolic host name such as *macalester.edu* to its equivalent 32-bit IP address 141.140.1.5. The DNS is a massive database, distributed over literally thousands of machines that,

I Can't Believe We've Run Out

When the Internet was started in the early 1970s, its designers selected a 32-bit addressing scheme believing, quite reasonably, that the 2^{32} = 4 billion+ available addresses would last for a long, long time. Well, that long, long time unexpectedly arrived on February 4, 2011 when the Internet Corporation for Assigned Names and Numbers (ICANN) announced that it had just handed out the very last unused block of network addresses. It had run out!

Fortunately, this is not yet a catastrophic situation because the careful recovery and reallocation of addresses previously handed out but never actually assigned will allow the current addressing scheme to continue functioning for quite a few more years. (As of mid-2016 there were still about 8–10 million network addresses available for assignment.) However, as ICANN likes to say, "four billion addresses is simply not enough for seven billion people." In addition, there are hundreds of millions of devices that have been assigned a network IP address as discussed in the Special Interest Box "The Internet of Things" earlier in this chapter. For that reason, Internet engineers have created a "next generation" set of IP protocols, called IPv6.

The transition from the current IPv4, with its 32-bit address, to IPv6, with a 128-bit address field, will certainly solve the "lack of addresses" problem. The new Internet protocol provides for 2^{128} = 300 undecillion unique addresses—that's a 3 followed by 36 zeros. The designers were determined never to run out of addresses again! However, because of the time and expense involved in converting to the new 128-bit IPv6 addresses, as of 2017, a significant number of communication companies and ISPs had not switched to this new addressing scheme, and it will likely still be a few years before the final conversion to IPv6 becomes a reality.

in total, contain the host name-to-IP address mappings for the more than 1 billion host computers on the Internet. When you use a symbolic host name, such as *mySchool.edu* or *myCompany.com,* this character string is forwarded to a computer called a *local name server* that checks to see if it has a data record containing the numeric IP address for this symbolic name. If so, it returns the corresponding 32-bit binary value. If not, the local name server forwards it to a remote name server (and possibly another, and another, ...) until it locates the name server that knows the correct IP address.

Let's use the diagram shown earlier to see how the Network layer operates:

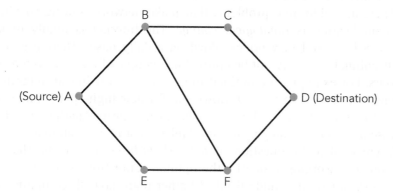

Assume A wants to send a message to D. First, node A uses the DNS to obtain the 32-bit IP address of node D, which it inserts into its message. Because there is no direct path from A to D, the message is sent along a multi-hop path reaching from A to D. (Each of these direct machine-to-machine hops uses the Data Link layer protocols described in the previous section.) In this example, there are four possibilities—ABCD, AEFD, ABFD, and AEFBCD—and the process of selecting one specific path is called routing.

Routing algorithms are highly complex because of the massive volume of data that must be maintained and the enormous amount of processing required to determine the optimal route, called the *shortest path*. The shortest path between two nodes is not necessarily the shortest path in length, but the path via which the message can travel the fastest (maybe it should be called the *quickest path*). To determine the shortest path between every pair of nodes, we need to know the time delay between every connected pair of nodes in the network. In the previous example, this is the time to get from A to B, from B to C, from A to E, and so on. For small networks, it is feasible to have all this data available at any one time, but for networks like the Internet, with its billions of nodes and links, this is an unimaginably huge amount of data to obtain and keep current.

Even if we were somehow able to collect all this data, we are still not finished. Now we must determine exactly which path to select. One possible algorithm is to determine the time required to send a message along *every* path from a source to a destination and then pick the one with the smallest delay. For example, to determine the optimal path from A to D, we could start out by summing the individual delays from A to B, B to C, and C to D, which would give us the time to get from A to D using the route A → B → C → D. We now repeat this process for every other path from A to D and pick the smallest.

However, in Section 3.5, we showed that, as the number of network nodes increases, the solution time for these "brute force" algorithms grows exponentially. Therefore, this method is infeasible for any but the tiniest networks. Fortunately, there are much better algorithms that can solve this problem in $\Theta(N^2)$ time, where N is the number of nodes in the network. (The Internet uses a method called *Dijkstra's shortest path algorithm*.) For large networks, where $N = 10^8$ or 10^9, an $\Theta(N^2)$ algorithm might require on the order of 10^{16} or 10^{18} calculations to determine the best route from any node to another—still an enormous amount of work.

There are additional problems that make network routing so difficult. One complication is *topological change*. The Internet is highly dynamic, with new links and new nodes added on a daily basis. Therefore, a route that is optimal now may not be optimal in a couple of days or even a couple of hours. For example, the optimal route from A to D in our diagram may currently be A → B → C → D. However, if a new high-speed line is added connecting nodes E and D, this might change the shortest path to A → E → D. Because of frequent changes, routing tables must be recomputed often.

There is also the question of *network failures*. It may be that when everything is working properly, the optimal route from A to D is A → B → C → D. But what if node B fails? Rather than have all communications between A and D suspended, it would be preferable for the network to switch to an alternative route that does not pass through node B, such as A → E → F → D. This ability to dynamically reroute messages allows a WAN to continue operating even in the presence of node and link failures.

The Network layer has many other responsibilities not mentioned here, including network management, broadcasting, and locating mobile nodes that move around the network. The Network layer is truly a complex piece of software.

With the addition of the Network layer to our protocol stack, we no longer have just a bit pipe or a message pipe, but a true end-to-end "network delivery service" in which messages are delivered between any two nodes in the network, regardless of their location, as illustrated in Figure 7.19.

7.3.4 Transport Layer

Imagine that 123 Main St. is a large, multistory office building with thousands of tenants. When you address a letter to an employee who works in this building, it is not enough to write:

Joe Smith
123 Main St.
My Town, Minnesota

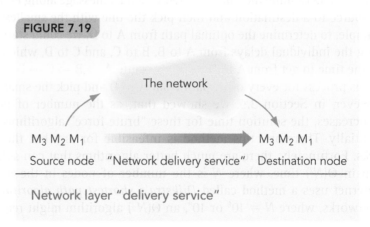

FIGURE 7.19

The network

M₃ M₂ M₁ ————————————————→ M₃ M₂ M₁

Source node   "Network delivery service"   Destination node

Network layer "delivery service"

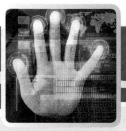
Practice Problems

Given the following six-node wide area network for which the numbers attached to the links are a measure of the "delay" in using that link (e.g., some lines could be more heavily used than others and therefore have a longer wait time), answer the following questions:

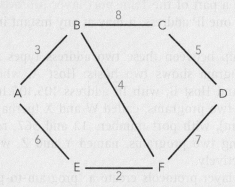

1. What is the shortest path from node A to node D, where *shortest path* is defined as the path with the smallest sum of the delays on each individual link? Explain exactly how you went about finding that path.

2. Do you think the algorithm you used in Practice Problem 1 works if we redraw the graph so it has 26 nodes rather than 6 and about 50 links rather than 10? Why or why not?

3. What if the link connecting node F to node D fails? What is now the shortest path from node A to node D? Could the failure of any single link in this network prevent nodes A and D from communicating?

4. What if the delay from node A to node E were reduced from six units to four? Would that change the shortest path from A to D?

5. If node B crashed and was unable to send or receive messages, would there be any other nodes in the network that would be unable to communicate?

This identifies the correct building, but how do the people in the central mailroom locate "Joe Smith" from among the thousands of people who work there? We need to provide a more descriptive address, one that not only identifies the correct building but also exactly where inside this building Mr. Smith works:

Joe Smith

Acme Services Inc., Suite 2701

123 Main St.

My Town, Minnesota

The same situation exists on the Internet. Every host computer has an IP address that uniquely identifies it. However, there may be multiple application programs running on that one machine, each one "doing its own thing." When a message comes in, how do we know which application program it is for and where to deliver it?

We need a second level of address that identifies not only a specific machine but also a specific program running on that machine. This "program identifier," usually just a small integer value, is called a port number, and it serves the same role as the address line "Acme Services Inc., Suite 2701." Assigning port numbers to programs and remembering which program goes with which port is a part of the Transport layer protocols. Although each host computer has one IP address, it may at any instant in time have many active ports.

The relationship between these two address types is shown in Figure 7.20. This diagram shows two hosts: Host A, whose IP address is 101.102.103.104, and Host B, with IP address 105.106.107.108. Host A is currently running two programs, called W and X (perhaps a web browser and an email client), with port numbers 12 and 567, respectively, while Host B is executing two programs, named Y and Z, with port numbers 44 and 709, respectively.

The Transport layer protocols create a "program-to-program" delivery service, in which we don't simply move messages from one host to another, but from a specific program at the source to a specific program at the destination.

In the example in Figure 7.20, it is the job of the Network layer protocol to deliver the message from the host with IP address 101.102.103.104 to the host with IP address 105.106.107.108, at which point its responsibilities are over. The Transport protocol at the destination node examines the newly arrived message to determine which program should get it, based on the port number field inside the message. For example, if the port number field is 709, then the information in the message is forwarded to application

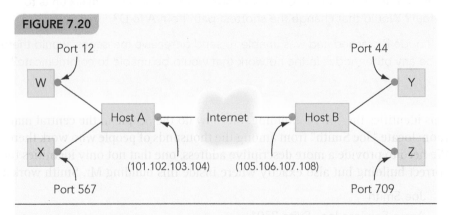

FIGURE 7.20

Relationship between IP addresses and port numbers

program Z. (What program Z does with this information and exactly what that message means are not part of the Transport protocols but rather the Application protocols discussed in the following section.)

How does a program (such as W or X) learn the port number of another program (such as Y or Z) running on a remote machine somewhere out in the network? The answer is that all important applications on the Internet use *well-known port numbers*. Just as it is widely known in the United States that directory assistance is found at 555-1212 and police and fire emergencies are reported to 911, fixed integer values are assigned to certain applications, and those values are made known to every machine on the Internet. For example, the HTTP protocol, which allows us to access remote webpages (and which we discuss in the following section), always uses port 80 for its communications. If you want to get a webpage from another machine, you simply talk to the program on that remote machine that is listening for messages on port 80.

Figure 7.22 later in the chapter lists the port numbers of some common Internet applications. A database of all well-known port assignments is maintained online by IANA, the Internet Assigned Numbers Authority.[1] The only time you need to get a new port number is when you are developing a new application program.

The other primary responsibility of the Transport layer has to do with errors and reliability. When we introduced the Data Link layer in Section 7.3.2, we said that one of its tasks is to take the inherently unreliable physical channel underneath it and turn it into an efficient and error-free channel. That same type of relationship exists between the Transport layer and the layer underneath it, namely, the Network layer.

The Network layer of the Internet, IP, is an inherently unreliable communication channel. IP uses what is called a *good faith* transmission model. That means that it tries very hard to deliver a message from source to destination, but it does not guarantee either correct or ordered delivery. In this sense, IP is like the post office. The post office does a very good job of delivering mail, and the overwhelming majority of letters do get through. However, the post office does not guarantee that every letter you send will arrive, and it does not guarantee that letters will arrive either within a specific time period or in exactly the same order that they were originally posted. If you need these features, you have to use some type of "special handling" service such as registered mail or express mail.

In a sense, the Transport layer represents just this type of "special handling" service. Its job is to create a high-quality, error-free, order-preserving, end-to-end delivery service on top of the unreliable delivery services provided by IP. On the Internet, the primary transport protocol is TCP (Transport Control Protocol). (There is another transport protocol called *UDP* for *User Datagram Protocol* that does not provide such a high level of service. We will not be discussing it here.)

---

[1] This database can be accessed on the IANA website, *www.iana.org*.

TCP requires that the two programs at the source and destination node initially establish a connection. That is, they must first inform each other of the impending message exchange, and they must describe the "quality of service" they want to receive. This connection does not exist in a hardware sense—there is no "wire" stretched between the two nodes. Instead, it is a logical connection that exists only as entries in tables. However, TCP can make this logical connection behave exactly as if there were a real connection between these two programs. This logical view of a TCP connection is shown in Figure 7.21.

Once this connection has been established, messages can be transmitted from the source program to the destination program. Programs P1 and P2 appear to have a direct, error-free link between them. In reality, however, their communications travel via the Network layer protocol from P1 to A, B, C, D, and finally to P2, using the services of the Data Link protocol for each link along the way.

TCP uses the same ARQ algorithm described in our discussion of the Data Link level. The receiving program must acknowledge every message correctly received. If a message is lost in the network and does not arrive, the sending program does not receive an acknowledgment and eventually resends it. Every message is ultimately delivered to the application program waiting for it and, therefore, this TCP connection does function like an error-free channel.

Every message sent on this TCP connection contains a sequence number—1, 2, 3,.... If messages are received out of order (say message 3 comes in before message 2 because of errors along the route), then TCP simply holds the later message (message 3) until the earlier message (message 2) correctly arrives. At that time, it can deliver both messages to

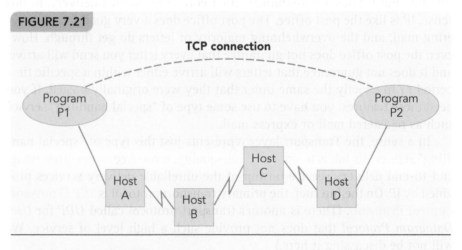

FIGURE 7.21

Logical view of a TCP connection

the application program in the proper order. From the destination's point of view, this TCP connection always delivers messages in the proper order.

With these four protocol layers in place, we now have a complete end-to-end delivery service. The network can transmit a message from a program anywhere in the network to another program anywhere in the network—and can do it correctly, efficiently, and in the proper order. The only thing left to specify is the *content* of those messages; that is, what does a program want to say to another program? Essentially we are asking the question: "What types of applications do we want to give to our network users and exactly how do we implement them?" We answer that fundamental question as we look at the very top layer of our protocol stack—the Application layer.

7.3.5 Application Layer

The Application layer protocols are the rules for implementing the end-user services provided by a network, and they are built on top of the four protocol layers described in previous sections. These services are the reason that networks exist in the first place, and the appearance of globally popular applications (often called *killer apps*) has fueled the rapid growth of networking and the Internet—email in the 1970s, chat rooms in the 1980s, the web and ecommerce in the 1990s, and social networking in the 21st century. Figure 7.22 lists a few of the important application protocols on the Internet upon which these killer apps are built.

It is not possible in this one section to discuss all the protocols listed in Figure 7.22. Instead, we will use the HTTP protocol, which is used by the web to access and deliver webpages, to serve as a general model for how Application layer services are typically built on top of the TCP/IP protocol stack.

FIGURE 7.22

Acronym	Name	Application	Well-Known Port
HTTP	Hypertext Transfer Protocol	Accessing webpages	80
SMTP	Simple Mail Transfer Protocol	Sending email	25
POP3	Post Office Protocol	Receiving email	110
IMAP	Internet Message Access Protocol	Receiving email	143
FTP	File Transfer Protocol	Accessing remote files	21
TELNET	Terminal Emulation Protocol	Accessing remote terminals	23
DNS	Domain Name System	Translating symbolic host names to IP addresses	42

Some popular application protocols on the Internet

A single webpage is identified by a symbolic string called a Uniform Resource Locator, abbreviated URL. URLs have three parts, and they look like this:

protocol:// host address/page

The first part, *protocol*, indicates the type of information contained in this webpage. The most common format is *hypertext*, and we access it using the Hypertext Transfer Protocol (HTTP). The second part of the URL is the *host address* of the machine where the page is stored. This is the symbolic host name first discussed in Section 7.3.3. The third and last part of the URL is the *page* identification, which is usually a file stored on the specified machine. Thus, a typical URL might look like the following:

http://www.macalester.edu/about

This identifies a hypertext ("http") document stored in a file called *about* located on a host computer whose symbolic name is *www.macalester.edu*. (*Note*: "http" is the default protocol. Thus, the previous URL can also be written as *www.macalester.edu/about*.)

Before you can transfer a webpage, you must first establish a connection between the client program (the web browser run by the user) and port 80, the port number of the web server located at the node where the webpage resides, in this example *www.macalester.edu*. The network uses the TCP protocol described in Section 7.3.4 to establish this connection. Thus, you can clearly see how the HTTP application protocol is built on top of the TCP/IP protocol stack just described.

Once you have established the TCP connection, an HTTP *request message* is sent from the client to the server, specifying the name of the webpage that you wish to access. A second HTTP message type, called a *response message*, is returned from the server to the client along the same TCP connection. The response contains a status code specifying whether or not the request was successful and, if it was, it includes a copy of the requested page.[2]

Let's illustrate how these pieces work together using a simple example. Imagine you are using a web browser such as Chrome, Safari, or Firefox, and have just clicked on, touched, or entered the following URL:

http://www.macalester.edu/about

The following sequence of events now takes place:

1. Your browser scans the URL and extracts the host name of the machine to which it must connect–*www.macalester.edu*. (Let's disregard the issue of how this symbolic name is converted to its corresponding 32-bit or 128-bit binary IP address.)

2. Your browser asks TCP to establish a connection between itself and port 80 (the web server) of the machine called *www.macalester.edu*.

---

[2] We have probably all had the experience of seeing return code 404: Page Not Found, which means the requested document does not exist on that server.

3. When the TCP connection between your browser and the web server is established, your browser scans the URL to identify the page you want to access. In this case, it is */about*. Your browser constructs an HTTP 'GET' message, which requests the contents of that webpage. This GET message looks something like the following:

    GET /about HTTP/1.2

    Host: www.macalester.edu

    This message says that we want a copy of the webpage */about* located at *www.macalester.edu*, and it should be accessed using the http protocol, version 1.2. (An actual GET message is quite a bit more complex and includes a number of additional fields not shown here.)

4. The GET message in Step 3 is transmitted across the Internet from the client's web browser port at the source node to the web server port at the destination node using the services of TCP/IP as well as the Data Link and Physical layer protocols.

5. When the GET message arrives at the destination, it is delivered to the web server (which is listening on port 80). The web server locates the file named in the GET message (*/about*) and creates a response message containing a copy of the contents of that file. This response message looks something like the following:

    HTTP/1.2 200

    Connection: close

    Date: Monday, 26 Mar 2018

    Content Length: 53908

    Content Type: text/html

    … (the actual contents of the webpage go here) …

    This response message says that the server successfully found the file (code 200), and it contains 53,908 bytes of text. It also says that after the webpage has been sent, the TCP connection between the browser and the server will be closed. Finally, there is a copy of the entire webpage. (Again, some fields in the response message have been omitted for clarity.)

6. The HTTP response message in Step 5 is transmitted across the Internet from the web server back to the port of the client's web browser using the services of TCP/IP as well as the Data Link and Physical layer protocols.

7. The message is delivered to your web browser, and the page is displayed on the screen. The TCP connection between the two programs is terminated.

Something similar to this occurs every time you click on a new URL. This sequence of events is diagrammed in Figure 7.23.

FIGURE 7.23

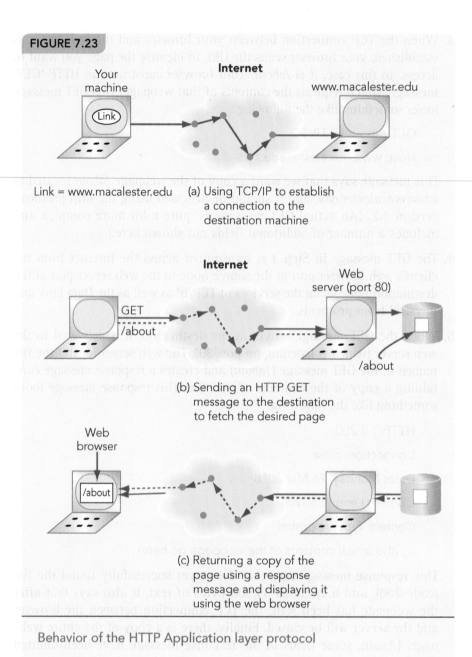

Link = www.macalester.edu   (a) Using TCP/IP to establish a connection to the destination machine

(b) Sending an HTTP GET message to the destination to fetch the desired page

(c) Returning a copy of the page using a response message and displaying it using the web browser

Behavior of the HTTP Application layer protocol

7.4 Network Services and Benefits

At the beginning of this chapter, we said that networks have the potential to create enormous social change. Now that we have looked at how they are designed and built, let's briefly examine the services they can offer and their impact on society.

Laboratory Experience 11

We have just completed a rather long and complex discussion of how a computer network functions. The chapter presented a good deal of technical material that some people may find fairly difficult to grasp. To help clarify these ideas, this Laboratory Experience illustrates network behavior using a software package called a *network simulator*. This simulator allows you to observe and control many of the technical concepts introduced in this section, concepts such as packets, messages, error detection, error correction, and routing.

7.4.1 Interpersonal Communications

Email (electronic mail) has been the single most popular application of networks for the last 35 years. It is estimated that about 400 billion email messages are transmitted across the Internet *every day*! When the Internet was first developed, its designers thought it would be an ideal way for scientists and engineers to access important software packages and data files stored on remote computers. However, the first Internet "killer app" was rather unexpected and something quite different—email.

Email is *convenient*. You can send a message whenever you want, and it waits for the recipient to log on and read at his or her convenience. Email is *fast*. A message from the United States typically arrives anywhere in the world in a few seconds, even though it may have to pass through 15 or 20 nodes along the way (using the packet-switched protocols described in the previous section). Email supports *multimedia*. The contents of your electronic messages are not limited to characters but can also include a range of *attachments*, including photographs, text, graphics, video, and sound. Finally, email is a *broadcast medium*. A computer can send a letter to a thousand recipients as easily as it can send it to one. (This feature has led to an explosive growth in spam—unsolicited bulk email. It is estimated that 70% of all email on the Internet today is spam.)

An interesting email-related application that flourished during the 1980s and 1990s was the bulletin board system, usually abbreviated BBS. A bulletin board is a shared public file where anyone can post messages and everyone is free to read the postings of others. It was an electronic version of the bulletin boards commonly seen in grocery stores, cafés, and public libraries. Today BBSs have evolved into Internet forums and chat rooms that support the real-time exchange of messages. Another popular form of message exchange is texting (also known as SMS, for Short Message Service) that allows for the rapid exchange of short messages, often using wireless cell phone technology. Today, roughly 100 billion text messages are sent on the Internet every day, and texting might be the latest killer app!

7.4.2 Social Networking

While some early email messages did contain technical content, even more were of the "Wanna meet for lunch today?" variety. Linking people together for purposes of social interaction has been a popular use of computer networks since their earliest days. Following the enormous success of email in the early 1970s, there were many other attempts to foster online communities. In 1980, a system called *Usenet* was developed. It was similar to a BBS with the added feature of having *newsgroups*—subgroups with a mutual interest in one specific topic, such as space flight, Chinese cooking, or Minnesota Vikings football. BBSs and Usenet were popular from the 1980s until the mid-1990s when they began to be replaced by web-based applications with a similar goal—allowing people to exchange thoughts, ideas, opinions, and stories. However, the web's powerful graphics capabilities and hypertext linking features allowed the scope of that sharing to increase dramatically, from text to all types of sound, graphics, videos, and imaging, and from the simple exchange of messages to advanced features such as mobile access, online profiles, trust-based recommendation systems, "friending" controls, blog postings, contact lists, privacy management, and geosocial networking that organize users on the basis of geographic location. The applications that support these types of social exchanges are called social networks.

The use of web-based social networks has grown to the point where they are now some of the most well-known and widely used applications on the Internet, and there is hardly a person who is not thoroughly familiar with them and, more likely, a registered member of one or more. *Facebook*, developed in 2004 by Mark Zuckerberg while a student at Harvard, currently has 1.97 billion active users worldwide (about 24% of the Earth's population), and it receives over 1 billion visits per month. Other highly popular social media sites include YouTube (1 billion users), Wei'xin or WeChat in English (889 million users), QZone (595 million users), Instagram (600 million users), Tumblr (550 million users), and Twitter (319 million users).[3]

However, social networks are not without their issues, many of them serious and potentially dangerous. For example, the information you post on a social networking site can be used by people in ways that you never intended. Strangers may use the information contained in a profile to violate your privacy. Those who want to harm you could post false information to ruin your reputation or limit your access to high-quality education and employment. We will discuss some of the ethical and legal issues related to social networking in Chapter 17.

7.4.3 Resource Sharing

Another important network service is resource sharing, the ability to share *physical resources*, such as a 3-D printer or massive terabyte storage device, as well as *logical resources*, such as software and data, among multiple users.

---

[3] "Leading Social Networks WorldWide as of April 2017 Ranked by Number of Active Users." *Statista.com/statistics/272014/global-social-networks-ranked-by-number-of-users/.*

The prices of computers and peripherals have been dropping for many years, so it is tempting to think that everyone can buy their own specialized I/O units or mass storage devices. However, that is not always a cost-effective way to configure computer systems. For example, a high-volume color laser printer may be used infrequently. Buying everyone in the office his or her own printer would leave most of the printers idle for long periods of time and would cost huge amounts for all the toner cartridges. It would be far more efficient to have a few shared printers, called print servers, which can be accessed whenever needed. Similarly, if a group of users requires access to a data file or a piece of software, it may make sense to keep a single copy on a set of shared network disks, called a file server. A network file server can be a cost-effective way to provide backup services as well as make it easier to access information from multiple devices such as your desktop computer at work, your tablet computer at home, and your smartphone on the road.

The style of computing wherein some nodes provide shared services while the remaining nodes are users (or clients) of those services is called, naturally enough, client/server computing. We have named two examples—print servers and file servers—but there are many others, such as mail servers, compute servers, and web servers. The philosophy behind the client/server model is that we use a network to share resources that are too widespread, too expensive, or used too infrequently to warrant replication at every node. A diagram of the client/server model of computing is shown in Figure 7.24. (We discuss the next generation of client/server computing, called the cloud computing model, in Section 7.5)

Information sharing is another important service, and a network is an excellent way to access scientific, medical, legal, and commercial data files stored on systems all over the world. (In fact, it was the need to share information efficiently among hundreds of physicists that led to the development of the World Wide Web in the early 1990s.) For example, information can be distributed among the geographically dispersed sites of a multinational corporation and shared as needed, using a distributed database. Webpages can

FIGURE 7.24

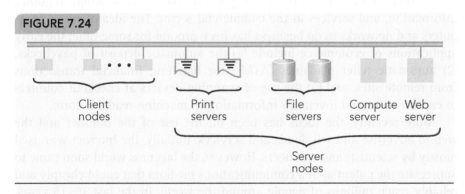

The client/server model of computing

be exchanged between remote systems. Files can be transmitted anywhere in the world using FTP, which is mentioned in Figure 7.22.

Many network sites now provide a service called a data warehouse. These nodes integrate massive amounts of information from a number of disparate sources and allow it to be electronically searched for specific facts or documents. Frequently, these sites focus on a single specialized topic, such as geopolitical data, stock price trends, real estate records, movie trivia, or information on case law and legal precedents. These single-subject data warehouses are often called data marts. Today, it is far more common for students, scientists, business people, and politicians to search for information in data marts than in the stacks of a physical library.

Another important resource-sharing service is the ability to support collaborative group efforts in producing a shared document such as a user's manual, grant application, or design specification. Workers on a project can communicate via the network; hold virtual conferences; check electronic calendars and schedule meetings automatically; and share, discuss, and edit documents online. A rapidly growing network application is *collaborative software*, also known as groupware. This is software that facilitates the creative efforts of individuals connected by a network and working on a single, shared project. One popular form of groupware is called a wiki (the Hawaiian word for fast or quick), which is a set of webpages that everyone is free to access, add to, or modify. One of the most successful examples of a wiki is *Wikipedia*, an online encyclopedia written, reviewed, and maintained by about 76,000 active volunteers working independently. Wikipedia currently includes 5.4 million English-language articles as well about 39 million other entries in 285 different languages from Polish to Portuguese, French to Finnish, Tajik to Tagalog. (By comparison, the *Encyclopedia Britannica* has about 0.5 million articles.) Currently, just the English pages in Wikipedia are viewed at the rate of 5.8 million per hour.

7.4.4 Electronic Commerce

Electronic commerce (or just ecommerce) is a general term applied to any use of computers and networking to support the paperless exchange of goods, information, and services in the commercial sector. The idea of using computers and networks to do business has been around for some time; the early applications of ecommerce include (1) the automatic deposit of paychecks, (2) automatic teller machines (ATMs) for handling financial transactions from remote sites, and (3) the use of scanning devices at checkout counters to capture sales and inventory information in machine-readable form.

More recently, the focus has been on the use of the Internet and the web to advertise and sell goods and services. Initially, the Internet was used mostly by scientists and engineers. However, the business world soon came to appreciate the potential of a communications medium that could cheaply and reliably reach millions of people around the world. In the last 10–15 years, traffic on the Internet has changed from primarily academic and professional to heavily commercial.

Today, about 8% of retail sales in the United States is handled online, up from less than 1% in 2001. This amounts to about $335 billion annually. Worldwide, online retail sales were $1.25 trillion in 2013 and growing at an annual rate of about 18%. Furthermore, using sites such as eBay, Amazon, and Craigslist, individuals, not just corporations, can reach a national or even international audience to buy and sell their products.

We will have much more to say about ecommerce and commercial uses of the Internet in Chapter 14.

7.5 Cloud Computing

In Section 7.4.3 we outlined reasons for the development of the client/server model shown in Figure 7.24. It is not cost effective to replicate expensive and infrequently used hardware, software, or data resources on every machine on your campus, office, or research center. Because of the economies of scale, it is far cheaper for an organization to purchase a shared resource (such as a server) and make it available on demand to users (clients) via a local area network. For over two decades the client/server model was the most widely used technique for sharing computational resources.

However, this model is not without problems, many of them quite serious. For example, the client/server approach can require large up-front capital expenditures to purchase the server, buy the software needed to access it, create the appropriate physical space, and install the system. The new server may incur significant operating costs for network connections, power, cooling, spare parts, staff training, documentation, and repair. When clients request enhanced services, your organization either has to purchase the necessary upgrades or design, implement, and test these new services using in-house technical staff. Finally, you must purchase enough capacity to handle the maximum theoretical needs of the entire client community. Otherwise, when a user requests a service he or she could be turned down because the system is overloaded. Unfortunately, providing sufficient capacity for peak needs leaves servers underutilized a majority of the time.

Because of these shortcomings, a new model for shared access to computing resources has begun to emerge, a model called cloud computing. (The term comes from the cloud diagram used to represent this model, as shown in Figure 7.25.) Cloud computing behaves much like the client/server model of Figure 7.24 in that there are server nodes that provide services and client nodes that access those services. However, with cloud computing the servers no longer need to be local to the client population, and they no longer must be provided by your own organization.

A client requests the services of a server via a communication network such as the Internet using a desktop computer, laptop, tablet, or mobile device, but the client has no idea of where the physical server is or even if the server is a single device or part of a larger server farm—an integrated collection of machines providing services over a network that would not be possible using only a single device. The logical concept of a computational resource

FIGURE 7.25

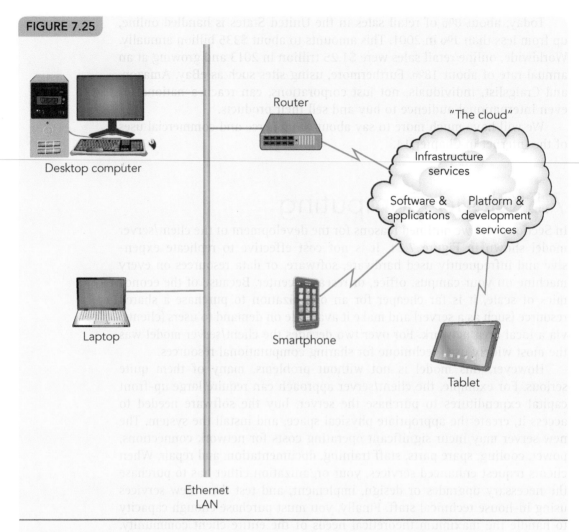

Model of cloud computing

(hardware, software, data) has been divorced from the physical realization of how that service is provided (its location, manufacturer, ownership, or technical structure). The term for the separation of a service from the entity (or entities) providing that service is virtualization, and it is one of the fundamental properties of cloud computing. For example, you use the concept of virtualization whenever you back up a smartphone or tablet to "the cloud." You have no idea where this data is going, how it is being stored, or who is managing the storage. You don't even know if it is being stored in a single location or distributed to multiple machines around the globe. You only know that it has been stored securely, and that you will be able to retrieve it if and when it is needed. Contrast this approach with how you backed up the hard drive on your desktop just a few years back. You would copy the information to a flash drive or an external hard drive that you purchased for this task and for which you took full responsibility to keep safe and secure.

The philosophy of cloud computing is to sell hardware, software, and data capabilities as complete, prepackaged services in which the technical details of networking, management, support, and implementation are hidden from users, who simply request and receive designated services at a specified cost. The user is freed from the messy and often quite complex details about how that service is being provided.

There are many types of cloud services provided by a huge number of cloud computing companies, but the services typically fall into one of three categories. The simplest and most basic is *infrastructure services*, where a provider offers access to shared resources that users do not wish to purchase and maintain themselves, resources such as storage and data backup facilities or access to specialized input/output devices. This is the type of service you use whenever you back up a tablet or smartphone to the cloud rather than to your own desktop or laptop. *Application services* provide shared access to software packages such as email, games, accounting, finance, or document creation. By sharing these software resources users are freed from the costs associated with buying, maintaining, and upgrading these expensive packages. This is the type of cloud service you exploit if you use Google Mail to manage your email or Google Drive to collaborate with others in writing and editing shared documents. The most sophisticated form of cloud computing is *platform and development services*. Companies that create new software such as apps for the Apple iPhone often need sophisticated and expensive development platforms to design, code, and test their new applications. Cloud computing can provide, in a totally transparent way, a powerful software development environment that includes such tools as language translators, debuggers, testers, efficiency metrics, and documentation systems—basically everything a programmer could possibly need to create and market new software packages.

The cloud computing approach to shared resources in Figure 7.25 offers a number of advantages over the client/server model in Figure 7.24. It has the potential to *lower costs* since users pay for only what they need and what they use, not for what they have to buy. Cloud computing providers argue that by purchasing computing and communication services, rather than installing them on site, users are able to focus on their core mission (e.g., education, health, research) rather than on purchasing, maintaining, and upgrading expensive computing infrastructures. Cloud computing provides *elasticity of demand* as your needs fluctuate. Since implementation details of the server are hidden, a service provider is free to dynamically allocate more (or fewer) resources to match current needs. An organization no longer has to purchase sufficient capacity to meet peak client needs, a situation that may occur infrequently. Cloud computing also can offer *wider access* to shared resources. Since a server is no longer tethered to your private local area network, it can typically be accessed anywhere in the world over the Internet using a smartphone, tablet, or laptop. Finally, some advanced computing and communications services might simply be too expensive for an organization to provide for themselves. Enhanced capabilities such as automatic backups and data replication (offering increased *reliability*) or advanced firewalls and data encryption (offering improved *security*) are just two examples of the many services available from cloud computing providers.

In the past two chapters we have described how system software can create a virtual environment that is easier for users to operate and understand. In the last 50 or so years, that virtual environment has grown ever more powerful and provided users with greater access to an enormous range of resources. The next step in that ongoing process is cloud computing. With cloud computing, not only are the resources of a single system and shared local servers accessible in a transparent way, the entire communications network as well as a global network of computational facilities becomes available in a totally transparent manner. With the simple push of a key, click of a mouse, tap of a finger, or voice command, a plethora of powerful services is available to a user without any concern about who is providing this service or where it is happening. This is certainly a most powerful virtual environment in which to work.

7.6 A History of the Internet and the World Wide Web

In the preceding sections, we discussed the technical characteristics and services of networks in general. However, to most people, the phrase *computer network* isn't a generalized term but a very specific one—the global Internet and its most popular component, the World Wide Web.

In this section, we highlight the history, development, and growth of the Internet and the World Wide Web. Much of the information in the following pages is taken from the original 1997 article "A Brief History of the Internet," written by its original designers and available on the web.[4]

7.6.1 The Internet

The Internet is an idea that has been floating around for more than 50 years. The concept first took shape during the early 1960s and was based on the work of computer scientists at MIT and the RAND Corporation in the United States and the NPL Research Laboratory in Great Britain. The first proposal for building a computer network was made by J. C. R. Licklider of MIT in August 1962. He wrote his colleagues a memo titled (somewhat dramatically) "The Galactic Network," in which he described a globally interconnected set of computers through which everyone could access data and software. He convinced other researchers at MIT, including Larry Roberts and Leonard Kleinrock, of the validity of his ideas. From 1962 to 1967, they and others investigated the theoretical foundations of wide area networking, especially such fundamental technical concepts as protocols, packet switching, and routing.

In 1966, Roberts moved to the Advanced Research Projects Agency (ARPA), a small research office of the U.S. Department of Defense charged

---

[4]Leitner, B., Cerf, V., Kahn, R., Kleinrock, L., Lynch, D., Postel, J., Roberts, L., and Wolff, S. (December 10, 2003). A Brief History of the Internet. See *http://www.isoc.org/internet/history/brief.shtml*.

with developing technology that could be of use to the U.S. military. ARPA was interested in packet-switched networking because it seemed to be a more secure form of communications during wartime. ARPA funded a number of network-related research projects, and in 1967 Roberts presented the first research paper describing ARPA's plans to build a wide area packet-switched computer network. For the next two years, work proceeded on the design of the network hardware and software. The first two nodes of this new network, called the ARPANET, were constructed at UCLA and the Stanford Research Institute (SRI), and in October 1969, the first computer-to-computer network message was sent. (The very first Internet transmission was sent by a UCLA student programmer named Charles Kline, and it contained the single word *login*. The network then crashed!) Later that same year two more nodes were added (the University of California-Santa Barbara and the University of Utah), and by the end of 1969, the budding four-node network was off the ground.

The ARPANET grew quickly during the early 1970s, and it was formally demonstrated to the scientific community at an international conference in 1972. It was also in late 1972 that the first killer app was developed—electronic mail. It was an immediate success and caused an explosion of growth in people-to-people traffic rather than the people-to-machine or machine-to-machine traffic that dominated usage in the first few years.

The success of the ARPANET in the 1970s led other researchers to develop similar types of computer networks to support information exchange within their own scientific area: HEPNet (High Energy Physics Network), CSNET (Computer Science Network), and MFENet (Magnetic Fusion Energy Network). Furthermore, corporations started to notice the success of the ARPANET and began developing proprietary networks to market to their customers: SNA (Systems Network Architecture) at IBM and DECNet from Digital Equipment Corporation. The 1970s were a time of rapid expansion of networks in both the academic and the commercial communities.

Farsighted researchers at ARPA, in particular Robert Kahn, realized that this rapid and unplanned proliferation of independent networks would lead to incompatibilities and prevent users on different networks from communicating with each other, a situation that brings to mind the problems that national railway systems have sharing railcars because of their use of different gauge track. Kahn knew that to obtain maximum benefits from this new technology, all networks need to communicate in a standardized fashion. He developed the concept of internetworking, which stated that any WAN is free to do whatever it wants *internally*. However, at the point where two networks meet, both must use a common addressing scheme and identical protocols—that is, they must speak the same language.

This is the same concept that governs the international telephone system. Every country is free to build its own internal phone system in whatever way it wants, but all must agree to use a standardized worldwide numbering system (country code, city code), and each must agree to send and receive telephone calls outside its borders in the format standardized by the worldwide telephone regulatory agency.

Figure 7.26 is a diagram of a "network of networks." It shows four WANs called A, B, C, and D interconnected by a device called a gateway that makes the internetwork connections and provides routing between different WANs.

To allow the four WANs of Figure 7.26 to communicate, Kahn and his colleagues needed to create (1) a standardized way for a node in one WAN to identify a node located in a different WAN and (2) a universally recognized message format for exchanging information across WAN boundaries. Kahn, along with Vinton Cerf of Stanford, began working on these problems in 1973, and together they designed the solutions that became the framework for the Internet. Specifically, they created both the hierarchical host naming scheme that we use today and the TCP/IP protocols that are the "common language" spoken by networks around the world. (These protocols were discussed in Sections 7.3.3 and 7.3.4.)

During the late 1970s and early 1980s, work proceeded on implementing and installing TCP/IP on not only mainframe computers but also the PCs and desktop machines that were starting to appear in the marketplace. It is a tribute to the power and flexibility of the TCP/IP protocols that they were able to adapt to a computing environment quite different from the one that existed when they were first created. Originally designed to work with the large mainframe computers of the 1970s, they were successfully implemented in a new computing environment—desktop PCs connected by LANs. (Later they were again successfully moved to the computing environments of the 21st century—tablets, smartphones, and wireless communications.)

By the early 1980s, TCP/IP was being used all around the world. Even networks that internally used other communication protocols implemented TCP/IP to exchange information with nodes outside their own community.

FIGURE 7.26

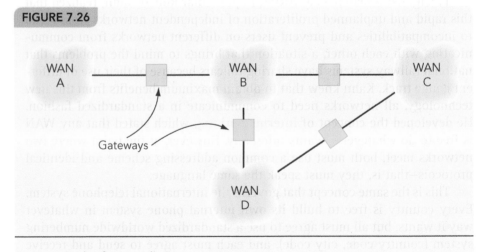

A network of networks

With TCP/IP becoming a *de facto* networking standard, a global addressing scheme, and a growing set of important applications, the infrastructure was in place for the creation of a truly international network. By the early 1980s the Internet, in its modern form, had slowly begun to emerge.

Although many of the technical problems had been solved, networking had yet to make a significant impact on the general population for one important reason: To access the ARPANET you needed a research grant from the U.S. Department of Defense (DOD). In the early 1980s, the people using the Internet were almost exclusively physicists, engineers, and computer scientists at a select set of secure military bases and academic research centers. For example, in 1982, 13 years after its creation, there were only 235 computers connected to the ARPANET.

One last step was needed, and it was taken by the National Science Foundation (NSF) in 1984. In that year, the NSF initiated a project whose goal was to bring the advantages of the Internet to the *entire* academic and professional community, regardless of discipline or relationship with the DOD. The NSF planned and built a national network called *NSFNet*, which used TCP/IP technology identical to the ARPANET. This new network interconnected six NSF supercomputer centers with dozens of new regional networks set up by the NSF. These new regional networks included thousands of users at places like universities, government agencies, libraries, museums, medical centers, and even high schools. Thus, by the mid-1980s, this emerging "network of networks" had grown to include many new sites and, even more important, a huge group of first-time users, such as students, faculty, librarians, museum staff, politicians, civil servants, and urban planners, to name just a few.

At about the same time, other countries began developing wide area TCP/IP backbone networks like NSFNet to interconnect their own universities, research centers, and government agencies. As these national networks were created, they were linked into this expanding network, and the user population continued to expand. For the first time since the development of networking, the technology had begun to have an impact on the wider community. A diagram of the state of internetworking in the late 1980s is shown in Figure 7.27.

Some time in the late 1980s, the term ARPANET ceased to be used because, as Figure 7.27 shows, the ARPANET was now only one of many networks belonging to a much larger collection. (By 1990, the collection had grown to 300,000 computers on 3,000 separate networks.) People began referring to the entire set of interconnected networks as "the Internet," though this name was not officially adopted by the U.S. government until October 24, 1995.

Once the public had easy access, the Internet became an immediate success and grew rapidly. By the middle of 1993, it included 1.8 million host computers and roughly 5 to 10 million active users, and its size was doubling every year. In fact, it had become so successful that the NSF decided it was time to get out of the "networking business." The goal of the NSF is to fund basic research, not to operate an ongoing commercial enterprise. In April 1995, NSFNet closed up shop. The exit of the U.S. government from the networking arena created business opportunities for new firms called Internet service providers (ISPs) that offered the Internet access once provided by ARPANET and NSFNet.

FIGURE 7.27

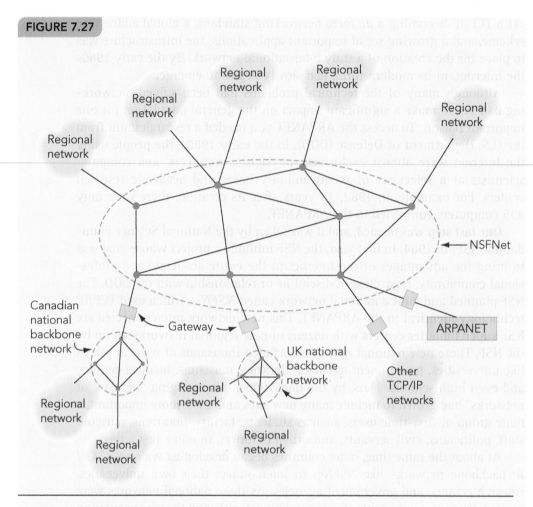

State of networking in the late 1980s

By early 2017, the Internet had grown to more than 1.06 billion computers and 3–4 billion users located in just about every country in the world, and the extraordinary growth of the Internet continues to this day. Figure 7.13 in Section 7.2.4 shows a graph of the number of host computers connected to the Internet.

The Internet has been one of the biggest success stories in moving research out of the laboratory and into the wider community. What began as the wild idea of a few dedicated researchers has grown, in only 50 years, into a global communications infrastructure moving trillions of bits of data among billions of people. It has adapted time and time again—to changes in usage (from research and academic to commercial and entertainment), changes in hardware (from mainframes to laptops, tablets, and smartphones), and changes in scale (from hundreds of nodes to billions of nodes).

The Internet continues to undergo massive growth and change, this time from the most important new killer app developed for the Internet since email—the World Wide Web.

7.6.2 The World Wide Web

Tim Berners-Lee, a researcher at CERN, the European High Energy Physics Laboratory in Geneva, Switzerland, first developed the idea for a hypertext-based information distribution system in 1989. Because physics research is often done by teams of people from different universities, he wanted to create a way for scientists throughout Europe and North America to easily exchange information such as research articles, journals, and experimental data. Although they could use existing Internet services such as FTP and email, Berners-Lee wanted to make information sharing easier and more intuitive for people unfamiliar with computer networks.

Beginning in 1990, Berners-Lee designed and built a system using the concept of hypertext, a collection of documents interconnected by pointers, called *links*, as shown in Figure 7.28. Traditional documents are meant to be read linearly from beginning to end, but users of hypertext documents (called *pages* in web parlance) are free to navigate the collection in whatever order they want, using the links to move freely from page to page. Berners-Lee reasoned that the idea of hypertext matched up very well with the concept of networking and the Internet. Hypertext documents could be stored on the machines of the Internet, and a link would be the name of a page along with the IP address of the machine where that page is stored. He called his hypertext link a URL, an acronym for Uniform Resource Locator, and it is the worldwide identification of a webpage located on a specific host computer on the Internet.

FIGURE 7.28

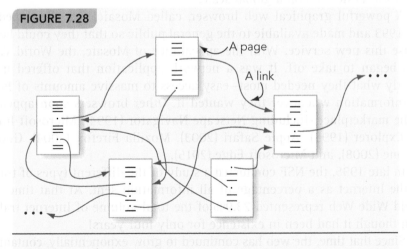

Hypertext documents

Geography Lesson

The Internet is a truly "global phenomenon," affecting the way people work, shop, and communicate throughout the world. Consider that, whereas the United Nations has 192 member states, the Domain Name System (DNS) of the Internet includes entries for 239 countries, territories, and possessions. The DNS includes standardized domain names for such places as (you may want to get out your atlas) Comoros (.km), Nauru (.nr), Pitcairn (.pn), Kiribati (.ki), Mayotte (.yt), Guinea Bissau (.gw), and St. Pierre and Miquelon (.pm). As of 2017, the smallest DNS domains are .td, the Republic of Chad and .sj, Svalbard and Jan Mayen Islands. They both contain exactly zero host computers!

Berners-Lee named his new information system the World Wide Web, and it was completed and made available to all researchers at CERN in August 1991, the date that marks the birth of the web. It became an instant success, and traffic on the CERN web server increased by 1,000% in its first two years of use. In April 1993, the directors of CERN, realizing the beneficial impact that the web could have on research throughout the world, announced that, effective immediately, all web technology developed at CERN would be freely available to everyone without fees or royalties. For many people, this important announcement really marks the emergence of the World Wide Web on a global scale.

A powerful graphical web browser, called Mosaic, was developed in late 1993 and made available to the general public so that they could begin to use this new service. With the appearance of Mosaic, the World Wide Web began to take off. It was a network application that offered users exactly what they needed most—easy access to massive amounts of helpful information whenever they wanted it. Other browsers soon appeared in the marketplace, including Netscape Navigator (1994), Microsoft Internet Explorer (1995), Apple Safari (2003), Mozilla Firefox (2004), Google Chrome (2008), and Microsoft Edge (2015).

In late 1995, the NSF conducted a study of the different types of traffic on the Internet as a percentage of all information sent. At that time, the World Wide Web represented 23.9% of the total volume of Internet traffic, even though it had been in existence for only four years!

Since that time, the web has continued to grow exponentially, containing roughly 1.2 billion active websites by 2017. It is by far the fastest growing component of the Internet. (Although today only about 38% of all web traffic originates from living human beings! The other 62% of traffic comes from *bots*, software applications designed to carry out automated tasks such as indexing webpages.) The web's colorful graphics and simple point-and-click method of accessing information has made it the most important method of delivering the capabilities of networking to everyone—from toddlers to senior citizens and kindergarten students to PhDs. For many people, the web *is* the Internet.

Net Neutrality

Imagine you are building a new dream home and have connected it to your city's public water system. Having made this connection you turn on the tap only to get an agonizingly slow drip, while your next door neighbor has a powerful flow from every outlet. What could possibly cause such a disparity in service?

What if you learned that your neighbor had paid a bit more each month to get better water service, even though it could negatively impact the amount of water available to others? You would be furious because the water company is a *public* utility that is supposed to provide equal levels of service to all customers.

That is exactly the argument raging right now with regard to the Internet. The term net neutrality means that a public information network such as an Internet service provider (ISP) should treat all users, all platforms, and all content equally—essentially it should be operated like the water, electric, and gas companies, as publicly regulated utilities. The proponents of this concept argue that if net neutrality were the law of the land, all users would be able to exchange information freely and openly without worrying about regulations, restrictions, and controls imposed on them by a third party such as their ISP. However, opponents of net neutrality say that providing a tiered level of Internet service is no different than creating high-speed lanes on a public roadway where people pay tolls to avoid heavy traffic and get to their destination more quickly. Essentially opponents of net neutrality want to create a "fast lane" on the Internet to provide top-level service for their best customers.

The Federal Communications Commission (FCC) held numerous hearings on the advantages and disadvantages of net neutrality and whether or not to permit paid prioritization of communication services. In April 2017 the Chairman of the FCC put forward a proposal to terminate all federal regulations regarding net neutrality that had been in place since 2014. This plan created a good deal of disagreement and unhappiness, and only time will tell what will eventually happen.

7.7 Conclusion

Computer networking has changed enormously in the 50 years that it has been around. From a specialized communication system devoted to academic research, it has blossomed into a worldwide information system. What was once the esoteric domain of a few thousand scientists is now used by billions of people, the vast majority of whom have no formal training in computer science. From providing access to technical databases and research journals, it has become a way for the average citizen to shop, chat, stay informed, and be entertained. There is every reason to believe that the Internet will continue to grow and evolve as much in the coming years as it has in the past.

The most pressing issue facing the Internet today is not better technology or new killer apps. Those issues have been and will continue to be addressed and solved. The biggest concern today is how the growth and direction of networking will be managed and controlled. In its early days, the Internet was run by a core group of specialists without a financial stake in its future, and its management was relatively simple. Now that it is a global phenomenon that affects billions of people and generates hundreds of billions of dollars in revenue, the Internet is being pulled and tugged by many new constituencies and stakeholders, such as corporations, politicians, lawyers, advertisers, government agencies, and manufacturers. The important question now is who will speak for the Internet in the future and who will help shape its destiny. As the designers of the Internet warned at the end of their paper (see footnote 4 on page 382) on the history of networking:

> *If the Internet stumbles, it will not be because we lack for technology, vision, or motivation. It will be because we cannot set a direction and march collectively into the future.*

EXERCISES

1. Show how a modem would encode the 5-bit binary sequence 11001 onto an analog carrier by

    a. Modifying its amplitude (the height of the carrier wave)

    b. Modifying its frequency (the number of waves per second)

2. A modem can also modify the *phase* of a carrier wave to encode binary data. Find out what the phase of a signal is and determine how it can be modified so that it can encode the same 5-bit signal 11001 used in Exercise 1.

3. Explain why noise and interference have a more serious impact on an analog transmission line (like a telephone link) than on a digital transmission line.

4. Determine the total time it takes to transmit an uncompressed grayscale image (with 8 bits/pixel)

from a screen with a resolution of 1,280 × 840 pixels using each of the following media:

  a. A 56 Kbps modem

  b. A 1.5 Mbps DSL line

  c. A 100 Mbps Ethernet link

5. Assume that we need to transmit a 1,440 × 900 uncompressed color image (using 16 bits per pixel) over a computer network in less than 0.01 second. What is the minimal necessary line speed to meet this goal?

6. a. Assume there are one million books in your campus library. Approximate (to the nearest order of magnitude) how many bytes of data there are if all these books were stored online and accessible across a computer network.

  b. How long does it take to transfer the entire collection of books if the data rate of the transmission medium is 10 Mbps, the speed of the original Ethernet? How long does it take if we have a line with a speed of 1 Gbps? (This value represents the time needed to download your entire campus library.)

7. Why is an address field needed in the Ethernet LAN protocol? Can you think of a useful situation in which you might want either to omit the address field entirely or to use some "special" address value in the address field?

8. After reviewing the description of the Ethernet protocol in Section 7.3.2, how do you think this protocol behaves in a very heavily loaded network—that is, a network environment where there are lots of nodes attempting to send messages? Explain what behavior you expect to see and why.

9. The Ethernet is a distributed LAN protocol, which means that there is no centralized control node and that the failure of a single node can never bring down the entire network. However, can you think of any advantage to the creation of a centralized LAN in which one node is in charge of the entire network and makes all decisions about who can send a message and who must wait? Explain.

10. Agree or disagree with the following assertion and state why:

    In an Ethernet network, even though there are collisions, every message is guaranteed to be delivered in some maximum amount of time T.

11. a. Assume there is a wide area network with N nodes, where $N \geq 2$. What is the *smallest* number of point-to-point communication links such that every node in the network is able to talk to every other node? (*Note:* A network in which some nodes are unable to exchange messages with other nodes because there is no path between them is called *disconnected.*)

  b. If you are worried about having a disconnected network, what type of interconnection structure should you use when configuring your network?

12. In Exercise 11, you determined the minimum number of links needed to ensure that every one of the N nodes in a network can communicate with every other node. However, most networks have far more than this minimum. What are the advantages of having these "extra" links in the network?

13. What happens to the store-and-forward protocol of Figure 7.9 if a packet M is repeatedly sent from node A to node B but never correctly arrives at B? (Perhaps the link from A to B is broken.) What modifications can we make to this protocol to handle this situation?

14. The ARQ algorithm described in Section 7.3.2 is quite inefficient because the sending node must stop sending until it receives an explicit ACK from the receiving node. Can you design a modification to the ARQ protocol that makes it more efficient by not requiring the sender to stop and wait each time it sends a message? Describe your revised protocol in detail.

15. How could we broadcast a message using an ARQ algorithm? That is, how do we send the same message to 100 different nodes on a WAN?

16. Given the following diagram, where the numbers represent the time delays across a link:

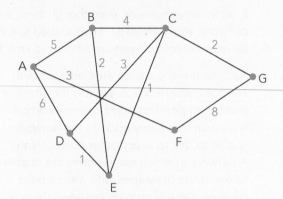

a. How many simple paths (those that do not repeat a node) are there from node A to G?

b. What is the *shortest path* from node A to node G? What is the overall delay?

c. If node E fails, does that change the shortest path? If so, what is the new shortest path?

17. Here is a simple heuristic (approximation algorithm) for routing a message from node A to node B in a reasonable amount of time. The algorithm assumes that every node in the network has at least two outgoing links.

Assume A has n outgoing links, $n \geq 2$, with delays to the nodes on the other end of a_1, $a_2, \ldots, a_n$. Select the link with the shortest delay and send the message on that line. If the message arrives at node B, you are done. Otherwise, repeat this process until the message does arrive at its intended destination, but do *not* send the message directly back to the node from where it just came. That is, if the message was sent from A to C, then C should not return the message to A. In this case, choose the second-lowest delay value for the outgoing line.

Will this heuristic always deliver the message from node A to node B? If not, explain why.

18. What are some of the specific responsibilities performed by the device called a gateway (diagrammed in Figure 7.26) that is placed between two different types of networks to allow them to communicate?

19. In Section 7.3.4, we said that the Transport layer turns the inherently unreliable Network layer into an error-free delivery service. However, the Network layer uses the services of the Data Link layer, which is guaranteed to correctly deliver messages on a point-to-point link. For example, assume we have the following four-node network:

If the Network layer is sending a message from A to D via B, it can be sure that a message sent by the Data Link layer from A to B will always correctly get to B, and a message sent from B to D will always correctly get to D. How then is it possible for the Network layer to be unable to correctly deliver a message from A to D?

20. What are the advantages of breaking up a single logical message into a number of fixed-sized packets and then sending each one of those packets independently through the network?

21. Look at the home page of the Internet Society (*www.internetsociety.org*) and read about one of the designers of the original ARPANET— Larry Roberts, Leonard Kleinrock, Vinton Cerf, Robert Kahn, John Postel, or others. Learn about the early days of networking and the contributions that these individuals made to the ultimate development of the Internet. The home page of the Internet Society has links to many other places that provide a wealth of fascinating information about networks in general and the Internet and the web in particular.

22. Purchasing services from a cloud provider has many advantages, as was discussed in Section 7.5. However, the cloud can also create problems with regard to your business or research environment. For each of the following areas, discuss problems that could occur when you purchase cloud services to handle your company's data storage backup.

a. Internet outages

b. Data security

c. Data inflexibility

d. Customer support

CHALLENGE WORK

The TCP/IP protocols are the heart and soul of the Internet, and they describe the fundamental rules that govern all communications in the network. Read more about the TCP/IP protocols and write a report describing their basic characteristics and giving a simple overview of the way that they work.

One of the best places to go for this information is a set of documents called RFCs (Request for Comments). These are a series of documents produced by the Internet Engineering Task Force (IETF) that describe virtually all aspects of the Internet's behavior, including its protocols. Some RFCs contain enormously detailed technical specifications of the workings of the Internet, while others are more informational or tutorial (even humorous) in nature. A good place to start is RFC 1180, "A TCP/IP Tutorial." A complete set of all the Internet RFCs is located at *www.faqs.org/rfcs*, and it can be searched using the searchable database located at that website.

Information Security

AFTER STUDYING THIS CHAPTER, YOU WILL BE ABLE TO:

- Explain the difference between authentication and authorization
- Explain the use of a hash function to encrypt passwords on a computer system
- Describe cyber-attacks including viruses, worms, Trojan horses, DoS attacks, and phishing, and explain how they differ from each other
- Describe ways to increase the security of information on your computer and online
- Encrypt and decrypt messages using simple Caesar ciphers and matrix-based block ciphers
- Describe the overall process used by symmetric encryption algorithms such as DES
- Describe the overall process used by RSA public-key encryption
- Explain why web transmission protocols such as SSL and TLS use multiple forms of encryption to secure data transfer over the web
- Explain the importance of computer security for networked embedded systems

8.1 Introduction

Information security means protecting data from those who do not have permission to access it. Information security could cover information locked in your filing cabinet, stuffed somewhere in your purse or wallet, or lying around on your desk. But today it usually means electronic information, such as data stored on your computer's hard disk, in the cloud, on your flash drive, or on your smartphone, or data transmitted across wired or wireless network connections.

In the early days of computing, large mainframe computers were considered showpieces and displayed prominently in a company for everyone to see. When management realized the folly of this situation, the mainframes were moved to secure rooms, frequently on secure floors or even in separate buildings. Only authorized persons had access. Now that there is a machine on virtually every desktop, a laptop or tablet in many briefcases, and a cell phone in every pocket, that kind of physical security is impossible to attain, but you can

take some obvious precautionary steps: Don't leave your laptop or tablet lying around; lock or secure your workstation when you leave the room; don't share your password with anyone; and don't lose your cell phone!

However, the danger of someone swiping your laptop or smartphone pales in comparison with the security risks created by the Internet and the web. As our virtual environment expands, we celebrate the ability to reach out from our desktop, laptop, or handheld device to the rest of the world, receiving information, entertainment, and communications from thousands of sources. But we may be less aware of the potential for thousands of sources around the world to reach into our machines and our lives to do us harm or steal our information.

Security can be breached at many different points in the "virtual machine" we have presented in the last few chapters. Flaws in systems programs can be exploited, operating system protections can be circumvented, and computer networks (wired or wireless) present all kinds of opportunities for viewing, manipulating, or destroying data. Consequences can range from simple annoyance to serious identity theft to major economic losses or threats to national security. Because there are so many ways in which security can be compromised, and the consequences can be so serious, information security has become an extremely important topic in computer science research and practice.

8.2 Threats and Defenses

You no doubt are aware of the possible threats to the security of your personal property, such as your car or the contents of your home or apartment. That's why you probably have auto and home or renter's insurance. Aside from fire, flood, or other accidents, someone can steal your property, causing financial harm and emotional distress. Your best defenses against this kind of theft are to employ locks and possibly an alarm system. The alarm system only comes into play in an active manner when security has already been breached, but the mere fact that a property has an alarm system can be a deterrent to break-ins. Although it's true that an experienced thief can quickly pick a lock, it's certainly easier to break into an unlocked house. Be it thieves or computer hackers, criminals tend to attack the most vulnerable and poorly guarded sites.

This section discusses the threat of individual computers being accessed by the wrong people and the threats to which a computer is exposed through network connections; in addition, it describes various defenses against these threats.

8.2.1 Authentication and Authorization

The first line of defense against the illicit use of, or threats to, computer resources and sensitive information is a strong authentication and authorization process.

Authentication. You want to start up your computer, access your online bank account, or pay a bill online. What's the first thing you must do in all these cases? Generally, it is to log on to your machine or to the appropriate webpage by giving your user ID and password. The authentication process to log on to your computer is managed by your machine's operating system, as you learned in Chapter 6. On the webpage, it is managed by the operating system and perhaps special security software of the web server computer. Authentication is the process of verifying that you really are the person who has the right to access a particular device, whether it is your local machine or the remote server. The operating system maintains a file of user IDs and corresponding passwords. When a user attempts to log on to the machine, the operating system reads the user ID and checks that the password matches the password for that user in the password file. Hackers breaking into a computer system look for a file of user IDs and passwords as the "Open, Sesame" for all locked doors.

If the user ID/password list were in the form of a simple two-column list like this:

```
Tijara      popsicle
Murphy      badboy2
Jaylynn     mom
   ...
```

then the entire system would be compromised if this password file were stolen or copied. To prevent this, the operating system encrypts the passwords—converts them into a representation that cannot be understood without the appropriate decryption algorithm. The encryption process that is used is called a hash function; this form of encryption is easy to apply but hard to undo. The hash function takes the password the user originally chooses,

The Metamorphosis of Hacking

The earliest use of the word *hack* appeared in English around 1200 and meant "to cut roughly, cut with chopping blows," and the term *hacker* meant "one who hacks." At MIT in 1955, the term was used at a meeting of the Tech Model Railroad Club to request that "anyone working or hacking on the electrical system turn the power off to avoid fuse blowing." From there the term *hacker* evolved to mean a "computer nerd" who seemed to know all the incomprehensible details about how computers worked and could fix anything that might go wrong. Over time, however, this term took on a much more negative connotation. Today, a **hacker** is a person who knows how to (and does) gain unauthorized access to a computer with malicious intent. Hacking is illegal and punishable under the law by fines or imprisonment, but as computers become ever more important in our society, hacking has become rampant.

Hacking is no longer the province solely of individuals. Just as there are organized auto theft rings that operate on a national or even international scale, there are organized hacking groups. Computer hacking on a large scale costs governments and businesses billions of dollars per year in terms of lost business, stolen information, and, more intangibly, loss of trust. Computer attacks from one country on the computing resources of another country with intent to damage or destroy computer systems or steal sensitive information are no longer mere "hacking" but cross over into the realm of **cyberwarfare**–politically motivated information theft or hardware damage for the purpose of sabotage, espionage, or even influence in democratic elections.

chops it up, and stirs it around according to a given formula. As a very simple example, suppose the hash function process is the following:

1. Take each letter in the password and replace it with a number representing its place in the alphabet (a → 1, b → 2, etc.). Leave each digit in the password alone. For example, Murphy's password, "badboy2", would become

   2 1 4 2 15 25 2

2. Add up these digits to get a single integer. In this example,

   2 + 1 + 4 + 2 + 15 + 25 + 2 = 51

3. Divide the integer from Step 2 by 7 and determine the remainder. In this example, dividing 51 by 7 gives a remainder of 2 (51 equals 7 × 7 with 2 left over).

4. Add 1 to the remainder from Step 3, then multiply this value by 9. In this example, the result equals (2 + 1) × 9 = 27.

5. Reverse the digits in the integer from Step 4 and then replace each digit with the corresponding letter of the alphabet. The result for this example is 72, which becomes gb.

The encrypted password file would contain an entry of

Murphy   gb

and the original password "badboy2" has been discarded.

Now when Tom Murphy attempts to log on, he enters "Murphy" as his user ID and types in his password "badboy2". The operating system applies this exact same hash function to the password just entered and compares the encrypted result to the encrypted value "gb" stored in the password file for that user ID. If there is a match, Tom is recognized as an authorized user and allowed access to the computer. If the results do not match, access is denied.

You may have had the experience of forgetting your password to an online account at, let's say, Ninth Street Bank, and asked for help. The people in charge of Ninth Street Bank's web server will email you a temporary password that will allow you to log on and then require you to reset your password to something you choose (which will change your entry in the password file). You might find this annoying and wonder why they didn't just send you your original password. As we've just seen, the system at Ninth Street Bank doesn't actually know your original password, only its encrypted form and—as we are about to see—this isn't enough information to regenerate the original password.

The benefit of encryption is that, with a well-designed hashing function, possession of the encrypted password file does not make it possible to recover a user's original password (e.g., "badboy2") from the encrypted password ("gb"). This is true even if the details of the mathematical operations performed by the hashing function are known, as they often are for a particular operating system. In our simple hash function, you could reverse Steps 5 and 4, but not Step 3. For example, the following seven-character alphabetic string:

chjbup5

also hashes to the two-character string "gb", so clearly the process is not reversible, and the thief cannot determine whether the original password is "badboy2", "chjbup5", or any one of the hundreds or thousands of words that also produce the value *gb*.

But this appears to raise another problem. What if Fred and Alice each have different passwords that hash to the same encrypted value or they coincidentally chose the same original password? In general, this is not a problem—both Fred and Alice can log on to their own personal accounts using their respective passwords. But if Fred stole the password file and saw that his password and Alice's password hashed to the same value, he would have a better than random chance of guessing Alice's password; he would certainly try his own password with Alice's user ID, and he would be successful if indeed the passwords were the same.

To solve this problem, some operating systems keep a third entry for each user in the password file, namely, the exact time at which the user created the password. This *timestamp* gets appended to the original password, and the result is then run through the encryption algorithm and stored as the encrypted password in the password file. That way, two identical passwords do not hash to the same value because the probability that they were created at the exact same instant in time is infinitesimally small. This also solves the problem of two nonidentical passwords that otherwise would hash to the same value. When someone attempting to log on gives his or her password, the operating system consults the password file, appends the timestamp for that user ID to the password just entered, encrypts the result, and compares it with the encrypted password entry for that user ID in the password file.

Even with all of these safeguards in place, there are still ways in which the operating system's authentication process is vulnerable to hacking. Consider Ravi, who has not stolen the password file but nevertheless knows Alice's user ID and wants to hack into Alice's account. Because Ravi knows Alice personally, he might try to guess her password. He might try her nickname, the name of her pet poodle, or the title of her favorite band. Of course, he could also try "alice", "123456", or—a perennial favorite—"password". Many systems set "password" as the default value, and if Alice hasn't changed (or been required to change) her password, this will get Ravi into Alice's account. Failing at these attempts, Ravi might use a brute force attack by trying all possible passwords. Suppose there are n possible characters that can be used in a password (at least uppercase and lowercase letters and the 10 digits are possibilities). To try all possible passwords of length k or less would require

$$n^1 + n^2 + \ldots + n^k = \frac{n(n^k - 1)}{n - 1}$$

attempts. On the average, Ravi might be successful after about

$$(n^1 + n^2 + \ldots + n^k) / 2$$

attempts, but this will be very time consuming (see Exercise 5 at the end of this chapter). In addition, most systems have a lockout after some number of failed tries, which would foil this brute force approach.

For someone who has stolen the password file, a better way to find a password is by using password-cracking software. For a given user ID (which our villain knows because the user ID is not encoded), password-cracking software first tries all words in its built-in dictionary, encrypting each with the well-known hash function and comparing the result with the password file. Such software is amazingly fast and can try millions of potential passwords per second. If this fails, it then goes on to more sophisticated techniques such as word list substitutions for common phrases. With knowledge of the hash algorithm, the software might use a *rainbow table*, a precomputed list of passwords and their hash values, so checking for a particular hash value just requires a search of the hash values in the table. A brute force attack is only used as a last resort.

Surprisingly, the easiest way to obtain someone's password is not to steal the password file (hard to do) or to guess that person's password (time consuming), but to use social engineering. Social engineering is the process of using people to get the information you want. If Ravi wants Alice's password, he might just ask her! In a business setting, he might get a chance to snoop around her office and find the yellow sticky note containing her password attached to her monitor or stuck beneath her keyboard. He might violate "password etiquette" and watch over her shoulder while she logs on. (This *shoulder surfing* method is often used to steal PIN numbers at ATM machines.) Or he could try an indirect approach; he could call Alice's (gullible) assistant and, posing as an IT technician, explain that Alice has called the IT service group about some computer problems she is experiencing and that to fix them, he needs Alice's password. Most companies try to educate their employees about the dangers of social engineering.

Your best defense against someone guessing your password is to be smart about how you choose and use your password. Most website operating systems impose rules about legal passwords (must be at least some minimum length, must include at least one digit and one special character, and so forth). Also, the user may be required to create a new password every so often. Managing passwords might be a bit of a hassle, but security measures are always a balancing act between user convenience and user protection. Consider using a password manager (password vault), a central site that securely stores all your passwords in encrypted form, leaving only the one vault password for you to remember.

User IDs and passwords are the most common authentication mechanism, but other security measures can be used in addition. Many systems ask you to preselect answers to a list of *security questions* about personal information that you will know but others might not (the first name of your maternal grandmother, the city in which you went to high school, etc.). Then after you present your user ID and password, you must respond with the correct answer to one of these questions. Some laptops, tablets, and smartphones now use *biometric information*, for example, fingerprint scans or facial recognition. Some company networks use a dual authentication scheme that works as follows: The legitimate user enters his or her user ID and password. Each user has a small device (or perhaps a smartphone app) that then generates a random sequence of digits, which is good only for a few seconds, that the user must enter. Some websites present the user with an image of text written with distorted letters and the user then has to type the correct text into a textbox on the webpage. Such distorted letters are recognizable by humans but not by computers, so the idea here is to determine that the user is indeed human and thus prevent a machine from voting

Practice Problems

1. Using the hash function described in this section, verify that the password "chjbup5" also hashes to "gb".

2. Assume Judy uses the password "judy" for her account (in violation of the guidelines in the Special Interest Box, "Password Pointers"). Using the simple hashing function presented in this section, to what value does her password hash?

3. If someone were to attempt to log on to Judy's account (from Practice Problem 2) using the password "mike", would he or she be granted access? Explain why or why not.

4. A hacker believes he has obtained a copy of the password file for a system that uses the hash function described in this section. One of the encrypted password entries is "mt". What can the hacker conclude about this file?

in a survey or filling out a form. A more elaborate version of visual recognition presents the user with a series of images and instructions such as "click on the images that show mountains."

Authorization. The intent of authentication is to allow the operating system to determine that you are the person you say you are. Once you are authenticated, there might still be operations that you are not permitted to carry out. Authorization governs what an authenticated user is allowed to do. Enforcing authorization rules is also one of the jobs of the operating system, as discussed in Chapter 6. On your own machine, you may have administrative privileges and be able to see everything on the machine. However, on your banking website, you can only see your own account information, and you are not allowed to change your balance or your interest rate.

The operating system maintains access control lists (also called permissions) that specify exactly what a user is allowed to do with each data file. Depending on who the users are, they have various levels of privilege, such as the following:

- Read access (can read a particular file)

- Write access (can modify a particular file)

- Execute access (can run a particular program file)

- Delete access (can delete a particular file)

A careful operating system will check every access every time by every user.

8.2.2 Threats from the Network

Once your handheld device, personal computer, business computer, or web server is connected to the Internet, there are many more possibilities for harm. Attacks can come from anonymous sources anywhere in the world via intermediate nodes that maintain varying levels of security. Recall from Chapter 7 that to send data across a network from the source at point A to the destination at point E, the packet may have to go through intermediate nodes B, C, and D. Also, if you remember that the Internet is not governed by one entity or one set of security guidelines, then it becomes rather clear what a difficult task maintaining "Internet security" can be.

Most of these security threats come in the form of malware (malicious software) that can attack an individual computer. The most common attacks to individual computers are by viruses, worms, Trojan horses, and denial of service.

Virus. A virus is a computer program that, like a biological virus, infects a host computer and then spreads. It embeds itself within another program or file. When that program or file is activated, the virus copies itself and attacks other files on the system. The results may be as simple as taunting pop-up messages, but could also include erratic behavior or drastic slowdown of the computer, corrupted or deleted files, loss of data, or system crashes. The virus is spread from one machine to another by passing on the infected file, perhaps on a flash drive. By far the most common mechanism for spreading a virus, however, is through email attachments. An infected file is attached to an email message and sent out to 100 people, for example. Anyone who downloads and opens the attachment causes the virus to replicate the infected file and perhaps send it out as an email attachment to the first 100 people in that person's personal address book. In this way, a virus can potentially spread like wildfire across the Internet.

Worm. A worm is very similar to a virus, but it can send copies of itself to other nodes on a computer network without having to be carried by an infected host file. It is a self-replicating piece of software that can travel from node to node without any human intervention. In its most benign form, a worm can clog the Internet so that legitimate traffic is slowed or shut out completely. In addition, the worm might also subvert the host systems it passes through so that, at a later time, those systems can be controlled by the worm's author and used to send spam (junk email), deface webpages, or perform other mischief.

Trojan Horse. A Trojan horse (in the software world, as opposed to Greek mythology) is a computer program that does some legitimate computational task but also, unbeknownst to the user, contains code to perform the same kinds of malicious attacks as viruses and worms—corrupt or delete files, slow down the computer, and the like. It might also upload or download files, capture the user's address book to send out spam, hide a keystroke logger that captures the user's passwords and credit card numbers (and sends them to someone else), or even put the computer under someone else's remote control at some point in the future. A computer can become infected by a Trojan horse when the user downloads infected software. In fact, even visiting an infected website can, behind the scenes, download a Trojan horse (an attack called a drive-by exploit or drive-by download).

Denial of Service. A denial-of-service (DoS) attack is typically directed at a business or government website. The attack automatically directs browsers, usually on many machines, to a single web address at roughly the same time. The result causes so much network traffic to the targeted site that it is effectively shut down to legitimate users. Although such an attack is seldom directed toward an individual's computer, the resulting effect can still

Beware the Trojan Horse

Tiny Banker Trojan (also known as Tinba, short for Tiny Banker) is a relatively new example of Trojan horse malware that first appeared in 2012. As the name suggests, it targets online banking customers, both individuals and businesses. It is not the first such Trojan horse, but one of its most distinguishing features is that the Tinba package is indeed tiny in size, only 20 kilobytes, much smaller—and therefore harder to detect—than previous packages, some of which ran to as large as 20 megabytes, 1000 times larger. Tinba is downloaded when a user visits an infected website.

Once on the user's machine, Tinba can capture keystrokes for login data. More than that, it reads the network traffic to determine if the user is in the process of logging on to an online bank account. If so, it captures information from the bank website such as the bank title and logo, then pops up a window (supposedly from the bank) that asks the unwary user to confirm account information, such as account number, security codes, even credit card information, which it then sends off to one of its four controlling computers. If that domain is down, it switches to one of the remaining three, meaning that it has three backups for receiving the captured data. (Never reply to such a popup window; your bank will never reach out to you in this manner. Close the window and immediately run your antivirus software to scan your machine.) Finally, Tinba turns the user machine into part of a *botnet* (see page 405 for a definition of this term).

In 2014, the source code for Tinba was published, and since then more sophisticated capabilities and protections have been added to Tinba and its variants. These include measures designed to avoid detection by antivirus software, such as increased encryption and the ability to update itself and its controlling servers. Tinba has "represented" major banking sites in the United States and around the world.

Your Money or Your Files

We mentioned earlier that cyberspace hacking is now frequently carried out by organized criminal groups, often operating on an international scale. And some of the schemes perpetrated, such as *ransomware*, are downright amazing.

Ransomware invades the user's computer, often by means of an infected email attachment. It then encrypts files on that computer, usually with a strong enough encryption algorithm that only the author of the malware software, who holds the decryption key, can unlock the files. The user is then presented with a "ransom note" demanding payment in order to release the files. Next, a screen appears with detailed instructions on how to pay the ransom and the timeframe within which it must be paid. Of course, even if the user decides to pay the ransom, the attacker might not release the files. Alternatively, the user might be warned that without payment, the files (which have by then also been sent to the server of the perpetrator) may be posted online and publicly released. The only credible defense against ransomware is a good, up-to-date backup system.

Ransomware has been aimed at individuals, corporations, federal agencies, and especially hospitals and other medical centers. Medical centers are particularly targeted because the threat to destroy or make public patient medical data often induces a prompt payment of the ransom. On May 12 2017, more than 75,000 ransomware attacks were carried out in more than 99 countries. In the U.K., many hospitals that are part of the National Health Service were attacked, forcing ambulances to go to alternate sites. Ransomware attacks grew from 4 million in 2015 to 638 million in 2016.[1] The typical "going rate" per infected computer is a few hundred dollars, often to be paid via *bitcoin* (we'll talk more about bitcoin in Chapter 14.) Nonetheless, some experts estimate that the annual profit in the ransomware business exceeds $500 million, and will soon reach $1 trillion per year. Some major corporations are purchasing bitcoin in order to be able to provide a rapid response to a possible ransomware attack.

In 2016, a new ransomware package named Locky made its appearance in a major way. On the first day it appeared, millions of emails were sent out with attachments carrying the Locky malware. By the following month, more than 50,000 infections had been detected. In addition to its aggressive spam campaign, Locky has several features that make it particularly dangerous:

- The spam email is often configured to appear as if it comes from an address on the user's network.

- As it busily works to encrypt data files, it postpones encrypting those most recently used so as to delay detection and allow the encryption process to be completed.

- Locky uses two of the most sophisticated encryption algorithms, RSA and AES, discussed later in this chapter.

[1]https://thejournal.com/articles/2017/02/07/report-number-of-ransomware-attacks-grew-nearly-17-times-larger-in-2016.aspx

inconvenience individual users of the targeted website. (Spam can accomplish a similar, but less targeted effect, by flooding the Internet with junk email messages that consume available bandwidth and clog mail servers.) If many machines are perpetrating this mischief, it's called a *distributed denial-of-service attack*, or *DDoS*. A DDoS may use thousands of machines, enabling much heavier attack traffic and at the same time making it harder to track down and disable all of the attacking machines. Many times, these machines are personal computers that were infected at some point by a Trojan horse. Then at a later time, the Trojan horse is activated in all these machines, putting them under the command of a single controller. This collection of machines is sometimes called a zombie army or botnet (short for "ro*bot net*work" because the machines act like robots under someone else's control).

Recently, however, DDoS attacks have relied less on massive botnets and instead have used a more sophisticated technique known as a reflection and amplification attack. This type of attack relies on integral features of the Internet, such as the Domain Name System (DNS; see Chapter 7). Queries to DNS servers are short, but these servers respond by sending much larger amounts of data back to the source of the query. The attacking computers alter the source address of the query so that it appears that the source is the DNS server itself. This results in the server receiving a torrent of information back from itself, amplifying the effect of the attacker machines by a factor of as much as 300 times the bandwidth (transmission rate) of the original query.

Phishing. Phishing is not a direct attack on a computer. Instead, phishing is a practice used to illegally obtain sensitive information such as credit card numbers, account numbers, and passwords. An email is sent claiming to be from a legitimate organization such as a bank, credit card company, online retailer, government agency, or social media site asking the recipient to click a link to update or verify his or her account information. Often the message contains a warning that your account will be suspended or canceled if you fail to provide this information (although this personal information is already on file with the legitimate organization if indeed you do have an account there). The link takes the unwary user to a fake website that appears to be legitimate and captures the information the user enters. Despite the fact that no legitimate bank or other financial organization ever operates this way, many people fall for this scheme and become victims of identity theft.

If you receive such a message, never follow the link or reply to the message; instead, delete the message immediately. If you want to check an account's status, open a separate browser window and access your account information as you normally would. Check that the web address area displays https:// and shows an icon of a green locked padlock, which indicates that the information will be securely transmitted, and that the site being visited is the one you intended to visit rather than a counterfeit site. If you click on the green locked padlock, you can probably see more information about the source/ownership of the webpage you are viewing and the security of the network connection.

The term *phishing* came about because perpetrators cast out bait, in the form of phony email messages, to a large number of potential victims in

Defense against the Dark Arts

You may feel at this point that you should just unplug your computer from the Internet or disable your wireless capability. The good news is that by following a few simple guidelines you can protect yourself against almost all the attacks discussed so far.

- Be sure your computer has up-to-date **antivirus software** from a reputable company. Such software can detect worms, viruses, and Trojan horses by the distinctive "signatures" those programs carry. It cleans your machine of infected files.

- Be sure your computer has up-to-date **firewall software** from a reputable company. Firewall software guards the access points to your computer, blocking communications to or from sites you don't permit and preventing certain operations from being initiated across the Internet.

- Be sure your computer has up-to-date **antispyware** from a reputable company. Antispyware routinely scans your computer for any "spyware" programs that may have infected your machine—programs that capture information on what websites you have visited and what passwords and credit card numbers you have used.

- Set your browser to use a pop-up blocker. A *pop-up* is a small window that "pops up" on the webpage your browser is currently displaying. Most pop-ups are simply annoying advertising, but some contain links, perhaps disguised as "Close" buttons, that download a virus to your machine.

- Always install the latest **security patches** or updates to your operating system; better yet, set your machine to install automatic updates.

- Don't send personal or financial information in response to any email ("My wealthy Nigerian uncle left me a fortune that I am willing to share with you but I need your account number . . . ").

the hope that one or two will "bite" and fall for this scam. If the emails are targeted toward specific individuals or groups (*spear phishing*), the email content is "personalized" and the chances of success are higher. The cost to mount a phishing attack is minimal, so even a tiny number of "bites" brings a profit. The average phishing site is left online for less than three days, making it difficult to catch those responsible.

Practice Problem

Do some research on the Morris worm, the first major computer worm. Who wrote it, when was it released, how did it spread, how much damage was it estimated to have caused (in dollar amounts), and what happened to the originator of the worm?

The Anti-Phishing Working Group (APWG) is an industry and law enforcement association focusing on helping eliminate identity theft resulting from phishing (*www.antiphishing.org*). It provides discussion forums, maintains statistics, and tests promising technology solutions. According to APWG statistics, 1,220,523 phishing attacks occurred in 2016, representing a 65% increase over 2015.

8.2.3 White Hats vs. Black Hats

"White hats" are the security experts who try to keep us safe in cyberspace. "Black hats" are the bad guys (or gals!) who try to ferret out computer system weaknesses for financial gain, control, or outright destruction. These two groups are locked in constant battle. As we as a society grow more and more dependent on online services, the opportunities for reward increase, and therefore so do the number of attempts to breach system defenses. The technology of attacks (and defenses) changes rapidly and keeps gaining in sophistication. The defenders have the harder job; as is often pointed out with respect to security (or warfare in general), the attacker needs to find only one weakness, but the defender must defend all possible points of entry.

8.3 Encryption

Much of the focus of information security is to devise defenses so that the "bad guys" can't steal our information. If, despite all these precautions, personal files on a computer or sensitive data packets on a network are illegally accessed and fall into the wrong hands, we can still protect their contents through the process of encryption. Essentially, the purpose of encryption is to make information meaningless even if someone does manage to steal it. We've already discussed encryption of the password file by the operating system as a security measure, in case the password file is stolen. In this section, we discuss various other encryption mechanisms, which apply to both stored and transmitted data.

You've Been Hacked

According to a report from a business advisory firm,[2] an estimated 15.4 million Americans were victims of identity theft in 2016, about 1 in every 16 adults. Identity theft occurs when personal information (name, address, telephone number, birth date, password, email address, credit and debit card numbers and expiration dates, and so forth) is stolen and used to commit fraud. Most of this stolen information was obtained not from computers owned by individual victims, but from corporate or government servers or point-of-sale computers. Here are some examples from 2016.

Who	When	What
U.S. Department of Justice	February 2016	Personal data on 10,000 Department of Homeland Security employees and 20,000 FBI employees
Omni Hotels and Resorts	January–June 2016	50,000 customers' credit and debit card data
Verizon Enterprise Solutions	March 2016	1,500,000 customers' contact information
Equifax W-2 Express	May 2016	431,000 Kroger employees' Social Security numbers and birth dates
Los Angeles County	May 2016	Personal data on 756,000 who had contact with branches of Los Angeles county government (through Auditor, Child Support Services, Mental Health, Probation, and many others)
Eddie Bauer	August 2016	Over 2 million customers' credit and debit card data
Michigan State University	November 2016	400,000 names, Social Security numbers, and MSU identification numbers of some current and former students and employees

In addition to potential financial or legal consequences, these organizations and others that have been similarly attacked have lost some level of trust from their customers, whether or not those customers ultimately suffered personal identity theft as a result. Trust is hard to regain, so this in turn represents a difficult-to-quantify but nonetheless real financial loss. Although institutions are generally loath to admit they have been hacked, they will suffer even greater backlash if they fail to promptly notify individuals that their personal information, account information, or credit card data may have been stolen.

---

[2]https://www.usatoday.com/story/money/personalfinance/2017/02/06/identity-theft-hit-all-time-high-2016/97398548/

8.3.1 Encryption Overview

Cryptography is the science of "secret writing." A message (*plaintext*) is encoded (encrypted) before it is sent, for the purpose of keeping its content secret if it is intercepted by the wrong parties. The encrypted message is called *ciphertext*. The ciphertext is decoded (decrypted) back to plaintext when it is received, in order to retrieve the original information. More formally, encryption is the process of using an algorithm to convert information into a representation that cannot be understood or utilized by anyone without the appropriate decryption algorithm; decryption is the reverse of encryption, using an algorithm that converts the ciphertext back into plaintext. Encryption and decryption date back thousands of years. The most famous instances of cryptography occur in military history, beginning with Julius Caesar of the Roman Empire, who developed the Caesar cipher, discussed in the next section. In more modern times, the military importance of cryptography was illustrated by the German Enigma code cracked by the Allies during World War II.[3]

Encryption and decryption are inverse operations because decryption must "undo" the encryption and reproduce the original text. (An exception is hash function encoding, used for password encryption, which is a one-way code and does not involve decryption.) There are many encryption/decryption algorithms, and of course both the sender and the receiver must use the same system.

A symmetric encryption algorithm requires the use of a secret key known to both the sender and the receiver. The sender encrypts the plaintext using the key. The receiver, knowing the key, is easily able to reverse the process and decrypt the message. One of the difficulties with a symmetric encryption algorithm is how to securely transmit the secret key so that both the sender and the receiver know what it is; in fact, this approach seems to simply move the security problem to a slightly different level, from transmitting a message to transmitting a key.

In an asymmetric encryption algorithm, also called a public key encryption algorithm, the key for encryption and the key for decryption are quite different, although related. Person A can make an encryption key public, and anyone can encrypt a message using A's public key and send it to A. Only A has the decryption key, however, so only A can decrypt the message. This approach avoids the difficulty of secret key transmission, but it introduces a new problem: The relationship between the decryption key and the encryption key must be sufficiently complex that it is not possible to derive the decryption key from knowledge of the public encryption key.

---

[3] In May 2011, the British National Museum of Computing reconstructed one of the early British decryption machines, using circuits from old telephone exchanges. See *http://www.tnmoc.org/explore/colossus-gallery*

8.3.2 Simple Encryption Algorithms

Caesar Cipher. A Caesar cipher, also called a *shift cipher*, involves shifting each character in the message to another character some fixed distance farther along in the alphabet. Specifically, let s be some integer between 1 and 25 that represents the amount of shift. Each letter in the message is encoded as the letter that is s units farther along in the alphabet, with the last s letters of the alphabet shifted in a cycle to the first s letters. For example, if $s = 3$, then A is encoded as D, B is encoded as E, X is encoded as A, and Z is encoded as C. The integer s is the secret key. Decoding a message, given knowledge of s, simply means reversing the shift. For example, if $s = 3$, then the code word DUPB is decoded as ARMY.

The Caesar cipher is an example of a stream cipher; that is, it encodes one character at a time. This makes it easy to encode just by scanning the plaintext and doing the appropriate substitution at each character. On the other hand, there are only 25 possible keys, so a ciphertext message could easily be decoded by brute force, that is, by simply trying all possible keys.

In addition, the Caesar cipher is a *substitution cipher*, whereby a single letter of plaintext generates a single letter of ciphertext. We can replace the simple shift mechanism of the Caesar cipher with a more complex substitution mechanism, for example:

```
A    B    C    D    E ...
|    |    |    |    |
Z    A    Y    B    X ...
```

(Can you guess the substitution algorithm being used?) However, in any simple substitution cipher, the structure of the plaintext is maintained in the ciphertext—letter frequency, occurrence of double letters, frequently occurring letter combinations, and so forth. With a sufficiently long message, an experienced *cryptanalyst* (code breaker) can use these clues to recover the plaintext.

Block Cipher. In a block cipher, a group or block of plaintext letters gets encoded into a block of ciphertext, but not by substituting one character at a time for each letter. Each plaintext character in the block contributes to more than one ciphertext character, and each ciphertext character is the result of more than one plaintext letter. It is as if each plaintext character in a block gets chopped into little pieces, and these pieces are scattered among the ciphertext characters in the corresponding block. This tends to destroy the structure of the plaintext and make decryption more difficult.

As a simple example, we'll use a block size of 2 and an encoding key that is a 2×2 arrangement of numbers called a *matrix*. Here A and B

$$A = \begin{bmatrix} 1 & 2 \\ 3 & 4 \end{bmatrix} \qquad B = \begin{bmatrix} 5 & 1 \\ 2 & 1 \end{bmatrix}$$

are matrices. We can define an operation of matrix multiplication as follows. The product $A \times B$ will also be a 2×2 matrix, where the element in row i, column j of $A \times B$ is obtained by multiplying each element in row i of A by its corresponding element in column j of B and adding the results. So to obtain the element in row 1, column 1 of the result, we multiply the row 1 elements of A by the corresponding column 1 elements of B and add the results:

$$\begin{bmatrix} 1 & 2 \\ 3 & 4 \end{bmatrix} \times \begin{bmatrix} 5 & 1 \\ 2 & 1 \end{bmatrix} = \begin{bmatrix} 9 & \\ & \end{bmatrix}$$

$$1 * 5 + 2 * 2 = 5 + 4 = 9$$

To obtain the element in row 1, column 2 of the result, we multiply the row 1 elements of A by the corresponding column 2 elements of B and add the results:

$$\begin{bmatrix} 1 & 2 \\ 3 & 4 \end{bmatrix} \times \begin{bmatrix} 5 & 1 \\ 2 & 1 \end{bmatrix} = \begin{bmatrix} 9 & 3 \\ & \end{bmatrix}$$

The completed product $A \times B$ is $\begin{bmatrix} 9 & 3 \\ 23 & 7 \end{bmatrix}$.

However, for encryption purposes, we are going to modify this definition. When we add up the terms for each element, whenever we exceed 25, we will start over again, counting from 0. In this scheme, $26 \rightarrow 0$, $27 \rightarrow 1$, $28 \rightarrow 2, \ldots, 52 \rightarrow 0$, and so on.

Not every 2×2 matrix can serve as an encryption key; we need an *invertible matrix*. This is a matrix M for which there is another matrix M' such that

$$M' \times M = \begin{bmatrix} 1 & 0 \\ 0 & 1 \end{bmatrix}$$

For example, $\begin{bmatrix} 3 & 5 \\ 2 & 3 \end{bmatrix}$ is invertible because for $M' = \begin{bmatrix} 23 & 5 \\ 2 & 23 \end{bmatrix}$

$$M' \times M = \begin{bmatrix} 23 & 5 \\ 2 & 23 \end{bmatrix} \times \begin{bmatrix} 3 & 5 \\ 2 & 3 \end{bmatrix} = \begin{bmatrix} 79 & 130 \\ 52 & 79 \end{bmatrix}$$

$$\rightarrow \begin{bmatrix} 1 & 0 \\ 0 & 1 \end{bmatrix} \text{ (remember that any value} > 25$$
$$\text{gets wrapped around).}$$

This property is what allows M' to reverse the effect of M. Also, part of our encryption algorithm is a simple substitution (mapping) S that maps letters into numbers; we'll let S be really simple here: $S(A) = 1$, $S(B) = 2, \ldots,$ $S(Z) = 26$. Obviously S is reversible, and we'll call the reverse mapping S': $S'(1) = A$, $S'(2) = B, \ldots, S'(26) = Z$.

To encode our message, we break it up into two-character blocks. Suppose the first two characters form the block $(D\ E)$. We apply the S mapping to this block to get $(4\ 5)$. Now we multiply $(4\ 5) \times M$ by treating $(4\ 5)$ as the row of some matrix (and remember to wrap around if the result exceeds 25):

$$(4\ 5) \times \begin{bmatrix} 3 & 5 \\ 2 & 3 \end{bmatrix} = (4 * 3 + 5 * 2 \quad\quad 4 * 5 + 5 * 3)$$

$$= (22\ 35) \rightarrow (22\ 9)$$

Practice Problems

1. Using a Caesar cipher with $s = 5$, encrypt the message
   NOW IS THE HOUR.

2. A messenger tells you that the secret key for today for the Caesar cipher is
   $s = 26$. Should you trust the messenger? Why, or why not?

3. a. Using the matrix $M = \begin{bmatrix} 3 & 5 \\ 2 & 3 \end{bmatrix}$ of this section, encrypt the two-character
   block (M Q).

   b. Decrypt the results of Part a.

Finally, apply the S' mapping to get from digits back to characters: $S'(22\ 9) = (V\ I)$. This completes the encoding, and $(V\ I)$ is the ciphertext for the message block $(D\ E)$. Notice that the digit 4 (i.e., the plaintext letter D) contributed to both the 22 (V) and the 9 (I), as did the digit 5 (i.e., the plaintext letter E). This *diffusion* (scattering) of the plaintext within the ciphertext is the advantage of a block cipher.

For decoding, we reverse the previous steps. Starting with the cipher-text $(V\ I)$, we first apply S to get (22 9). We then multiply (22 9) by M', the inverse of the encoding key (remembering to wrap around if the result exceeds 25):

$$(22\ 9) \times \begin{bmatrix} 23 & 5 \\ 2 & 23 \end{bmatrix} = (22 * 23 + 9 * 2 \qquad 22 * 5 + 9 * 23)$$

$$= (524\ 317) \rightarrow (4\ 5)$$

Finally, we apply S' to get back—voilà!—the plaintext $(D\ E)$.

Figure 8.1 summarizes the steps. Again, the matrix M is the secret encryption key, from which the decryption key M' can be derived.

FIGURE 8.1

Encoding
   1. Apply S mapping to plaintext block.
   2. Multiply result times M, applying wraparound.
   3. Apply S' to the result.

Decoding
   1. Apply S mapping to ciphertext block.
   2. Multiply result times M', applying wraparound.
   3. Apply S' to the result.

Steps in encoding and decoding for a block cipher

Laboratory Experience 12

The software for this Laboratory Experience uses a block
cipher of block size 2. You will be able to encrypt and decrypt messages.
The encryption key is again a matrix, but the encryption algorithm is quite different from that of the block cipher discussed in this section.

8.3.3 DES

Both of the previous encryption algorithms—the Caesar cipher and an elementary block cipher—are too simplistic to provide much real security. DES
(Data Encryption Standard) is an encryption algorithm developed by IBM
in the 1970s for the U.S. National Bureau of Standards (now called the U.S.
National Institute of Standards and Technology, or NIST), and is certified as
an international standard by the International Organization for Standardization, or ISO (the same organization that certifies the MP3 digital audio
format, as discussed in Chapter 4). One might expect this internationally
standard algorithm to rest upon some extremely complex and obscure operations, but the DES algorithm actually uses very simple operations—however, it uses them over and over.

DES was designed to protect electronic information, so the plaintext is a
binary string of 0s and 1s, just as it is stored in a computer. As we learned in
Chapter 4, this means that ordinary text has already undergone an encoding
using ASCII or Unicode to convert characters to bit strings. This encoding,

Hiding in Plain Sight

Steganography is the practice of hiding the very existence of
a message. It's an old idea; an ancient Greek ruler was said to have sent a
(not very urgent) message by tattooing the message on the shaved head of
one of his slaves and then sending the slave off after his hair had grown back.
The message was revealed on the other end by once more shaving the messenger's head.   (Continued)

These days, steganography has again come into favor in the form of hidden text within images posted on the web. As we learned in Chapter 4, a colored digital image is composed of individual pixels; in the usual RGB format, 8 bits are allocated for each of the red, green, and blue color components. This allows for $2^8 = 256$ variations of intensity for each color, from 0 to 255. Let's say the red component in a pixel has the following 8-bit value:

11010010 (= 2 + 16 + 64 + 128 = 210)

The least significant bit (the rightmost 0) contributes the least to the color intensity. If this bit is changed from 0 to 1, the red component becomes

11010011 (= 1 + 2 + 16 + 64 + 128 = 211)

Such a tiny change (1/256th of the original red color) would not be detectable to the human eye viewing the image.

A text file can be hidden in an image file by changing (if needed) the least significant bit of each byte of the image file to match the binary form of the characters in the text. For example, if the first letter of the text file to be hidden is "A", with ASCII code 01000001, then the first 8 bytes of the image file would be modified (if needed) so that the least significant bits are 0, 1, 0, 0, 0, 0, 0, and 1. To the naked eye, the image appears unaltered.

In the following set of images, the image on the left is the original. The image on the right uses steganography to hide 668 KB of text, over 140 double-spaced pages. Can you see any difference?

A standard Windows file compare sees a lot of difference:

```
C:\Temp>fc Ocean01.bmp Ocean02.bmp
Resync Failed.  Files are too different.
```

In 2011, German Federal Criminal Police arrested a suspected al-Qaeda member who was found to be concealing a memory stick. It contained a pornographic video, which in turn contained, hidden via steganography, 141 separate text files reviewing the success of past al-Qaeda operations and laying out plans for future operations.

Original image

Steganographic image

however, is not for the purposes of secrecy and has nothing to do with the cryptographic encoding we are talking about in this chapter.

DES is a block cipher, and the blocks are 64 bits long, meaning that 64 plaintext bits at a time are processed into 64 ciphertext bits. The key is a 64-bit binary key, although only 56 bits are actually used. The algorithm begins by sending the plaintext 64-bit string through an initial *permutation* (rearrangement). The algorithm then cycles through 16 "rounds." Each round i performs the following steps:

1. The incoming 64-bit block is split into a left half L_i and a right half R_i. A copy of the right half R_i gets passed through unchanged to become the left half of the next round, L_{i+1}.

2. In addition, the 32 bits in the original right half get permuted according to a fixed formula and then expanded to 48 bits by duplicating some of the bits. Meanwhile, the 56-bit key is also permuted (the result is passed on as the key to the next round) and then reduced to 48 bits by omitting some of the bits. These two 48-bit strings are matched bit by bit, using an XOR (exclusive OR) gate for each bit. Figure 8.2 shows the standard symbol for an XOR gate, along with its truth table.

3. The resulting 48-bit string undergoes a substitution and reduction to emerge as a 32-bit string. This string is permuted one more time, and the resulting 32-bit string is matched bit by bit, using XOR gates, with the left half L_i of the input. The result is passed to the next round as the new right half R_{i+1}.

After all 16 rounds are complete, the final left and right halves are recombined into a 64-bit string that is permuted one more time, and the resulting 64-bit string is the ciphertext. Figure 8.3 outlines the steps involved in the DES algorithm.

Two important points about the DES algorithm: The first is that every substitution, reduction, expansion, and permutation is determined by a well-known set of tables. So, given the same plaintext and the same key,

FIGURE 8.2

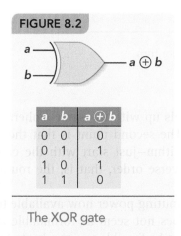

a	b	a ⊕ b
0	0	0
0	1	1
1	0	1
1	1	0

The XOR gate

FIGURE 8.3

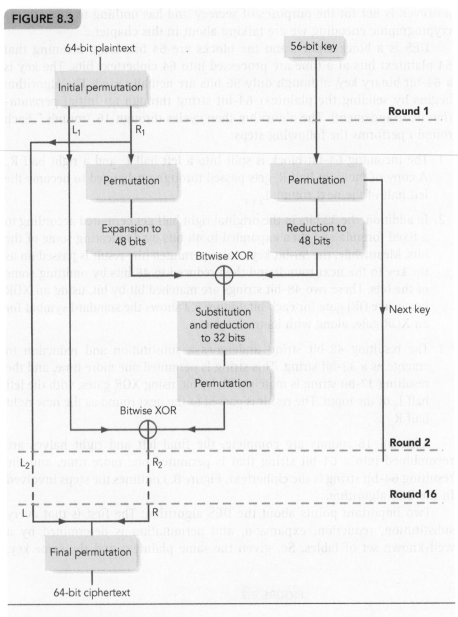

The DES encryption algorithm

everyone using DES ends up with the same ciphertext. The "secret" part is the 56-bit initial key. The second point is that the same algorithm serves as the decryption algorithm—just start with the ciphertext and apply the sequence of keys in reverse order, that is, the round-16 key first and the original secret key last.

With increased computing power now available to those trying to break a code, a 56-bit key does not seem as formidable as when DES was first introduced. It might even be feasible to use a brute force method and try all

2^{56} (72,057,594,037,927,936) possible keys. In 1998, the Electronic Frontier Foundation, a nonprofit civil-liberties organization, used a PC connected to a large array of custom chips to respond to a challenge in the form of a DES ciphertext message posed by RSA Laboratories, the research component of RSA Security, a leading electronic security company. Their system could test 88 billion keys per second and it found the correct 56-bit key in less than three days. If a system could evaluate 100 billion keys per second (using, for example, a massively parallel supercomputer like those described in Section 5.4), it would take only a little more than a week to try every possible secret key. *Triple DES* improves the security of DES; it requires two 56-bit keys (which can be thought of as a 112-bit key length), and runs the DES algorithm three times: Encode using key 1, decode the result using key 2, encode the result using key 1 again.

Concerns about the eventual breakdown of DES in the face of ever-increasing computing power prompted NIST in 1997 to request proposals for a successor encryption scheme. The result was AES (Advanced Encryption Standard), which was adopted for use by the U.S. government in 2001. AES is based on the Rijndael (pronounced Rindahl) algorithm, named for the two Belgian cryptographers who designed it, Vincent Rijmen and Joan Daemen. Like DES, AES uses successive rounds of computations that mix up the data and the key. The key length can be 128, 192, or even 256 bits, and the algorithm appears to be very efficient.

8.3.4 Public-Key Systems

The encryption algorithms we have discussed so far have all been symmetric encryption algorithms, requiring that both the sender and the receiver have knowledge of the secret key. Our final example is an asymmetric, or public-key, encryption algorithm. Remember that the main difficulty with a symmetric algorithm is how to securely transmit the secret key. In a public-key system, the encryption key for messages to go to a particular receiver is broadcast to everyone, but the decryption key cannot be derived from it and is known only by the receiver.

The most common public-key encryption algorithm is RSA, named for its developers, Ron Rivest, Adi Shamir, and Len Adleman at MIT (founders of RSA Security, mentioned above). This algorithm, developed in 1977, is based on results from the field of mathematics known as *number theory*.

A *prime number* is an integer greater than 1 that can only be written as the product of itself and 1. For example, 2, 3, 5, 7, 11, ... are prime numbers; you can only write 7, for example, as $7 = 1 \times 7$, the product of 1 and 7. The numbers 4, 6, 8, 10, and 12, for example, are not prime because they can be factored in a nontrivial way:

$$4 = 2 \times 2 \qquad 6 = 2 \times 3 \qquad 8 = 2 \times 2 \times 2$$
$$10 = 2 \times 5 \qquad 12 = 2 \times 2 \times 3$$

Any positive integer is either a prime number or a number that can be written in a unique way as a product of prime factors. For example, $12 = 2 \times 2 \times 3$

is the product of three prime factors. The success of RSA encryption is based on the fact that it is extremely difficult to find the prime factors for n if n is a large number. That is, it is easy to multiply prime factors together to get a result, such as $2 \times 3 \times 7 \times 7 \times 13 \times 17 \times 23 \times 23 = 34{,}371{,}246$. However, it is far more difficult to be given the value $34{,}371{,}246$ and asked to find all its prime factors. So although information encrypted using RSA is technically not secure, it is secure in practice because of the large amount of computation necessary to find the prime factors of the encoding key.

Here's how RSA works. Two large prime numbers p and q are chosen at random (where "large" means 200 or so digits). Then their product $n = p \times q$ is computed. The product $m = (p - 1) \times (q - 1)$ is also computed. Next, a large random number e is chosen in such a way that e and m have no common factors other than 1. This step guarantees the existence of a unique integer d between 0 and m, such that when we compute $e \times d$ using the same sort of wraparound arithmetic we used in the block encoding scheme—that is, whenever we reach m, we start over again counting from 0—the result is 1. There are computationally efficient ways to produce p, q, e, and d.

For example, suppose we pick $p = 3$ and $q = 7$ for our two prime numbers (a trivially small case). Then,

1. $n = p \times q = 3 \times 7 = 21$

2. $m = (p - 1) \times (q - 1) = 2 \times 6 = 12$

3. Choose $e = 5$ ($e = 5$ and $m = 12$ have no common factors)

4. Then $d = 5$ because $e \times d = 5 \times 5 = 25 = 2 \times 12 + 1$, so when we compute $e \times d$ using wraparound arithmetic with respect to 12, we get 1.

Now the number pair $(n,\ e)$ becomes the public encryption key, and d is the decryption key. Let's suppose that the plaintext message has been converted into an integer P, using some sort of mapping from characters to numbers. The encryption process is to compute P^e using wraparound arithmetic with respect to n (when you reach n, make that 0). Continuing with our example, suppose $P = 3$. Then the ciphertext is computed as

5. $3^5 = 243 = 11 \times 21 + 12 \rightarrow 12$

(Note that the sender uses both parts of the public key, n and e, to compute the ciphertext.) The receiver decodes the ciphertext C by computing C^d using wraparound arithmetic with respect to n. In our example,

6. $12^5 = 248832 = 11849 \times 21 + 3 \rightarrow 3$

Of course, our example has a major problem in that d is the same as e. Obviously, in a real case, you want e and d to be different. The whole point is that even though n and e are known, the attacker must determine d, which involves finding the prime factors p and q of n. There is no known computationally efficient algorithm to carry out this task.

Quantum Computing vs. RSA

RSA encryption begins by multiplying two large prime numbers p and q to get the product n. The security of data encrypted via RSA depends on the computational difficulty (that is, time to perform this task) of reversing this process, that is, finding the two prime factors of n. The faster this can be done, the more feasible it becomes to "crack" an RSA-encrypted ciphertext.

Shor's algorithm, developed in 1994, uses quantum computing to solve the factorization problem (see the Special Interest Box "Quantum Computing" in Chapter 5). The difficulty is that this algorithm requires an "idealized" quantum computer, one with a sufficiently large number of qubits (the computational unit of a quantum computer, much as the bit is the computational unit of a conventional computer). It turns out that building a quantum computer with a large number of qubits is difficult because such systems rapidly "deteriorate."

In 2016, a team of researchers from MIT and the University of Innsbruck (in Austria) developed a new quantum computer architecture. As proof of concept, this team was able to factor 15 into 3 × 5 using Shor's algorithm with a machine using 5 qubits rather than the 15 qubits normally required. In addition to reducing the number of qubits required, thus speeding up the computation, the architecture itself is scalable, meaning that, theoretically, the number of qubits can be arbitrarily large. The consequence is that in future, when such machines become available, RSA will no longer be a secure encryption algorithm.

Practice Problem

You receive a message "17" that was sent using the RSA public encryption key (21, 5) of the example in this section. Decode this to find the original numeric message. (You might want to use a spreadsheet to help with this computation.)

8.4 Web Transmission Security

One area about which the public is very security conscious is in making online purchases, which require the purchaser to send his or her name, address, and—most worrisome of all—credit card number across a network. One method for achieving secure transfer of information on the web is SSL (Secure Sockets Layer). This is a series of proprietary protocols developed by Netscape Communications (Netscape was an early web browser) in the mid-1990s. The TLS (Transport Layer Security) protocol, first defined in 1999, is based on SSL and is nearly identical to SSL but with a few technical improvements. The major difference is that TSL is nonproprietary and is a standard supported by the Internet Engineering Task Force (IETF), an open organization of individuals concerned with "the evolution of the Internet architecture and the smooth operation of the Internet."[4]

Both TLS and SSL are in use and are supported by all web browsers. Technically, TSL/SSL fits between the Transport layer, with its TCP protocols, and the Application layer, with its HTTP protocols (both discussed in the previous chapter). When you see a closed lock icon at the top or bottom of your web browser page, or when a web address begins with HTTPS, instead of HTTP, then you can be assured that the communication between your browser and the web server (the vendor's web computer) is secure and protected by TLS or SSL. TLS/SSL allows a client (the purchaser's web browser) and a web server to agree on the encryption methods to be used, exchange the necessary security keys, and authenticate the identity of each party to the other. (Here we are again with *encryption* and *authentication*, the two pillars of security we've seen before.)

Now that you know a bit more about encryption, you might ask what encryption algorithm TLS/SSL uses; is it DES encryption or the newer, stronger RSA encryption? Surprisingly, it is both. One of the problems with the RSA algorithm is the computational overload for encryption/decryption. What often happens is that RSA is used in the initial stage of communication between client and server. For example, in response to a client request, the server may send the client its public key along with a public-key certificate (also known as a digital certificate). This is a certificate issued by a trusted third-party certificate authority; it's like a letter of introduction that attests that the server belongs to the organization the browser thinks it is talking to.

The client, using RSA and the public key of the server, encodes a short message containing the keys for a symmetric encryption algorithm. Because only keys are being encrypted, the message is short and the encryption can be done quickly with little RSA overload. The server receives and decodes this message and responds to the client with a message encoded using the symmetric key. The client and the server have now established a secure exchange of keys (one of the issues with a symmetric encryption algorithm) and can complete the transaction using, for example, DES. Figure 8.4

---

[4]*www.ietf.org/about*

FIGURE 8.4

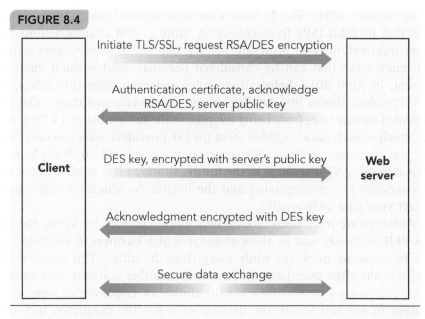

Initiate TLS/SSL, request RSA/DES encryption →

← Authentication certificate, acknowledge RSA/DES, server public key

Client

DES key, encrypted with server's public key →

Web server

← Acknowledgment encrypted with DES key

Secure data exchange ↔

A typical TLS/SSL session

illustrates the major steps in this process, although the technical details may require a few additional transmissions between the client and the server. The exchange of setup information between the client and the server, preparatory to exchanging real data, is known as a handshake.

Another way to obtain network security is to transmit via a Virtual Private Network (VPN). When you have an account with a VPN provider, then you can use the software provided by that VPN to connect to one of their servers (and later disconnect). This connection is made via an encrypted connection (sometimes called a *VPN tunnel*) so that all traffic back and forth between your device and that server is encrypted. The VPN server assigns a unique IP address to your device. For subsequent data traffic from your device, your ISP sends that traffic through the Internet to the VPN server for further processing, but that traffic is encrypted. Therefore, the ISP can neither read that data nor know what subsequent service you are asking the VPN server to perform, such as connecting you to some website. All traffic between the VPN server and the rest of the Internet sees only your assigned IP address.

One of the disadvantages of using a VPN is that your Internet traffic may be a bit slower than otherwise, because it goes through the VPN server. However, we have already mentioned two advantages of using a VPN:

1. Your device's IP address is "hidden" behind the IP address assigned by the VPN server, so web traffic cannot easily be connected directly to you, that is, to the device you are using.

2. All network traffic between you and the VPN server is encrypted, so at least that leg of the journey is secure.

In October 2016, The Federal Communications Commission adopted rules that prohibit ISPs from collecting, storing, and sharing/selling customer information (web browsing history, app usage history, geolocation, and much more that can be considered personal data) without customer consent. In April 2017, before these rules had even gone into effect, the U. S. President signed into law legislation that overturned those rules and prevented similar rules from being adopted in the future. Using a VPN means that much of such data is hidden from the ISP providers, who can only "see" that you are connected to a VPN server. Hence there will no doubt be more interest in using VPN services in the future, although it should be noted that VPN services are not regulated and the lengths to which providers go to protect your data vary greatly.

Although we have been talking here about commercial VPNs, the idea of a VPN originally was to allow employees of a business to securely connect to corporate networks while away from the office. This usage is still in effect, but often goes hand-in-hand with another software tool called a Remote Desktop Protocol (RDP). RDP allows an employee at some other location to see and utilize the desktop of a specific computer, including using files and software applications available on that computer.

8.5 Embedded Computing

Up to now, we have primarily treated security as if it were always a matter between your personal computer and the rest of the world. But there are many other places where computing devices interact with the rest of the world.

Embedded computers are computational devices such as chips, processors, or computers that are embedded within another system. Unlike a general-purpose computer that can be programmed to do many different things, embedded computers usually perform just one or two tasks as part of the system in which they occur. Frequently this means they are small devices that you never see, and the ability to package more and more transistors on a single chip has contributed to the growth of embedded computers. Where are they found?

- In your car
- In your home thermostat
- In your home alarm system
- In your cell phone
- In your digital clock or watch
- In your iPod or MP3 player
- In your video game console
- In your TV remote controller

- In your digital camera

- In your credit card

- In your microwave

- In your car's navigation system

- In your car's emergency and vehicle diagnostics system (for example, General Motors OnStar)

- In a plane's flight control system

- In a bank ATM

- In a hospital patient monitoring system

Well, you get the idea—embedded computers are everywhere! It is estimated that 98% of all new CPUs (central processing units) are used in embedded systems.

Embedded computers differ from conventional computers in other ways as well. Input and output are usually not via keyboard and screen, respectively; instead, input may be data sent from sensors within the surrounding system, and output may be commands to control devices within the system. The embedded computer has very limited memory and processing capacity. And its response time is often in the "real-time" category (a plane's flight control system has to respond instantly, so does the patient monitoring system, and you hope your antilock brakes do that as well). For these same safety-critical systems, reliability is a key requirement.

But reliability is not the same as security. Security comes into the picture when these embedded systems become networked or even Internet-enabled. Your car's navigation system gets updates from the web, the home alarm system connects over a network to the alarm company, the electric company may connect with your thermostat to raise the temperature slightly during peak air-conditioning load times, and sensors that monitor manufacturing processes communicate to streamline the production flow. The challenge is how to build security into network-enabled embedded computers that have little extra memory, often have energy constraints, and have no system administrator at hand to deal with security updates or breaches.

The term *the Internet of Things* originated in 1999. As mentioned in Chapter 7, the Internet of Things (IoT) refers to the idea that in the future, many of the objects we interact with daily will be connected (or at least connectable) to the Internet, often by means of RFID tags that can sense their environment and both send and receive data. The future is now here! In 2017, an estimated 20 billion devices were already part of the IoT.

This technology has many positive uses: medical monitoring, inventory control, home appliance and security management, traffic monitoring, industrial robot management, and so forth. An agricultural application we might not think of uses RFID ear tags for livestock to track and safeguard herds (see Figure 8.5). A home assistant can recognize voice commands and

FIGURE 8.5

©davesimon / Shutterstock.com

Scottish Highland cow with RFID
ear tag

even hold a conversation ("What's the weather report for today?" "What is Tom Hanks' latest movie?").

But at the same time, there are many potential privacy risks: If all this data is floating around, then it can be captured, scanned, and perhaps manipulated by government agencies, criminal organizations, or others with less-than-honorable intent. Your home assistant can record everything it hears in your living room and store it in the cloud, which certainly raises questions about personal privacy.

On the other end of the size spectrum, computer systems control much of the world's vital infrastructure such as utility plants, electric grid systems, transportation, telecommunications, and financial markets, to say nothing of defense and military installations. It is not hard to imagine terrorist groups and perhaps hostile foreign powers contemplating attacks on one of these systems.

In February 2013, President Obama issued an executive order (Executive Order 13636: Cybersecurity Framework) for the development of a set of industry standards and best practices that could serve as a basis for organizations to measure and manage their cybersecurity risks. Exactly one year later, as a result of collaboration with representatives from industry, government, and academia, the National Institute of Standards and Technology issued the Framework for Improving Critical Infrastructure Cybersecurity, version 1.0. The framework guides organizations through tasks of identifying and protecting

Mischief-Makers in the Internet of Things

In October 2016, the largest denial-of-service attack to date was perpetrated on a company called Dyn. Dyn controls much of the Internet domain-name structure, and bringing this company to its knees also caused Internet disruption for many U.S. and European companies. This DDoS attack was carried out by something called the Mirai botnet. But this botnet is not composed of compromised computers; instead it uses compromised devices from the Internet of Things. (That's right, your web-enabled home refrigerator might have been part of this attack!) Taking advantage of the multitude of devices on the IoT, this attack at its peak used an estimated 100,000 devices.

Mirai builds its list of insecure IoT devices to incorporate into the botnet by randomly scanning the Internet and trying various user ID/password combinations. IoT devices frequently have default (and hardwired, that is, can't be changed) combinations set by their manufacturers. In fact, Mirai uses a list of 60 such combinations that are tried on any device, combinations such as *admin/password* or *guest/12345*. How do we know this? Because shortly before this massive DDoS attack, the source code for the Mirai malware was publicly released, thus making additional attacks using Mirai or a variant even more likely.

resources critical to their business goals and of detecting, responding to, and recovering from attacks. Still, there is concern that such a voluntary policy does not go far enough to protect essential national infrastructure.

Safeguarding vital infrastructure is a complex but extremely important issue, and much work remains to be done. This is not just a U.S. issue, but a concern of every industrialized nation.

8.6 Conclusion

In this chapter, we've looked at components of information security, both on an isolated local computer and on a machine exposed to the network. Whether it's an individual's personal data, proprietary corporate information, sensitive government data, or military infrastructure, all are under threat. Still, a bit of caution and common sense can go a long way. As the well-worn watchword says, "Security: It's Everybody's Business."

8.7 Summary of Level 3

We have seen that the hardware described in Chapters 4 and 5 is, by itself, nearly unusable. Working directly with the hardware components of a Von Neumann machine—processors, memory, ALU—is impossible for any but the most technically knowledgeable users. To make the system accessible, the system software must create a people-oriented *virtual machine* or *virtual environment* that is easy to understand and use. In addition to ease of use, this virtual environment provides a number of other services, including resource management, security, access control, and efficient resource use. A great deal of work has been done to try to identify and create an optimal virtual environment.

Operating systems—a critical component of the virtual environment—have evolved from early batch systems through multiprogramming and time-sharing to the current network and real-time operating systems. Most modern operating systems allow us to use a large collection of machines, called a computer network, almost as easily as if it were a single logical system. Network technology has expanded our virtual environment to encompass a worldwide grid of interconnected computers. More and more, the computer user on a networked system can deal only with *what* operations need to be done, not with where or how they can be done. Perhaps they are being done "in the cloud." The future of computer systems definitely lies in the direction of more abstract and more powerful virtual environments.

As our virtual environment has expanded, our most important asset—our data—is increasingly at risk for theft or destruction by clever intruders with malicious intent. Constant vigilance is required to maintain information security so that our virtual environment is not only user-friendly but also safe.

Now that we have created a vastly more usable environment in which to work, what do we want to do with it? Well, we probably want to write programs that solve important problems. In the next level of the text, we will begin our study of the software world.

EXERCISES

1. The following are three possible logon scenarios. Explain why option (c) below is preferable in terms of system security.

   a. Welcome to XYZ computing
      Enter username: jones
      Invalid username
      Enter username:

   b. Welcome to XYZ computing
      Enter username: smith
      Enter password: password
      Invalid access
      Enter username:

   c. Enter username: smith
      Enter password: password
      Invalid access
      Enter username: smith
      Enter password: FpQr56
      Welcome to XYZ computing

2. Using the hash function described in Section 8.2.1, find the encrypted forms of the following passwords:

   a. fido

   b. blank

   c. ti34pper

3. Consider a password hash function that works as follows on a system where the password must contain only letters:

   Step 1. Take each letter in the password and replace it with a number representing its place in the alphabet.
   Step 2. Take each number from Step 1, multiply it by 2, and add 1.
   Step 3. Combine the resulting numbers, separated by 0s, into a single string. This string is the encrypted password.

   a. Given the user password "user", what would this hashing algorithm produce as the final encrypted password?
   b. Comment on this hashing algorithm in terms of the security it provides for user passwords.

4. The default passcode on a cell phone is usually 4 digits, each 0–9.

   a. How many different passcodes are possible?
   b. If you can enter a 4-digit passcode in one second, about how long would it take you to try all possible passcodes?

5. Password characters on a certain system are limited to 26 uppercase letters [A ... Z], 26 lowercase letters [a ... z], 10 digits [0 ... 9], and 3 special symbols [#, $, %]. Suppose a password-cracking tool can generate and test 10,000,000 character strings (potential passwords) per second. Could all possible passwords of length 10 or less be generated and tested in under one week's time? (Use a spreadsheet to help find the answer.)

6. *Merriam-Webster's Collegiate Dictionary*, 11th ed. (Merriam-Webster, Inc., 2003), contains over 225,000 entries. Using a password-cracking tool that can process 1.7 million words per second, how long would it take to test each word in the dictionary as a possible password?

7. A virus attacks a single user's computer and within one hour embeds itself in 50 email attachment files sent out to other users. By the end of the hour, 10% of these have been opened and have infected their host machines. If this process continues, how many machines will be infected at the end of 5 hours? Can you find a formula for the number of machines infected after n hours?

8. A certain individual has a Hilton account, a RitzCarlton account, and a Marriott International account. The following email message is sent to this individual. Point out clues that should alert this individual that he or she is the victim of a phishing attack.

> We here at Marriott appreciate your loyalty as a customer. We want to make things more easy for you when you travel, so we have partnered with Hilton and Ritz-Carlton to create a unified rewards program. Now when you stay at any of these fine brand hotels, you will earn award points that can apply to a future stay at any of the three hotels. For you we will quick set this up, just click on the link below to get started:
>
> *www.Mariott.com*

9. Read about one of the following. Decide whether there seems to be enough evidence to put it in the category of cyberwarfare:

   a. Stuxnet
   b. 2007 – Estonia
   c. Titan Rain
   d. Operation Hangover
   e. Operation Cleaver

10. *Risk analysis* is one way to monitor security in an organization. Risk analysis can be a time-consuming process; it involves a number of steps, some of which require "educated guessing." Nevertheless, the process alone raises awareness of security issues even if no immediate actions are taken as a result. The steps are:

    i. Identify assets (infrastructure, people, hardware, software, reputation, etc.).

    For the rest of this list, we'll concentrate on a single asset.

    ii. Determine vulnerability (what event or events might happen to the asset. For example, the building could catch fire, the website could be hacked, etc.).

    For the rest of this list, we'll concentrate on a single asset vulnerable to a single event.

    iii. Estimate the probability per year of this event (based on past data, expert estimates, etc.). Take current security measures into account.

    iv. Estimate the expected cost if this event occurs (cost to repair or replace, cost of lost business, etc.).

    v. Compute risk exposure = cost estimate × probability estimate.

    vi. Identify any additional security measure X that would help protect against this event, determine what it would cost, and do a calculation of the risk exposure with the additional security measure X in place.

    vii. Do a cost-benefit analysis:
    (Risk exposure without X – Risk exposure with X) – Cost of X

    You have a small web-based business that uses a single server to manage your webpage and your customer information. Over the past four years, your website has been hacked and taken down twice. You estimate that the cost of this event is $600 to clean the server and reload the webpage and $12,000 in lost business while the server is down.

    a. You could purchase a backup server for a cost of $3,000, which you estimate would reduce the probability per year of losing your website to 0.2. Would this be a cost-effective security measure?

    b. What if you reevaluate the probability per year with the backup server to be 0.3. Does this change your answer?

11. Using a Caesar cipher with $s = 5$, decode the received message RTAJ TZY FY IFBS.

12. The centurion who was supposed to inform you of s was killed en route, but you have received the message MXX SMGX UE PUHUPQP in a Caesar cipher. Find the value of s and decode the message.

13. You receive a message that was encoded using a block encoding scheme with the encoding matrix

$$M = \begin{bmatrix} 3 & 2 \\ 7 & 5 \end{bmatrix}$$

a. Verify by computing $M' \times M$ that $M' =$

$$\begin{bmatrix} 5 & 24 \\ 19 & 3 \end{bmatrix}$$

(Remember to wrap around if a value is > 25.)

b. Decode the ciphertext message MXOSHI.

14. The DES algorithm combines two bit strings by applying the XOR operator on each pair of corresponding bits. Compute the 6-bit string that results from $100111 \oplus 110101$.

15. To decode a message encrypted using DES requires finding the key from among the 2^{56} possible 56-bit binary keys. Although you might find the key early on, the worst case is that you have to test all 2^{56} possible DES keys.

a. How long would this take using the gaming PC described in the Special Interest Box "The Tortoise and the Hare" in Chapter 3? Assume that a single key can be tested in one floating-point operation.

b. How long would this take using the Chinese Sunway TaihuLight supercomputer described in the Special Interest Box "The Tortoise and the Hare" in Chapter 3? Assume that a single key can be tested in one floating-point operation.

16. Using the RSA encryption algorithm, pick $p = 11$ and $q = 7$. Find a set of encryption/decryption keys e and d.

17. Using the RSA encryption algorithm, let $p = 3$ and $q = 5$. Then $n = 15$ and $m = 8$. Let $e = 11$.

a. Compute d.
b. Find the code for 3.
c. Decode your answer to Part (b) to retrieve the 3.

18. If a message is encrypted using AES with a key length of 256 bits, the brute force approach to decryption involves generating each of the 2^{256} possible keys in turn until one is found that decodes the encrypted message. Quantum computing was discussed in Chapter 5. Using a quantum computer, how many qubits are required to represent all 2^{256} possible keys simultaneously?

CHALLENGE WORK

1. In this chapter, we discussed hash functions (hash algorithms) as a means to protect passwords. Another application is *message integrity*: A hash algorithm is applied to a message and the resulting hash is appended to the original message when it is transmitted. Upon receipt, the message is rehashed to produce a new hash that is compared with the original. If the two hashes match, it is deemed that the message has not been altered in transmission. This is based on the assumption that any change in the message would produce a change in the hash. The standard hash algorithm for message integrity has been SHA-1 (Secure Hash Algorithm-1).

a. Read about how the basic assumption was challenged in 2005 by a Chinese cryptographer named Xiaoyun Wang, who found a shorter way to produce two different messages that hash to the same value under SHA-1.

b. Prompted by the work of Xiaoyun Wang, in 2007 NIST (the National Institute of Standards and Technology) launched a five-year competition to produce a new and more secure hash algorithm. Read about the resulting SHA-3 or Keccak algorithm that became a Federal Information Processing Standard in 2015.

2. Find information about a well-known computer virus or worm. Answer as many of the following questions as you can, and be sure to list your sources.

    a. What is the name of the virus or worm?
    b. When did it first appear?
    c. Who wrote it?
    d. How was it spread?
    e. What systems did it attack?
    f. What were its observable effects?
    g. What are the technical details on how it worked?
    h. What was the "cure"?
    i. Did it spawn "copycat" attacks?
    j. What was its economic impact?
    k. Was the perpetrator found, arrested, convicted?

3. The Vigenère cipher was first proposed in the 16th century. At its heart is the Vigenère table (shown on the next page), where each row represents a Caesar cipher of the letters of the alphabet shown in the row of column headers. The shift for row A is $s = 0$, for row B it is $s = 1$, for row C it is $s = 2$, etc. Thus in row C, the column header A is shifted two characters to become C, B becomes D, and so forth. The key to the Vigenère cipher is a secret word or phrase known only to the sender and the receiver. Each letter in the key is used to encode a letter in the plaintext by finding in the table the row of the key letter and the column of the plaintext letter; their intersection is the ciphertext letter for that plaintext letter. When every letter in the key has been used, the key is repeated.

For example, suppose the key is

SONG

and the plaintext message is

MEETATNOON

Because the key is shorter than the plaintext, it will have to be used several times:

SONGSONGSO
MEETATNOON

The first character of the ciphertext is found at the intersection of row S and column M; it is E. The second character of the ciphertext is found at the intersection of row O and column E; it is S. The complete ciphertext is

ESRZSHAUGB

To decode a received message, you reverse this process. Again matching the key characters to the ciphertext characters,

SONGSONGSO
ESRZSHAUGB

find the ciphertext character in the key character's row; the plaintext character is the corresponding column heading. Thus in row S, the E occurs in column M, so M is the corresponding plaintext.

You receive the following ciphertext message that you know was encoded using the Vigenère cipher with a secret key of PEANUTS:

DREVZUQAENQ

Decode the ciphertext to find the plaintext.

	A	B	C	D	E	F	G	H	I	J	K	L	M	N	O	P	Q	R	S	T	U	V	W	X	Y	Z
A	A	B	C	D	E	F	G	H	I	J	K	L	M	N	O	P	Q	R	S	T	U	V	W	X	Y	Z
B	B	C	D	E	F	G	H	I	J	K	L	M	N	O	P	Q	R	S	T	U	V	W	X	Y	Z	A
C	C	D	E	F	G	H	I	J	K	L	M	N	O	P	Q	R	S	T	U	V	W	X	Y	Z	A	B
D	D	E	F	G	H	I	J	K	L	M	N	O	P	Q	R	S	T	U	V	W	X	Y	Z	A	B	C
E	E	F	G	H	I	J	K	L	M	N	O	P	Q	R	S	T	U	V	W	X	Y	Z	A	B	C	D
F	F	G	H	I	J	K	L	M	N	O	P	Q	R	S	T	U	V	W	X	Y	Z	A	B	C	D	E
G	G	H	I	J	K	L	M	N	O	P	Q	R	S	T	U	V	W	X	Y	Z	A	B	C	D	E	F
H	H	I	J	K	L	M	N	O	P	Q	R	S	T	U	V	W	X	Y	Z	A	B	C	D	E	F	G
I	I	J	K	L	M	N	O	P	Q	R	S	T	U	V	W	X	Y	Z	A	B	C	D	E	F	G	H
J	J	K	L	M	N	O	P	Q	R	S	T	U	V	W	X	Y	Z	A	B	C	D	E	F	G	H	I
K	K	L	M	N	O	P	Q	R	S	T	U	V	W	X	Y	Z	A	B	C	D	E	F	G	H	I	J
L	L	M	N	O	P	Q	R	S	T	U	V	W	X	Y	Z	A	B	C	D	E	F	G	H	I	J	K
M	M	N	O	P	Q	R	S	T	U	V	W	X	Y	Z	A	B	C	D	E	F	G	H	I	J	K	L
N	N	O	P	Q	R	S	T	U	V	W	X	Y	Z	A	B	C	D	E	F	G	H	I	J	K	L	M
O	O	P	Q	R	S	T	U	V	W	X	Y	Z	A	B	C	D	E	F	G	H	I	J	K	L	M	N
P	P	Q	R	S	T	U	V	W	X	Y	Z	A	B	C	D	E	F	G	H	I	J	K	L	M	N	O
Q	Q	R	S	T	U	V	W	X	Y	Z	A	B	C	D	E	F	G	H	I	J	K	L	M	N	O	P
R	R	S	T	U	V	W	X	Y	Z	A	B	C	D	E	F	G	H	I	J	K	L	M	N	O	P	Q
S	S	T	U	V	W	X	Y	Z	A	B	C	D	E	F	G	H	I	J	K	L	M	N	O	P	Q	R
T	T	U	V	W	X	Y	Z	A	B	C	D	E	F	G	H	I	J	K	L	M	N	O	P	Q	R	S
U	U	V	W	X	Y	Z	A	B	C	D	E	F	G	H	I	J	K	L	M	N	O	P	Q	R	S	T
V	V	W	X	Y	Z	A	B	C	D	E	F	G	H	I	J	K	L	M	N	O	P	Q	R	S	T	U
W	W	X	Y	Z	A	B	C	D	E	F	G	H	I	J	K	L	M	N	O	P	Q	R	S	T	U	V
X	X	Y	Z	A	B	C	D	E	F	G	H	I	J	K	L	M	N	O	P	Q	R	S	T	U	V	W
Y	Y	Z	A	B	C	D	E	F	G	H	I	J	K	L	M	N	O	P	Q	R	S	T	U	V	W	X
Z	Z	A	B	C	D	E	F	G	H	I	J	K	L	M	N	O	P	Q	R	S	T	U	V	W	X	Y

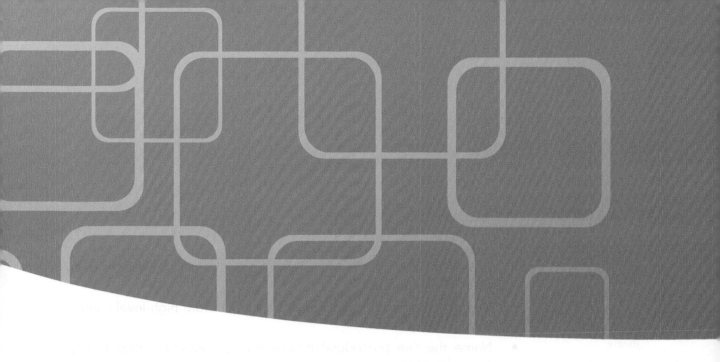

n Level 4, we return to our original focus on algorithms as the heart of computer science. Algorithms are devised to solve problems. Computer programs express these algorithms using the capabilities of a programming language, harnessing the power of the hardware and the system software to bring algorithms to life.

Chapter 9 presents a framework for comparing several important programming languages: Ada, C++ (pronounced C plus plus), C# (pronounced C sharp), Java, and Python. A more detailed introduction to each of these languages can be found in five separate online chapters that accompany this text.[1]

Other programming languages and different language design philosophies are introduced in Chapter 10. Chapter 11 explains how high-level programming language statements are translated into low-level machine language statements that can be executed by the hardware. Chapter 12 demonstrates that, in spite of all the power of modern hardware and software, and no matter how clever we may be in designing algorithms, problems exist that have no algorithmic solution.

---

[1] For information on accessing the online chapters, refer to the Special Interest Box on page 439.

Introduction to High-Level Language Programming

AFTER STUDYING THIS CHAPTER, YOU WILL BE ABLE TO:

- Explain the advantages of high-level programming languages over assembly language
- Describe the general process of translation from high-level source code to object code
- Name the five procedural programming languages used in the examples of this chapter
- Explain the favorite number and data cleanup examples for each programming language
- Explain why the software development life cycle is necessary for creating large software programs
- List the steps in the software development life cycle, explain the purpose of each, and describe the products of each
- Explain how agile software development differs from the traditional waterfall model

9.1 The Language Progression

As of the end of Chapter 8, we have a complete and workable computer system. We have created a virtual environment in which we imagine that we are communicating directly with the computer, even though we are using a language (assembly language) that is far more suited to human communication than is (binary) machine language. We have learned about the system software needed to create and support this virtual environment, including the assembler that translates assembly language programs into machine language, as well as the operating system that accepts requests to load and execute a program and coordinates and manages the other software tools needed to accomplish this task. Our system also includes the network technologies and protocols that extend the virtual world across our campus, throughout our office building, and around the world, and we are aware of the need for protection against the security threats to which we are exposed as our virtual world widens.

But this puts us somewhat ahead of our story. In Chapter 6, we talked about the progression from machine language to assembly language, but today, using computers to solve problems usually involves writing programs in a high-level programming language. This section continues our discussion of the progression of programming languages from assembly language (where we left off in our language story) to high-level languages.

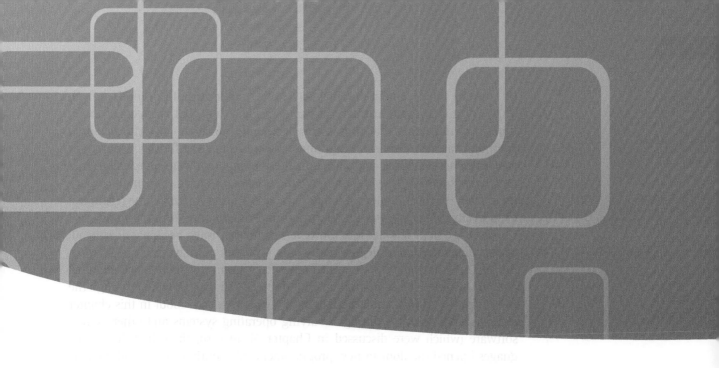

9.1.1 Where Do We Stand and What Do We Want?

At the end of Chapter 6, we were back in the "early days" of computing—the 1950s—when assembly language had just come into existence. As a step up from machine language, it was considered a reasonable programming environment because the people writing computer programs were for the most part technically oriented. Many had backgrounds in engineering or (as it would later be called) computer science. They were familiar with the inner workings of a computer and were accustomed to dealing with difficult problems steeped in mathematical notation, so the tedious precision of assembly language programming did not deter them. Also, because assembly language is so closely tied to machine language, assembly language programmers could see the kinds of processor activity that assembly language instructions would generate. By being sufficiently clever in their choice of instructions, they could often shave a small amount off the execution time or amount of memory that their programs required. For example, the following sequence of assembly language instructions:

```
            LOAD    X
            ADD     ONE
            STORE   X
              .       .
              .       .
              .       .
    ONE:    .DATA    1
```

could be replaced by the single instruction

```
            INCREMENT X
```

This is not the sort of performance improvement obtained by changing from a sequential search algorithm to a binary search algorithm. Instead, it is a fine-tuning improvement that may save a few millionths of a second, or even a few seconds if these instructions occur inside a loop that is executed many times. But remember that in this era, people did not have powerful personal computers at their disposal. Programmers were competing for the resources of a mainframe computer, and although these computers were physically large and very expensive, they did not have the processing speed or memory capacity of even the most modest of today's systems. Conserving machine resources, even in tiny amounts, was an important part of computer programming.

Over the next few decades, however, computer usage became widespread, permeating society to a degree that would probably not have been believed in the 1950s. "Nontechie" types needed to write programs too, and they demanded a more user-friendly programming environment. This was provided through the use of high-level programming languages (which we talk about in this chapter and the next) and also through evolving operating systems and other system software (which were discussed in Chapter 6). In turn, these high-level languages opened the door to new programmers. Also during this period, incredible technological strides made machines so powerful that conserving resources was no longer the critical issue it once was, and the overhead of execution time occasioned by the use of high-level programming languages became acceptable.

Let's review some of the aspects of assembly language programming that made people look for better alternatives. Suppose our task is to add two integers. In the assembly language of Chapter 6, the following instructions would have to be included after the instructions that assign legitimate data values to B and C.

```
        LOAD      B
        ADD       C
        STORE     A
          .         .
          .         .
          .         .
A:      .DATA     0
B:      .DATA     0
C:      .DATA     0
```

The three .DATA statements reserve storage for signed integers, generate the binary representation of the integer value 0 to occupy those storage locations initially, and ensure that the labels A, B, and C are bound to those memory locations. But at this point in the execution of our assembly language program, the initial 0 values for B and C have been written over by legitimate data values. The LOAD statement then copies the current contents of the memory location labeled B into the ALU register R, the ADD statement adds the current contents of the memory location labeled C to what is currently in register R, and the STORE instruction copies the contents of R (which is now $B + C$) into the memory location labeled A.

To perform a simple arithmetic task, we had to manage all the data movement of the numbers to be combined as well as the resulting answer. This is a microscopic view of a task—we'd like to be able to say something like "add B and C, and call the result A," or better yet, something like

"$A = B + C$." But each assembly language statement corresponds to at most one machine language statement (you may recall from Chapter 6 that the pseudo-op .DATA statements do not generate any machine language instructions). Therefore, individual assembly language statements, though easier to read, can be no more powerful than the operations of the underlying instruction set. For the same reason, assembly language programs are machine specific. An assembly language statement that runs on machine X is nothing but a slightly "humanized" variant of the machine language statement for X, and it will not execute on a machine Y that has a different instruction set. Indeed, machine Y's assembler won't know what to do with such a statement.

Finally, assembly language instructions are rather stilted. STORE A does not sound much like the sort of language we customarily speak, though STORE is certainly more expressive than its binary machine language counterpart. To summarize, assembly language has the following disadvantages:

- The programmer must "manually" manage the movement of data items between and among memory locations and registers (although such data items can be assigned mnemonic names).

- The programmer must take a microscopic view of a task, breaking it down into tiny subtasks—ADD, COMPARE, INCREMENT—that direct what is going on in individual memory locations and registers.

- An assembly language program is machine specific.

- Statements are not natural-language-like (although operations are given mnemonic code words as an improvement over a string of bits).

We would like to overcome these deficiencies, and *high-level programming languages* were created to do just that. Thus, we have the following expectations of a program written in a high-level language:

- The programmer need not manage the details of the movement of data items within memory or pay any attention to exactly where those items are stored.

- The programmer can take a macroscopic view of tasks, thinking at a higher level of problem solving (add B and C, and call the result A). The "primitive operations" used as building blocks in algorithm construction (see Chapter 1) can be larger.

- Programs are portable rather than machine specific.

- Programming statements are closer to natural language and use standard mathematical notation.

High-level programming languages are often called third-generation languages, reflecting the progression from machine language (first generation) to assembly language (second generation) to high-level language. They are another step along the continuum shown in Chapter 6, Figure 6.3. This also suggests what by now you have suspected: We've reached another layer of abstraction, another virtual environment designed to further distance us from the low-level hardware components of the machine.

9.1.2 Getting Back to Binary

There is a price to pay for this higher level of abstraction. When we moved from machine language to assembly language, we needed a piece of system software—an assembler—to translate assembly language instructions into binary machine language instructions (object code). This was necessary because the computer itself—that is, the collection of electronic devices—can respond only to machine language instructions. Now that we have moved up another layer with regard to the language in which we communicate, we need a different type of translator to convert our high-level language instructions into machine language instructions. This new type of translator is called a *compiler*. Rather than doing the entire translation job right down to object code, a compiler often translates high-level language instructions (source code) only into assembly language (the hard part of the translation). It then turns the final (simple) translation job over to an assembler that finishes the task by converting the assembly language into binary, exactly as we showed in Chapter 6.

Some tasks (e.g., sorting and searching) need to be performed often, as part of solving other problems. The code for such a useful task can be written as a group of high-level language instructions and thoroughly tested to be sure it is correct. Then the object code for the task can be stored in a code library. A program can just request that a copy of this object code be included along with its own object code. A piece of system software called a linker inserts requested object code from code libraries into the object code for the requesting program. The resulting object code is often called an executable module. Thus, a high-level program might go through the transitions shown in Figure 9.1. Compare this with Figure 6.4.

FIGURE 9.1

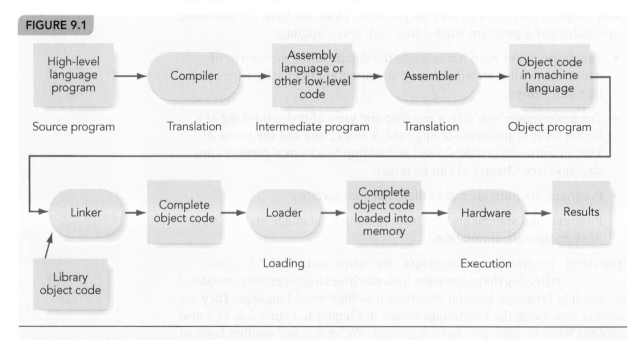

Transitions of a high-level language program

The work of the compiler is discussed in more detail in Chapter 11. Let us note here, however, that the compiler has a much tougher job than the assembler. An assembler has a one-for-one translation task because each assembly language instruction corresponds to at most one machine language instruction. A single high-level programming language instruction, on the other hand—precisely because a high-level language is more expressive than assembly language—can "explode" into many assembly language instructions.

9.2 A Family of Languages

Most of today's popular high-level programming languages fall into the same philosophical family; they are procedural languages (also called imperative languages). A program written in a procedural language consists of sequences of statements that manipulate data items. The programmer's task is to devise the appropriate step-by-step sequence of "imperative commands"—instructions in the programming language—that, when carried out by the computer, accomplish the desired task.

Procedural languages follow directly from the Von Neumann computer architecture described in Chapter 5, an architecture characterized by sequential fetch-decode-execute cycles. A random access memory stores and fetches values to and from memory cells. Thus, it makes sense to design a language whose most fundamental operations are storing and retrieving data values. For example,

```
a = 1;          //store the value 1 in location a
c = a + b;      //retrieve a and b, add, store the result
                //in location c
```

Even though a high-level programming language allows the programmer to think of memory locations in abstract rather than physical terms, the programmer is still directing, via program instructions, every change in the value of a memory location.

Ada, C++, C#, Java, and Python Online Chapters

To explore programming through the lens of a particular programming language, and to get a sense of what programming in a high-level language is like, try one or more of the online language chapters found on the companion site for this text (*www.cengage.com*) and in the MindTap. Each chapter includes language-specific exercises and practice problems.

The languages we have chosen to discuss from this procedural language family are Ada, C++, C#, Java, and Python. These languages differ in the rules (the syntax) for exactly how statements must be written and in the meaning (semantics) of correctly written statements. Rather than fill up pages and pages of this book with the details of each of these languages, we've created online chapters for you to investigate the language(s) of your choice (or your instructor's choice) in much more detail than you will see here. See the Special Interest Box on the previous page for information on accessing these online chapters.

9.3 Two Examples in Five-Part Harmony

At this point you might (or might not) have studied one or more of the online chapters for Ada, C++, C#, Java, or Python. In either case, you might be interested to see how these languages are similar and how they differ. In this section, we'll look at two sample problems and their solutions in each of the five languages. Don't be overly concerned about the details; just try to get the "big picture" in each of these solutions.

9.3.1 Favorite Number

Our first problem is trivially simple. Nonetheless, it will allow you to observe some of the significant syntactic differences in these five languages. A pseudocode version is shown in Figure 9.2.

Next, we show this same algorithm implemented in Ada (Figure 9.3), C++ (Figure 9.4), C# (Figure 9.5), Java (Figure 9.6), and Python (Figure 9.7). The program code in each figure is easily recognizable as a formalized version of the pseudocode—it uses some mechanism to get the user's favorite number, then sets the value of n to $n + 1$, and finally writes the output. The syntax, however, varies with the language. In particular, each language has its own way of reading input (from the keyboard), performing a computation, and writing output (to the screen). There's also a variation in the amount of "startup" code required to get to the actual algorithm implementation part. Each language has a notation (--, //, or #) that denotes a program comment, and each language has its own set of special "punctuation marks." For example, four of the five languages (Python being the exception) require a semicolon to terminate an executable program statement.

FIGURE 9.2

1. Get value for the user's favorite number, n
2. Increase n by 1
3. Print a message and the new value of n

Pseudocode algorithm for favorite number

FIGURE 9.3

```
--Ada program for the
--favorite number algorithm

WITH TEXT_IO;

PROCEDURE FavoriteNumber IS
  PACKAGE INT_IO IS NEW TEXT_IO.INTEGER_IO(INTEGER);

       n : INTEGER;                --user's favorite number

BEGIN
  --Get the user's favorite number
  TEXT_IO.PUT("What is your favorite number? ");
  INT_IO.GET(n);

  --Compute the next number
  n := n + 1;

  --Write the output
  TEXT_IO.NEW_LINE;
  TEXT_IO.PUT("My favorite number is 1 more than that, ");
  INT_IO.PUT(n, 4);
  TEXT_IO.NEW_LINE;
  TEXT_IO.NEW_LINE;
END FavoriteNumber;
```

Ada program for favorite number

FIGURE 9.4

```
//C++ program for the
//favorite number algorithm

#include <iostream>
using namespace std;

void main()
{
    int n;     //user's favorite number

    //get the user's favorite number
    cout << "What is your favorite number? ";
    cin  >> n;
```

C++ program for favorite number (*continues*)

FIGURE 9.4 (CONTINUED)

```cpp
     //compute the next number
     n = n + 1;

     //write the output
     cout << endl;
     cout << "My favorite number is 1 more than that, "
          << n << endl;
     cout << endl << endl;
}
```

C++ program for favorite number

FIGURE 9.5

```csharp
//C# program for the
//favorite number algorithm

using System;

namespace InvitationCSharp

{
    class FavoriteNumber
    {
        static void Main(string[] args)
        {
            int n;  //user's favorite number

            //get the user's favorite number
            Console.Write("What is your favorite number? ");
            n = Convert.ToInt32(Console.ReadLine());

            //compute the next number
            n = n + 1;

            //write the output
            Console.WriteLine();
            Console.Write("My favorite number is ");
            Console.WriteLine("1 more than that, " + n);
            Console.WriteLine();
            Console.WriteLine();
        }
    }
}
```

C# program for favorite number

FIGURE 9.6

```java
//Java program for the
//favorite number algorithm

import java.util.*;
public class FavoriteNumber
{
    public static void main(String[] args)
    {
        int n;             //user's favorite number
        Scanner inp = new Scanner(System.in);    //to read input

        //get the user's favorite number
        System.out.print("What is your favorite number? ");
        n = inp.nextInt();

        //compute the next number
        n = n + 1;

        //write the output
        System.out.println();
        System.out.println("My favorite number is 1 more "
            + "than that, " + n);
        System.out.println();
        System.out.println();
    }
}
```

Java program for favorite number

FIGURE 9.7

```python
#Python program for the
#favorite number algorithm

#get the user's favorite number
n = int(input("What is your favorite number? "))

#compute the next number
n = n + 1

#write the output
print()
print("My favorite number is 1 more than that,", n)

#finish up
input("\n\nPress the Enter key to exit");
```

Python program for favorite number

9.3.2 Data Cleanup (Again)

Now that you've seen a bare-bones sample for each language, let's implement a solution to a considerably more interesting problem. In Chapter 3, we discussed several algorithms to solve the data cleanup problem. In this problem, the input is a set of integer data values (answers to a particular question on a survey, for example) that may contain 0s, although 0s are considered invalid data. The output is to be a clean data set where the 0s have been eliminated. Figure 9.8 is a copy of Figure 3.16. It shows the pseudocode for the converging-pointers data cleanup algorithm, the most time- and space-efficient of the three data cleanup algorithms from Chapter 3.

Our pseudocode does not specify the details of how to "get values." In the favorite number example, the single input value was entered at the keyboard. The survey data, however, is probably already stored in an electronic file. It might have been collected via an online survey that captured the responses or via paper forms that have been scanned to capture the data in digital form. Designing our programs to read input data from a file, however, is a bit more than we want to get into, so we'll again assume the input data is typed in at the keyboard.

The pseudocode algorithm of Figure 9.8 is implemented in Ada (Figure 9.9), C++ (Figure 9.10), C# (Figure 9.11), Java (Figure 9.12), and Python (Figure 9.13).

As with the previous, simpler example, you can see that each program follows the outline of the pseudocode algorithm. Each language supports if statements and while loops. The extent of the while loop is denoted by curly

---

FIGURE 9.8

1. Get values for *n* and the *n* data items
2. Set the value of *legit* to *n*
3. Set the value of *left* to 1
4. Set the value of *right* to *n*
5. While *left* is less than *right* do Steps 6 through 10
6.   If the item at position *left* is not 0 then increase *left* by 1
7.   Else (the item at position *left* is 0) do Steps 8 through 10
8.   Reduce *legit* by 1
9.   Copy the item at position *right* into position *left*
10.   Reduce *right* by 1
11. If the item at position *left* is 0, then reduce *legit* by 1
12. Stop

The converging-pointers algorithm for data cleanup

FIGURE 9.9

```ada
--Ada program for the converging-pointers
--data cleanup algorithm

WITH TEXT_IO;

PROCEDURE DataCleanup IS
  PACKAGE INT_IO IS NEW TEXT_IO.INTEGER_IO(INTEGER);

    maxList : constant := 50;   --maximum list size
    n : INTEGER;                --max number of data elements
                                --in list
    data : array(0..maxList - 1) of INTEGER; --create the empty
                                             --list
    i : INTEGER;               --index variable
    left : INTEGER;            --algorithm left pointer into
                               --the list
    right: INTEGER;            --algorithm right pointer
                               --into the list
    legit: INTEGER;            --counts number of legitimate
                               --(nonzero) data values

BEGIN
  --Get the values for n and the n data items
  TEXT_IO.PUT("How many numbers are in the list? (maximum is ");
  INT_IO.PUT(maxList,2);
  TEXT_IO.PUT(") ");
  INT_IO.GET(n);

  i := 0;
  TEXT_IO.PUT("Enter the first number: ");
  INT_IO.GET(data(i));

  while i < n - 1
   loop
    i := i + 1;
    TEXT_IO.PUT("Enter next number: ");
    INT_IO.GET(data(i));
   end loop;

  --Set the value of legit, left, and right
  legit := n - 1;
  left := 0;
  right := n - 1;

  TEXT_IO.NEW_LINE;
  TEXT_IO.PUT("The original list is: ");
```

Ada converging-pointers algorithm (*continues*)

FIGURE 9.9 (CONTINUED)

```
i := 0;
while i <= legit
 loop
   INT_IO.PUT(data(i), 4);
   i := i + 1;
 end loop;
TEXT_IO.NEW_LINE;
TEXT_IO.NEW_LINE;

--move the pointers together,
--swapping value at right for 0 at left

while left < right
 loop
   if data(left)/= 0
    then
     left := left + 1;
    else
     legit := legit - 1;
     data(left) := data(right);
     right := right - 1;
   end if;
 end loop;
if data(left) = 0
 then
   legit := legit - 1;
end if;

--final output
TEXT_IO.PUT("The cleaned list is: ");

i := 0;
while i <= legit
 loop
   INT_IO.PUT(data(i), 4);
   i := i + 1;
 end loop;
TEXT_IO.NEW_LINE;

END DataCleanup;
```

Ada converging-pointers algorithm

braces { } in three of the languages, by *loop ... end loop* in Ada, and (although this is less evident) by a colon and indentation in Python. There are several different ways of creating the memory space to hold the list of data values. And, as we saw before, each language does I/O (from keyboard to screen) using different syntax, and requires different "startup" code. But the output of each version looks like Figure 9.14, where boldface indicates user input.

FIGURE 9.10

```cpp
//C++ program for the converging-pointers
//data cleanup algorithm

#include <iostream>
using namespace std;

void main()
{
    const int MAXLIST = 50;          //maximum list size
    int n;               //max number of data elements in list
    int data[MAXLIST]; //create the empty list
    int i;               //index variable
    int left, right;     //algorithm pointers into the list
    int legit;           //counts number of legitimate (nonzero)
                         //data values

    //Get the values for n and the n data items
    cout << "How many numbers are in the list? ";
    cout << "(maximum is " << MAXLIST << ") ";
    cin >> n;

    i = 0;
    cout << "Enter the first number: ";
    cin >> data[i];

    while (i < n - 1)
    {
        i = i + 1;
        cout << "Enter next number: ";
        cin >> data[i];
    }

    //Set the value of legit, left, and right
    legit = n - 1;
    left = 0;
    right = n - 1;

    cout << endl;
    cout << "The original list is" << endl;

    i = 0;
    while (i <= legit)
    {
        cout << data[i] << " ";
        i = i + 1;
    }
    cout << endl << endl;

    //move the pointers together,
    //swapping value at right for 0 at left
```

C++ converging-pointers algorithm (*continues*)

FIGURE 9.10 (CONTINUED)

```
    while (left < right)
    {
        if (data[left] != 0)
            left = left + 1;
        else
        {
            legit = legit - 1;
            data[left] = data[right];
            right = right - 1;
        }
    }
    if (data[left] == 0)
            legit = legit - 1;

    //final output
    cout << "The cleaned list is" << endl;
    i = 0;
    while (i <= legit)
    {
        cout << data[i] << " ";
        i = i + 1;
    }
    cout << endl << endl;

}
```

C++ converging-pointers algorithm

FIGURE 9.11

```
//C# program for the converging-pointers
//data cleanup algorithm

using System;

namespace InvitationCSharp
{
    class DataCleanup
    {
        static void Main(string[] args)
        {
            const int maxList = 50;       //maximum list size
            int n;                        //max number of data
                                          //elements in list
            int[] data = new int[maxList]; //create the empty
                                           //list
            int i;                        //index variable
```

C# converging-pointers algorithm (*continues*)

FIGURE 9.11 (CONTINUED)

```
int left, right;            //algorithm pointers
                            //into the list
int legit;                  //counts number of
                            //legitimate
                            //(nonzero) data
                            //values

//Get the values for n and the n data items
Console.Write("How many numbers are in the list? ");
Console.Write("(maximum is " + maxList + ") ");
n = Convert.ToInt32(Console.ReadLine());

i = 0;
Console.Write("Enter the first number: ");
data[i] = Convert.ToInt32(Console.ReadLine());

while (i < n - 1)
{
    i = i + 1;
    Console.Write("Enter next number: ");
    data[i] = Convert.ToInt32(Console.ReadLine());
}

//Set the value of legit, left, and right
legit = n - 1;
left = 0;
right = n - 1;

Console.WriteLine();
Console.WriteLine("The original list is");

i = 0;
while (i <= legit)
{
    Console.Write(data[i] + " ");
    i = i + 1;
}
Console.WriteLine();
Console.WriteLine();

//move the pointers together,
//swapping value at right for 0 at left

while (left < right)
{
    if (data[left] != 0)
        left = left + 1;
    else
```

C# converging-pointers algorithm (*continues*)

FIGURE 9.11 (CONTINUED)

```
                {
                    legit = legit - 1;
                    data[left] = data[right];
                    right = right - 1;
                }
            }
            if (data[left] == 0)
                legit = legit - 1;

            //final output
            Console.WriteLine("The cleaned list is");
            i = 0;
            while (i <= legit)
            {
                Console.Write(data[i] + " ");
                i = i + 1;
            }
            Console.WriteLine();
            Console.WriteLine();
        }
    }
}
```

C# converging-pointers algorithm

FIGURE 9.12

```
//Java program for the converging-pointers
//data cleanup algorithm

import java.util.*;
public class DataCleanup
{
    public static void main(String[] args)
    {
        final int MAXLIST = 50;          //maximum list size
        int n;                           //max number of data
                                         //elements
                                         //in the list
        int[] data = new int[MAXLIST];   //create the empty list
        int i;                           //index variable
        int left, right;                 //algorithm pointers
                                         //into the list
        int legit;                       //counts number of
                                         //legitimate (nonzero)
                                         //data values
```

Java converging-pointers algorithm (*continues*)

FIGURE 9.12 (CONTINUED)

```java
Scanner inp = new Scanner(System.in);  //to read input


//Get the values for n and the n data items
System.out.print("How many numbers are in the list? ");
System.out.print(" (maximum is " + MAXLIST + ") ");
n = inp.nextInt();

i = 0;
System.out.print("Enter the first number: ");
data[i] = inp.nextInt();

 while (i < n - 1)
 {
     i = i + 1;
     System.out.print("Enter next number: ");
     data[i] = inp.nextInt();
 }

 //Set the value of legit, left, and right
 legit = n - 1;
 left = 0;
 right = n - 1;

 System.out.println();
 System.out.println("The original list is");

 i = 0;
 while (i <= legit)
 {
     System.out.print(data[i] + " ");
     i = i + 1;
 }
 System.out.println();
 System.out.println();

 //move the pointers together,
 //swapping value at right for 0 at left

while (left < right)
{
    if (data[left] != 0)
        left = left + 1;
    else
    {
        legit = legit - 1;
        data[left] = data[right];
        right = right - 1;
    }
}
```

Java converging-pointers algorithm (*continues*)

FIGURE 9.12 (CONTINUED)

```java
        if (data[left] == 0)
            legit = legit - 1;

        //final output
        System.out.println("The cleaned list is");
                i = 0;
        while (i <= legit)
        {
            System.out.print(data[i] + " ");
            i = i + 1;
        }

        System.out.println();
    }
}
```

Java converging-pointers algorithm

FIGURE 9.13

```python
#Python program for the converging-pointers
#data cleanup algorithm

#Get the values for n and the n data items
n = int(input("How many numbers are in the list: "))
data = []   #create an empty list

i = 0
number = int(input("Enter first number: "))
data.append(number)   #append a value to the data list
while i < n - 1:
    i = i + 1
    number = int(input("Enter next number: "))
    data.append(number)

#Set the value of legit, left, and right
legit = n - 1
left = 0
right = n - 1

print()
print("The original list is")
i = 0
while i <= legit:
    print(data[i],end=" ")
    i = i + 1
print()
```

Python converging-pointers algorithm (*continues*)

FIGURE 9.13 (CONTINUED)

```
print()

#move the pointers together,
#swapping value at right for 0 at left

while left < right:
    if data[left] != 0:
        left = left + 1
    else:
        legit = legit - 1
        data[left] = data[right]
        right = right - 1
if data[left] == 0:
    legit = legit - 1

#final output
print("The cleaned list is")
i = 0
while i <= legit:
    print(data[i], end=" ")
    i = i + 1

#finish up
input("\n\nPress the Enter key to exit");
```

Python converging-pointers algorithm

FIGURE 9.14

```
How many numbers are in the list? (maximum is 50) 10
Enter the first number: 0
Enter next number: 24
Enter next number: 16
Enter next number: 0
Enter next number: 36
Enter next number: 42
Enter next number: 23
Enter next number: 21
Enter next number: 0
Enter next number: 27

The original list is
0 24 16 0 36 42 23 21 0 27

The cleaned list is
27 24 16 21 36 42 23
```

Output from the various data cleanup implementations

Each of the five languages supports many more programming features than are shown in these simple examples. Consult the online language chapters for more in-depth programming concepts (including functions, parameter passing, object-oriented programming, and graphical programming) supported by each of these languages.

9.4 Feature Analysis

If you have studied one (or more) of the online chapters for Ada, C++, C#, Java, or Python, then the "features" of that programming language will be familiar to you. You can compare them with the features of the other languages by scanning Figure 9.15 starting on page 456. If you haven't studied any of these languages in detail, the figure will still give you a brief reference on each of them. Figure 9.15 compares only the features that are included in the online chapter for each language, so it should not be viewed as a comprehensive list of features for any of these languages.[2]

9.5 Meeting Expectations

At the beginning of this chapter, we gave four expectations for programs written in a high-level programming language. Now that we have been introduced to the essentials of writing programs in such a language, it is time to see how well these expectations have been met.

1. *The programmer need not manage the details of the movement of data items within memory or pay any attention to exactly where those items are stored.* The programmer's only responsibilities are to declare (or in the case of Python, create) all constants and variables the program will use. This involves selecting identifiers—that is, symbolic names—to represent the various data items and indicating the data type of each, either in the declaration statement or, in the case of Python, in an assignment statement. The identifiers can be descriptive names that meaningfully relate the data to the problem being solved. Data values are moved as necessary within memory by program instructions that simply reference these identifiers, without the programmer knowing which specific memory locations contain which values, or what value currently exists in an ALU register. The concepts of memory address and movement between memory and the ALU, along with the effort of generating constant data values, have disappeared.

2. *The programmer can take a macroscopic view of tasks, thinking at a higher level of problem solving.* Instead of moving data values here and there and carefully orchestrating the limited operations available at the machine language or assembly language level, the programmer can, for example, write the formula to compute the circumference of a circle given

---

[2]For example, each of these languages supports a for-loop (counting loop), but this was not discussed in the online chapters and is not included in Figure 9.15.

its radius. The details of how the instruction is carried out—how the data values are moved about and exactly how the multiplication of real number values is done—are handled elsewhere. Compare the power of conditional and looping instructions—which are tools for algorithmic problem solving and resemble the operations with which we constructed algorithms in pseudocode—with the assembly language instructions LOAD, STORE, JUMP, and so on, which are tools for data and memory management.

3. *Programs written in a high-level language will be portable rather than machine specific.* Program developers use a variety of approaches to make their programs portable to different platforms. For programs written in most high-level languages, the program developer runs through the entire translation process to produce an executable module (complete object code) as shown in Figure 9.1, and it is the executable module that is sold to the user, who runs it on his or her own machine. The program developer doesn't usually give the user the source code to the program, for a multitude of reasons. First, the program developer does not want to give away the secrets of how the program works by revealing the code to someone who could make a tiny modification and then sell this "new" program. Second, the program developer wants to prevent the user from being able to change the code, rendering a perfectly good program useless, and then complaining that the software is defective. And finally, if the program developer distributes the source code, then all users must have their own translators to get the executable module needed to run on their own machines.

The developer can compile the program on any kind of machine as long as there is a compiler on that machine for the language in which the program is written. However, there must be a compiler for each (high-level language, machine-type) pair. If the program is written in C++, for example, and the program developer wants to sell his or her program to be used on a variety of computers, he or she needs to compile the same program on a Windows PC using a C++ compiler for the PC, on a Mac using a C++ compiler for the Mac, and so on, to produce all the various object code versions. The program itself is independent of the details of each particular computer's machine language because each compiler takes care of the translation. This is the "portability" we seek from high-level language programs.

Even the availability of the appropriate compiler may not guarantee that a program developed on one type of machine can be compiled on a different type of machine. Each programming language has a certain core of instructions that are considered standard. Any respectable compiler for that language must support that core. In fact, national and international standards groups such as ANSI (American National Standards Institute) and ISO (International Organization for Standardization), which develop standards for an incredible number of things, also develop standards for programming languages. Compilers are thus built to support "ANSI-standard language X." However, there are often useful features or types of instructions that are not considered a standard part of the language and that some compilers support and some do not. If a program is

FIGURE 9.15

Feature	Ada	C++	C#
Comment	--	//	//
Include object code from code libraries	WITH WITH TEXT_IO;	#include <> #include <iostream> using namespace std;	using using System;
Statement terminator	;	;	;
Statement continuation character	N/A	N/A	N/A
Block delimiter	keyword pairs BEGIN ... END loop ... end_loop then ... else ... endif	{...}	{...}
Free format	yes	yes	yes
Case sensitive	no	yes	yes
Reserved words	yes (BEGIN, INTEGER, FLOAT, ...)	yes (void, double, ...)	yes (void, double, ...)
Identifiers	letters, digits, or underscore; must begin with a letter; cannot be a reserved word	letters, digits, or underscore; cannot begin with a digit; cannot be a reserved word	letters, digits, or underscore; cannot begin with a digit; cannot be a reserved word
Named constants	yes	yes	yes
Declarations	before use, in declarative portion of procedure or function speed : INTEGER;	before use, generally at the top of a function int speed;	before use, generally at the top of a function int speed;
Strong typing	yes	yes	yes
Implicit (automatic) typecasting	no	yes—int to double in input, assignment, arithmetic expressions	yes—int to double in input, assignment, arithmetic expressions
Explicit typecasting	yes FLOAT(number)	yes double(number)	yes Convert.To Double(number)
Primitive data types			
Integer	INTEGER	int	int
Decimal	FLOAT	double	double
Character	CHARACTER	char	char
String			

Feature analysis of five high-level languages (examples in blue) (*continues*)

FIGURE 9.15 (CONTINUED)

Java	Python
//	#
import import java.util.*;	import import math
;	end of line unless followed by statement continuation character
N/A	\
{...}	: followed by indentation
yes	no, due to indentation signifying blocks of code
yes	yes
yes (class, public, ...)	yes (if, while, ...)
letters, digits, or underscore; cannot begin with a digit; cannot be a reserved word	letters, digits, or underscore; cannot begin with a digit; cannot be a reserved word
yes	no
before use, generally at the top of a method int speed;	no—variable is created when a value is assigned to it
yes	no—variable assumes data type of value assigned to it
yes—int to double in input, assignment, arithmetic expressions	yes—assignment statement sets data type of variable; int to float in arithmetic expressions
yes (double)number	yes float(number)
int	int
double	float
char	
	string

Feature analysis of five high-level languages (examples in blue) (*continues*)

FIGURE 9.15 (CONTINUED)

Feature	Ada	C++	C#
Composite data type	array	array	array
Literal string	yes—enclose in " "	yes—enclose in " "	yes—enclose in " "
String concatenation	&		+
Input from keyboard	INT_IO.GET(...); requires I/O package for integers FLO_IO.GET (...); requires I/O package for floating-point numbers TEXT_IO.GET(...)	cin >> cin >> number;	Console.ReadLine() returns a string; typecast to numeric data type if needed
Output to screen	INT_IO.PUT(...); requires I/O package for integers FLO_IO.PUT(...); requires I/O package for floating-point numbers TEXT_IO.PUT(...);	cout << cout << number;	Console.Write(string); or Console.WriteLine(string);
Output formatting	yes FLO_IO.PUT(time, 5, 2, 0);	yes cout.setf(ios::fixed); cout.precision(2);	yes time.ToString("#.##")
Assignment operator	:=	=	=
Arithmetic operators	+, -, *, /, mod, **	+, -, *, /, %	+, -, *, /, %
Comparison operators	=, <, <= , >, >=, /=	==, <, <=, >, >=, !=	==, <, <=, >, >=, !=
Boolean operators	and, or, not	&&, ||, !	&&, ||, !
Control structures			
Conditional	if ... or if ... then then ... ... else endif; ... end if;	if ( ) or if ( ) {...} {...} else {...}	if ( ) or if ( ) {...} {...} else {...}
Looping	while ... or loop loop ... ... exit when ... ; end loop; end loop;	while ( ) or do {...} {...} while( );	while ( ) or do {...} {...} while( );

Feature analysis of five high-level languages (examples in blue) (*continues*)

FIGURE 9.15 (CONTINUED)

Java	Python
array	list
yes—enclose in " "	yes—enclose in " "
+	+
use the Scanner class method Scanner inp = new Scanner(System.in); number = inp.nextInt();	input ("prompt") returns a string; typecast to numeric data type if needed
System.out.print(string); or System.out.println(string);	print(string)
yes import java.text.*; DecimalFormat p = new DecimalFormat("0.00"); System.out.println(p.format(time));	yes print("%5.2f" % time)
=	=
+, -, *, /, %	+, -, *, /, //, %
==, <, <=, >, >=, !=	==, <, <=, >, >=, !=
&&, ||, !	and, or, not

if ( ) or if ( )
{...}   {...}
else
{...}
	if ... : or if ... :
	   ... ...
	else:
	   ...
	(colon and indentation required)

while ( ) or do
{...}   {...}
        while ( );
	while ... : or while True:
	   ... ...
	        if ... :
	           break
	(colon and indentation required)

Feature analysis of five high-level languages (examples in blue) (*continues*)

FIGURE 9.15 (CONTINUED)

Feature	Ada	C++	C#
Modularity	via functions and procedures, which are nested within other functions or procedures	via functions	via functions
Local scope	yes—variables declared within functions or procedures are known only there	yes—variables declared within functions are known only there	yes—variables declared within functions are known only there
Arguments/ Parameters	yes—must match in number, order, data type	yes—must match in number, order, data type	yes—must match in number, order, data type
Parameter passing	default: pass by value (or use *in* in parameter list) Use *out* or *in out* in parameter list for pass by reference	default: pass by value Use & in parameter list for pass by reference	default: pass by value Use *ref* in both parameter list and argument list for pass by reference
Math-like module (computes and returns a single value)	keyword FUNCTION in header, give returned data type in function header, return statement with computed expression in function body	give returned data type in function header, return statement with computed expression in function body	give returned data type in function header, return statement with computed expression in function body
Procedure-like module	keyword PROCEDURE in header	use *void* in function header	use *void* in function header
Object-oriented programming	supported via tagged record type	supported	required—everything is part of a class
Class terminology	object properties; primitive operations	member variables, member functions	member variables, member functions
Scope	object properties are private, primitive operations are public	public—known everywhere private—known only within class protected—known within class and subclass	public—known everywhere private—known only within class protected—known within class and subclass
Module invocation	module-identifier(object-identifier, argument list)	object-identifier.function-identifier(argument list)	object-identifier.function-identifier(argument list); static function can be invoked without an object
Inheritance	yes	yes	yes
Separate compilation	yes	yes	yes

Feature analysis of five high-level languages (examples in blue) (*continues*)

FIGURE 9.15 (CONTINUED)

Java	Python
via methods	via functions
yes—variables declared within methods are known only there	yes—variables declared within functions are known only there
yes—must match in number, order, data type	yes—must match in number and order; parameters will pick up passed data type
pass by value	the effect of pass by value is achieved if the function invocation is a stand-alone statement (changing the parameter value by an assignment statement creates a new local variable and does not change the original argument value); the effect of pass by reference is to invoke the function on the right side of an assignment statement and send the changed value(s) back via a return statement
give returned data type in method header, return statement with computed expression in method body	return statement with computed expression in function body
use *void* in method header; no values returned to invoking module	use no return statement or use return statement with multiple values where function invocation is on the right side of assignment statement
required—everything is part of a class	supported
instance variables, instance methods	attributes, methods
public static instance method—known everywhere, public instance method—known everywhere, private instance variable or instance method—known only within class	class methods are public class attributes are public by default; they are "semi-private" if declared with __ before the identifier, but still can be referenced anywhere if class name is used, as in swimmingPool_Circle__radius

for public static:
  class-identifier.method-identifier(argument list)
for public:
  object-identifier.method-identifier(argument list)
	object-identifier.method-identifier(argument list); "self" must be first parameter in method parameter list

yes	yes
required—must have separate file for each class	yes

Feature analysis of five high-level languages (examples in blue)

written to take advantage of some of these extra features that are available on a particular compiler—often referred to as extensions, or "bells and whistles"—the program might not work with a different compiler that does not support these extensions. The price for using nonstandard features is the risk of sacrificing portability.

The standardization process (for anything, including a programming language) is necessarily a slow one because it seeks to satisfy the interests of a number of groups, such as consumers, industry, and government. If official standardization comes too late, it must bow to what may have become a de facto standard by common usage. If standardization is imposed too early, it may thwart the development of new ideas or technology.

Newer languages such as Java and C# were developed specifically to run on a variety of hardware platforms without the need for a separate compiler for each type of machine. A compiler for Java or C# translates the source code program into very low-level code (called *bytecode* in Java and *Microsoft Intermediate Language* in C#). The resulting programs are not machine-language code for any real machine, but rather for an "idealized" virtual machine. The machine language for this virtual machine can easily be translated into any specific machine language. The program developer only needs to do one compilation to produce low-level virtual machine code and then distribute this virtual machine code to the various users. The final translation/execution of this virtual code into the machine language of a particular user's machine is done by a small piece of software on the user's machine (a Java bytecode interpreter for Java or a Just In Time compiler for C#).

The Python language takes a still different approach to portability. A Python program is *interpreted* rather than compiled, which means that it is translated from source code into object code every time it is executed. As a consequence, each user's machine has to have a Python interpreter, but such an interpreter is available for virtually every operating system, and is small, quick, and free. Python is an open source programming language. The open source philosophy is based on the belief that better software is developed if a large group of individuals can examine and modify the code; essentially, "the more eyes, the merrier." The open source movement has attracted many skilled and dedicated people who, usually working for free, are motivated by the goals of producing high-quality software and working cooperatively with like-minded individuals. In the spirit of open source code development, Python developers are happy to send their source code to users. (Other well-known open source programming projects include the online encyclopedia Wikipedia and the Mozilla Firefox browser.)

4. *Programming statements in a high-level language will be closer to natural language and will use standard mathematical notation.* High-level languages provide us with statements that give natural implementations of pseudocode instructions such as "while condition do something ..." or "if condition do something ...." Although pseudocode is still somewhat stilted, it is nonetheless close to natural language. We can also use standard mathematical notation such as $A + B$ and $A > B$.

9.6 The Big Picture: Software Engineering

Because any high-level language program ultimately must be translated by a compiler or interpreter, there are very stringent syntax rules about punctuation, use of keywords, and so on for each program statement. If something about a program statement cannot be understood by the compiler, then the compiler cannot translate the program into machine language; if the compiler cannot translate the program, you get an error message and the program's instructions cannot be executed. For novice programmers this can happen many times during the development of new software. This obstacle leads beginning programming students to conclude that the bulk of the effort in the software development process should be devoted to implementation—that is, restating an algorithm in terms of computer code and ridding that code of all syntax errors so that it finally executes.

In fact, implementation represents a relatively small part of the software development life cycle—the overall sequence of steps needed to complete a large-scale software project. Studies have shown that on big projects (system software such as operating systems or compilers, for example, or large applications such as a program to manage an investment company's portfolio), the initial implementation of the program may occupy only 10–20% of the total time spent by programmers and designers. About 25–40% of their time is spent on problem specification and program design—important planning steps that must be completed prior to implementation. Another 40–65% is spent on the tasks that follow implementation—reviewing, modifying, fixing, and improving the original code and writing finished documentation. Although there is no universal agreement on the exact sequence of steps in the software development life cycle, Figure 9.16 summarizes one possible breakdown. We'll discuss each of these steps shortly.

FIGURE 9.16

1. Before Implementation
   a. Feasibility study
   b. Problem specification
   c. Program design
   d. Algorithm selection or development, and analysis
2. Implementation
   a. Coding
   b. Debugging
3. After Implementation
   a. Testing, verification, and benchmarking
   b. Documentation
   c. Maintenance

Steps in the software development life cycle

Beginning programming students might not see or appreciate the entire software development life cycle because the programming assignments usually solved in introductory classes are extremely and unrealistically small. This can create a skewed and misleading view of the software development process. It is somewhat akin to a civil engineering student building a matchstick bridge that is just a couple of inches long; a multitude of new problems must be addressed when that task is scaled up to a full-sized, real-life bridge.

9.6.1 Scaling Up

The programs that students write in an introductory course may have 50–100 lines of code. Even by the end of the course, programs are usually not longer than a few hundred lines. However, real-world programs are often orders of magnitude larger. Compilers or some operating systems contain many thousands of lines. Truly large software systems, such as the NASA Space Shuttle ground control system and the data management system of the U.S. Census Bureau, may require the development of millions of lines of code. To give you an idea of how very large that is, a printed listing of a 1-million-line program would be almost 17,000 pages long—about the size of 50 books. The difference in complexity between a million-line software package and a 100-line homework assignment is equivalent to the difference in scale between a 300-page novel and a single sentence!

Figure 9.17 categorizes software products in terms of size, the number of programmers needed for development, and the duration of the development effort. These numbers are very rough approximations, but they give you an idea of the size of some widely used software packages. Analogous building construction projects are also listed.

Virtually all software products developed for the marketplace are neither trivial nor small. Most fall instead into either the Medium or the Large category of Figure 9.17. The Very Large and Extremely Large categories are enormous intellectual enterprises. It would be impossible to develop correct and maintainable software systems of that size without extensive planning and design, just as it is impossible to build a 50-story skyscraper without paying a great deal of attention to initial project planning and project management. Neither endeavor can be carried out by a single individual; a team development effort is essential in building software, just as in constructing buildings. Such projects also entail estimation of costs and budgets, personnel management, and scheduling issues, which are typical concerns for large engineering projects, and therefore the term software engineering is often applied to these large-scale software development projects.

9.6.2 The Software Development Life Cycle

Each step in the software development life cycle, as shown in Figure 9.16 and described in the following paragraphs, has its own purpose and activities. Each should also result in a written document that reflects past decisions and guides future actions. Keep in mind that every major software

FIGURE 9.17

Category	Typical Number of People	Typical Duration	Product Size in Lines of Code	Examples	Building Analogy
Trivial	1	1–2 weeks	< 500	Student homework assignments	Small home improvement
Small	1–3	A few weeks or months	500–2,000	Student team projects, advanced course assignments	Adding on a room
Medium	2–5	A few months to 1 year	2,000–10,000	Research projects, simple production software such as assemblers, editors, recreational and educational software	Single-family house
Large	5–25	1–3 years	10,000–100,000	Most current applications—word processors, spreadsheets, operating systems for small computers, compilers, iPhone apps	Small shopping mall
Very Large	25–100	3–5 years	100,000–1 M	Airline reservations systems, inventory control systems for multinational companies	Large office building
Extremely Large	> 100	> 5 years	> 1 M	Large-scale real-time operating systems, advanced military work, international telecommunications networks	Massive skyscraper

Size categories of software products

project is developed as a team effort, and these documents help keep various members of the team informed and working toward a common goal.

1. *The feasibility study*—The feasibility study evaluates a proposed project and compares the costs and benefits of various solutions. One choice might be to buy a new computer system for this project. Even though the cost of computer hardware has dropped dramatically, computers are still significant purchases. In addition to the costs of the machine itself, there may be costs for peripherals such as 3-D printers or telecommunications links. The costs of software (purchased or produced in-house); equipment maintenance; salary for developers or consultants, technical support people, and data entry

clerks—these must all be factored in, as must the costs incurred in training new users on the system. The overall cost of using a computer to solve a problem can be much higher than expected, and it can also be more than the value of the information produced. Other options should also be considered. Thus, the feasibility study should address the following question:

Vital Statistics for Real Code

The Windows operating system was created by Microsoft Corporation. Development of this system (originally called the Interface Manager) began in 1981. Subsequently renamed Microsoft Windows, the system was not released until November 1985, after 55 person-years of effort. Since then, there have been a number of evolutions. Each new version provided more and more services with a resulting expansion in the number of lines of source code (SLOC). Here is some sample data, including, for comparison, information from Chapter 6 (Special Interest Box, "Now That's Big") on Mac OS X Tiger 10.4, and on the Linux kernel version 4.1 operating system. (Google's Android operating system, common on many mobile phones, is based on the Linux kernel.)

Name	Release Date	Estimated SLOC (in millions)
Windows 3.1	1992	2.5
Windows 95	1995	8.0
Mac OS X Tiger 10.4	2005	86.0
Windows 7	2009	39.5
Windows 10	2015	50
Linux kernel v. 4.1	2015	20

Operating systems are not the only software packages that fall into the "massive skyscraper" (Extremely Large) category of Figure 9.17. Here are three other examples:

Name	Estimated SLOC (in millions)
Facebook	61
Software in a modern high-end automobile	100
Google Software Services (web search engine, Gmail, YouTube, etc.)	2000

(Continued)

This creeping code growth is a little more striking when viewed visually:

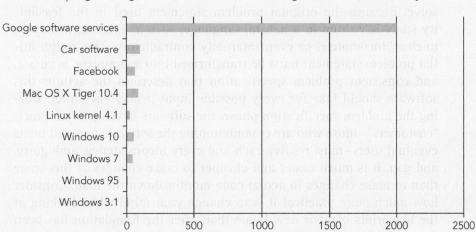

The complexity of software projects of this magnitude is breathtaking. Not only technical capabilities, but also planning, teamwork, communication, and management skills are vital to successful completion.

What are the relative costs and benefits of the following choices?

- Buying a new computer system and writing or buying software
- Writing new software for an existing computer system
- Purchasing the needed resources from a "cloud computing" provider (see Chapter 7)
- Outsourcing the work to a contractor
- Revising the current manual process for solving this problem
- Cutting back the scope of the project to better align it with existing resources
- Cancelling the project entirely and doing without the information that would be generated

At the end of the feasibility study, a *feasibility document* expresses the resulting recommendations. The creation of this document can be a very complex process involving considerations that are the provinces of business, law, management, economics, psychology, and accounting as well as computer science. The purpose of the feasibility study is to make all project stakeholders aware of the costs, risks, and benefits of various development paths as a guide to deciding which approach to use.

2. *Problem specification*—If it is determined that the project is feasible and will benefit from a computer solution, and that software development is to go forward, we move on to the problem specification

phase. Problem specification involves developing a clear, concise, and unambiguous statement of the exact problem the software is to solve. Because the original problem statement used in the feasibility study is written in a natural language, such as English, it may be unclear, incomplete, or even internally contradictory. This rough initial problem statement must be transformed into a complete, accurate, and consistent problem specification that describes the actions this software should take for every possible input it may encounter. During the problem specification phase, the software developers and their "customers"—those who are commissioning the software and will be its eventual users—must resolve each and every inconsistency, ambiguity, and gap. It is much easier and cheaper to make changes at this stage than to make changes in actual code months down the road. Consider how much more practical it is to change your mind when looking at the blueprints of your new home than after the foundation has been dug and the walls have started to go up.

The *problem specification document* expresses the final and complete problem specification and guides the software developers in all subsequent decisions. The specification document describes exactly how a program is to behave in all circumstances—not only in the majority of cases, but even under the most unusual and unexpected conditions. It contains a description of the data to be input to the program, the desired results to be computed, and instructions on how these results are to be displayed as output. It may also include limitations on the time allotted to produce those computations or on the amount of memory the program requires.

Once agreed to by the developer and the customer, the problem specification document becomes essentially a legal contract describing what the developer promises to provide and what the customer agrees to accept. Like a contract, it usually includes a delivery schedule and a price, and it is signed by both the customer and the developer.

3. *Program design*—Now that it is clear *what* is to be done, the program design phase is the time to plan *how* it is to be done. In a traditional programming approach, the divide-and-conquer strategy (also called top-down decomposition) comes into play. Tasks are broken down into subtasks, which are broken down into sub-subtasks, and so on, until each piece is small enough to code comfortably. These pieces work together to accomplish the overall job. In an object-oriented programming approach, the appropriate objects are identified, together with their data and the subtasks they must perform. This allows classes to be designed with variables to store the data, and functions (also called *methods*) to carry out these subtasks. Objects from these classes cooperate to accomplish the total job.

The larger the project, the more crucial it is to think of it in terms of smaller building blocks, or helpful classes, that are created separately and then properly assembled to solve the problem at hand. Although small programs of 50–100 lines can be thought of in one piece, 100,000-line programs cannot. However, it is possible to treat a 100,000 line program as a collection of about 1,000–2,000 smaller pieces, each containing about 50–100 lines.

The *program design document* breaks the problem into subtasks and sub-subtasks, or into various classes. Some of this design may be documented graphically, through structure charts or through class diagrams that give the properties and functions of each class. Modules that carry out subtasks in a traditional design, or that carry out some service that the objects of a class provide, are ultimately translated into separate sections of code. There must also be a complete specification of each module: what it is to do, what information it needs to know in order to do it, and what the rest of the program needs to get from it when it is done. This information must be sufficiently detailed that a programmer can use the description as a guide to writing code for the module in the language of choice.

Program design is one of the most creative and interesting parts of the overall software development life cycle. It is related to coding in roughly the same way that designing an airplane is related to riveting a wing.

4. *Algorithm selection or development, and analysis*–Once the various subtasks have been identified, algorithms must be found to carry them out. For example, one subtask may be to search a list of numbers for some particular value. In Chapters 2 and 3, we examined two different algorithms for searching–sequential search and binary search. If there is a choice of algorithms, the programmer must determine which is more suitable for this particular task and which is more efficient. It may also be the case that a totally new algorithm has to be developed from scratch. This, too, is a very creative process. Documentation of this phase includes a description of the algorithms chosen or developed, perhaps in pseudocode, an analysis of their efficiency (as we did in Chapter 3), and a rationale for their use.

5. *Coding*–Coding is the process of converting the detailed designs into computer code. If the design has been carefully developed, this should be a relatively routine job. Perhaps reusable code can be pulled from a program library, or a useful class can be employed. Coding is the step that usually comes to mind when people think of software development. However, as we have shown, a great deal of important preparatory work precedes the actual production of code. Inexperienced programmers may think that they will save time by skipping the earlier phases and getting right to coding. The opposite is usually true. In all but the most trivial of programs, tackling coding without first doing problem specification, program design, and algorithm selection or development ultimately leads to more time being spent and a poorer outcome. The coding phase also results in a written document, namely, the listing of the program code itself.

6. *Debugging*–Debugging is the process of locating and correcting program errors, and it can be a slow and expensive operation that requires as much effort as writing the program in the first place. Errors can occur because

a program statement fails to follow the correct rules of syntax, which makes the statement unrecognizable by the compiler and results in an error. Though irritating, these syntax errors are accompanied by messages from the compiler that help to pinpoint the problem. Other errors, called runtime errors, occur only when the program is run using certain sets of data that result in some illegal operation, such as dividing by zero. The system software also provides messages to help detect the cause of runtime errors. The third, and most subtle, class of errors is logic errors. These are errors in the algorithm used to solve the problem. Some incorrect steps that result in wrong answers are performed, but there are no error messages to help pinpoint the problem. Indeed, the first step in debugging a logic error is to notice that the answers are wrong. For example, if our algorithm calls for us to add 317 to the value of A, but we accidently translate this as:

$$A = A + 371;$$

our mistake will not produce an error message as the statement is syntactically correct and semantically meaningful. The only way we know there is an error is to notice that an incorrect value has been stored in A.

Debugging has always been one of the most frustrating, agonizing, and time-consuming steps in the programming process. Extensive time spent on debugging usually means that insufficient time was spent on carefully specifying, organizing, and structuring the solution. If the design is poor, then the resulting program is often a structural mess, with convoluted, hard-to-understand logic. On the other hand, devoting careful attention to the design phases can help reduce the amount of debugging and speed up the completion of the project.

Careful documentation of the debugging process includes notes on the problems found and on how the code was changed to solve them. This may prevent later changes from reintroducing old errors.

7. *Testing, verification, and benchmarking*—Even though a program produces correct answers for 1, 5, or even 1,000 data sets, how can we be sure that it is 100% correct and will work on all data? One approach, called empirical testing, is to design a special set of test cases, called a test suite, and run the program using this special test data. Test data that is carefully chosen to exercise all the different logic paths through a program can help uncover errors. In a conditional statement, for example, one set of data should make the Boolean expression true, so that one block of code is executed. Another set of data should make the same Boolean expression false, so that the other block of code is executed. The quantity of the test data per se does not matter; what matters is that the data covers all the various possibilities that could occur when the program is run. The goal of empirical testing is to make sure that every statement in the program has been executed at least once or, even better, multiple times. Having said that, we should note that in all but the most trivial of programs, it is not feasible to "test all the cases" because there are so many different

possibilities. The best that can be said is that the more thorough the testing, the higher the level of our confidence that the program is correct.

It's not a good plan to wait until the complete program is "finished" before testing takes place. In a program of any size, there are too many places where an error could occur, so the debugging process is extremely difficult at such a late stage. Unit testing takes place on each module (subtask code) as it is completed. As these tested modules are combined to work together, integration testing is done to see that the modules communicate the necessary data between and among themselves and that all modules work together smoothly. And if anything is changed on an already-tested module, regression testing is done to be sure that this change hasn't introduced a new error into code that was previously correct. Thus, testing should not be viewed as a separate and distinct phase of software development that occurs at the very end; instead, it is something that is going on simultaneously with the development of code.

A second, and totally different, approach to confirming a program's correctness is to use mathematical logic. Program verification can be used to prove that if the input data to a program satisfies certain conditions, then, after the program has been run on this data, the output data satisfies certain other conditions. This process is a formal proof, much like the proof of a mathematical theorem that condition B follows from condition A. However, verification is not a magic wand that gives us blanket assurance that a program will behave exactly as we want; it only works if we know that the input conditions will indeed be true and that the output conditions indeed reflect what the program was supposed to produce. Furthermore, the program verification process can be difficult and time consuming. That's why program testing is used much more than formal program verification to reduce the risk of program errors.

In addition to correctness, the problem specification may require that the finished program meets certain performance characteristics such as the amount of time it takes to compute the results. *Benchmarking* the program means running it on many data sets to be sure its performance falls within those required limits. At the completion of testing (or verification) and benchmarking, we should have a correct and efficient program that is ready for delivery. Of course, all of the testing, verification, and benchmarking results are committed to paper (well, at least to a digital document) as evidence that the program meets its specifications.

8. *Documentation*—Program documentation is all of the written and online material that makes a program understandable. This includes internal documentation, which is part of the program code itself. Good internal documentation consists of choosing meaningful names for program identifiers, using plenty of comments to explain the code, and separating the program into short modules, each of which does one specific subtask. External documentation consists of any materials assembled to clarify the program's design and implementation. Although we have put this step rather late in the software development process, note that each preceding

step produces some form of documentation. Program documentation goes on throughout the software development life cycle. The final, finished program documentation is written in two forms. Technical documentation enables programmers who later have to modify the program to understand the code. Such information as problem specification documents, design documents, structure charts or class diagrams, descriptions of algorithms, and program listings fall in this category. User documentation helps users run the program. Such documentation includes online tutorials, answers to frequently asked questions (FAQs), help systems that the user can bring up while the program is running, and perhaps (less and less often) written users' manuals.

9. *Maintenance*—Programs are not static entities that, once completed, never change. Because of the time and expense involved in developing software, successful programs are used for a very long time. It is not unusual for a program to still be in use 20 or 30 years after it was written. (Microsoft Word was first developed and released in 1983!) In fact, the typical life cycle for a medium- to large-sized software package is 1–3 years in development and 5–20 years in the marketplace. During this long period of use, errors may be uncovered, new hardware or system software may be purchased on which the program has to run, user needs may change, and the whims of the marketplace may fluctuate. The original program must be modified and brought out in new versions to meet these changing needs. Program maintenance, the process of adapting and improving an existing software product, may consume as much as 65% of the total software development life cycle budget. If the program has been well planned, carefully designed, well coded, thoroughly tested, and well documented, then program maintenance is a much easier task. Indeed, it is with an eye to program maintenance (and to reducing its cost) that we stress the importance of these earlier steps.

   Maintenance should not really be viewed as a separate step in the software development life cycle. Rather, it involves repetition of some or all of the steps previously described, from a feasibility study through implementation, testing, and updated documentation. Maintenance reflects the fact that the software development life cycle is truly a *cycle*, during which it may be necessary to redo earlier phases of development as our software changes, grows, and matures.

9.6.3 Modern Environments

Development Environments. Modern software development environments have had a great impact on the software development life cycle process. Regardless of the programming language used, most programmers now work within an integrated development environment, or IDE. The IDE lets the programmer perform a number of tasks within the shell of a single application program, rather than having to use a separate program for each task. Consider some of the system software tasks described in Section 6.2: Use a *text editor* to create a program; use a *file system* to store the program; use a *language translator* to translate the program to machine language; and if the program does not work correctly, use a *debugger* to help locate the errors.

A modern programming IDE provides a text editor, a file manager, a compiler, a linker and loader, and tools for debugging, all within this one integrated piece of software. This can significantly speed up program development.

Many IDEs enable programmers to quickly create sample graphical user interfaces (GUIs) called prototypes that can be shown to prospective users in the initial stages of software development. These prototypes do not have any functionality, but they can give users a good idea of what the final software package will look like—much like seeing a small-scale mock-up of a proposed new building before it is actually built. This rapid prototyping process allows any misunderstandings or miscommunications between user and programmer to be identified and corrected early in the development process.

Finally, there are software packages that track requirements from the initial specification through the design process to final code, to make sure that nothing gets lost along the way. These packages may also support graphical design of the various program elements, such as classes, and facilitate their translation into code.

Code Repositories. Software development is not a one-time thing. Even a single developer, for anything but a trivial piece of code, makes changes. And huge software projects involve teams of many people working on and interacting with various sections of code. There will be progressive versions as the project develops, hence the need for a version control system to manage the project as changes are made. Anyone who wants to make a change must be sure he or she is working on the latest version of the code. The user "checks out" a file from the version control system, edits it, and submits the revised file back to the version control system; in the meantime, while the file is "checked out," no one else can edit it. Alternatively, multiple users may simultaneously change a single file and the version control system warns of potential conflicts when the edited files are "merged." Also, there is a need for past versions to be maintained in some organized way so if some bug is found, it can be traced back through earlier versions to see when it first occurred. The version control system manages all of the details of this code repository (all the various versions and details about when, why, and by whom changes were made).

There are many version control systems, including Git, an open-source version control package created in 2005 by Linus Torvalds, the developer of the Linux operating system (who slyly named the system using British slang for a silly or stupid person). Git excels at managing large projects efficiently while being simple to use, even on your own personal machine. GitHub is a cloud-based storage facility for code repositories, which can be designated as private or public. It provides backup for files and, even in private repositories, can allow collaborators to see, use, and change these files, thereby enhancing distributed code development where programmers may be in different locations and different time zones. Public cloud-based code repositories, which anyone can view, use, and change, are particularly useful for open-source code development. As of April 2017, GitHub had almost 20 million users and hosted 57 million code repositories.

9.6.4 Agile Software Development

The software development process described in Section 9.6.2 is also known as the waterfall model of software development. Think of a series of waterfalls moving a river down and down through various plateaus. In the software development process, these plateaus would be the feasibility study, problem specification, program design, and so on—all the steps we outlined in Section 9.6.2. This imagery suggests that software development is a completely sequential process, that is, one step must be completed before moving on to the next, and that previous steps are never revisited. The waterfall model was originally developed to describe manufacturing processes, in which a step such as "cut sheet metal" definitely had to be completed (and never revisited) before "weld the seams."

Software development is much more fluid, and in fact there is a lot of wiggle room in the waterfall model. The program design phase may bring out issues that require revisiting the problem specification, the debugging phase obviously requires some amount of recoding, and testing and documentation are done throughout the process. Thus, the "pure" waterfall model of software development is seldom used in favor of a more flexible approach that is instead guided by the waterfall model.

Around 2001, a new software development model known as agile software development started to be used. The Merriam-Webster online dictionary defines the word *agile* as "marked by ready ability to move with quick easy grace; having a quick, resourceful and adaptable character." This suggests flexibility, nimbleness, and the ability to adjust to changes. Let's revisit a phrase or two from our discussion of the waterfall model: "The problem specification document expresses the final and complete problem specification and guides the software developers in all subsequent decisions .... Once agreed to by the developer and the customer, this document becomes essentially a legal contract describing what the developer promises to provide and what the customer agrees to accept." Sounds like a done deal.

The whole agile software development philosophy is a recognition that problem specifications are never a "done deal," that there are bound to be changes, that the development team must be "agile" in its response to these changes, and that the customer should be involved in working with the development team throughout the design process. Agile software development is actually a whole suite of methods and processes that help to promote this flexible and ready response to meet a shifting and ever-changing target.

One of the principles of agile software development, pair programming has even made its way into some college computer science classes. Pair programming involves two programmers (students) at a single workstation. At any given point in time, one is writing code and the other is actively observing. The observer watches each line of code for possible errors but also is thinking about the overall approach, what problems may lie ahead, and possibly spotting improvements that could be made. The roles of the two individuals are switched frequently. The emphasis is on cooperation, not competition. Pair programming, if done well, actually produces better code more quickly than a single programmer, but of course there is the added cost of two people working together. So for any particular project, the relative costs and benefits of pair programming should be weighed.

Software Engineering Failures

It is easy to find numerous instances of software failures, with consequences ranging from temporary inconvenience to huge financial losses, or even to loss of life. Many of these failures can be attributed to a specific coding error, but usually a thorough investigation also reveals a much broader spectrum of errors.

The Mars Exploration Program, begun by NASA (National Aeronautics and Space Administration) in 1993, is a U.S. effort to understand and explore the planet Mars. As part of this program, the Mars Climate Orbiter was launched in December, 1998; its purpose was to study the climate and atmosphere of Mars. However, when the Mars Climate Orbiter entered the Martian atmosphere, it had evidently moved much closer to the planet's surface than its projected entry path; as a result, the propulsion system overheated and the engine burned out. It is believed that the $125 million vehicle was destroyed in the atmosphere.

According to the official NASA report, the "root cause" was an embarrassing mismatch between the English units (pound-secs) output by one software module and used as input to another software module that—by NASA software interface specifications—expected metric units (Newtons-secs). This second software module used the English unit quantities as if they were in metric units (1 pound force = 4.45 Newtons), and this discrepancy drove the trajectory down. According to the chairman of the Mars Climate Orbiter Mission Failure Investigation Board, "The failure review board has identified other significant factors that allowed this error to be born, and then let it linger and propagate to the point where it resulted in a major error in our understanding of the spacecraft's path as it approached Mars." The report

(Continued)

went on to list the following contributing factors (quoted from the report), among others:

- *The systems engineering function within the project that is supposed to track and double-check all interconnected aspects of the mission was not robust enough, exacerbated by the first-time handover of a Mars-bound spacecraft from a group that constructed it and launched it to a new, multi-mission operations team.*

- *Some communications channels among project engineering groups were too informal.*

- *The small mission navigation team was oversubscribed and its work did not receive peer review by independent experts.*

- *The process to verify and validate certain engineering requirements and technical interfaces between some project groups, and between the project and its prime mission contractor, was inadequate.*

These are failures of the software engineering process that allowed a coding error to go undetected.

On a happier note, NASA's Mars Exploration Rover vehicle Opportunity landed on the surface of Mars on January 24, 2004, with an expected mission lifespan of 90 days. On January 24, 2017, 13 years after landing, Opportunity was still rolling around on Mars, collecting and transmitting scientific data!

9.7 Conclusion

In this chapter, we have seen how the use of a high-level language overcomes many of the disadvantages of assembly language programming, creating a more comfortable and useful environment for the programmer. In a high-level language, the programmer need not manage the storage or movement of data values in memory. The programmer can think about the problem at a higher level, use program instructions that are both more powerful and more natural-language-like, and write a program that is much more portable among various hardware platforms. The online language chapters (on Ada, C++, C#, Java, and Python) spell out the mechanisms used by each language to give the programmer these more powerful problem-solving abilities. In this chapter, we've seen two small sample programs in each language plus a brief comparison of some of the features of these languages.

We also discussed the entire software development life cycle, noting that for large, real-world programs, software development must be a managed discipline. Coding is but a small part of the software development process.

The high-level languages we have investigated so far all belong to the procedural language family. In the next chapter, we'll look briefly at several additional procedural languages as well as other languages that take quite a different approach to problem solving.

EXERCISES

Each online language chapter has its own set of exercises. See the Special Interest Box on page 439 for instructions on accessing the online chapters.

CHALLENGE WORK

1. Write a program in the language of your choice to implement the sequential search algorithm of Chapter 3, Figure 3.1, except that instead of searching a list of telephone numbers for a particular number, have the program search a list of integers for a particular integer. Use the same input mechanism as in the data cleanup programs of Section 9.3.2 to get the list of integers to be searched. Then get the target number to be searched for. The program should output "Successful search, the value is in the list" or "Unsuccessful search, the value is not in the list." Be sure to test your program for both outcomes.

2. In Chapter 8, we learned about a simple encryption algorithm called a Caesar cipher. Write a program in the language of your choice to implement the Caesar cipher algorithm.

   a. Write a main function (method, procedure) that collects a message from the user and writes it out again. Assume for simplicity that the message contains no more than 10 characters and that only the 26 uppercase letters of the alphabet are used. Use an array of 10 elements to store the message. Ask the user to enter no more than 10 characters, one per line, and to terminate the message by entering some special character such as "%." Use a variable to keep track of the number of array elements actually used (which could be fewer than 10 if the message is short) so that

   you do not write out meaningless characters stored at the end of the array.

   b. Because you will be writing out the contents of the message array several times, write a helper function (method, procedure) *WriteMessage* to do this task. Now rewrite your main function so that it uses *WriteMessage* to write out the message array.

   c. Write a function (method, procedure) to modify the array to represent the encoded form of the message using a Caesar cipher. Have the main function ask for the shift amount. Pass this information, along with the message array and the number of array elements actually used, to the encoding function. To get from one character to the character *s* units along in the alphabet, you can simply add s to the original character. This works for everything except the end of the alphabet; here you will have to be a bit more clever to cycle back to the beginning of the alphabet once the shift is applied. Have the main function invoke the encoding function and then invoke *WriteMessage* to write out the encoded form of the message.

   d. Write a function (method, procedure) to modify the array containing the encoded message back to its original form. This function also needs as arguments the number of array elements used and the value of the shift amount, as well as the array itself. The body of the function should accomplish the reverse of the encoding function. Have the main function invoke the decoding function and then write out the decoded form of the message, which should agree with the original message.

e. Test your program with different values for *s* and different word lengths.

3. In Chapter 7, we learned about the *routing problem* in computer networks, which consists of finding the optimal path from a source node to a destination node. Each hop along a path represents a communication channel between two nodes that has an associated "cost"; the cost might actually be a monetary cost to use a leased line, but it could also be a cost in terms of the volume of traffic the line typically carries. In either case, the "shortest path" is the one with the lowest cost. As mentioned in Chapter 7, the Internet uses Dijkstra's shortest path algorithm to solve this problem. If node *x* is the source node and receives a message for node *y*, then *x* only needs to know the shortest path from itself to node *y*. But an alternative is to have a centralized site periodically compute the "all-pairs shortest path" from any node to any other node, and then broadcast that information to all nodes in the network. The algorithm for the all-pairs shortest path, called *Floyd's algorithm*, is simpler to implement than Dijkstra's algorithm.

A two-dimensional array (table) is used to represent the nodes in the network. If there are *n* nodes in the network, the array is *n* × *n* in size. The entry in position *i, j* of the array is the length (cost) of the line from *i* to *j*. For example, the following network has five nodes, numbered 0 through 4.

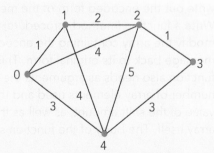

It is represented by the 5 × 5 array shown here.

	0	1	2	3	4
0	0	1	4	∞	3
1	1	0	2	∞	4
2	4	2	0	1	5
3	∞	∞	1	0	3
4	3	4	5	3	0

The entry in row 1, column 4 is 4 because the length of the line between node 1 and node 4 is 4. The entry in row 0, column 3 is ∞ because there is no direct line between nodes 0 and 3. All the entries on the "main diagonal" (positions [0,0], [1,1], [2,2], [3,3], and [4,4]) are 0 because there is a 0-length link from a node to itself.

Floyd's algorithm operates on the array A of the graph. A pseudocode description of the algorithm is:

set the value of k to 0
while (k <= n − 1) do
    set the value of i to 0
    while (i <= n − 1) do
        set the value of j to 0
        while (j <= n − 1) do
            if A [i, k] +A [k, j] < A [i, j]
                A [i, j] = A [i, k] + A [k, j]
        end of the j-loop
    end of the i-loop
end of the k-loop

When this algorithm terminates, the entry in position [*i, j*] of the array represents the length of the shortest path between nodes *i* and *j*, although this algorithm does not say what the intermediate nodes on the shortest path are.

Write a program in the language of your choice to solve the all-pairs shortest path problem for a graph with five nodes. The program gets the values for each row of the array from the user, runs Floyd's algorithm, and writes out the resulting array. Use 500 for "infinity," which assumes all legitimate line lengths are less than 500.

Try your program for the graph shown here. From the output of your program, what is the length of the shortest path from node 2 to node 4? By looking at the graph, what are the nodes on this path?

4. Exercise 1 asks you to write a program to search a list of integers for a particular value. Your program asks the user to enter the list at the keyboard, the same mechanism we have used for collecting data in the examples of this chapter. It is more realistic to read the list from a preexisting data file stored on the computer's hard drive. Ask your instructor how to read a file in the language of your choice, then create a data file of random integers and write the sequential search program again, this time using file input data. Output can be to the screen, as before.

5. Again create a data file of random integers. Then write a program in the language of your choice to implement the selection sort algorithm of Figure 3.6 using file input

data. Write a separate function (method, procedure) to find the location of the largest number in the unsorted section of the list (see Figure 2.14) and have your main function call that as needed. Write your sorted list to another data file.

6. Read more about software engineering and write a short paper on one or more of the following topics:

- Black-box and white-box testing
- CASE tools
- Code refactoring
- Code review
- Configuration management
- Data dictionary
- Data modeling
- Extreme programming (XP)
- JAD (Joint Application Development) sessions
- Quality assurance
- Rapid prototyping
- Requirements tracing
- Software design patterns
- Software metrics
- Stubs and drivers

The Tower of Babel: Programming Languages

AFTER STUDYING THIS CHAPTER, YOU WILL BE ABLE TO:

- Explain why so many programming languages exist
- List four key procedural languages and the main purpose for the development of each
- Describe the purpose of each special-purpose language: SQL, HTML, JavaScript, and R
- Describe the alternative paradigms for programming languages: functional, logic, and parallel
- Name a functional programming language and a logic programming language
- Describe how logic programming languages work, and explain what facts, rules, and inference are
- Explain how the MIMD model of parallel processing could be used to find the largest number in a list

10.1 Why Babel?

The biblical story of the Tower of Babel takes place at a time when "the whole earth had one language and the same words." The people began to build a city with a mighty tower when, suddenly, everyone began speaking in different tongues and could no longer communicate. They became confused, abandoned the tower, and scattered "over the face of all the earth." A shared enterprise was impossible to pursue without the mutual understanding fostered by a common language, and (the message this story was intended to convey) the power of what people could do was thus forever limited.

Similarly, it might seem that having all computer programs written in the same programming language would have an appealing simplicity. Chapter 9 gave a brief comparison of five general-purpose programming languages: Ada, C++, C#, Java, and Python. By now, you may have also studied one or more of these languages in some depth through the online language chapters. But again, why aren't all programs written in the best one of these languages? Or does each of these languages have some things it can't do that some of the other languages can do? If so, then why aren't all programs written in some "superlanguage" that overcomes these deficiencies?

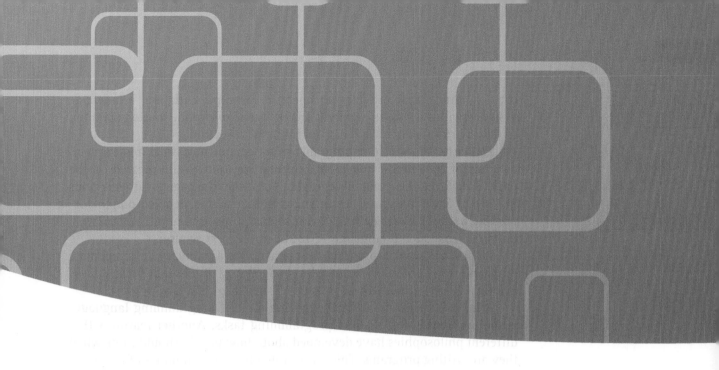

There are multiple programming languages not so much because there are tasks that one language cannot do but because each language was designed to meet the specific needs of one particular area of application. Consequently, one language might be better suited than others for writing certain kinds of programs. The situation is somewhat analogous to the automobile market. The basic automotive needs of the country probably could be served by a single car model and a single truck model. So why do we have seemingly endless models from which to choose? The answer lies partly in competition: Automotive companies are all trying to claim a share of the market. More than that, though, the answer lies in the variety of ways we use our automobiles. Although a luxury car could be used for off-roading, it is not designed for that use; a four-wheel-drive vehicle does the job better, more safely, and more efficiently. Although a sports car could be used to haul Little Leaguers home from the ball game, it is not designed for that use; an SUV serves this purpose better. The diversity of tasks for which we use our automobiles has promoted a variety of automotive models, each designed to handle a particular range of tasks.

The same thing applies to programming languages. For example, we *could* use C++ to write programs for solving engineering problems (and it has indeed been so used). However, C++ was not designed with engineering applications in mind. Although C++ supports the basic arithmetic operations of addition, subtraction, multiplication, and division by providing simple operators $(+, -, *, /)$ to do these tasks, there is no operator for exponentiation—that is, raising a value to a power. Computing $2.84^{1.8}$ in a C++ program, for example, can certainly be done but it requires some effort.[1] Calculations involving exponents are performed hundreds of times in many engineering and other numerical-based applications, so why not

---

[1] The C++ expression for $2.84^{1.8}$ is exp(1.8*log(2.84)), or, somewhat shorter, pow(2.84, 1.8), using functions available in the math library that are linked in with a #include <cmath> directive.

use a language that provides an operator for exponentiation, a language designed with such tasks in mind? Ada has such an exponentiation operator, as does Fortran, which we'll discuss in the next section.

Similarly, suppose our program writes complicated sales reports with columns of figures and blocks of information strategically located on the page. Specifying the exact placement of output on the page is rather tedious in C++ or Java. Why not use a language that allows detailed output formatting because it was designed with such a purpose in mind? Again, we'll briefly discuss such a language—COBOL—in the next section.

What if we want a program to interact with a database, to manipulate graphics, or to act as a hyperlinked webpage? Any of these specialized tasks is probably best done with a language designed for just that purpose.

A major reason, then, for the proliferation of programming languages is the proliferation of distinct programming tasks. Another reason is that different philosophies have developed about how people should think when they are writing programs. This has resulted in several families of programming languages that take quite different approaches from the ones we've looked at so far, and we'll see some of these approaches in Section 10.4.

10.2 Procedural Languages

As mentioned earlier, all the languages of Chapter 9 (Ada, C++, C#, Java, and Python) are *procedural languages*. Programs written in such languages differ in the way the statements must be arranged on a line and in how variables can be named. They differ in the details of assigning a new value to a variable, in the mechanisms the language provides for directing the flow of control through conditional and looping statements, and in the statement forms that control input and output. They also differ in the way programs can be broken down into modules to handle separate tasks and in how those modules share information. We noted some of these syntactical differences in the Feature Analysis table (Figure 9.15) of Chapter 9. But all procedural language programs tell the computer in a step-by-step fashion how to manipulate the contents of memory locations. In a general sense, then, the languages are quite similar, just as French, Spanish, and Italian are all members of the family of Romance languages. In this section we concentrate not on syntactical differences, but on the history and "intent" of some of the most important procedural languages—important in that, of the many programming languages that have come and gone over the years, these became widely used. The languages of Chapter 9 are included here, but there are additional languages as well.

10.2.1 Plankalkül

What? OK, this language never became widely used. In fact, it was never even implemented. It's a programming language designed by Konrad Zuse who, you may recall from Chapter 1, built a computer in Germany during World War II. The manuscript describing this programming language was completed in 1945 but was not published until 1972. The manuscript contained a number of complex algorithms written in Plankalkül (the name, in German, means "formal planning system"). The language itself, although burdened with obscure notation, contained a number of sophisticated concepts that, had they been known earlier, might have changed the development of programming languages. As the very first attempt to design a high-level programming language for computers, Zuse's proposal was a very important milestone in the field of computing, although it never received the attention it deserved.

10.2.2 Fortran

The name Fortran derives from *For*mula *Tran*slating System. The very name indicates its affiliation with "formulas" or engineering-type applications. Developed in the mid-1950s by a group at IBM headed by John Backus, in conjunction with some IBM computer users, the first commercial version of Fortran was released in 1957. This makes Fortran the first high-level programming language that was actually implemented. Early computer users were often engineers who were solving problems with a heavy mathematics or computational flavor. Fortran has some features ideally suited to these applications, such as the exponentiation operator we mentioned earlier, as well as the ability to carry out extended-precision arithmetic with many decimal places of accuracy, and the ability to work within the complex number system. Updated versions of Fortran have been introduced over the years, incorporating new data types, new statements to direct the flow of control, and the ability to use recursion (recursion is discussed later in this chapter). Object-oriented programming is supported in later versions of the language.

Early versions of Fortran required all variable identifiers to be uppercase. Also it did not allow the use of mathematical symbols such as < to compare two quantities; the keypunches that were used to create the punched cards on which early Fortran programs were submitted to the computer had no such symbols. Thus the condition we would usually write now as

```
number < 0
```

would have been expressed as

```
NUMBER .LT. 0
```

There was no while loop mechanism. The effect of a while loop was obtained by using an IF statement together with GO TO statements. The pseudocode

```
input number
while (number >= 0)
{
    .

    .

    .

    input number
}
```

would have been accomplished by

```
      READ(*,*) NUMBER
  10  IF (NUMBER .LT. 0) GO TO 20
            .

            .

            .

      READ(*,*) NUMBER
      GO TO 10
  20  ...
```

READ is the Fortran implementation of "input," so the first line inputs a value for *NUMBER*. If *NUMBER* is less than 0, the GO TO statement transfers control to statement 20. If *NUMBER* is greater than or equal to 0, something is done and then another value for *NUMBER* is obtained. Control is then redirected by the second GO TO statement back to statement 10 where the new value is tested. Directing the flow of control by GO TO statements is similar to using the various JUMP statements in the assembly language of Chapter 6, and it reflects the fact that Fortran's developers were, after all, working from assembly language.

Fortran was designed to support numerical computations. This led to concise mathematical notation (aside from the early < dilemma just mentioned) and to the availability of a number of mathematical functions within the language. Another design goal was to optimize the resulting object code, that is, to produce object code that took as little space and executed as efficiently as possible. (Remember that when Fortran was developed, machine resources were scarce and precious.) Fortran allows external libraries of well-written, efficient, and thoroughly tested code modules that are separately compiled and then drawn on by any program that wants to use their capabilities. Because of Fortran's extensive use as a programming language over the years, a large and well-tested Fortran library collection exists, so in many cases programmers can use existing code instead of having to write all code from scratch. This feature is sometimes highly touted for newer languages, but Fortran designers got there first.

The next revision of the ISO (International Organization for Standardization) Fortran standard is Fortran 2015, scheduled for publication in 2018.

10.2.3 COBOL

The name COBOL derives from *CO*mmon *B*usiness-*O*riented *L*anguage. COBOL was developed in 1959 and 1960 by a group headed by Admiral Grace Murray Hopper of the U.S. Navy. Fortran and COBOL were the dominant high-level languages of the 1960s and 1970s. COBOL was designed to serve business needs such as managing inventories and payrolls. In such applications, summary reports are important output products. Much of the processing in the business world concerns updating "master files" with changes from "transaction files." For example, a master inventory file contains the names, manufacturers, and quantities on hand of items in

Old Dog, New Tricks #1

Fortran was first introduced in 1957. In the history of computing, this is roughly the Jurassic Age, but Fortran is no extinct dinosaur. Instead, it is a chameleon, changing with the times. Fortran now runs on PCs, tablets, and even smartphones while still providing the power to help supercomputers tackle some of the most computationally intensive problems ever. Fortran programs can present a graphical user interface to help the user easily operate the program and perhaps visualize the results.

Parallelism is especially useful for speeding up the kinds of calculations on huge arrays that often occur in scientific and engineering problems, Fortran's traditional domain. An *array* is a block of numerical data, and manipulation of array values often occurs in such tough numerical problems as climate modeling, computational fluid dynamics, and computational economics. Fortran now includes the ability to use *coarrays*, in which arrays can be split between multiple processors for parallel processing, and the communication between these processors is easily managed. Problems with real-time response requirements in the areas of signal processing and image processing are also appropriate for parallelism; Fortran programs often beat more "sophisticated" languages in raw speed.

inventory; a transaction file has the names and quantities of items sold out of inventory or delivered to inventory over some period of time. The master file is updated from the transaction file on a daily or weekly basis to reflect the new quantities available, and a summary report is printed. The user doesn't interact directly with the COBOL program; rather, the user prepares the master file (once) and the transaction file (regularly).

In the design of COBOL, particular attention was paid to input formatting for data being read from files and to output formatting both for writing data to a file and for generating business reports with information precisely located on the page. Therefore, much of a COBOL program may be concerned with formatting, described by "PICTURE clauses" in the program. COBOL was also designed such that programs describe what they are doing in natural language phrases. As a result, COBOL programs can be rather verbose.

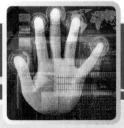

Practice Problems

1. Write a Fortran condition to test whether the value of *ITIME* is less than or equal to 7. Use early Fortran syntax.

2. Using the if/then/else construct introduced in Chapter 2, rewrite the following Fortran code fragment so that it does not require any GO TO statements:

```
      IF (X .LT. 3) GO TO 10
      A = 1
      GO TO 20
   10 A = 2
      GO TO 30
   20 B = 3
   30 . . .
```

3. In the code fragment of Practice Problem 2, suppose that *X* has the value 2, *A* has the value 7, *B* has the value 1, and that statement 30 is

```
   30 A = A + B
```

What is the final value of *A*?

COBOL programs are highly portable across many different COBOL compilers, are quite easy to read, and are very well suited to manipulating large data files. Because COBOL has been around for a long time, there is a huge base of existing COBOL applications. Nonetheless, the continuing importance of COBOL as a commercial programming language had perhaps been overlooked by those outside the business world until the "Year 2000 problem" came along. The Y2K problem (K stands for *kilo*, or "thousand") dealt with a lurking time bomb in legacy code (old computer code that is still in use), primarily COBOL code. When these programs were written, their authors never imagined their longevity. In addition, computer memory was at a premium, so efficiency was the order of the day. Why store four digits of a date (1967, say) when two digits (67)—the "19" prefix was assumed—would be sufficient and take less space? In the new millennium, "02" should mean "2002," but in these programs it would be interpreted incorrectly as "1902."

Making code Y2K-compliant was technically simple: Just change every date reference to four digits instead of two. It was the magnitude of the task that was staggering because it was necessary to locate each line of code where a date entry needed to be changed. Huge sums of government and corporate money were spent to address the problem and, despite dire predictions on the potential consequences of Y2K, it proved to be a "nonevent"—probably because of the massive effort made to address the problem.

So, does post-Y2K mark the death of COBOL? Absolutely not! All this money was not spent on fixing code that businesses planned to throw away. On the contrary, the majority of business transactions, for retail point-of-sale systems, banking, insurance, payroll, ATMs, hospital systems, and government systems are still done on COBOL code that has now been updated and is likely to continue to run for the foreseeable future. Even in 2016, the Social Security Administration relied on more than 60 million lines of COBOL code.

The current international standard for COBOL was published in 2014.

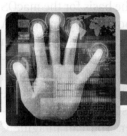

Practice Problem

Write statements in your choice of language from Chapter 9 that are equivalent to the following COBOL statements:

```
MOVE INPUT-NUMBER TO OUTPUT-NUMBER.
ADD INPUT-NUMBER TO SUM-OF-VALUES.
```

Uncle Sam Wants *Who*?

A Y2K-like problem arose in June 2014 after the Pennsylvania Department of Motor Vehicles completed a computer-generated transfer to the U.S. Selective Service of some 400,000 records it had on file. (Males in the United States between the ages of 18 and 25 must register with the Selective Service for possible military draft.) These included records for males born 1993–1997. However, the state agency uses only a 2-digit indicator for the year of birth, so this transfer also included records for males born 1893–1897. The Selective Service duly sent letters out to those in both groups ordering them to register for the military draft or face fines and imprisonment. Many of the more than 14,000 letters to the 1893–1897 group reached bewildered relatives of these no-doubt long-dead gentlemen. Oops!

10.2.4 C/C++

C was developed in the early 1970s by Dennis Ritchie at AT&T Labs. It was originally designed for systems programming, in particular for writing the operating system UNIX. UNIX had been developed at Bell Labs a short time before and was originally written primarily in assembly language. Ritchie sought a high-level language in which to rewrite the operating system in order to gain all the advantages of high-level languages: ease of programming, portability, and so on.

Since that time, C has become a popular general-purpose language for two major reasons. One is the close relationship between C and UNIX. UNIX has been implemented on many different computers (and is the basis for the macOS operating system). UNIX provides many "tools" that support C programming. A second reason for C's popularity is its efficiency—that is, the speed with which its operations can be executed. This efficiency derives from the fact that C programs can make use of low-level information such as knowledge of where data are stored in memory. In this respect, C is closer to assembly language than are other high-level languages, yet it still has the powerful statements and portability to many machines that high-level languages offer. You can imagine C humming along as a high-level language but then, every once in a while when efficiency is really important, slipping into a low-level, machine-dependent configuration. One of the goals of a high-level language is to provide a level of abstraction that shields the programmer from any knowledge of the actual hardware/memory cells used during program execution, as depicted in Figure 10.1(a). C provides this outlook, unless the programmer wants to make

FIGURE 10.1

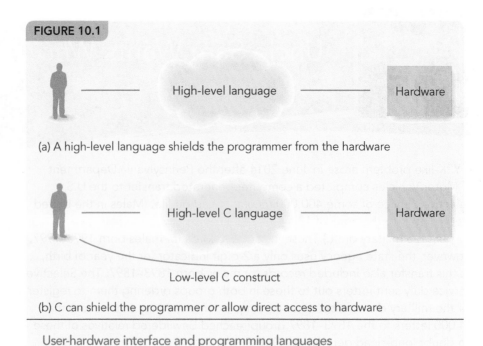

(a) A high-level language shields the programmer from the hardware

(b) C can shield the programmer *or* allow direct access to hardware

User-hardware interface and programming languages

use of the low-level constructs available in C that give him or her a direct view of the actual hardware, which Figure 10.1(b) depicts.

For example, suppose *number* is a variable in a C program with the value 234. The value of *number* is stored in some specific memory location with address, say, 1000 (Figure 10.2). The notation *&number* in that same program refers to the memory address where the value of *number* is stored, in this case, 1000. Note the distinction between the content of a memory cell and the address of that cell. Here *number* refers to the value 234, but *&number* refers to the address 1000. It is possible to write a C program statement that passes *&number* as an argument to an output function so that the program actually writes out the memory address value (1000). The ability to work with an actual memory address is not available in most other high-level languages.

C not only provides a way to see the actual memory address where a variable is stored, it also gives the programmer some control over the address where information is stored. C includes a data type called *pointer*. Variables of pointer type contain—instead of integers, real numbers, or characters—memory addresses. For example, the statement

```
int* intPointer;
```

declares *intPointer* as a pointer variable that will contain the address of a memory cell containing integer data. The assignment

```
intPointer = (int*) 800;
```

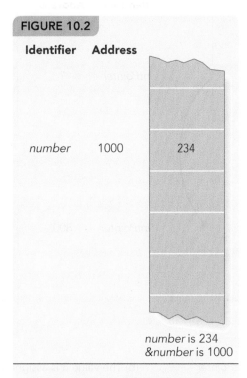

FIGURE 10.2

Identifier	Address	
number	1000	234

number is 234
&number is 1000

C allows access to a memory cell address as well as to its content

assigns the memory address 800 to be the value of *intPointer*. Figure 10.3(a) illustrates this situation: The pointer variable *intPointer* is stored at some unknown memory address, but the content of *intPointer* is the memory address 800. The value stored at the address contained in *intPointer*, in this case stored at 800, is denoted by **intPointer*. In other words, **intPointer* is the value contained in the address to which *intPointer* points. We can find out what this value is by writing out **intPointer*. We can also assign an integer value, say 3, to be the content of memory address 800 by the statement

```
*intPointer = 3;
```

which results in Figure 10.3(b). We have controlled the content of a specific memory location, and now we know exactly what is stored in memory location 800. Similarly, if *number* is an integer variable that has been stored somewhere in memory, then the statement

```
*intPointer = number;
```

results in the value of *number* being stored in memory cell 800.

This capability for low-level memory manipulation resembles the assembly language programming of Chapter 6. It is fraught with the

FIGURE 10.3

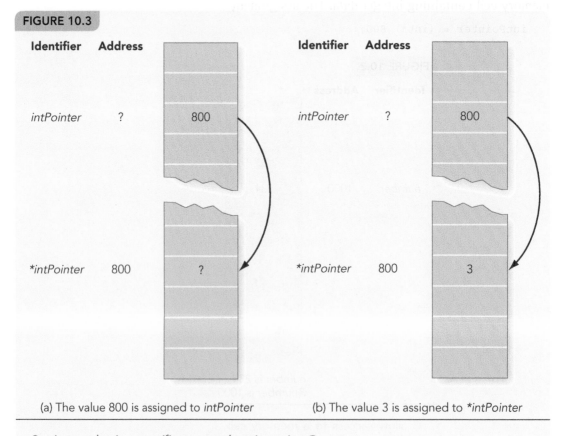

(a) The value 800 is assigned to *intPointer*   (b) The value 3 is assigned to **intPointer*

Storing a value in a specific memory location using C

same problems we sought to avoid by going to high-level languages in the first place; specifically, the programmer is assuming responsibility for what is stored where. For example, what if memory cell 800 in our example is not a memory cell allocated to this program? Perhaps something needed by another program, or even by the operating system, has been overwritten. However, the fact that it enables the programmer to reach down into the machine level is precisely why C is useful for writing system software such as operating systems, assemblers, compilers, and input/output controllers.

A program that interacts with an I/O device is called a device driver. Consider, for example, the problem of writing a device driver for the mouse on a PC or laptop. If the mouse is a wired mouse, it is connected to a USB port on the computer that reads changes in the mouse position by changes in voltage levels. In the case of a wireless mouse, the mouse sends radio frequency or Bluetooth signals about the mouse position to a receiver in the computer. In either case, this data is stored in fixed locations in memory that are allocated by the operating system. The job of the mouse driver is to translate this data to specific locations on the screen so that any application software that uses the mouse, such as a word processor, does not have to interact with low-level hardware information (abstraction again!). The mouse driver program has to access the specific memory locations where the mouse location data has been stored. A language like C provides such a capability.

C is the most widely used language for writing system software because it combines the power of a high-level language with the ability to circumvent that level of abstraction and work at the assembly-language-like level. But C is also used for a great deal of general-purpose computing.

The C++ language was developed in the early 1980s by Bjarne Stroustrup, also at AT&T Labs. C++ is in fact a "superset" of C, meaning that all of the C language is part of C++. Everything that can be done in C—including the ability to change the contents of specific memory locations—can be done in C++. But C++ adds many new features to C, giving it more sophistication and cleaner ways to do certain tasks. The most significant extension of C that C++ provides is the ability to do object-oriented programming.

C++ was first commercially released by AT&T in 1985. Like many other languages, C++ has evolved over time. The standardization process for the language took more than 10 years, in part because of this evolution. In November 1997, the combined C++ subcommittees of ANSI and ISO submitted their C++ standards draft, part of a document of some 800 pages, for final ISO approval. The standards were finally approved in 1998. Standardization, object orientation, and a strong collection of library code have helped to make C++ one of the most popular of the modern "industrial-strength" languages.

The newest C++ international standard is C++ 14, published in 2014, but at the time of this writing, a major revision (C++ 17) is expected to receive final approval in 2017, with work on C++ 20 to begin right after that.

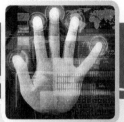

Practice Problems

1. Suppose a C/C++ program uses a variable called *Rate*. Explain the distinction in the program between *Rate* and *&Rate*.

2. Suppose that *Rate* is an integer variable in a C/C++ program with the value 10 and that *intPointer* is a pointer variable for integer data. *Rate* is stored at memory address 500. After the statement

   ```
   intPointer = &Rate;
   ```

   is executed, what is the value of **intPointer*?

3. The following statement is executed after the statement in Problem 2.

   ```
   *intpointer = 29;
   ```

   What is the value of *&Rate* now? What is the value of *Rate* now?

10.2.5 Ada

Probably more than any other language we have mentioned, Ada has a long and interesting development history. It began in the mid-1970s when the various branches of the U.S. armed services set about trying to develop a common high-level programming language for use by defense contractors. They began by specifying the requirements that the language would have to meet, including such characteristics as efficiency, reliability, readability, and maintainability.

The original set of requirements, first circulated for discussion in 1975, was known as "Strawman." Successively tighter and more thorough requirements bore the names "Woodenman" and "Tinman." The Tinman requirements were approved in 1976, and many existing programming languages were evaluated in the light of these requirements. All were found wanting, and it became clear that a new language would have to be developed. The "Ironman" specification, issued in 1977, became the standard against which to measure a new language. A design competition was held, and the requirements were further specified in "Steelman."

The eventual language-design winner was chosen in 1979, and the new language was christened Ada, after Ada Augusta Byron Lovelace, daughter of the poet Lord Byron and later the wife of Lord Lovelace. Ada was trained in mathematics and science at the wish of her mother, who sought to steer Ada away from the mental instability and moral lapses she despised in Lord Byron. Lady Ada Lovelace is regarded as the world's first programmer on the basis of her correspondence with Charles Babbage and her published notes on his work with the Analytical Engine (see the Special Interest Box on Charles Babbage and Ada Augusta Byron in Chapter 1).

Ada, like C++, is a large language, and it was adopted not only by the defense industry, where its use was mandated by the U.S. Department of Defense, but also for other technological applications and as a general-purpose language as well. Ada is known for its multiprocessing capability—the ability to allow multiple tasks to execute independently and then synchronize and communicate when directed. It is also known as a strongly object-oriented language.

The Department of Defense "Ada mandate" was terminated in 1997, but by then Ada was well established as a programming language supporting good software engineering practice, safety, and reliability. Today, Ada is still strong in the transportation industry (aircraft, helicopters, subway systems, and European high-speed train control systems) and in safety monitoring systems at nuclear reactors, as well as in financial and communication systems. Its proponents tout Ada as "the language designed for building systems that really matter." The newest international Ada standard was adopted in 2012.

SPARK 2014 is a programming language that is a well-defined subset of Ada 2012. SPARK aims to build upon the strengths of Ada while eliminating some of its ambiguities and security concerns. SPARK goes

Practice Problem

What do you think is accomplished by the following Ada program?

```
with ada_io; use ada_io;
procedure simple is
begin
    for i in 1..10 loop
        put(i);
        put(' ');
    end loop;
    new_line;
end;
```

even farther than Ada in support for critical systems development. For example, SPARK supports "contracts" that assert conditions that should be true before a module of code is executed and conditions that should be true as a result of that execution, plus a tool that can analyze the code to verify correctness of these conditions.

10.2.6 Java

Unlike Fortran, COBOL, C, C++, and Ada, which were carefully developed as programming languages, Java was almost an accident. In early 1991, Sun Microsystems Inc. created a team of top-notch software developers and gave them free rein to do whatever creative thing they wanted. The somewhat secret "Green Team" isolated itself and set to work mapping out a strategy. Its focus was on the consumer electronics market. Televisions, VCRs, stereo systems, laser disc players, and video game machines all operated on different CPUs. Over the next 18 months, the team worked to develop the graphical user interface (GUI), a programming language, an operating system, and a hardware architecture for a handheld, remote-control device called the *7 that would allow various electronic devices to communicate over a network. The *7 was designed to be small, inexpensive, easy to use, reliable, and equipped with software that could function over the multiple hardware platforms of the consumer electronics market at that time.

Armed with this technology, Sun went looking for a business market but found none. In 1993, Mosaic, the first graphical Internet browser, was created at the National Center for Supercomputing Applications, and the World Wide Web began to emerge. This development sent the Sun group in a new direction, where its capabilities with platform independence, reliability, security, and GUI paid off: The group wrote a web browser using the programming language (later named Java) of the *7. The web browser was released in 1995, and the first version of the Java programming language itself was released in 1996. After that, Java gained market share among programming languages at quite a phenomenal rate.

Java applications are complete stand-alone programs that reside and run on a self-contained computer; these are the kinds of programs we illustrated in Chapter 9, and Java applications are everywhere. As a modern example, Twitter handles over 400 million tweets per day, and much of its core service software is written in Java. Java's development went hand in hand with the development of web browsers. Java applets (small applications) are programs designed to run from webpages. Applets are embedded in webpages on central servers; when the user views a webpage with a Java-enabled browser, the applet's code is temporarily transferred to the user's system (whatever that system may be) and interpreted/executed by the browser itself. Java applets bring audio, video, and real-time user interaction to webpages, making them "come alive" and become much more than static hyperlinked text. For example, a Java applet might display a streaming ticker tape of stock market quotes or a form that allows you to book an airline reservation online. Due to security issues, however, most web browsers no longer support Java applets, but instead use a technology called Java Web Start (or JAWS) where Java code (even for full-fledged Java applications) is accessed from the web via the user's browser, but is executed in a restricted environment outside the web browser itself. Existing Java applets can be converted to Web Start applications.

Java applications also can run on the processor of Android smart-phones. (Google Android is the operating system on the majority of the world's smartphones; Android phones represented about 88% of the total number of units shipped in the third quarter of 2016.) Android apps are usually written in Java, and there are more than 2.2 million apps, by far the majority of them free. Java has certainly made its way into many hands (or many pockets).

Java is an object-oriented language based on C++, but it avoids some of the features that can make C/C++ programs error-prone. For example, in C++ we could declare an array of 12 integers by

```
int hits[12];
```

The equivalent statement in Java is

```
int hits[] = new int[12];
```

Both Java and C++ number individual array locations beginning with 0, so there is no *hits[12]* in either case. In C++, you can write an assignment statement such as

```
hits[12] = 5;
```

that destroys the contents of some memory location outside the array, and the program will go merrily on its way. Such an assignment in Java would cause a runtime error.

One of the main features of Java is its portability; recall that platform independence was one of the goals of the original Sun "Green Team." In most languages, source code gets compiled into the object code for a particular machine, which means that the developer who wants to dis-tribute executable code needs to compile the source code on each target platform, using the appropriate compiler. The Java programmer, however, compiles source code just once, into low-level code called Java bytecode, which is then distributed to the various users. Bytecode is not itself the language of any real machine, but it can be easily translated into any specific machine language. This final translation/execution of bytecode is done by software called a Java bytecode interpreter, which must be present on each user machine. This approach is workable because the Java bytecode interpreter is a small piece of software.

Oracle Corporation acquired Sun Microsystems in 2010. The Java lan-guage is not defined by any international standards organization, so the de facto standard is whatever version of Java is currently supported by Oracle. OpenJDK is an open source version of Java for the Linux operating system.

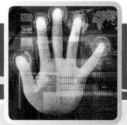

Practice Problem

Output in Java is handled by requesting the predefined Java System.out object to invoke a println() function. Also, the + operator stands for string concatenation. What is the output after execution of the following Java statement if *number* has the value 7?

```
System.out.println("The answer is" + number);
```

10.2.7 Python

The Python language was originally created in the early 1990s by Guido van Rossum at Stichting Mathematisch Centrum in the Netherlands. Its development is now overseen by the Python Software Foundation, but Van Rossum still has the final stamp of approval on "official" features of the language. However, unlike most of the other languages mentioned here, Python is an open source language. The source code is freely available and can be used, distributed, or modified by anyone. Python's advocates claim that having a community of people interested in using and improving the language has led to a better design than would have resulted from standardized or proprietary code.

Python is an *interpreted language*, meaning it is translated from source to object code at every execution. Python was originally used for system administration tasks and as a web interface language. But with the development of an extensive library of supporting code, Python has become a powerful language for more general use. As an example, SciPy is an open-source Python library with code designed to support scientific and engineering computing needs.

Python's main distinguishing feature among the procedural family of languages is its ease of use. No doubt this accounts for its increasing use as the "first" programming language, that is, the language taught in introductory college programming courses. A survey conducted in July 2014 showed that of the top 39 U.S. universities (according to the annual *U.S. News and World Report* rankings), 69% were using Python as their introductory programming language, overcoming the dominance Java held for many years as the language taught in the first programming course.

The syntax rules for Python are relaxed and intuitive, making it easy to develop programs rapidly. However, this lack of rigidity can put the responsibility for careful usage on the programmer rather than on the compiler/interpreter.

The latest version of Python, as of this writing, was released in December 2016.

10.2.8 C# and .NET

In June 2000, Microsoft introduced the C# language (pronounced "C sharp"). This language is a successor in spirit to C++, but it is a totally new language. Therefore, it has no backward-compatibility issues, as C++ had with C. C# is designed to make some improvements over C++ in safe usage, and it shares many features with Java. As an example of potentially unsafe usage, a C++ program can dynamically grab additional memory for its use during program execution, but the programmer is responsible for releasing that memory when the program no longer needs it to reduce the possibility of running out of memory. In C#, however, this process of garbage collection—reclaiming memory no longer needed by the program—is handled automatically.

Practice Problem

The following are some sample programming statements (from Ada, C++, C#, Java, and Python) to output the programmer's typical first message of Hello World:

a. `System.out.print("Hello World");`

b. `WITH TEXT_IO;`
   `TEXT_IO.PUT("Hello World");`

c. `print("Hello World")`

d. `using System;`
   `Console.Write("Hello World");`

e. `#include <iostream>`
   `using namespace std;`
   `cout << "Hello World";`

Given our claims about the simplicity of Python syntax, which of these would you judge to be the Python output statement?

The "Popularity" Contest

There is a website that keeps track, on a monthly basis, of the most "popular" programming languages. According to this site, "popularity" is not about the best language or the one with the most lines of code that have been written. It is based mainly on data gleaned from web searches about the number of practicing programmers, courses taught, and third-party vendors. Nonetheless, it is an interesting site. Visit

www.tiobe.com/index.php/content/paperinfo/tpci/index.html

to see how your favorite language rates at the moment. For May 2017, some of the languages we have discussed (or will mention later) were rated as follows:

Language	Rating
Java	1
C	2
C++	3
Python	4
C#	5
Visual Basic .NET	6
Swift	13
R	14
Go	16
COBOL	25
Ada	29
Fortran	30
Scheme	34
Prolog	35

A different view of language popularity can be obtained from the following website *http://stackoverflow.com/insights/survey/2016* that shows the results of a survey of more than 50,000 software developers. The most popular languages for 2016 were, in order, JavaScript, SQL, Java, and C#. We'll talk about JavaScript and SQL in Section 10.3.

It is impossible to discuss C# without discussing the Microsoft .NET Framework that supports C# and other programming languages. The .NET Framework is essentially a giant collection of tools for software development. It was designed so that traditional text-based applications, GUI applications, and web-based programs can all be built with equal ease. For example, the .NET Framework provides a whole library of classes for building GUIs with menus, buttons, text boxes, and so forth. And it is the .NET Framework (actually a part of the .NET Framework called the *Common Language Runtime* or *CLR*) that handles garbage collection for a C# program or for any other language that uses the .NET platform. All .NET programs—in whatever language—are compiled into Microsoft Intermediate Language (MSIL) code. Like Java bytecode, MSIL is not tied to any particular platform. The final step of compiling MSIL code into object code is done by a just-in-time (JIT) compiler (part of the CLR) on the user's machine. So, like Java, the developer achieves portability across multiple platforms because source code is compiled only once, into the MSIL.

There is one notable difference between the Java approach and the .NET approach. The Java bytecode translator is an interpreter, meaning that the first statement in a program is translated into object code and then executed, at which point the interpreter moves to the next statement and repeats these two operations, and so forth through the whole program. At the end of program execution, no object code is retained and the next time the program executes, the interpreter must repeat this task. The just-in-time compiler, on the other hand, senses when a particular module of MSIL code is being called, translates that module into object code, and then executes it. At the end of program execution, the object code for that module is still there, and if the program executes again with no changes, it can be run directly without invoking the JIT compiler. This difference between interpreted and compiled code leads to more efficient program execution.

Many programming languages have been adapted to fit into the .NET Framework, including Ada, Fortran, COBOL, C++, C# (of course), and Visual Basic .NET (see the Special Interest Box, "Old Dog, New Tricks #2" on the next page). That means applications written in any of these languages have access to the tools provided within the .NET Framework and, because all of these languages compile to MSIL, applications can be written that mix and match modules in various languages. Thus, the choice of which language to use becomes less an issue of language capability and more a matter of personal preference and familiarity.

In April 2003, only three years after the first release of C# and .NET, C# and the *CLI* (*Common Language Infrastructure*)—a significant subset of the .NET tools—were adopted as ISO standards. Edition 2 of the C# language specification was approved by ISO in 2006, but the latest version of C# is Edition 6, released in 2015. C# continues to grow in popularity as a programming language.

Old Dog, New Tricks #2

Headline News, May 1, 1964, 4:00 A.M.

Dartmouth College professor John Kemeny and a student programmer sit at neighboring computer terminals and both type RUN, executing their simple programs written in the BASIC programming language. Programming for the people is born!

During the 1960s, programming was a rather difficult task relegated to technical professionals or, in the academic world, to advanced undergraduate engineering, math, and physics majors. Dartmouth mathematics professors John Kemeny and Thomas Kurtz wanted a programming language easy enough for anyone to learn, including high school and even elementary school students. They designed BASIC (Beginner's All-purpose Symbolic Instruction Code). Here is the first BASIC program shown in the May 1964 Instruction Manual for BASIC.[2]

```
LET X = (7 + 8)/3
PRINT X
END
```

This effort of a "programming language for the people" was very successful. BASIC was supplied with most microcomputers throughout the 1980s, and as such it introduced many people, in and out of school, to simple programming ideas. (One of the earliest BASIC compilers for microcomputers was developed by a then-tiny company called Microsoft, headed by 20-year-old Harvard University dropout Bill Gates.) But by 1990, after other much more powerful languages had appeared, BASIC had faded from view.

BASIC got a new lease on life and a whole new look when Microsoft released Visual Basic in 1991. Visual Basic supplied tools to create a sophisticated GUI application by simply dragging components such as buttons and text boxes from a Toolbox onto a form, and then writing BASIC code to allow those components to respond to events, such as the click of a button. This type of easy "drag and drop" programming made Visual Basic a very popular language for rapid prototyping of Windows applications. Subsequent versions of Visual Basic produced an ever-more-powerful language. Now Visual Basic .NET is a fully object-oriented language that, like the other .NET languages, can take advantage of all the built-in .NET Framework tools. Old languages that can evolve with the times need never die!

---

[2] www.dartmouth.edu/basicfifty/basic.html

Practice Problem

A running Visual Basic program produces the following GUI:

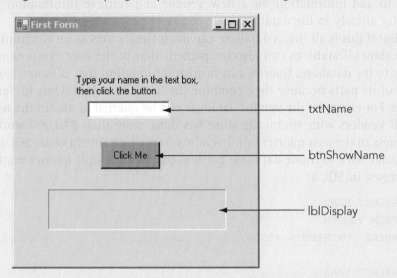

The user types a name in the text box called *txtName*, then clicks the button called *btnShowName*. This "click event" is handled by the following Visual Basic module. Explain what you think happens when this module is executed.

```
Private Sub btnShowName_Click(ByVal sender As System.Object,
                ByVal e As System.EventArgs)
        lblDisplay.Text = txtName.Text
End Sub
```

10.3 Special-Purpose Languages

Although each of the procedural languages we have mentioned has its own strengths and weaknesses, all are more or less *general-purpose languages* that can address different types of problems. In this section, we visit four *special-purpose languages* that were each designed for only one particular task. These four are merely representative; many other specialized languages exist.

10.3.1 SQL

Our first specialized language is *SQL*, which stands for *S*tructured *Q*uery *L*anguage. SQL is designed to be used with databases, which are collections of related facts and information. We'll do some work with databases in Chapter 14, but here is the general idea. A database stores data; the user of the database must be able to add new data and to retrieve data already stored. For example, a database contains information on vendors with which a retail store does business. For each vendor, the database contains the name, address, and phone number of the vendor, the name of the product line the vendor sells, and the amount of stock purchased from that vendor during the previous business quarter. The database user should be able to add information on a new vendor and retrieve information on a vendor already in the database.

But if this is all that a database can do, it simply acts as an electronic filing cabinet. Databases can also be queried—that is, the user can pose questions to the database. Queries can furnish information that is more than the sum of its parts because they combine the individual data items in various ways. For example, the vendor database can be queried to obtain the names of all vendors with whom the store has done more than $40,000 worth of business in the past quarter or all vendors from a certain zip code. SQL is the language used to frame database queries. Our two example queries might be expressed in SQL as

```
SELECT NAME
FROM VENDOR
WHERE PURCHASE > 40000;

SELECT NAME
FROM VENDOR
WHERE ZIP = "55416";
```

SQL was developed by IBM, and in 1986, it was adopted by the American National Standards Institute (ANSI) as the standard query language in the United States; it has since been adopted by the ISO as an international standard. Even database systems that provide users with easier—even graphical—ways to frame queries are simply using a front end that eventually translates the query into an equivalent SQL statement.

An SQL query does not give specific directions as to how to retrieve the desired result. Instead, it merely describes the desired result. This makes SQL similar in flavor to a logic programming language, which we'll see in a later section.

10.3.2 HTML

HTML stands for *HyperText Markup Language*. It is used to create HTML documents that, when viewed with web browser software, become webpages. An HTML document consists of the text to be displayed on the webpage, together with a number of special characters called tags that achieve formatting, special effects, and references to other HTML documents. Although we speak of "HTML programming," that's a bit of a stretch. The program is just giving the web browser instructions on how to interpret and display text; there's no computation or processing going on as we think of with programming in general.

HTML tags are enclosed in angle brackets (< >) and often come in pairs. The end tag, the second tag in the pair, looks like the begin tag, the first tag in the pair, but with an additional / in front.

The overall format for an HTML document is

```
<html>
  <head>
    <title> stuff to go in the title bar </title>
  </head>
  <body>
    stuff to go on the page
  </body>
</html>
```

Here we see the paired tags for the document as a whole (<html>, </html>), the head (<head>, </head>), the title (<title>, </title>)—framing what appears in the title bar or title tab when the web browser displays the page, and also what will be displayed in a list of search-engine results—and the body (<body>, </body>)—framing what is on the page itself.

Of course, other material needs to go between the beginning and ending "body" tags, or the page will be blank. Figure 10.4 shows an HTML document, and Figure 10.5 shows how the webpage actually looks when viewed with a web browser. By comparing the two, you can probably understand the

FIGURE 10.4

```
<html>
  <head>
    <title>First Page</title>
  </head>

  <body>
    <h1>This is an H1 heading</h1>
    <p>This text is <strong>IMPORTANT</strong> and
        this text is <em>emphasized</em></p>
    <p>Below is a bulleted list:</p>
    <ul>
        <li>First item</li>
        <li>Second item</li>
    </ul>
    <p>Here is a link to another Web page,
        <a href="http://PBS.org">PBS</a></p>
    <p>And here is an image:</p>
        <img src="flower1.jpg"
        alt="Sunflowers in a field">
  </body>
</html>
```

HTML code for a webpage

FIGURE 10.5

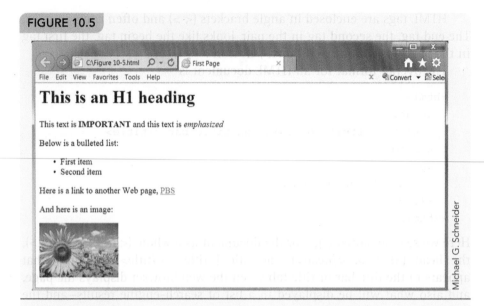

Body of webpage generated by the HTML code in Figure 10.4

meaning of the tags used, as explained in Figure 10.6.[3] Technically, *href* is an attribute of the "a" tag that indicates a link to another document, in this case the home page of the well-known PBS website. Similarly, *src* is an attribute of the "img" tag that gives the "source" for the image. In Figure 10.4, the source is just the image filename, meaning that the image file is in the same folder as the HTML code file; if the image file were elsewhere, the source would have to show the pathname where the image file can be found. The second attribute

FIGURE 10.6

HTML Tag	Purpose
h1	Create H1 heading (bold with largest font size)
p	New paragraph
strong	Important
em	Emphasized
ul	Unordered list (bulleted list)
li	List item
a href = "..."	Provides hyperlink address
img src = "..."	Gives the source (location) for the image file

Some HTML tags

---

[3]In HTML5, the <strong> and <em> tags indicate that the enclosed text should be "important" or "emphasized" in some way. The webpage text is usually displayed as bold or italic text, respectively, so it might seem that there is little difference between <strong> and <b> (bold), or between <em> and <i> (italic). But a screen reader for visually impaired persons cannot deal with a direction about the font style, whereas a <strong> or <em> tag would indicate some change of voice for importance or emphasis.

Laboratory Experience 13

This Laboratory Experience will give you practice in HTML programming. Due to powerful web editor software, you don't have to know HTML in order to create a webpage, but HTML is what lies "under the hood" of all webpages—even Facebook!—so this will give you an insight into the basics of webpage creation. You will also learn how to use your web browser to perform simple file transfers from special computers called FTP servers. This will enable you to access a wealth of software and data files in the public domain.

of the img tag, the *alt* attribute, is displayed if the image file cannot be located. The text in the *alt* attribute is also used by assistive technologies for visually impaired persons, who would otherwise be unable to "see" the image.

Early word processors required the user to type in various codes manually to mark text for boldface, italic, and so forth. Later, more sophisticated word processors with GUI interfaces reduced these tasks to point and click. The same has come to pass with HTML code. HTML documents themselves are simply text files that can be created using any text editor by typing the appropriate tags. But web editor software makes it possible to create HTML code by, for example, highlighting text and clicking a button to insert a pair of tags that surround the highlighted text.

10.3.3 JavaScript

A *scripting language* is a "lightweight" language that is interpreted (translated, then executed, statement by statement). Scripting language code fragments can be embedded in webpages to make those pages active rather than static. JavaScript is such a language; keep in mind that JavaScript is not the same as the full-blown Java programming language we discussed earlier.

Consider the HTML page from the previous section. When this page is displayed by the web browser, the user has no interaction with the page except possibly to click on the hypertext link to go to another page. In particular, the image on the page is fixed. The webpage can be made a little more interesting if the image changes when the user hovers the mouse over the current image. In fact, let's switch back and forth between the original image and a second image as the user moves the mouse into and out of the image area of the page. To accomplish this, we'll use a JavaScript function called *imageSwitch()*. The JavaScript code will be placed within <script></script> tags to alert the browser that these statements are to be interpreted as JavaScript commands.

The *imageSwitch()* function must accomplish two tasks. One is to reset the *src* attribute of the "img" tag. But we have to say what image tag we are modifying, so in the original image tag we'll add an *id* attribute. Basically, we

Beyond HTML

The tags in HTML are, as we have seen, specified. The tag pair <p> </p>, for example, is used for marking the enclosed text as a paragraph. The writer of the HTML document cannot invent new tags. *XML* (*eXtensible Markup Language*) is a newer markup language. It is a "metalanguage," that is, a markup language for markup languages. Using XML, the writer can create his or her own tags; an XML document is not about displaying information but about how to structure and interpret information to be displayed. An XML document usually also contains or refers to a *schema* that describes the data, and the body of the XML document can then be checked against the schema to be sure that it is a well-formed document. All modern browsers support mechanisms that translate XML documents into HTML documents for display. XML allows for flexible document interchange across the web; for example, in May 2003, the National Library of Medicine announced a "Tagset" for journal articles to provide a single format in which journal articles that originate from many different publishers and societies can be archived. XML-based file formats now form the basis for office productivity tools such as Microsoft Office, Apple iWork, and Google Docs; for example, the file extension .docx for a Word document indicates that it is using an XML file format, and similarly with .xlsx for Excel spreadsheets and .pptx for PowerPoint slides.

Some other XML standards are shown in the following table; all of these facilitate exchange, within a community of special interests, of documents or other data that might otherwise have differing vocabulary or formats.

Name	Data to be exchanged
BeerXML	Beer brewing data
LandXML	Data of interest to land developers, civil engineers, and surveyors
LegalXML	Documents between courts and attorneys, court transcripts, electronic contracts
RailML	Railway industry data
RecipeML	Recipe ingredients (facilitates automated conversions from one type of measurement to another)

are giving the image a name; we'll call it *mainImage*. This name is not the name of an actual visual image (a picture); it's the name of the image element on the page that holds a picture as determined by its *src* attribute. In the original image tag, we'll also add two additional attributes that are event handlers, that is, they respond to the events of the user moving the mouse over the image element (a MouseOver event) or moving the mouse away from the image element (a MouseOut event). For either of those two events, we want to call the *imageSwitch()* function. Figure 10.7 shows the new image tag for the page.

The *imageSwitch()* function itself uses a variable called *nextPicName* that contains the image filename for the new picture, the one being switched to. The image element *src* attribute will be set to the value of this variable. The code is

```
document.getElementById("mainImage")
            .src=nextPicName;
```

This statement locates the appropriate image element by its id (even though in this case there is only one image element on the page) and assigns *nextPicName* to its *src* attribute.

The second task of the *imageSwitch()* function is to make sure that *nextPicName* is updated to the appropriate value in preparation for the next image switch. This is accomplished by an if/then/else statement, one of the basic algorithmic constructs we introduced in Chapter 2. The code is straightforward: If we just changed to the flower2.jpg image, then we should be ready next time to change to the flower1.jpg image, and vice versa.

```
if (nextPicName=="flower2.jpg")
{
      nextPicName = "flower1.jpg";
}
else
{
      nextPicName = "flower2.jpg";
}
```

We are almost done. The only remaining thing is to initialize the *nextPicName* variable. We'll use another JavaScript function called *startValue()* to do that task. Because the page loads with the *flower1.jpg* image showing, the *nextPicName* value (the new image value) should be *flower2.jpg*. In the HTML body, we'll use the "onload" event handler to invoke the *startValue()* function to get things started.

Figure 10.8 shows the complete HTML page with the embedded JavaScript.

FIGURE 10.7

```
<img src="flower1.jpg" id="mainImage"
          alt="Sunflowers in a field"
          onMouseOut="imageSwitch()"
          onMouseOver="imageSwitch()">
```

The new HTML <img> (image) tag

FIGURE 10.8

```html
<html>
  <head>
    <title>First Page</title>

    <script language = "JavaScript">

    function startValue()
    {
      nextPicName = "flower2.jpg";
    }

    function imageSwitch()
    {
      //switch photo to nextPicName
      document.getElementById("mainImage")
          .src=nextPicName;

      //set up for the next switch
      if(nextPicName=="flower2.jpg")
      {
          nextPicName = "flower1.jpg";
      }
      else
      {
          nextPicName = "flower2.jpg";
      }
    }
    </script>

  </head>

  <body onload="startValue()">
    <h1>This is an H1 heading</h1>
    <p>This text is <strong>IMPORTANT</strong> and
        this text is <em>emphasized</em></p>
    <p>Below is a bulleted list:</p>
    <ul>
        <li>First item</li>
        <li>Second item</li>
    </ul>
    <p>Here is a link to another Web page,
        <a href="http://PBS.org">PBS</a></p>
    <p>And here is an image:</p>
    <img src="flower1.jpg" id="mainImage"
        alt="Sunflowers in a field"
        onMouseOut="imageSwitch()"
        onMouseOver="imageSwitch()">
  </body>
</html>
```

JavaScript embedded in an HTML page

PHP

Webpages that are designed using HTML are generally static, that is, their content looks the same each time the page is opened in your browser. However, when you visit your favorite online store, the content is different with each visit, reflecting, for example, items on sale or the newest products. These are dynamic webpages (their content changes) that are stored on the web server of the online merchant. Dynamic pages are often tied to a behind-the-scenes product database. If a new product becomes available or a price changes because of a sale, the change is made in one place in the underlying database. Whenever any dynamic page tied to the database is requested from the server, the latest database information is loaded into the page before it is sent back to your web browser, and your browser then displays it. The HTML for the various pages does not have to be constantly rewritten to incorporate the new data.

PHP (which originally stood for Personal Home Pages but now stands for PHP: Hypertext Preprocessor) is a *server-side scripting language*, that is, its programs run on the web server computing system rather than on the user's own machine. Like JavaScript, PHP is embedded within HTML code in webpages hosted on a server. PHP is particularly adept at making database connections for dynamic webpages. The PHP code, when executed, sets up a connection to the database and formats HTML code on the page to include the new data values. According to a March 2017 survey, over 82% of the websites whose server-side programming languages were known were using PHP.

Practice Problems

1. Describe the result of executing the following SQL query on the vendor database.

```
SELECT NAME
FROM VENDOR
WHERE CITY = "CHICAGO";
```

2. Given the following HTML statement, what does the corresponding line of text on the webpage look like?

```
<p>These are the <em>times</em> that try
<strong>men's souls</strong></p>
```

3. Type the HTML code of Figure 10.4 into a text editor such as Notepad. Save the file with an .html extension. Find a small .jpg image (it need not be sunflowers!) and store it in the same folder as the .html file. Then double-click the .html file to bring it up in your browser. Does it look like Figure 10.5?

10.3.4 R

R is a specialized programming language designed for statistical computing and graphics. The name "R" comes at least in part from the first names of the two authors of the language, Ross Ihaka and Robert Gentleman. Like Python, R is an open source language. A group called the R Core Team controls modifications to the core code, but many code libraries have been contributed by users. The first version of R was released in 2000; the latest version, R.3.3, was released in March 2017.[4]

Given a set of data, you can ask R to compute the maximum value, minimum value, mean, median, standard deviation, and other more sophisticated statistical functions. Many of these computations can be done in a spreadsheet, but having an R program allows multiple data sets to be run efficiently and repeatedly. R has become more popular with the rapid development of the field of "data science" (we'll talk more about data science in Chapter 14).

Here is an example using R on a trivially small data set. A medical research team is concerned about medical conditions X and Y, and has gathered data from surveys at six different sites. The data from each site consists of the percentage of the survey population that exhibits condition X, condition Y, are smokers, are overweight, or have low income levels. This data was entered into a spreadsheet and then saved as a .csv (comma-delimited) file. One of the advantages of R over many other languages is the ease with which tabular data in such a file can be loaded into memory and then displayed. Only two simple commands are required. Here, boldface indicates what the user types:

> **mydata <- read.csv("MedData.csv")**

> **head(mydata, n = 6)**

---

[4] The R code shown in this section was run on Microsoft R Open 3.3.2, available for free download at https://mran.microsoft.com/download.

R responds immediately with the resulting display of data:

```
    X Y       Smoker   Overweight   Low_Income
1 4 2          28         19            32
2 6 2          31         22            28
3 3 4          24         31            35
4 5 7          18         25            25
5 2 6          32         29            34
6 4 5          41         35            37
```

Another one-word command produces a lot of statistical results:

> **summary(mydata)**

```
       X              Y            Smoker        Overweight       Low_Income
Min.   :2.00   Min.   :2.000  Min.   :18.00  Min.   :19.00  Min.   :25.00
1st Qu.:3.25   1st Qu.:2.500  1st Qu.:25.00  1st Qu.:22.75  1st Qu.:29.00
Median :4.00   Median :4.500  Median :29.50  Median :27.00  Median :33.00
Mean   :4.00   Mean   :4.333  Mean   :29.00  Mean   :26.83  Mean   :31.83
3rd Qu.:4.75   3rd Qu.:5.750  3rd Qu.:31.75  3rd Qu.:30.50  3rd Qu.:34.75
Max.   :6.00   Max.   :7.000  Max.   :41.00  Max.   :35.00  Max.   :37.00
```

Here we see the *minimum* and *maximum* values for each of the five attributes of interest over the six sites. These results also show the *mean* (often called the average), and the *median* (roughly half of the six data values are above the median value and the other half are below if the six data values were sorted in order). The 1st Quartile value is a value such that roughly 25% of the sorted data values are below it and the 3rd Quartile value is a value such that roughly 75% of the sorted data values are below it, although these are quite meaningless on such small data samples.

The medical research team is interested in any correlation between these five attributes; *correlation* measures the extent to which two attributes increase or decrease more or less together. A correlation value can range between -1.0 and $+1.0$. Negative values mean that the two attributes being compared change in the opposite way–when one goes up, the other tends to go down, and vice versa; positive values mean that the two attributes change in the same way as each other–when one value goes up (or down), the other also tends to go up (or down).

The R command

> **cor(mydata)**

produces the following result:

	X	Y	Smoker	Overweight	Low_Income
X	1.0000000	-0.34232660	-0.1450953	-0.4756067	-0.68604993
Y	-0.3423266	1.00000000	-0.2110973	0.5264281	-0.07828438
Smoker	-0.1450953	-0.21109734	1.0000000	0.4399277	0.67869945
Overweight	-0.4756067	0.52642809	0.4399277	1.0000000	0.66617525
Low_Income	-0.6860499	-0.07828438	0.6786995	0.6661752	1.00000000

Obviously, X values correlate 100% with X values, and similarly for the other four attributes. Here it appears that conditions X and Y have no correlation (−0.34232660). However, condition Y has a moderate correlation (0.5264281) with being overweight, and both smoking and being overweight have a somewhat strong correlation with low income (0.67869945 and 0.66617525, respectively). Correlation does not mean cause, that is even if Y had a very high correlation with being overweight, that would not mean that condition Y is caused by being overweight or vice versa.

Finally, R makes it easy to visualize large data sets in many ways. The following two commands cause R to produce the colorful bar graph seen in Figure 10.9.

```
> barplot(as.matrix(mydata), main = "Survey Data", ylab = "Percent",
names.arg=c("X", "Y", "Smoker", "Overweight", "Low_Income"),
beside=TRUE, col=rainbow(6))
```

```
> legend("topleft", c("Site 1", "Site 2", "Site 3", "Site 4", "Site 5",
"Site 6"), cex=0.8, bty="n", fill=rainbow(6))
```

FIGURE 10.9

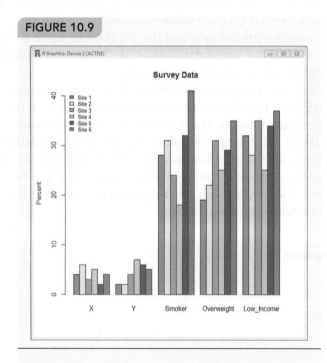

R bar chart

10.4 Alternative Programming Paradigms

Computer scientists are fond of the word *paradigm*. A paradigm is a model or mental framework for representing or thinking about something. The paradigm of procedural programming languages says that a sequence of detailed instructions is provided to the computer. Each instruction accesses or modifies the contents of a memory location. If the computer carries out these instructions one at a time, then the final result of all the memory cell manipulations is the solution to the problem at hand. This sounds suspiciously like our definition of an algorithm in Chapter 1 ("a well-ordered collection of unambiguous and effectively computable operations that when executed produces a result . . ."). In fact, programming in a procedural language consists of

- Planning the algorithm

- Capturing the "unambiguous and effectively computable operations" as program instructions

In a procedural programming language, then, we must pay attention to the details of exactly how the computer is going to accomplish the desired task in a step-by-step fashion. In object-oriented programming, the procedural paradigm still holds, but the step-by-step instructions may be split into multiple small sets that are encapsulated within classes.

In this section, we look at programming languages that use alternatives to the procedural approach—languages based on other paradigms. It is as though · we have studied French, Spanish, and Italian (different but related languages) and are now about to embark on a study of Arabic, Japanese, or sign language—languages totally different in form, structure, and alphabet. Alternative paradigms for programming languages include viewing a program's actions as:

- A combination of various transformations on items (functional programming)

- A series of logical deductions from known facts (logic programming)

- Multiple subtasks of the same problem being performed simultaneously by different processors (parallel programming)

We'll look briefly at each of these alternative programming paradigms, focusing on the different conceptual views rather than on the details of language syntax. In short, this chapter won't make you an expert programmer, or even a novice programmer, in any of these languages, but you'll have a sense of some of the different approaches to programming languages that have been developed.

10.4.1 Functional Programming

Functional programming had its start with the design of the LISP (*LISt Processing*) programming language by John McCarthy at MIT in 1958. This makes LISP second only to Fortran in longevity.

A functional programming language views every task in terms of (surprise!) functions. Unlike the more general usage of the word function in some procedural programming languages, *function* in this context means something like a mathematical function—a recipe for taking an argument (or possibly several arguments) and doing something with them to compute a single value. More formally, when the arguments are given values, the function transforms those values, according to some specified rule, into a corresponding resulting value. Different values for the arguments can produce different resulting values. The doubling function $f(x) = 2x$ transforms the argument 3 into 6 because $f(3) = 2*3 = 6$, and it transforms the argument 6 into 12 because $f(6) = 2*6 = 12$. In the grand sense, we can think of a program as a function acting on input data (the arguments) and transforming them into the desired output.

In a functional programming language, certain functions, called *primitive functions* or just *primitives*, are defined as part of the language. Other functions can be defined and named by the programmer. We will look at examples using Scheme, a functional programming language that was derived from LISP in the late 1970s.

To define the doubling function using Scheme, we can say

```
(define (double x)
    (* 2 x))
```

The keyword *define* indicates that we are defining a new function. The function name and its list of arguments follow in parentheses. The function name is *double*, and *x* is its single argument. The definition says that when this function is invoked, it is to multiply ('*') the argument value *x* by 2. Having defined the function, we can now invoke it in a program by giving the function name, followed by a list of values for the arguments of the function. (For the *double* function, there is only one number in the list of argument values because there is only one argument.) Scheme responds immediately to a function invocation by displaying the result, so the following interaction occurs as the user invokes the *double* function with various argument values (boldface indicates what the user types).

(double 4)
8
(double 8)
16

Here's the definition of another function:

```
(define (square x)
    (* x x))
```

which says that the function named *square*, when invoked, is to multiply the single argument value by itself. Thus a dialog with Scheme could be

(square 3)
9

Functions, once defined, can be used in the definition of other functions. This can lead to nested tasks that must be performed. The function *polynomial*, defined by

```
(define (polynomial x)
     (double (square x)))
```

is the function that we would write mathematically as $g(x) = 2x^2$. Using this function, the dialog could be

(polynomial 3)

18

When the *polynomial* function is invoked with the argument 3, Scheme consults the function definition and sees that this is really

```
(double (square 3))
```

Thus, the polynomial function must invoke the *double* function, and it is to invoke that function with an argument value of (square 3). Therefore, the first thing to do is to invoke the *square* function with an argument value of 3. The result is $3^2 = 9$. This 9 then gets used as the argument value for the double function, resulting in 18. The total computation is equivalent to $g(3) = 2(3)^2 = 2(9) = 18$.

Here we've defined one function (*polynomial*) in terms of another function (*double*) acting on the result of applying a third function (*square*). In functional programming languages, we can build complex combinations of functions that use the results of applying other functions, which use the results of applying still other functions, and so on. In fact, functional programming languages are sometimes called applicative languages because of this property of repeatedly applying functions.

As the name LISP suggests, LISP processes lists of things and so does Scheme. The arguments to functions, then, are often lists. As a trivial case, "nothing" can be thought of as an empty list, which is called *nil*. We will use four primitive list-processing functions available in Scheme, namely,

list
car
cdr
null?

The first function is called *list*. This function can have any number of arguments, and its action is to create a list out of those arguments. Therefore,

(list 3 4 5)

evaluates to the list 3, 4, 5, which we write as

```
(3  4  5)
```

Two other list-processing functions are called *car* (pronounced as when it means an automobile) and *cdr* (pronounced "could-er"). (The names have historical significance from the distant past. Car stands for "Contents of Address Register," and cdr stands for "Contents of Decrement Register."

These registers were part of the architecture of the IBM 704 computer on which LISP was originally implemented.) The *car* function takes a nonempty list as its argument and produces as a result the first element in that list. Therefore, a dialog with Scheme could consist of

(car (list 3 4 5))

3

The *cdr* function takes a nonempty list as its argument and produces as a result the list that remains after the first element has been removed. Therefore,

(cdr (list 3 4 5))

evaluates to the list

(4 5)

As a special case, when the *cdr* function is applied to an argument consisting of a one-element list, the empty list is produced as the result. Thus,

(cdr (list 5))

evaluates to the list *nil*. Note that the *car* function applied to a list evaluates to a single list element, whereas the *cdr* function applied to a list evaluates to another, shorter list.

The final primitive list-processing function is *null?*, which has a single list as its argument and evaluates to true if the list is *nil* (empty) and to false if the list is nonempty. Armed with these primitives, we can at last write a little Scheme program (Figure 10.10) to add numbers.

Dialog with the program in Figure 10.10 could result in

(adder (list 3 4 5))

12

Let's see how this works. Our function *adder* was defined to have one argument, symbolically denoted in the definition by *input-list*. Now we're invoking this function where the argument has the value of (*list* 3 4 5); that is to say, the function is to operate on (3 4 5). The *cond* function (short for "conditional") is acting like an if-else statement: It is equivalent to

```
if (null? input-list)
   total = 0;
else
   total = (car input-list) + (adder(cdr input-list));
```

FIGURE 10.10

```
(define (adder input-list)
  (cond ((null? input-list) 0)
     (else (+ (car input-list)
        (adder (cdr input-list))))))
```

Scheme program to add numbers

The condition "null? input-list" is evaluated and found to be false because *input-list* at this point is (*list* 3 4 5) or (3 4 5). The else clause is executed, and it says to add two quantities. The first of these two quantities is (*car input-list*), which is (*car* (*list* 3 4 5)), or 3. Thus, 3 is to be added to the second quantity. The second quantity is the result of invoking the *adder* function on the argument (*cdr input-list*), which is (*cdr* (*list* 3 4 5)), or (4 5). The value, as constructed so far, is therefore

    3 + (*adder* (*list* 4 5))

Now the program invokes the *adder* function again, this time with an argument of (*list* 4 5) instead of (*list* 3 4 5). Once again we test whether this list is *nil* (it isn't), so we add together

    (*car* (*list* 4 5)) + (*adder* (*cdr* (*list* 4 5)))

or

    4 + (*adder* (*list* 5))

The *adder* function is invoked again with an argument of (*list* 5). The list still is not *nil*, so we add together

    (*car* (*list* 5)) + (*adder* (*cdr* (*list* 5)))

or

    5 + (*adder nil*)

A final invocation of the *adder* function, this time with the *nil* list as its argument, takes the other branch of the *cond* statement, which results in 0. Altogether, then, we've done

    (*adder* (*list* 3 4 5))

or

    (*adder* (3 4 5)) =
        3 + (*adder* (4 5)) =
        3 + 4 + (*adder* (5)) =
        3 + 4 + 5 + (*adder nil*) =
        3 + 4 + 5 + 0 = 12

The definition of the *adder* function involves the *adder* function again, this time acting on a shorter list. Note in our example how we invoke the *adder* function repeatedly—first on (3 4 5), then on (4 5), next on (5), and finally on *nil*. Something that is defined in terms of "smaller versions" of itself is said to be recursive, so the *adder* function is a recursive function.

Recursion is one of the features of functional languages that makes possible short and elegant solutions to many problems. Although recursion is a dominant mode of operation in functional languages, many procedural languages also support recursion, so that's not the major argument for using a functional language. Then what is the benefit of going to a functional language?

A functional language allows for clarity of thought; data values are transformed by flowing, as it were, through a stream of mathematical functions. The programmer has no concern about where intermediate values are stored, nor indeed about how a "list" could occupy many memory cells. Another layer of abstraction has been offered to the programmer—the rarefied layer of pure mathematics. Because functions are described in a mathematical way by what they do to an item of data rather than by how they modify memory cells in the process of doing it, the possibility of side effects is eliminated. A side effect occurs when a function, in the course of acting on its argument values to produce a result value, also changes other values that it has no business changing. Implementing a function in a procedural language, where the major mode of operation is modification of memory cells, opens the door to potential side effects.

It's All in How You
Look, Look, Look, . . . at It

We used recursion to define the function to add a list, as follows: Add the first list element to the result of adding the rest of the list elements together. The recursive way of thinking takes a bit of getting used to. For example,

- Reading a book can be defined as reading the first page followed by reading the rest of the book.
- Climbing a ladder can be defined as climbing the first rung followed by climbing the rest of the ladder.

Having learned to program in a procedural language, some people are initially uncomfortable with the recursive style of functional languages. It might seem as if mysterious things are going on in the background and suddenly there's a result.

Consider the following scenario. You are standing in a long line at the grocery store, and you'd like to know exactly how many people are ahead of you.

Solution #1: You step out of line to get a better view and count the number of people. Your algorithm is something like:

```
count = 0
while there is an uncounted person
    pick the next uncounted person
    increment count
stop
```

This is an iterative (looping) solution.

Solution #2: You ask the person in line ahead of you how many people are in line ahead of him. When he responds, you add 1 to his count, and that's the number of people ahead of you. You have to have faith that all the people in line ahead of you know how to do the same process, and that when the person ahead of you finally responds, he'll be giving you the correct answer for how many people are ahead of him. This is a recursive solution. Here's how it works in more detail.

You   Jose   Anna   Tom

You ask Jose how many people are ahead of him. He tells you to wait, and he asks Anna, "How many people are ahead of you?" Anna asks Jose to wait, and she asks Tom, "How many people are ahead of you?" Tom can answer this question, so he tells Anna, "There are 0 people ahead of me." Anna adds 1 (to account for Tom), then tells Jose, "There is 1 person ahead of me." Jose adds 1 to this count (to account for Anna), then tells you, "There are 2 people ahead of me." Finally receiving this news from Jose, you add one (to account for Jose), and then you know there are 3 people ahead of you. You just ask the correct question, wait for a bit, and then there's your answer (unless you are the special *base case* of Tom, who actually has to provide the first answer).

Practice Problems

1. To what does each of the following evaluate?

   a. **(cdr (list 1 2 3 4))**

   b. **(car (cdr (list 4 5 6)))**

2. Define a function in Scheme that adds 3 to a number.

Laboratory Experience 14

This Laboratory Experience will guide you through some functional programming exercises. You'll see that a higher level of problem solving is possible than in procedural languages, where you have to write step-by-step instructions to manipulate data values by way of specific memory locations. You will need your own LISP or Scheme interpreter; a free Scheme interpreter is available to download at *www.gnu.org/software/mit-scheme/* or you can run Scheme online at *www.biwascheme.org/*

10.4.2 Logic Programming

Functional programming gets away from explicitly instructing the computer about the details of each step to be performed; instead, it specifies various transformations of data and then allows combinations of transformations to be performed. Logic programming languages go a step further toward not specifying exactly how a task is to be done. In logic programming, various facts are asserted to be true, and on the basis of these facts, a logic program can infer or deduce other facts. When a *query* (a question) is posed to the program, it begins with the storehouse of facts and attempts to apply logical deductions, in as efficient a manner as possible, to answer the query. Logic programming languages are sometimes called declarative programming languages (as opposed to procedural languages) because their programs, instead of issuing step-by-step procedural commands, make declarations or assertions that various facts are true.

A logic program relates to a domain of interest in which the declarations make sense (such as medicine, literature, or chemistry), and the queries are related to that domain. Logic programming has been used to write expert systems. In an *expert system* about a particular domain, a human "expert" in that domain contributes facts based on his or her knowledge and experience. A logic program using these facts as its declarations can then make inferences that are close to those the human expert would make.

The best-known logic programming language is Prolog, which was developed in France at the University of Marseilles in 1972 by a group headed by A. Colmerauer. Prolog stands for *PRO*gramming in *LOG*ic. Prolog programs consist of *facts* and *rules*. A Prolog fact expresses a property about a single object or a relationship among several objects. For example, let's write a Prolog program in the domain of American history. We are interested in which

U.S. presidents were in office when certain events occurred and in the chronology of those presidents' terms in office. Here is a short list of facts (declarations):

```
president(lincoln, gettysburgaddress).
president(lincoln, civilwar).
president(nixon, firstmoonlanding).
president(jefferson, lewisandclark).
president(kennedy, cubanmissilecrisis).
president(fdr, worldwarII).
before(jefferson, lincoln).
before(lincoln, fdr).
before(fdr, kennedy).
before(kennedy, nixon).
```

The interpretation of these facts is fairly obvious. For example, the declaration

```
president(jefferson, lewisandclark).
```

asserts or declares that Jefferson was the U.S. president during the Lewis and Clark expedition. And

```
before(kennedy, nixon).
```

asserts that Kennedy was president before Nixon. (There are a number of versions of Prolog available; the version we use requires that identifiers for specific items begin with lowercase letters and have no internal blanks or underscores.)

This list of facts constitutes a Prolog program. We interact with the program by posing queries; this is the way Prolog programs are executed. For example, the user could make the following query (boldface indicates what the user types):

?before(lincoln, fdr).

which represents the question "Was Lincoln president before FDR?" Prolog responds

```
before(lincoln, fdr).
true
```

because "before(lincoln, fdr)" is a fact contained in the program.

Here's some further dialogue with Prolog using this same program.

?president(lincoln, civilwar).
```
president(lincoln, civilwar).
true
```
?president(bush, iraq).
```
president(bush, iraq).
false
```

The first query corresponds to a declaration in the program, and the second does not. The "false" response does not signify that the statement is indeed false, only that its truth value cannot be confirmed because it is not part of the collection of facts in the program.

More complicated queries can be phrased. A query of the form "A, B" is asking Prolog whether fact A and fact B are both in the program. Thus, a query such as

?president(lincoln, civilwar), before(lincoln, fdr).

produces a "true" response because both facts are in the program. The interpretation is that Lincoln was president during the Civil War and that Lincoln was president before FDR.

So far, Prolog appears to be little more than some sort of retrieval system that does lookups on a table of facts. But Prolog can do much more. Variables can be used within queries, and this is what gives Prolog its power. Variables must begin with uppercase letters. The query

?president(lincoln, X).

is asking for a match against facts in the program of the form

president(lincoln, "something")

In other words, X can stand for anything that is in the "president" relation with Lincoln. The responses are

```
president(lincoln, X).
X = gettysburgaddress
X = civilwar
```

because both

```
president(lincoln, gettysburgaddress).
president(lincoln, civilwar).
```

are facts in the program.

Let's describe what it means for one president to precede another in office. It may appear that the *before* relation already takes care of this. Certainly if "before(X, Y)" is true, then President X precedes President Y. However, in our sample program,

```
before(lincoln, fdr).
before(fdr, kennedy).
```

are both true, but that does not tell us that Lincoln precedes Kennedy (which is also true). Of course, we could add another *before* fact to cover this case, but that is an *ad hoc* patch. Instead, let's add further declarations to the program to define the *precedes* relation. We already know that two presidents in the *before* relation should also be in a *precedes* relation. Furthermore, from the previous example, it would appear that if X is before Z and Z is before Y, then "precedes(X, Y)" should also be true. But we can say more than that: if X is before Z and Z precedes Y, then "precedes(X, Y)" should be true. This extension means that Jefferson precedes Kennedy because

before(fdr, kennedy)

implies   precedes(fdr, kennedy)

                    before(lincoln, fdr)
                    precedes(fdr, kennedy)
    implies   precedes(lincoln, kennedy)

and

                    before(jefferson, lincoln)
                    precedes(lincoln, kennedy)
    implies   precedes(jefferson, kennedy)

Using this reasoning, we have derived three new "precedes" facts that were not in the original list of facts.

Thus, we want to say that there are two ways in which X can precede Y:

precedes(X, Y) if before(X, Y)
precedes(X, Y) if before(X, Z) and precedes(Z, Y)

We can make declarations in our Prolog program that express the *precedes* relation, but this time the declarations are stated as rules rather than as facts. A Prolog rule is a declaration of an "if A then B" form, which means that if A is true (A is a fact), then B is also true (B is a fact). The actual Prolog declarations follow; think of the notation B :- A as meaning "if A then B."

```
precedes(X, Y) :- before(X, Y).
precedes(X, Y) :- before(X, Z), precedes(Z, Y).
```

The rule for *precedes* includes *precedes* as part of its definition; it is therefore a recursive rule.

Our Prolog program now consists of the facts and rules shown in Figure 10.11.

FIGURE 10.11

```
president(lincoln, gettysburgaddress).
president(lincoln, civilwar).
president(nixon, firstmoonlanding).
president(jefferson, lewisandclark).
president(kennedy, cubanmissilecrisis).
president(fdr, worldwarII).

before(jefferson, lincoln).
before(lincoln, fdr).
before(fdr, kennedy).
before(kennedy, nixon).

precedes(X, Y) :- before(X, Y).
precedes(X, Y) :- before(X, Z), precedes(Z, Y).
```

A Prolog program

Here's some further dialogue, using the new program. Be sure you understand why each query receives the response or responses it does.

?precedes(fdr, kennedy).
```
precedes(fdr, kennedy).
true
```
?precedes(lincoln, nixon).
```
precedes(lincoln, nixon).
true
```
?precedes(lincoln, X).
```
precedes(lincoln, X).
X = fdr
X = kennedy
X = nixon
```

Let's add one final declaration to the program—a declaration that says that event X occurred earlier than event Y if X took place during President R's term in office, Y took place during President S's term in office, and President R precedes President S. (Do you agree with this definition of the *earlier* relation?) Here's the rule:

```
earlier(X, Y) :- president(R, X), president(S, Y),
                 precedes(R, S).
```

Then a final query of

?earlier(worldwarII, X).

produces the responses
```
earlier(worldwarII, X).
X = firstmoonlanding
X = cubanmissilecrisis
```

In this simple example, it is easy to check that the responses to our queries are correct, and it is also not difficult to do the necessary comparisons with the program declarations to see how Prolog was able to arrive at its responses. The interesting thing to note, however, is that the program consists solely of declaratives (facts and rules), not instructions about what steps to take in order to produce the answers. The program provides the raw material, and in the logic programming paradigm, this raw material is inspected more or less out of our sight, and without our detailed instructions, to deduce the answers to a query. Figure 10.12 illustrates the situation. The programmer builds a knowledge base of facts and rules about a certain domain of interest; this knowledge base constitutes the program. Interaction with the program takes place by posing queries—sometimes rather complex queries—to an inference engine (also called a *query interpreter*). The inference engine is a piece of software that is supplied as part of the language itself; that is, it is part of the compiler or interpreter, not something the programmer has to write. The inference engine can access the knowledge base, and it contains its own rules of deductive reasoning based on symbolic

FIGURE 10.12

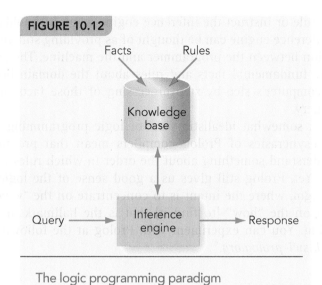

The logic programming paradigm

logic. For example, a Prolog inference engine processing the program in Figure 10.11 would conclude that

```
precedes(fdr, kennedy)
```

is true from the rule of the form "if before(X, Y) then precedes(X, Y)",

```
precedes(X, Y) :- before(X, Y).
```

together with the fact

```
before(fdr, kennedy).
```

because it is a rule of deductive reasoning (known as modus ponens) that "if A then B" together with "A" must result in "B." The programmer need not

Practice Problems

Using the Prolog program of Figure 10.11, what is the result of each of the following queries?

1. ?before(jefferson, kennedy).

2. ?president(X, lewisandclark).

3. ?precedes(jefferson, X).

supply this rule or instruct the inference engine when it should be applied. Thus, the inference engine can be thought of as providing still another layer of abstraction between the programmer and the machine. The programmer supplies the fundamental facts and rules about the domain but does not direct the computer's step-by-step processing of those facts and rules to answer a query.

This is a somewhat idealistic view of logic programming; in actuality, the idiosyncrasies of Prolog compilers mean that programmers do need to understand something about the order in which rules of logic will be applied. Yet, Prolog still gives us a good sense of the logic programming paradigm, where the intent is to concentrate on the "what" [is true] rather than on the "how" [to find it] that is the hallmark of procedural programming. You can experiment with Prolog at the following website: *http://swish.swi-prolog.org.*[5]

10.4.3 Parallel Programming

The complex scientific problems of the 21st century, such as climate change prediction, drug design and development, water sustainability, understanding of biological systems, greenhouse gas management, and many more are classified as "Grand Challenges." These are defined as "fundamental problems in science or engineering, with broad applications, whose solution would be enabled by the application of the high performance computing resources that could become available in the near future."[6] Solutions to Grand Challenge problems may require new algorithms, new data management and analysis techniques, new computational models, and increased technical communication and cooperation among diverse communities. But they will also require heavy-duty computational power. As noted in Chapter 5, problems such as these are testing the limits of the Von Neumann model of sequential processing. Parallel processing offers the promise of providing the computational speed required to solve such important large-scale problems.

Parallel processing is really a catchall term for a variety of approaches to computing architectures and algorithm design. Let's review the MIMD (*multiple instruction stream/multiple data stream*) model of parallel architecture introduced in Chapter 5: Interconnected processors independently execute their own program on their own data, communicating as needed with other processors. The MIMD model includes a number of different structures, such as multicore computing, in which multiple processors are packaged together on a single integrated circuit, and cluster computing, in which independent systems such as mainframes, desktops, or laptops are interconnected by a local area network (LAN) such as the Ethernet or a wide area network (WAN) such as the Internet.

---

[5] Toy Prolog, recommended in previous editions of this text, is no longer available. The syntax used here is slightly different than that for Toy Prolog.
[6] "A Research and Development Strategy for High Performance Computing," Executive Office of the President, Office of Science and Technology Policy, Nov. 20, 1987.

The algorithms with which we are most familiar, like those introduced in Chapters 2 and 3, operate sequentially because they were originally designed for Von Neumann-type execution. To reap the full benefit of a parallel architecture, we need to develop totally new algorithms that exploit this collection of processing resources. After all, it does not do any good to have 100 people available to help with a project if only one is doing any useful work, while the other 99 sit idle. (In contrast to other sections of this chapter, this one does not describe a specific parallel programming language. Instead, we introduce and discuss some general principles of parallel languages and algorithms.)

Chapter 5 suggested a parallel processing solution using 1,000 processors for our old problem of locating a single telephone number in a reverse telephone directory of 350,000,000 entries. Let's look at how a parallel programming language might manage these computing resources. We now assume that we have 1,001 independent processors to assist with this task. We designate one processor, say ID number 1001, to handle input/output while the remaining ones, those with ID numbers 1 to 1000, are assigned to the search task. The job of the input/output processor is to input the 350,000,000-element reverse phone directory, partition it into 1,000 separate chunks each of size 350,000, and send these chunks to the 1,000 search processors along with the NUMBER we are looking for. After distributing this data, the input/output processor waits for one of the search processors to find the designated phone number (and the corresponding name) and send the name back. It then prints this result (or, more likely, speaks or displays it) and terminates. This MIMD data allocation strategy is diagrammed in Figure 10.13.

Now, in parallel, the 1,000 search processors execute the sequential search algorithm (here called SEQSEARCH) on their chunk of data, called *YOURLIST*, to see if *NUMBER* is contained in this segment. However, they do not have to do this in instruction-by-instruction lockstep; instead, each

FIGURE 10.13

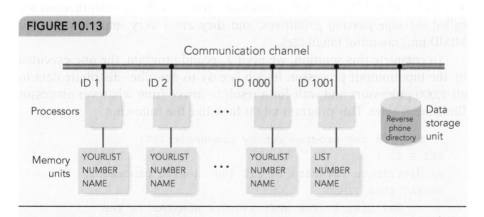

Model of MIMD processing

processor executes independently. Here is the outline of the program that each of the 1,000 search processors will run:

```
// this is the program run by processors numbered 1
// to 1000.
// These are the ones carrying out the search task.
YOURLIST = LIST[1..350000]  // the sublist of
                            // numbers to be searched
NUMBER                      // the one number we
                            // are searching for
 . . .
RECEIVE YOURLIST, NUMBER FROM PROCESSOR 1001
 . . .
// Each processor now executes the following
// instructions at its own rate
FOUND EQUALS FALSE
SEQSEARCH (YOURLIST, NUMBER, FOUND, NAME)
IF FOUND
    SEND NAME TO PROCESSOR 1001
ELSE
    DO NOTHING
END
HALT
```

Each search processor initially waits for a message from the input/output processor (ID 1001) that contains *YOURLIST* (its particular sublist), and *NUMBER* (the number for which we are searching). This is achieved via the RECEIVE instruction. When the message arrives, the processor executes the sequential search algorithm to determine if *NUMBER* is located within its 350,000-element sublist. If *NUMBER* is located within that list, then SEQSEARCH will exit with *FOUND* set to true, and that processor will SEND the corresponding *NAME* to processor 1001. If *NUMBER* is not found, the variable *FOUND* will remain false, and that processor will "Do nothing" and halt. The SEND/RECEIVE commands used to exchange information are called *message-passing primitives*, and they are a very important part of MIMD programming languages.

To complete this solution, we need a second program, the one executed by the input/output processor. Its job is easy to describe—distribute data to all 1,000 processors and wait for a result to arrive from whatever processor finds the answer. This program might look like the following:

```
// this is the program run by processor 1001
SET P TO 1
// distribute the data to all 1000 search processors
REPEAT 1000 TIMES
    SET LIST TO THE NEXT 350,000 NUMBERS IN THE
      REVERSE TELEPHONE DIRECTORY
    SEND LIST, NUMBER TO PROCESSOR P
    ADD 1 TO P
```

```
END LOOP
RECEIVE NAME FROM ANY PROCESSOR
OUTPUT THE NAME
HALT
```

Note that not every processor uses the same program. In this case, there are two programs, one for the 1,000 search processors and one for the input/output processor. Furthermore, even though 1,000 processors are executing the same program, they are not all executing the same sequence of instructions. For example, if *NUMBER* occurs exactly one time in the reverse phone directory, then 999 processors will execute the ELSE clause and "do nothing." The one processor that does find *NUMBER* will SEND the corresponding name to processor 1001. Also note that every processor needed access to *NUMBER*, but there is no global shared memory. Instead, processor 1001 explicitly SENDs this value to every other processor, using message-passing primitives.

This reverse telephone directory search is a rather simplified example of MIMD parallelism for three reasons. First, there were only two distinct programs, and 1,000 of the 1,001 processors were executing the same one. In many MIMD algorithms, there are many more distinct programs. The situation here is equivalent to having 1,001 people building a house and having 1,000 of those 1,001 doing the exact same task. In most cases, there will be carpenters, roofers, plumbers, masons, and so forth, all performing their own specific tasks.

The second reason why this is a simplified example is that there is little communication between processors. In this algorithm, processors receive data at the start of the program and (possibly) send a result at the end. There is no communication during the computation itself. However, in most MIMD algorithms, there is message passing going on throughout the computation for such purposes as sharing intermediate computations, exchanging temporary data, and providing status information. For example, in the home-building analogy mentioned previously, the people putting up the walls must communicate their status (progress) to the roofers, who are waiting for wall construction to finish before they can begin. This example is simple for a third reason—it does not deal with the possibility that *NUMBER* is not in the phone book. If that occurs, all 1,000 search processors will execute the ELSE clause and "Do nothing." The input/output processor will be sitting and waiting to RECEIVE a result that never will be SENT. (We ask you to think about how to solve this problem in an upcoming Practice Exercise.)

An example of more sophisticated MIMD parallel processing is the divide-and-conquer model. In this approach, the problem is successively partitioned into smaller and smaller parts and sent off to other processors, until each one has only a trivial job to perform. Each processor then completes that trivial operation and returns its result to the processor that sent it the task. These processors in turn do a little work and give the results back to the processors that gave them the tasks, and so on, all the way back to the originating processor. In this model, there is far more communication between processors.

For example, the task of finding the largest number in a list can be solved in a MIMD parallel fashion using the divide-and-conquer model. (The sequential version of this algorithm was presented in Chapter 2.) The original list of numbers is assigned to the top-level processor, which partitions the list into two parts and sends each half to a different processor. Each of these two processors divides its list in half and hands it off to yet two other processors, and so on, creating the pyramid effect shown in Figure 10.14.

At the bottom of the pyramid is a collection of processors that only have to find the largest number in a one-element list, a trivial task. They each pass this result up to their "parent" processor, which selects the larger of the two numbers it receives and passes that value up to its parent. All the way up the pyramid, each processor has only to select the larger of the two numbers it receives from its "children." When the processor at the top of the pyramid completes this task, the problem of finding the overall largest number has been solved.

Using a single processor, finding the largest of N numbers takes $\Theta(N)$ time because each of the N numbers in the list must be examined exactly once. (This order of complexity was introduced and discussed in Chapter 3.) However, the parallel approach diagrammed in Figure 10.14 traverses the pyramid from top to bottom and then back to the top. Because the N numbers are divided into two halves at each step, until the lists are of length one, this down-and-up-the-pyramid process requires $(2 * \lg N)$ steps, and a parallel solution to the "Find Largest" algorithm is $\Theta(\lg N)$. (Logarithmic efficiency was discussed in Section 3.4.2; recall that $\lg N$ means $\log_2 N$.) This can lead to enormous speedup in the solution time because the function $\lg N$ grows at a much slower rate than N. For example, if $N = 1,000,000$, then using a sequential approach to finding the largest number takes on the order of 1,000,000 steps, whereas our parallel solution needs only on

FIGURE 10.14

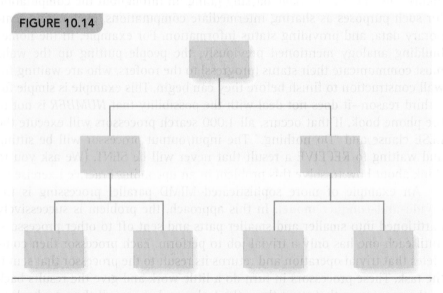

The divide-and-conquer approach using multiple processors

the order of 2 * lg 1,000,000 = 40 steps, a potential speedup of 25,000! (Of course, it also needs a whole lot of processors!)

We would expect the use of parallelism to reduce processing time because subtasks are being executed concurrently. However, one potential roadblock to achieving these higher levels of speedup is the amount of communication traffic between processors, both to distribute code and data and to share status and results. At some point, an increase in the number of processors can become more of a hindrance than a help, due to the extra data communication required. This is analogous to having too many people serve on a committee. The work involved in keeping everyone informed can slow down rather than speed up the work. In that case, it could actually be more efficient to have fewer people working on the task. One of the most important areas of research in parallel processing is the design and development of efficient parallel algorithms that keep processors busy, minimize communications, and significantly speed up the overall execution time.

New Dogs, New Tricks

Section 9.1 described the evolution of sequential programming languages from machine language to assembly language to high-level languages like C++, Java, and Python. A similar evolution is happening with parallel programming languages. The early parallel languages required programmers to personally manage many aspects of parallelism—allocating data to local memory units, distributing programs, and sending and receiving messages. That is not unlike low-level assembly languages that required programmers to format data and manage memory, tasks that humans do not do very well. However, just as assembly languages evolved into high-level languages in which compilers perform these mundane tasks, the field of parallel programming languages is also evolving. A language called ParaSail (Parallel Specification and Implementation Language), whose design began in 2009, is targeted toward multicore chips. Instead of trying to add parallel programming features to an existing non-parallel programming language, ParaSail began as an inherently parallel language in which most of the parallel tasks are carried out automatically and are transparent to the programmer. That is, execution proceeds in parallel by default, and the programmer actually has to work hard to force sequential processing. In addition, ParaSail rules out constructs from other languages that make parallel processing potentially unsafe. The latest release of ParaSail was in November 2016.

Practice Problems

1. Explain how parallel processing can be used to evaluate the expression

   $$A + B + C + D$$

   If each addition operation takes one "time slot," what savings can be achieved by using parallel processing instead of sequential processing?

2. Explain how you could get the parallel reverse telephone directory lookup problem to work correctly even if the desired NUMBER is not in the directory.

10.5 New Languages Keep Coming

After our discussion of many programming languages that fall into several distinct language categories, you might think that surely all programming needs have been met with existing languages. But new languages and new paradigms continue to be developed, perhaps in the hope of finding the "silver bullet" of an easy-to-use, efficient, general-purpose computing language that enforces good programming practices to allow quick production of error-free code on all computing platforms.

Here are three more programming languages that are relatively new. It remains to be seen whether they will stand the test of time and become widely used "standard" languages.

10.5.1 Go

Go, sometimes referred to as *golang*, is a programming language developed at Google. One of the people involved in its development was Ken Thompson, a recipient, along with Dennis Ritchie, of the 1983 A. M. Turing Award (see Chapter 12) for the development of UNIX.

What prompted the development of yet another programming language? Here is a quote from the FAQ (Frequently Asked Questions) page at *http://golang.org/doc/faq*:

> Go was born out of frustration with existing languages and environments for systems programming. Programming had become too difficult and the choice of languages was partly to blame. One had to choose either efficient compilation, efficient execution, or ease of programming; all three were not available in the same mainstream language. Programmers who could were choosing ease over safety and efficiency by moving to dynamically typed languages such as Python and JavaScript rather than C++ or, to a lesser extent, Java.

Go is an attempt to combine the ease of programming of an interpreted, dynamically typed language with the efficiency and safety of a statically typed, compiled language. It also aims to be modern, with support for networked and multicore computing. Finally, it is intended to be *fast*: it should take at most a few seconds to build a large executable on a single computer. To meet these goals required addressing a number of linguistic issues…a new language was called for.

Go is an open source language; the source code is available for anyone to examine and use, and changes or additions can be proposed. As noted in the quote, two of the target areas for Go applications are systems programming and programming for multicore machines. Although Go is a completely new language, it certainly borrows a lot from C/C++. As a result, you can probably understand exactly what the following Go program does:

```
package main
import "fmt"
func main() {
    fmt.Println("The first few perfect squares are:")
    for i := 1; i < 6; i++ {
        fmt.Println(i*i)
    }
}
```

Go was named by the TIOBE Index (see the Special Interest Box, "The 'Popularity' Contest," earlier in this chapter) as the Language of the Year in 2016, that is, the "programming language that gained the most popularity in a year." The latest version of Go at this writing is release 1.8; it was available as of February 2017.

Go is Going Places

Go supports many internal Google projects, but it has also been adopted by external users:

- Dropbox is a company that offers cloud storage services. In July 2014, Dropbox announced it had migrated critical Python code to Go partly to improve speed of execution. The result was about 200,000 lines of Go code. Dropbox engineers found that they needed some new code libraries, which they ultimately released to the open source community for testing, use, and possible improvement by others.
- Uber, an on-demand transportation company, operates in 580 cities worldwide. Uber has defined specific geographic areas, called

(Continued)

"geofences." The first thing that happens when a client requests a car-and-driver via mobile phone is to locate the geofence from which the client is calling. Hundreds of thousands of geofence lookups are needed per second, and Uber requires that 99% of them be done in less than 100 milliseconds. In 2015, Uber wrote a new system to handle this task using the Go language in part because Go could provide high throughput (could handle this volume of tasks) with low latency (delay). As proof of its success, on New Years Eve in 2015, the new system handled a peak load of 170,000 queries per second with a 99% response time of less than 50 milliseconds.

- Netflix, the well-known streaming video company, now serves customers in over 190 countries. Its computer systems must hold personalized data for its more than 81 million members, as well as manage member signup, browsing, and what Netflix calls the "playback experience." One of the concerns, as with Uber, is the amount of latency (delay) in processing client requests. In 2016 Netflix built a new system, written in Go, that acts as an intermediary between the client and the systems that access all the stored data. Go was chosen for lower latency than Java while handling tens of thousands of client connections, and was found to be more productive for developers than C.

10.5.2 Swift

In June 2014, Apple announced a new programming language at its annual Worldwide Developers Conference. The language is called *Swift*, and it was designed for building apps on the iOS and macOS operating systems, in others words, for the iPhone/iPad and the Mac. Apple developers had long been using Objective-C, an object-oriented version of the C language. Swift borrows much from Objective-C, and can work alongside Objective-C, but with faster performance. It also adds some modern programming constructs and attempts to make it harder to do "unsafe" things. This announcement was for the beta release only, meaning that the code was available to registered Apple developers but not yet to the general public. In July 2015, Lyft, an on-demand transportation company, announced that its mobile app for iOS platforms had been completely rewritten in Swift. In September 2015, Apple announced the first public Swift version, Swift 1.0. Originally a proprietary language, that is, the implementation of the language is controlled solely by the vendor (Apple in this case), Swift became open source software in December 2015, and now runs on Linux machines as well as all Apple products. While the rise in the use of Swift was initially driven by Apple apps, the ability to run Swift programs on low-cost Linux servers that support many web apps will increase its usage as a programming language.

By March 2017, less than two years after its first publicly released version, Swift had entered the "top 10" language group for the first time on the language popularity site *www.tiobe.com/index.php/content/paperinfo/tpci/index.html*. The latest version of Swift was released in September 2016.

10.5.3 Milk

In September 2016, researchers at MIT's Computer Science and Artificial Intelligence Laboratory announced a new programming language called Milk.[7] This language is geared to the "big data" that is of interest in many applications that attempt to detect connections and patterns between data points. Often, while the pool of data is huge, only selected points in the data are of interest at any one time; the technical term is that the data of interest is "sparse"—widely scattered throughout the large dataset.

In Chapter 5 we learned that fetching data from memory is a slow process compared to CPU actions, and that speedup is obtained by using *caching*. Caching relies on the *principle of locality* so that when an item of data is requested from main memory, that item plus items stored nearby are all read into the high-speed cache memory on the theory that such items are likely to be used again in the near future. Clearly caching based on this principle of locality is inefficient for sparse data.

Milk assumes the use of multicore processors, each with local cache memory. When a core processor is instructed to fetch a data item from main memory, it does not do so immediately. Instead, it adds the memory address of that item to a growing list in its local cache. When the lists get long enough, the cores pool their address lists, which the Milk compiler then reorganizes into new lists so that addresses "near" each other are grouped together. The new lists are redistributed to the core processors, each of which then accesses (and caches) the data on its particular new list. In that way, only needed data items are fetched from main memory. The three steps can overlap so that, for example, in a particular core a new address request list can be building while a previously distributed access list is being executed. To accomplish these effects, a few Milk directives have to be added within loops in programs that randomly request data items from a large dataset. The benefit appears to be that programs run 3-4 times faster.

As these last three example languages clearly demonstrate, even though the field of programming language design is now well over 50 years old, it is still a fertile area of creative research.

10.6 Conclusion

There is an entire spectrum of programming languages, each with its own features that make it more suitable for some types of applications than for others. A number of well-known languages (Fortran, COBOL, C, C++, Ada, Java, C#, Python) fall into the traditional, procedural paradigm. Procedural languages can be object-oriented, leading to a different program design perspective and the promise of software reuse. Some languages (such as SQL, HTML, JavaScript, and R) are designed as special-purpose tools. Still others rely on combinations of function evaluations (a functional language—Scheme), logical deductions from specified facts (a logic

---

[7] Milk is named in honor of Cilk, an early parallel programming language also developed at MIT.

programming language—Prolog), or a parallel programming approach. And new languages continue to be developed. Figure 10.15 lists the languages we have discussed, along with other major languages. A few words about this figure are in order. It is hard to pinpoint a date for a programming language.

FIGURE 10.15

Name	Date	Type
Fortran	1957	Procedural
COBOL	1960	Procedural
BASIC	1964	Procedural
Pascal	1971	Procedural
C	1974	Procedural
Ada	1979	Procedural/Parallel
Go	2009	Procedural/Concurrent
C++	1983	Object oriented
Visual Basic	1988	Object oriented
Python	1990	Object oriented
Java	1995	Object oriented
C#	2000	Object oriented
SQL	1986	Database queries
Perl	1987	Text extraction/reporting
HTML	1994	Hypertext authoring
R	2000	Statistics and graphing
LISP	1958	Functional
Scheme	1975	Functional
Scala	2004	Functional
F#	2005	Functional
Prolog	1972	Logic
Datalog	1977	Logic
Fortran 2008	2008	Parallel
Chapel	2010	Parallel
ParaSail	2011	Parallel
Julia	2012	Parallel
Ruby	1995	Scripting language/object oriented
JavaScript	1996	Scripting language
VBScript	1996	Scripting language
PHP	1997	Server-side scripting language
JSP	1999	Server-side scripting language
ASP.NET	2002	Server-side scripting language

Some programming languages at a glance

Should it be when the language was proposed or developed, when it was first commercially used, or when it became standardized? It is also sometimes hard to pigeonhole a language as to paradigm. Although we've tried to make clear distinctions in this chapter, many newer languages combine features drawn from several approaches, making them "multi-paradigm." Finally, your favorite language may have been omitted. (By all means, add it to the table.) At any rate, it is certain that the programming language world has been and continues to be a "Tower of Babel."

The trend in programming language design is to develop still higher levels of abstraction. This allows the human programmer to think in bigger pieces and in more novel or conceptual ways about solving the problem at hand. We would like eventually to be able to write programs that contain only the instruction "Solve the problem." Yet, we must remember that code written in any high-level programming language is still of no use to the computer trying to execute that code. No matter how abstract and powerful the language for front-end communication with the computer, the machine itself is still toiling away at the level of binary digits, absolute memory addresses, and machine language instructions. The services of an appropriate translator must be employed to take the code down into the machine language of that computer. The workings of a translator will be discussed in Chapter 11.

EXERCISES

1. What is the output from the following section of Fortran code?

   ```
       ISUM = 0
       I = 1
   20 IF (I .GT. 4) GO TO 30
          ISUM = ISUM + I
          I = I + 1
          GO TO 20
   30 WRITE(*,*) ISUM
   ```

2. Exponentiation is expressed in Fortran by **; that is, 3**2 means 3^2. If *I* has the value 7 and *J* has the value 3, what is the value of the following Fortran expression?

   ```
   ((I - J)**2)/2
   ```

3. Fortran has a three-way IF statement of the form IF(*expression*) n1, n2, n3 where expression is a numeric expression and n1, n2, n3 are statement numbers. Control transfers to statement n1 if *expression* is negative, to statement n2 if *expression* equals 0, and to n3 if *expression* is positive. What is the output of the following section of Fortran code if *I* has the value 3 and *MAX* has the value 4?

   ```
   IF (I - MAX) 10, 20, 30
   10 WRITE(*,*) 2*I
   20 WRITE(*,*) I*I
   30 WRITE(*,*) I**MAX
   ```

4. What is the value of *RESULT* after execution of the following COBOL code? Assume that *VALUE1* has the value 100.

   ```
   MOVE VALUE1 TO VALUE2.
   ADD 1 TO VALUE2.
   ADD VALUE1 TO VALUE2.
   ADD VALUE1 TO VALUE2 GIVING
      RESULT.
   ```

5. What is true after the following statements in a C program have been executed?

```
int* intPointer;
intPointer = (int*) 500;
*intPointer = 10;
```

6. Write a section of C code that stores in memory location 1000 the integer value currently in *SAM*.

7. The following section of Ada code conveys the services that a "teller" object can perform. What are these services?

```
task type teller is
  -- Entries to do simple
  -- transactions and return status
     entry deposit (id : cust_id;
       val : in money; stat : out
       status);
     entry withdraw (id : cust_id;
       val : in money; stat : out
       status);
     entry balance (id : cust_id;
       val : out money; stat :
       out status);
end teller;
```

8. In the following two Java output statements,

```
System.out.println("Hello. Welcome
  to this program.");
System.out.print("Tell me your
  favorite number: ");
```

why do you think the first uses *println* and the second uses *print*?

9. In Python, indentation is used to indicate the extent of a block of code. What is the output of the following Python code?

```
first = 3
second = 5
if first < second:
   print ("second is bigger")
else:
   print ("but this time ")
print ("first is bigger")
```

10. In C#, && is the symbol for the Boolean AND operation, and || is the symbol for the Boolean OR operation. What is the truth value of the following Boolean expressions?

a. (3 <= 3) && (7 > 5)
b. (3 < 3) || (7 > 5)
c. (4 < 1) && (3 > 2)

11. Which procedural language might be most appropriate for a program to do each of the following applications and why?

a. Compute trajectories for a satellite launcher.
b. Monitor an input device feeding data from an experiment to the computer.
c. Process the day's transactions at an ATM (automated teller machine).

12. Describe the result of executing the following SQL query on the vendor database described in Section 10.3.1:

SELECT NAME
FROM VENDOR
WHERE CITY = "DALLAS"
AND AMOUNT < 10000;

13. In the vendor database described in Section 10.3.1, the user wants to know all of the cities where there are vendors from whom the store bought more than $10,000 worth of stock the previous business quarter. Write an SQL query for this information.

14. Describe the text on a webpage that results from the HTML statement:

```
<p> The <span style="color: red;">red
</span>dog chased the <span style=
"color:brown;">brown</span> cow across
the <span style="color: green;">green
</span> field.</p>
```

15. Using a text editor (such as Notepad) and two image files of your own, create the HTML page shown in Figure 10.8. Save the file with an .html extension, then double-click to open it in your web browser. Does it behave as you expect?

16. What is the result of the following Scheme expression?

```
(car (cdr (cdr (list 16 19 21))))
```

17. Write a Scheme function that returns a list consisting of the first two values in the input list but in the opposite order.

18. Consider the following Scheme function:

```
(define (mystery input-list)
  (cond ((null? input-list) 0)
    (else (+ 1 (mystery (cdr
      input-list))))))
```

What is the result of invoking the function as follows?

(mystery (list 3 4 5))

Explain what this function does in general.

19. Write a Scheme function to evaluate the polynomial $2x^3 - 5x + 1$. Include the code for all the subfunctions you use.

20. Consider the following Scheme function:

```
(define (unknown n)
  (cond ((= n 1) 1)
    (else (* n (unknown (- n 1))))))
```

The condition (= n 1) means "If $n = 1$...". What is the result of the following function invocation?

(unknown 4)

21. After the rule

```
earlier(X, Y) :- president(R, X),
president(S, Y), precedes(R, S).
```

is added to the Prolog program of Figure 10.11, what is the result of each of the following queries?

a. **?earlier(lewisandclark, civilwar).**

b. **?earlier(worldwarII, firstmoonlanding).**

c. **?earlier(X, worldwarII).**

22. Here is the beginning of a Prolog program about a family. The facts are

```
male(eli).
male(bill).
male(joe).
female(mary).
female(betty).
female(sarah).
parentof(eli, bill).
```

```
parentof(mary, bill).
parentof(bill, joe).
parentof(bill, betty).
parentof(bill, sarah).
```

The declaration

```
male(eli).
```

asserts that Eli is male, and

```
parentof(eli, bill)
```

asserts that Eli is Bill's parent. Draw a "family tree" based on these facts.

23. Add to the Prolog program of Exercise 22 a rule to define "father of".

24. Add to the Prolog program of Exercise 22 a rule to define "daughter of".

25. a. Add to the Prolog program of Exercise 22 a rule to define "ancestor of".

b. After this rule is added, determine the result of the query

?ancestorof(X, sarah).

26. Go to the Prolog simulator website at *http:// swish.swi-prolog.org*.

Load the Prolog program of Figure 10.11 and run it, making some of the queries used in Section 10.4.2.

27. Suppose the symbolic arrangement of Figure 10.14 is used in a divide-and-conquer algorithm to compute the largest element in a list of eight elements. Assume that the time to partition a list in half and pass it to subprocessors is $0.003n$ msec, where n is the size of the list to be partitioned. Assume that the time to compare two values and find the larger of the two is 1 Msec. Assume that the time to pass the larger value back to a parent processor is 0.001 Msec. Compute the time required to do this task compared with doing it on a sequential processor that uses the Find Largest algorithm of Chapter 2, which also involves a series of comparisons of two values and finding the larger of the two.

CHALLENGE WORK

1. Visual Basic .NET (see the Special Interest Box "Old Dog, New Tricks #2") supplies a "toolbox" that makes creation of a graphical user interface a simple matter of dragging and dropping the objects you want (e.g., buttons, labels, and text boxes) onto a form object. The resulting Windows-based programs operate in an *event-driven mode*. Instead of proceeding from beginning to end under the control of the program instructions, an event-driven program starts up and then waits for some "event" to occur. An event is generally caused by some user action such as clicking on a button. Each of the form objects can have a code module to respond to such events.

   The illustration below shows a simple Visual Basic .NET form that contains two text boxes, a label, and a button. The user types his or her first name and last name into the two text boxes. When the user clicks the button, the name is displayed in the label as

   Lastname, Firstname

   If you have Visual Basic .NET (available in Microsoft Visual Studio), open a new Visual Basic Windows Application. Drag objects from the Toolbox to create a form that looks like the one shown below. Give each of these objects a meaningful name by changing its Name property in the Properties window. Use the Text property of each object to set what that object displays (the text boxes and label should initially be blank and the button should say "Name Writer").

   The only code required is a response to the button's Click event. Double-click the button and then write a code statement that concatenates—in the correct order—the Text properties of the two text boxes, together with a comma, and assigns the result to the Text property of the label. Run your program (press the function key F5 on the keyboard) to test it. (*Hints*: Visual Basic uses & as the concatenation operator. A form object's property is referenced by giving the name of the object, followed by a dot, followed by the property name, as in lblOutput.Text.)

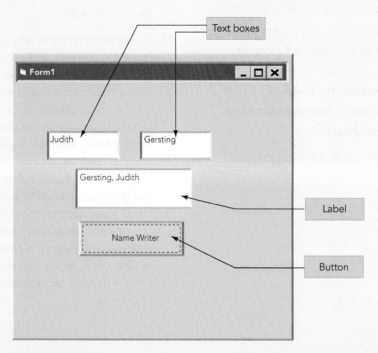

2. Using a text editor (such as Notepad) and three image files of your own, create the HTML page shown in Figure 10.8. Save the file with an .html extension and be sure it runs properly in your browser. Change the JavaScript so that the image cycles through picture 1 to picture 2 to picture 3 to picture 1, and so forth, as the user moves the mouse into and out of the image area. (*Hint*: Check the web for the JavaScript if...else if...else statement.)

3. There are small examples online of programs written in Go. Go (no pun intended!) to *http://golang.org* and in the Examples drop-down box below the code window, select Fibonacci Closure. Click Pop Out to get a bigger window to see the code. The Fibonacci sequence is a famous sequence of numbers invented by Leonardo Fibonacci in the year 1202 to model the population growth of rabbits. The first two numbers in the sequence are 1, 1. Successive numbers in the sequence are obtained by adding the two previous numbers. For example, the third Fibonacci number is the sum of the first two Fibonacci numbers, $1 + 1 = 2$.

   a. Write the first six numbers in the Fibonacci sequence.

   b. Compile and run the Fibonacci Closure Go program. What is the output?

   c. Some of the Go syntax is similar to C/C++. How does Go indicate comments?

d. One bit of C/C++ syntax is missing from Go. On the FAQ page, what does it say about ending statements with semicolons?

e. Can you guess the semantics (meaning) of the following statement?

```
a, b := 0, 1
```
What about the next statement?

```
a, b = b, a+b
```
(*Note*: You can modify and recompile/rerun the code to test possible equivalent statements.)

4. (*Note*: This exercise assumes you have completed Exercise 26.) We mentioned that "idiosyncrasies of Prolog compilers mean that programmers do need to understand something about the order in which rules of logic will be applied." In the program of Figure 10.11, replace the line:

```
precedes(X, Y) :- before(X, Z),
   precedes(Z, Y).
```
with

```
precedes(X, Y) :- precedes(Z, Y),
   before(X, Z).
```

It would seem that A and B should be equivalent to B and A; in fact these two Boolean expressions have the same truth table. But what happens when you use the Prolog interpreter to make a simple query such as:

```
?precedes(fdr, kennedy).
```

What does this tell you about the way the Prolog inference engine works?

AFTER STUDYING THIS CHAPTER, YOU WILL BE ABLE TO:

- List the phases of a typical compiler and describe the purpose of each phase

- Demonstrate how to break up a string of text into tokens

- Understand grammar rules written in BNF and use them to parse statements

- Explain how semantic analysis uses semantic records to determine meaning

- Show what a code generator does

- Explain the historical importance of code optimization, and why it is less central today

- Give an example of local code optimization and an example of global code optimization

11.1 Introduction

Although the high-level languages you learned about in the previous two chapters vary greatly in structure and behavior, they all share one feature: No computer in the world can understand them. There are no "Java computers" or "C++ processors" that can directly execute programs written in the high-level languages of Chapters 9 and 10. In Chapter 6, you learned that assembly language must first be translated into machine language prior to execution. High-level languages must also be translated into machine language prior to execution—in this case by a special piece of system software called a *compiler*. Compilers for languages like those discussed in Chapters 9 and 10 are very complex programs. They contain tens of thousands of lines of code and may require dozens or hundreds of person-years to complete. Unlike the assemblers of Chapter 6, these translators are not easy to design or implement.

There is a simple explanation for the vast difference in complexity between assemblers and compilers. Assembly language and machine language are related *one to one*; that is, one assembly language instruction produces exactly one machine language instruction. Therefore, translation is really a replacement process in which the assembler looks up a symbolic value in a table (either the op code table or the symbol table) and replaces it by its numeric equivalent:

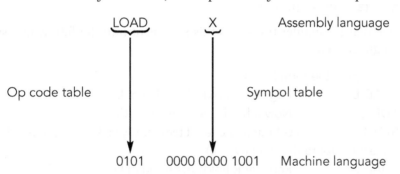

This is equivalent to translating English into Spanish by looking up each individual English word in an English/Spanish dictionary and replacing it with exactly one Spanish word:

This is a simple way to do translation, and this approach does work for assemblers. Unfortunately, it does not work for most English sentences. Often, a single English word must be translated into a multiword Spanish phrase or vice versa. This same problem exists in the translation of high-level programming languages like Java, C++, or Python.

The relationship between a high-level language and machine language is not one to one but *one to many*. That is, one high-level language statement, such as an assignment or conditional statement, usually produces *many* machine language or assembly language instructions. For example,

Java	**Assembly Language**
a = b + c − d; →	LOAD B
	ADD C
	SUBTRACT D
	STORE A

To determine which machine language instructions must be generated, a compiler cannot simply look up a name in a table. Instead, it must do a thorough linguistic analysis of the structure (syntax) and meaning (semantics) of each high-level language statement before deciding what to do. This is far more difficult than table lookup. In fact, building a compiler for a modern high-level programming language can be one of the most difficult system software projects.

When performing a translation, a compiler has two distinct goals. The first is *correctness*. The machine language code produced by the compiler must do exactly what the high-level language statement describes, and nothing else. For example, here is a typical Java assignment statement:

```
A = (B + C) - (D + E);
```

Assume that a compiler translates this statement into the following assembly language code:

```
-- Compute the term (B + C)
LOAD B         -- Register R holds the value of B
ADD C          -- Now it holds the result (B + C)
STORE B        -- Let's store the result temporarily in B (see comments below)
-- Next compute the term (D + E)
LOAD D         -- Register R holds the value of D
ADD E          -- Now it holds the result (D + E)
STORE D        -- Let's store the result temporarily in D (see comments below)
-- Finally, subtract the two terms and store the result in A
LOAD B         -- This loads (B + C)
SUBTRACT D     -- This is (B + C) − (D + E)
STORE A        -- Put the result in A. We are done translating the statement
```

This translation is *wrong*. Although the code does evaluate the expression (B + C) − (D + E) and store the result into A, it does two things it should not do. The translated program destroys the original contents of the variables B and D when it does the first two STORE operations. This is *not* what the Java assignment operator is supposed to do, and this compiler has produced an incorrect machine language translation of the original high-level language statement.

In addition to correctness, a compiler has a second goal. The code it produces should be reasonably *efficient and concise*. Even though memory costs have come down and processors are much faster, programmers will not accept gross inefficiencies in either execution speed or size of the compiled program. They might not care whether a compiler eliminates every wasted nanosecond or every unnecessary memory cell, but they do want it to produce reasonably fast and efficient machine language code. For example, to compute the sum $2x_0 + 2x_1 + 2x_2 + ... + 2x_{50000}$, an inexperienced programmer might write something like the following:

```
sum = 0.0;
i = 0;
while (i <= 50000)      {
        sum = sum + (2.0 * x[i]);
        i = i + 1;
}
```

This loop includes the time-consuming multiplication operation $(2.0 * x[i])$. By the rules of arithmetic, this operation can be moved outside the loop and done just once. A "smart" compiler should recognize this and translate the previous fragment of code as though it had been written:

```
sum = 0.0;
i = 0;
while (i <= 50000)      {
        sum = sum + x[i];
        i = i + 1;
}
sum = sum * 2.0;
```

By restructuring the loop, a smart compiler eliminates 49,999 unnecessary multiplications.

As you can see, we have our work cut out for us in this chapter. We want to describe how to construct a compiler that can read and interpret high-level language statements, understand what they are trying to do, correctly translate their intentions into machine language without any errors or unexpected side effects, and do all of this efficiently and concisely. Now you can appreciate why building a compiler is such a major undertaking.

The remainder of this chapter gives an overview of the steps involved in building a compiler for a procedural, Java-like, or C++-like language. No single chapter could investigate the subtleties and complexities of this huge subject. We can, however, give you an appreciation for some of the issues and concepts involved in designing and implementing this important piece of system software.

11.2 The Compilation Process

The general structure of a compiler is shown in Figure 11.1. Because there is a good deal of variability in the design and organization of a compiler, this diagram should be viewed as a generalized model rather than an exact description of how all compilers are structured.

The four phases of compilation listed in Figure 11.1 are the following:

- *Phase I: Lexical analysis*—The compiler examines the individual characters in the source program and groups them into syntactical units, called tokens, that will be analyzed in succeeding stages.

FIGURE 11.1

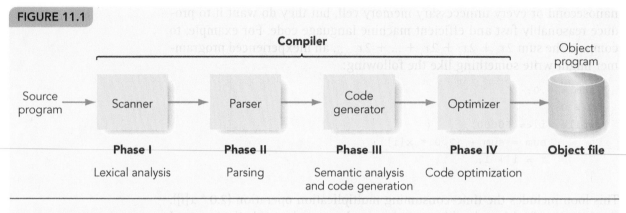

General structure of a compiler

This operation is analogous to grouping letters into words prior to analyzing natural language text.

- *Phase II: Parsing*—The sequence of tokens formed by the scanner is checked to see whether it is syntactically correct according to the rules of the programming language. This phase is roughly equivalent to checking whether individual words in a natural language text are connected together in a way that forms grammatically correct sentences.

- *Phase III: Semantic analysis and code generation*—If the high-level language statement is structurally correct, then the compiler analyzes its meaning and generates the proper sequence of machine language instructions to carry out the intended actions.

- *Phase IV: Code optimization*—The compiler takes the generated code and sees whether it can be made more efficient, either by making it run faster, having it occupy less memory, or possibly both.

When these four phases are complete, we have a correct and efficient machine language translation of the original high-level language *source program*. In the final step, this machine language code, called the *object program*, is written to an *object file*. We have reached the stage labeled "Machine language program" from Chapter 6, Figure 6.4, and the resulting object program can be handled in exactly the fashion shown there. That is, it can be loaded into memory and executed by the processor to produce the desired results.

The overall sequence of operations performed on a high-level language program is summarized in Figure 11.2. The following sections take a closer look at each of the four phases of the compilation process.

11.2.1 Phase I: Lexical Analysis

The program that performs lexical analysis is called a lexical analyzer, or more commonly a scanner. Its job is to group input characters into units

FIGURE 11.2

FIGURE 11.2

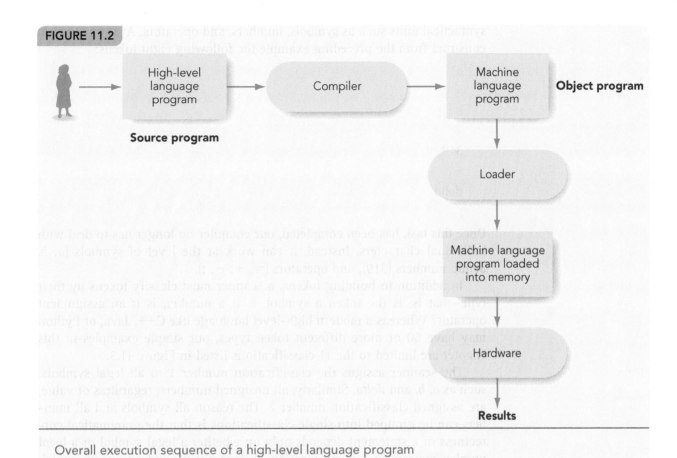

Overall execution sequence of a high-level language program

called tokens—syntactical units that are treated as single, indivisible entities for the purposes of translation. For example, take a look at the following assignment statement:

```
a = b + 319 - delta;
```

You probably see an assignment statement containing some symbols (*a*, *b*, *delta*), a number (319), and some operators (=, +, −, ;). However, your eyes and your brain have already done a great deal of processing to recognize and mentally create these objects, just as they do a great deal of processing to create words, sentences, and paragraphs from the individual characters on this page. In the assignment statement shown previously, high-level linguistic objects such as symbols and numbers do not yet exist. Initially, there are only the following 21 characters:

tab, a, blank, =, blank, b, blank, +, blank, 3, 1, 9, blank, −, blank, d, e, l, t, a, ;

It is the task of the scanner to discard nonessential characters, such as blanks and tabs, and then group the remaining characters into high-level syntactical units such as symbols, numbers, and operators. A scanner would construct from the preceding example the following eight tokens:

a

=

b

+

319

−

delta

;

Once this task has been completed, our compiler no longer has to deal with individual characters. Instead, it can work at the level of symbols (a, b, delta), numbers (319), and operators (=, +, −, ;).

In addition to building tokens, a scanner must classify tokens by their type—that is, is the token a symbol, is it a number, is it an assignment operator? Whereas a modern high-level language like C++, Java, or Python may have 50 or more different token types, our simple examples in this chapter are limited to the 11 classifications listed in Figure 11.3.

The scanner assigns the classification number 1 to all legal symbols, such as a, b, and delta. Similarly, all unsigned numbers, regardless of value, are assigned classification number 2. The reason all symbols and all numbers can be grouped into single classifications is that the grammatical correctness of a statement depends only on whether a legal symbol or a legal number appears in a given location. It does not depend on exactly which symbol or which number is actually used. For example, given the following model of an assignment statement:

"symbol" = "symbol" + "number";

FIGURE 11.3

Token Type	Classification Number
symbol	1
number	2
=	3
+	4
−	5
;	6
= =	7
if	8
else	9
(	10
)	11

Typical token classifications

it is possible to determine that a given assignment statement is syntactically correct, regardless of which specific "symbol" and "number" are actually used (as long as they are all legal in the programming language being used).

Using the token types and classification values shown in Figure 11.3, it is now possible to describe exactly what a scanner must do:

The input to a scanner is a high-level language statement from the source program. Its output is a list of all the tokens contained in that statement, as well as the classification number of each token found.

Here are some examples (using the classification values shown in Figure 11.3):

Input:	a = b + 319 - delta;	
Output:	**Token**	**Classification**
	a	1
	=	3
	b	1
	+	4
	319	2
	−	5
	delta	1
	;	6

Input:	if (a == b) xx = 13; else xx = 2;	
Output:	**Token**	**Classification**
	if	8
	(	10
	a	1
	==	7
	b	1
	)	11
	xx	1
	=	3
	13	2
	;	6
	else	9
	xx	1
	=	3
	2	2
	;	6

Regardless of which programming language is being analyzed, every scanner performs virtually the same set of operations: (1) It discards blanks and other nonessential characters and looks for the beginning of a token; (2) when it finds the beginning, it puts characters together until (3) it detects the end of the token, at which point it classifies the token and begins looking for the next one. This algorithm works properly regardless of what the tokens look like.

We can see this process more clearly by looking at an algorithm for grouping natural language characters into words:

This Is English.
Este es Espanol.
Kore wa Nihongo desu.

Even though these three sentences are written in very different languages—English, Spanish, and Japanese—the algorithm for constructing words is identical: (1) Discard blanks until you find a nonblank character; (2) group characters together until (3) you encounter either a blank or the character ".". You have now built a word. Go back to Step 1 and repeat the entire sequence to locate the next word. This is essentially the same algorithm that is used to build a lexical scanner for high-level programming languages.

11.2.2 Phase II: Parsing

During the parsing phase, a compiler determines whether the tokens recognized by the scanner during Phase I fit together in a grammatically meaningful way. That is, it determines whether they are a syntactically

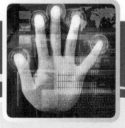

Practice Problems

1. Using the token types and classification numbers given in Figure 11.3, determine the output of a scanner given the following input statements:

   a. `x = x + 1;`
   b. `if (a + b42 == 0) a = zz - 12;`

2. Do you think a scanner would classify the following sequence of symbols as a single token or as multiple tokens? Give a reason for your choice.

   a. abc–def
   b. abc_def
   c. abc def (there is exactly one space between the c and the d)

3. The following character sequence is illegal in virtually all programming languages:

   `X = ; (14 hello`

   What would you expect a scanner to do if it encounters such a sequence?

4. Explain what will happen if the user writes the following assignment statement:

   `else = a + b;`

legal statement of the programming language. This step is analogous to diagramming a sentence. For example, to prove that the sequence of words

The man bit the dog.

is a correctly formed sentence, we must show that the individual words can be grouped together structurally to form a proper English language sentence:

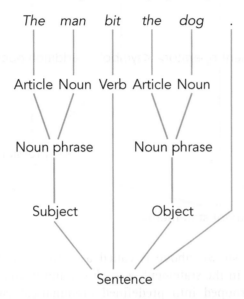

If we are unable to diagram the sentence, then it is not correctly formed. For example, when we try to analyze the sequence, "The man bit the", here is what happens:

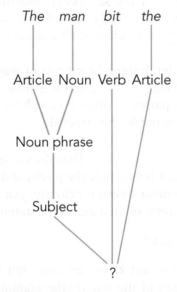

At this point in the analysis, we are stuck because there is no object for the verb "bit." We cannot diagram the sentence and must conclude that it is not properly formed.

The same thing happens with statements in a programming language, which are roughly analogous to sentences in a natural language. If a compiler is able to "diagram" a statement such as $a = b + c$, it concludes that the statement is structurally correct:

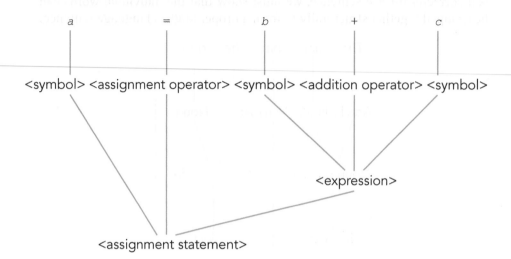

The structure shown above is called a **parse tree**. It starts from the individual tokens in the statement, a, $=$, b, $+$, and c, and shows how these tokens can be grouped into predefined grammatical categories such as <symbol>, <assignment operator>, and <expression> until the desired goal is reached—in this case, <assignment statement>. (We will explain shortly why we are writing the names of these grammatical categories inside the angle brackets "<" and ">".) The successful construction of a parse tree is proof that this statement is correctly formed according to the rules of the language. If a parser cannot produce such a parse tree, then the statement is not correctly formed.

In the field of compiler design, the process of diagramming a high-level language statement is called **parsing**, and it is done by a program called a **parser**. The output of a parser is either a completed parse tree or an error message if such a tree cannot be constructed.

Grammars, Languages, and BNF. How does a parser know how to construct the parse tree? What tells it how the pieces of a language fit together? For example, in the statement shown previously, you might wonder how the parser knows that the format of an assignment statement in our language is

<symbol> = <expression>

The answer is that it does not know; we must tell it. The parser must be given a formal description of the *syntax*—the grammatical structure—of the language that it is going to analyze. The most widely used notation for representing the syntax of a programming language is called BNF, an acronym for **Backus-Naur Form**, named after its designers John Backus and Peter Naur.

In BNF, the syntax of a language is specified as a set of rules, also called productions. The entire collection of rules is called a grammar. Each individual BNF rule looks like this:

left-hand side ::= "definition"

The *left-hand side* of a BNF rule is the name of a single grammatical category, such as <symbol>, <expression>, or <assignment statement>. The BNF operator ::= means "is defined as," and "definition," which is also called the *right-hand side*, specifies the grammatical structure of the symbol appearing on the left-hand side of the rule. The definition may contain any number of objects. For example, here is a BNF rule that defines how an <assignment statement> is formed:

<assignment statement> ::= <symbol> = <expression>

This rule says that the syntactical construct called <assignment statement> is defined as a <symbol> followed by the token = followed by the syntactical construct called <expression>. To have a structurally correct assignment statement, these three objects must all be present in exactly that order.

A BNF rule that gives one possible definition for the English language construct called <sentence> follows.

<sentence> ::= <subject> <verb> <object> .

This BNF rule says that a <sentence> is defined as a <subject> followed by a <verb> followed by an <object> and ending with a period. It is this rule that allowed us to correctly parse the sentence "The man bit the dog." since "The man" is a <subject>, "bit" is a <verb>, "the dog" is an <object>, and there is a period at the end.

Finally, the simple BNF rule

<addition operator> ::= +

says that the grammatical construct <addition operator> is defined as the single character +.

If a parser is analyzing a statement in a language and it sees exactly the same sequence of objects that appears on the right-hand side of a BNF rule, it is allowed to replace them with the one grammatical object on the left-hand side of that rule. For example, given our BNF rule for <assignment statement>:

<assignment statement> ::= <symbol> = <expression>

if a parser encounters the three objects <symbol>, =, and <expression> next to each other in the input, it can replace them with the object appearing on the left-hand side of the rule—in this case, <assignment statement>. In a sense, the parser is constructing one branch of the parse tree, which looks like this:

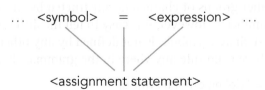

We say that the three objects, <symbol>, =, and <expression>, *produce* the grammatical category called <assignment statement>, and that is why a BNF rule is also called a production.

BNF rules use two different types of objects, called terminals and non-terminals, on the right-hand side of a production. Terminals are the actual tokens of the language recognized and returned by a scanner. The terminals of our language are the 11 tokens listed in Figure 11.3:

<symbol>	==
<number>	if
=	else
+	(
−	)
;	

The important characteristic of terminals is that they are not defined any further by other rules of the grammar. That is, there is no rule in the grammar that explains the "meaning" of such objects as <symbol>, =, +, and *if.* They are simply elements of the language, much like the words *man, bit,* and *dog* in our earlier example.

The second type of object used in a BNF rule is a nonterminal. A nonterminal is not an actual element of the language but an intermediate grammatical category used to help explain and organize the language. For example, in the analysis of the English sentence "The man bit the dog.", we used grammatical categories called article, noun, verb, noun phrase, subject, and object. These categories help us understand the structure of the sentence and show that it is correctly formed, but they are not actual words of the sentence being studied.

In every grammar, there is one special nonterminal called the goal symbol. This is the nonterminal object that the parser is trying to produce as it builds the parse tree. When the parser has produced the goal symbol using all the elements of the sentence or statement, it has proved the syntactical correctness of the sentence or statement being analyzed. In our English language example, the goal symbol is the nonterminal object <sentence>. In our assignment statement example, it is, naturally, <assignment statement>. When this nonterminal goal symbol has been produced, the parser has finished building the tree, and the statement has been successfully parsed. The collection of all statements that can be successfully parsed is called the language defined by a grammar.

All nonterminals are written inside angle brackets; examples include <expression> and <assignment statement>. Some terminals are also written in angle brackets when they do not represent actual characters of the language but rather groups of characters constructed by the scanner, such as <symbol> or <number>. However, it is easy to tell the difference between the two. A terminal such as <symbol> is not defined by any other rule of the language. That is, there is no rule anywhere in the grammar that looks like this:

<symbol> ::= "definition of a symbol"

Terminal symbols are like the words and punctuation marks of a language, and a parser does not have to know anything more about their syntactical structure to analyze a sentence.

However, nonterminals are constructed by the parser from more elementary syntactical units. Therefore, nonterminals such as <expression> and <assignment statement> must be further defined by one or more rules that specify exactly how this nonterminal is constructed. For example, there must exist at least one rule in our grammar that has the nonterminal <expression> as the left-hand side. This rule tells the parser how to form expressions from other terminals and nonterminals:

> <expression> ::= "definition of expression"

Similarly, there must be at least one rule that specifies the structure of an assignment statement:

> <assignment statement> ::= "definition of assignment statement"

We can summarize the difference between terminals and nonterminals by saying that terminals never appear on the left-hand side of a BNF rule, whereas nonterminals must appear on the left-hand side of one or more rules.

The three symbols <, >, and ::= used as part of BNF rules are termed metasymbols. This means that they are symbols of one language (BNF) that are being used to describe the characteristics of another language. In addition to these three, there are two other metasymbols used in BNF definitions. The vertical bar, |, means OR, and it is used to separate two alternative definitions of a nonterminal. This could be done without the vertical bar by just writing two separate rules:

> <nonterminal> ::= "definition 1"
>
> <nonterminal> ::= "definition 2"

However, it is sometimes more convenient to use the | character and write a single rule:

> <nonterminal> ::= "definition 1" | "definition 2"

For example, the rule

> <arithmetic operator> ::= + | − | * | /

says that an arithmetic operator is defined as either a +, or a −, or an *, or a /. Without the | operator, we would need to write four separate rules, which would make the grammar much larger. Here is a rule that defines the nonterminal <digit>:

> <digit> ::= 0 | 1 | 2 | 3 | 4 | 5 | 6 | 7 | 8 | 9

We will see many more examples of the use of the OR operator.

The final metasymbol used in BNF definitions is the Greek character lambda, Λ, which represents the null string—nothing at all. It is possible that a nonterminal can be "empty," and the symbol Λ is used to indicate this. For example, the nonterminal <signed integer> can be defined as an

Practice Problems

1. Write a single BNF rule that defines the nonterminal <Boolean operator>. (Assume that the three possible Boolean operators are AND, OR, and NOT.)

2. Create a BNF grammar that describes all one- or two-character identifiers that begin with the letter *i* or *j*. The second character, if present, can be any letter or digit. What is the goal symbol of your grammar?

3. Write a BNF grammar that describes Boolean expressions of the form

   (var op var)

   where *var* can be one of the symbols *x*, *y*, and *z*, and *op* can be one of the three relational operators ==, >, and <. The parentheses are part of the expression.

4. Using the grammar created in Practice Problem 3, show the parse tree for the expression $(x > y)$.

5. Using the grammar created in Practice Problem 3, show what happens when you try to parse the illegal expression $(x ==)$.

6. Modify your grammar from Practice Problem 3 so that the enclosing parentheses are optional. That is, Boolean expressions can be written as either (var op var) or var op var.

7. Do the symbols "Λ" (Greek lambda) and " " (blank) have the same meaning and can they be used interchangeably? Explain why or why not.

optional sign preceding an integer value, such as +7 or −5 or 8. To define the idea of an optional sign in BNF, we could say:

   <signed integer> ::= <sign> <number>
   <sign> ::= + | − | Λ

which says that <sign> may be either a + or a −, or it may be omitted entirely.

Parsing Concepts and Techniques. Given this brief introduction to grammars, languages, and BNF, we can now explain how a parser works. A parser receives as input the BNF description of a high-level language and a sequence of tokens recognized by the scanner. The fundamental rule of parsing follows.

If, by repeated applications of the rules of the grammar, a parser can convert the complete sequence of input tokens into the goal symbol, then that sequence of tokens is a syntactically valid statement of the language. If it cannot convert the input tokens into the goal symbol, then this is not a syntactically valid statement of the language.

To illustrate this idea, here is a three-rule grammar:

Number	Rule
1	<sentence> ::= <noun> <verb>.
2	<noun> ::= bees | dogs
3	<verb> ::= buzz | bite

The grammar contains five terminals: bees, dogs, buzz, bite, and the character "." (a period). It also contains three nonterminals: <sentence>, <noun>, and <verb>. The goal symbol is <sentence> because it is the one nonterminal that does not appear on the right-hand side of any other rule. Given this three-rule grammar, we can provide a sequence of tokens such as *dogs, bite,* and "." and have the parser attempt to transform these tokens into the goal symbol <sentence> using the three BNF rules given above:

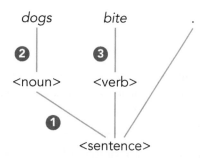

In this case, the parse was successful. (The numbers in the diagram indicate which rule is being applied.) Thus, "dogs bite." is a syntactically valid sentence of the language defined by this three-rule grammar. However, the following sequence of tokens:

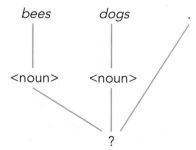

leads to a dead end. We have not yet produced the goal symbol <sentence>, but there is no rule in the grammar that can be applied to the sequence <noun> <noun> ".". That is, no sequence of terminals and nonterminals in the parse tree constructed so far matches the right-hand side of any rule. This means that "bees dogs." is not a valid sentence of this language.

Grammars for "real" high-level languages like C++, Python, or Java are very large, containing many hundreds of productions; therefore, it is not feasible to use these grammars as examples in our discussions. Even a grammar describing individual statements can be quite complex. For example, the BNF description of a Java assignment statement, complete with variables, constants, operators, parentheses, and function calls, can easily require 20 or 30 rules. Therefore, the following examples all use highly simplified "toy" languages to keep the level of detail manageable and enable us to focus on important concepts.

Our first example is a grammar for a highly simplified assignment statement in which the only operator is +, numbers are not permitted, and the only allowable variable names are x, y, and z. A first attempt at designing a grammar for this simplified assignment statement is shown in Figure 11.4.

If the input statement is $x = y + z$, then the parser can determine that this statement is correctly formed because it can construct a parse tree (Figure 11.5). The parse tree of Figure 11.5 is the output of the parser, and

FIGURE 11.4

Number	Rule
1	<assignment statement> ::= <variable> = <expression>
2	<expression> ::= <variable> | <variable> + <variable>
3	<variable> ::= x | y | z

First attempt at a grammar for a simplified assignment statement

FIGURE 11.5

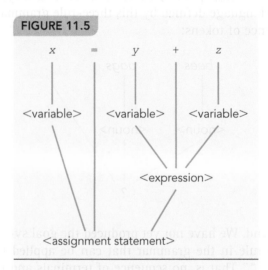

Parse tree produced by the parser

it is the information that is passed on to the next stage in the compilation process.

Building a parse tree like the one in Figure 11.5 is not as easy as it may appear. Often two or more rules of a grammar may be applied to the current input string, and the parser is not sure which one to choose. For example, assume that a grammar contains the following two rules:

Number	Rule
1	<t1> ::= A B
2	<t2> ::= B C

and that the statement being parsed contains the three-character string … A B C …. We could apply either Rule 1:

```
          ... A    B    C ...
               \   /
                \ /
               <t1>
```

or Rule 2:

```
          ... A    B    C ...
                    \   /
                     \ /
                    <t2>
```

One of these choices might be correct, whereas the other might lead down a grammatical dead end, and the parser has no idea which is which.

You are probably not aware that a similar situation occurs in the example shown earlier in Figure 11.5. Assume that the parser reaches this position in building the parse tree for the statement $x = y + z$:

In Figure 11.5, the parser next groups the three objects <variable>, +, and <variable> into an <expression> using Rule 2. However, at this point the parser has other options. For example, it could choose to parse the nonterminal <variable> generated from the symbol y to <expression> using Rule 2 and then parse the sequence <variable> = <expression> to <assignment statement> using Rule 1. This produces the following parse tree:

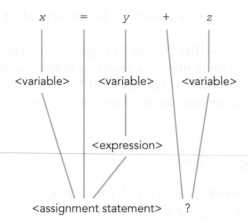

Unfortunately, this is the wrong choice. Although the parser does generate the goal symbol <assignment statement>, it does not use all of the tokens contained in the statement. An extra plus sign and <variable> are not used. (It accidentally parsed the assignment statement $x = y$ instead of $x = y + z$.) The parser has gone down the wrong path and reached a point where it is unable to continue. It must now go back to the point where it made the incorrect choice and try something else. For example, it might choose to parse the nonterminal <variable> generated from z to <expression> using Rule 2. Unfortunately, this is also a dead end; it produces the sequence <variable> + <expression>, which does not match the right-hand side of any rule.

The process of parsing is a complex sequence of applying rules, building grammatical constructs, seeing whether things are moving toward the correct answer (the goal symbol), and, if not, "undoing" the rule just applied and trying another. It is much like finding one's way through a maze. You try one path and if it works, fine. If not, you back up to where you made your last choice and try another, hoping that this time it will lead in the right direction.

This sounds like a haphazard and disorganized way to analyze statements, and in fact, it is. However, "real" parsing algorithms don't rely on a random selection of rules, as our previous discussion may have implied. Instead, they try to be a little more clever in their choices by looking ahead to see whether the rule they plan to apply will or will not help them to reach the goal. For example, assume we have the following input sequence:

A B C

and this grammar:

    <goal> ::= <term> C
    <term> ::= A B | B C

We have two choices on how to parse the input string. We can either group the two characters A B to form a <term>, or we can group B C instead. A random choice causes us to be wrong about half the time, but if a parser is clever and looks ahead, it can do a lot better. It is easy to see that grouping B C to produce the nonterminal <term> leads to trouble, because there is no rule telling us what to do with the sequence A <term>. We quickly come to a dead end:

```
A    B    C
 \    \  /
       <term>
  \      /
     ?
```

However, by choosing to group the tokens A B into <term> instead of B C, the parser quickly produces a correct parse tree:

```
A    B    C
 \  /      |
  <term>   |
      \    |
       <goal>
```

There are many well-known look-ahead parsing algorithms that use the ideas just described. These algorithms "look down the road" a few tokens to see what would happen if a certain choice is made. This helps keep the parser moving in the right direction, and it significantly reduces the number of false starts and dead ends. These algorithms can do very efficient parsing, even for large languages with hundreds of rules.

There is another important issue in the design of grammars. Let's assume we attempt to parse the following assignment statement:

```
x = x + y + z
```

using the grammar in Figure 11.4. No matter how hard we try to build a parse tree, it is just not possible:

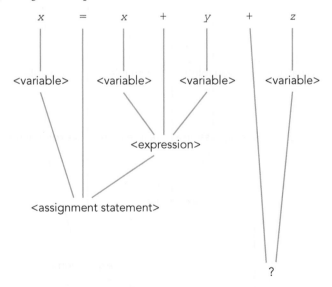

All other attempts lead to a similar result.

The problem is that the grammar in Figure 11.4 does not correctly describe the desired language. We wanted a language that allowed expressions containing an *arbitrary number* of plus signs. However, the grammar of Figure 11.4 describes a language in which expressions may contain at most a single addition operator. More complicated expressions such as $x + y + z$ cannot be parsed, and they are erroneously excluded from our language.

One of the biggest problems in building a compiler for a programming language is designing a grammar that:

- Includes every valid statement that we want to include in the language, and

- Excludes every invalid statement that we do not want to include in the language.

In this case, a statement that should be a part of our language ($x = x + y + z$) was excluded. If this statement were contained in a program, the parser would not recognize it and the user would receive an error message for a statement that is not really in error. The grammar in Figure 11.4 is wrong in the sense that it does not define the language that we want.

Let's redo the grammar of Figure 11.4 so that it describes an assignment statement that allows expressions containing an arbitrary number of occurrences of the plus sign. That is, our language will include such statements as

```
x = x + y + z
x = x + y + x + y + x + z + z
```

This second attempt at a grammar is shown in Figure 11.6.

The grammar in Figure 11.6 does recognize and accept expressions with more than one plus sign. For example, here is a parse tree for the statement $x = x + y + z$:

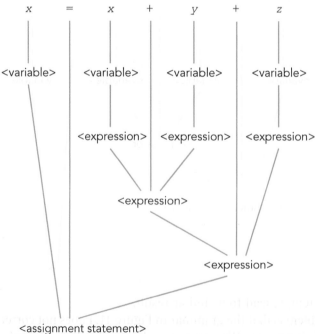

FIGURE 11.6

Number	Rule
1	<assignment statement> ::= <variable> = <expression>
2	<expression> ::= <variable> | <expression> + <expression>
3	<variable> ::= x | y | z

Second attempt at a grammar for assignment statements

Note that Rule 2 of Figure 11.6 uses the nonterminal <expression> on both the left-hand and the right-hand side of the same rule. In essence, the rule defines the nonterminal symbol <expression> in terms of itself. This is called a recursive definition, and its use is very common in BNF. It is recursion that allows us to describe an expression not just with one or two or three or … plus signs but with an *arbitrary* and *unbounded* number, as shown here.

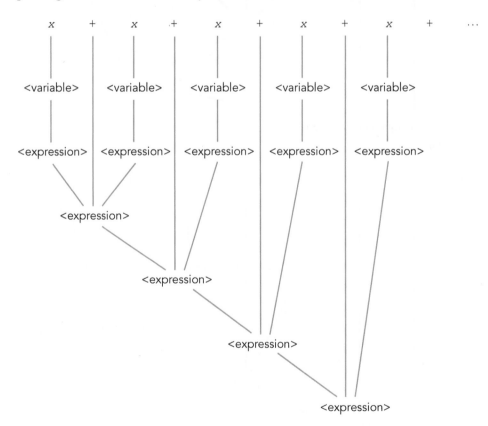

We have solved one problem: that of making sure our grammar defines a language that includes expressions with multiple addition operators. Unfortunately, though, while one problem has disappeared, another one has arisen, and the grammar of Figure 11.6 is still not quite correct.

To demonstrate this new problem, let's take the same statement that we have been analyzing:

```
x = x + y + z
```

and construct a second parse tree using the grammar of Figure 11.6. Both trees are shown in Figure 11.7.

FIGURE 11.7

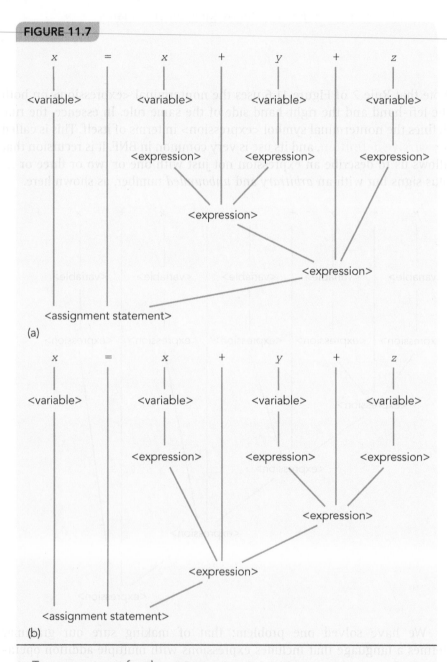

Two parse trees for the statement x = x + y + z

Using this assignment statement and the grammar in Figure 11.6, it is possible to construct *two* distinct parse trees. This might not seem to be a problem because the construction of a parse tree has been used only to demonstrate that a statement is correctly formed. Building two parse trees implies that the parser has demonstrated correctness in two different ways, perhaps twice as good.

However, a parse tree not only serves to demonstrate that a statement is correct, it also assigns it a specific *meaning,* or *interpretation.* The next phase of compilation uses this parse tree to understand what a statement means, and it generates code on the basis of that meaning. The existence of two different parse trees implies two different interpretations of the same statement, which is disastrous. A grammar that allows the construction of two or more distinct parse trees for the same statement is said to be ambiguous.

This problem can occur in natural languages as well as programming languages. Consider the following ambiguous sentence:

I saw the man in the store with the dogs.

This sentence has two distinct meanings depending on how we choose to parse it:

Interpretation 1:	I saw the man in the *store* (with the dogs).
Meaning:	The man I viewed was in a pet store that sells dogs.
Interpretation 2:	I saw the *man* in the store (with the dogs).
Meaning:	The man I viewed was walking his dogs and was inside some type of store.

These two interpretations say very different things, so the sentence leaves us confused about what the speaker meant. In the areas of languages and grammars, ambiguity is decidedly not a desirable property.

The two parse trees shown in Figure 11.7 correspond to the following two interpretations of the assignment statement $x = x + y + z$.

$x = (x + y) + z$ (Do the operation $x + y$ first.)
$x = x + (y + z)$ (Do the operation $y + z$ first.)

Because addition is associative—that is, $(a + b) + c = a + (b + c)$—in this case the ambiguity does not cause a serious problem. However, if the statement were changed slightly to

$x = x - y - z$

then these two different interpretations lead to completely different results:

$x = (x - y) - z$ which evaluates to $x - y - z$
$x = x - (y - z)$ which evaluates to $x - y + z$

We now have a situation in which a statement could mean one thing using compiler C on machine M and something totally different using compiler C′ on machine M′, depending on which parse tree it happens to construct.

FIGURE 11.8

Number	Rule
1	<assignment statement> ::= <variable> = <expression>
2	<expression> ::= <variable> | <expression> + <variable>
3	<variable> ::= x | y | z

Third attempt at a grammar for assignment statements

This contradicts the spirit of machine independence, which is a basic characteristic of all high-level languages.

To solve the problem, the assignment statement grammar must be rewritten a third time so that it is no longer ambiguous. This new grammar is shown in Figure 11.8. To see that the grammar of Figure 11.8 is not ambiguous, try parsing the statement $x = x + y + z$ in the two ways shown in Figure 11.7. You will see that one of these two parse trees cannot be built (see Problem 2 in the next set of Practice Problems).

Figure 11.9 shows the BNF grammar for a simplified version of an *if-else* statement that allows only a single assignment statement in the two separate clauses and allows the *else* clause to be omitted. The <Boolean expression> can include at most a single use of the relational operators $==$, $<$, and $>$. The nonterminal <assignment statement> is defined in the same way as in Figure 11.8. Figure 11.10 then shows the parse tree for the statement

```
if (x == y) x = z; else x = y;
```

using the grammar of Figure 11.9.

Even though this *if-else* statement has been greatly simplified, its grammar still requires seven rules. The parse trees for actual conditional statements can become quite large and "bushy."

FIGURE 11.9

Number	Rule
1	<if statement> ::= if (<Boolean expression>) <assignment statement> ; <else clause>
2	<Boolean expression> ::= <variable> | <variable> <relational> <variable>
3	<relational> ::= == | < | >
4	<variable> ::= x | y | z
5	<else clause> ::= else <assignment statement> ; | Λ
6	<assignment statement> ::= <variable> = <expression>
7	<expression> ::= <variable> | <expression> + <variable>

Grammar for a simplified version of an *if-else* statement

FIGURE 11.10

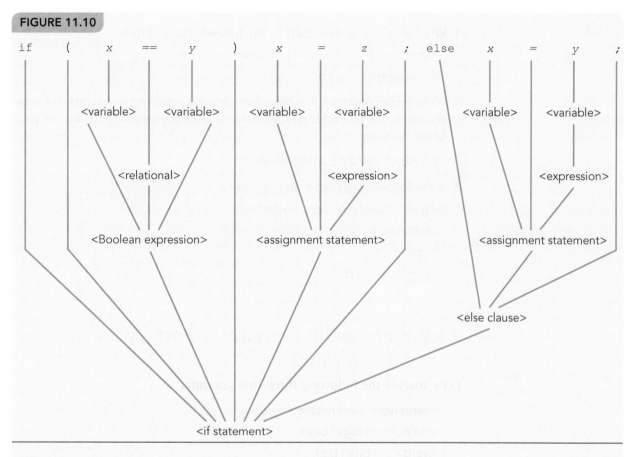

Parse tree for the statement if (x = = y) x = z; else x = y;

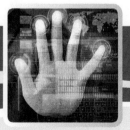

Practice Problems

1. Using the grammar of Figure 11.8, show the parse tree for the assignment statement

   x = x + y

2. Using the grammar of Figure 11.8, show the parse tree for the assignment statement

   x = x + y + z

3. Using the grammar of Figure 11.9, show the parse tree for the statement

   if (x > y) x = y;

(Continued)

4. What language is described by the following pair of rules?

    <string> ::= <character> | <character> <string>

    <character> ::= a | b

5. Write a BNF grammar that describes strings containing any number of repetitions of the character pair AB. That is, all of the following strings are part of the language:

    AB ABAB ABABAB ABABABABAB ...

6. Is the following grammar ambiguous?

    <goal> ::= <left> <op> <right>

    <left> ::= a | b

    <op> ::= *

    <right> ::= c | d

11.2.3 Phase III: Semantics and Code Generation

Let's analyze the following three-rule grammar:

    <sentence> ::= <noun> <verb>.

    <noun> ::= dogs | bees

    <verb> ::= bite | bark

The language defined by this grammar contains exactly four sentences:

    dogs bite.

    dogs bark.

    bees bite.

    bees bark.

For each of these four sentences, we can construct a parse tree showing that it is (structurally, at least) a valid sentence of the language:

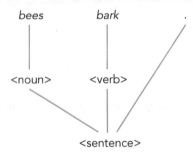

There is one problem, though. Although the sentence "bees bark." is structurally valid, it makes no sense whatsoever! During parsing, a compiler deals only with the *syntax* of a statement—that is, its grammatical structure. At that point, the only "correctness" that a compiler can determine is grammatical correctness with respect to the syntactical rules of the language. In this limited sense the sentence "bees bark." is perfectly correct. Another example of this limitation is the sentence, "The man bit the dog." This sentence is structurally correct, but its meaning is somewhat unusual!

The next phase of translation, during which a compiler examines the semantics of a programming language statement, deals with this issue. It analyzes the meaning of the tokens and tries to understand the *actions* they perform. If the statement is meaningless, as "bees bark." is, then it is semantically rejected, even though it is syntactically correct. If the statement is meaningful, then the compiler translates it into machine language.

It is easy to give examples of English-language sentences that are syntactically correct but semantically meaningless:

The orange artichoke flew through the pink eight-legged elephant.

But what are semantically meaningless statements in high-level programming languages?

One possibility is the following assignment statement:

```
sum = a + b;
```

This is obviously correct syntactically, but what if the variables *sum*, *a*, and *b* are declared as follows:

```
real a;
char b;
int sum;
```

What does it mean to add a character to a real number? What would possibly be the result of adding the letter 'Q' to 3.1416? In most cases, this operation has no meaning, and perhaps it should be rejected as semantically invalid.

To check for this semantic error, a compiler must look at the parse tree to see whether there is a branch that looks something like this:

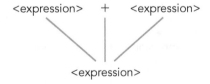

If there is such a branch, then the compiler must examine the data types of the two expressions to see whether they "make sense." That is, it must determine whether addition is defined for the data types of the two expressions.

The compiler does this by examining the semantic records associated with each nonterminal symbol in the grammar, such as <expression> and <variable>. A semantic record is a data structure that stores information about a nonterminal, such as the actual name of the object that it represents and its data type. For example, the nonterminal <variable> might have been constructed from a character variable named CH. This relationship is represented by a link between the nonterminal <variable> and a semantic record containing the name CH and its data type, char. Pictorially, we can represent this link as:

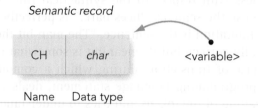

Semantic record

CH	char

<variable>

Name   Data type

The initial semantic records in our parse tree are built by the compiler when it sees the declarations of new objects; that is, when it sees declarations such as char CH;. Additional semantic records are constructed as the parse tree grows and new nonterminals are produced. Thus, a more realistic picture of the parse tree for the expression $a + b$ (assuming both are declared as integers) would look like this:

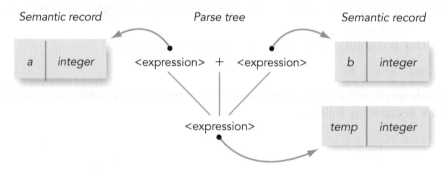

Semantic record   *Parse tree*   *Semantic record*

a	integer

<expression> + <expression>

b	integer

<expression>

temp	integer

This parse tree says that we are adding two <expression>s that are integer variables named *a* and *b*. The result is an <expression> stored in the integer variable *temp*, a name picked by the compiler. Because addition is well defined for integers, this operation makes perfectly good sense, and the compiler can generate machine language instructions to carry out this addition. If, however, the parse tree and its associated semantic records looked like this:

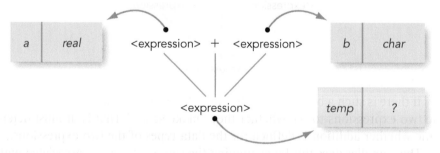

a	real

<expression> + <expression>

b	char

<expression>

temp	?

the compiler determines that this is not a meaningful operation because addition is not defined between a real number and a character. The compiler rejects this parse tree for semantic rather than syntactical reasons.

Thus, the first part of code generation involves a pass over the parse tree to determine whether all branches of the tree are semantically valid. If so, then the compiler can generate machine language instructions. If not, there is a semantic error, and generation of the machine language is suppressed because we do not want the processor to execute meaningless code. This step is called semantic analysis.

Following semantic analysis, the compiler makes a second pass over the parse tree, not to determine correctness (it has already done that), but to produce the translated machine language code. Each branch of the parse tree represents an action, a transformation of one or more grammatical objects into other grammatical objects. The compiler must determine how that transformation can be accomplished in machine language. This step is called code generation.

Let's work through the complete semantic analysis and code generation process using the parse tree for the assignment statement $x = y + z$, where x, y, and z are all integers. The example uses the instruction set shown in Chapter 6, Figure 6.5.

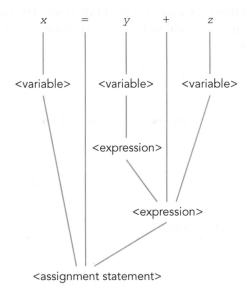

Typically, code generation begins at the productions in the tree that are nearest to the original input tokens. The compiler takes each production and, one branch at a time, translates that production into machine language operations or data generation pseudo-ops. For example, the following branch in the parse tree:

can be implemented by allocating space for the variable y using the .DATA pseudo-op

    Y: .DATA   0

In addition to generating this pseudo-op, the compiler must build the initial semantic record associated with the nonterminal <variable>. This semantic record contains, at a minimum, the name of this <variable>, which is *y*, and its data type, which is integer. (The data type information comes from the *int* declaration, which is not shown.) Here is what is produced after analyzing and translating the first branch of the parse tree:

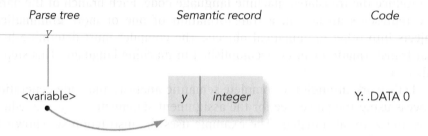

Parse tree	Semantic record	Code

Identical operations are done for the branches of the parse tree that produce the nonterminal <variable> from the symbols *x* and *z*, leading to the following situation:

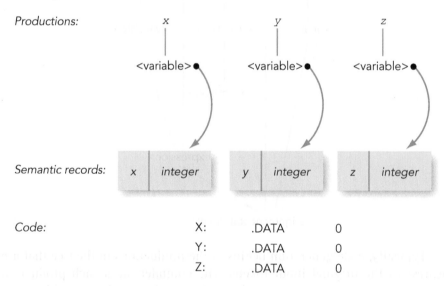

Productions:

Semantic records:

Code:
```
X:      .DATA      0
Y:      .DATA      0
Z:      .DATA      0
```

The production that transforms the nonterminal <variable> generated from *y* into the nonterminal <expression>

does not generate any machine language code. This branch of the tree is really just the renaming of a nonterminal to avoid the ambiguity problem discussed earlier. This demonstrates an important point: Although most branches of a parse tree produce code, some do not. Although no code is produced, the compiler must still create a semantic record for the new nonterminal <expression>. It is identical to the one built for the nonterminal <variable>.

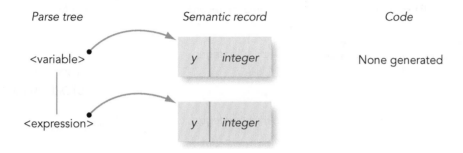

The branch of the parse tree that implements addition:

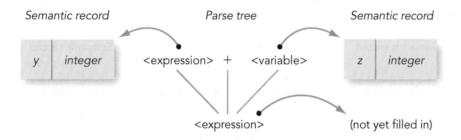

can be translated into machine language using the assembly language instruction set presented in Section 6.3.1. The compiler loads the value of <expression> into a register, adds the value of <variable>, and stores the resulting <expression> into a temporary memory location. This can be accomplished using the LOAD, ADD, and STORE operations in our instruction set. The names used in the address field of the instructions are determined by looking in the semantic records associated with the nonterminals <expression> and <variable>. The code generated by this branch of the parse tree is

```
LOAD     Y
ADD      Z
STORE    TEMP
```

TEMP is the name of a memory cell picked by the compiler to hold the result (Y + Z). Whenever the compiler creates one of these temporary variables, it must also remember to allocate memory space for this new variable using the DATA pseudo-op

```
TEMP:    .DATA    0
```

In addition, the compiler records the name (TEMP) and the data type (*integer*) of the result in the semantic record associated with this new nonterminal called <expression>. Here is what is produced by this branch of the parse tree:

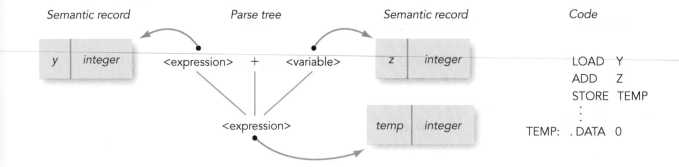

The final branch of the parse tree builds the nonterminal called <assignment statement>:

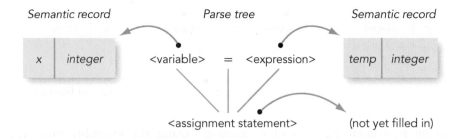

This production is translated into machine language by loading the value of the <expression> on the right-hand side of the assignment operator, using a LOAD instruction, and storing it, via a STORE operation, into the <variable> on the left-hand side of the assignment operator. Again, the names used in the address fields of the machine language instructions are obtained from the semantic records associated with <variable> and <expression>. The machine language code generated by this branch of the parse tree is

```
LOAD      TEMP
STORE     X
```

The compiler must also build the semantic record associated with the newly created nonterminal <assignment statement>. The name (*x*) and the data type (*integer*) of the variable on the left-hand side of the assignment operator are copied into that semantic record because the value stored in that variable is considered the value of the entire assignment statement.

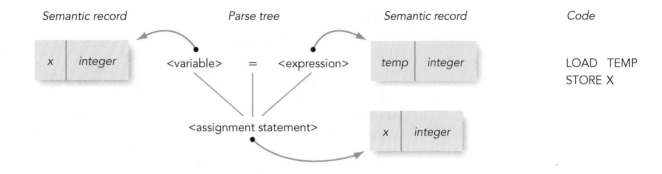

Our compiler has now analyzed every branch in the parse tree, and it has produced the following translation. (We have separated the pseudo-ops and executable instructions for clarity.)

```
          LOAD       Y
          ADD        Z
          STORE      TEMP
          LOAD       TEMP
          STORE      X
           .
           .
           .
X:        .DATA      0
Y:        .DATA      0
Z:        .DATA      0
TEMP:     .DATA      0
```

This is an exact translation of the assignment statement $x = y + z$.

Figure 11.11 shows the code generation process for the slightly more complex assignment statement $x = x + y + z$. The branches of the parse tree are labeled and referenced by comments in the code. (The parse tree was constructed using the grammar shown in Figure 11.8.)

The code of Figure 11.11 could represent the end of the compilation process because generating a correct machine language translation was our original goal. (*Note*: We have shown the output of the compiler in assembly language, not binary machine language. This assembly language result could easily be converted to machine language using the assembler techniques described in Chapter 6.) However, we are not quite finished. In the beginning of the chapter, we said that a compiler really has *two* goals: correctness and efficiency. The first goal has been achieved, but not necessarily the second. We have produced correct code, but not necessarily good code. Therefore, the next and final operation is *optimization*, where the compiler polishes and fine-tunes the translation so that it runs a little faster or occupies a little less memory.

FIGURE 11.11

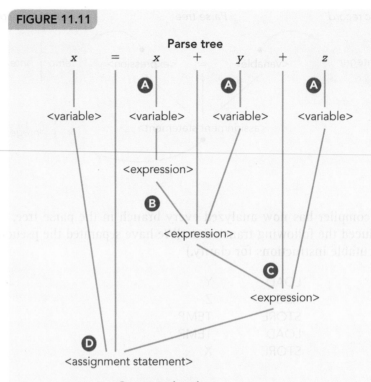

Parse tree

Generated code

```
--Here is the code for the production labeled B
       LOAD   X
       ADD    Y
       STORE  TEMP    -- Temp holds the expression (x + y)
--Here is the code for the production labeled C
       LOAD   TEMP
       ADD    Z
       STORE  TEMP2   --Temp2 holds (x + y + z)
--Here is the code for the production labeled D
       LOAD   TEMP2
       STORE  X        --X now holds the correct result
                       --The remainder of the program goes here
--These next three pseudo-ops are generated by the productions labeled A
X :     .DATA  0
Y :     .DATA  0
Z :     .DATA  0
--The pseudo-ops for these temporary variables are generated
by productions B and C
TEMP :  .DATA  0
TEMP2 : .DATA  0
```

Code generation for the assignment statement x = x + y + z

Practice Problem

Go through the code generation process for the simple assignment statement
$x = y$ where x and y are integers. The parse tree for this statement is

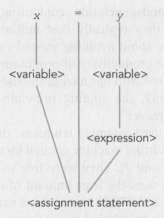

For each branch in the tree, show what semantic records are created and what
code is generated.

11.2.4 Phase IV: Code Optimization

As you learned in Chapter 10, the first high-level language and compiler
was Fortran, which appeared in 1957. (It was created by John Backus, the *B*
of BNF.) At that time, everyone programmed in assembly language because
nothing else was available. Given all the shortcomings of assembly language, you might think that programmers would have flocked to Fortran

Laboratory Experience 15

In this Laboratory Experience, you will be able to observe how a compiler
actually translates a program written in the type of high-level statements you
learned about in Chapter 9. You will observe as a compiler carries out each of
the phases of translation described in the preceding sections. You can view
the original source code, the translated object code, and the symbol table
produced by the compiler.

and thanked their lucky stars that it was available. After all, it is certainly a lot easier to understand the statement $a = b + c$ than the rather cryptic sequence LOAD B, ADD C, STORE A.

In fact, programmers did not accept this new language very quickly. The reason had nothing to do with the power and expressiveness of Fortran. Everyone admitted that it was far superior to assembly language in terms of clarity and ease of use. The problem had to do with efficiency—the ability to write highly optimized programs that contained no wasted microseconds or unnecessary memory cells.

In 1957 (early second-generation computing), computers were still enormously expensive; they typically cost millions of dollars. Therefore, programmers cared more about avoiding wasted computing resources than simplifying their job. The productivity of programmers earning $2 per hour was unimportant compared with optimizing the use of a multimillion-dollar computer system. In 1957, the guiding principle was "Programmers are cheap, hardware is expensive!"

When programmers used assembly language, they were working on the actual machine, not the virtual machine created by the system software (and described in Chapters 6 and 7). They were free to choose the instructions that ran most quickly or used the least amount of memory. For example, if the INCREMENT, LOAD, and STORE instructions execute in 1 μsec, whereas an ADD takes 2 μsec, then translating the arithmetic operation $x = x + 3$ as

```
INCREMENT   X          -- x + 1     This takes 1 μsec
INCREMENT   X          -- x + 2     This takes 1 μsec
INCREMENT   X          -- x + 3     and this takes 1 μsec
```

requires 3 μsec to execute. This code runs 25% faster than if it had been translated as

```
LOAD    X          -- This takes 1 μsec
ADD     THREE      -- x + 3 This takes 2 μsec
STORE   X          -- and this takes 1 μsec
        .
        .
        .

THREE:  .DATA   3
```

which takes 4 μsec to execute and requires an additional memory cell to hold the integer constant 3. When programmers wrote in assembly language, they were free to choose the first of these sequences rather than the second, knowing that it is faster and more compact. However, in a high-level language like Fortran, a programmer can only write $x = x + 3$ and hope that the compiler is "smart enough" to select the faster of the two implementations.

Because efficiency was so important to programmers of the 1950s and 1960s, these early first- and second-generation compilers spent a great deal of time doing code optimization. In fact, Backus himself did not regard language design as a difficult problem, but merely a prelude to the real problem: designing a compiler that could produce efficient programs. These compiler pioneers were quite successful in solving many of the problems of optimization, and early Fortran compilers produced object programs that ran nearly as fast as highly optimized assembly language code produced by top-notch programmers. After seeing these startling results, programmers of the 1950s and 1960s were eventually won over. They could gain the benefits of high-level languages—a powerful virtual environment—without any loss of efficiency. The code optimization techniques developed by Backus and others were one of the most important reasons for the rapid acceptance of high-level programming languages during the early years of computer science.

However, conditions have changed dramatically since 1957. Because of impressive reductions in hardware costs, code optimization no longer plays the central role it did 50 or 60 years ago. Programmers rarely worry about saving a few memory cells when even an inexpensive tablet has 64 GB of memory. Similarly, as processor speeds increase to 1–10 Gflops (billions of floating-point instructions per second), removing a few instructions becomes much less important. For example, eliminating the execution of 1,000 unnecessary instructions saves only 0.000001 second on a 1 Gflop machine. Therefore, compilers are no longer judged solely on whether they produce highly optimized code.

Whereas hardware costs are dropping, programmer costs are rising dramatically. A powerful high-speed graphics workstation can be purchased for as little as $1,000, but the programmers developing software for that system may earn 75 to 150 times that in annual salary. The operational phrase of the 21st century is the exact opposite of what was true in the 1950s: "Hardware is cheap, people are expensive!" The primary goal in compiler design today is to provide a wide array of compiler tools that simplify the programmer's task and increase his or her productivity. This includes such tools as visual development environments that use graphics and video to let the programmer see what is happening, sophisticated online debuggers to help programmers locate and correct errors, and reusable code libraries, which contain a large collection of prewritten and fully debugged program units. When a compiler is embedded within a collection of supporting software development routines such as debuggers, editors, toolkits, and libraries, it is called an integrated development environment (IDE). It is these types of programmer productivity optimizations, rather than computer speed and memory optimizations, that have taken center stage in language and compiler design. Often, these sophisticated IDEs are provided transparently to software developers via the cloud computing techniques described in Section 7.5.

However, this does not mean that code optimization is no longer of any importance or that programmers will tolerate any level of code inefficiency. A little bit of effort by a compiler can often pay large dividends in reduced memory space and lower running time. Thus, optimization algorithms are still included, at least to some level, as a component of modern compilers.

There are two types of compiler optimizations: local optimization and global optimization. The former is relatively easy and is part of virtually all compilers. The latter is more difficult and is often omitted from all but the most sophisticated and expensive production-level *optimizing compilers.*

In local optimization, the compiler looks at a very small block of instructions, typically from one to five. It tries to determine how it can improve the efficiency of this local code block without regard for what instructions come before or after. It is as though the compiler has placed a tiny "window" over the code, and it optimizes only the instructions inside this optimization window:

```
   .
   .
   .
instruction
┌──────────┐
│instruction│
│instruction│   ←────── The optimization window
│instruction│
└──────────┘
instruction
   .
   .
   .
```

Here is a list of some possible local optimizations:

1. Constant evaluation—Arithmetic expressions are fully evaluated at compile time if possible, rather than at execution time.

   High-level statement: x = 1 + 1;
   Nonoptimized code: LOAD ONE   *Optimized code:* LOAD TWO
                            ADD ONE   STORE X
                            STORE X

2. Strength reduction—Slow arithmetic operations are replaced with faster ones. For example, on most computers increment is faster than addition, and addition is faster than multiplication, which in turn is faster than division. Whenever possible, the compiler replaces an operation with one that is equivalent but executes more quickly.

   High-level statement: x = x * 2;   //x times 2 is equivalent to x + x
   Nonoptimized code: LOAD X   *Optimized code:*   LOAD X
                            MULTIPLY TWO   ADD X
                            STORE X   STORE X

3. Eliminating unnecessary operations—Instructions that are correct, but not necessary, are discarded. For example, because of the nondestructive read principle, when a value is stored from a register into memory, its value is still in the register, and it does not need to be reloaded. However, because the code generation phase translates each statement individually, there may be some unnecessary LOAD and STORE operations:

   High-level statement: x = y
                          z = x;
   Nonoptimized code: LOAD Y   -- This is x = y *Optimized code:* LOAD Y
                        STORE X   STORE X
                        LOAD X   -- This is z = x   STORE Z
                        STORE Z

The code in Figure 11.11 contains two opportunities for local optimizations:

- There are unnecessary LOAD and STORE operations. For example, the first four instructions in Figure 11.11 read

```
LOAD       X
ADD        Y
STORE      TEMP
LOAD       TEMP
```

  The STORE and LOAD operations on Lines 3 and 4 are both unnecessary because the sum (X + Y) is still in register R.

- The code uses two memory cells called TEMP and TEMP2 to hold temporary values. Neither of these variables is needed.

Locally optimized code for the assignment statement $x = x + y + z$ is shown in Figure 11.12. It uses only 7 instructions and data generation pseudo-ops rather than the 13 of Figure 11.11, a savings of about 45%.

The second type of optimization is global optimization, and it can be much more difficult. In global optimization, the compiler looks at large segments of the program, not just small pieces, to determine how to improve performance. The compiler examines large blocks of code such as *while* loops, *if* statements, and procedures to determine how to speed up execution. This is a much harder problem, both for a compiler and for a human programmer, but it can produce enormous savings in time and space. For example, earlier in the chapter we showed a loop that looked like this:

```
sum = 0.0;
i = 0;
while (i <= 50000) {
    sum = sum + (2.0 * x[i]);
    i = i + 1;
}
```

FIGURE 11.12

```
        LOAD    X
        ADD     Y
        ADD     Z
        STORE   X     --X now holds the correct result
        .
        .             --The remainder of the program goes here
        .
X:      .DATA   0
Y:      .DATA   0
Z:      .DATA   0
```

Optimized code for the assignment statement x = x + y + z

"Now I Understand," Said the Machine

Chapter 6 showed that translating assembly language into machine language is relatively easy. This chapter demonstrated that translating high-level programming languages into machine language is more difficult, but it still can be done. What about the next step—the translation of natural languages such as English, Spanish, or Chinese into machine language?

Getting computers to understand and use natural language is a far more difficult problem than translating programming languages like Java and C++. In fact, for many years **natural language understanding** was viewed as the single most difficult research problem in computer science. Demonstrated success was always "just over the next hill," and for many years true natural language understanding remained an unattainable goal. Many in computer science were pessimistic about the possibility of ever giving a computer true language understanding capabilities. However, that pessimism was shown to be unfounded when, in February 2011, a computer program called Watson, developed by artificial intelligence and natural language researchers at IBM, defeated two human players in a game of *Jeopardy!* The computer was presented with the same questions as the human contestants, Ken Jennings and Brad Rutter, the two most successful players in the game's history. Watson had to parse and understand English sentences that might include puns, similes, metaphors, and obscure pop culture references, then search its vast database to find the correct answer, and "buzz in" before either of the two human contestants. Watson won the game and the first place prize of $1 million. For the last half dozen years IBM researchers have continued to refine and improve the natural language and data access algorithms used on that TV show. Today, Watson and its sophisticated language capabilities are being used in over 45 different countries and 20 different industries, doing things like assisting physicians with medical diagnostics, improving online customer support by quickly and efficiently responding to user questions, translating news feeds in real time, and even chatting with management of the Toronto Raptors to help them select the best players in the NBA draft.

By moving the multiplication operation outside the loop, it is possible to eliminate 49,999 unnecessary and time-consuming operations. A good optimizing compiler would analyze the entire loop and restructure it as follows:

```
sum = 0.0;
i   = 0;
while (i <= 50000) {
```

```
      sum = sum + x[i];
      i = i + 1;
   }
   sum = sum * 2.0;
```

Such restructuring requires the ability to look at more than a few instructions at a time. The compiler cannot look at only a small "optimization window" but must be able to examine and analyze large segments of code. It requires a compiler that can see the "big picture," not just a small scene. Seeing this big picture is difficult, and many compilers are unable to do the type of global optimizations just discussed.

We close this section with one extremely important fact about code optimization: It *cannot* make an inefficient algorithm efficient. As we learned in Chapter 3, the efficiency of an algorithm is an inherent characteristic of its structure; It is not something programmed in by a programmer or optimized in by a compiler. A sequential search program, written by a team of world-class programmers and optimized by the best compiler available, will not run as fast as a nonoptimized binary search program written by first-year computer science students. Code optimization should not be seen as a way to create fast, efficient programs. That goal is achieved when we decide which algorithm to use. Optimization is more like the "frosting on the cake," whereby we take a good algorithm and make it just a tiny bit better.

11.3 Conclusion

This chapter has touched on some of the many issues involved in compiler design. Topics such as syntax, grammars, parsing, semantics, and optimization are rich and complex, each worthy of an entire book rather than one brief chapter. In addition, there are many topics not mentioned here that play an important role in compiler design:

- Integrated development environments (IDEs) and support tools

- Compilers for alternative languages, such as functional, object-oriented, or parallel languages

- Language standardization

- Top-down versus bottom-up parsing algorithms

- Error detection and recovery

The key point is that, unlike the assemblers of Chapter 6, a compiler is hard to build, and compilers for languages like C++, Python, and Java are large, complicated pieces of software. John Backus reported that the construction of the first Fortran compiler in 1957 required about 18 person-years of effort to design, code, and test. Even though we know much more today about how to build compilers, and numerous support tools are available to assist in this effort, it still requires a large team of programmers working months or years to build a correct and efficient compiler for a modern high-level programming language.

This chapter and the previous two chapters looked at the implementation phase of software development. They focused on the languages used to write programs and the methods used to translate programs into instructions that can be executed by the hardware. However, there are limits to computing. Chapter 12 will show that, no matter how powerful your hardware capabilities and no matter how sophisticated and expressive your programming language, there are some problems that simply cannot be solved algorithmically.

EXERCISES

1. Identify the tokens in each of the following statements. (You do not need to classify them; just identify them.)

   a. if (a == b1) a = x + y;
   b. delta = epsilon + 1.23 − sqrt(zz);
   c. print(Q);

2. Assume that we are working in a programming language that allows underscores (_) in variable names. When a scanner sees a character string such as AB_CD, is it more likely to classify this string as the single five-character token AB_CD or as three separate tokens: AB, _, CD? Explain your answer.

3. In some programming languages, a comment can be enclosed either in braces { } or in the symbols (* *). How do you think a scanner would group the four symbols {, }, (*, *) for purposes of classification? That is, would each symbol be given its own classification number or would some share classifications?

4. Using the token types and classification values given in Figure 11.3, show the output of a scanner when it is presented with each of the following statements:

   a. limit = begin + end
   b. a = b − 1;

   c. if (c == 50) x = 1; else y = x + 44;
   d. thenelse == error −

5. a. Write a BNF grammar that describes the structure of a nonterminal called <number>. Assume that <number> contains an optional + sign followed by exactly two decimal digits, the first of which cannot be a 0. Thus 23, +91, and +40 are legal, but 9, +01, and 123 are not.

   b. Using your grammar from Exercise 5a, show a parse tree for the value +90.

6. a. Write a BNF grammar that describes the structure of U.S. telephone numbers, which can be either (xxx)xxx-xxxx or xxx-xxxx, where x can be any digit from 0 to 9.

   b. Modify your grammar from Exercise 6a so that (1) the middle digit of an area code must be either a 0 or a 1, (2) the first digit of an area code cannot be a 0 or a 1, and (3) the first digit of the seven-digit phone number cannot be a 0 or a 1.

   c. Using your grammar from either Exercise 6a or 6b, show a parse tree for the phone number (612)555-1212.

7. a. Write a BNF grammar for identifiers that consist of an arbitrarily long string of letters and digits, the first one of which must be a letter.

   b. Using your grammar from Exercise 7a, show a parse tree for the identifier AB5C8.

8. Assume that we represent dollar amounts in the following way:

   $number.numberCR

   The dollar sign and the dollar value must be present. The cents part (including both the decimal point and the number) and the CR (which stands for CRedit and is how businesspeople represent negative numbers) are both optional, and *number* is a variable-length sequence of one or more decimal digits. Examples of legal dollar amounts include $995, $99CR, $199.95, and $500.000CR.

   a. Write a BNF grammar for the dollar amount just described.
   b. Modify your grammar so that the cents part is no longer an arbitrarily long sequence of digits but is exactly two digits, no more and no less.
   c. Using your grammar from either Exercise 8a or 8b, show a parse tree for $19.95CR.

9. Describe the language defined by the following grammar:

   <goal> ::= <letter> | <letter> <next>
   <next> ::= , <letter>
   <letter> ::= A

10. How does the language defined by the following grammar differ from the language defined by the grammar in Exercise 9?

    <goal> ::= <letter> | <letter> <next>
    <next> ::= , <letter> | <letter> <next>
    <letter> ::= A

11. a. Create a BNF grammar that describes simple Boolean expressions of the form

    var AND var
    var OR var

    where *var* is one of the symbols *w*, *x*, *y*, and *z*.

    b. Modify your grammar from Exercise 11a so that the Boolean expressions can be of the form

    expr AND expr
    expr OR expr

    where *expr* is either a simple variable (*w*, *x*, *y*, or *z*) or an expression of the form

    (var == var)   (var < var)   (var > var)

    c. Modify your grammar one more time to allow a Boolean expression to have an *arbitrary* number of terms connected by either AND or OR. That is, your expressions can be of the form

    expr AND expr OR expr OR expr AND expr....

12. Using the grammar of Figure 11.8, show a parse tree for the statement

    y = x + y + y + z

    Is your parse tree unique? If not, how many other parse trees exist for this statement? What does the existence of these different trees imply about the meaning of this assignment statement?

13. What is the language defined by the following pair of BNF rules?

    <number> ::= <digit> | <digit> <number>
    <digit> ::= 0 | 1

    Where have you seen this language before?

14. Write a BNF grammar that describes an arbitrarily long string of the characters *a*, *b*, and *c*. The string can contain any number of occurrences of these three letters (including none) in any order. The strings "empty", a, accaa, abcabccba, and bbbbb are all valid members of this language.

15. What are the different interpretations of the following English language sentence?

    I bought a shirt in the new store that was too large.

16. Write a BNF grammar to describe the following hypothetical input statement:

    input(var, var, … , var);

    The statement begins with the word *input*, followed by a left parenthesis, and then one or more variables, each variable separated from the one after it by a comma. The entire statement ends with a right parenthesis and a semicolon. Variable names are arbitrarily long strings of digits and letters, the first of which must be a letter.

17. Discuss what other information, in addition to name and data type, might be kept in a semantic record. From where would this other information come?

18. Referring to the parse tree shown in Figure 11.11, why is the production to the left of the = sign that transforms *x* into the nonterminal <variable> not labeled with an A? Does this production generate any code?

19. Assume that our language specifically permits you to assign an integer value to a real variable. The compiler handles this *mixed mode* by generating code to perform data conversion from an integer to a real representation. Consider the following declarations:

    int x;
    real y;

    The assignment statement *y* = *x* is legal in this language. Explain how a compiler handles the previous assignment statement. You do not have to show the exact code that would be generated; just describe how a compiler deals with the statement, and show at what point in the code generation process the compiler discovers that it needs to produce the data conversion instructions.

20. Explain how the concept of *algebraic identities* could be exploited during the code optimization phase of compilation. An algebraic identity is a relationship that is true for all values of the unknowns. For example,

    x + 0 = x for all values of x.
    x * 0 = 0 for all values of x.

    Describe other identities and explain how they could become part of the optimization phase. Is this considered local or global optimization?

21. Assume that we wrote the following pairs of assignment statements:

    Delta = 2.9 + (a + b + c * 3) / (x − 5.7);

    Epsilon = (a + b + c * 3) + sqrt(3.1 * y);

    How can a compiler optimize the execution of these two statements? Is this considered local or global optimization?

22. If we assume that all mathematical operations take 5 nsec (5 billionths of a second) to execute, how much time does your optimization from Exercise 21 actually save? What does this value say about the importance of compiler optimizations?

23. How do you think a compiler translates into machine language a branch in the parse tree that looks like the following?

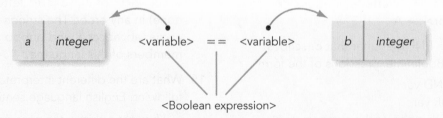

Show the code that can be generated from this production and the semantic record created for the new nonterminal symbol <Boolean expressions>.

CHALLENGE WORK

1. Our discussion on lexical analysis in Section 11.2.1 may lead you to believe that every lexical analyzer is unique and built "from scratch." In fact, it is quite rare to write a scanner when building a compiler for a new language because there exists a special program called a *scanner generator* that can, with the appropriate input, act as a "universal scanner" for any language. To use a scanner generator, we need to provide only a formal linguistic description of the tokens in our language and their classification. This description is input to the scanner generator, which then locates and classifies tokens according to the description provided. Thus, instead of writing a program called a scanner, you provide data to an already written program called a scanner generator.

   One of the most widely used scanner generators is a program called *lex*, and it has been used to build dozens of compilers, assemblers, and other linguistic interfaces. Read about scanner generators in general and lex in particular. Find out how they work and the techniques for describing the structure and classification of tokens. Then show how you formally describe in lex the following token types:

   a. Identifiers
   b. Signed integers
   c. Signed real numbers

   If your installation has lex available, enter your formal descriptions and have lex locate tokens of each of these types.

2. The techniques described in Challenge Exercise 1 also work for the parsing phase of the compilation process. That is, instead of writing a parsing program, we can provide data to an already written program that will do the job for us. A special program called a *parser generator*, also called a *compiler-compiler*, can act as a universal parser for any language that can be described using BNF notation. To use a parser generator, you simply input the productions of the grammar of your language and the sequence of tokens to be parsed. The output of the parser generator is a parse tree if the sequence of tokens is legal according to your productions or an error message if it is not.

   The most widely used parser generator is a program called *yacc*, an acronym for "Yet Another Compiler-Compiler." Yacc, like lex, has been used to build a great number of compilers. Read about parser generators and yacc, and write a report describing how yacc works and how you formally represent BNF productions. If you have yacc available at your installation, enter the BNF rules for <assignment statement> and let yacc parse the statement

   ```
   x = y + z;
   ```

Models of Computation

AFTER STUDYING THIS CHAPTER, YOU WILL BE ABLE TO:

- Explain the purpose of constructing a model
- List the required features of a computing agent
- Describe the components of a Turing machine, and explain how it is a good model of a computing agent
- List the features of an algorithm, and explain how a Turing machine program matches them
- Simulate the operation of a simple Turing machine on specific inputs
- Construct a simple Turing machine from a specification, both writing the rules and drawing the state diagram
- State the Church-Turing thesis and explain what it means
- Justify why computer scientists believe the Church-Turing thesis is true
- Explain what an unsolvable problem is
- Describe the halting problem, what its inputs and outputs are
- Outline the proof that the halting problem cannot be solved by any Turing machine

12.1 Introduction

The central topic of this book has been, in one way or another, algorithmic problem solving. We've discussed the concept of an algorithm, how to represent algorithms, their correctness and efficiency, the hardware that executes algorithms, the levels of abstraction in which a programmer deals with algorithms, and, finally, the system software that translates these abstractions back to the elementary hardware level. It might seem as though algorithms, and the problems solvable by algorithms, represent the entire scope of the computer science universe.

However, one of the most fundamental ideas in mathematics and computer science is that *there are problems that do not have any algorithmic solution*! Be sure you understand why this is such a powerful statement. There are many problems for which no algorithmic solution has yet been found, but for which we might find one if we were clever enough to discover it. Indeed, such new discoveries are being made all the time. But there are also problems for which no algorithmic solution exists; it does not

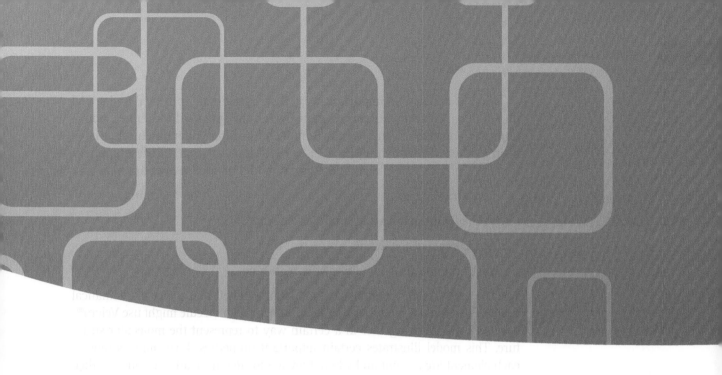

matter how inventive we may be, how much time we spend looking, or how remarkable our hardware or software; *no algorithms will ever be found that solve these problems.*

We will prove this statement later in this chapter by actually finding such a problem. This is a difficult task because failing to find an algorithmic solution to a problem does not prove that one does not exist. It might only mean that we have not yet been able to discover such an algorithm. Instead, we must show that no one can ever find such an algorithm—that one does not exist.

Algorithms, as noted in Chapter 1, are carried out by computing agents (such as people, robots, and computers). Throughout most of this book, we've assumed that the computing agent is a real computer. Ordinarily, we would choose to execute an algorithm on the most modern, high-speed computer available, with all the bells and whistles we could possibly find. But to show that something cannot be done by *any* computer, we want the bells and whistles to get out of the way so we can concentrate on the fundamental nature of "computerness." What we need is a simple, "idealized" computer—something easy to work with yet theoretically as powerful as the real thing. We need a *model* of a computer; indeed, to consider algorithms in general, we need a model of a computing agent.

12.2 What Is a Model?

Model cars, model trucks, model airplanes, and dolls (model people) are forever popular with children. Children use these toys to "play" at being grown up—at being drivers, pilots, and parents—because the toys capture the spirit of the objects they model. A model car looks like a car. The more expensive the model, the more realistic its features. But although the model captures the essence of a car, it is smaller in scale, omits many of the details of a real car, and does not have the full functionality of a real car.

Models are also an important way of studying many physical and social phenomena. Weather systems, climate cycles, the spread of epidemics, population demographics, and chemical molecules—all are phenomena that have been studied via modeling. (In fact, we will look at some of these applications in Chapter 13.) Like a model car, a model of such a phenomenon

1. Captures the essence—the important properties—of the real thing;

2. Probably differs in scale from the real thing;

3. Omits some of the details of the real thing; and

4. Lacks the full functionality of the real thing.

The model might be a physical model or a pencil-and-paper mathematical model. For example, a physical model of a chemical molecule might use Velcro®-covered balls stuck together in a certain way to represent the molecular structure. This model illustrates certain important properties: how many atoms of each element are present and where they are located in relation to one another. It is much larger than the real molecule, does not display the details of the chemical bonding, and is certainly not a real molecule. An alternative "physical" model—a computer visualization—is shown in Chapter 13, Figure 13.12.

A simple example of a mathematical model is the equation for the distance d that a moving vehicle travels as the product of rate r and time t:

$$d = r \times t$$

A calculation that a vehicle traveling at a constant rate of 60 miles per hour for 2 hours will cover a distance of 120 miles can be done in an instant by simply plugging values into the equation. But this equation is a simplification of reality because it assumes that the rate, that is, the speed of the vehicle, is constant throughout the entire two-hour period, so this result is only an approximation. Because this is not a physical model, it does not have a size as such, but there is a difference in time scale from the actual moving vehicle.

What can be gained by studying models if they do not behave in exactly the same way as the real thing? For one thing, they can enhance our understanding of the real system being modeled. By changing some aspect within the model, we can immediately see the effects of that change. These changes might be very costly, difficult, or dangerous to make in the real phenomena. The benefit is that models give us a safe and controlled environment to play with "what ifs"—what might be the effect if this or that factor in the real system were changed? The answers can be used to guide future decisions. Models can also provide environments for learning and practicing interactions with various phenomena. An aircraft flight simulator, for example, can give the trainee pilot realistic experience in a danger-free setting. Finally, not only can models give us information about existing phenomena, they also can be used as design tools. A model of a new design may reveal major flaws without the time, expense, and potential danger of building a prototype. (We will look more closely at these applications of models in Chapter 13.)

Whether a model is used to predict the behavior of an existing system or as a test bed for a proposed design, the information it provides is only as good as the assumptions made in building the model. If the model does not incorporate the major aspects of the system being studied, if relationships are represented incorrectly, or if so much detail has been omitted as to make the model a totally inaccurate representation, then little faith can be placed in the results it produces.

12.3 A Model of a Computing Agent

12.3.1 Properties of a Computing Agent

To construct a good model of the "computing agent" entity—one that enables us to explore the capabilities and limitations of computation in the most general sense—we must make certain that we capture the fundamental properties of a computing agent while suppressing lower-level details. This means we must decide which features are central to a computing agent and which are relatively incidental and can be ignored. For example, a computing agent must be able to follow the instructions in an algorithm. The instructions must be presented in some form that the computing agent can comprehend, but it does not matter whether the instructions are presented in English or Japanese, as binary strings, or even as pictures.

Likewise, the computing agent must be able to receive any data pertinent to the task. When we dealt with real computers, we described this as an input task, but the ability to accept input is central to any computing agent—whether a human being or a programmable thermostat. The instructions and data must be stored somewhere during the execution of the algorithm. In addition, they must be retrievable, whether from a computer's memory, the thermostat microprocessor's memory, a human being's memory, or a written sheet of paper.

The computing agent must be able to act in accordance with algorithm instructions. These instructions may take into account the present situation or state of the computing agent, as well as the particular input item being processed. In a real computer, a conditional operation may say, "If condition A then do B else do C." Condition A may involve the value of some variable or variables that have already been read into memory; we may think of the contents of memory (i.e., how the various bits are set) as the present state of the computer. The thermostat microprocessor may have an instruction that says, "If the temperature is greater than 74 degrees and I am programmed to keep the temperature at or below 74 degrees, then turn the cooling control to ON." Here the action of the thermostat depends on both the input of the current temperature from its temperature sensor and the "state" of its programming, just as a human being carrying out the algorithm of ordering lunch from a menu reacts both to the "input" (what items are on the menu) and to his or her present state of hunger.

Finally, the computing agent is expected to produce output because the outcome of an algorithm must be an observable result. The computer

Practice Problems

1. The mathematical model of the relationship between distance, rate, and time gives a better approximation of reality if it is applied over smaller time segments, assuming a constant rate within each time segment. Use the following data to approximate the distance traveled over a two-hour period.

Time period	Rate during that period
1:00–1:30 p.m.	58 mph
1:30–2:00 p.m.	61 mph
2:00–2:30 p.m.	57 mph
2:30–3:00 p.m.	62 mph

2. Describe a situation (besides aircraft pilot training) in which a simulator would be useful as a training device.

3. What factors might a model of groundwater pollution need to include? What are the advantages of a good model? Are there potential disadvantages to using such a model?

displays results on a screen, prints them on a sheet of paper, or writes them to a file; the thermostat displays the ON signal for the cooling system; the human being speaks or writes.

To summarize, we require that any computing agent be able to do all of the following:

1. Accept input.

2. Store information in memory and retrieve it from memory.

3. Take actions according to algorithm instructions; the choice of what action to take may depend on the present state of the computing agent, as well as on the input item presently being processed.

4. Produce output.

Of course, a real computer has all of these capabilities and is an example of a computing agent, as are a human being and a programmable thermostat. The thermostat, however, has a very limited set of primitive operations it can perform, so it can react only to a very limited algorithm. The computer, although it has a limited set of simple primitives, is a general-purpose computing agent because, as we have seen in the previous chapters, those primitives can be combined and organized to accomplish complex tasks. The "primitive operations" available to human beings haven't been fully explored, but in many ways they seem to exceed those of a computer, and we would certainly classify a human being as a general-purpose computing agent.

In the next section, we will discuss one particular model for a computing agent. It will have the four required properties just specified, and it will represent a general-purpose computing agent able to follow the instructions of many different algorithms.

12.3.2 The Turing Machine

We think of "computing" as a modern activity—something done by electronic computers. But interest in the theoretical nature of computation far predates the advent of modern computers. By the end of the 19th century, mathematicians were interested in formalizing the nature of proof, with two goals in mind. First, a formal basis for mathematical proofs would guarantee the correctness of a proof because the proof would contain no intuitive statements, such as "It is clear that..." or "We can now see that...." Second, a formal basis for proofs might allow for mechanical theorem-proving, where correct proofs could be generated simply by following a set of rules. In 1931, the Austrian logician Kurt Gödel looked at formal systems to describe the ordinary arithmetic of numbers. He demonstrated that in any reasonable system, there are true statements about arithmetic that cannot be proved using that system. This led to interest in finding a way to recognize which statements are indeed unprovable in a formal system—that is, in finding a computational procedure (what we have called an algorithm) to recognize such statements. This in turn led to an investigation of the nature of computation itself, and a number of mathematicians in the mid-1930s proposed various models of computational procedures, along with models of computing agents to carry out those procedures. We will look at the model proposed by Alan Turing.

Alan Turing,
Brilliant Eccentric

Alan Turing (1912–1954) was a brilliant British mathematician and a colorful individual. Stories abound about his "absentminded professor" demeanor, his interest in running (through the streets of London with an alarm clock flopping about, tied to his belt by a piece of twine), and his fascination with a children's radio show whose characters he would discuss daily with his mother. Convicted of homosexual acts in 1952, he chose drug treatment over prison, primarily

(Continues)

because he feared a prison term would impede his intellectual work. There was a Broadway play (*Breaking the Code*) written about him, years after his death by suicide. In 2014, a film about Turing's life, *The Imitation Game* starring British actor Benedict Cumberbatch, was released. It was the highest-grossing independent film of 2014, and in 2015 was nominated for eight Academy Awards and nine British Academy of Film and Television Arts awards.

Turing made three distinct and remarkable contributions to computer science. First, he devised what is now known as the Turing machine, using it—as we will see in this chapter—to model computation and to discover that some problems have no general computable solution. Second, during World War II, his team at the British Foreign Office built the Colossus machine, which used cryptanalysis, the science of code breaking, to break the secret code used on the German Enigma machine. The details of this work, carried out in a Victorian country mansion called Bletchley Park, were kept secret until many years later. Breaking the code enabled the British to gain access to intelligence about German military movements, which contributed significantly toward winning the war. Third, after the war Turing investigated what it means for machines to "think." We'll discuss his early contribution to *artificial intelligence* in Chapter 15.

Starting in 2011, a restoration project began on the by-then decrepit buildings of Bletchley Park. Because of the secrecy surrounding the work there during the war, there were no photographs of the building interiors. The restoration team contacted some veterans of Bletchley Park to help supply authentic details. In June 2014, the restored Bletchley Park was opened to the public by the Duchess of Cambridge, wife of Britain's Prince William, who walked through one of the restored code breaking "huts" where her paternal grandmother had worked during World War II and talked with a Bletchley Park veteran who had been a colleague of her grandmother.

A Turing machine is a theoretical model of computation that includes a (conceptual) tape extending infinitely in both directions. The tape is divided into cells, each of which contains one symbol. The symbols must come from a finite set of symbols called the tape alphabet. The tape alphabet for a given Turing machine always contains a special symbol b (for "blank"), usually both of the symbols 0 and 1 (zero and one), and sometimes a limited number of other symbols, let's say X and Y, used as placeholders or markers of some kind. At any point in time, only a finite number of the cells contain nonblank symbols. Figure 12.1 shows a typical tape configuration, with three nonblank cells containing the alphabet symbols 0, 1, 1, respectively.

The tape is used to hold the input to the Turing machine. We know that input must be presented to a computing agent in a form it can understand; for a Turing machine, this means that the input must be expressed as a finite string of nonblank symbols from the tape alphabet. The Turing machine writes its output on the tape, again using the same alphabet of symbols. The tape also serves as memory.

FIGURE 12.1

·	·	·	b	b	0	1	1	b	b	·	·	·

A Turing machine tape

The rest of the Turing machine consists of a unit that reads one cell of the tape at a time and writes a symbol in that cell. There is a finite number k of "states" of the machine, labeled 1, 2, ... , k, and at any moment the unit is in one of these states. A state can be thought of as a certain condition; the Turing machine may reach this condition partly on the basis of its history of events, much as your "hungry state" is a condition reached because of the meals you have skipped recently.

Figure 12.2 shows a particular Turing machine configuration. Using the tape of Figure 12.1, the machine is currently in state 1 and is reading the cell containing the symbol 0, so the 0 is what the machine is seeing as the current input symbol.

The Turing machine is designed to carry out only one type of primitive operation. Each time such an operation is done, three actions take place:

1. Write a symbol in the cell (replacing the symbol already there).
2. Go into a new state (it might be the same as the current state).
3. Move the "read head" one cell left or right.

The details of the actions (what to write, what the new state is, and which direction to move) depend on the current state of the machine and on the contents of the tape cell currently being read (the input). Turing machine instructions describe these details. Each instruction tells what to do for a specific current state and current input symbol, as follows:

if (you are in state i) and (you are reading symbol j) then

> write symbol k onto the tape
>
> go into state s
>
> move in direction d (where d can be either right or left)

FIGURE 12.2

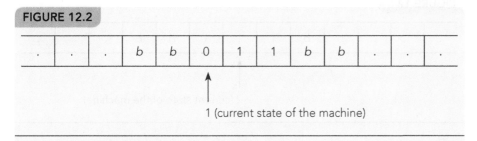

·	·	·	b	b	0	1	1	b	b	·	·	·

1 (current state of the machine)

A Turing machine configuration

The Turing machine's single primitive operation is to check its current state and the current input symbol being read, look for an instruction that tells what to do under these circumstances, and then carry out the three actions specified by that instruction. For example, one Turing machine instruction might say

> if (you are in state 1) and (you are reading symbol 0) then
>> write symbol 1 onto the tape
>> go into state 2
>> move right

If a Turing machine is in the configuration shown in Figure 12.2 (where the current state is 1 and the current input symbol is 0), then this instruction applies. After the machine executes this instruction, its next configuration is shown in Figure 12.3, where the previous 0 symbol has been overwritten with a 1, the state has changed to state 2, and the read head has moved one cell to the right on the tape.

Let's develop a shorthand notation for Turing machine instructions. There are five components:

- Current state
- Current symbol
- Next symbol
- Next state
- Direction of move

We'll write these five things in that order, enclosed in parentheses.

(current state, current symbol, next symbol, next state, direction of move)

The instruction that we talked about earlier,

> if (you are in state 1) and (you are reading symbol 0) then
>> write symbol 1 onto the tape
>> go into state 2
>> move right

FIGURE 12.3

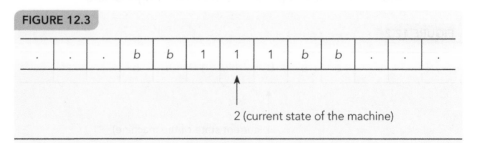

2 (current state of the machine)

The next Turing machine configuration after executing one instruction is therefore represented by the 5-tuple:

(1,0,1,2,R)

Similarly, the Turing machine instruction

(2,1,1,2,L)

stands for

if (you are in state 2) and (you are reading symbol 1) then

write symbol 1 onto the tape

go into state 2

move left

In following this instruction, the machine writes in the current cell the same symbol (1) as was already there and remains in the same state (state 2) as before. It also moves one cell to the left.

A Turing machine can execute a whole sequence of instructions. A clock governs the action of the machine. Whenever the clock ticks, the Turing machine performs its primitive operation; that is, it looks for an instruction that applies to its current state and the symbol currently being read and then follows that instruction. Instructions may be used more than once.

We have glossed over a couple of important details. What if there is more than one instruction that applies to the current configuration? Suppose, as in Figure 12.2, that the current state is 1, that the current symbol is 0, and that

(1,0,1,2,R)

(1,0,0,3,L)

both appear in the same collection of instructions. These instructions are in conflict. Should the Turing machine write a 1, go to state 2, and move right, or should it write a 0, go to state 3, and move left? We can eliminate this ambiguity by requiring that a set of instructions for a Turing machine can never contain two or more instructions that begin with the same two values, as in the following:

$(i, j, -, -, -)$

$(i, j, -, -, -)$

On the other hand, what if there is no instruction that applies to the current state and current symbol for the machine? That is, we are currently in state a reading symbol b, but there is no instruction of the form $(a, b, -, -, -)$. In this case, we specify that the machine halts, doing nothing further. This is the stopping condition for a Turing machine.

We impose two additional conventions on the Turing machine regarding its initial configuration when the clock begins. The start-up state is always state 1, and the machine is always reading the leftmost nonblank cell on the tape. This ensures that the Turing machine has a fixed and definite starting point.

Now let's do a sample Turing machine computation. Suppose the instructions available to a Turing machine are

1. $(1,0,1,2,R)$
2. $(1,1,1,2,R)$
3. $(2,0,1,2,R)$
4. $(2,1,0,2,R)$
5. $(2,b,b,3,L)$

Also suppose the Turing machine's initial configuration is again that of Figure 12.2, reprinted here:

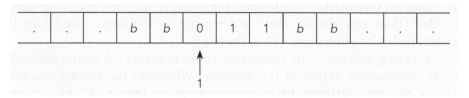

This satisfies our convention about starting in state 1 at the leftmost nonblank cell on the tape. The Turing machine looks for an appropriate instruction for its current state, 1, and its current input symbol, 0, which means it looks for an instruction of the form $(1,0,-,-,-)$. Instruction 1 applies; this was our sample instruction earlier, and the resulting configuration agrees with Figure 12.3:

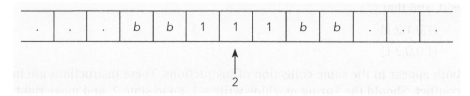

At the next clock tick, with current state 2 and current symbol 1, the Turing machine looks for an instruction of the form $(2,1,-,-,-)$. Instruction 4 applies and, after the appropriate actions are performed, the resulting configuration is

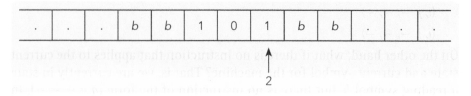

Instruction 4 applies again and results in

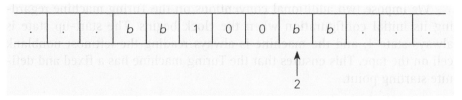

Instruction 5 now applies, leading to

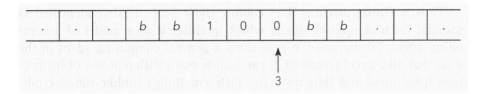

At this point, the machine is in state 3 reading the symbol 0. Because there are no instructions of the form (3,0,–,–,–), the machine halts. The Turing machine computation is complete.

   Although we numbered this collection of instructions for reference, the Turing machine does not necessarily execute instructions in the order of this numbering. Some instructions may not be executed at all, and some may be executed more than once. The sequence of instructions used depends on the input written on the tape.

   As we have seen, the Turing machine (despite its name) is not a machine at all. It is a theoretical model of the pencil-and-paper type designed to capture the essential features of a computing agent. So, how well does the Turing machine stack up against our list of required features for a computing agent?

1. *It can accept input*–The Turing machine can read symbols on its tape.

2. *It can store information in memory and retrieve it from memory*–The Turing machine can write symbols on its tape and, by moving around over the tape, can go back and read those symbols at a later time. The tape serves as the Turing machine memory.

3. *It can take actions according to algorithm instructions, and the choice of action to take may depend on the present state of the computing agent and on the input item presently being processed*–Certainly the Turing machine satisfies this requirement insofar as Turing machine instructions are concerned; the present state and present symbol being processed determine the appropriate instruction, and that instruction specifies the actions to be taken.

4. *It can produce output*–The Turing machine writes symbols on its tape in the course of its normal operation. If (when?) the Turing machine halts, what is written on the tape at that time can be considered output.

In the Turing machine computation that we just finished, the input was the string of symbols 011 (ignoring the surrounding blanks) and the output was the string of symbols 100. Starting with the same input tape but with a different set of instructions could result in different output; similarly, starting with the same instructions but with a different input tape could result in different output. Given the benefit of hindsight, we could say that we wrote this particular set of instructions to carry out the task of transforming the string 011 into the string 100. Writing a set of Turing machine instructions to allow a Turing machine to carry out a certain task is similar to writing a computer program in a programming language, such as those discussed in

Chapters 9 and 10, to allow a real computer to carry out a certain task. We call such a collection of instructions a Turing machine program.

Thus, a Turing machine does capture those properties we identified as essential for a computing agent, which qualifies it as a model of a computing agent. Furthermore, it represents a general computing agent in the sense that, like a real computer, it can follow many different sets of instructions (programs) and thus do many different things (unlike the one-job-only thermostat). By its very simplicity of operation, it has eliminated many real-world details, such as exactly how symbols are read from or written to the tape, exactly how data are to be encoded into a string of symbols from the alphabet to be written on the tape, exactly how a string of symbols on the tape is to be interpreted as meaningful output, and exactly how the machine carries out the activities of "changing state." In fact, the Turing machine is such a simple concept that we may wonder how good a model it really is. Did we eliminate too many details? We'll answer the question of how good a model the Turing machine is later in the chapter.

A Turing machine is different in scale from any real computing agent in one respect. A Turing machine can, given the appropriate instructions, move right or left to the blank portion of the tape and write a nonblank symbol. When this happens, the machine has gobbled up an extra cell to use for information storage purposes—that is, as memory. Depending on the instructions, this could happen over and over, which means that there is *no limit* to the amount of memory available to the machine. Any real computing agent has a limit on the memory available to it. In particular, a real computer, though it has a certain amount of internal memory and has access to external memory in the form of disks, tapes, or online storage, still has such a limit.

This difference in scale means that a Turing machine (elementary device though it may seem to be) actually has more capability in one respect than any real computer that exists or ever will exist. Therefore, we must be careful about the use of the Turing machine model and the conclusions we draw

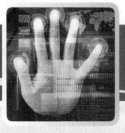

Practice Problems

1. Given the Turing machine instruction $(2,b,1,3,L)$ and the configuration

		b	1	1	b	b		

↑
2

   draw the next configuration.

2. A Turing machine has the following instructions:

(1,0,0,2,R)

(2,1,1,2,L)

(2,0,1,2,R)

(1,b,1,1,L)

For each of the following configurations of this Turing machine, draw the next configuration.

a.
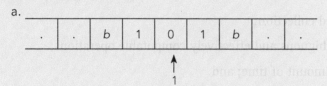

b.
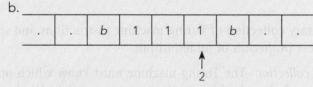

c.
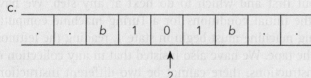

d.
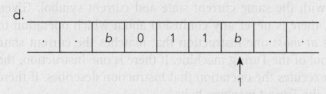

3. Consider a Turing machine that has the following two instructions:

(1,1,0,2,R)

(2,1,1,1,R)

Determine its output when it is run on the following tape. (Remember that a Turing machine starts in state 1, reading the leftmost nonblank cell.)

.	.	b	1	1	1	b	.	.

4. Using the Turing machine from Practice Problem 3, determine its output when it is run on the following tape.

.	.	b	1	0	0	b	.	.

from it about "real" computing (i.e., computing on a real computer). If we find some task that a Turing machine can perform (because of its limitless memory), it *might* not be a task that a real computer could perform.

12.4 A Model of an Algorithm

An algorithm is a collection of instructions intended for a computing agent to follow. If we accept the Turing machine as a model of a computing agent, then the instructions for a Turing machine should be a model of an algorithm. Remember from our definition in Chapter 1 that an algorithm must

1. Be a well-ordered collection;

2. Consist of unambiguous and effectively computable operations;

3. Halt in a finite amount of time; and

4. Produce a result.

Let's consider an arbitrary collection of Turing machine instructions and see whether it exhibits these properties of an algorithm.

1. *Be a well-ordered collection*—The Turing machine must know which operation to carry out first and which to do next at any step. We have already specified the initial conditions for a Turing machine computation: that the Turing machine must begin in state 1, reading the leftmost nonblank cell on the tape. We have also insisted that in any collection of Turing machine instructions, there cannot be two different instructions that both begin with the same current state and current symbol. Given this requirement, there is never any confusion about which operation to do next. There is *at most* one instruction that matches the current state and current symbol of the Turing machine. If there is one instruction, the Turing machine executes the operation that instruction describes. If there is no instruction, the Turing machine halts.

2. *Consist of unambiguous and effectively computable operations*—Recall that this property is *relative to the computing agent*; that is, operations must be understandable and doable by the computing agent. Each individual Turing machine instruction describes an operation that (to the Turing machine) is unambiguous, requiring no additional explanation, and any Turing machine is able to carry out the operation described. After all, Turing machine instructions were explicitly designed for Turing machines to execute.

3. *Halt in a finite amount of time*—For a Turing machine to halt when executing a collection of instructions, it must reach a configuration where no appropriate instruction exists. This depends on the input given to the Turing machine—that is, the contents initially written on the tape. Consider the following set of Turing machine instructions:

   (1,0,0,1,*R*)

   (1,*b*,*b*,1,*R*)

and suppose the tape initially contains, as its nonblank portion, the single symbol 1. The initial configuration is

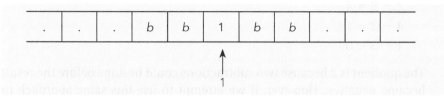

and the machine halts immediately because there is no applicable instruction. On the other hand, suppose the same set of instructions is used with a starting tape that contains the single symbol 0. The Turing machine computation is then

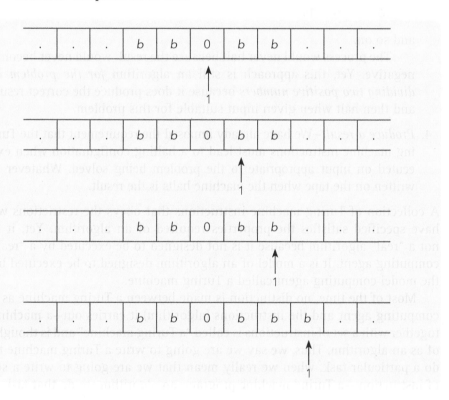

We can see that the second instruction applies indefinitely and that this Turing machine will never halt.

Typically, an algorithm is designed to carry out a certain type of task. Let us agree that *for input appropriate to that task*, the instructions must be such that the Turing machine does indeed eventually halt. If the Turing machine is run on a tape containing data that are not appropriate input for the task of interest, it need not halt.

This may seem to be a change in our definition of an algorithm, but it simply confirms that there is always a "universe of discourse" connected with the problem we are trying to solve. For example, we can use a simple algorithm for dividing one positive integer by another positive integer using repeated subtraction until the result is negative. Thus, $7 \div 3$ can be computed using this algorithm as follows:

$$7 - 3 = 4$$
$$4 - 3 = 1$$
$$1 - 3 < 0$$

The quotient is 2 because two subtractions could be done before the result became negative. However, if we attempt to use this same approach to compute $7 \div (-3)$, we get

$$7 - (-3) = 10$$
$$10 - (-3) = 13$$
$$13 - (-3) = 16$$
$$16 - (-3) = 19$$

and so on.

The process would never halt because the result would never become negative. Yet, this approach is still an algorithm *for the problem of dividing two positive numbers* because it does produce the correct result and then halt when given input suitable for this problem.

4. *Produce a result*—We have already imposed the requirement that the Turing machine instructions must lead to a halting configuration when executed on input appropriate to the problem being solved. Whatever is written on the tape when the machine halts is the result.

A collection of Turing machine instructions that obeys the restrictions we have specified satisfies the properties required of an algorithm. Yet, it is not a "real" algorithm because it is not designed to be executed by a "real" computing agent. It is a model of an algorithm, designed to be executed by the model computing agent called a Turing machine.

Most of the time, no distinction is made between a Turing machine as a computing agent and the instructions (algorithm) it carries out—a machine together with a set of instructions is called "a Turing machine" and is thought of as an algorithm. Thus, we say we are going to write a Turing machine to do a particular task, when we really mean that we are going to write a set of instructions—a Turing machine program, an algorithm—to do that task.

12.5 Turing Machine Examples

Because the Turing machine is such a simple device, it may seem nearly impossible to write a program for a Turing machine that carries out any interesting or significant task. In this section, we look at a few Turing machines that, though they do not accomplish anything earthshaking, should convince you that Turing machines can do some rather worthwhile things.

12.5.1 A Bit Inverter

Let's assume that the only nonblank portion of the input tape for a particular Turing machine consists of a string of bits (0s and 1s). Our first Turing machine moves along its tape from left to right inverting all of the bits—that is, changing 0s to 1s and 1s to 0s. (Recall that our sample Turing machine computation inverted the bits in the string 011, resulting in the string 100. Do you think that machine is a bit inverter? What if the leftmost nonblank symbol on the input tape is a 1?)

The Turing machine must begin in state 1 on the leftmost nonblank cell. Whatever the current symbol that is read, the machine must invert it by printing its opposite. Machine state 1 must, therefore, be a state in which 0s are changed to 1s and 1s are changed to 0s. This is exactly what we want to happen everywhere along the tape, so the machine never needs to go to another state; it can simply move right while remaining in state 1. When we come to the final blank, we want to halt. This can be accomplished by making sure that our program does not contain any instruction of the form

    $(1, b,-,-,-)$

We have now described the Turing machine algorithm in words, but let's represent it more precisely. In the past, we've used pseudocode to describe algorithms. Here we'll use an alternative form of representation that corresponds more closely to Turing machine instructions. A state diagram is a visual representation of a Turing machine algorithm, where circles represent states, and arrows represent transitions from one state to another. Along each transition arrow, we show three things: the input symbol that caused the transition, the corresponding output symbol to be written, and the direction of movement. For the bit inverter Turing machine, we have only one state and hence one circle in the state diagram, shown in Figure 12.4.

The arrow originating in and returning to state 1 marked $1/0/R$ says that when in state 1 (the only state) reading an input symbol of 1, the machine should print the symbol 0, move right, and remain in state 1. The arrow marked $0/1/R$ says that when in state 1 reading an input symbol of 0, the machine should print the symbol 1, move right, and remain in state 1.

FIGURE 12.4

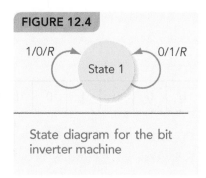

State diagram for the bit inverter machine

The complete Turing machine program for the bit inverter is

1. $(1,0,1,1,R)$ Change the symbol 0 to 1.

2. $(1,1,0,1,R)$ Change the symbol 1 to 0.

(We've added a comment to each instruction to explain its purpose.) Here's a sample computation using this machine, beginning with the string 1101 on the tape:

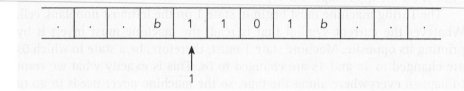

Using instruction 2,

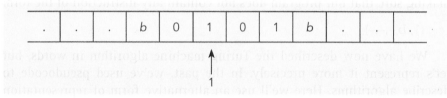

Using instruction 2 again,

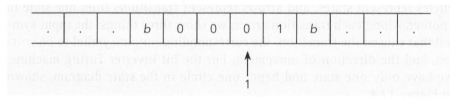

Using instruction 1,

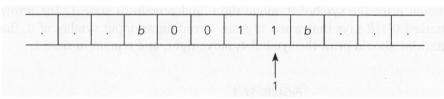

Using instruction 2,

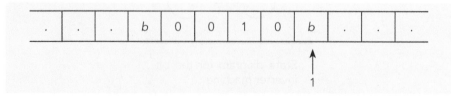

and the machine halts with the inverted string 0010 as output on the tape.

Practice Problems

1. Is the Turing machine shown here equivalent to the one shown in Figure 12.4, that is, will it produce the same output given the same input? Why or why not?

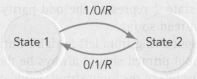

1/0/R

State 1   State 2

0/1/R

2. Explain exactly what would happen to the Turing machine of Practice Problem 1 if it were given a completely blank tape as input.

Bit inversion might seem like a trivial task, but recall that in Chapter 4 we introduced an electronic device called a NOT gate that is essentially a bit inverter and is one of the components of a real computer.

12.5.2 A Parity Bit Machine

An extra bit, called an *odd parity bit,* can be attached to the end of a string of bits. The odd parity bit is set such that the total number of 1s in the whole string of bits, including the parity bit, is odd. Thus, if the string preceding the parity bit has an odd number of 1s, the parity bit is set to 0 so that there is still an odd number of 1s in the whole string. If the string preceding the parity bit has an even number of 1s, the parity bit is set to 1 so that the number of 1s in the whole string is odd. As an example, the following string of bits includes as its rightmost bit an odd parity bit:

    1 1 0 0 0 1 0 1 0 1

The parity bit is set to 1 because there are four 1s (an even number) in the string before the parity bit; the total number of 1s is five (an odd number). Another example of odd parity is the string

    1 0 1 1 0 0

where the parity bit (the rightmost bit) is a 0 because three 1s (an odd number) appear in the preceding string. Our job here is to write a Turing machine that, given a string of bits on its input tape, attaches the correct odd parity bit to the right end.

We know from Chapter 4 that information in electronic form is represented as strings of bits. Parity bits are used to detect errors that occur as a result of electronic interference when transmitting such strings (see Exercise 25, Chapter 4).

If a single bit (or any odd number of bits) is changed from a 1 to 0 or from a 0 to 1, then the parity bit is incorrect, and the error can be detected. A correct copy of the information can then be retransmitted. Again, we are devising a Turing machine for a significant real-world task.

Our Turing machine must somehow "remember" whether the number of 1s processed so far is even or odd. We can use two states of the machine to represent these two conditions. Because the Turing machine begins in state 1, having read zero 1s so far (zero is an even number), we can let state 1 represent the even parity state, where an even number of 1s has been read so far. We'll let state 2 represent the odd parity state, where an odd number of 1s has been read so far.

We can read the input string from left to right. Until we get to the end of the bit string, the symbol printed should always be the same as the symbol read because none of the bits in the input string should change. But every time a 1 bit is read, the parity should change, from even to odd or from odd to even. In other words, the state should change from 1 to 2 or from 2 to 1. Reading a 0 bit does not affect the parity and therefore should not change the state. Thus, if we are in state 1 reading a 1, we want to go to state 2; if we are in state 1 reading a 0, we want to stay in state 1. If we are in state 2 reading a 1, we want to go to state 1; if we are in state 2 reading a 0, we want to stay in state 2.

When we come to the end of the input string (when we encounter the first blank cell), we write the parity bit, which is 1 if the machine is in state 1 (the even parity state) or 0 if the machine is in state 2 (the odd parity state). Then we want to halt, which is accomplished by going into state 3, for which there are no instructions. The state diagram for our odd parity bit machine is given in Figure 12.5.

FIGURE 12.5

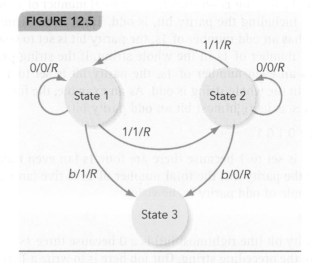

State diagram for the odd parity bit machine

The Turing machine program is as follows:

1. $(1,1,1,2,R)$ Even parity state reading 1, change state.

2. $(1,0,0,1,R)$ Even parity state reading 0, don't change state.

3. $(2,1,1,1,R)$ Odd parity state reading 1, change state.

4. $(2,0,0,2,R)$ Odd parity state reading 0, don't change state.

5. $(1,b,1,3,R)$ End of string in even parity state, write 1 and go to state 3.

6. $(2,b,0,3,R)$ End of string in odd parity state, write 0 and go to state 3.

Let's do an example. The initial string is 101, which contains an even number of 1s. Therefore, we want to add a parity bit of 1 and have the final output be the string 1011. Because this final string contains three 1 bits, it has the correct parity. Here's the initial configuration:

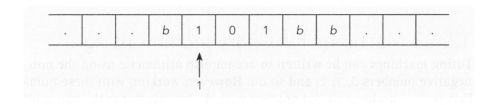

Using instruction 1,

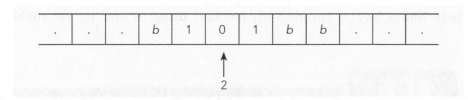

Using instruction 4,

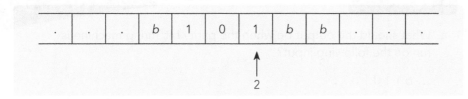

Using instruction 3,

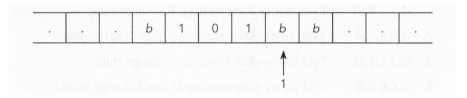

and finally using instruction 5 to write the parity bit, we get

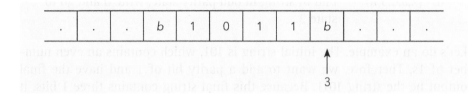

whereupon the machine halts.

12.5.3 Machines for Unary Incrementing

Turing machines can be written to accomplish arithmetic using the non-negative numbers 0, 1, 2, and so on. However, working with these numbers poses a problem we did not face with the bit inverter or the parity bit machine. In those examples, we were manipulating only bits (i.e., 0s and 1s), already part of the Turing machine alphabet of symbols. We can't put numbers like 2, 6, or 754 in cells of the Turing machine tape because these symbols are not part of the tape alphabet. Therefore, our first task is to find a way to encode such numbers using 0s and 1s. We could

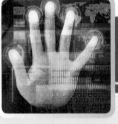

Practice Problem

1. a. What should the output be when the parity bit Turing machine is run on the following input?

    ...b1101b...

   b. Now run the parity bit Turing machine on this tape and see whether you get the answer you expected from Practice Problem 1a.

use binary representation, as a real computer does. Instead, let us agree on a simpler unary representation of numbers (unary representation means that we will use only *one* symbol, namely 1). In unary representation, any unsigned whole number n is encoded by a sequence of $n + 1$ 1s. Thus,

Number	Turing Machine Representation
0	1
1	11
2	111
3	1111
.	.
.	.
.	.

(You may wonder why we don't simply use 1 to represent 1, 11 to represent 2, and so on. This scheme would mean using no 1s to represent 0, and then the machine could not distinguish a single 0 on the tape from nothing—all blanks—on the tape.)

Using this unary representation of numbers, let's write Turing machines to accomplish some basic arithmetic operations. We can write a Turing machine to add 1 to any number; such a machine is often called an *incrementor*. (Recall from Chapter 5 that the program counter in a Von Neumann architecture uses an incrementor to bump up the address for the next instruction to be executed.) Using the unary representation of numbers just described, we need only stay in state 1 and travel over the string of 1s to the right-hand end. When we encounter the first blank cell, we write a 1 in it and go to state 2, which has no instructions, in order to halt. Figure 12.6 shows the state diagram.

The Turing machine for the incrementer is

1. $(1,1,1,1,R)$ Pass to the right over the 1s.

2. $(1,b,1,2,R)$ Add a single 1 at the right-hand end of the string and change to state 2.

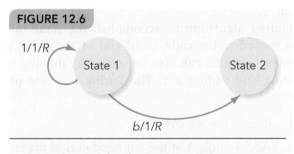

FIGURE 12.6

1/1/R

State 1   State 2

b/1/R

State diagram for the incrementer

Here's a quick sample computation:

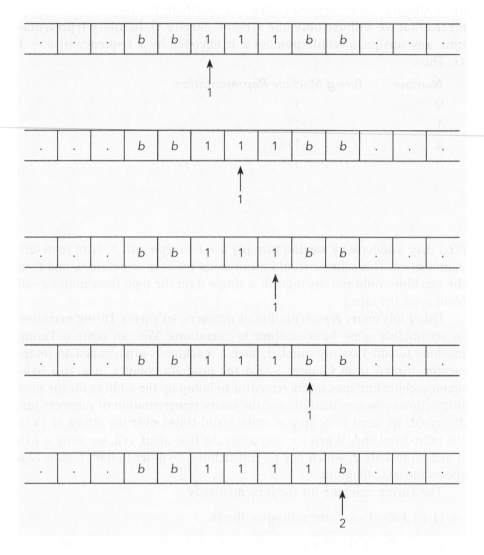

at which point the machine halts. The output on the tape is the unary representation of the number 3. The machine has thus incremented the input, 2, to the output, 3.

Here is another algorithm to accomplish the same task. The preceding algorithm moved to the right-hand end of the string and added a 1. But the increment problem can also be solved by moving to the left-hand end of the string and adding a 1. The Turing machine program for this algorithm is

$(1,1,1,1,L)$ Pass to the left over 1s.

$(1,b,1,2,L)$ Add a single 1 at the left-hand end of the string and change to state 2.

If we apply this algorithm to the same input tape, the computation is

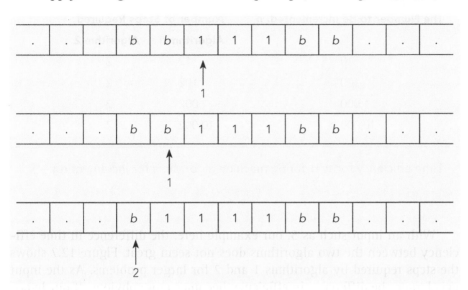

Once again, 2 has been incremented to 3. But whereas the first computation took four operations—that is, four applications of Turing machine instructions—the second computation took only two.

Let's compare these two algorithms in terms of their time and space efficiency. We'll take the execution of a single Turing machine instruction as a unit of work, so we measure the time used by a Turing machine algorithm by the number of instructions executed. The "space" a Turing machine algorithm takes on any given input is the number of nonblank cells on the tape that are used during the course of running the program. The input itself occupies some nonblank cells, so the interesting question is how many additional cells the algorithm uses in the course of its execution.

Suppose that the number 5 is to be incremented using algorithm 1. The initial input tape contains six 1s (the unary representation for 5). The machine moves to the right, over all the 1s on the tape, until it encounters the first blank cell. It writes a 1 into the blank cell and then halts. One instruction is executed for each move to the right. By the time the blank cell is reached, the first instruction has been executed six times. One final execution, this time of the second instruction, completes the task. Altogether, seven steps are required, two more than the number 5 we are incrementing. One "extra" step comes because of the unary representation, with its additional 1, and a second "extra" step writes over the blank cell. Therefore, it is easy to see that if the problem is to increment the number n, then $n + 2$ steps would be required using algorithm 1. Algorithm 2 does a constant number of steps (two) no matter what the size of n. Both algorithms use $n + 2$ cells on the tape: $n + 1$ for the initial input and one more for incrementing. The algorithms are equivalent in space efficiency, but algorithm 2 is more time efficient.

FIGURE 12.7

The Number to Be Incremented, n	Number of Steps Required	
	Algorithm 1	Algorithm 2
10	12	2
100	102	2
1,000	1,002	2
10,000	10,002	2

Time efficiency for two Turing machine algorithms for incrementing

With an input such as 5, our example here, the difference in time efficiency between the two algorithms does not seem great. Figure 12.7 shows the steps required by algorithms 1 and 2 for larger problems. As the input gets larger, the difference in efficiency becomes more obvious. If our hypothetical Turing machine actually existed and could do, say, one step per second, then to increment the number 10,000, algorithm 1 would take 2 hours, 46 minutes, and 42 seconds. Algorithm 2 could do the same job in 2 seconds! This significant difference gives a definite edge to algorithm 2 as the preferable solution method for this problem. Using the notation of Chapter 3, algorithm 1 is a linear time $\Theta(n)$ algorithm, whereas algorithm 2 is a constant time $\Theta(1)$ algorithm.

Although we can compare two Turing machine algorithms for the same task, we can't really compare the efficiency of a Turing machine algorithm with an algorithm that runs on a "real" computer. For one thing, the data representation is probably different (numbers aren't written in unary form). But more to the point, the basic unit of work is different. It takes many Turing machine operations to do a trivial task because the entire concept of a Turing machine is so simplistic. Turing machines, as we saw in our few examples, work by carefully moving, changing, and keeping track of individual 0s and 1s. Given such a limited range of activities, a Turing machine must exert a lot of effort to accomplish even mildly interesting tasks.

12.5.4 A Unary Addition Machine

A Turing machine can be written to add two numbers. Again using unary representation, let's agree to start with the two numbers on the tape separated by a single blank cell. When the Turing machine halts, the tape should contain the unary representation of the sum of the two numbers. The separating blank should be gone. If we erase the leftmost 1 and then fill in the separating blank with a 1, this has the effect of sliding the entire first number one cell to the right on the tape. Also, both numbers are originally written on the tape using unary representation, which means that there are two extra 1s on the tape, one for each number. When we are finished, we want to have only one extra 1, for the unary representation of the sum. Therefore, a second 1 should be removed from the tape. Our plan is to erase the two leftmost 1s on the tape, proceed rightward to the separating blank, and replace the blank with a 1.

For example, suppose we want to add 2 + 3. The original tape representation (rather than drawing the individual cells, we'll just show the tape contents) is

$$...b\,b\,\underline{1\ 1\ 1}\,b\,\underline{1\ 1\ 1\ 1}\,b\,b\,...$$
$$23$$

and the final representation should be the unary representation for the number 5,

$$...b\,b\,b\,b\,\underline{1\ 1\ 1\ 1\ 1}\,b\,b\,...$$
$$5$$

Our algorithm will accomplish this transformation in stages. First, we erase the leftmost 1:

$$...\,b\,b\,b\,1\,1\,b\,1\,1\,1\,1\,b\,b\,...$$

We then erase a second 1 from the left end (see Exercise 26 at the end of this chapter for the case when there is no "second 1"):

$$...\,b\,b\,b\,b\,1\,b\,1\,1\,1\,1\,b\,b\,...$$

and then move to the right and change the separating blank to a 1:

$$...\,b\,b\,b\,b\,\underline{1\ 1\ 1\ 1\ 1}\,b\,b\,...$$
$$5$$

The Turing machine begins in state 1, so we use that state to erase the leftmost 1 and move right, changing to state 2. The job of state 2 is to erase the second 1 and move right, changing to state 3. State 3 must move across any remaining 1s until it encounters the separating blank, which it changes to a 1 and then goes into a "halting state" with no instructions, state 4. A state diagram (Figure 12.8) illustrates the desired transitions to next states.

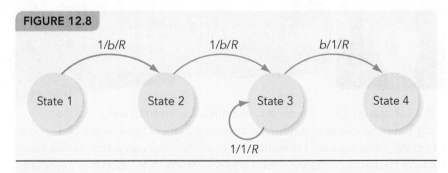

FIGURE 12.8

State diagram for the addition machine

Here is the Turing machine program:

1. $(1,1,b,2,R)$ Erase the leftmost 1 and move right.
2. $(2,1,b,3,R)$ Erase the second 1 and move right.
3. $(3,1,1,3,R)$ Pass over any 1s until a blank is found.
4. $(3,b,1,4,R)$ Write a 1 over the blank and halt.

Try "running" this machine on the preceding $2 + 3$ addition problem to see exactly how it works.

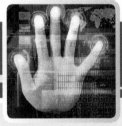

Practice Problems

1. Set up the input and run the addition Turing machine to compute $3 + 4$.

2. a. Write a Turing machine that, when run on the tape

   $$\ldots b\,1\,1\,1\,0\,b\,\ldots$$

   produces an output tape of

   $$\ldots b\,1\,1\,1\,0\,1\,b\,\ldots$$

   b. Does your machine from Problem 2a, when run on a tape containing k 1s followed by a single 0, produce k 1s followed by a single 0 and a single 1? If not, rewrite your machine so that it solves this more general problem.

Laboratory Experience 16

In this Laboratory Experience, you will run a Turing machine simulator. Using Turing machine algorithms that we have developed in the text, you can set up the input tape and then run the machine. You can watch as the Turing machine passes from state to state and see which instruction it is executing at each step. You can also see whether the input tape is modified at any step, and how (or whether) the machine reaches a halting configuration.

12.6 The Church–Turing Thesis

Just how good is the Turing machine as a model of the concept of an algorithm? We've already seen that any Turing machine exhibits the properties of an algorithm, and we've even produced Turing machine algorithms for a couple of important tasks. But perhaps we were judicious in our choice of tasks and happened to use those for which Turing machine instructions could be devised. We should ask whether there are other tasks that are "doable" by an algorithm but not "doable" by a Turing machine.

Of course, the answer to this question is yes. A Turing machine cannot program a DVR or shampoo hair, for example—tasks for which algorithms were given in Chapter 1. But suppose we limit the task to one for which the input and output can be represented symbolically, that is, using letters and numbers. Symbolic representation is, after all, how we traditionally record information such as names, addresses, telephone numbers, pay rates, yearly profits, temperatures, altitudes, growth rates, and so on. Taking a symbolic representation of information and manipulating it to produce a symbolic representation of other information covers a wide range of tasks, including everything done by "traditional" computing. Now let's ask a modified version of our previous question: Are there symbol manipulation tasks that are "doable" by an algorithm but not "doable" by a Turing machine?

The answer to this question is generally considered to be "No", as stated by the Church–Turing thesis, named for Alan Turing and another famous mathematician, Alonzo Church.

The Church–Turing thesis makes quite an extraordinary claim. It says that any symbol manipulation task that has an algorithmic solution can also be carried out by a Turing machine executing some set of Turing machine instructions. Processing the annual Internal Revenue Service records, for example, or calculating positions for global navigation satellite systems such as GPS can be done (according to this claim) using Turing machines. The thought of writing a Turing machine program to process IRS records is mind-boggling, but our examples may have convinced you that it is possible. Although such a program can be written, one can hardly imagine how many centuries it would take to execute, even with a very rapid "system clock." But the Church–Turing thesis says nothing about how efficiently the task will be done, only that it *can* be done by some Turing machine.

There are really two parts to writing a Turing machine for a symbol manipulation task. One part involves encoding symbolic information as strings of 0s and 1s so that it can appear on Turing machine tapes. This is not difficult, and we know that real computers store all information, including graphical information, in binary. The other part is the heart of the challenge: Given that we can get the input encoded onto a Turing machine tape, can we write the Turing machine instructions that produce the encoded form of

DEFINITION

Church–Turing thesis: If there exists an algorithm to do a symbol manipulation task, then there exists a Turing machine to do that task.

The Turing Award

The most prestigious technical award in the field of computer science, presented by the Association for Computing Machinery, is the annual Turing Award (officially the A. M. Turing Award), named in honor of Alan Turing. It is sometimes called the "Nobel Prize" of computing, and is given to an individual selected for "major contributions of lasting importance to computing." Some of the individuals we've mentioned in this book have been recipients of the Turing Award, which was first given in 1966:

1971:   John McCarthy (Chapter 10)

1977:   John Backus (Chapters 10 and 11)

1983:   Dennis Ritchie, Ken Thompson (Chapter 10)

2002:   Ron Rivest, Adi Shamir, and Len Adleman (Chapter 8)

2004:   Vinton Cerf and Robert Kahn (Chapter 7)

2005:   Peter Naur (Chapter 11)

Other recipients of the award have made contributions in areas we have discussed or will discuss in later chapters:

1972:   Edsger Dijkstra for fundamental contributions to programming as a high, intellectual challenge (Chapters 9 and 10)

1975:   Allen Newell as one of the founding fathers of artificial intelligence (AI), beginning his work in this area in 1954 (Chapter 15)

1981:   Edgar F. Codd for fundamental contributions to database management systems (Chapter 14)

1982:   Stephen A. Cook for exploring the class of problems that in Chapter 3 we called "suspected intractable"

1986:   John Hopcroft and Robert Tarjan for their work on analysis of algorithms (Chapter 3)

1990:   Fernando J. Corbato for pioneering work on general-purpose, time-shared mainframe operating systems (Chapter 6)

1999:   Frederick P. Brooks, Jr., for landmark contributions to computer architecture, operating systems, and software engineering (Chapters 5, 6, 9)

2008:   Barbara Liskov for contributions to practical and theoretical foundations of programming language and system design (Chapters 6 and 9)

2010: Leslie Valiant for transformative contributions to the theory of computation (Chapter 12)

2013 Leslie Lamport for fundamental contributions to the theory and practice of distributed and concurrent systems (Chapter 6)

2014 Michael Stonebraker for fundamental contributions to the concepts and practices underlying modern database systems (Chapter 14)

2015 Martin Hellman and Whitfield Diffie for inventing and promulgating both asymmetric public-key cryptography, including its application to digital signatures, and a practical cryptographic key-exchange method (Chapter 8)

2016 Sir Tim Berners-Lee for inventing the World Wide Web, the first web browser, and the fundamental protocols and algorithms allowing the web to scale (Chapter 7)

the correct output? Figure 12.9 illustrates the problem. The bottom arrow is the algorithmic solution to the symbol manipulation task we want to emulate. To perform this emulation, we must first encode the symbolic input into a bit string on a Turing machine tape (upward-pointing left arrow), write the Turing machine that solves the problem (top arrow), and, finally, decode the resulting bit string into symbolic output (downward-pointing right arrow). The Church–Turing thesis asserts that this process can always be done.

What exactly is a *thesis*? According to the dictionary, it is "a statement advanced for consideration and maintained by argument." That sounds less than convincing—hasn't the Church–Turing thesis been proved? No, and that's why it is called a thesis, not a theorem. Theorems are ideas that can be proved in a formal, mathematical way, such as "the sum of the interior angles of a triangle equals 180°." The Church–Turing thesis can never be proved because— despite all our talk about algorithms and their properties—the definition of

FIGURE 12.9

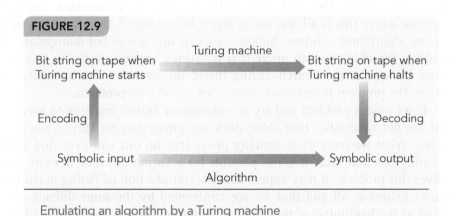

Emulating an algorithm by a Turing machine

an algorithm is still descriptive, not mathematical. It would be like trying to "prove" that an ideal day at the beach is sunny and 85°F. We might all agree on this, but we'll never be able to "prove" it. Well, then, the Church–Turing thesis makes a remarkable claim and can never be proved! Sounds pretty suspicious—what are the arguments on its behalf? There are two.

One argument is that early on, when the thesis was first put forward, whenever computer science researchers described algorithmic solutions for tasks, they also tried to find Turing machines for those tasks. They were always successful; no one was ever able to put forth an algorithm for a task for which a Turing machine was not eventually found. This does not mean that no such task exists, but it lends weight to a body of evidence in support of the thesis.

A second argument on behalf of the thesis is the fact that a number of other mathematicians attempted to find models for computing agents and algorithms. All of these proved to be equivalent to Turing machines and Turing machine programs in that whatever could be done by these other computing agents running their algorithms could also be done by a Turing machine running a Turing machine program, and vice versa. This suggests that the Turing machine captures all of these other ideas about "algorithms."

The Church–Turing thesis is now widely accepted by computer scientists. They no longer feel it necessary to write a Turing machine when they talk about an algorithmic computation. After describing an algorithm to carry out some task, they simply say, "Now let T be the Turing machine that does this task." You may make your own decision about the Church–Turing thesis, but in this book we will go along with convention and accept it as true. We therefore accept the Turing machine as an ultimate model of a computing agent and a Turing machine program as an ultimate model of an algorithm. We are saying that Turing machines define the limits of computability—that which can be done by symbol manipulation algorithms. What can be done by an algorithm is doable by a Turing machine, and what is not doable by a Turing machine cannot be done by an algorithm. In particular, if we find a symbol manipulation task that no Turing machine can perform (in its elementary way of moving around over a tape of 0s and 1s), then there is no algorithm for this task, and no real computer, no matter how sophisticated, will ever be able to do it either. That's why the Turing machine is so important. You can now see where this is all leading in terms of our search for a problem that has no algorithmic solution. Suppose we can find a (symbol manipulation) problem for which we can prove that no Turing machine exists to solve it. Then, because of the Church–Turing thesis, no algorithm exists to solve it either. The problem is an uncomputable or unsolvable problem.

If we pose a problem and try to construct a Turing machine to solve it but are not successful, that alone does not prove that no Turing machine exists. What we must do is actually prove that no one can ever find such a Turing machine—that it is not possible for a Turing machine to exist that solves this problem. It may appear that the introduction of Turing machines hasn't helped at all and that we are confronted by the same dilemma we faced at the beginning of this chapter. But Alan Turing, in the late 1930s, found such a problem and proved its unsolvability.

12.7 Unsolvable Problems

The problem Turing found is an ingenious one that itself involves Turing machine computations. A Turing machine that is executing an algorithm (a collection of Turing machine instructions) to solve some task must halt when begun on a tape containing input appropriate to that task. On other kinds of input, the Turing machine may not halt. It is easy enough for us to decide whether any specific configuration of a given Turing machine is a halting configuration. If a Turing machine program consists of the following four instructions:

$(1,0,1,2,R)$

$(1,1,0,2,R)$

$(2,0,0,2,R)$

$(2,b,b,2,L)$

then the configuration

is a halting configuration because there is no instruction of the form $(2,1,-,-,-)$. It is also easy to see that this configuration will arise if the Turing machine is begun on the tape

$\dots b\,0\,1\,b\,b\,b\dots$

Similarly, we can see that if the Turing machine is begun on the tape

$\dots b\,1\,b\,b\,b\dots$

then it will never halt. Instead, after the first step (clock tick), the machine will cycle forever between the two configurations

In a more complicated case, however, if we know the Turing machine program and we know the initial contents of the tape, then it may not be so easy to decide whether the Turing machine will eventually halt when begun on that tape. Of course, we can always simply execute the Turing machine—that is, carry out the instructions. We don't have all day to wait for the answer, so we'll set a time-out for our Turing machine system clock. Let's say we are willing to wait for 1,000 clock ticks. If we come to a halting configuration within the first 1,000 steps, then we know the answer: This Turing machine, running on this input tape, halts. But suppose we do not come to a halting configuration within the first 1,000 clock ticks. Can we say that the machine will never halt? Should we wait another 1,000 clock ticks? 10,000 clock ticks? Just running the Turing machine doesn't necessarily enable us to decide about halting. Here is the problem we propose to investigate:

> *Decide, given any collection of Turing machine instructions together with any initial tape contents, whether that Turing machine will ever halt if started on that tape.*

This is a clear and unambiguous problem known as the halting problem. Does it have a Turing machine solution? Can we find one single Turing machine that will solve every instance of this problem—that is, one that will give us the answer "Yes, halts" or "No, never halts" for every (Turing machine, initial tape) pair?

This is an uncomputable problem; we will show that no Turing machine exists to solve this problem. Remember that we said it was not sufficient to look for such a machine and fail; we actually have to prove that no such machine can exist. The way to do this is to assume that such a Turing machine does exist and then show that this assumption leads to an impossible situation, so such a machine could not exist after all. This approach is called a proof by contradiction.

Assume, then, that *P* is a Turing machine that solves the halting problem. On the initial tape for *P* we have to put a description—using the binary digits 0 and 1—of a collection *T* of Turing machine instructions, as well as the initial tape content *t* on which those instructions run. This is the encoding part of Figure 12.9. Translating Turing machine instructions into binary form is tedious but not difficult. For example, we can use unary notation for machine states and tape symbols, designate the direction in which the read unit moves by 1 for *R* (right) and 11 for *L* (left), and separate the parts of a Turing machine instruction by 0s. Let's use *T** to symbolize the binary form of the collection *T* of Turing machine instructions. *P* is then run on a tape containing both *T** and *t*, so the initial tape for *P* looks like the following, where *T** and *t* may occupy many cells of the tape:

$$\ldots b\, b\, T^*\, b\, t\, b\, b \ldots$$

Our assumption is that *P* will always give us an answer ("Yes, halts" or "No, never halts"). *P*'s yes/no answer would be its output—what is written on the tape when *P* halts; therefore, *P* itself must always halt. Again, because the output is written on *P*'s tape, it also has to be in binary form, so let's say that a single 1 and all the rest blanks represent "yes," and a single 0 and all the rest blanks represent "no." This is the decoding part of Figure 12.9. To summarize:

When begun on a tape containing T* and t

> *P halts with 1 on its tape exactly when T eventually halts when begun on t*
> *P halts with 0 on its tape exactly when T never halts when begun on t*

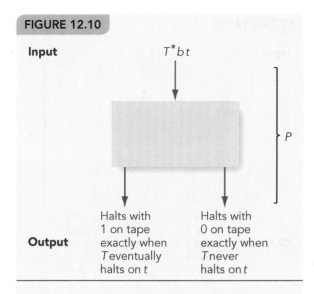

FIGURE 12.10

Input T^*bt

P

Output Halts with 1 on tape exactly when T eventually halts on t

Halts with 0 on tape exactly when T never halts on t

Hypothetical Turing machine P running on T^* and t

Figure 12.10 is a pictorial representation of the actions of P when started on a tape containing T^* and t.

When P halts with a single 1 on its tape, it does so because there are no instructions allowing P to proceed in its current state when reading 1. For example, P might be in state 9, and there is no instruction of the form

$$(9,1,-,-,-)$$

for machine P. Let's imagine adding more instructions to P to create a new machine Q that behaves just like P except that when it reaches this same configuration, it moves forever to the right on the tape instead of halting. To do this, pick some state not in P, say 52, and add the following two new instructions to P:

$$(9,1,1,52,R)$$
$$(52,b,b,52,R)$$

Figure 12.11 represents Q's behavior when started on a tape containing T^* and t.

Finally, we'll create a new machine S. This machine first makes a copy of what appears on its input tape. (This is a doable, if tedious, task. The machine must "pick up" a 0 or 1 by going to a particular state, move to another part of the tape, and write a 0 or 1, depending on the state. It travels back and repeats the process; however, each time it picks up a 0 or 1, it must mark the tape with some marker symbol, say X for 0 and Y for 1, so that it doesn't try to pick it up again. At the end of the copying, the markers must be changed back to 0s and 1s.) After S is finished with its copying job, it uses the same instructions as machine Q.

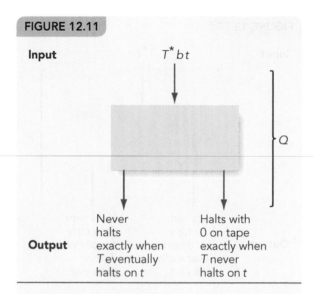

FIGURE 12.11

Input $\quad T^* b t$

Q

Output
Never halts exactly when *T* eventually halts on *t*

Halts with 0 on tape exactly when *T* never halts on *t*

Hypothetical Turing machine *Q* running on *T** and *t*

Now what happens when machine *S* is run on a tape that contains *S**, the binary representation of *S*'s own instructions? *S* first makes a copy of *S** and then turns the computation over to *Q*, which is now running on a tape containing *S** and *S**. Figure 12.12 shows the result; this figure follows from Figure 12.11 where *T** and *t* are both *S**.

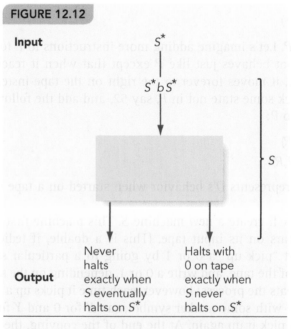

FIGURE 12.12

Input $\quad S^*$

$S^* b S^*$

S

Output
Never halts exactly when *S* eventually halts on *S**

Halts with 0 on tape exactly when *S* never halts on *S**

Hypothetical Turing machine *S* running on *S**

Figure 12.12 represents the behavior of *S* running on input *S**. The final outcome is either (left output)

S running on input S* never halts

> *exactly when S halts running on S*—this is a contradiction*

or (right output)

S running on input S* halts with 0 on the tape

> *exactly when S never halts running on S*—also a contradiction*

(Perhaps you'll need to read this several times while looking at Figure 12.12 to convince yourself of what we have said.) We have backed ourselves into a corner here, but that's good. This is exactly the impossible situation we were hoping to find.

We assumed that there was a Turing machine that could solve the halting problem, and this assumption led to an impossible situation. The assumption is therefore incorrect, and no Turing machine can exist to solve the halting problem. Therefore, no algorithm can exist to solve this problem. The halting problem is an example of an unsolvable or uncomputable problem.

The halting problem seems rather abstract; perhaps we don't care whether it is unsolvable. However, real computer programs written in real programming languages to run on real computers are also symbol manipulation algorithms and, by the Church–Turing thesis, can be simulated by Turing machines. This means that the unsolvability of the halting problem has practical consequences. For example, we know that some C++, Java, and Python programs can get stuck in infinite loops. It would be nice to have a program that you could run ahead of time on any C++, Java, or Python program, together with its input, that would tell you, "Uh-oh, if you run this program on this input, it will get into an infinite loop," or "No problem, if you run this program on this input, it will eventually stop." The unsolvability of the halting problem says that no such program is possible. Other unsolvable problems, related to the halting problem, have the following practical consequences:

- No program can be written to decide whether any given program always stops eventually, no matter what the input.

- No program can be written to decide whether any two programs are equivalent (will produce the same output for all inputs).

- No program can be written to decide whether any given program run on any given input will ever produce some specific output.

This last case means it is impossible to write a general automatic program tester—one that for any program can check whether, given input *A*, it produces correct output *B*. That is why program testing plays such an important role in the software development life cycle described in Chapter 9.

It is important to note, however, that these problems are unsolvable because of their generality. We are asking for *one* program that will decide

Couldn't Do, Can't Do, Never Will Be Able to …

Unsolvable problems are not confined to problems about running programs (Java programs, C++ programs, Python programs, or Turing machines). In Chapter 11, we talked about grammars that can be described in Backus-Naur Form (BNF) and about how a compiler parses a programming language statement by applying the rules of its grammar. We noted that ambiguous grammars are not suitable for programming languages because they can allow multiple interpretations of a statement. It would be nice to have a test (an algorithm) to decide whether any BNF grammar is ambiguous. This is an unsolvable problem—no such algorithm can exist. Deciding whether any two such grammars produce the same language is also unsolvable.

One of the earliest "decision problems" was posed by the British mathematician David Hilbert in 1900. Consider quadratic equations of the form

$$ax^2 + bx - c = 0$$

where a, b, and c are integers. We can easily decide whether any one such equation has integer solutions by applying the quadratic formula to solve the equation. But consider more general polynomial equations in several unknowns, such as

$$ax^4 + by^2 + cz^6 + dw^4 + e = 0$$

where the unknowns are x, y, z, and w and the coefficients (a, b, c, d, and e) are integers. Is there an algorithm to decide whether any such equation has integer solutions? In 1970, this problem was shown to be unsolvable.

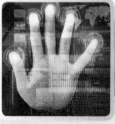

Practice Problems

1. Explain how a proof by contradiction is done.
2. a. Write in your own words a description of the halting problem.

    b. Write a paragraph that describes the proof of the unsolvability of the halting problem.

Laboratory Experience 17

Using the same Turing machine simulator as before, you can now design and run your own Turing machine algorithms for simple problems. You will add states to an initially empty machine by describing the purpose of the new state and adding instructions for that state. You then run your machine on an appropriate input tape to see whether it behaves as intended.

something about *any* given program. It may be very easy to write a program *A* that can make a decision only about a specific program *B* by utilizing specialized properties of *B*. (*Analogy*: If I ask you to be ready to write "I love you" in English, you can do it; if I ask you to be ready to write "I love you" in any language I might later specify, you can't do it.)

12.8 Conclusion

We began this chapter by proposing that there exist problems for which no solution algorithm exists. To prove such a statement, we looked for appropriate models of "computing agent" and "algorithm" that would enable us to concentrate on the fundamental nature of computation. After developing a list of properties inherent in any computing agent, we defined the Turing machine, noted that it incorporates these properties, and accepted it as a model of a computing agent. A Turing machine program incorporates the properties of an algorithm described in Chapter 1, so we accepted it as a model of an algorithm. Are these good models? Do they capture everything that is fundamental about computing and algorithms? After looking at a few Turing machines devised to do some simple tasks, we stated our position with a resounding *yes* in the form of the Church–Turing thesis: Not only is a Turing machine program an example of an algorithm, but also every symbolic manipulation algorithm can be done by a Turing machine (we believe). This leap of faith—putting total confidence in Turing machine programs as models of algorithms—allows us to define the boundaries of computability. If it can't be done by a Turing machine, then it is not computable. Thus, the real value of Turing machines as models of computability is in exposing problems that are uncomputable—problems for which no algorithmic solution exists no matter how intelligent we are or how long we keep looking. As a practical matter, recognizing uncomputable problems certainly saves time; we are less likely to devote our lives to searching for algorithms that can never be. As a philosophical matter, it is important to know that computability has its limits, beyond which lies the great abyss of the uncomputable!

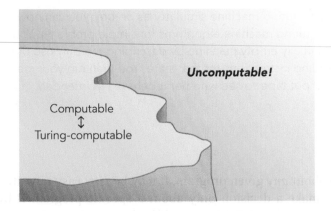

12.9 Summary of Level 4

In Level 4, we examined the use of procedural programming languages as a means for expressing algorithms at a high level of abstraction. Other high-level languages exist, including special-purpose languages, and those that follow other philosophies, such as functional languages and logic-based languages. Because algorithms written in high-level languages ultimately run on low-level hardware, program translators must convert from one level of algorithmic expression to another. We've looked at the series of tasks that a language compiler must perform to carry out this conversion. This final chapter of Level 4 proved that there are limits to computability—that there exist problems that can never be solved algorithmically.

With all of the hardware and software mechanisms in place to implement algorithmic problem solutions, we are ready to proceed to the next level—the level of applications—to see some of the ways in which computers (and algorithms) are being put to use.

The first application we examine relates very closely to what we have discussed in this chapter—building models. In Chapter 13, we will discuss simulation models that help us solve important problems such as predicting the weather, creating new medicines, tracking our economy, and designing safe and efficient airplanes.

EXERCISES

In this set of exercises, when writing Turing machine algorithms, include comments for each instruction or related group of instructions. The comments should convey information in terms of the algorithm the Turing machine is accomplishing. Thus, the instruction

(1,0,0,1,R)

might have a comment such as, "Pass to the right over all the 0s," not a comment such as, "In state 1 looking at a 0, write a 0, stay in state 1, and move right," which provides no additional information.

1. Describe what factors might be included in a model for the spread of an epidemic.

2. Say an automobile manufacturer designs a new car using a sophisticated and detailed computer simulation, but no prototype vehicles, and the automobile is later found to have a defect. Do you think the manufacturer is accountable? Is the manufacturer accountable if it builds prototypes that do not reveal the defect, but it does not do a simulation?

3. Give an example of a potential use of computerized models in

   a. The pharmaceutical industry
   b. The food processing industry
   c. The insurance industry

4. Which of the following can be considered computing agents and why?

   a. A clock radio
   b. A vacuum cleaner
   c. A video camera
   d. A programmable calculator

5. Given the Turing machine instruction

(1,1,0,2,L)

and the configuration

... b 1 0 b ...

1

draw the next configuration.

6. A Turing machine contains only the following instructions:

(1,1,1,1,R)

(1,b,1,2,R)

Can this machine ever reach the following configuration? Explain your answer.

... b 0 1 b ...

1

7. Is the following a legitimate Turing machine? Why or why not?

(1,1,0,2,R)

(1,0,0,3,R)

(2,1,1,2,R)

(3,0,0,3,R)

(2,0,0,4,L)

(3,0,1,4,L)

(4,1,1,5,R)

(4,0,0,5,R)

8. Find the output for the Turing machine

   $(1,1,1,2,R)$
   $(1,0,0,2,R)$
   $(1,b,1,2,R)$
   $(2,0,0,2,R)$
   $(2,1,0,1,R)$

   when run on the tape

   $\ldots b\,1\,0\,0\,1\,b\ldots$

9. Find the output for the Turing machine

   $(1,1,1,2,L)$
   $(2,b,0,3,L)$
   $(3,b,1,4,R)$
   $(4,0,1,4,R)$

   when run on the tape

   $\ldots b\,1\,b\ldots$

10. Describe the behavior of the Turing machine

    $(1,1,1,2,R)$
    $(2,0,0,1,L)$

    when run on the tape

    $\ldots b\,1\,0\,1\,b\ldots$

11. Describe the behavior of the Turing machine

    $(1,1,1,1,R)$
    $(1,0,0,2,L)$
    $(2,1,0,2,L)$
    $(2,b,1,3,L)$
    $(3,b,b,1,R)$

    when run on the tape

    $\ldots b\,1\,0\,1\,b\ldots$

12. Describe the behavior of the following Turing machine on any input tape containing a binary string:

    $(1,1,1,1,R)$
    $(1,0,0,1,R)$
    $(1,b,1,1,R)$

13. Write a Turing machine that, when run on the tape

    $\ldots b\,1\,1\,1\,1\,1\,b\ldots$

    produces an output tape of

    $\ldots b\,0\,1\,1\,1\,1\,b\ldots$

    You can accomplish this using only one instruction.

14. Say a Turing machine is supposed to change any string of 1s to a string of 0s. For example,

    $\ldots b\,1\,1\,1\,b\ldots$

    should become

    $\ldots b\,0\,0\,0\,b\ldots$

    Will the following Turing machine do the job? Why or why not?

    $(1,1,0,2,R)$
    $(2,1,0,3,R)$
    $(3,1,0,4,R)$

15. a. Write a Turing machine that, when run on the tape

    $\ldots b\,1\,1\,1\,1\,1\,b\ldots$

    produces an output tape of

    $\ldots b\,1\,1\,1\,1\,0\,b\ldots$

    b. Write a Turing machine that, when run on any tape containing a unary string, changes the rightmost 1 to 0 and then halts. (If your solution to Exercise 15a was sufficiently general, you will not have to change it here.)

16. Write a Turing machine to perform a *unary decrement* (the opposite of an increment). Assume that $n > 0$.

17. Write a Turing machine to perform a unary decrement. Assume that n may be 0, in which case a single 0 should be output on the tape to signify that the operation results in a negative number.

18. Write a Turing machine that operates on any binary string and changes it to a string of the same length with all 1s. It should, for example, change the tape to

    $\ldots b\,0\,1\,1\,0\,1\,0\,b\ldots$

    to

    $\ldots b\,1\,1\,1\,1\,1\,1\,b\ldots$

However, you must write instructions that allow your Turing machine to work on *any* binary string, not just the one shown here.

19. Write a Turing machine that operates on any string of 1s and changes it to a string of alternating 1s and 0s.

20. The parity-bit Turing machine of Section 12.5.2 uses an odd parity bit scheme. Write a Turing machine that uses an even parity bit scheme.

21. Write a Turing machine that *efficiently* adds 3 to any unary number.

22. Write a Turing machine that begins on a tape containing a single 1 and never halts but successively displays the strings

    $\ldots b\,1\,b\,\ldots$
    $\ldots b\,0\,1\,0\,b\,\ldots$
    $\ldots b\,0\,0\,1\,0\,0\,b\,\ldots$
    and so on.

23. Write a Turing machine that operates on the unary representation of any number and decides whether the number is 0; your machine should produce an output tape containing the unary representation of 1 if the number was 0 and the unary representation of 2 if the number was not 0.

24. Write a Turing machine that takes any unary string of an even number of 1s and halts with the first half of the string changed to 0s. (*Hint*: You may need to use a "marker" symbol such as X or Y to replace temporarily any input symbols you have already processed and do not want to process again; at the end, your program must "clean up" any marker symbols.)

25. Write a Turing machine that takes as input the unary representation of any two different numbers, separated by a blank, and halts with the representation of the larger of the two numbers on the tape. (*Hint*: You may need to use a "marker" symbol such as X or Y to replace temporarily any input symbols you

have already processed and do not want to process again; at the end, your program must "clean up" any marker symbols.)

26. The Turing machine described in Section 12.5.4 to add two unary numbers was designed to erase the two leftmost 1s on the tape, move to the right to the blank separating the two numbers, and replace the blank with a 1. If the first of the two numbers being added is 0, then there are not two 1s before the separating blank. Does the algorithm still work in this case?

27. Draw a state diagram for a Turing machine that takes any string of 1s and changes every third 1 to a 0. Thus, for example,

    $\ldots b\,1\,1\,1\,1\,1\,1\,b\,\ldots$
    becomes
    $\ldots b\,1\,1\,0\,1\,1\,0\,b\,\ldots$

28. Draw a state diagram for a Turing machine that increments a binary number. Thus, if the binary representation of 4 is initially on the tape,

    $\ldots b\,1\,0\,0\,\ldots$
    then the output is the binary representation of 5,

    $\ldots b\,1\,0\,1\,\ldots$
    or if the initial tape contains the binary representation of 7,

    $\ldots b\,1\,1\,1\,b\,\ldots$
    then the output is the binary representation of 8,

    $\ldots b\,1\,0\,0\,0\,b\,\ldots$

29. Analyze the time and space efficiency of the following Turing machine operating on a unary string of length n.

    $(1,1,1,1,R)$

    $(1,b,b,2,L)$

    $(2,1,0,2,L)$

    $(2,b,b,3,R)$

    $(3,0,1,3,R)$

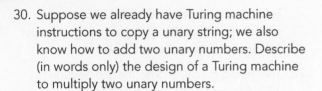

30. Suppose we already have Turing machine instructions to copy a unary string; we also know how to add two unary numbers. Describe (in words only) the design of a Turing machine to multiply two unary numbers.

31. Two other Turing machine unary addition algorithms follow.

    1. Fill in the separating blank with a 1, go to the far right end, and erase two 1s.

    2. Erase a 1 on the left end, fill in the separating blank with a 1, and erase a 1 on the right end.

    a. Do both of these algorithms work correctly?

    b. Write the Turing machine for each of these algorithms.

    c. Informally, which of the three addition algorithms (the one given in the chapter and these two) seems most time efficient?

    d. Suppose that the numbers to be added are n and m. The original tape contains the unary representation of n, followed by a blank, followed by the unary representation of m.
       Write exact expressions in terms of n, m, or both for the time efficiency of each of the three algorithms. Does this confirm your answer from Exercise 31-2c?

    e. Again assuming that the numbers to be added are n and m, write an exact expression for the space efficiency of each of the three algorithms.

We have considered Turing machines as computation devices, turning input to output according to some specific requirement. Turing machines can also be used as **recognizers**, deciding whether the string of characters initially on its tape matches a certain pattern. The following problem uses a Turing machine in this way.

32. A *palindrome* is a string of characters that reads the same forward and backward, such as radar or IUPUI. Write a Turing machine to decide whether any binary string is a palindrome by halting with a blank tape if the string is a palindrome and halting with a nonblank tape if the string is not a palindrome.

    Note: The world's longest single-word palindrome is the Finnish word for "lye dealer":

    Saippuakivikauppias
    Other palindromes include:
    Slap a ham on Omaha pals
    Do geese see god
    A man a plan a canal Panama

Recall from Chapter 11 that the job of the parser in a compiler is also to recognize strings that match patterns, where the patterns are given by means of a grammar expressed in BNF notation. Exercises 33–36 use BNF grammar notation.

33. The following BNF grammar defines a set of binary strings.

    <string> ::= <one> | <one><string>

    <one> ::= 1

    a. Describe the language defined by this grammar.

    b. Write a Turing machine to decide whether any binary string is a string in this language by halting with a blank tape if the string is in the language and halting with a nonblank tape if the string is not in the language.

34. The following BNF grammar defines a set of binary strings.
    <string> ::= <zero><zero><string> | <one>
    <zero> ::= 0
    <one> ::= 1

    a. Describe the language defined by this grammar.

    b. Write a Turing machine to decide whether any binary string is a string in this language by halting with a blank tape if the string is in the language and halting with a nonblank tape if the string is not in the language.

35. The following BNF grammar defines a set of binary strings.

    <string> ::= <zero><A><zero>
    <A> ::= <zero><B><zero>
    <B>::= <one> <B>| <one>
    <zero> ::= 0
    <one> ::= 1

    a. Describe the language defined by this grammar.
    b. Write a Turing machine to decide whether any binary string is a string in this language by halting with a blank tape if the string is in the language and halting with a nonblank tape if the string is not in the language.

36. The following BNF grammar defines a set of binary strings.

    <string> ::= <zero><one> | <zero><string><one>
    <zero> ::= 0
    <one> ::= 1

    a. Describe the language defined by this grammar.
    b. Write a Turing machine to decide whether any binary string is a string in this language by halting with a blank tape if the string is

    in the language and halting with a nonblank tape if the string is not in the language.

37. Your boss gives you a computer program and a set of input data and asks you to determine whether the program will get into an infinite loop running on these data. You report that you cannot do this job, citing the Church–Turing thesis. Should your boss fire you? Explain.

38. What is the significance of the unsolvability of the halting problem?

39. The *uniform halting problem* is to decide, given any collection of Turing machine instructions, whether that Turing machine will halt for every input tape. This is an unsolvable problem. Which of the three practical consequences of unsolvability problems described in Section 12.7 follows from the uniform halting problem?

40. The *10-step halting problem* is to decide, given any collection of Turing machine instructions, together with any initial tape contents, whether that Turing machine will halt within 10 steps when started on that tape. Explain why the 10-step halting problem is computable.

CHALLENGE WORK

1. Several alternative definitions of Turing machines exist, all of which produce machines that are equivalent in computational ability to the Turing machine defined in this chapter. One of these alternative definitions is the *multitrack Turing machine*. In a multitrack Turing machine, there are multiple tapes. The machine reads a cell from each of the tapes and, on the basis of what it reads, it writes a symbol on each tape, changes state, and moves left or right. Diagram (a) on the next page shows a two-track Turing machine currently in state 1 reading a 1 on the first tape and a 0 on the second tape.

   An instruction for this Turing machine has the following form:

   (current state, current first tape symbol, next first tape symbol, current second tape symbol, next second tape symbol, next state, direction of move)

   An instruction of the form (1,1,0,0,0,2,*R*) applied to the machine configuration of diagram (a) results in the configuration shown in diagram (b) on the next page.

(a)

.	.	.	b	b	1	1	1	b	b	.	.	.
.	.	.	b	b	0	1	1	0	b	.	.	.

↑
1

(b)

.	.	.	b	b	0	1	1	b	b	.	.	.
.	.	.	b	b	0	1	1	b	b	.	.	.

↑
2

As in the original Turing machine definition, some conventions apply. Each tape can contain only a finite number of nonblank symbols, and the leftmost nonblank symbols must initially "line up" on the two tapes. The read head begins in this leftmost nonblank position in state 1. At any time, if no instruction applies to the current machine configuration, the machine halts.

a. Design a two-track Turing machine that compares two binary strings and decides whether they are equal. If the strings are equal, the machine halts in some fixed state; if they are not equal, the machine halts in some other fixed state.

b. Solve this same problem using the Turing machine defined in this chapter.

c. Prove the following statement: Any computation that can be carried out using a regular Turing machine can be done using a two-track Turing machine.

d. On the basis of Challenge Exercise 1a and 1b, make an argument for the following statement: Any computation that can be carried out using a two-track Turing machine can be done using a regular Turing machine.

2. Read some biographical information on Alan Turing and write a report on his life, concentrating particularly on his contributions in computability theory, cryptography, and artificial intelligence.

Chapter 17   Social Issues

Chapters 13, 14, 15, 16   Applications

Chapters 9, 10, 11, 12   The Software World

Chapters 6, 7, 8   The Virtual Machine

Chapters 4, 5   The Hardware World

Chapters 2, 3   The Algorithmic Foundations of Computer Science

Level 4 focused on programming languages and software development. In this section, entitled *Applications*, we answer the question, What kind of programs do we want to write? Now that we have introduced the hardware (Level 2) and software (Levels 3, 4) tools that implement algorithms, we will take a look at the specific types of computational problems we might wish to address.

Of course, there are far too many applications to survey them all; indeed, there is hardly an area of society that has not been significantly influenced and changed by the rapid growth of information technology. Therefore, rather than trying to briefly survey a large number of applications, we will, instead, examine a few important applications in depth. These applications exemplify the enormous effect that computing has on our work and on our daily lives.

13

Simulation and Modeling

AFTER STUDYING THIS CHAPTER, YOU WILL BE ABLE TO:

- Describe the purpose of modeling in science
- List the benefits of a computational model over a physical model
- Explain the trade-off between accuracy and complexity in models
- Define different types of simulation models, including discrete and continuous, deterministic and stochastic
- Describe how a discrete event simulation works
- Explain the purpose of scientific visualization
- List some common methods of scientific visualization

13.1 Introduction

The computational devices of the 19th and early 20th centuries were used to solve important mathematical and scientific problems of the day. We saw this in the historical review of computing in Chapter 1: Charles Babbage's Difference Engine evaluated polynomial functions; Herman Hollerith's punched-card machines carried out a statistical analysis of the 1890 census; ENIAC computed artillery ballistic tables; and Alan Turing's Colossus cranked away at Bletchley Park, breaking the "unbreakable" German Enigma code. The users of these early computing devices were almost exclusively mathematicians, physicists, and engineers.

Today, there is hardly a field of study or aspect of society—from art to zoology, business to entertainment—that has not been profoundly changed by information technology and telecommunications. Now we use computers in many "nonscientific" ways, such as buying and selling products (a topic we investigate in Chapter 14), playing games (the focus of Chapter 16), surfing the web, listening to music, and sharing photos and videos with friends.

However, the physical, mathematical, engineering, and economic sciences are still some of the largest users of computing and information technology. In this chapter, we investigate perhaps the single most important scientific use of computing—computational modeling. This application is having a major impact on many quantitative fields, including chemistry, biology, medicine, meteorology, ecology, geography, and economics.

13.2 Computational Modeling

13.2.1 Introduction to Systems and Models

The *scientific method* entails observing the behavior of a system and formulating a hypothesis that tries to understand and explain that behavior. We then design and carry out experiments on the system to either prove or disprove the validity of our hypothesis. This is the fundamental way of gaining new scientific knowledge and understanding.

Scientists often work with a model of a system rather than experimenting on the "real thing." Models were discussed in Chapter 12, where the Turing machine was presented as a model of a computing agent. A model is a representation of the system being studied, which we claim behaves much like the original. If that claim is valid, then we can experiment on the model and use the results to understand and explain the behavior of the actual system. For example, *physical models* (small-scale replicas) have been in use for many years, and we are all familiar with the idea of testing a model airplane in a wind tunnel to understand how the full-sized aircraft would behave. Small-scale mockups of a building give architects a sense of how the full-scale structure will function in its surroundings.

In this chapter, we are not interested in physical models but in computational models, also called simulation models. In a computer simulation, a physical system is not modeled as a small-scale replica but as a set of mathematical equations and/or algorithmic procedures that capture the fundamental properties and behaviors of a system. This computational model is then translated into a computer program written in one of the high-level languages described in Chapters 9 and 10 and executed on the Von Neumann computer described in Chapters 4 and 5.

Why construct a simulation model? Why not simply study the system itself, or a physical replica of the system? There are many reasons:

- *Existence*—The system might not yet exist, so it is not possible to experiment directly on the actual system. In fact, we might be using a model to help us with the construction of the system.

- *Physical realization*—The system is not constructed from entities that can be represented by physical objects. For example, it may be a social system (such as welfare policies or labor practices) that can only be simulated on a computer.

- *Safety*—It might be too dangerous to experiment on the actual system or a physical replica. For example, you would not want to try out a new monetary policy that could economically devastate a population or build a nuclear reactor using a new and unproven technology.

- *Speed of construction*—It might take too much time to construct a physical model. Sometimes it is faster to design and build a computer simulation.

- *Time scale*—Some physical systems change too slowly or too quickly. For example, an elementary particle in a high-speed accelerator may decompose in 10^{-15} seconds. At the other end of the time scale, some ecosystems take thousands of years to react to a modification. A simulation can easily model fractions of a second or billions of years because time is simply a parameter in an equation.

- *Ethical behavior*—Some physical models have serious moral and ethical consequences, perhaps the best known being the use of animals in medical research. In this case, a computational model could eliminate a great deal of suffering.

- *Ease of modification*—If we are not happy with the design of a physical model, we need to construct a brand-new one. In a simulation, we only need to change some numerical parameters and rerun the existing model.

This last advantage—ease of modification—makes computational modeling a particularly attractive tool for designing totally new systems. We initialize the model, observe its response, and if we are not satisfied, modify the parameters and run the model again. We repeat this process over and over, always trying to improve system performance. Only when we think we have created the best design possible would we actually build it. This "interactive" approach to design, called computational steering, is usually infeasible using physical models, as it would take too much time and require too many rebuilds. This interactive design methodology is diagrammed in Figure 13.1.

Computational models are therefore an excellent way to design new systems and to study and improve the behavior of existing systems. Virtually every branch of science and engineering makes use of models, and it is not unusual today to see chemists, biologists, economists, and physicians conducting fundamental research at their computer screens rather than in the laboratory.

FIGURE 13.1

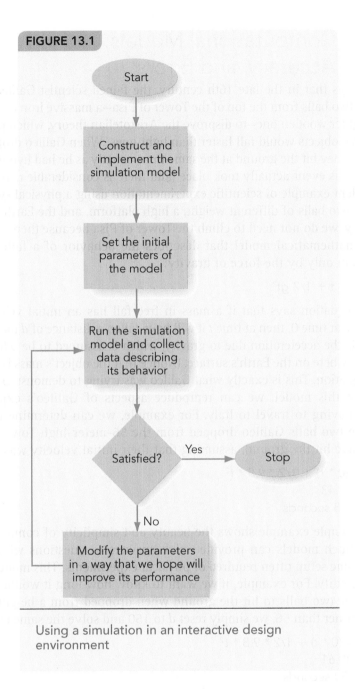

Using a simulation in an interactive design
environment

Computational models often use advanced mathematical techniques that
are far beyond the scope of this text (and solving them often requires the
large-scale parallel computers described in Section 5.4). Therefore, in the
following pages we often must rely on rather simple examples, far simpler
than the models you will encounter in the real world. However, even these
simple examples illustrate the enormous power and capabilities of computational modeling.

13.2.2 Computational Models, Accuracy, and Errors

Legend says that in the late 16th century, the famed scientist Galileo Galilei dropped two balls from the top of the Tower of Pisa—a massive iron cannonball and a lighter wooden one—to disprove the Aristotelian theory, which predicted that heavy objects would fall faster than light ones. When Galileo dropped the two balls, they hit the ground at the same time, exactly as he had hypothesized. Whether this event actually took place (and there is considerable debate), it is an excellent example of scientific experimentation using a physical system, in this case two balls of different weight, a high platform, and the Earth below.

Today, we do not need to climb the Tower of Pisa because there is a well-known mathematical model that describes the behavior of a falling mass acted upon only by the force of gravity:

$$d = v_{init}\, t + 1/2\, gt^2$$

This equation says that if a mass in free fall has an initial velocity v_{init} meters/sec at time 0, then at time t it will have fallen a distance of d meters. The factor g is the acceleration due to gravity, which is assumed to be 9.8 meters/sec^2 everywhere on the Earth's surface. (Notice that the object's mass is not part of the equation. This is exactly what Galileo was trying to demonstrate.)

Using this model, we can reproduce aspects of Galileo's experiment without having to travel to Italy. For example, we can determine the time when the two balls Galileo dropped from the 56-meter-high Tower of Pisa would have hit the ground, assuming that their initial velocity was 0.0:

$$56 = (0 * t) + 1/2 * 9.8 * t^2$$
$$t^2 = 11.43$$
$$t = 3.38 \text{ seconds}$$

This simple example shows the beauty and simplicity of computational models. Such models can provide quick answers to questions without the cumbersome setup often required of physical experiments. This model is also easy to modify. For example, if we want to know how long it would take for those same two balls to hit the ground when dropped from a height of 150 meters, rather than 56, we simply reset d to 150 and solve the same equation:

$$150 = (0 * t) + 1/2 * 9.8 * t^2$$
$$t^2 = 30.61$$
$$t = 5.53 \text{ seconds}$$

To use a physical model, Galileo would have had to scour the 16th-century world to find a 150-meter-high tower. (He would have had to travel 1,740 kilometers to Lincoln Cathedral in England, then the tallest building in the world at 159 meters.)

Unfortunately, computer modeling is not quite as simple as we have just described, and there are a number of issues that must be addressed and solved to make this technique workable.

The first issue is achieving the proper balance between *accuracy* and *complexity*. Our model must be an accurate representation of the physical system, but at the same time, it must be simple enough to implement as a program or a set of equations and solve on a computer in a reasonable amount of time. Often this balance is not easy to achieve, as most real-world systems are acted upon by a large number of external factors. We need to decide which of those factors are important enough to be included in our model and which can safely be omitted without jeopardizing the validity of our conclusions.

For example, the model of a falling body given earlier is inaccurate because it does not account for the effects of air resistance. (It is only an appropriate model if the object is falling in a vacuum.) Whereas the effect of air resistance on a cannonball is minimal, imagine dropping a feather! The model would produce inaccurate results, and our conclusions about how the system behaves would be totally wrong. It is obvious that we need to incorporate the effects of air resistance into our model if we have any hope of producing worthwhile and useful results.[1]

Our model also assumes that the Earth is a perfect sphere and that the acceleration due to gravity is constant everywhere along its surface. That assumption is not quite true. The Earth is a "slightly squashed" sphere with a radius of 6,378 km at the equator and 6,357 km at the poles. This means the acceleration due to gravity is a tiny bit greater at the North and South Poles (9.83 m/sec^2) than at the equator (9.78 m/sec^2), because the poles are 21 km closer to the center of the Earth. It also changes from the top of Mount Everest to the depths of Death Valley. Is this something for which we should account? Is this effect important when constructing a model of a freely falling body? In this case, probably not—because the miniscule error resulting from this approximation will almost certainly not affect our conclusions.

This is how computational models are built. We include the truly important factors that act upon our system so that our model is an accurate representation but omit the unimportant factors that add little to our understanding and only make the model harder to build and solve. As you might imagine, identifying these factors and distinguishing the important from the unimportant can be a daunting task.

Another problem with building simulations is that we may not know, in a mathematical sense, exactly how to describe certain types of systems and behaviors. The gravitational model given earlier is an example of a continuous model. In a continuous model, we write out a set of explicit mathematical equations that describes the behavior of a system as a continuous function of time t. These equations are then solved on a computer system to produce the desired results. Unfortunately, there are many systems that cannot be modeled using precise mathematical equations because researchers have not yet discovered exactly what those equations should be. Simply put, science is not yet sufficiently knowledgeable about how some systems function to characterize their behavior using explicit mathematical formulae.

---

[1] The resistance of the air, called *drag*, is given by the equation $D = KrV^2A\ /\ 2.0$, where K is the coefficient of drag, r is the air density, V is the velocity of the object, and A is the reference area of the object. Now you can begin to see why computational models can quickly become so complex.

In some cases, what makes these systems difficult to model is that they contain stochastic components, that is, parts of the system that display *random behavior*, much like the throw of the dice or the drawing of a playing card. In these cases, we cannot say with mathematical certainty what will happen to our system because it is the very essence of randomness that we can never know exactly which event will occur next. An example of this is a model of a business in which customers walk into the store at random times. In these cases, we need to build models that use *statistical approximations* rather than exact equations. We will present one such example in the following section.

In summary, computational modeling is a powerful but complex technique for designing and studying systems. However, building a good computational model can be a difficult task that requires us to capture all the important factors that influence the behavior of a system. If we are able to successfully build such a model, then we have at our disposal a powerful tool for studying the behavior of that system. This is how a good deal of quantitative research is done today. Simulation is also an interesting area of study within computer science itself. Researchers in this field create new techniques, both algorithms and special-purpose languages, that allow users to design and implement computer models more quickly and easily.

13.2.3 An Example of Model Building

As we mentioned at the end of the previous section, there are many ways to build a model, but most of them require mathematical techniques that are far beyond the scope of this text. In this section, we construct a model using a method that is relatively easy to understand and does not require a lot of complex mathematics. It is called *discrete event simulation*, and it is a very popular and widely used technique for building computational models.

In discrete event simulation, we do not model time as continuous, like the falling body model in the last section, but as *discrete*. That is, we model the behavior of a system only at an explicit and finite set of times. The moments we model are those times when an event takes place, an event being any activity that changes the state of our system. For example, if we are modeling the operation of a department store, an event might be a new customer entering the store, a customer purchasing an item, or a customer departing the building.

When we process an event, we change the state of the simulated system in the same way that the actual system would change if this event had occurred in real life. In the case of a department store, this might mean that when a customer arrives we add one to the number of customers currently inside the store or, if a customer buys an item, we decrease the number of these items on the shelf. Furthermore, the processing of one event can cause new events to occur at some time in the future. For example, a customer coming into a store creates a later event related to that customer leaving the store. When we are finished processing one event, we move on to the next, skipping those times in between when nothing is happening—that is, when there are no events scheduled to occur.

Figure 13.2(a) shows system S and three events scheduled to occur within system S: event E_1 at time 9:00, event E_2 at time 9:04, and event E_3 at time 9:10. Because E_1 is the event currently being processed, the variable *current time*, which functions like a "simulation clock," has the value 9:00. Let's assume that E_1 causes a new event, E_4, to be created and scheduled for time 9:17. We add this new event to the list of all scheduled events. When we are finished processing event E_1, we remove it from the list and determine the next event scheduled to occur in system S, in this case E_2. We move *current time* ahead to 9:04, skipping over the time period 9:01–9:03, because nothing of interest happens, and begin processing E_2. The new list of events scheduled for system S is shown in Figure 13.2(b).

We repeat this sequence—process an event, remove it from the list, add newly created events to the list, move on to the next event—as long as desired. The variable *current time* keeps advancing as we process the events in strict time order. Typically the simulation is terminated when *current time* reaches some upper bound. For example, in a department store we might choose to run the model until closing time. When the simulation is complete, the program displays a set of results that characterizes the system's behavior and allows the user to examine these results at his or her leisure.

Let's apply this modeling technique to an actual problem. Assume that you have been hired as a consultant by the owner of a new fast-food restaurant, McBurgers, currently under construction. The owner wants to determine the proper number of checkout stations that will be needed in the new store. This is an important business decision because if there are too few checkout stations, the lines will get long and customers will become irritated and leave. If there are too many checkout stations, money will be wasted paying for unnecessary construction costs, equipment, and personnel. You could just

FIGURE 13.2

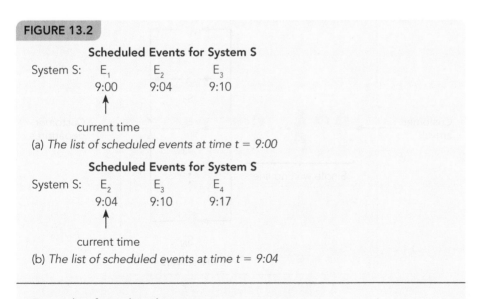

Scheduled Events for System S

System S: E_1 E_2 E_3
            9:00   9:04   9:10

            ↑
            current time
(a) *The list of scheduled events at time t = 9:00*

Scheduled Events for System S

System S: E_2 E_3 E_4
            9:04   9:10   9:17

            ↑
            current time
(b) *The list of scheduled events at time t = 9:04*

Example of simulated events

make an educated guess at the optimal number but, because you took a computer science class in college, you decide the best way to advise your client is to construct a simulation model of the new restaurant and use this model to determine the optimal number of servers.

The system being simulated is shown in Figure 13.3. Customers enter the restaurant and wait in a single line for service. If any of the N servers is available, where N is an input value provided by the user, the first customer in line goes to that station, places an order, waits until the order is processed, pays, and departs. During that time, the server is busy and cannot help anyone else. When the server is finished with a customer, he or she can immediately begin serving the next person, if someone is in line. If no one is waiting, then the server waits until a new customer arrives.

To create this model, we must first identify the events that can change the state of our system and thus need to be included in the model. In this example, there are only two: (1) a new customer arriving, and (2) an existing customer departing after receiving his or her food and paying. An arrival changes the system because either the waiting line grows longer by one, or, if there is no waiting line, an idle cashier becomes busy. A departure changes the system because the cashier serving that customer either begins serving a new customer or becomes idle because no one is in line.

For each of these two events, we must design an algorithm that describes exactly what happens to our system when that event occurs. Figure 13.4 shows the algorithm for the new customer arrival event.

Let's examine this algorithm in detail. When a new customer arrives, we record the current simulation time. The arrival time of each new customer is

FIGURE 13.3

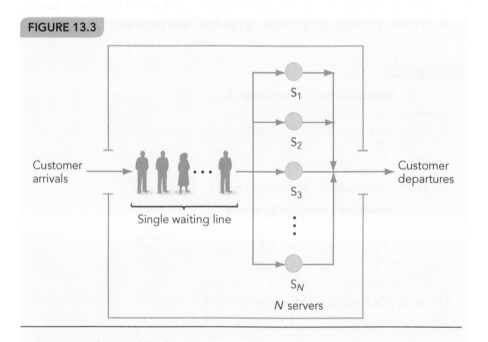

System to be modeled

FIGURE 13.4

New customer arrival
> Record the time that this customer entered the restaurant
> Check if any one of the N servers S_1, S_2, ... , S_N is currently idle
> If all of the servers are busy then
>> Put this customer at the end of the waiting line
>> Increase the length of the waiting line by 1
> Else (server S_i is idle)
>> Mark that server S_i is now busy
>> Determine how long it will take to serve this customer, call that value T_{serve}
>> Schedule a customer departure event for (*current time* + T_{serve})
>> Increase the total time that server S_i has worked by T_{serve}
> End of new customer arrival

New customer arrival algorithm

stored in a variable associated with that specific customer until that individual is served and departs. As we mentioned earlier, when the simulation is finished we want to display a set of results that allows the user to determine how well the system has performed. The total time a customer spends in the restaurant (waiting time + service time) is a good example of this type of result. If this value is large, we are not doing a good job serving customers, and we need to increase the number of servers so customers don't wait so long. A key part of any simulation model is collecting important data about the system so that we can understand and analyze its performance.

The next operation in the new customer arrival algorithm of Figure 13.4 is to determine if there is an idle server. If not, the customer goes to the end of the waiting line (no special treatment here at McBurgers), and the length of the waiting line is increased by 1. If there is an idle server, then the customer goes directly to that server, who is then marked as busy. (*Note*: If more than one server is free, the customer can go to any one because our model assumes that all servers are identical. We could also construct a model in which not all servers are identical and some provide a special service.)

Now we must determine how much time is required to service this customer. This is a good example of what we termed a *stochastic*, or *random*, component of a simulation model. Exactly what a customer orders and how much time it takes to fill that order are random quantities whose exact values can never be known with certainty in advance. However, even though it behaves in a random fashion, it is possible that this value, called T_{serve} in Figure 13.4, follows a pattern called a statistical distribution, a mathematical equation specifying the probability that a random variable takes on a certain value. If we know this pattern, then the computer can generate a sequence of random numbers that follows this pattern, and this sequence will accurately model the time it takes to serve customers in real life.

How can we discover this pattern? One way is to know something about the statistical distribution of quantities that behave in a similar way. For example, if we know something about the distribution of service times for customers in a bank or a grocery store, then this information might help us understand the pattern of service times at our hamburger stand. Another way is to observe and collect data from an actual system similar to ours. For example, we could go to other fast-food restaurants and measure exactly how long it takes them to service their customers. If these restaurants are similar to ours, then the McBurgers owner might be able to discover from this data the statistical distribution of the variable T_{serve}.

There are other ways to work with statistical distributions, but we will leave this complex topic to courses in statistics. In this example, we simply assume that the statistical distribution for the customer service time, T_{serve}, has been discovered and is shown in the graph in Figure 13.5.

The graph in Figure 13.5 states that 5% of the time a customer is served in less than 1 minute; 15% of the time it takes 1–2 minutes; 40% of the time it takes 2–3 minutes; 30% of the time it takes 3–4 minutes; and, finally, 10% of the time it takes 4–5 minutes. It never requires more than 5 minutes to serve a customer. We can model this distribution using the algorithm shown in Figure 13.6.

First, we generate a random integer v that takes on one of the values 1, 2, 3, ..., 100 with equal likelihood. This is called a uniform random number. We now ask if v is between 1 and 5. Because there are five numbers in this range, and there were 100 numbers that could originally have been generated, the answer to this question is yes 5% of the time. This is the same percent of time that customers spend from 0 to 1 minute being served. Therefore, we generate another uniform random value, this time a real number between 0.0 and 1.0, which is the value of T_{serve}, the customer service time.

If the original random value v is not between 1 and 5, we ask if it is between 6 and 20. There are 15 integers in this range, so the answer to this question is

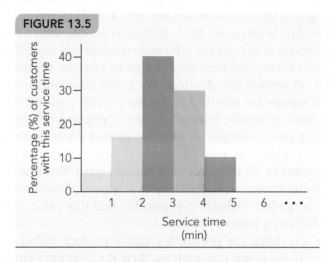

FIGURE 13.5

Statistical distribution of customer service time

FIGURE 13.6

Generate a uniform random integer value v between 1 and 100
If v is in the range 1–5, then
    Set T_{serve} to a uniform random number between 0.0 and 1.0
Else if v is in the range 6–20, then
    Set T_{serve} to a uniform random number between 1.0 and 2.0
Else if v is in the range 21–60, then
    Set T_{serve} to a uniform random number between 2.0 and 3.0
Else if v is in the range 61–90, then
    Set T_{serve} to a uniform random number between 3.0 and 4.0
Else
    Set T_{serve} to a uniform random number between 4.0 and 5.0

Algorithm for generating random numbers that follow the distribution given in Figure 13.5

yes 15% of the time, exactly the fraction of time that customers spend 1–2 minutes being served. If the answer is yes, we generate a T_{serve} value that is in the range 1.0 to 2.0. This process is repeated for all possible values of service time.

Once the value of T_{serve} has been generated, we use this value to determine exactly when this customer leaves the store (*current time* + T_{serve}) as well as to update the total amount of time the server has spent serving customers. This last computation allows us to determine the percentage of time during the day that each server was busy.

The value assigned to T_{serve} using the algorithm of Figure 13.6 exactly matches the statistical distribution graph shown in Figure 13.5. If this graph is an accurate representation of customer service time, then our model is an accurate depiction of what happens in the real world. However, if the graph of Figure 13.5 is not an accurate representation of customer service time, then our model is incorrect and will produce wrong answers. This is a good example of the well-known computer science dictum garbage in, garbage out—the results you get from a simulation model are only as good as the data and the assumptions put into the model.

We can now specify how to handle the second type of event contained in our model, customer departures. The algorithm to handle a customer leaving the restaurant is given in Figure 13.7.

When a customer is ready to leave, we determine the total time this customer spent in the restaurant. The variable *current time* represents the time now, which is the time of this customer's departure. We recorded the time this customer first arrived on Line 2 of Figure 13.4, and we can retrieve the contents of the variable storing that information. The difference between these two numbers is the total time this customer spent in the restaurant, including both waiting time and service time. We use this result, averaged over all customers, to determine if we are providing an adequate level of service.

If there is another customer in line, the server begins serving that customer in exactly the same way as described earlier. If no one is waiting, then

FIGURE 13.7

Customer departure from server S_i
    Determine the total time that this customer spent in the restaurant
    If there is someone in line then
        Take the next customer out of line and decrease the waiting line size by one
        Determine how long this new customer will take to be served,
            and call that value T_{serve}
        Schedule a customer departure event for (*current time* + T_{serve})
        Increase the total time that server S_i has worked by T_{serve}
    Else
        Mark this server as idle
End customer departure

Algorithm for customer departure event

the server becomes idle and has nothing to do until a new customer arrives. (We don't want this to happen too often because then the restaurant owner will be paying the salary of someone with little to do.)

We have now described the two main events that change our system: someone arriving at the restaurant and someone leaving the restaurant. The only thing left is to initialize our parameters and get the model started. To initialize the model, we must do the following four things:

- Set the current time to 0.0 (we begin our simulation at time 0).

- Set the waiting line size to 0 (no one is in line when the doors open).

- Get a value for N, the number of servers, and make them all idle.

- Determine the total number of customers to be served and exactly when they will arrive.

The last value—customer arrival times—are like the service times discussed earlier in that they are stochastic, or random, values that cannot be known in advance. We cannot possibly know exactly when each new customer will walk in the front door. However, if we can determine the statistical distribution of the time interval between the arrival of any two customers, then we can generate a set of random intervals, called $T_{interval}$, that will allow us to model customer arrivals. It would also allow us to examine what would happen if our restaurant became more (or less) busy. We could simulate that effect by simply decreasing (or increasing) the average value of the time interval between customers.

Assume we have a graph like Figure 13.5 that specifies the statistical distribution of the time interval that elapses between the arrivals of two successive customers. (That is, it might say something like 10% of the time two customers arrive within 0–15 seconds of each other, 20% of the time they arrive within 15–30 seconds of each other, and so on.) We schedule our first customer to arrive at time 0.0, just as the doors open. We then use an algo-rithm like the one in Figure 13.6 to generate a random value that matches the distribution of interarrival times. Call this value $T_{interval}$. This represents the amount of time that will elapse until the next customer arrives. Because the first customer arrived at time 0.0, we schedule the next one to arrive at $(0.0 + T_{interval}) = T_{interval}$. We repeat this for as many customers as desired, scheduling each one to arrive at $T_{interval}$ time units after the previous one. Our sequence of customer arrivals will look something like this:

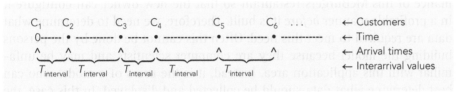

The main program to run our McBurgers simulation model is given in Figure 13.8. It allows the user to provide two inputs: M, the total number of customers to model, and N, the number of servers. Each one of the M customer arrivals is handled by the arrival algorithm of Figure 13.4. Each arrival event generates a customer departure event that is handled by the

---

FIGURE 13.8

Main part of the simulation model
    Set *current time* to 0
    Set the waiting line size to 0
    Get an input value for N, the number of servers
    Set all N servers, $S_1, S_2, \ldots, S_N$ to idle
    Get an input value for M, the total number of customers
    Schedule M customer arrivals and put them on the list of events
        Each arrival occurs $T_{interval}$ time units after the previous one
    While there is still a scheduled event on the list do
        Get the next event on the list
        Move *current time* to the time of this event
        If this is a customer arrival event
            Execute the arrival algorithm of Figure 13.4
        Else
            Execute the departure algorithm of Figure 13.7
        Remove this event from the list of all scheduled events
    End of the loop
    Print out a set of data that describes the behavior of the system
Stop

The main algorithm of our simulation model

departure algorithm of Figure 13.7. This simulation does not terminate at a specific point in time but, instead, when there are no more events to be processed—that is, when every one of the M customers scheduled to arrive has been served and has departed.

The last issue that we must address is how to implement the second-to-last line of Figure 13.8, the one that reads, "Print out a set of data that describes the behavior of the system." Looking back at Figure 13.1, we see that one of the responsibilities of a simulation is to "collect data describing its behavior." Our model must collect data that accurately measures the performance of this McBurgers restaurant so that the new owner can configure it in a profitable manner *before* it is built. Therefore, we need to determine what data are required to meet this need. Often this cannot be done by the persons building the model because they are computer scientists and may be unfamiliar with this application area. Instead, it is the *users* of a model who can best determine what data should be collected and displayed. In this case, the user is the restaurant owner. Thus, model building is often a cooperative effort between technical specialists in the area of software development and those knowledgeable about the unique characteristics of the system being modeled.

Let's assume that we have talked to the restaurant owner and determined that the information he or she most needs to know is the following:

- The average time that a customer spends in the restaurant, including both waiting in line and getting served

- The maximum length of the waiting line

- The percentage of time that servers are busy serving customers

From this data, the owner should be able to determine whether the system is functioning well. For example, if our model determines that a server is busy only 10% of the time (about 48 minutes in an 8-hour workday), we can probably reduce the number of servers without affecting service, saving a good deal in salary costs. On the other hand, if the average time that a customer spends in the restaurant is 1 hour or there are times when there are 100 people in line, then we had better increase the number of servers if we want to avoid bankruptcy (or riots)!

This model will likely be used in the interactive design approach first diagrammed in Figure 13.1. The owner will enter his or her best estimate for the arrival time and service time distributions and then select a value for N, the number of servers. The computer will run the simulation, processing all M customers, and then print the results, perhaps something like the following:

Servers	Average Waiting Time (min)	Maximum Line Length	Server Busy Percentage (%)
2	63.3	35	100.0

With only two servers, our customers waited on average more than one hour to be served, there were dozens of people in line, and both servers were busy every second of the day—not very good performance! The owner would certainly try to improve on this performance, perhaps by having 6 servers, rather than only 2. He or she resets the parameter N to 6 and reruns the model, which now produces the following:

Servers	Average Waiting Time (min)	Maximum Line Length	Server Busy Percentage (%)
6	2.75	1	43

Now the owner may have erred too far in the other direction. Our customers are being well served, waiting only a couple of minutes, and the line is tiny, never having more than a single person. However, on the average our six servers are busy only 43% of the time—meaning they are idle about 4.5 hours during an 8-hour workday. Could we provide the same high level of service to our customers with fewer servers? To answer this question, the owner might try rerunning the model with $N = 3$, 4, or 5, a compromise value between these two extremes. The owner may also want to study how well this number of servers works when the restaurant gets slightly more or less busy. This is how a simulation model is used—run it repeatedly under different assumptions, examine the results, and use these results to reconfigure the system being modeled so its performance is enhanced.

This completes the development of our McBurgers simulation but is not the end of its usefulness. In the next Laboratory Experience, you are going to "play" with this model by selecting a range of values for customer arrival and service times. You then take on the role of the McBurgers owner and determine the optimal number of servers to use for the selected configuration. Working with a simulation in an interactive design environment demonstrates the enormous power and capabilities of computational models.

The restaurant modeled in this section is about as simple a system as we could present, yet it still took about 10 pages to describe its design.

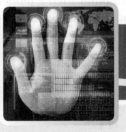

Practice Problems

1. In the McBurgers new customer arrival algorithm, describe the consequences of accidentally omitting the instruction "Mark that server S_i is now busy."

2. In the McBurgers customer departure algorithm, describe the consequences of accidentally omitting the instruction "Mark this server as idle."

3. Suppose we try to simplify our model by assuming that every customer requires exactly two minutes of service to complete his or her purchase. How do you think this would affect the conclusions that we could draw from our model?

4. Are there other parameters that you might have included if you were building a model of a fast-food restaurant?

Laboratory Experience 18

In this Laboratory Experience, you will work with a simulation model of a McBurgers restaurant that is similar to the one presented in this section. You will play the role of the restaurant owner who is trying to determine the correct number of servers for a specific pattern of customer arrivals and service times. You will configure your restaurant, run the model, see how well you provided service to your customers, and then reconfigure the restaurant to try to improve its performance and its profit. The software allows you to set parameters for (1) the total running time of the simulation, (2) the average service time of each customer, (3) the probability that a new customer will arrive, and (4) the number of servers. It will then run the model exactly as you have described and, upon completion, produce the following output: (1) the number of customers remaining in line when the simulation terminated, (2) the average time that a customer spent in the restaurant, and (3) the average percentage of time that the servers were busy over the entire simulation.

Your goal in this simulation is to determine the set of parameters that optimizes behavior of the overall system.

A computational model of "El Niño" Pacific Ocean currents, the human heart, or a strand of DNA would certainly be far more complex than the simulation of a hamburger joint! Real-world models are mathematically intricate, highly detailed, and difficult to build. However, if we are able to build such a model or if we have access to such a model, then we have a powerful tool that can significantly enhance our ability to do high-quality research and design.

13.3 Running the Model and Visualizing Results

The McBurgers restaurant model developed in Section 13.2.3 is much simpler than most real-world computer models for two reasons. First, it is computationally small. The process of running it and producing results does not require much in the way of hardware resources. For example, assume that we model $M = 1,000$ customers, a reasonable daily value for a large restaurant. Each customer generates one arrival event (Figure 13.4) and one departure event (Figure 13.7), for a total of 2,000 events that must be processed by the computer before the simulation is completed and the results displayed. The execution of 2,000 events is a miniscule amount of work that could be handled by even the smallest laptop or tablet in just a few seconds or, more likely, fractions of a second. Most real-world models require much more computational work to produce their results.

For example, the U.S. Department of Energy's National Energy Research Scientific Computing Center (NERSC) at Lawrence Berkeley National Laboratory has developed a powerful climate system model. Using this model, simulating one year of global climatic change requires about 10^{18} computations—one quintillion operations. A single Von Neumann machine could not handle this almost unimaginably large amount of work. A typical laptop computer executes roughly 5 billion instructions per second. At this rate, completing one year of simulated time in the model would require about six-and-a-half years of real time—we would not get our results until the actual time period being simulated had long since passed! Even a high-speed desktop system that executes 50 billion instructions per second would require over seven months of nonstop computing to produce a single result.

Massive models like this one can be executed only on the large-scale parallel machines described in Chapter 5. For example, the NERSC climate model was executed on a massively parallel Cray XC40 supercomputer containing 11,000 separate processors, and with a peak computation rate of about 10 petaflops, or 10^{16} floating point operations per second. At this rate, one year of climatic change can be modeled in less than two minutes!

This latter example is far more typical of the amount of computational work required by large, real-world simulations. It is not unusual for a model to perform 10^{16}, 10^{17}, 10^{18}, or more operations just to produce a single result—amounts far beyond the capabilities of individual single-, dual-, or quad-processor machines. The increasing interest in building complex computational models is one of the main reasons behind the development of larger and more powerful supercomputers. For example, the massively parallel Chinese Sunway TaihuLight supercomputer mentioned in Chapters 3 and 5, which runs at a rate of 93 petaflops, will be executing computational models in the areas of climate change, neural imaging, and nuclear weapons testing.

The second reason why the McBurgers model in Section 13.2.3 is so unrealistic is that it produces only a tiny amount of output. After each run is complete, the model generates only three lines of output, such as those shown below and in the previous section:

Servers	Average Waiting Time (min)	Maximum Line Length	Server Busy Percentage (%)
6	2.75	1	43

Because the number of servers in a restaurant might range from one up to a few dozen, the total volume of output this model would ever produce is about 20–60 lines, less than a single page. With such a small amount of output, our model can display its results using a simple text format, as shown in the lines above. A user will have no difficulty reading and interpreting this output.

Unfortunately, most simulations do not produce a few dozen lines of output, but rather tens or hundreds of thousands of lines, perhaps even millions. For example, assume the NERSC climate model described earlier displayed the temperature, humidity, barometric pressure, wind velocity, and wind direction at 50-mile intervals over the entire surface of the Earth for every simulated day the model is run. After one year of simulated time, it will have produced roughly 500 million data values—about 10 million pages of output! If these values were displayed as text, it would overwhelm its users, who wouldn't have a clue how to deal with this mountain of paper.

Text, when it is presented in such large amounts, does not lend itself to easy interpretation or understanding. The field of scientific visualization addresses the issue of how to visualize large volumes of scientific data in a way that highlights its important characteristics and simplifies its interpretation and analysis. This is an enormously important part of computational modeling because without it we would be able to construct models and execute them, but we would not be able to interpret their results.

The term *scientific visualization* is often treated as synonymous with the related term computer graphics, but there is an important difference. The field of computer graphics is concerned with the technical issues involved in information display. That is, it deals with the actual algorithms for rendering a screen image—light sources, shadows, hidden surfaces, shading, contours, and perspective. (We will be discussing these operations in Section 16.2.) Scientific visualization, on the other hand, is concerned with how to display a large data set in a way that maximizes its clarity and user comprehension. It is concerned with issues such as *data presentation*—determining the optimal format for presenting data; *data extraction*—determining which values are important and should be included and which values can be omitted; and *data manipulation*—converting the data to other forms or to different units that make the information easier to understand and interpret. Once we have decided exactly how we want to display the data, then scientific visualization software typically uses a computer graphics package to display an image on a screen or printer.

For example, assume we have built a computer model of the ocean tides at some point along the coast. Our model predicts the height of the tide every 30 seconds in a 24-hour day, based on such factors as lunar phase, water depth, wind speed, and wind direction. If this information were printed as text, it might look something like the following:

Time	Height (feet)
12:00:00 A.M.	43.78
12:00:30 A.M.	43.81
12:01:00 A.M.	43.84
12:01:30 A.M.	43.88
12:02:00 A.M.	43.92
12:02:30 A.M.	43.97
.	.
.	.
.	.
11:57:00 P.M.	45.08

11:57:30 P.M.	45.04
11:58:00 P.M.	45.01
11:58:30 P.M.	44.99
11:59:00 P.M.	44.97
11:59:30 P.M.	44.95

There are 2,880 lines of output, which at 60 lines per page would produce almost 50 printed pages. Trying to extract meaning or locate significant features from these long columns of numbers would certainly be a formidable, not to mention boring, task.

What if, instead, we displayed these two columns of values as a two-dimensional graph of time versus height? The output could also include a horizontal line showing the average water height during this 24-hour period. This latter value is not part of the original output but can easily be computed from these values and included in the output—an example of a data manipulation carried out to enhance data interpretation. Now the output of our model might look something like the graph in Figure 13.9.

FIGURE 13.9

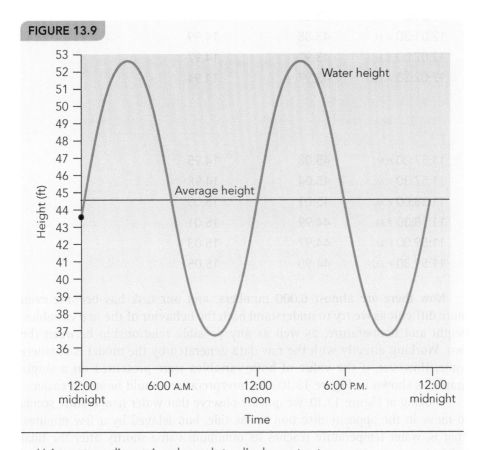

Using a two-dimensional graph to display output

Using the graph in Figure 13.9, it is a lot quicker and easier to identify the interesting features of the model's output. For example,

- There appear to be two high tides and two low tides during this 24-hour time period.

- The high tide is about 8 feet above the average water level, whereas the low tide is about 8 feet below the average water level.

It is possible to extract the same information from a textual representation of the output, but it would take much more time. Interpreting the graph of Figure 13.9 is a great deal easier than working directly with the raw data. The use of visualizations becomes more and more important as the amount of output increases and grows more complex. For example, what if in addition to tidal height our model also predicted the water temperature and displayed its value every 30 seconds. Now the raw data produced by the model might look like this:

Time	Height (feet)	Temperature (°C)
12:00:00 A.M.	43.78	15.03
12:00:30 A.M.	43.81	15.02
12:01:00 A.M.	43.84	15.01
12:01:30 A.M.	43.88	14.99
12:02:00 A.M.	43.92	14.97
12:02:30 A.M.	43.97	14.94
.	.	.
.	.	.
.	.	.
11:57:00 P.M.	45.08	14.95
11:57:30 P.M.	45.04	14.98
11:58:00 P.M.	45.01	15.00
11:58:30 P.M.	44.99	15.01
11:59:00 P.M.	44.97	15.03
11:59:30 P.M.	44.95	15.05

Now there are almost 6,000 numbers, and our task has become even more difficult as we try to understand both the behavior of the *two* variables, height and temperature, as well as any possible relationship between the two. Working directly with the raw data generated by the model is cumbersome. However, if the value of both variables were presented on a single graph, as shown in Figure 13.10, the interpretation would be much easier.

Looking at Figure 13.10, we quickly observe that water temperature seems to move in the opposite direction as the tide, but delayed by a few minutes. That is, water temperature reaches its minimum value shortly after the tidal height has reached its maximum value, and vice versa. This is exactly the type of information that could be of help to a researcher. Without the graphical visualization in Figure 13.10, we may have overlooked this important relationship.

FIGURE 13.10

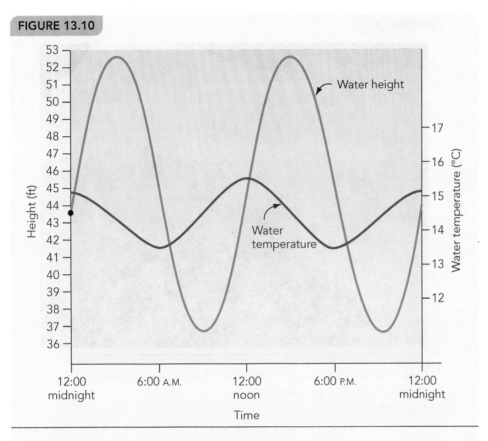

Using a two-dimensional graph to display and compare two data values

The graphs in Figures 13.9 and 13.10 are both two-dimensional, but many real-world models study the behavior of three-dimensional objects, for example, an airplane wing, a gas cloud, or the Earth's surface. The results produced by these models are also three-dimensional, such as the spatial coordinates of a point on that airplane wing or on a gas molecule. Therefore, it is common for the output of a computational model to be displayed as a three-dimensional image rather than the two-dimensional graphs shown earlier. For example, Figure 13.11 shows output from a model of a portion of the Earth's surface overlaid with colors that represent the intensity of a forest fire at a particular moment in time. The hottest areas are shown in yellow and red, while cooler areas are displayed in blue and green. Such three-dimensional digital elevations make it easy to locate important topographical features, such as mountains, valleys, and rivers and areas where we should place our maximum effort. This type of output would be extremely useful when, for example, planning the movement of equipment to fight the fire or directing airplanes on where to drop fire retardant chemicals. Given the same information in a textual format, it would take a far, far greater amount time to extract the identical information.

FIGURE 13.11

Three-dimensional image of the Earth's surface with overlay
showing status of a forest fire
Source: NASA

As a second example, suppose that medical researchers are using a
simulation model to study the behavior of the chemical compound methyl
nitrite, CH_3NO_2, a potential carcinogen found in our air and drinking water.
Assume that their molecular model produces the following textual output:

Molecule Number	Element	Location			Bonded To
		x	y	z	
1	O	1.7	1.0	0.0	3, 4
2	O	3.0	0.0	0.0	3
3	N	2.6	0.3	1.0	1, 2
4	C	0.0	0.0	0.0	1, 5, 6, 7
5	H	−0.5	0.5	0.5	4
6	H	0.5	0.5	0.5	4
7	H	−0.5	−0.5	0.5	4

This is an accurate textual description of a methyl nitrite molecule. The
output specifies the seven atoms in the molecule, the spatial (x, y, z) coordinates of the center of each atom in the molecule, and the identity of all
other atoms to which this one has a chemical bond. This is all the information required to understand the structure of this molecule. However, most of

us would find it hard to form a mental image of what this molecule actually looks like using just this table.

What if, instead, our model took this textual description of methyl nitrite and used it to create and display the three-dimensional image of Figure 13.12?

It is certainly a lot easier to work with the visualization in Figure 13.12 than with the original textual description. For example, if our model changed the shape or structure of this molecule, say by simulating a chemical reaction or the breaking of a chemical bond, we would be able to observe this change on our computer screen, significantly increasing our understanding of exactly what is happening. In the table-based representation, we would only see changing numerical values without any clue as to what these changes represent chemically or structurally.

The image in Figure 13.12 makes use of two other features found in many visualizations—color and scale. These characteristics allow us to display information in a way that makes the image more understandable by someone looking at the diagram. In this example, color represents the element type—blue for hydrogen, yellow for carbon, purple for oxygen, and red for nitrogen. The relative size of each sphere represents the relative size of each of the atoms.

The clever use of visual enhancements such as color and scale can make an enormous difference in how easy or hard it is to interpret the output of a computer model. For example, the image displayed in Figure 13.13 models the dispersion and height of tsunami waves following a hypothetical earthquake near Japan.

In this example, color indicates projected wave heights across the Pacific Ocean. The largest wave heights, shown in purple, are expected near the earthquake epicenter off the Japanese coast. Progressively smaller waves are indicated in red, orange, and yellow. Using images like Figure 13.13, it is easy to see the areas likely to be most impacted, information that helps relief organizations determine where the greatest assistance is needed. If, instead of these color-coded images, we were given only page after page of

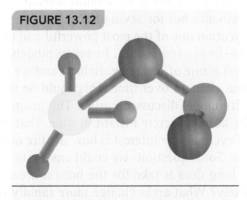

FIGURE 13.12

Three-dimensional model of a methyl nitrite molecule

FIGURE 13.13

Visualization of projected tsunami wave heights
Source: NOAA Center for Tsunami Research

numerical values, it would take much longer to extract this vital information. Here is another example, along with the forest fire status model of Figure 13.11, in which enhancing the comprehension of a model's output is not just for convenience but for saving lives!

Finally, we mention one of the most powerful and useful forms of scientific visualization—image animation. In many models, time (whether continuous or discrete) is one of the key variables, and we want to observe how the model's output changes over time. This could be the case, for example, with the forest fire model discussed earlier. The image in Figure 13.11 is a picture of the fire at one discrete instant in time. That may be of value, but what might be of even greater interest is how the fire moves and disperses as a function of time. Some questions we could answer using this time-varying model are: How long does it take for the hottest areas (yellow and red) to dissipate completely? What areas change more rapidly from hot to cool?

To answer these and similar questions, we need to generate not one image like Figure 13.11, but many, with each image showing the state of the system at a slightly later point in time. If we generate a sufficient number of these images, then we can display them rapidly in sequence, producing a visual animation of the system's behavior over time.

Obviously we cannot show an animation in this book, but Figure 13.14 shows two images (out of 365) from a program that models the total amount of ozone present in the Earth's atmosphere over a one-year period. The model computes the ozone levels for each day of the year and displays the results graphically, with green and blue representing acceptable ozone levels and red representing a dangerously low level. These 365 images can be displayed in sequence to produce a "movie" showing how the ozone level changes throughout the year.

The amount of output needed to produce these 365 images was probably in the range of tens or hundreds of billions of data values. If this volume of data were displayed as text, a user would be overwhelmed, and the truly important characteristics of the data would be buried deep within this mass of numbers, much like the proverbial "needle in a haystack." However, using the visualization techniques highlighted in this section—two- and three-dimensional graphics, color, scale, and animation—key features of the data, such as the presence of a significant ozone hole (the red area) over the Antarctic on day 292, can be quickly and easily located.

This is precisely why scientific visualization techniques are so important. Their goal is to take a massive data set and present it in a way that is more informative and more understandable for the user of that data. Without this understanding, there would be no reason to build computational models in the first place.

FIGURE 13.14

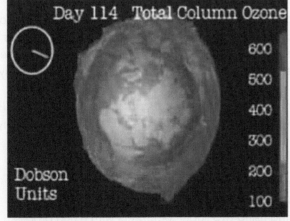

(a) *On Day 114*

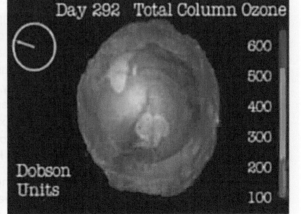

(b) *On Day 292*

Use of animation to model ozone layers in the atmosphere

Source: Lloyd A. Treinish/IBM Thomas J. Watson Research Center

13.4 Conclusion

Computational modeling is a fascinating and highly complex subject, and one that will become even more important in the coming years as computers increase in power and researchers gain experience in designing and building models.

Constructing models of complex systems requires a deep understanding of both mathematics and statistics so, as we have mentioned a number of times, they can be rather difficult to build. However, even if you are not directly involved in building computer models, it is quite likely that you will be *working with* these types of models in your research, development, or design work. Simulation is affecting many fields of study. For example, in this chapter we looked at models drawn from physics (the falling body equations), economics (the McBurgers simulation), chemistry (the molecular model of methyl nitrite), cartography (a map of the Earth's surface), meteorology (tides, climatic changes), and ecology (forest fire dispersion,

The Mother of All Computations!

In May 2014, a research group from the Physics department of MIT reported in the journal *Nature* that they had completed the most detailed and realistic computer simulation ever built to study the formation of the universe. The model, called *Illustris*, tracked the evolution of the cosmos from a few hundred thousand years after the Big Bang up to the current time, 13.8 billion years later. Illustris uses equations drawn from physics, astronomy, hydrodynamics, chemistry, and mathematics to study a cube of simulated space that is 350 light years on each side and that contains tens of thousands of galaxies. The model, executed on supercomputers in France and Germany, simulated the expansion of galaxies, the gravitational pull of matter, the formation of stars and black holes, and the motions of cosmic gases.

It took five years for the software teams in the United States, France, and Germany to design, program, and test Illustris, and it required three months of nonstop parallel computing using two supercomputers with 8,000 processors each to execute the approximately 10^{21} (one sextillion, or one billion trillion) operations needed to simulate 14 billion years of galactic evolution. Researchers estimated that if this model were run on a high-perforamce desktop computer, it would have taken about 1,500 years to complete. You can read more about this enormous simulation project at *www.illustris-project.org/about/*

ozone depletion). We could just as easily have selected examples from the fields of medicine, geology, biology, pharmacology, or urban planning. For those who work in scientific or quantitative fields like these, computational modeling is rapidly becoming one of the most important tools available to the researcher. It is also a vehicle for amusing and entertaining us through the creation of simulated fantasy worlds and alien planets where we can relax, explore, and play. We'll discuss this exciting role of simulation in Chapter 16.

Even though simulation is an important scientific application, you are probably more familiar with the many uses of computers in the commercial sector—paying bills online, remotely accessing financial data, and buying and selling products on the web. These commercial applications, often grouped together under the generic term *electronic commerce*, or *ecommerce*, will be discussed at length in Chapter 14.

EXERCISES

1. You are probably familiar with the idea of a two-dimensional spreadsheet, like the ones created in Microsoft Excel. Would you call this type of spreadsheet a "computational model"? State why or why not, and justify your answer.

2. Look up the definition of the terms *computer-aided design* (abbreviated CAD) and *computer-aided manufacturing* (CAM). Find out what they mean, how they are used, and how they relate to the ideas presented in this chapter.

3. Rather than using a general-purpose programming language like the ones discussed in Chapter 9, models are often constructed using *simulation languages* designed specifically for this application.

(These languages fall into the category of "special-purpose languages" mentioned in Chapter 10.) Examples of simulation languages include:

- SIMULA
- GPSS (General Purpose System Simulation)
- Simscript

Read about one of these languages and discuss what features make it well suited for implementing simulation models.

4. In Section 13.2.2, we specified two inaccuracies in the equation describing a body falling under the influence of gravity: the problems of air resistance and the fact that the Earth is not a perfect sphere. Are there additional inaccuracies contained in this mathematical model? Do you think that these

other factors should be included in our falling body model? Explain why you believe they do or do not need to be included.

5. In this chapter, we described a way to model a statistical distribution by using random numbers generated by a computer. How do you think it is possible for a computer to generate a truly random number that successfully passes all tests for randomness? Read about random number generators and discuss the algorithms that they use.

6. In Section 13.2.3, we specified the statistical distribution for the service time in our McBurgers restaurant: 5% of customers were served in less than 1 minute, and so forth. Do you think this is an accurate distribution of service times in real-world take-out restaurants? Why or why not? If this distribution is not an accurate portrayal of the customer service time, what are the implications of this inaccuracy on our model?

7. Describe how the customer arrival and departure event algorithms (Figures 13.4, 13.7) and the main algorithm (Figure 13.8) of our McBurgers simulation would change if we changed the system in each of the following three ways:

   a. Instead of a single waiting line, we have N waiting lines, one for each of the N servers in the restaurant. That is, our model now behaves as shown:

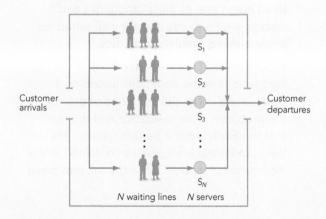

Customer arrivals — Customer departures

S_1
S_2
S_3
S_N

N waiting lines N servers

   b. The waiting line has a maximum length of MAX. If the length of the waiting line is currently less than MAX, then the customer gets into line in exactly the same way as in the current model. However, if the waiting line has a length equal to MAX, then the customer leaves the store without being served.

   c. Each customer is assigned a priority when first entering the store (a value from 1 to 10), and if there is no server currently available, the customer goes into the waiting line in priority order. That is, a customer gets into line ahead of all people with lower priority and behind everyone with an equal or higher priority.

8. In the McBurgers simulation, our model assumes that the arrival distribution of customers is the same throughout the entire day. Do you think this is a realistic assumption? If not, explain how you could modify the model to make it a better representation of customer arrivals in real life.

9. Do you think that inclusion of the following parameters in the McBurgers model would or would not increase the accuracy of the model and its ability to predict real-world behavior?

   a. Age of the customer
   b. Sex of the customer
   c. Height of the customer

10. Assume that you want to model a bus system in which passengers purchase tickets and travel from city A to one of four other cities, either B, C, D, or E. An important part of the model is determining to which city a specific passenger is traveling, a random variable. How might you go about creating a statistical distribution that accurately specifies to which of these four cities a passenger will buy a ticket and travel?

11. Do you think a computational model of elementary particles being created and destroyed by collisions in a high-speed accelerator would be discrete or continuous?

12. a. Assume our model requires 10^{14} computations to simulate one hour of activity. We run the program on a desktop computer with a computation speed of 800 MIPS (millions of instructions per second). How long will it take to simulate one day of activity in the model?
    b. How fast a computer (in terms of MIPS) do we need to use if we want to complete the simulation of one day in five minutes of computing time?

13. We discussed the use of color and scale to enhance and highlight aspects of a data set being studied. In addition to these two features, suggest other ways to visually enhance the output of a model that will help to clarify its interpretation.

14. In this chapter, we focused our discussions primarily on the uses of modeling in the physical sciences, life sciences, economics, and engineering. However, the use of models is certainly not limited to these areas. Read about how simulation models are currently used to conduct research in the social sciences and humanities, such as the fields of anthropology, sociology, and political science. Write a report describing the uses of computational modeling in one of these fields.

15. Read about how simulation models are being used in your own specific field of study, and write a report on exactly what these models do and what type of research is being done using them.

CHALLENGE WORK

In this Challenge Exercise, you are going to build a computational model, much like the McBurgers simulation of Section 13.2.3. To do this, follow the same design steps that were used in this example, namely:

- Specify the events that can change the state of your system.
- For each event, specify an algorithm that shows how the system changes when this type of event occurs.
- Specify the main algorithm that will initialize your system, get the simulation started, and run the simulation until it has completed.

You do not need to specify your solution in a high-level programming language (unless you want to). Instead, you can write your algorithms using the pseudocode presented in Chapter 2 and shown in Figure 2.9.

The system that you are going to model is a small airport with a single runway that handles both takeoffs and landings. This system is diagrammed on the next page.

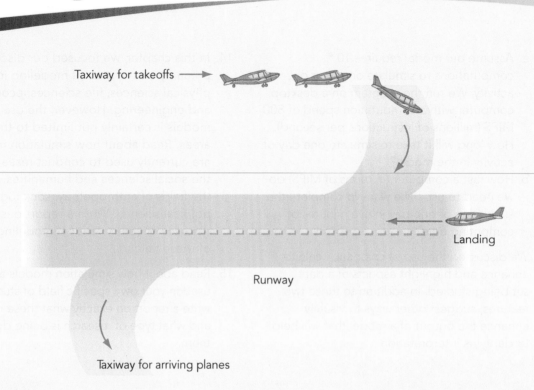

All planes take off and land from right to left. In this model, departures are created, and these newly created flights taxi to the beginning of the runway, take off, and leave the system. Arrivals are created, and these new flights land, taxi off the far end of the runway, and leave the system. Only one plane at a time can use the runway, and because planes currently in the air may be low on fuel, arriving flights have priority to use the runway over departing flights. That is, if a flight is ready to depart and another flight is ready to land, the landing flight is the one that gets to use the runway and the departing flight must wait in line.

The purpose of this model is to determine, for a given rate of flight arrivals and departures, how long a plane must wait to take off or land and the maximum number of planes in the arrival and departure lines. This type of information would be of great help to a transportation engineer trying to decide whether a second runway will be needed as the airline traffic increases.

AFTER STUDYING THIS CHAPTER YOU WILL BE ABLE TO:

- Explain the issues, pros, and cons of whether to create an ecommerce website

- List the components of online transactions, and explain what is involved in each step

- List one other ecommerce model besides the online retailer selling to the general public and explain how it works

- List one other electronic payment system besides traditional credit cards and explain how it works

- Describe the relational database model

- Frame simple queries in SQL to retrieve information from one or more tables in a relational database

- Define data mining

- List three sources data brokers use to collect data on individuals

- Give an example of data science used "for the greater good"

14.1 Introduction

As mentioned in Chapter 7, the Internet has been around for quite a while (since 1969), but it did not have much of an impact on our everyday lives until the appearance of the World Wide Web in the early 1990s. Increasingly, the web is our primary source of information about a variety of topics as well as a purveyor of goods and services from businesses "in the cloud." These days, if you own just about any type of business, you need to have a web presence. For example:

- Your business provides a service, such as landscaping, that does not sell products directly to retail customers. However, you use the web for advertising.

- Your business provides a service for which follow-up information is important. For example, you are a shipping company and you use your website to allow customers to track their shipments.

- Your business provides a service that enables customers to engage in online transactions, such as banking, that are not retail sales.

Ecommerce, Databases, and Data Science

AFTER STUDYING THIS CHAPTER, YOU WILL BE ABLE TO:

- Explain the issues, pros, and cons of whether to create an ecommerce website
- List the components of online transactions, and explain what is involved in each step
- List one other ecommerce model besides the online retailer selling to the general public and explain how it works
- List one other electronic payment system besides traditional credit cards and explain how it works
- Describe the relational database model
- Frame simple queries in SQL to retrieve information from one or more tables in a relational database
- Define data mining
- List three sources data brokers use to collect data on individuals
- Give an example of data science used "for the greater good"

14.1 Introduction

As mentioned in Chapter 7, the Internet has been around for quite a while (since 1969), but it did not have much of an impact on our everyday lives until the appearance of the World Wide Web in the early 1990s. Increasingly, the web is our primary source of information about a variety of topics as well as a purveyor of goods and services from businesses "in the cloud."

These days, if you own just about any type of business, you need to have a web presence. For example,

- Your business provides a service, such as landscaping, that does not sell products directly to retail customers. However, you use the web for advertising.

- Your business provides a service for which follow-up information is important. For example, you are a shipping company and you use your website to allow customers to track their shipments.

- Your business provides a service that enables customers to engage in online transactions, such as banking, that are not retail sales.

- Your company sells products or materials to other companies rather than to the general public. You maintain a *B2B* (*business-to-business*) web presence to streamline transactions between you as the seller and other businesses as buyers.

- Your company is a retail business, and you maintain a *B2C* (*business-to-consumer*) website. You do this to advertise your products and to allow the general public to shop and to make online purchases.

In this chapter, we'll talk mostly about the last scenario—selling retail products to the general public. This is how most consumers interact with and experience the web's commercial capabilities.

Databases are an important component of any ecommerce business, in fact of any business. We'll discuss databases in more detail later in this chapter.

Then, we'll look at the relatively new world of *data science*: some of the tools it uses, privacy considerations that arise because information about us is likely to be stored in many databases, and finally some examples of how the use of data science can improve, or even save, lives.

14.2 Ecommerce

Assume that you run a retail rug business—let's call it "Rugs-For-You"—out of a traditional store, that is, a store with a physical building, display windows, aisles with merchandise, and salespeople. In addition to your traditional store, you have decided to establish a web presence for your business where customers can visit, view area rugs for sale, ask questions, make a selection, purchase a rug, and arrange to have it delivered to them, all in a quick, easy, and secure electronic environment. In other words, you have decided to expand your retail business into the ecommerce world.

Shopping on the Web

The Census Bureau of the U.S. Department of Commerce estimated ecommerce retail sales in the United States for the first quarter of 2017 to be $105.7 billion, an increase of 14% from the first quarter of 2016. In the first quarter of 2017, ecommerce sales accounted for 8.5% of total U.S. retail sales as opposed to just 1% in 2001. The growth in ecommerce sales, and its increasing percentage of total retail sales, continues unabated. This trend is having an effect on traditional brick-and-mortar stores. In just the first quarter of 2017, well-known retail brands such as Radio Shack, JCPenney, Macy's, Sears, and many others announced store closings as a result of reduced store traffic and profitability.

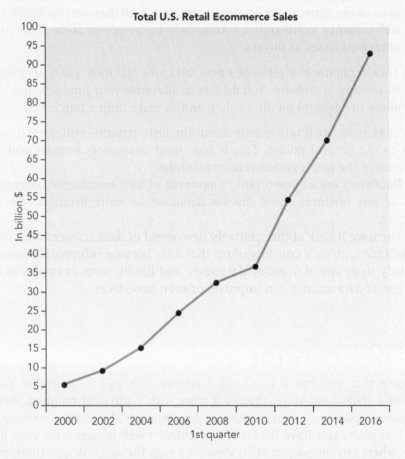

Fun Facts: During the 2016 holiday shopping season, November 1–December 19, Amazon shipped over a billion items. It sold a watch every 1.5 seconds, enough running shoes to run 18,603 times around the globe, and enough KitchenAid mixers to make 7.5 million cookies all at the same time.

In this section, we'll look at some of the many considerations involved in such a decision. Some of these are technical; some are purely business; many are a combination of the two.

14.2.1 Decisions, Decisions

In Chapter 10, we talked about HTML, the language used to build webpages. As a small business owner, you might not know much about HTML, to say nothing of the many other technologies used in creating webpages, such as XML (see the Special Interest Box "Beyond HTML" in Chapter 10). However, you can hire someone who knows these technologies, ask that person to put together some webpages for your store, and presto, you're in ebusiness! But maybe not for long.

Opening an online store requires at least as much planning as building another physical store location—in fact, probably more, because it is a different medium in which to do business.

The first question you need to answer is: What is your vision for this new part of your overall commercial enterprise? Put another way: What is the business objective you are trying to achieve? Do you want to

- Broaden your customer base?

- Recapture customers you are losing to competitors with online stores?

- Better serve your existing customer base?

- Better integrate departments or functions within your existing business, so that the shipping department and the accounting department, for example, work off the same order form?

Any or all of these might be legitimate reasons for moving into ecommerce, but have you considered the risks involved with this decision?

- Will you just move your in-store customers online and achieve no overall gain?

- When you expose yourself to online competition, will you have something unique to offer?

- Does your existing customer base need or want anything that you don't or can't provide in your traditional business environment? What part of your existing customer base will never shop online?

- Are the employees in your shipping and accounting departments in agreement with this idea, or do they feel threatened by change?

And we haven't even mentioned the costs involved with this decision:

- Do you have all the necessary hardware (computers), software, and infrastructure (network connectivity) to host a business website? If not, what will it cost you to acquire or lease them?

- Do you have the personnel and skills you need to build and maintain a website? If not, what will it cost to acquire new personnel or retrain existing personnel?

- Do you have the legal expertise on your staff to manage issues such as (1) protecting your intellectual property; (2) navigating regulations, tariffs, and taxes in the many geographic regions where you will now be doing business (including perhaps overseas); and (3) legally handling customer data collected online? If not, what will it cost you to acquire this expertise?

- Do you know the potential costs of diverting resources away from your existing traditional business?

- Will you have adequate security to protect sensitive online data from hackers who will attempt to steal information such as credit card numbers? (In 2013, Target suffered one of the biggest retail hacks to date, with the theft of personal data from 70 million customer accounts plus 40 million customers' credit and debit card data. If it can happen to the likes of Target, it can happen to Rugs-For-You.)

Let's assume that you and your company officers have assessed the objectives, the risks, and the costs, and you feel that overall your bottom line will improve by going online. What should happen next?

Once you decide to move into the ecommerce arena, there are still many questions to be answered and decisions to be made. The first major decision is choosing between *in-house development* (doing the work within your own company), *outsourcing* (hiring an outsider to do the work), or, for small retail businesses, using an off-the-shelf software package designed to host an online retail enterprise right out of the box. In fact, this is not a single decision but a whole host of decisions.

- *Personnel*—Are you going to use your existing staff to develop this ebusiness, either because they already have the necessary skills or because they will be retrained? Will you hire new personnel with the needed skills? Or will you turn the entire job over to an ASP (application service provider) who, for a fee, will design your website and manage it or host it on an ongoing basis?

- *Hardware*—You will need at least one web server machine to host your website. You may need additional computers to store your customer database information, to support program development, to provide backup capabilities in case of hardware malfunctions, and to supply the appropriate network connections and security. Do you have these machines? Will you buy them? Will you lease space on someone else's commercial web server? Or will you use a cloud computing service, which can supply computer assets that expand or shrink according to your needs?

- *Software*—You will also need a substantial amount of new software, such as programs to process the customer orders that you hope will come pouring in; to interact with your accounting, shipping, and inventory control software; and to manage and store customer information. Will you use commercial software or develop your own proprietary software that can be modified whenever your business needs change?

Of course, if you decide to turn everything over to an ASP, you will have little or no control over these hardware and software decisions. Similarly, if you decide to use off-the-shelf software, you have no further software decisions beyond choices the software package may allow.

14.2.2 Anatomy of a Transaction

What draws a customer to online shopping? The number-one attraction is probably *convenience.* Your online store is open 24 hours a day, 365 days a year. People can shop from the comfort of home, save time, and avoid the hassles of traffic. It is also easy to comparison shop merely by hopping from one website to another. But this also means that your competition is just a mouse click or a finger tap away. Your goals are to

- Draw potential customers to your site.

- Keep them there.

- Set up optimum conditions for them to complete a purchase.

Figure 14.1 illustrates the major components of an online purchase, which we have broken down into nine steps. Next, we'll elaborate on these steps, with an eye to the three goals just mentioned.

Step 1: Getting There. How can you get customers to your website? Technically, once the customer enters the web address (the URL - Uniform

FIGURE 14.1

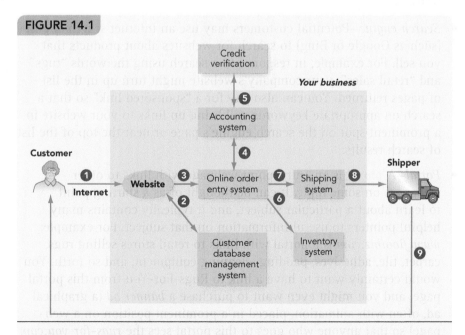

A typical online transaction in nine steps

Resource Locator) into his or her browser's address bar, the process to reach your website works exactly as described in Section 7.3.5. But how does your potential customer learn your URL in the first place? There are many possibilities:

- *Conventional advertising*—You post your homepage URL on flyers, in print and TV advertisements, on letterhead, and on any other traditional promotional materials you may produce.

- *Obvious domain name*—You want your domain name (your homepage URL) to relate so closely to your business name that potential customers can easily guess it if they don't have it in front of them. Who wouldn't try *www.mcdonalds.com* to reach this well-known fast-food giant? Of course, Rugs-For-You might not be quite that well known. Domain names are registered by companies, called *registrars*, that are accredited for this purpose by ICANN (Internet Corporation for Assigned Names and Numbers), a nonprofit corporation that took over the task of domain name management from the U.S. government in 1998. When a domain name is registered, it becomes part of the DNS so that web browsers can find your IP address and get to your site. A list of these accredited registrars can be obtained from *www.internic.net/regist.html*. A number of websites allow you to determine whether a particular domain name has already been registered. In addition to registering your "real" domain name (*rugs-for-you.com*), you would be wise to register obvious spelling variants (*rugs-for-u.com, rugs-4-u.com*, etc.) if they are available, so that all roads lead to your website.

- *Search engine*—Potential customers may use an Internet search engine (such as Google or Bing) to search for websites about products that you sell. For example, in response to a search using the words "rugs" and "retail sales", your company's website might turn up in the list of pages returned. You can also pay for a "sponsored link" so that a search on appropriate keywords will bring up links to your website in a prominent spot on the search engine's page or near the top of the list of search results.

- *Portal*—A portal is an entry-point webpage with links to other webpages on some topic. It can be thought of as a starting point to learn about a particular subject, and it typically contains many helpful pointers to useful information on that subject. For example, *www.floorbiz.com* is a portal with links to retail stores selling rugs, carpet, tile, adhesives, padding, cleaning equipment, and so forth. You would certainly want to have a link to Rugs-For-You from this portal page, and you might even want to purchase a *banner ad* (a graphical ad, often with animation, placed in a prominent position on a webpage) so that anyone who goes to this portal sees the *rugs-for-you.com* link right away.

A Rose by Any Other Name...

Cybersquatting, also called *domain squatting*, is the practice of registering a domain name that uses the name or trademark of an existing business, with the intent to resell the name to that business at a profit or to capitalize on that name for some other purpose. A 1999 federal law called the Anti-Cybersquatting Consumer Protection Act (ACPA) makes cybersquatting illegal in the United States. International disputes may be brought before the World Intellectual Property Organization (WIPO), a United Nations agency. In 2016, the WIPO heard over 3000 cases, a record number and a 10% increase over 2015. Since beginning this practice in 1999, the WIPO has received over 36,000 cases involving over 66,000 domain names. More than 80% of the cases settled in WIPO in the past five years were decided in favor of those who charged they were the victims of cybersquatting.

In June 2011, ICANN announced a new policy for "personalized" domain names. Top-level domain names, that is, the suffixes at the end of URLs, had been limited to two-character country codes plus the familiar .com, .org, .edu, and so forth. The new policy allowed for suffixes that are brand-specific or industry-specific names. This opened the door to over 1900 applications in 2012, and by 2016 there were over 1200 approved new top-level domain names, including .hotels, .wine, and .rugby. Disputes over these domain names have formed a growing percentage of the WIPO cases, 16% in 2016.

In 2013, future-president Donald Trump sued a Brooklyn man who had registered four domain names: trumpmumbai.com, trumpindia.com, trumpbeijing .com, and trumpbudhabi.com and had developed actual websites using those domain names. Trump sought $100,000 in damages for each of the four domain names and in 2014 was awarded total damages of $32,000, not by the WIPO but by the U. S. District Court in Brooklyn. (There actually is a Trump Tower in Mumbai, and if you enter *trumpmumbai.com* in your web browser, you will now reach the Trump Organization homepage showing a picture of this building.)

Step 2: Do I Know You? Regular customers at your traditional store are treated with special care. You might mail them promotional offers that you think will be of interest to them, and the salespeople know them when they walk into the store and greet them by name. You pay particular attention to their needs because, after all, return customers are the heart and soul of your business. How will your online store provide this type of personalized attention?

Some sites ask users to register and then log in when they revisit the site. These sites consult the database of registered customers and recall pertinent information—for example, how the customer browsed the site previously and what the customer bought. What the return customer sees is tailored to reflect this information.

Other sites that do not require a customer login might still greet the customer with "Welcome, John," for example, and arrange a webpage with items tied to John's apparent interests, based on his last purchase. This type of website personalization can be accomplished by means of *cookies*. A cookie is a small text file that the web server sends to the user's browser and that gets stored on the user's computer or handheld device. It contains personal information about the user, such as name, address, time of visit, and what was looked at or bought. On the customer's next visit to that same site, the browser sends the cookie back to the server (along with the page request) so the server can create a customized page just for this shopper— "Hello John, we are having a sale on new area rugs." This does more than merely create a friendly, personalized atmosphere. It also allows the server to record information for later use. For example, cookies enable a customer to put items into his or her online shopping cart and return at a later time to find them still there. It's possible to configure a web browser to not accept cookies, but cookies cannot execute on the client machine and are harmless. They just take up a little space.

You can provide incentives and benefits for return customers—product support for items already purchased, special promotions ("John, would you like some stain guard for that new rug you just bought? Click here for our special offer!"), free shipping, a clearly stated return policy (including the ability to return items to your traditional brick-and-mortar store if more convenient), and a chance to register complaints or ask questions online (to which you should pay attention and respond). In addition, you should provide links to Facebook, Twitter, Pinterest, or other appropriate social media sites for further interaction with your customers. And certainly you should provide a toll-free number where your customers can speak with a real, live person.

Online customers, both new and returning, can leave your site in the blink of an eye or, more precisely, the click of a mouse button or tap of a finger. Your website must invite them in, entice them to stay, and make their path toward purchase so convenient that there is no reason not to buy from you. This is what makes designing a webpage so much more than just an HTML programming exercise! Let's assume that a customer has successfully navigated your website, selected an item to purchase, and is ready for Step 3.

Step 3: Committing to an Online Purchase. Customers are understandably hesitant to transmit sensitive information such as their credit card number, or even their name and address, over the web. Your site must provide a secure environment for transmitting this information, and that security comes in two pieces: encryption and authentication. *Encryption* encodes the data to be transmitted into a scrambled form, using a scheme agreed on between the sender and the receiver. Although encryption provides for the secure transmission of data, this is of little use if the data is not being sent to the correct party. *Authentication* is the process of verifying the identity of the receiver of the data. In Step 3 of our online transaction process, the sender is the customer (actually the customer's web browser) placing an order and sending confidential personal and financial information, and the receiver is the retailer's web server. In Chapter 8, we discussed how the SSL (Secure Sockets Layer) and TLS (Transport Layer Security) protocols provide encryption and authentication for web transactions. There you learned that the web server can pass to the browser a certificate of authentication issued by a trusted third party.

However, these behind-the-scenes security measures do nothing to reassure the customer. The website can display a visual seal assuring the customer that the site has been authenticated and meets high security standards. A secure webpage has the protocol heading *https* in the address bar, rather than *http*, with the *s* signifying a site under the protection of SSL. Customers may also see a little green padlock graphic on the webpage to indicate a secure site, and the browser address bar may turn green. Most customers won't go any farther than this, but hovering the mouse over the lock or the green area may display a tag that reads, for example, "verified by: Verisign, Inc."[1] Clicking or tapping the lock or the green area will display information similar to Figure 14.2; selecting More Information tells you whether you have visited this website previously, technical details on the encryption used, and so forth.

FIGURE 14.2

> You are connected to
> **rugs-for-you.com**
> which is run by
> ### Rugs-For-You, Inc.
> Somewheresville
> Tennessee, US
>
> Verified by: VeriSign, Inc.
>
> 🔒 The connection to this website is secure.
>
> More Information...

Secure site assurance

---

[1] Verisign, now part of Symantec Corp., is one of the leading providers of web security products.

Steps 4 and 5: Payment Processing. Let's assume that your customers will pay with credit cards, the most common online option. (Various other modes of online payment are discussed later in this chapter.) The online order form communicates with your accounting system (Step 4), which might verify the customer's credit and process this transaction with the credit company (Step 5) on the fly, that is, while the customer waits. This way, the customer can be alerted and given another chance to enter information if there is an error. In addition, you do not have to store the customer credit card number in your database, which reduces your security risk.

Another option is to collect information on the customer's order, including an email address (Step 4), close the order process, and then evaluate the customer's credit and complete the transaction offline (Step 5). Once the transaction is completed, an email confirmation is sent to the customer. To use this option, you must maintain customer credit card information.

Steps 6–9: Order Fulfillment. Once your customer's credit is approved, your order-entry system must alert your inventory system to decrement the number of items in stock by whatever quantity the user has purchased (Step 6) and must also contact your shipping system to arrange for shipping (Step 7). The shipping system works with the shipping company you use (Step 8) to pick up and deliver the purchase to the customer (Step 9).

14.2.3 Designing Your Website

Your website must be designed with your customers in mind. It has to be fresh and up to date, ever changing, and always displaying the latest product information. One of your earliest decisions is your website *taxonomy*—how information is classified and organized so customers can easily find what they want. At *rugs-for-you.com*, you could organize your site by rug manufacturer, color, size, material, or rooms in the house.

Your customers should always know where they are on your website. As we mentioned in Chapter 7, hypertext allows a user to move easily from page to page by simply clicking or tapping a link. However, after a few clicks, it is easy to become totally lost and not know where you are or how to get back. A site map or a navigation bar can provide a high-level overview of your site architecture, plus make it easy to navigate (that is, move from page to page) through the site. A good rule of thumb is that the customer should be able to get from any page in your website to any other page in four clicks or fewer. And your webpages should include the ability to search the site for a specific item, either by name or by product number.

You need electronic "shopping carts" and order checkout forms. Keep in mind that customers want to feel in control (especially of their money!). Be sure that as customers step through the ordering process, they are always informed about the current order—items being ordered, quantity, price, and so on—and about what will happen with the next button press or click. It is also important to give customers the option to go back and change something or to clearly indicate to customers that, following the next click, the order will be final and no further changes will be possible.

Give customers shipping options so that they can make the best trade-off between cost and speed of delivery. Send email to confirm orders, and send follow-up emails or text messages when orders are shipped.

You may also want to offer extras to your customers. Put up a *FAQ* (*frequently asked questions*) page and links to contact customer service, review new products, or connect with other customers. Allow customers to track their shipment with an order number. Post news and press releases about your business or products. And again, configure your site in a personalized way for return customers. All of these measures can help improve customer satisfaction, build customer relationships, and bring people back to your website time and time again. The suggestions and ideas listed above are part of your online *CRM* (*customer relationship management*) strategy.

At the same time that you want to cram all this content into your webpages, your site must adhere to good design principles. It must look professional and uncluttered. Make good use of white space—it can draw attention to the items you want emphasized. All of your pages should have a consistent look and feel and a consistent set of navigation tools; this can be accomplished by designing a master template page from which all pages are derived.

Your webpages need to be designed to be displayed on different machines (desktops, laptops, tablets, phones) with different operating systems and browsers (Internet Explorer, Safari, Chrome, Firefox, Edge). Not all browsers render every HTML element in exactly the same way. Users may run monitors at different screen resolutions and have widely varying communication speeds, from tens of thousands to tens of millions of bits per second. Your web design should use only those features that you know will work satisfactorily on virtually every machine and browser that your customers are likely to use. Adhere to ADA (Americans with Disabilities Act) requirements for web accessibility. One of the most common issues in webpage accessibility relates to images, charts, and photographs. Blind users or users with low vision have several assistive technologies available to them, but these technologies can only read text. Therefore a visual element on a webpage needs a corresponding text tag in the HTML code so that the browser will display text describing the image.

As you can see from our brief discussion, designing webpages, or at least a successful set of commercial webpages, is a difficult and complex task. It involves not only computer science skills (HTML, XML, HTTP, TCP/IP, networking, databases), but also a knowledge of such fields as art, graphics design, business, management, and consumer psychology, to name but a few. It is easy to create just any webpage, but much more difficult to create a really good one.

Less Is More

Good webpage design does not necessarily involve complexity.
The goal should be a page that is uncluttered, clean, attractive, informative, and easy to use. The Google home page, one of the best-known—and most effective—webpages, is a model of striking simplicity:

Google

Google Search   I'm Feeling Lucky

Finally, in addition to your own business website, you need a presence on social networking sites. Create a Facebook page, post on Twitter and YouTube, and put links on your own website so people can easily find, follow, friend, like, watch, and tweet you. People now expect to be able to post user reviews, provide product feedback, and share opinions and experiences. Companies gain valuable information through this social media process, which used to be obtained through more costly invitation-only "focus groups."

14.2.4 Behind the Scenes

Your business maintains a number of other computer applications in addition to your online order-entry system. In Figure 14.1, you saw that there are accounting, inventory control, and shipping systems as well as a customer database, and that's just to deal with customers. You also have systems that deal with your suppliers to manage orders, shipments, billing, and payments. Finally, you have personnel systems to deal with your employees—payroll, insurance, Social Security. Some of these systems may be brand new and just installed (like your new website), whereas others may be legacy code that has been around for dozens of years.

Practice Problems

1. Locate a portal page for at least one of the following topics: health care, environmental issues, fantasy sports, higher education, or the alternative energy industry.

2. Take a look at the website of a major online retailer such as Amazon.com, Apple.com, or Walmart.com and identify some characteristics of its site that you find helpful and some things that you find annoying or troublesome.

Obviously, these systems are not all independent of one another, and some must collaborate quite closely. However, these systems may have been developed by different vendors (some functions may even be done by hand) and may run on different machines using totally different protocols and formats from those on your new website. Because of this, once the website is up and running, you may need to invest in middleware—software that allows separate, existing programs to communicate and work together seamlessly. Middleware does such things as translate between incompatible data representations, file formats, and network protocols to allow otherwise disparate systems to exchange information. Think of middleware as a "translator" that allows for meaningful communications between, say, one businessperson who speaks just Chinese and another fluent only in Turkish.

Finally, as soon as you have your enterprise humming along smoothly as an ecommerce site, you will need an effective disaster recovery strategy. What are your plans for backing up critical data? What is your plan to keep your online business open even when your server fails? Will you be able to survive a massive natural disaster? What will you do if a hacker breaks into your website and steals customer information? Without a plan, you are never more than one electrical storm, one malicious user, or one disk failure away from catastrophe.

14.2.5 Other Ecommerce Models

The ecommerce model we have been discussing is that of an online retailer selling products or services over the web to the general public, but there are other models.

eBay. One of the most successful alternative ecommerce models is *eBay*, founded in 1995 and now a huge international business. As of April 2017, eBay had almost 169 million active registered users, and at any given time there are over 800 million items on sale. The most expensive item ever purchased was a 405-ft luxury yacht, which was purchased in 2006 by a Russian billionaire for $168 million. One of the weirdest was a cornflake in the shape of the state of Illinois, which sold in 2008 for $1,350.

Unlike the traditional retailer/customer relationship, eBay facilitates peer-to-peer relationships in an "auction" mode. Anyone can post an item to be sold at auction on eBay. The item must conform to eBay's policies (for example, it can't be a prescription drug, stolen property, or used cosmetics). Restrictions for this multinational company are aligned with regional or country laws. The seller selects the appropriate category for the item, writes a description, includes shipping details and costs, and sets the opening bid price and duration of the bidding period. eBay collects a fee to list an item and a second fee if the item sells.

As a buyer on eBay, you see the current maximum bid for an item and the time left for bidding. You enter the maximum amount you are willing to pay, which is not revealed to the seller or to other bidders, and the system raises your bid just enough to make you the highest bidder, up to your maximum price. If the bidding exceeds your maximum price, you are notified that you have been outbid and you have an opportunity to enter a new maximum price. If the current maximum bid is yours and there is no further bidding, then you have purchased the item, possibly at a lower price than your maximum price. Safeguards are in place to protect both the buyer and the seller, for example, seller ratings, privacy policies, and standardized electronic payment mechanisms. A "fixed-price" selling option is also available.

eBay was a precursor to the growing peer-to-peer (collaborative consumption) economy that now includes companies such as Uber, Lyft, Airbnb, and others.

Craigslist. Craigslist is an online classified ad site. Actually, it is a network of local sites for various cities or areas. Each such site gives postings for local items for sale, job opportunities, housing options, personal ads, discussion forums, and so on. Begun in 1995 as a modest list of San Francisco events circulated to friends of the founder, Craig Newmark, Craigslist now has over 700 local sites in 70 countries, from Ahmedabad, India, to Zamboanga in the Philippines. Craigslist users post about 80 million new classified ads each month, and the sites receive about 50 billion page views per month. Craigslist supports 13 languages: Catalan, Danish, Dutch, English, Filipino, French, German, Italian, Norwegian, Portuguese, Spanish, Swedish, and Turkish. Unfortunately, there have been several cases of crimes committed and scams perpetrated based on contacts established through Craigslist (the Craigslist online community site includes information about how to detect and avoid scams, *www.craigslist.org/about/scams*), but the overall effect is a sense of local community and people-to-people trust.

Groupon. Groupon has some similarities to Craigslist, but is less peer-to-peer in nature. The name is a shortened form of "group coupon." Groupon's first site, in Chicago, was launched in November 2008. As of March 2017, it served over 500 local markets in 15 countries and had sales in 2016 of $3.1 billion. Here's how it works: A local business offers a coupon through

Groupon for a great deal—on museum admission, a spa session, a restaurant meal, or whatever. The coupon offer is featured on the local Groupon site for a single day. The business specifies a minimum number of customers who must purchase the coupon. If that number is not met, the deal is off; no one gets a coupon and no one gets charged. If that minimum is met, the deal is on and additional customers can purchase the coupon. Coupons are emailed or texted the next day to customers who purchased them. Groupon splits the coupon charge with the business, so the business spends no out-of-pocket money to advertise unless a minimum number of customers is already guaranteed.

14.2.6 Electronic Payment Systems

In addition to new models of ecommerce, there are electronic payment systems that are alternatives to a customer paying an online merchant by a traditional credit card.

PayPal. To use this online payment service, the customer must have a PayPal account that is tied to a credit card, debit card, or bank account; the PayPal account can be funded by a bank transfer. If a site accepts payment via PayPal, then the customer can choose to pay from his or her PayPal account balance, or from the associated bank account or credit card. PayPal provides other services as well, such as the ability to securely send money to someone else who has a PayPal account.

As of the first quarter of 2017, PayPal had 203 million active registered accounts and was available in more than 200 markets around the world. It supports transactions in multiple currencies, such as the U.S. dollar, the Polish zloty, and the Thai baht. In 2016, PayPay processed 6.1 billion transactions, averaging out to about 193 transactions per second.

Apple Pay. Apple Pay, and similar systems such as Android Pay and Samsung Pay, are mobile payment systems. First announced by Apple in 2014, Apple Pay is a *digital wallet*. To get started, on newer versions of the Apple iPhone or on the Apple Watch, you open the Wallet and add your credit card information. Apple contacts your bank to see that this is a valid credit card issued to you, and that completes the setup process. To use Apple Pay at a merchant with a contactless card reader, just hold your phone or watch near the reader and when an image of your card appears on the screen, use Touch ID or your passcode to authenticate your transaction. An increasing number of banks/credit cards and merchants accept Apple Pay.

Apple Pay, and similar systems, put a big focus on security. The credit card information you entered in the setup process does not stay on your phone; instead Apple Pay uses that information to create a device-specific account number that is stored on your phone. Then when you use Apple Pay for a purchase, Apple creates a one-time payment number and a dynamic security code that are both encrypted and sent for processing to the bank issuing your credit card. The merchant never sees information about your credit card, you don't have to sign anything, and Apple keeps no record of what you bought, from whom you bought it, or what you paid for it.

Bitcoin. Bitcoin is more than a payment system. Rather it is a form of money—sort of. Consider the U.S. dollar. It was originally based on the gold standard, meaning that a certain amount of gold could be redeemed for your dollar bill, the idea being that the gold was what made your dollar bill valuable, and therefore useful for the payment of debt or the purchase of goods. In 1971, the United States dropped the gold standard, and today your dollar bill is valuable only because the U.S. government says it is, and that it must be accepted as "legal tender" within the United States. Only the U.S. government can print U.S. dollar bills or any other U.S. currency.

In contrast, bitcoin is never printed, it isn't highly regulated by any country or other entity such as the Federal Reserve Board or the European Central Bank, and no entity guarantees its value. Yet you can buy and sell bitcoin at an online bitcoin exchange service and you can use your bitcoin to make purchases from the increasing number of online businesses that accept bitcoins as a medium of payment. How does that work? Bitcoin is accepted as legitimate currency in large part because of the security obtained from two mechanisms we discussed in Chapter 8, namely, *public-key encryption* and *hashing*.

The idea for bitcoin originated in 2008 in a report by an anonymous individual(s) using the pseudonym Satoshi Nakamoto. Bitcoin is managed by a decentralized network of computers. All bitcoin transactions are recorded in a public ledger called the *blockchain*, which frequently gets updated and distributed to the bitcoin network. Each user has one or more anonymous bitcoin addresses that are actually public keys, with associated private keys. Obtaining a private key from its corresponding public key is not computationally feasible.

Suppose that X has some amount of bitcoin available and wants to transmit that to Y (perhaps to a merchant as payment for a purchase). X constructs a transaction that includes the value v in bitcoin of the transaction, the public key for Y, information from the blockchain about the previous transaction (or transactions) that transferred v bitcoins to X, and a digital signature that bitcoin software creates using X's private key. X then sends the transaction to Y's public key (bitcoin address). Y uses another piece of bitcoin software that reads the signature to verify that this transaction comes from the owner of X's public key. This validates the transaction, which then can be broadcast to the entire network.

Now here is where it gets interesting. Individuals (or conglomerates) called *bitcoin miners* pick up new transactions on the network, validate them, and eventually include them in a new block to be added to the blockchain. For this work, the miner is rewarded with additional, newly created bitcoin. This is how bitcoin comes into existence. The new block includes more than just these new transactions; it also includes a small random number and the *block header* of the previous block in the chain, which is the result of applying a standard hash function to that block. Then the same standard hash function is applied to this entire new block to create its block header. Powerful software allows this to be accomplished quickly and easily.

So, what's the work, you ask? The rules are that the miner can only add the new block if the value of its hash is smaller than the value of the block header (the hash) for the previous block; if that's not the case, the miner has to choose a new random number and repeat the hash. The first one to succeed gets to broadcast the new block to the network and, once the network agrees that the block is correct, it gets added to the blockchain and the miner collects the reward. On the average, the blockchain is updated every 10 minutes.

Finally, note that each blockchain header is derived in part from the previous blockchain header. If anyone attempts to tamper with a transaction or add a new transaction to a block, that block's hash value (header) will no longer be correct, and neither will the header of any subsequent block. Anyone can check a block by recomputing its hash value; if the result does not agree with that block's header, then something in that block or an earlier block has been tampered with. In fact, a newly created block is checked by everyone on the network and if it fails that test, it is ignored, not added to the blockchain, and the miner receives no reward.

To sum up, here are the advantages of bitcoin:

- Transactions are anonymous but completely transparent (verifiable).

- There is no "middle man," such as a credit card or a bank, with associated fees.

- The results are immutable (tamper-proof).

Blockchain: A New Revolution?

Blockchain is the basis of bitcoin cybercurrency, which clearly has the potential to revolutionize the banking industry—or perhaps even eliminate banking as we know it. But this relatively new technology is starting to be explored for other uses. Basically, any transfer of assets can benefit from the transparency and immutability of blockchain technology. Think of selling/buying stocks and bonds, valuable.art, or real estate without the expense of brokerage firms, auction houses, or real estate companies. Think of transferring commodities, important documents, digital media, or intellectual property. Many people feel that digital access to these distributed networks will open doors to much of the world's population that currently has no access to financial markets of any kind. On the other hand, such developments will mean the loss of many jobs we have today.

14.3 Databases

The management and organization of data have always been important problems. It is likely that a strong impetus for the development of written language was the need to record commercial transactions ("On this day Procrastinus traded Consensius 4 sheep for 7 barrels of olive oil"). From there, it is only a short step to recording inventories ("Procrastinus has 27 sheep"), wages paid, profits gained, and so on. As the volume of data grows, it becomes more difficult to keep track of all the facts, harder to extract useful information from a large collection of facts, and more difficult to relate one fact to another. With the 1890 U.S. census (Chapter 1), Herman Hollerith demonstrated the advantages that can accrue from mechanizing the storage and processing of large amounts of data.

We talked about the online customer database as part of your expansion into ecommerce, but databases are probably a key part of your business whether you have an online presence or not. You have a set of data to maintain about your employees (names, addresses, pay rates, Social Security numbers, etc.), another set of data to maintain about your suppliers (names, addresses, products, orders, etc.), and yet another set of data to maintain about your business itself (sales, expenses, taxes, etc.). Previously, such items of data were recorded by hand, but they are now maintained in electronic databases. The important thing about an electronic database is that it is more than a storehouse of individual data items; these items can easily be extracted, sorted, and even manipulated to reveal new information. To see how this works, let's examine the structure of a file containing data.

14.3.1 Data Organization

As you learned in Chapters 4 and 5, the most basic unit of data is a single *bit*, a value of 0 or 1. A single bit rarely conveys any meaningful information. Bits are combined into groups of eight called *bytes*; each byte can store the binary representation of a single character or a small integer number. A byte is a single unit of addressable memory. A single byte is often too small to store meaningful information, so a group of bytes is used to represent a string of characters—say, the name of an employee in a company—or a larger numerical value such as an employee ID. Such a group of bytes is called a field. A collection of related fields—say, all the information about a single employee— is called a record, a term inherited from the pencil-and-paper concept of "keeping records." Related records—say, the records of all the employees in a single company—are kept in a data file. (*File* is another term inherited from the familiar *filing cabinet*.) And finally, related files make up a database. Thus,

Bits combine to form bytes.
Bytes combine to form fields.
Fields combine to form records.
Records combine to form files.
Files combine to form databases.

FIGURE 14.3

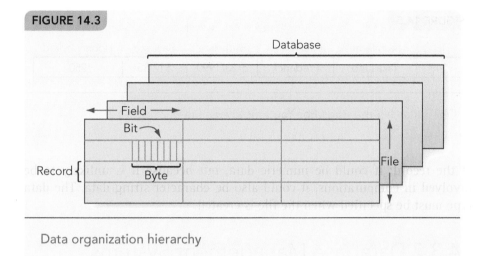

Data organization hierarchy

Figure 14.3 shows this hierarchical organization of data elements. (This figure was drawn to look neat, but files in a database are almost never all the same size or "shape.")

Bits and bytes are too fine a level of detail for what we will discuss in this section. Also, for the moment, let's assume for simplicity that the database consists of only a single file. Figure 14.4 illustrates a single file made up of five records (the rows), each record composed of three fields (the columns). The various fields can hold different types of data. One field in each record might hold character strings; another field in each record might hold integer data.

Each record in a file contains information about an item in the "universe of discourse" that the file describes. In our example, we assume that the universe of discourse is the set of employees at Rugs-For-You and that each record corresponds to a single employee. An individual employee record, with six different fields, is shown in Figure 14.5. Here it is clear that the *LastName* and *FirstName* fields hold character strings. The type of data being stored in the *ID* field is not clear to us as human beings from looking

FIGURE 14.4

	Field 1	Field 2	Field 3	
Record 1				
Record 2				File
Record 3				
Record 4				
Record 5				

Records and fields in a single file

FIGURE 14.5

ID	LastName	FirstName	Birthdate	PayRate	HoursWorked
149	Takasano	Frederick	5/23/1990	$12.35	250

One record in the Rugs-For-You Employees file

at the record; it could be numeric data, but because it is unlikely to be involved in computations, it could also be character string data. The data type must be specified when the file is created.

14.3.2 Database Management Systems

A **database management system (DBMS)** manages the files in a database.[2] We know that such files actually consist of collections of individual records. However, Edgar F. Codd (mentioned in Chapter 12 as a Turing Award winner for his work in database management systems) proposed the conceptual model of a file as simply a two-dimensional table. In this **relational database model**, the *Employees* file at Rugs-For-You would be represented by the *Employees* table of Figure 14.6.

With the change from records in a file to a conceptual table representing data comes some changes in terminology. The table represents information about an **entity**, a fundamental distinguishable component in the Rugs-For-You business—namely, its employees. A row of the table contains data about one instance of this entity—that is, one employee—and the row, in relational database terms, is called a **tuple** (in Figure 14.6, each row is

FIGURE 14.6

Employees

ID	LastName	FirstName	Birthdate	PayRate	HoursWorked
116	Kay	Janet	3/29/1980	$16.60	94
123	Perreira	Francine	8/15/1993	$ 8.50	185
149	Takasano	Frederick	5/23/1990	$12.35	250
171	Kay	John	11/17/1978	$17.80	245
165	Honou	Morris	6/9/1997	$ 6.70	53

Employees table for Rugs-For-You

---

[2] Database examples and exercises in this chapter were run using Access in Microsoft Office 365 ProPlus on the Windows 10 operating system, and Access 2010 and 2013 on Windows 7. Students could also use Microsoft SQL Server 2016 Express with SQL Server Management Studio v17 (both are free downloads).

a 6-tuple, containing six pieces of information). How the tuples (rows) are ordered within the table is not important. Each category of information (*ID*, *FirstName*, and so on, in our example) is called an attribute. The heading above each column identifies an attribute; the order of the attributes (columns) is also not important, but of course must be the same for each tuple in the table. The table thus consists of tuples of attribute values. (In other words, in the relational model, files are thought of as tables, records as tuples, and fields as attributes.) A primary key is an attribute or combination of attributes that uniquely identifies a tuple. In our example, we are assuming that *ID* is a primary key; *ID* is underlined in the heading in Figure 14.6 to indicate that it is the primary key for this table. Social Security numbers were previously used as primary keys to uniquely identify tuples that involve people, but because of privacy issues, most employers construct a unique internal identification number for each employee. Obviously, neither *Last-Name* nor *FirstName* can serve as a primary key—there are many people with the last name Smith and many people with a first name of Michael or Judith.

The computer's operating system functions as a basic file manager. As we learned in Chapter 6, the operating system contains commands to list all of the files on the hard drive, to copy or delete a file, to rename a file, and so forth. But a database management system, unlike a simple file manager, works at the level of individual fields in the individual records of the file; in more appropriate terminology, we should say that it works at the level of individual attribute values of individual tuples in the relational table. For example, a simple file system could not tell you specific information about the employee with ID number 123. However, given the *Employees* table of Figure 14.6, a database management system could be given the instruction shown here:

```
SELECT ID, LastName, FirstName, Birthdate, PayRate,
  HoursWorked
FROM Employees
WHERE ID = 123;
```

This command asks the system to retrieve all the information about the employee with ID 123. Because *ID* is the primary key, there can only be one such employee, and this is a relatively easy task. But the following request to locate all the information about an employee with a given last name,

```
SELECT ID, LastName, FirstName, Birthdate, PayRate,
  HoursWorked
FROM Employees
WHERE LastName = "Perreira";
```

is done just as easily, even though the *LastName* attribute may not uniquely identify the tuple. If multiple employees in the table have the same name, all of the relevant tuples will be returned.

If only some of the attributes are wanted, an instruction such as

```
SELECT LastName, PayRate
FROM Employees
WHERE LastName = "Perreira";
```

produces just the last name and pay rate for the employee(s) with the given last name.

Database management systems usually require specialized *query languages* to enable the user or another application program to *query* (ask questions of) the database in order to retrieve information. The three preceding SELECT examples are written in a language called SQL (Structured Query Language), a special-purpose language used for posing questions to a database management system. We briefly discussed SQL in Chapter 10.

To appreciate the power of SQL, consider the following simple SQL queries for more complicated tasks:

```
SELECT *
FROM Employees
ORDER BY ID;
```

This query says to retrieve *all* of the attribute values (the asterisk is shorthand notation for listing all attributes) for all the tuples (because there is no further qualification) in the *Employees* table sorted in order by *ID*. Thus, we have effectively sorted the tuples in the relational table using a single command. This is a significant gain in productivity over the step-by-step process of comparing items and moving them around used by the sorting algorithms in Chapter 3. (Of course, what happens internally is that SQL invokes its own sorting algorithm, perhaps even one of those described in Chapter 3. However, the user is shielded from the details of this algorithm and is allowed to work at a more abstract level.) The query

```
SELECT *
FROM Employees
WHERE PayRate > 15.00;
```

gets all the tuples for employees above a certain pay rate. Here we've searched all the tuples on a particular attribute without having to specify the details of the search, as we had to do when coding the sequential search or binary search algorithms of Chapter 3. Again, underneath this SQL command the system has invoked a sequential, binary, or other type of search algorithm, but we are insulated from this level of detail and allowed to think at a higher (and more productive) level of abstraction.

To manage a relational table over time, it must be possible to add new tuples to the table (which is how the existing tuples got into the table in the first place), delete tuples from a table, and change information in an existing tuple. These tasks are easily handled by the SQL commands INSERT, DELETE, and UPDATE.

In order to explore further the power of a DBMS, let's expand our Rugs-For-You database to include a second relational table. The *InsurancePolicies* table shown in Figure 14.7 contains information on the insurance plan type and the date of issue of the policy for an employee with a given ID.

In the *InsurancePolicies* table, there is a *composite primary key* in that both *EmployeeID* and *PlanType* are needed to identify a tuple uniquely because a

FIGURE 14.7

InsurancePolicies

EmployeeID	PlanType	DateIssued
171	B2	10/18/1998
171	C1	6/21/2006
149	B2	8/16/2012
149	A1	5/23/2010
149	C2	12/18/2015

InsurancePolicies table for Rugs-For-You

given employee may have more than one insurance plan (for example, both health and disability insurance plans), and a given insurance plan may be held by more than one employee. Both attributes are underlined in the column headings in the figure, showing that they form a composite primary key. It is clear from Figure 14.7 that this composite primary key is needed for the current employees of Rugs-For-You, but even if that were not the case, the design of the database should use this composite primary key because it is a reasonable assumption that it might be needed in the future. It is also true that an employee may have no plan; in Figure 14.7, there is no tuple with ID 116, although there is an employee with ID 116. Each value of *EmployeeID* in the *InsurancePolicies* table exists as an *ID* value in a tuple of the *Employees* table, where it is a primary key. Because of this, the *EmployeeID* attribute of the *InsurancePolicies* table is called a foreign key into the *Employees* table. This foreign key establishes the relationship that employees may have insurance plans.

The database management system can relate information between various tables through these key values—in our example, the linkage between the foreign key *EmployeeID* in the *InsurancePolicies* table and the primary key *ID* in the *Employees* table. Thus, the following query will give us information about Frederick Takasano's insurance plan, even though Frederick Takasano's name is not in the *InsurancePolicies* table:

```
SELECT LastName, FirstName, PlanType
FROM Employees, InsurancePolicies
WHERE LastName = "Takasano"
AND FirstName = "Frederick"
AND ID = EmployeeID;
```

This query uses the Boolean AND operation we encountered in Chapter 4 in our discussion on Boolean logic. The query is an instruction to the database management system to retrieve the *LastName* and *FirstName* attributes from the *Employees* table and the *PlanType* attribute from the *InsurancePolicies* table by looking for the tuple with *LastName* attribute value

"Takasano" and *FirstName* attribute value "Frederick" in the *Employees* table, and then finding the tuple(s) with the matching *EmployeeID* value in the *InsurancePolicies* table. It is the last term in the WHERE clause of the query (the last line) that causes the two tables to be joined together by the match between primary key and foreign key.

The result of executing the entire query is

```
Takasano Frederick B2
Takasano Frederick A1
Takasano Frederick C2
```

Now let's see how this works. The FROM clause, line 2 in the query, picks out the tables to be used in order to answer the query. (These are the only two tables in the database at the moment, but there could be more.) The rest of the query illustrates the use of three relational database operations:

- Join—Match tuples from two different relational tables using the specified attributes. The

  ```
  ID = EmployeeID
  ```

  part of the query is doing a *join* operation. The result of the join would be the temporary table

ID	LastName	FirstName	Birthdate	PayRate	Hours Worked	EmployeeID	PlanType	DateIssued
149	Takasano	Frederick	5/23/1990	$12.35	250	149	B2	8/16/2012
149	Takasano	Frederick	5/23/1990	$12.35	250	149	A1	5/23/2010
149	Takasano	Frederick	5/23/1990	$12.35	250	149	C2	12/16/2015
171	Kay	John	11/17/1978	$17.80	245	171	B2	10/18/1998
171	Kay	John	11/17/1978	$17.80	245	171	C1	6/21/2006

- Restrict—Pick out tuples that meet a certain condition. The

  ```
  WHERE LastName = "Takasano"
  AND FirstName = "Frederick"
  ```

  part of the query is doing a *restrict* operation, which has the following effect on the previous table (note that two tuples have been eliminated):

ID	LastName	FirstName	Birthdate	PayRate	Hours Worked	EmployeeID	PlanType	DateIssued
149	Takasano	Frederick	5/23/1990	$12.35	250	149	B2	8/16/2012
149	Takasano	Frederick	5/23/1990	$12.35	250	149	A1	5/23/2010
149	Takasano	Frederick	5/23/1990	$12.35	250	149	C2	12/16/2015
~~171~~	~~Kay~~	~~John~~	~~11/17/1978~~	~~$17.80~~	~~245~~	~~171~~	~~B2~~	~~10/18/1998~~
~~171~~	~~Kay~~	~~John~~	~~11/17/1978~~	~~$17.80~~	~~245~~	~~171~~	~~C1~~	~~6/21/2006~~

- Project—Pick out certain attributes (columns) from a set of tuples. The

```
SELECT LastName, FirstName, PlanType
```

part of the query is doing a *project* operation, which has the following effect on the previous table (note that most attribute columns have been eliminated):

ID	LastName	FirstName	Birthdate	PayRate	Hours Worked	EmployeeID	PlanType	DateIssued
149	Takasano	Frederick	5/23/1990	$12.35	250	149	B2	8/16/2012
149	Takasano	Frederick	5/23/1990	$12.35	250	149	A1	5/23/2010
149	Takasano	Frederick	5/23/1990	$12.35	250	149	C2	12/16/2015
171	Kay	John	11/17/1978	$17.80	245	171	B2	10/18/1998
171	Kay	John	11/17/1978	$17.80	245	171	C1	6/21/2006

leaving

```
Takasano Frederick B2
Takasano Frederick A1
Takasano Frederick C2
```

as before.

The correspondence between primary keys and foreign keys is what establishes the relationships among various entities in a database and makes a *join* operation possible. The SQL command to create a table requires specification of the various attributes by name and data type, identification of the primary key, identification of any foreign keys, and identification of the tables into which these are foreign keys. This information is used to build the actual file that stores the data in the tuples.

We've now done a fairly complex query involving two different tables. It is easy to see how these ideas can be expanded to multiple tables, linked together by relationships represented by foreign keys and their corresponding primary keys. Figure 14.8 shows an expansion of the Rugs-For-You database to include a table called *InsurancePlans* that contains, for each type of insurance plan, a description of its coverage and its monthly cost. *PlanType* is the primary key for this table. This makes *PlanType* in the *InsurancePolicies* table a foreign key into the *InsurancePlans* table, as shown in Figure 14.8. This linkage would allow us to write a query to find, for example, the monthly cost of Mr. Takasano's insurance (see Practice Problem 2 at the end of this section).

Using multiple tables in a single database reduces the amount of redundant information that must be stored; for example, a stand-alone insurance file for Rugs-For-You employees would probably have to include employee names as well as IDs. It also minimizes the amount of work required to maintain consistency in the data (if Francine Perreira gets married and changes her name, the name change need only be entered in one place). But most important of all, the database gives the user, or the user's application software, the ability to combine and manipulate data easily in ways that would be very difficult if the data were kept in separate and unrelated files.

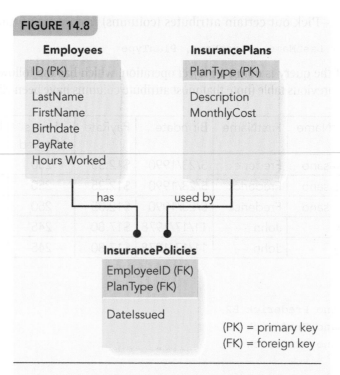

FIGURE 14.8

Employees

ID (PK)

LastName
FirstName
Birthdate
PayRate
Hours Worked

InsurancePlans

PlanType (PK)

Description
MonthlyCost

has   used by

InsurancePolicies

EmployeeID (FK)
PlanType (FK)

DateIssued

(PK) = primary key
(FK) = foreign key

Three entities in the Rugs-For-You database

As we have seen by looking at some queries, SQL is a very high-level language in which a single instruction is quite powerful. In terms of the language classifications of Chapter 10, it is also a nonprocedural language. A program written in SQL merely asks for something to be done (sort all tuples in some order, search all tuples to match some condition); it does not contain a specific sequence of instructions describing *how* it is to be done.

14.3.3 Other Considerations

Existing tuples in a relational database table can be modified or deleted, and new tuples can be added to a table. These operations must be done with care to be sure the data remains correct and consistent throughout the database. In database terminology, the *integrity* of the data must be preserved. There are three integrity rules that, if enforced during additions, modifications, or deletions, will help in this goal. The entity integrity rule says that no primary key value, or no component of a composite primary key value, can be missing ("null") in a tuple. The reason is, if the primary key uniquely identifies a tuple, then a tuple with (part of) its primary key missing might not be uniquely identifiable. The data integrity rule specifies that values for a particular attribute must come from the appropriate category of information for that attribute. In the Rugs-For-You *InsurancePolicies* table, for example, any values for the *PlanType* attribute must be designations for valid plan types, and any values for the *DateIssued* must be valid dates. Finally, the referential integrity rule specifies that any value of a foreign key attribute in a given table must match a value in the corresponding primary keys of the related table. For example, we can't add a tuple to the *InsurancePolicies* table of the Rugs-For-You database with an *EmployeeID* value that does not exist in the *Employees* table. Most database systems enforce the integrity rules by default.

Performance issues definitely affect the user's satisfaction with a database management system; a slow response to a query is at best annoying and at worst unacceptable to the person waiting for the result. Large files are maintained on disk in secondary storage rather than being brought in total into main memory. Accessing a record in the file involves at least one disk input/output (I/O) operation, which is a much slower process than accessing information stored in main memory, sometimes as much as three or four orders of magnitude slower.

Creating small additional records to be stored along with the file, although consuming extra storage, can significantly reduce access time. The smaller structure stored with the file may even be organized in a treelike manner that is a generalization of the tree structure we used in Chapter 3 to visualize the binary search. Following the branches of the tree can quickly lead to information about the location in the file of the record with a particular primary key value. A good DBMS incorporates the services of a sophisticated file manager to organize the disk files in an optimal way in order to minimize access time to the records.

SQL, NoSQL, NewSQL

Throughout this database section we have been talking about relational databases, where a file is thought of as a rather rigid two-dimensional table, there are various connections between "related" tables, and queries are processed using SQL. *NoSQL* databases are designed to give high performance on massive clusters of data and rely on various structures other than tables. Driven by Big Data (see Section 14.4) and real-time web applications, such systems are intended to be highly scalable, highly distributed, flexible, and error-resilient. *NewSQL* databases are sort of a combination of the two; they do rely on SQL and achieve the consistency required for traditional transaction-process activities, while featuring the scalability of NoSQL systems. Neither NoSQL nor NewSQL systems are overall replacements for standard relational databases, but they are alternative choices depending on the application/data of interest.

A distributed database allows the physical data to reside at separate and independent locations that are electronically networked together. The user at site A makes a database query that needs access to data physically stored at site B. The database management system and the underlying network make the necessary links and connections to get the data from where it is currently stored to the node where it is needed. To the user, it looks like a single database on his or her own machine, except perhaps for increased access time when the data has to travel across a network.

Practice Problems

1. Using the *Employees* table of Figure 14.6, what is the result of the following SQL query?

   ```
   SELECT ID, PayRate
   FROM Employees
   WHERE LastName = "Takasano";
   ```

2. Complete the following SQL query to find the monthly cost of Frederick Takasano's insurance; because *PlanType* is an attribute of both *InsurancePolicies* and *InsurancePlans*, we must include the table name as well.

   ```
   SELECT LastName, FirstName, _____
   FROM Employees, InsurancePlans, InsurancePolicies
   WHERE LastName = _____
   AND ID = EmployeeID
   AND InsurancePolicies.PlanType = _____;
   ```

3. Using the *InsurancePolicies* table of Figure 14.7, write an SQL query to find all the employee IDs for employees who have insurance plan type B2.

4. Assuming that no other changes are made to any of the three tables in the Rugs-For-You database, what integrity constraint is violated if the tuple with ID 171 is deleted from the *Employees* table?

Laboratory Experience 19

If you have a commercial database package available, you can work through the exercises in this Laboratory Experience using an expanded Rugs-For-You database. You will write SQL queries similar to the ones discussed in this section and will also learn how to use SQL to carry out some computations.

14.4 Data Science

We are surrounded by data, and the amount of data is growing exponentially. According to International Data Corporation (IDC), the "global datasphere," that is, the amount of data that existed in the world in 2017, was 25 zettabytes, which measured in bytes is 25 followed by 21 zeroes, or 25 trillion gigabtyes. Wow. And IDC estimates that by the year 2025, this figure will be 160 zettabytes.

Much of this data is trivial, but a lot is critically important. How do we make sense of it all? How can we locate truly useful information from this vast ocean of data? How can we make use of it to improve living conditions, find solutions to major health problems, protect the environment, and an endless stream of other important questions?

Because of the massive amounts of data, we need skills to analyze important segments of data, extract information from them, and apply that information to solve problems from how to increase potato production to how to cure cancer.

First, we'll look at some common terms. The first three are often used interchangeably, so the descriptions given here would not be universally agreed upon.

- *Big Data*—A term that expresses that we now have huge amounts of data available, as mentioned earlier.

- *Data analysis*—The process of finding the right data sets, putting the data into the right format, and writing queries to extract information from the data, much as we did with the Rugs-For-You database.

- *Data science*—Data science incorporates many of the tasks of data analysis, but also involves knowledge of the enterprise in order to formulate useful queries, along with the use of sophisticated statistics and visualization techniques. Data science also involves interpreting the results in terms of the enterprise and predicting future strategies likely to achieve a desired goal.

- *Data warehouse*—A data warehouse is a collection of databases that contain current and archived data used for research and analysis purposes rather than to manage day-to-day business transactions such as inventory control or payroll data.

14.4.1 Tools

One of the major objectives of data science is to analyze large amounts of data (often obtained from data warehouses) to extract and interpret previously hidden patterns contained therein. This process is called data mining. In other words, data mining is used to discover previously hidden patterns that a big data set might contain. This sounds rather magical.

Data mining is part of an overall process consisting of several steps:

1. Determine what problem you are trying to solve: What information do you hope to unearth from your large data set?

2. Review the condition of the data you have. Are there several data sets? If so, do they all have the same structure, for example, does each tuple have the same attributes? Are there any tuples with missing or obvious "outlier" attribute values that should be eliminated?

3. Determine a model to represent your data in some way that will help bring out patterns. You want to use these patterns to classify your existing data and help determine which attributes are the strongest predictors of a given outcome. It is this step that is the data mining part: creation of a model.

4. Evaluate your model. Are the results predicted borne out by further data? Would a different model give better results?

Let's look at an extremely simple example. You are the loan manager at Gringotts Third Bank, and you must decide who gets approved for a loan, that is, who is a high risk (likely to default on some payments) and who is a low risk (very likely to repay the loan on time). Past experience at the bank has produced the data shown in Figure 14.9.

What is the problem you want to solve? You would like to use the attributes of Employed (yes or no), Gender (male or female), and Married (yes or no) to predict Risk (high or low). What is the condition of the data (aside from being a ridiculously small data set)? All attributes have reasonable values.

What model should we use? This is the hard part because there are many ways to create a data mining model, some involving quite complex mathematics or statistics. We are going to use a rather simple model called a *decision tree*. (Recall that we used tree structures in Chapter 3 to represent the actions of the binary search algorithm and the possible paths in a graph to find Hamiltonian circuits.) A decision tree for data mining uses the input attributes (in our problem, Employed, Gender, and Married) as nodes in the tree; at each node, the branches below it represent the possible values. The

FIGURE 14.9

ID	Employed	Gender	Married	Risk
1	Y	M	Y	Low
2	Y	F	N	Low
3	N	M	N	High
4	Y	M	Y	Low
5	Y	F	Y	Low
6	N	F	N	High
7	Y	M	N	High
8	N	M	N	High
9	Y	F	N	Low
10	Y	M	Y	Low

Existing data for bank loan risk

leaves of the tree (the nodes at the bottom of the tree) represent the values for the target attribute, which here is Risk.

We'll make the root of the tree, that is, the top-most node, the attribute Employed. So the beginning of the tree is shown in Figure 14.10(a). Now as it happens, all tuples in Figure 14.9 who are not employed are at high risk, so we don't have to consider any further attributes for them and this terminates the N branch of Employed. For those that are employed, we next consider Gender (Figure 14.10(b)). The three employed females in Figure 14.9 are all at low risk, so that terminates another branch, but we have to consider the marital status of employed males (Figure 14.10(c), which is the complete decision tree).

According to this model, any new unemployed person looking for a loan, regardless of gender or marital state, will be turned down, whereas any employed female will get a loan, regardless of her marital state. But a male, in order to get loan approval, must be both employed and married.

It is easy to see how to turn this model into an algorithm that can be implemented in some programming language. Then, when a new customer applies for a loan at Gringotts Third Bank, you can just collect the desired attribute values, plug the results into your computer program, and come out with the risk factor. In other words, you now have an algorithmic solution to your problem. But reliance on algorithmic predictions has risks:

1. Is the model the algorithm implements too simplistic? Of course, our bank loan model is an unrealistically simple model, based as it is on a very small data set. And there are many other attributes that might influence the applicant's creditworthiness, such as age, income, savings, amount of debt, amount of loan requested, term of loan requested, and so forth.

Data modeling is never done with 10 items of data, but with millions or billions of data items. Often a large part of the available data, say 70–80%, is used as training data, that is, to build the model. Then the model is tested against the remaining existing data to see whether it will be a good predictor.

2. Is the data used to train the model biased, thereby leading to biased decision-making by the algorithm? (See the Special Interest box, "Algorithm Bias.")

FIGURE 14.10

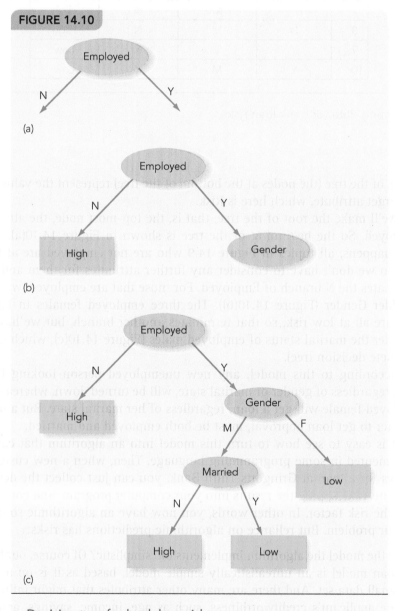

Decision tree for bank loan risk

Algorithm Bias

As data science becomes more pervasive, the consequences of biased decision algorithms, that is, decision algorithms based on biased input, become more apparent. For example,

"According to a 2013 article published by Sonja B. Starr, a professor of law at the University of Michigan Law School, nearly every state has adopted some type of risk-based assessment tools to aid in [criminal] sentencing. The primary concern related to these tools revolves around the use of computerized algorithms, which provide risk scores based on the result of questions that are either answered by defendants or pulled from criminal records, and whether such tools may ultimately penalize racial minorities by overpredicting the likelihood of recidivism in these groups."[3]

In January 2017, The ACM (Association for Computing Machinery) U.S. Public Policy Council issued a statement on Algorithmic Transparency and Accountability, noting that using algorithms for automated decision-making that affects individuals can result in harmful discrimination. The statement contains guidelines for institutions creating or using such algorithms.[4]

---

[3] "It's Not the Algorithm, It's the Data," Kirkpatrick, K., Communications of the ACM, February 2017, pgs. 21–23.
[4] https://techpolicy.acm.org/?p=6156.

Other tools for data science incorporate statistics and visualization to observe patterns, trends, and relationships buried in a large data set. In Chapter 10, we briefly discussed the use of the programming language R (see pages 510–512), which is specifically designed for statistical computing and graphics. There we analyzed a trivially small data set that looks like this, where surveys from six sites contributed information on the percentage of the survey population that exhibits medical condition X, medical condition Y, are smokers, are overweight, or have low income levels.

```
X Y Smoker Overweight Low_Income
4 2   28       19          32
6 2   31       22          28
3 4   24       31          35
5 7   18       25          25
2 6   32       29          34
4 5   41       35          37
```

Practice Problem

Draw the resulting decision tree if the following tuple is added to Figure 14.9:

11	Y	F	N	High

R provided us with an easy way to obtain basic statistical information such as the minimum, maximum, and average over the six sites for each of the attributes X, Y, Smoker, Overweight, and Low_Income. R also revealed that condition Y has a moderate correlation with being overweight, and both smoking and being overweight have a somewhat strong correlation with low income, where correlation means that these attributes increase or decrease more or less together. And R produced a graphical visualization of the data values for each of the six sites in the form of a bar chart. (Such information can also be obtained, although not quite as easily, using a spreadsheet.)

14.4.2 Personal Privacy

We learned that a database management system can easily make connections among different files, and even among data stored at different locations, so one might wonder, How difficult is it to electronically link information in the IRS database with information in the FBI database, the Social Security database, credit card databases, banking databases, and so on? Building these types of massive, integrated government databases raises fewer technical questions than legal, political, social, and ethical ones. Remember that even the online customers of Rugs-For-You want assurances as to how their personal information is used. In general, issues of personal privacy and public safety are magnified enormously by the capabilities of networked databases, and privacy concerns arise because of the potential for information to be uncovered from massive databases using data mining techniques.

When does data mining become an actual privacy issue? Companies called data brokers collect data on virtually everyone and then in turn sell that data to clients, who use it primarily to target consumers with "personalized" advertising. Data brokers get their data from

- Public records (birth certificates, marriage certificates, death certificates, property records, bankruptcies, courthouse records, business ownership, professional listings, voter registrations, auto registrations);

- Publicly available data (telephone directories, business directories, newspapers, website tracking data, social networking sites, résumé sites, online forums); and

- Nonpublic data (consumer transaction data; cell phone records; information from mobile apps),

and they sell it to ... almost anyone willing to pay for it.

Many people are not even aware that data brokers exist. There is currently little regulation concerning what they cannot collect (except for medical records and data used to determine your credit rating or your eligibility for housing, employment, or insurance). Nor are they required to let you see what data they have collected about you.

The companies who purchase your data can use sophisticated data mining techniques to put together the separate little dots of information about you to form a startlingly complete picture, including your age, marital status, children's ages, ethnicity, income level, hobbies, education level, occupation, buying habits, and vacation destinations. They may even know your potential health conditions—do you do a lot of online searching for super-size clothes or for diet information?

What Your Smartphone Photo Knows

If you take a photo with your smartphone, the image file probably contains much more than just the image. This metadata (data about data, in this case, data about the image) may tell the local time when the photo was taken, the exact location where it was taken (GPS coordinates), information about the make and model of the camera, the size of the image file (in MB), and the dimensions of the image in pixels. All this metadata is transmitted as part of the image file when you email it or post it online. This makes it handy to catalog your photos or remind you where you were when a photo was taken, but if the photo is publicly viewed there may be privacy issues. For example, if a photo shows your lovely home (and gives its exact location), it may become a target for a break-in. (It is possible to disable the smartphone's location-information feature, but the details on how to do this vary by manufacturer. If this feature is totally disabled, then other smartphone apps such as driving directions will not work, either.)

According to its 2016 annual report, data broker Acxiom Corporation had by then collected data on over 700 million individuals, using that data to conduct over 1 trillion transactions per week with over 3000 clients. These clients come from all sectors of the economy, including financial services, retail, telecommunications, insurance, technology, healthcare, travel, entertainment, non-profit, and government. Acxiom's goal is to enable those clients "to reach audiences with highly relevant messages." Part of that goal is achieved by providing not just raw data, but categories of consumer "labels" such as "Expectant Parent," "Number of Bedrooms," "Delinquent Tax Flag," "Diabetic Focus," and many more. (Note that such data may be useful for political campaigns where the client is trying to influence not your purchase, but your vote.) Acxiom does allow consumers to see and correct information that Acxiom holds about them.

Advertising targeted to your individual profile can sometimes be helpful, such as information on sales of baby formula to expectant mothers. However, privacy experts fear that such classifications could lead to targeting vulnerable groups, for example, predatory loan offers to people with considerable debt or exclusions of high-risk patients from opportunities to purchase health services. In addition to this, you just might feel that some of your personal data should remain private.

Companies need not turn to a data broker to collect information. Retail companies such as Target, Amazon, grocery stores, and so forth can collect data about your shopping habits at the point of sale, then apply data mining to more effectively target advertising to your particular circumstances or interests.

14.4.3 For the Greater Good

We've perhaps painted a rather unsettling picture of data mining with respect to personal privacy. However, the main societal impact of data mining is the positive contributions it can make to science, medicine, ecology, and so many other fields. Without going into details, we'll give four diverse examples.

- The December 2016 issue of *The Journal of Infectious Diseases* was devoted entirely to the use of Big Data for infectious disease surveillance and modeling. One article discusses the possible use of global positioning data obtained from cell phone usage to reveal population movements that can help drive the spread of epidemic diseases.

- Data-mining techniques have been applied to data sets of housing prices. A research team in India in 2016 used data mining on previous market trends and home prices to develop a model that predicts future trends and prices. This has two-fold benefits. For consumers, given their housing priorities and budget constraints, this helps pinpoint the most suitable areas for house-hunting. For developers (home builders), this can guide development plans and help reduce financial risk.

- The aerospace industry is awash with data. The Boeing 787 Dreamliner is a long-haul, twin-engine jet plane that first entered commercial service in 2011. Due to the many sensors on the plane, a single flight can produce terabytes of data. But, quoting a Boeing engineer, "Big Data by itself doesn't produce any value. The value really comes from being able to look at the data through algorithms, machine learning, and data mining that help you pull out the information and then analyze the results and transform that data into right decisions." (This is pretty much our definition of data science!) For Boeing, data mining can help with design decisions, performance during flight, warnings of anomalous conditions, and many other aspects of safely and efficiently building, flying, and maintaining such complex machines.

- The "Ancientbiotics team" is a group of medievalists, microbiologists, medicinal chemists, parasitologists, pharmacists and data scientists from multiple universities and countries. Yes, medievalists—authorities on that period of time otherwise known as the European Middle Ages, from the 5th to the 15th centuries. This period is also known as the Dark Ages, implying ignorance or, at best, little social or scientific progress. Not so fast, says this team of researchers, who are using modern data science tools to extract information from medieval "recipes" for treating infections. This research can address a crucial issue, which is that current antibiotics are proving ineffective against microbes that have developed resistance to these drugs. If no solutions are found to this problem, it is estimated that by 2050, 10 million people will die annually from drug-resistant infections. The team translated a 1000-year-old recipe for treating eye infections, recreated the "potion," and tested it. To their astonishment, early lab results show that the resulting "antibiotic" is extremely effective in combatting MSRA, a very potent drug-resistant bacterium that is a major problem for modern hospitals. Now the team is on the hunt for other potential medicines from the Middle Ages.

14.5 Conclusion

In this chapter, we've looked at ecommerce—an important application of computing. You've learned that there is much more involved in a retail web business than simply creating a webpage, and that technical areas of computer science such as information security, networking, and databases play a critical role. You've also seen new models of ecommerce and electronic payment that have become hugely popular. We went on to examine in more detail how databases work. Finally, we looked at some aspects of data science, including some of the tools it uses, its impact on personal privacy, and its potential for problem-solving in many important areas.

In Chapter 15, we will look at another application of computer science, one that has long captured the public's attention through its depiction in science-fiction literature and movies—artificial intelligence.

EXERCISES

1. Find an example of what you consider an excellent retail website. Comment on

   a. The use of color and white space.
   b. The ease of navigation.
   c. The taxonomy.
   d. Whether the site displays its privacy policy.
   e. Whether the site displays a security assurance.
   f. Your experience walking through the online purchase process (of course, cancel before you commit to the final purchase!). Are you in control and informed at each step?

2. Find an example of what you would consider a poor retail website. Use the same list as for Exercise 1 and note the differences you find.

3. Depending on your web browser, you may be able to locate a folder or a file on your machine that contains cookies. Look through the folder or open the file. List references to three websites you have visited.

4. Using the *Employees* table of Figure 14.6, what is the result of the following SQL query?

   ```
   SELECT * FROM Employees
   WHERE HoursWorked < 100;
   ```

5. Write an SQL query that retrieves first and last names and pay rate, ordered by *PayRate*, from the *Employees* table of Figure 14.6.

6. Using the *Employees* table of Figure 14.6 and the *InsurancePolicies* table of Figure 14.7, what is the result of the following SQL query? (The # marks allow the date to be treated numerically.)

   ```
   SELECT ID, PlanType
   FROM Employees, InsurancePolicies
   WHERE Birthdate > #1/01/1980#
   AND ID = EmployeeID;
   ```

7. Using the *Employees* table of Figure 14.6 and the *InsurancePolicies* table of Figure 14.7, write an SQL query that retrieves first and last names, hours worked, and insurance plan types for all employees who have worked fewer than 100 hours.

8. Figure 14.8 describes the attributes in an *InsurancePlans* table. Write some possible tuples for this table.

9. Assuming the existence of an *InsurancePlans* table as described in Figure 14.8, write an SQL query that retrieves the employee first and last name, insurance plan type, and monthly cost for John Kay's insurance.

The following information applies to Exercises 10–14.

You are working for the ABC Clinic, a small medical clinic that is open 7 days per week. The clinic would like to generate a reminder telephone call to clinic patients the day before their scheduled appointments. A vendor has a software application that will do this, given the appropriate data from the clinic database. You have been asked to investigate how to obtain the necessary data from the clinic's relational database. You are to begin with a small test database.

The following figure shows the entities in the clinic database, namely, doctors, patients, and clinic appointments.

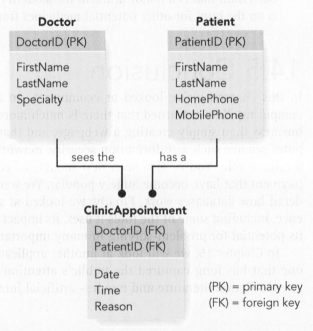

The following test data has been loaded into the tables. All fields are data type Text, that is the data are treated as character strings, except for AppDate and AppTime, which are type Date/Time.

Doctor

DoctorID	FirstName	LastName	Specialty
DO1	Vladimir	Yevgeny	Internal medicine
DO2	Nancy	Cooper	Internal medicine
DO3	Estelle	Villanueva	Dermatology
DO4	Anne	Davis	Gynecology
DO5	Michael	Roth	Pediatrics

Patient

PatientID	First Name	Last Name	Home Phone	Cell Phone
PA1	Craig	Martin	333-999-1212	333-410-9999
PA2	Gail	Perez	333-777-1212	333-410-7777
PA3	DuWayne	Martin	332-555-1212	332-317-1234
PA4	Gordon	Zhang	332-555-9999	332-217-4321

ClinicAppointment

Doctor ID	Patient ID	AppDate	AppTime	Reason
DO1	PA1	2/27/2018	11:30 AM	Infected finger
DO1	PA3	2/27/2018	1:00 PM	Chest pains
DO3	PA4	2/28/2018	10:30 AM	Poison ivy
DO4	PA2	2/28/2018	8:30 AM	Prenatal check

10. Write three SQL queries to display the full contents of each of the three tables.

11. Now write a query to return the information used by the reminder program. The query must take a date and return the doctor's first and last name, the patient's first and last name and both phone numbers, and the appointment time, so it can produce a voice message of the form:

"<Patient's name> **has an appointment with doctor** <Doctor's name> **at** <Appointment time> **on** <Appointment date>."

Write the query to obtain data for all patients for February 28, 2018. (*Hint*: Your query will need two Join operations. Also, there are attributes in both the *Doctor* and *Patient* tables with the same names. You will need to qualify them with their table names, for example, *Doctor.FirstName*.)

Show the results of your query.

12. Someone has suggested that if the clinic is going to remind the patients, they should also remind the doctors. The query must take the doctor's ID and a date and return the doctor's first and last name and the appointment time so it can produce a voice message of the form:

"**Doctor** <Doctor's name>, **you have an appointment at** <Appointment time> **on** <Appointment date>."

Write the query to obtain data for all appointments for DoctorID DO1 on 2/27/2018, ordered by appointment time. Show the results of your query.

13. What would it take to allow the patient to call in, give his or her patient ID, select a date using the touch pad on the phone, and have the system tell him or her by voice the time of the appointment on the date specified along with the doctor's name? The query must take the date and PatientID and return the doctor's first and last name, the patient's first and last name, and the appointment time and date so it can produce a voice message of the form:

"<Patient's name> **has an appointment with** <Doctor's name> **on** <Appointment date> **at** <Appointment time>."

Write the query for PatientID PA3 on 2/27/2018. Show the results of your query.

14. The following decision tree was obtained by data mining from 10,000 medical records concerning factors that may influence the incidence of a certain disease. The leaves of the decision tree reflect a low/high propensity to develop the disease where a low incidence is < 50% of the individuals in that classification, and a high incidence is ≥ 50%. The percentage is shown along with the low/high classification. Based on this decision tree, what would you conclude about the relative weight of age, obesity, or high blood pressure as a risk factor for developing this disease?

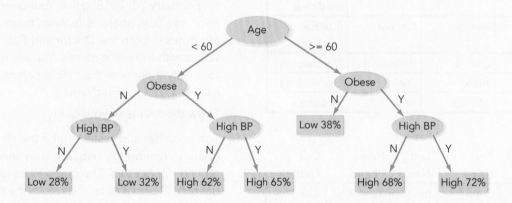

15. As mentioned earlier, a spreadsheet can provide a lot of statistical information on a data set. Using Excel, open a blank spreadsheet and enter the data shown here. Save the file.

X	Y	Smoker	Overweight	Low_Income
4	2	28	19	32
6	2	31	22	28
3	4	24	31	35
5	7	18	25	25
2	6	32	29	34
4	5	41	35	37

a. Using the Formulas tab in Excel, find functions to compute the minimum, median, average (mean), maximum for each of the data columns. Compare your results with the values produced by R (page 511). (You might want to format your cells to 2 decimal places for easier comparison.) Save the file.

b. Excel can create a chart of the data set similar to Figure 10.9. Select your data, then under the Excel Insert tab, select Column, then the first choice under 2-D Column. You should get a column chart, but comparing to Figure 10.9, it's not quite what you want. (Hint: Right-click in the chart area and choose Select Data. Make some adjustment there so your chart matches Figure 10.9, except the colors won't be as bright!) Save the file.

c. For more complex analysis, you will need to install the Data Analysis Tools as an Excel Add-In. To do this, go to File/Options and select Add-Ins. Find and select Analysis ToolPak, then click Go. In the Add-Ins dialog box, check the box for Analysis ToolPak and click OK. Finally, when you click the Data tab on your spreadsheet, you should see a Data Analysis group.

Click Data Analysis, select Descriptive Statistics, and click OK. To easily identify the Input Range (the data you want to work with), click the little worksheet button at the end of the Input Range textbox, drag your mouse over the data, then click the worksheet button again. Check the "Labels in First Row" box. Select the Output Range in the same way as you did the Input Range, then click Summary Statistics, and then OK. You should get the same results as you got in part (a), plus a whole lot more! Finally,

click Data Analysis, select Correlation, and follow the same steps as before. Compare your results with the last R table on page 512.

CHALLENGE WORK

1. Referring to the ABC Clinic database, Dr. Yevgeny has scheduled DuWayne Martin to return at the same time two days after his appointment on February 27 for another check on his chest pain. What happens when you try to add this record to the current *ClinicAppointment* table? Redesign the Clinic Appointment table so that you can add this record. After you add the record, write the SQL query to display the resulting *ClinicAppointment* table, ordered by appointment date, then appointment time. Show the results of your query.

2. Write a report on some aspect of data science as applied to a field of interest for you. What is the question (problem) to be answered (solved)? Give a nontechnical description of the data being used. Have any conclusions or solutions been reached? (*Hint*: You won't get far by just searching online for "data science"; try something like "data science [or data mining or Big Data] in psychology", for example.)

Artificial Intelligence

AFTER STUDYING THIS CHAPTER, YOU WILL BE ABLE TO:

- Describe the two types of artificial intelligence
- Explain the pros and cons of various knowledge representation methods
- Explain the parts of a simple neural network, how it works, and how it can incorporate machine learning
- Describe how intelligent state-space search algorithms work
- Give examples of possible usage for each of the following: swarm intelligence, intelligent agents, and expert systems
- Explain what a robot is, and list some tasks for which robots are currently suited
- Explain what a drone is, and list some tasks drones can perform

15.1 Introduction

Artificial intelligence (AI) is the branch of computer science that explores techniques for incorporating aspects of intelligence into computer systems. This definition, however, raises more questions than it answers. What really is "intelligence"? Is it a uniquely human attribute? If a computer system exhibits behavior that we might characterize as intelligent, does that make it truly intelligent? What sorts of behaviors demonstrate intelligence?

Alan Turing, whose investigations into the fundamental nature of computation led to the Turing machine (Chapter 12), was also interested in artificial intelligence. In 1950, before the term *artificial intelligence* was coined,[1] he proposed a test to measure the intelligent behavior of machines. The Turing test allows a human to interrogate two entities, both hidden from the interrogator (Figure 15.1). One entity is a human and the other a machine (a computer). The interrogator can ask the entities questions and receive their responses. The communication is carried on in some form that does not alone reveal which entity is the computer; for example, the interrogator's questions could be typed on a keyboard and the responses printed out. If, as a result of this questioning, the interrogator is unable to determine which entity is the human and which is

---

[1] John McCarthy, in 1955, was the first to use the term *artificial intelligence*. At that time he was a mathematics professor at Dartmouth College; in 1956 he organized the first Artificial Intelligence conference. He went on to start AI labs at MIT and Stanford, design the LISP programming language, and win the 1971 Turing Award.

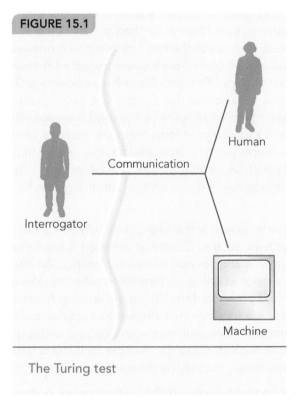

FIGURE 15.1

Human

Communication

Interrogator

Machine

The Turing test

the computer, then the computer has exhibited sufficiently human intelligence to pass the Turing test. This test does not explore the nature of human intelligence in a deep philosophical way; it merely says that if a machine exhibits behavior indistinguishable from that of a human, then how can we tell the difference—a question that has been explored more than once in science fiction.

We need to distinguish between *general artificial intelligence* and *narrow artificial intelligence*. The aim of general artificial intelligence is to model

Victory in the Turing Test?

Numerous Turing test competitions have been held over the years, but no computer had sufficiently convinced its interrogators of its "humanity" until June 2014. On the 60th anniversary of Alan Turing's death, a Turing test competition was held at the Royal Society in London. A *chatbot* (chatter robot or chatterbot) pretended to be a 13-year-old boy from Ukraine named Eugene Goostman. Goostman (let's call it by the name the chatbot claimed) held 30 five-minute sessions involving a total of 10 interrogators. And in 33% of these conversations, Goostman won, that is, "he" was proclaimed to be the human. The passing score for the test was 30%. Goostman had scored 29% in a 2012 competition, so evidently "he" had gotten a little smarter since then. More impressive, this was the first Turing test with open-ended questions allowed, rather than one in which questions were set ahead of time or could only pertain to a specific topic. The software powering Goostman was indeed remarkable. It was clever that the storyline had Goostman as an adolescent, presumably speaking English as a second language. This justified Goostman's lack of knowledge in some areas and perhaps some bad grammar. The software developers also incorporated a rather cocky attitude, a tendency to change the subject, and a little wackiness in Goostman's responses. All of this typical teenage behavior made a more convincing case for Goostman's "humanness."

But some AI experts claim that the Turing test really isn't a test of human intelligence, and that a win such as Goostman achieved is more misdirection and fakery than a demonstration of true human intelligence. An alternative challenge has been proposed based on something called the *Winograd schema* in honor of Stanford professor Terry Winograd, an early AI researcher. A Winograd schema is a sentence that involves two entities and a pronoun that refers back to one of the two entities; the challenge is to decide to which entity the pronoun refers. Such challenges are simple for humans based on life experience or common sense, but may be difficult for a computer. For example,

> *John couldn't see the stage with Billy in front of him because he is so short.*[2]
> Who is so short, John or Billy?

Obviously (responds the human), the "he" refers to John. Note that if "short" were changed to "tall," the answer would be Billy; this one-word change that switches the answer is also a required feature of a Winograd schema.

[2]Levesque, H., Davis, E., and Morgenstern, L., *The Winograd Schema Challenge.* See *http://www .aaai.org/ocs/index.php/KR/KR12/paper/view/4492/4924*

human intelligence, that is, all aspects of human intelligence, or at least as many as possible. This includes the capability for understanding natural language and nuances of meaning; the ability to accumulate knowledge and adapt that knowledge to apply it to new situations or problems; being able to interpret sensory information and then draw reasonable conclusions from it; a lot of "common sense"; and finally some amount of emotional empathy (remember how Commander Data of *Star Trek* fame always wanted an "emotion chip"?).

General artificial intelligence was the original thrust of artificial intelligence research. And much progress has been made in natural language understanding, machine learning, facial recognition, and other areas. Conversely, attempts to model human intelligence within a computer have in turn made contributions to *cognitive science*, the study of how humans think and learn. But just as we learned in Chapter 13 that a model cannot capture all aspects of the physical phenomenon it represents, so artificial intelligence cannot (yet) capture all aspects of human intelligence. Science fiction conjures scenarios of thinking and all-knowing computers controlling the world, but the advances in general artificial intelligence have been far more modest.

The most visible successes have occurred in the area of narrow artificial intelligence, which focuses on solving very particular kinds of problems. The skills involved here are more specific, often based on large amounts of data. Game playing, expert systems, robotics, and recommendation systems are areas of great success for narrow artificial intelligence systems. When you ask questions of Siri, Alexa, Cortana, or Google Assistant, those systems are accessing a giant database of possibly pertinent facts. No real human-like conversation is going to develop out of that. For example:[3]

> You: *"Siri I'm bleeding really bad can you call me an ambulance?"*
> Siri: *"From now on, I'll call you 'an ambulance.' OK?"*

15.2 A Division of Labor

To understand better what artificial intelligence is all about, let's consider a division of task types. Humans can perform a great variety of tasks, but we'll divide them into three categories, representative but by no means exhaustive:

- *Computational tasks*
  - Adding a column of numbers
  - Sorting a list of numbers into numerical order
  - Searching for a given name in a list of names
  - Managing a payroll
  - Calculating trajectory adjustments for a space shuttle

---

[3] http://www.quertime.com/article/30-really-funny-siri-responses-to-weird-questions/

- *Recognition tasks*
  - Recognizing your best friend
  - Understanding the spoken word
  - Finding the tennis ball in the grass in your back yard
- *Reasoning tasks*
  - Planning what to wear today
  - Deciding on the strategic direction a company should follow for the next five years
  - Running the triage center in a hospital emergency room after an earthquake

Algorithmic solutions exist for computational tasks (we devised algorithms for sorting and searching in the early chapters of this book). As humans, we can, in principle at least, follow these step-by-step instructions. Computational tasks are also tasks for which accurate answers must be found—sometimes very quickly—and that's where we as humans fall down. We make mistakes, we get bored, and we aren't very speedy. Computers are better (faster and more accurate) at performing computational tasks, provided they are given programs that correctly embody the algorithms. Throughout this book, with its emphasis on algorithms, we've been talking a great deal about designing procedures to solve computational tasks, learning how to translate these procedures into a programming language, and designing machines to execute the resulting programs.

Humans are often better at recognition tasks. We should perhaps expand the name of this task type to sensory/recognition/motor-skills tasks because we receive information through our senses (primarily seeing and hearing), we recognize or "make sense of" the information we receive, and we often respond to the information with some sort of physical response that involves controlled movement. Although we wait until elementary school to learn how to add, an infant just a few weeks old, on seeing its mother's face, recognizes that face and smiles; soon that infant understands the spoken word. You spot the tennis ball in the yard even though it is green and nestled in among other green things (grass, dandelions). You register whether the tennis ball is close or far away, and you manipulate your legs and feet to propel you in the right direction.

How do we do these things? Traditional step-by-step procedural algorithms don't seem to apply, or if they do, we have not yet learned what those algorithms are. Rather, it seems that we as humans succeed at these tasks by processing a huge amount of data and then matching the results against an even larger storehouse of data based on our past experiences. Consider the task of recognizing your best friend. You have, in effect, been shown a number of "pictures" of your friend's face that seem to be "burned into" your memory, along with pictures of the faces of everyone else you know well. When you see your friend, you sort through your mental picture file until you come to a match. It is a bit more complicated than that, however, because if you encounter your friend's sister, you might know who it is even though you have never met her before. If your friend has a different haircut or has started wearing glasses, you will most likely still recognize her or him, in spite of a changed appearance. It would seem that you do not need to find an exact match to one of the images in your mental picture file, but only a reasonably close approximation. Approximation, unlike the exactitude required in computational tasks, is good enough. These complex recognition tasks that we find so easy can be difficult for computers, although facial detection (to aid in focusing) is now a feature of some digital cameras and facial recognition is a part of some photo management software as well as programs used by law enforcement to identify criminals entering a building or boarding an airplane.

When humans perform reasoning tasks, they are also using a large storehouse of experience. This experience involves not just images but also cause-and-effect situations. You know that you should wear a coat when it's cold because you've experienced discomfort in cold weather when you didn't wear a coat. This could be considered "mere" commonsense reasoning, but getting a computer to mimic common sense, to say nothing of higher-order conceptual, planning, or reasoning tasks, is extremely challenging. There may be no "right" answer to such tasks, and the way humans arrive at their respective answers sometimes seems ambiguous or based at least in part on intuition, which may be just another name for knowledge or reasoning that we don't yet understand.

Figure 15.2 summarizes what we've outlined as the relative capabilities of humans and computers in these three types of tasks. Computers fall below humans when procedural algorithms either don't work or aren't known, and when there seems to be a high level of complexity and perhaps approximation or ambiguity. Artificial intelligence seeks ways to improve the computer's ability to perform recognition and reasoning tasks, and we'll look

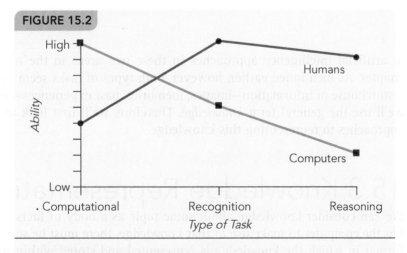

FIGURE 15.2

Human and computer capabilities

Predicted AI Milestones

In 2015, a group of academic and industry experts in artificial intelligence from around the world were asked to predict when they thought artificial intelligence would be able to outperform humans at various tasks. The average opinions on a few of these tasks were as follows:

Translate languages	2024
Assemble any LEGO kit	2024
Win at the game of Go[4]	2028
Drive a truck	2027
Write a *New York Times* best-seller	2049
Perform surgery	2053
All human jobs	2136

Of course, these are only predictions, so they must be taken with much skepticism. Still, do you suppose the citizens of 1900 would have predicted that the first commercial flight school would be opened 10 years later?

---

[4]Read more about artificial intelligence and the game of Go in Section 15.5.5 of this chapter.

at artificial intelligence approaches in these two areas in the rest of this chapter. As mentioned earlier, however, both types of tasks seem to require a storehouse of information—images, memories, past experiences—for which we'll use the general term *knowledge*. Therefore, we'll first look at various approaches to representing this knowledge.

15.3 Knowledge Representation

We can consider knowledge about some topic as a body of facts or truths. For the computer to make use of that knowledge, there must be some digital format in which the knowledge is represented and stored within the computer. (At the lowest level, of course, only 0s and 1s are stored within the computer, but strings of 0s and 1s are organized and interpreted at a higher level of abstraction—as integers or characters, for example.) For computational tasks, the relevant knowledge is often isolated numeric or textual items. This is the data that we've manipulated with procedural programs. What about more complex knowledge?

There are many workable representation schemes; let's consider four possibilities.

1. *Natural language*—A paragraph or a page of text that contains all the knowledge we are trying to capture is written in English, Chinese, Spanish, or some other natural language. Here is an example:

   Spot is a brown dog and, like any dog, has four legs and a tail. Also like any dog, Spot is a mammal, which means Spot is warm-blooded.

   Note that although this representational form is text, it is text in a different sense from the character strings that are used in computational tasks. Here it is not simply the strings of characters that are important but also the meaning that those strings of characters convey. When reading a natural language paragraph, we use our understanding of the richness of the language's vocabulary to extract the meaning. Some researchers believe that the words we read or hear do not actually communicate meaning, but merely act as "triggers" to meanings stored in our brains.

2. *Formal language*—A formal language sacrifices richness of expression for precision of expression. Attributes and cause-and-effect relationships are more explicitly stated. A formal language version of the foregoing natural language paragraph might look like this:

   Spot is a dog.

   Spot is brown.

   Every dog has four legs.

   Every dog has a tail.

   Every dog is a mammal.

   Every mammal is warm-blooded.

   The term *language* was used in Chapter 11 to mean the set of statements derivable by using the rules of a grammar. But here, the term formal language means the language of formal logic, usually expressed more symbolically than we have done in this example. In the notation of formal logic, we might use $dog(x)$ to symbolize that the symbolic entity x has the attribute of being a dog and $brown(x)$ to mean that x has the attribute of being brown. Similarly $four\text{-}legged(x)$, $tail(x)$, $mammal(x)$, and $warm\text{-}blooded(x)$ could symbolize that x has these various attributes. The specific entity Spot could be represented by S. Then $dog(S)$ would mean that Spot has the attribute of being a dog. Cause-and-effect relationships are translated into "if-then" statements. Thus, "Every dog has four legs" is equivalent to "For every x, if x is a dog, then x has four legs." An arrow symbolizes cause and effect (if-then); "If x is a dog, then x has four legs" would be written symbolically as

$$dog(x) \rightarrow four\text{-}legged(x)$$

To show that every x that has the dog property also has the four-legged property, we would use a *universal quantifier*, $(\forall x)$, which means "for every x." Therefore,

$$(\forall x)(dog(x) \rightarrow four\text{-}legged(x))$$

means "For every x, if x is a dog, then x has four legs" or "Every dog has four legs." Symbolically, the preceding six formal language statements become

Natural Language Statement	*Symbolic Representation*
Spot is a dog.	$dog(S)$
Spot is brown.	$brown(S)$
Every dog has four legs.	$(\forall x)(dog(x) \rightarrow four\text{-}legged(x))$
Every dog has a tail.	$(\forall x)(dog(x) \rightarrow tail(x))$
Every dog is a mammal.	$(\forall x)(dog(x) \rightarrow mammal(x))$
Every mammal is warm-blooded.	$(\forall x)(mammal(x) \rightarrow warm\text{-}blooded(x))$

The use of formal languages represents one of the major approaches to building artificial intelligence systems. Intelligent behavior is achieved by using symbols to represent knowledge and by manipulating these symbols according to well-defined rules. We'll see an example of this when we discuss expert systems later in this chapter.

3. *Pictorial*—Information can be stored in pictorial form as an image—a grid of pixels that have attributes of shading and color. Using this representation, we might have a picture of Spot, showing that he is brown and has four legs and a tail. We might have some additional labeling that says something like, "This is Spot, the dog." This visual representation might contain additional knowledge about Spot's appearance that is not embodied in the natural language paragraph or the formal language statements, but it would also fail to capture the knowledge that Spot is a mammal and that mammals are warm-blooded. It also wouldn't tell us that all dogs have four legs and a tail. (After all, a photo of a three-legged dog does not tell us that all dogs have three legs.)

4. *Graphical*—Here, we are using the term *graphical* not in the sense of "visual" (we have already talked about pictorial representation) but in the mathematical sense of a graph with nodes and connecting arcs. Figure 15.3 is such a graph, also called a semantic net, for our dog example. In the terminology of object orientation that was a feature of the programming language(s) of Chapter 9, the rectangular nodes represent classes or objects, the oval nodes represent properties, and the arcs

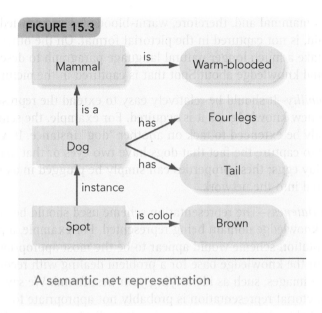

FIGURE 15.3

A semantic net representation

represent relationships. The "is a" relationship represents a subclass of a class that inherits properties from the parent class; "dog" is a subclass of "mammal," and any dog object inherits all the properties of mammals in general, such as being warm-blooded. Objects from the dog class may also have properties of their own. The "instance" relationship shows that something is an object of a class; Spot is a particular object from the dog class and may have a unique property not necessarily shared by all dogs. The "is", "has", "is color" relationships specify properties of a class (the "mammal" class or the "dog'" class) or of a specific object (Spot).

Any knowledge representation scheme that we select must have the following four characteristics:

1. *Adequacy*—The representation method must be adequate to capture all of the relevant knowledge. Because of its rich, expressive powers, a natural language representation will surely capture a lot of knowledge. However, it might be difficult to extract exactly what that knowledge is. You might have to wade through a lot of unnecessary verbiage (as we discussed in Chapter 2, this is the reason for using pseudocode instead of natural language to describe an algorithm), and you must also understand the nuances of meaning within the natural language. A formal language representation has the advantage of extracting the essentials.

2. *Efficiency*—We want the representational form to be minimalist, avoiding redundant information wherever possible. This means allowing some knowledge that is not explicitly represented to be inferred from the knowledge that is explicitly represented. In the preceding example, it is easy to infer from the natural language, the formal language, or the semantic net that because Spot is a dog, he has four legs and a tail and

also is a mammal and, therefore, warm-blooded. This knowledge, as we have said, is not captured in the pictorial format. On the other hand, it would take a much longer natural language paragraph to describe all the additional knowledge about Spot that is captured in the picture.

3. *Extendability*—It should be relatively easy to extend the representation to include new knowledge as it is acquired. For example, the semantic net can easily be extended to tack on another "dog" instance. It would also be easy to capture the fact that dogs have two eyes or that mammals do not lay eggs; these properties can simply be plugged in as new ovals connected into the network.

4. *Appropriateness*—The representation scheme used should be appropriate for the knowledge domain being represented. For example, a pictorial representation scheme would appear to be the most appropriate way to represent the knowledge base for a problem dealing with recognition of visual images, such as identifying your best friend. We saw before that a pictorial representation is probably not appropriate for the kind of knowledge about Spot that is difficult to display visually. The level of granularity needed for the intended application might also influence the appropriateness of a particular scheme. Is a given pictorial representation sufficient, or do we need to "zoom in" and expose more detail? The appropriate representational form for knowledge therefore depends on the knowledge to be captured and on the type of task for which the knowledge is to be used.

Practice Problems

1. Write a natural language paragraph that describes the concept of a hamburger. Now draw a semantic net that incorporates the same knowledge as your natural language description. Which one is easier for you to produce?

2. Convert the following natural language statements to formal symbolic representation, using the properties sandwich(x), hamburger(x), grilledCheese(x), onBread(x), vegetarian(x):

Every hamburger is a sandwich

Every grilled cheese is a sandwich

All sandwiches are on bread

Every grilled cheese is vegetarian

15.4 Recognition Tasks

If artificial intelligence aims to make computers "think" like humans, then it is natural to investigate and perhaps attempt to mimic the way the human brain functions. It is estimated that the human brain contains about 86 billion neurons. Each *neuron* is a cell capable of receiving stimuli, in the form of electrochemical signals, from other neurons through its many *dendrites* (Figure 15.4). In turn, it can send stimuli to other neurons through its single *axon*. The axon of a neuron does not directly connect with the dendrites of other neurons; rather, it sends signals over small gaps called *synapses*. Some of the synapses appear to send the neuron activating stimuli, whereas others seem to send inhibiting stimuli. A single neuron collects all the stimuli passing through all the synapses around its dendrites. The neuron sums the activating (positive) and inhibiting (negative) stimuli it receives and compares the result with an internal "threshold" value. If the sum equals or exceeds the threshold value, then the neuron "fires," sending its own signal down its axon to affect other neurons.

Each neuron can be thought of as an extremely simple computational device with a single on/off output. The power of the human brain lies in the vast number of neurons, the many interconnections between them, and the activating/inhibiting nature of those connections. To borrow a term from computer science, the human brain uses a connectionist architecture, characterized by a large number of simple "processors" with multiple interconnections. This contrasts quite noticeably with the Von Neumann architecture discussed in Chapter 5 that is still the basis for most computers today. In that model, there are a small number (maybe only one) of very powerful processors with a limited number of interconnections between them. Even the fast-

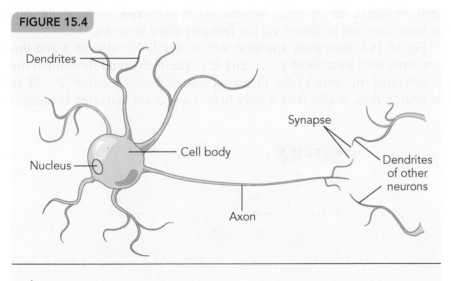

FIGURE 15.4

Dendrites

Nucleus

Cell body

Axon

Synapse

Dendrites
of other
neurons

A neuron

est parallel computer in the world as of 2016 had a little over 10.5 million processors rather than the 86 billion found in the human brain—about 0.01%.

In some areas of the brain, an individual neuron may collect signals from as many as 100,000 other neurons and send signals to an equally large number of neurons. This extensive parallelism is evidently required because of the relatively slow time frame within which a neuron fires. In the human brain, neurons operate on a time scale of milliseconds (thousandths of a second), as opposed to the nanoseconds (billionths of a second) in which computer operations are measured, a difference of 6 orders of magnitude. In a human processing task that takes about 1/10 second (recognition of your friend's face), the number of steps that can be executed by a single neuron would be on the order of 100. In the same time period, a typical computer processor could perform about 1 billion machine language operations. To carry out the complexity of a recognition task, then, requires the parallel activities of a large number of neurons executing cooperatively within this short time frame. In addition, massive parallelism supplies redundancy so that information is not stored only in one place but is shared within the network of neurons. Thus, the deterioration of a limited number of individual neurons (a process that happens constantly as biological cells wear out) does not cause a failure of the information processing capabilities of the network.

Artificial intelligence systems for recognition tasks have tried to mimic this connectionist approach. *Artificial neural networks*, usually just called neural networks, can be created by simulating individual neurons in hardware and connecting them in a massively parallel network of simple devices that act somewhat like biological neurons. Alternatively, the effect of a neural network may be simulated in software on an ordinary sequential-processing computer. In either case, each neuron has a threshold value, and its incoming lines carry weights that represent stimuli. The neuron fires when the sum of the incoming weights equals or exceeds its threshold value; the input lines are activated via the firing of other neurons.

Figure 15.5 represents a neuron with a threshold value of 3 and three input lines with weights of 2, -1, and 2, respectively. If all three input lines are activated, the sum of the incoming signals is $2 + (-1) + 2 = 3$ and the neuron fires. It also fires if only lines 1 and 3 are activated because the

FIGURE 15.5

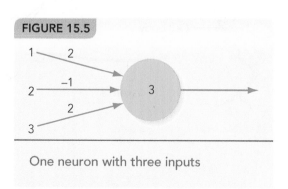

One neuron with three inputs

sum of the incoming signals is then $2 + 2 = 4 > 3$. Any other combination of activated input lines cannot carry sufficient stimulation to fire the neuron. (Real, biological neurons fire with intensities that vary through a continuous range but, as usual, our simplified computer representation of such analog values uses a set of discrete values.)

Figure 15.6 depicts a neural net with an input layer and an output layer of neurons. An input value x_i is presented to neuron N_j in the input layer via a line with signal strength $x_i \times w_{ij}$. The values of x_i are usually binary (0 or 1), so that this line carries a signal of either 0 when x is 0, or the weight w_{ij} when x_i is 1. The weights to the input neurons, as well as the weights from the input layer to the output layer, can be positive, negative, or zero.

In the neural network shown in Figure 15.7, we have eliminated connections of weight 0 and all remaining connections have weight 1. Here x_1 and x_2 have binary values of 0 or 1. If x_1 or x_2 or both have the value 1, then a signal of 1 is passed to one or both of the neurons in the input layer, causing one or both of them to fire, which causes the single neuron in the output layer to fire and produce an output of 1. If both x_1 and x_2 have

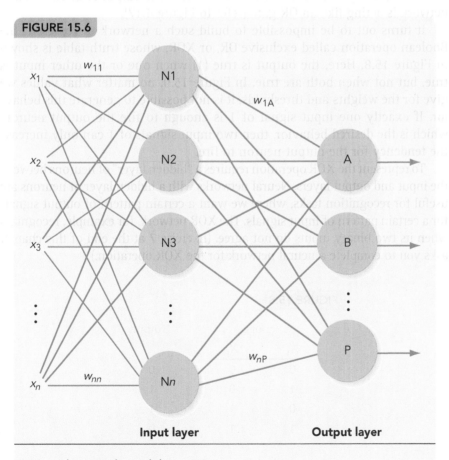

FIGURE 15.6

Input layer

Output layer

Neural network model

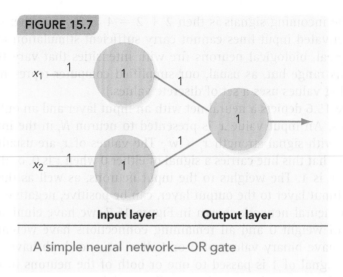

FIGURE 15.7

Input layer   Output layer

A simple neural network—OR gate

the value 0, then neither neuron in the input layer fires, the single neuron in the output layer does not fire, and the network output is 0. This neural network is acting like an OR gate (refer to Figure 4.17).

It turns out to be impossible to build such a network to represent the Boolean operation called exclusive OR, or XOR, whose truth table is shown in Figure 15.8. Here, the output is true (1) when one or the other input is true, but not when both are true. In Figure 15.9, no matter what values we give for the weights and thresholds, it is not possible to generate this behavior. If exactly one input signal of 1 is enough to fire the output neuron, which is the desired behavior, then two input signals of 1 can only increase the tendency for the output neuron to fire.

To represent the XOR operation requires a "hidden layer" of neurons between the input and output layers. Neural networks with a hidden layer of neurons are useful for recognition tasks, where we want a certain pattern of output signals for a certain pattern of input signals. The XOR network, for example, recognizes when its two binary inputs do not agree. (Exercise 7 at the end of this chapter asks you to complete a neural network for the XOR operation.)

FIGURE 15.8

Inputs		Output
X_1	X_2	
0	0	0
1	0	1
0	1	1
1	1	0

The truth table for XOR

FIGURE 15.9

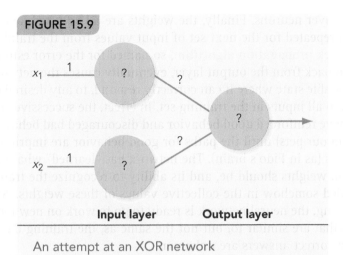

An attempt at an XOR network

Conventional computer processing works on a knowledge base where the information is stored as data in specific memory cells that can be accessed by the program as needed. In a neural network, both the knowledge representation and the "programming" are stored in the network itself as the weights of the connections and the thresholds of the neurons. If you want to build a neural network that performs in a certain way, how do you determine these values? In a simple network, trial and error can produce a solution, but such is not the case for a network with thousands of neurons. Fortunately, the right answer doesn't have to be found the first time. Remember that neural networks are modeled on the human brain; you learned to recognize your best friend through repeated "learning experiences" that modified your knowledge base until you came to associate certain features or characteristics with that individual.

Similarly, a neural network can learn from experience by modifying the weights on its connections (even making some connections "disappear" by assigning them 0 weights). A network can be given a set of weights and thresholds that is simply an initial educated guess. The network is then presented with training data, for which the correct outputs are known. The actual output from the network is compared with the correct output for one set of input values from the training data. For those output neurons that produce correct values, their threshold values and the weights on their inputs do not change. Output neurons that produce erroneous values can err in one of two ways. If an output neuron fires when it is not supposed to, then the positive (excitatory) input values coming into it are adjusted downward, and the negative (inhibitory) weights coming into it are adjusted upward. If it fails to fire when it is supposed to, the opposite adjustment is made. But before these adjustments take place, information on the errors is passed back from each erroneous output neuron to the neurons in the hidden layer that are connected to it. Each hidden-layer neuron adds these error counts to derive an estimate of its own error. This estimate is used to calculate the adjustments to be made on the weights of the connections coming to it from the input-layer neurons. Finally, the weights are all adjusted, and then the process is repeated for the next set of input values from the training data.

This back propagation algorithm, so named for the error estimates that are passed back from the output layer, eventually causes the network to settle into a stable state where it can correctly respond, to any desired degree of accuracy, to all inputs in the training set. In effect, the successive changes in weights have reinforced good behavior and discouraged bad behavior (much as we train our pets) until the paths for good behavior are imprinted on the connections (as in Fido's brain). The network has "learned" what the proper connection weights should be, and its ability to recognize the training data is embedded somehow in the collective values of these weights. At the end of its training, the neural network is ready to go to work on new recognition problems that are similar to, but not the same as, the training data and for which the correct answers are unknown.

This process is an example of machine learning, where, without specific step-by-step programming, computing agents learn and improve from past errors made on known training data. Then, when deemed sufficiently trained, they can be set loose on data with no known answers. Machine learning is also one of the tools of data science, where the objective is to discover previously unknown patterns in large amounts of data.

Neural networks have found their way into dozens of real-world applications. A few of these are handwriting recognition, speech recognition, identifying billing patterns indicative of credit card fraud, predicting the odds of susceptibility to cancer, analyzing magnetic resonance images in medicine, adapting mirror shapes for astronomical observations, and discovering the best routing algorithm in a large communications network (a problem we mentioned in Chapter 7). With the ever-decreasing cost of massively parallel networks, it appears that neural networks will continue to find new applications.

Brain on a Chip

In August 2014, IBM announced a new computer chip that mimics the way the brain works. The chip, called TrueNorth, consists of 4,096 "neurosynaptic" cores arranged in a 64 × 64 grid. Each core contains 256 programmable neurons (think of programming here as setting the neuron threshold to control whether the neuron fires) and 256 axons (think of these as input signals). Information travels from axons to neurons controlled by

programmable synapses (think of programming here as setting the weights on connection lines). Altogether the TrueNorth chip contains 5.4 billion transistors, over 1 million programmable neurons, and over 260 million programmable synapses. All this processing power consumes energy at about the rate of a hearing aid battery. And for scalability the chips can also be connected together. Talk about parallel processing!

This milestone chip is the result of work begun in 2008 funded by DARPA (Defense Advanced Research Projects Agency) under a program called Systems of Neuromorphic Adaptive Plastic Scalable Electronics, or SyNAPSE. An estimate, based on the number of neurons, is that TrueNorth has roughly the complexity of a honeybee's brain, which has approximately 960,000 neurons. So TrueNorth, while mimicking the way real neurons work in biological brains, has a long way to go to match human brainpower.

The trend in machine learning since 2012 has primarily been in so-called *deep learning.* Deep learning uses fairly standard computer architecture to simulate neural networks with multiple layers (that's where the "deep" comes in) and back propagation from the output layer all the way back to the input layer to improve accuracy, much as we have described. The focus is on developing neural networks for specific AI applications such as image recognition. However, in September 2016, IBM announced a breakthrough in the usefulness of TrueNorth. A new algorithm had been developed that allowed deep learning networks to be built on TrueNorth's brain-simulating hardware. The resulting new system has highly accurate image recognition capability while being scalable, much more energy efficient, and faster than traditional deep learning architectures.

Laboratory Experience 20

In this Laboratory Experience, you will train a neural network simulator for a character-recognition task. You can choose one or more characters to present to a neural network's input layer and then train the network to correctly recognize these characters. After the network is trained, you can input garbled variations of these characters that are similar to, but not identical to, the training data characters and test the network's ability to correctly identify them. You can vary the level of "garbling" in the input to see at what point the network fails in its recognition task.

Practice Problems

1. If input line 1 is stimulated in the following neural network (and line 2 is not stimulated), will the output line fire? Explain.

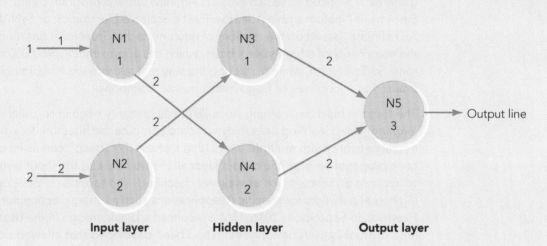

2. If the firing threshold on node N5 is changed from its current value of 3 to 5, under what conditions will it fire?

15.5 Reasoning Tasks

We noted that one of the characteristics of human reasoning seems to be the ability to draw on a large body of facts and past experience to come to a conclusion. In this section, we look at several ways in which artificial intelligence specialists are trying to get computers to emulate this characteristic.

15.5.1 Intelligent Searching

Earlier in this book, we presented two algorithms for searching—sequential search and binary search. These search algorithms look for a perfect match between a specific target value and an item in a list. The amount of work involved is $\Theta(n)$ for sequential search and $\Theta(\lg n)$ for binary search.

A *decision tree* for a search algorithm illustrates the possible next choices of items to search if the current item is not the target. In a sequential search, there is only one item to try next: the next item in the list. The decision tree for sequential search is therefore linear, as shown in Figure 15.10. A decision tree for a binary search (in which the search items are in sorted order), such as the one shown in Figure 15.11, reflects the fact that if the current item is

FIGURE 15.10

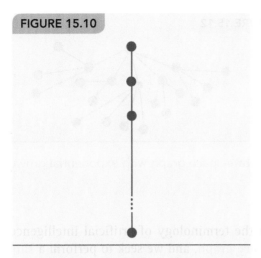

Decision tree for sequential search

FIGURE 15.11

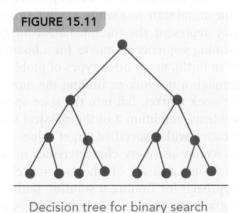

Decision tree for binary search

not the target, there are only two next choices: the midpoint of the sublist before this node or the midpoint of the sublist after this node. Furthermore, the binary search algorithm specifies which of the two nodes to try next.

The classical search problem benefits from two simplifications:

1. The search domain (the set of items being searched) is highly constrained. At each point in the search, if the target is not found, the choice of where to look next is determined.

2. We seek a perfect match, so the comparison of the target against the list item results in a binary decision—either they match or they do not.

Suppose, however, that condition 1 does not hold; the search domain is such that after any one node has been searched (unsuccessfully), there are an enormous number of potential next choices, and there is no algorithm to dictate which of these next choices is best. Figure 15.12 attempts to portray

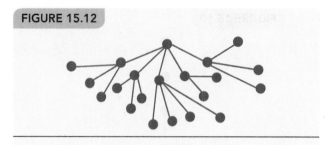

FIGURE 15.12

A state-space graph with exponential growth

this scenario. In the terminology of artificial intelligence, such a figure is called a state-space graph, and we seek to perform a state-space search to find a *solution path* through the graph. The idea is that each node of the graph represents a "state" of our problem, and we have some "goal state" or states in mind. For example, in a game of tic-tac-toe, our initial state is the empty game grid, and our goal state is a winning configuration. A solution path takes us from the initial state to a winning configuration, and the graph nodes along the way represent the intermediate configurations. In addition to finding a winning sequence of moves for a board game (tic-tac-toe, checkers, chess, and so forth), many other types of problems, such as finding the shortest path through a network or finding the most successful investment strategy in the stock market, fall into the state-space search category. In some of these problems, condition 2 of the classical search problem—that of seeking an exact match with a specified target value—is not present either. We simply want to acquire as many characteristics of the desired goal as possible, and we need some measure of when we are "close enough."

A *brute force* approach for finding a solution path traces all branches of the state-space graph so that all possible choices are tested and no test cases are repeated. This becomes a massive bookkeeping task because the number of branches grows exponentially. Given that time and computing resources are limited, an intelligent search needs to be employed. An intelligent search narrows the number of branches that must be tried and thereby puts a cap on the otherwise exponential growth of the problem. Intelligent searching involves applying some heuristic (which means, roughly, an "educated guess") to evaluate the differences between the present state and the goal state and to move us to a new state that minimizes those differences—namely, the state that maximizes our progress toward the goal state.

An intelligent chess-playing strategy, for example, is one that makes an appropriate first move and that, at each step, makes a move more likely than others to lead to a winning board configuration. Even a grand master of chess cannot pursue the brute force approach of mentally trying out all possible next moves, all the possible moves that follow from each of those moves, and so on, for very many steps. (In Section 1.2, we showed that using a brute force approach, a computer would require a billion billion billion years to make its first move!) Intelligent searching is required to prune the number of potential candidates to a reasonable size. There must be a deep storehouse of experience that can be "consulted" on the basis of the present configuration of the board. A grandmaster-level player may need a mental database of around 50,000 of these board configurations, each with its associated information about the best next move.

Building a machine that can beat a human at chess was long thought to be a supreme test of artificial intelligence—machines that "think." Successfully playing chess, it was believed, surely epitomized logical reasoning, true "intelligence." Chess is difficult for humans. Yet, the rules for chess are straightforward; it is simply the size of the state-space that is overwhelming. As artificial intelligence researchers delved deeper into supposedly "simpler" problems such as visual recognition or natural language understanding— things we humans do easily—it became clear that these were the harder challenges for machines. Playing chess came to be viewed as the last of the "easy" hard problems.

15.5.2 Swarm Intelligence

Recall that the connectionist architecture—neural networks—draws its inspiration from nature, namely, the human brain. Another approach to achieving a desired end, *swarm intelligence*, also draws its inspiration from nature, modeling the behavior of, for example, a colony of ants. Each ant is an unsophisticated creature with limited capabilities, yet acting as a collective, an ant colony can accomplish remarkable tasks. Ants can find the shortest route from a nest to a food source, carry large items, emigrate as a colony from one location to another, and form bridges. An ant "communicates" with other ants by laying down a scent trail, called a *pheromone trail*; other ants follow this trail and reinforce its strength by laying down their own pheromones. Given a choice, ants have a higher probability of following the strongest pheromone trail. Hence, the ant that took the shortest path to food and returned to tell about it lays down a trail that other ants follow and reinforce faster than the trail laid down by an ant that took a longer path. Because pheromone trails evaporate quickly, the collective intelligence of the colony is constantly updated to respond to current conditions of its environment.

The swarm intelligence model captures this collective behavior. Computer scientists create algorithms that simulate the process of having simple agents (analogous to the ants) operate independently and follow each other's "trails" to find the most efficient routes. This algorithmic approach is called Ant Colony Optimization (ACO) and has been used commercially in vehicle routing, job scheduling, and the sensing of biological or chemical contaminants. Studies have demonstrated the use of such simple agents in telecommunications networks to avoid the complexity of a centralized control system to compute and distribute routing tables within a network.

Robot Swarms

Several research groups are experimenting with swarms of tiny robots. These entities, like ants, have very limited capabilities as individuals, but they can communicate with one another and, as a collective, perform simple tasks. At Harvard's School of Engineering and Applied Sciences, over 1,000 robots, each only a few centimeters across, can collectively form themselves into any given 2-D shape once an image of that shape has been presented to them. Individual robots, using their limited processing power and the artificial intelligence algorithms they have been given, can sense the edge of the group, track their distance from the origin, avoid collisions, and even clear up little traffic jams until, finally, they have formed the desired shape. The image here shows the Kilobots with Harvard research scientist Michael Rubenstein. To see these Kilobots in action, go to *http://news.harvard.edu/gazette/story/2014/08/the-1000-robot-swarm*.

Wendy Maeda/The Boston Globe/Getty Images

Studies (with smaller swarms) at the Sheffield Centre for Robotics in the United Kingdom have produced robotic collectives that can organize themselves by order of priority, and can fetch an object by surrounding it and working together to push it across the floor. Scientists foresee uses for robot swarms in environmental cleanup, search and rescue operations, or even in noninvasive micromedicine.

15.5.3 Intelligent Agents

Swarm intelligence rests in the colony as a whole, which seems to acquire "knowledge" that is greater than the sum of its parts. At the opposite end of the spectrum are intelligent agents. An intelligent agent is a form of software technology that is designed to interact collaboratively with a user somewhat in the mode of a personal assistant. Imagine that you have hired your own (human) personal assistant. In the beginning, you must tell your assistant what to do and how you want it done. Over time, however, your assistant comes to know more about you and soon can anticipate which tasks need to be done and how to perform them, which items to bring to your attention, and so forth. Your assistant becomes more valuable as he or she becomes more self-directed, always acting with your best interests in mind. You, in turn, put more and more trust in your assistant.

Like the human personal assistant, an intelligent agent does not merely wait for user commands but begins to initiate communication, anticipate what is required, take action, and perform tasks on its own on the basis of its growing knowledge of your needs and preferences. Here are some examples that exist today:

- A personalized web search engine that allows you to profile items of interest to you and then automatically delivers appropriate information from the web. For example, you may request updated weather conditions for your geographic area, along with news items related to sports and European trade. At periodic time intervals, this push technology downloads your updated, personalized information to your screen (or smartphone) to be displayed whenever no other task is active.

- A more intelligent version of this personalized web searcher that enables you to rate each article it sends you and then dynamically adjusts the information that it sends in the future as it learns about your preferences.

- An even more intelligent search agent that not only narrows down choices from topics you have chosen but can suggest new, related topics for you to explore. This is accomplished by having your agent communicate with similar agents on the web, even when you are not online. If your agent knows of your interest in French cuisine, for example, it communicates with other agents to find those that represent users with the same interest. It may learn from these agents that many of their users are also interested in red wines. Your agent then judges whether these suggestions are coming from agents whose recommendations on the whole have been well received by you in the past. If so, it asks whether you also want information about red wines. If you do not agree to this proposal, your agent notes which agents made that suggestion and, on the next pass, gives less consideration to their ideas. The more agents that participate, the more accurate each one becomes at "understanding" the interests of its user.

- The intelligent agent that "lives" in your smartphone (Siri for iPhones, Google Assistant for Android phones and iPhones), able to answer questions, tell you where the nearest hospital is, make dinner reservations for you at your favorite restaurant, remind you of items on your calendar, and much more. Or the intelligent agent that "lives" in your living room (Alexa on Amazon's Echo device, Google Assistant on the Google Home device), able to check your flight status, track a package, play music, tell you a joke, and more.

- An ecommerce company that uses recommendation software (an intelligent agent) to welcome a returning customer to its webpage and make suggestions on future purchases based on what this customer or other customers have done in the past. "Customers who bought this item also bought...."

- A manufacturing plant that uses an intelligent agent to negotiate with suppliers on the price and scheduling of parts delivery to maximize efficiency of production.

Intelligent agent technology has been an area of interest in artificial intelligence for many years. However, intelligent agents need to display significantly greater learning capabilities and "common sense" before most users will trust them to make autonomous decisions regarding the allocation of time and money. Until then, they will be relegated to presenting suggestions to their human users. However, when a sufficient level of trust in intelligent agent technology has been achieved, and when human users are willing to allow their software to make independent decisions, we will take applications like the following for granted:

- *Financial agents* that negotiate with one another over the web for the sale and purchase of goods and services, using price/cost parameters set by the sellers and buyers (sort of an automated eBay)

- *Travel and tourism agents* (electronic, not human) that book airline flights, rent automobiles, and make hotel reservations for you on the basis of your destination, schedule, price range, and preferences

- *Office manager agents* that screen incoming email, put meetings on their users' schedules, and draft replies

15.5.4 Expert Systems

Although intelligent agents incorporate a body of knowledge to "filter" their choices and thereby appear to capture certain aspects of human reasoning, they still perform relatively limited tasks. Consider the more unstructured scenario of managing the triage center in a busy hospital emergency room. The person in charge draws on (1) past experience and training to recognize various medical conditions (which may involve many recognition subtasks), (2) understanding of those conditions and their probable consequences, and (3) knowledge about the hospital's capabilities and resources in general and at the moment. From this knowledge base, a chain of reasoning is followed that leads, for example, to a decision to treat patient A immediately in a particular fashion and to let patient B wait. We consider this to be evidence of quite general "logical reasoning" in humans.

Artificial intelligence simulates this kind of reasoning through the use of expert systems, also called *rule-based systems* or *knowledge-based systems*. (The latter term is a bit confusing because all "intelligent activity" rests on some base of knowledge.) An expert system attempts to mimic the human ability to engage pertinent facts and string them together in a logical fashion to reach some conclusion. An expert system must therefore contain these two components:

- A *knowledge base*—A set of facts about the subject matter

- An *inference engine*—A mechanism for selecting the relevant facts and for reasoning from them in a logical way

Note that the knowledge base contains facts about a *specific* subject domain to narrow the scope to a manageable size.

The facts in the knowledge base consist of certain simple assertions. For example, let's say that the domain of inquiry is U.S. presidents. Three simple assertions are

1. Lincoln was president during the Civil War.

2. Kennedy was president before Nixon.

3. FDR was president before Kennedy.

Another type of fact is a *rule*, a statement of the form *if… then…*, which says that whenever the clause following "if" is true, so is the clause following "then." For example, here are two rules that, taken together, define what it means for one president to precede another in office. In these rules, X, Y, and Z are variables.

I. If X was president before Y, then X precedes Y.

II. If X was president before Z and Z precedes Y, then X precedes Y.

What conclusions can be reached from this collection of three assertions and two rules? Assertion 2 says that Kennedy was president before Nixon. This matches the "if" clause of rule I, where X is Kennedy and Y is Nixon. From this, the "then" clause of rule I yields a new assertion, that Kennedy precedes Nixon, which we'll call assertion 4. Now assertion 3 says that FDR was president before Kennedy, and assertion 4 says that Kennedy precedes Nixon. This matches the "if" clause of rule II, where X is FDR, Z is Kennedy, and Y is Nixon. From this, the "then" clause of rule II yields a new assertion, that FDR precedes Nixon, which we'll call assertion 5. Hence,

4. Kennedy precedes Nixon.

5. FDR precedes Nixon.

are two new conclusions or assertions. These assertions were not part of the original knowledge base and were previously unknown. Instead, they were obtained from what was known through a process of logical reasoning. The knowledge base has been extended. We could also say that the system has *learned* two new pieces of knowledge.

If this example sounds familiar, it is because it is part of the example we used in Chapter 10 to illustrate the logic programming language Prolog. Prolog provides one means of implementing an inference engine for an expert system.

The inference engine is basically using the following pattern of reasoning:

Given that the rule
  If A then B
and the fact
  A
are both in the knowledge base, then the fact
  B
can be inferred or concluded.

This reasoning process, as we noted in Chapter 10, goes by the Latin name of *modus ponens*, which means "method of assertion." It gives us a method for making new assertions. We humans use this deductive reasoning process all the time, for example,

> I know that if my grade on the math final was below 50, then I will fail the course. My grade on the final was below 50. I can infer exactly what is going to happen!

However, it is also suitable for computerization because it is basically a matching algorithm that can be implemented by brute force trial and error. Systems like Prolog, however, apply some additional guidelines in their search for matches to speed up the process; that is, they employ a form of intelligent searching.

Inference engines for expert systems can proceed in several ways. *Forward chaining* begins with assertions and tries to match those assertions to the "if" clauses of rules, thereby generating new assertions. These may in turn be matched with "if" clauses, generating still more assertions. This is the process we used in our example. *Backward chaining* begins with a proposed conclusion and tries to match it with the "then" clauses of rules. If successful, it next looks at the corresponding "if" clauses of those rules and tries to match those with assertions, or with the "then" clauses of other rules. This process continues until all "if" clauses that arise have been successfully matched with assertions, in which case the proposed conclusion is justified, or until no match is possible, in which case the proposed conclusion is rejected. Backward chaining in our example would start with the proposed conclusion that FDR precedes Nixon, and the system would then work backward to justify this conclusion.

In addition to the knowledge base and the inference engine, most rule-based systems also have an explanation facility. This allows the user to see the assertions and rules used in arriving at a conclusion, as a sort of check on the path of reasoning or for the user's own enlightenment.

Of course, a rule-based system about some particular domain is only as good as the assertions and rules that make up the knowledge base. The builder of such a system acquires the information for the knowledge base by consulting "experts" in the domain and mining their expertise. This process, called knowledge engineering, requires a great deal of interaction with the human expert, much of it in the domain environment. If the domain expert is the manager of a chemical processing plant, for example, a decision to "turn down valve A whenever the temperature in pipe P exceeds 235°F and

Practice Problems

1. Given the assertion "Frank is bald" and the rule "If X is bald, then X is tall," what conclusion can be inferred? If Frank were known to be tall, would that necessarily imply that he was bald?

2. Given the assertion "Frank is not bald" and the rule "If X is bald, then X is tall," what conclusion can be inferred?

3. Given the assertion "Frank is bald" and the rule "If X is tall, then X is bald," what conclusion can be inferred?

4. Given the assertion "Frank is not bald" and the rule "If X is tall, then X is bald," what conclusion can be inferred?

valves B and C are both closed" may be such an ingrained behavior that the expert won't remember it as part of a question-and-answer session on "what you do on your job." It only emerges by on-site observation. For the hospital example, one might need to follow people around in the emergency room, observe their decisions, and later question them on why those decisions were made. It is also possible to incorporate probabilities to model the thinking process, for example, "If the patient has fever and stomach pains, the probability of appendicitis is 73% and the probability of gall bladder problems is 27%, therefore I first check for A and then for B."

Expert systems have been implemented in many domains, including specific forms of medical diagnosis, computer chip design, monitoring of manufacturing processes, financial planning, purchasing decisions for retail stores, automotive troubleshooting, and diagnosis of failures in electronic systems. They will no doubt be even more commonplace in the future.

15.5.5 The Games We Play

These days, the world of video game playing draws many enthusiasts. We will explore some of the computer technologies that make video games possible in the next chapter. But here, we want to trace the progression of the "artificial intelligence" needed to have the computer play (rather than just display) a game.

Board Games. Almost everyone is familiar with the simple pencil-and-paper game of tic-tac-toe. Two players draw Xs and Os, respectively, in the squares of a 3 × 3 grid. The first player to draw three of his or her symbol in a row (vertically, horizontally, or diagonally) wins. While the "X" player is trying to build such a row, the "O" player is trying to block it, and vice versa. For example, if the current configuration looks like this:

then the "O" player should write an O in the middle square to block X's diagonal. The rules are pretty simple, making it a good children's game. For experienced players, most games will end in a draw.

Writing a computer program to play tic-tac-toe is fairly easy. (The first-ever computer game was tic-tac-toe, written for the EDSAC computer in 1952; it played perfect games against human opponents. The first computer program Bill Gates wrote, at the age of 13, played tic-tac-toe.) The state-space graph (see Section 15.5.1) for tic-tac-toe is relatively small. Because there are nine positions, each of which can contain X, O, or blank, at first it seems that there are $3^9 = 19{,}683$ board configurations. However, many of these are essentially the same. For example, a single X in a corner square with all other cells blank occurs four ways because there are four corners, but these are all rotations of the same thing, so this is really only one configuration. Eliminating these similarities, there are only 765 distinct configurations. We want a solution path from the initially empty board to a winning configuration, and because of the small state-space, a brute force approach is feasible. If we assume that each player can write in any vacant cell, that the game is terminated with any three-in-a-row symbol or a full grid, and that configurations that are essentially the same are ignored, there are 26,830 possible games (paths through the state space). By following the simple strategies of trying to make three in a row while trying to block your opponent, and concluding the game when the outcome is determined, the number of paths through the state space is much smaller—1,145 games. These can be analyzed in their entirety to find a winning path.

Checkers is a board game with more complex rules than tic-tac-toe and a far larger state space; there are 5×10^{20} (500 billion billion) possible board configurations. The Chinook project, involving a group of computer scientists at the University of Alberta in Canada, headed by Professor Jonathan Schaeffer, began in 1989. This project was to develop a checkers-playing computer program. In April 2007, it was announced that Chinook was finally perfected. From the standard starting positions used in tournament play, Chinook can never lose; the best a skilled opponent can achieve is a draw. Multiple computers—as many as 200 at a time—worked simultaneously to carry out the 10^{14} (100 trillion) computations needed to determine how Chinook should make its moves so that it never loses.

The solutions to both tic-tac-toe and checkers are complete solutions—the "winning move" to make from any board position has been determined and has been built into the software. The game of chess is still more complex. As mentioned earlier, a computer that could play winning chess games was thought to be the pinnacle of artificial intelligence. In May 1997, international attention was focused on a historic chess match between world champion Garry Kasparov and the IBM chess-playing supercomputer known as Deep Blue. Kasparov and Deep Blue played neck and neck. Both relied on the respective strengths of their "species," Kasparov utilizing recognition and reasoning, and Deep Blue churning out its high-speed computations. In the final game, Kasparov lost the match by falling for a well-known trap. Kasparov's error, which was considered a major blunder for a player of his ability, probably reflected his weariness and the emotional strain of competing against an unexpectedly strong, utterly impassive foe. These human frailties, of course, were not shared by Deep Blue or its successor, Deep Junior, shown in Figure 15.13 playing against Kasparov in 2003.

Kasparov could evaluate up to three chess positions per second, or 540 in the 3 minutes allowed between moves; he selected which few positions to evaluate on the basis of his experience, study of successful strategies or tactical approaches, and intuition. Deep Blue could evaluate up to 200,000,000 chess positions per second, or 50 billion in 3 minutes, using its 512 communicating processors. But even Deep Blue could not pursue a true brute force approach of playing out to the bitter end every possible consequence of every potential move from a given configuration. Instead, its programmers provided a number

FIGURE 15.13

Man vs. computer

Source: Bebeto Matthews/Associated Press

of heuristics that helped "prune" the search tree to a manageable number of paths, in effect selecting what seemed to be the most promising moves.

The game of Go is an ancient Chinese board game played by two players using black-and-white stones placed on a (usually) 19 × 19 grid. Stones represent territory controlled by a player. Once put in place, they are never moved, but can be removed if "captured" by the opposing player. The object of the game is to control a maximum amount of territory. A stone surrounded by stones of the opposite color is subject to capture, which makes it advisable to keep your stones clustered closely together. But that defeats the object of increasing the territory you control. Although the rules of Go are simple, there is a great deal of strategy involved in successful play. Obstacles to success include the large size of the grid and the number of pieces on the grid, the fact that pieces generally remain on the board, the fact that a player has a huge number of moves at his or her disposal at any time, and the fact that a given move could be good or bad depending on the intent of the player. It is estimated there are 10^{761} possible Go games that can be played.

Recall that the AI experts (see the Special Interest Box "Predicted AI Milestones" earlier in this chapter) estimated that it would be 2028 before artificial intelligence would be able to win at the game of Go. However, in May 2017, only two years after these predictions were made, Google's AlphaGo software was pitted in a series of three Go matches against the world's top Go player at The Future of Go Summit held in China, the birthplace of Go. AlphaGo won the series in a clean sweep. (Before we celebrate the impressive artificial intelligence win, we should note the pretty remarkable fact that the human player, at the time of this competition, was a 19-year-old Chinese man named Ke Jie.)

AlphaGo did not play by memorizing gazillions of possible paths to victory at each step. Rather, it learned from experience as a result of playing a large number of games against itself (machine learning). After the final match, Ke Jie said "This Summit is one of the greatest matches that I've had. I believe, it's actually one of the greatest matches in history."

Google is retiring AlphaGo from the world of Go, but plans to put the team that developed AlphaGo to work on other grand challenges, such as reducing energy consumption or finding cures for certain diseases. Meanwhile, the high-level human Go players plan to study AlphaGo's innovative moves during the tournament to improve their own play.

Quiz Games. *Jeopardy!* is a popular American television quiz show. The show draws an estimated 25 million viewers per week who watch Alex Trebek, the host since 1984, throw "answers" at three contestants, who have to supply the corresponding "question." *Jeopardy!* took a startling new turn when, in 2011, an IBM supercomputer was one of the three contestants. Named Watson, after IBM's founder Thomas Watson, the computer got off to a slow start, but over three days of competition, bested two previous *Jeopardy!* champions, Ken Jennings and Brad Rutter.

In Figure 15.14, the Watson avatar is glowing proudly. But behind the scenes is the real Watson, consisting of 90 IBM Power 750 servers, each with 32 core processors and up to 256 GB of RAM (Figure 15.15). When Watson got a clue, processing algorithms analyzed the clue and then ran

FIGURE 15.14

IBM's Watson beats its human opponents on *Jeopardy!*
Source: Seth Wenig/AP

FIGURE 15.15

IBM's Watson supercomputer
Source: Courtesy of IBM

several different searches that could produce as many as 300–500 candidate answers. This phase used heavy-duty computing resources (note the large amount of main memory storage) and although several servers may have been working at once on the same clue, this was basically not a parallelized process. However, the next phase of "scoring" the candidate answers to decide on the best response was distributed across the cluster and done in parallel.

Certainly Watson had a huge database of facts at its disposal, but what the IBM researchers and their collaborators accomplished is much more than a massive search process. Web search engines conduct massive searches, but they basically do word matching and then present you with a list of potentially relevant documents or other artifacts to sift through yourself, although they do vast statistical analyses to attempt to improve relevance. Watson analyzed clues fraught with vagaries of English language—puns, humor, rhymes, riddles, plays on words—to understand their meaning.

Watson was not infallible. With a category of "U.S. cities" and the clue "Its largest airport is named for a World War II hero; its second largest for a World War II battle," Watson responded "What is Toronto?", although with a low level of confidence in its answer.[5] But before you feel smug, consider Watson's correct response in the category of "edible rhyme time" and the clue "A long, tiresome speech delivered by a frothy pie topping." It had to recognize that the clue consists of two parts, a long tiresome speech and a frothy pie topping. It had to find potential answers for each part, and then apply the constraint that the two answers must rhyme. Can you answer this—in under three seconds?[6]

Watson has evolved since its game-playing *Jeopardy!* days, now employing its natural language processing capabilities in many fields of interest (see the Special Interest Box, "'Now I Understand,' Said the Machine," in Chapter 11).

15.6 Robots and Drones

15.6.1 Robots

The term robot implies a device, which may or may not be humanlike in form, that has the ability to gather sensory information from its surroundings and to autonomously (without direct human instructions) perform mechanical actions of some sort in response. The term *robot* was used in a play written in 1921 by Czech author Karel Capek. The play was titled *R.U.R.*, short for *Rossum's Universal Robots*. In the play, a scientist invents robots that perform simple repetitive tasks to help people but who take over the world when their human owners try to use them to fight wars. The word *robot* comes from the Czech word *robota*, meaning slavelike labor. Robots have been part of science fiction ever since—think C-3PO and R2-D2 in the *Star Wars* movies.

---

[5] The correct response is "What is Chicago?"

[6] The correct response is "What is meringue harangue?"

Fact has not yet caught up with science fiction, but today there are a surprising number of applications of robots. Here's a partial list of the uses to which robots are put in manufacturing, science, the military, medicine, and the consumer marketplace:

- Assembling automobile parts
- Packaging food and drugs
- Placing and soldering wires in circuits
- Bomb disposal
- Exploration (the Mars Rovers)
- Underwater salvage
- Microsurgery
- Emergency search and rescue
- Fetching and packing items from warehouse storage

Robots currently perform many tasks that are too repetitive or dangerous for humans. Robots, of course, do not get bored, they can perform the same tasks with the same precision every time, and they can work in hostile environments.

We have all seen photos of robots performing manufacturing tasks; in Figure 15.16, robots are busy welding car frames. But what if the car itself is the robot? Google began developing an autonomous (self-driving) car in 2009. It used modified commercial automobiles fitted with lots of sensors and software. On top of these cars is a revolving turret called a *lidar* device, short for light detection and ranging. The lidar constructs a 3-D map of the car's environs, which the software then compares with a high-definition (at the one-inch level) map of the area in which the car is traveling.

In May 2014 Google revealed a new prototype autonomous car—one without a steering wheel, brake pedal, or accelerator pedal (see Figure 15.17; it was intentionally made to be cute so as not to frighten people). As of March 2016, the Google test cars had logged 1,500,000 autonomous driving miles with a remarkable safety record, but always with a trained human ready to take control if needed. In December 2016, Google spun off its autonomous car program as a new business called Waymo. Waymo then launched a program in Phoenix, Arizona, for public trials of their autonomous vehicles, that is, selected ordinary citizens are invited to use an autonomous vehicle for everyday uses such as driving to work, school, or the grocery store, and report on their experiences.

Now there are a number of companies, including traditional automakers, in various stages of designing and testing autonomous vehicles. By May 2016, sixteen states and Washington D.C. had passed legislation relating to autonomous vehicles, some creating study groups, some encouraging development and testing, and some permitting autonomous vehicles to be driven on public roads. In 2016, Florida became the first state to authorize the use of autonomous vehicles on public roads with no requirement for a

FIGURE 15.16

Robots welding car frames on an assembly line

FIGURE 15.17

Google's prototype autonomous car

human driver in the car. In May 2017, the governor of New York announced a one-year trial of autonomous cars on public roads in the state, which requires a human with a valid driver's license in the driver's seat as a precaution; someday we may see fully autonomous vehicles navigating the challenging traffic of Manhattan.

Wait—Where Am I?

Those who call on Uber for a ride in Pittsburgh might now find themselves passengers in an autonomous vehicle. Uber began testing its own autonomous vehicles in Pittsburgh in September 2016. These vehicles do have a steering wheel with a driver behind the wheel to take control of the car in an emergency, plus an engineer in the front seat to monitor the car's actions.

Pittsburgh was chosen as a test site because it is an old city with a complicated pattern of roads, lots of bridges, lots of potholes, lots of traffic, and its share of bad winter weather, so it provides quite a challenge for an autonomous vehicle.

Did we mention bridges? Uber cars tend to have difficulty with bridges, as in "disengaging"—dropping out of autonomous mode—in the middle of a long bridge. Why? Because at that point the landmarks by which the autonomous car judges its position relative to its internal map are too far away to see. Another unexpected difficulty occurred because some of the internal maps were compiled by driving around Pittsburg in the winter when there were no leaves on the trees, and when the autonomous car drove the same roads in spring when the trees had grown lots of leaves, the landmarks (trees) the car sensed no longer matched the internal maps.

More and more, however, robots are being developed to interact with humans in a less "robotic" and more "humanlike" way to perform tasks for disabled individuals, to watch over small children, and to entertain and provide companionship. Japan has an interest in developing "humanoid" robots to help care for its aging population.

One of the more well-known humanoid robots is ASIMO (Advanced Step in Innovative Mobility), built by Honda Motor Company, a Japanese corporation. As the name suggests, much of the focus of the design of this robot over earlier models was refinement of the robot's motion capabilities, extending the range of its arm movement and improving the smoothness and stability of its two-legged walking, including walking on uneven ground and navigating stairs. This jointed robot is designed to measure the forces acting on it at each step. If these forces get out of balance, threatening a fall, adjustments are made in the placement of the foot and the position of the torso to regain balance. One only has to watch a toddler learning to walk to see the challenges this represents. ASIMO was created in 2000, but its capabilities have developed over time, with better balance, smoother motions, and increased hand dexterity, including the ability to use both American and Japanese sign language. ASIMO can climb up and down stairs, hop on one foot forwards, backwards, and sideways, and run remarkably smoothly, if somewhat noisily, at a speed of 9 km/hour (almost 5.6 mph) (see Figure 15.18). ASIMO can open and close doors while passing through a doorway, walk down a hallway without bumping into people, guide office guests to a meeting room and serve refreshments on a tray, and unscrew a lid from a jar and pour its liquid contents into a cup without spilling. Moreover, ASIMO, based on input from its multiple sensors, can evaluate its environment and autonomously adapt its actions accordingly; it can also recognize faces and voices. ASIMO is an international celebrity, with public appearances worldwide. It has conducted the Detroit Symphony Orchestra, received a royal

FIGURE 15.18

AFP/Getty Images

Honda's ASIMO running

welcome in Dubai, and served (in 2017) as Grand Marshall of the Honda Indy Grand Prix auto race in Alabama where it taught one of the drivers some dance moves. ASIMO now is part of the Honda-sponsored Autopia attraction at Disneyland in California.

Research is ongoing in the field of robotics. Robotics involves the aspects of artificial intelligence we discussed earlier, namely, recognition tasks and reasoning tasks. Through some sort of elementary vision, auditory, or tactile system, the robot must not only gather sensory information but also filter out the possibly vast amount of data its surroundings might present to it to "recognize." That is, it must be able to make sense of the important features and discard the unimportant. Then the robot must make decisions—reason about—the information it has recognized to be able to take some action. There is also the additional challenge of the mechanics and electronics needed to make the robot respond physically.

Two strategies characterize robotics research. The deliberative strategy says that the robot must have an internal representation of its environment and that its actions in response to some stimuli are programmed into the robot based on this model of the environment. This strategy seems to reflect what we as humans think of as high-level cognitive reasoning—we have a mental model of our environment, we reflect on a stimulus from that environment, and make a reasoned decision about the next course of action. (This is a generalization of the expert system idea discussed earlier.)

The reactive strategy uses heuristic algorithms to allow the robot to respond directly to stimuli from its environment without filtering through some line of reasoning based on its internal understanding of that environment. This stimulus-response approach seems to reflect human subconscious behavior—holding out our hands to protect ourselves during a fall, for example, or drawing back from a hot flame. Proponents of the deliberative strategy argue that a robot cannot react meaningfully without processing the stimulus and planning a reaction based on its internal representation of the environment. Proponents of the reactive strategy say that such a requirement is too restrictive and does not allow the robot to respond freely to any or all new stimuli it might encounter. Note that we as humans use both our conscious thought processes and our subconscious reactions in our everyday life, so a combination of these strategies may be the most successful approach.

15.6.2 Drones

A drone (more properly called a *UAV* for *Unmanned Aerial Vehicle*) is an aircraft that is either under autonomous control via a computer system on board or is controlled by a human controller at a remote site. In other words, no pilot is on board.

The use of a UAV in the most general sense actually dates back much farther than we would expect, to the American Civil War, in which both Union and Confederate troops launched bomb-filled balloons. But the idea of a drone as we think of it today began in the 1960s during the Vietnam War, in which drones were used for reconnaissance missions.

Drones are still used primarily for military (or law enforcement) purposes today, but their use is expanding into other areas as well. A partial list of what drones are starting to do includes:

- Agricultural-related aerial photography. Drones can take photographs of a farm field row-by-row; each photo is tagged with GPS information. Using specialized software, the resulting data can be used to create fertilizer distribution plans, predict crop yield, and other useful information.

- Delivery of medical supplies or blood to remote areas, such as some Native American reservations or communities where natural disasters have knocked out access roads. Such a program has been underway in Rwanda since July 2016, and plans are underway to test this process in Maryland, Nevada, and Washington, once FAA approval is obtained.

- Surveys of livestock or wildlife. In February 2017 (summer in Antarctica), wildlife biologists were spying on penguins and humpback whales. Using drones is safer and cheaper than using helicopters or small planes. Drones could even be used to spot wildlife poachers (in, say, Africa, not Antarctica).

- Real-time reports on fires, floods, chemical spills, receding glaciers or volcanic activity. The Fire and Rescue Service in the town of Chorley, Lancashire, U.K., is using a drone for monitoring fires, floods, collapsed structures, and even searching for missing persons. The drone can be gotten up in the air quickly and can fly in high winds and poor weather.

- Pipeline inspections. Drones use high-resolution digital, infrared, and thermal imaging to detect and document possible hazard concerns in pipelines, such as methane or ethane gas leaks, pipe erosion, exposed pipes, vegetation overgrowth, and missing or damaged signs or markers. Again, the drone is a faster, safer, and less-expensive solution than helicopters or small aircraft.

- Urban traffic reports. Drones can be used to monitor urban traffic, report rush-hour traffic jams, and so forth. However, Dubai has another solution in mind for avoiding rush-hour traffic; beginning in July 2017, Dubai is scheduled to use one-passenger drones that can fly short, pre-programmed routes. It's sort of Uber-of-the-air, but with no drivers, although flights will be monitored by a ground crew.

Drones are usually not as big as a regular airplane or helicopter. In fact, small drones working together (swarm intelligence again) can get into places where a large vehicle cannot and obtain a more complete picture of the environment they are exploring. For example, human engineers currently inspect bridges for damage, a slow, dangerous, and far-from-foolproof method. Researchers at Tufts University are developing a system that will allow drones to improve the infrastructure problem of decaying bridges. The plan is to attach wireless sensors to bridge joints; these sensors can monitor bridge vibrations and detect changes that may signal structural damage. A group of drones can not only visually survey the bridge but also collect data from the sensors and send it to a central site for analysis, allowing decisions to be made on a priority list for bridge repair. These drones would communicate with each other to check one another's position and flight paths, and to autonomously regroup to collect more data on a suspicious location.

There is also interest in tiny drones. For example, swarms of insect-sized drones could be released in a disaster area to assess damage and search for survivors. Because of their size, they could penetrate hard-to-access areas of debris and transmit signals to (human or robotic) rescue workers. Insect-like drones are not just "small airplanes"—the flight dynamics of insects are much more complex because of an insect's ability to hover, fly in any direction, land on walls, and so forth.

A Japanese lab is researching the use of small drones to act as artificial "bees" (after all, "drone" is the term for a worker bee). Bees are crucial to the pollination of many important crops and flowering plants, but the bee population is in serious decline. The artificial bee is about the size of a hummingbird, but has a fuzzy strip made from paintbrush hairs that are coated with a gel sticky enough to trap pollen if the bee brushes up against a flower, yet not so sticky that the pollen isn't released when visiting another flower. Currently the artificial bee is "flown" by a human controller, but future plans include arming it with a visual recognition system so it can find flowers on its own.

The possible use for drones that has most captured public attention is package delivery. Amazon.com's plan is to use drones to deliver a package weighing up to 5 pounds to the customer within a 30-minute window. You would place your order online, step outside, and wait for a little buzzing drone to gently drop your order on your front porch. In fact, Amazon made its first package drop to a customer in England in December 2016.

Companies, including Amazon, that want to build or use drones for commercial purposes are lobbying for faster approvals by the Federal Aviation Administration. The FAA is proceeding with caution, and the rules adopted in 2016 require that UAVs can weigh no more than 55 pounds, must fly below 400 feet above ground or the top of a building, must fly below 100 miles per hour, cannot fly at night or over crowds of people, must have a human operator, and cannot fly beyond the operator's visual line of sight.

But aside from regulations, there are other issues to consider:

- How will the increasing number of drones work safely in crowded skies, especially if they are all flying below 400 feet? (X is a futuristic lab that is a subsidiary of Alphabet, the parent company of Google. X is working on software to manage "air traffic control" for drones. The system views current flight paths, anticipates when collisions might occur, and updates the drones' flight paths to avoid them.)

- Are they safe or will they crash into someone's home or car?

- What about privacy—what prevents a little drone from hovering outside your window and collecting data?

15.7 Conclusion

In this chapter, we have touched on three basic elements of artificial intelligence: knowledge representation, recognition problems, and reasoning problems. We've discussed common approaches to building artificial intelligence systems: connectionist architectures (neural networks), genetic or evolutionary approaches (swarm intelligence), and symbolic manipulation (expert systems). We have followed the progress of artificial intelligence in game playing and have also outlined some of the strategies and challenges in robotics design and the use of drones. Yet we have mentioned only a few of the many application areas of AI, a field that is finally beginning to realize its potential. Today we can use speech-recognition systems to control our phones, appliances, and computers by talking to them, exploit face-recognition software to assist the police with their crime-solving responsibilities, use a tablet PC with handwriting-recognition software, and ask a webpage to translate text from one language to another. In 10–20 years, artificial intelligence will be used in ways we have not even imagined today.

EXERCISES

1. a. Write a Winograd schema and the challenge question. Also give the correct answer. (See the Special Interest Box "Victory in the Turing Test?" earlier in this chapter.)

   b. Now change one word in your sentence from Exercise 1a so that the correct answer is different.

2. Suppose that in a formal logic, green(x) means that x has the attribute of being green, frog(x) means that x has the attribute of being a bullfrog, and J stands for the specific entity Jeremiah. Translate the following formal statements into English:

   a. frog(J)
   b. $(\forall x)(frog(x) \rightarrow green(x))$

3. Draw a semantic net that incorporates the knowledge contained in the following paragraph:

   > If I had to describe what distinguishes a table from other pieces of furniture, I guess I would say it has to have four legs and a flat top. The legs, of course, hold up the top. Nancy's table is made of maple, but mine is bigger and is walnut.

4. a. Use an English-like formal language to represent the knowledge explicitly contained in the following semantic net:

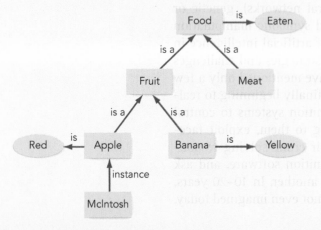

   b. Add to your list from Exercise 4a the knowledge that can be inferred from the semantic net.

5. In the following neural network, which combinations of input values cause node N3 to fire? Each input signal (x_1, x_2, x_3, x_4) can have a value of either 0 or 1.

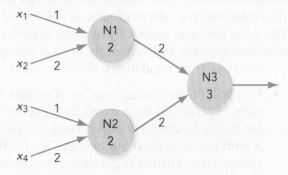

6. Assign weights and threshold values in the following neural network so that the output neuron fires only when x_1 and x_3 have the value 1 and x_2 has the value 0. Remember that weights can be negative.

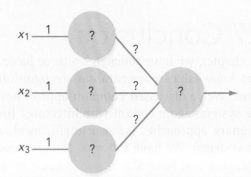

7. The truth table for the XOR operation is given in Figure 15.8. As noted in the text, a neural network for this operation requires a hidden layer of neurons. A partial solution to a neural network for XOR is shown at the top of the next page. In this solution, all neurons have a threshold value of 1 and the inputs x_1 and x_2 are binary. Finish this network by finding weights

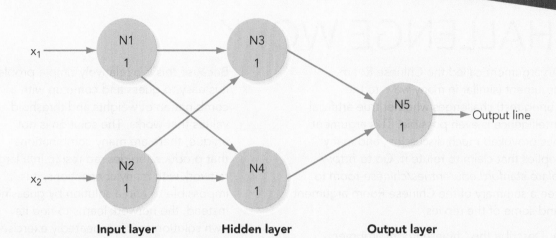

Input layer   **Hidden layer**   **Output layer**

for the connections and test that the resulting network implements the XOR operation. (*Hint*: All weights can be integer values.)

8. Find some literature or product information on a mobile device or tablet PC that allows pen-based handwritten entries. What sort of scheme does this system use for handwriting recognition? Does the system use a neural network? Does it require initial training on the user's handwriting?

9. Ant colonies are an example from nature of swarm intelligence. Find two other examples of swarm intelligence seen in nature.

10. You are a knowledge engineer and have been assigned the task of developing a knowledge base for an expert system to advise on mortgage loan applications. What are some sample questions you would ask the loan manager at a bank?

11. We described both forward chaining and backward chaining as techniques used by inference engines in rule-based systems. In Section 11.2.2, we described how a parser might analyze a programming statement to produce a parse tree. Does the method described in Chapter 11 correspond more closely to forward chaining or to backward chaining? Explain.

12. A rule-based system for writing the screenplays for mystery movies contains the following assertions and rules:

The hero is a spy.

The heroine is an interpreter.

If the hero is a spy, then one scene should take place in Berlin and one in Paris.

If the heroine is an interpreter, then the heroine must speak English.

If the heroine is an interpreter, then the heroine must speak Russian.

If one scene should take place in Berlin, then there can be no car chase.

If there can be no car chase, then there can be no crash scene.

If one scene should take place in Berlin, then the hero is European.

If one scene should take place in Paris, then the hero must speak French.

Can the following assertion be inferred? Explain.

The hero must speak French and there can be no crash scene.

13. In Exercise 12, is it possible to add the following assertion to the knowledge base? Why or why not?

The hero is American.

14. If you studied Prolog in Chapter 10 and have a Prolog interpreter available, try implementing the rule-based system of Exercise 12 in Prolog and pose the queries of Exercises 12 and 13.

CHALLENGE WORK

1. An argument called the Chinese Room argument (similar in many ways to the Turing test) challenges whether true artificial intelligence is even possible. This argument has provoked much discussion, and many replies that claim to refute it. Go to *http://plato.stanford.edu/entries/chinese-room* to see a summary of the Chinese Room argument and some of the replies.

    a. Describe the Chinese Room argument.

    b. Pick one of the replies and describe it. Does it seem to invalidate the Chinese Room argument?

2. A neural network is to be built that behaves according to the following truth table, which represents the Boolean AND operation. Input to the network consists of two binary signals; the single output line fires exactly when both input signals are 1.

Inputs		Output
x_1	x_2	
0	0	0
1	0	0
0	1	0
1	1	1

    a. Find values for the missing weights and threshold values for the neurons in the following diagram that cause the network to behave properly.

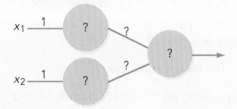

b. Because this is a relatively simple problem, it is easy to guess and come up with a combination of weights and threshold values that works. The solution is not unique; there are many combinations that produce the desired result. In a large network with many connections, it is impossible to find a solution by guessing. Instead, the network learns to find its own solution as it is repeatedly exercised on a set of training data. For networks with hidden layers, the back propagation algorithm can be used for training. For a general class of networks of the form shown in the next diagram, an easier training algorithm exists, as we will see. Note that in the diagram, the input signals are binary, and all neurons are assumed to have the same threshold value θ.

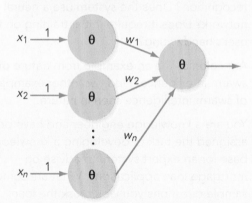

The following table sets up the notation needed to describe the training algorithm.

Symbol	Meaning
$X_1, X_2, \ldots$	Binary input values from the training set
y	The binary output value from the network

Symbol	Meaning
t	The target binary output value from the network for this set of input values
α	The "learning rate" for the network; a small positive value that controls how rapidly the weights change during training
$w_1, w_2, \ldots$	The current set of weights
θ	The current threshold value
$w_1', w_2', \ldots$	The next set of weights
θ'	The next threshold value

Initially, the network is given arbitrary values between 0 and 1 for the weights $W_1, W_2, \ldots$, and the threshold value θ. A set of input values $X_1, X_2, \ldots$ from the training data is then applied to the network. Because we are working with training data, the correct result t for this set of input values is known. The actual result from the network, y, is computed and compared with t. The difference between the two values is used to compute the next round of values for the weights and the threshold value, which are then tested on another set of values from the training data. This process is repeated until the weights and threshold value have settled into a combination for which the network behaves correctly on all of the training sets. The network is fully trained at this point.

Each new weight w_i' is computed from the previous weight by the formula

$$w_i' = w_i + \alpha\,(t - y)\,x_i \qquad \text{(A)}$$

and the new threshold value θ' is computed from the previous value by the formula

$$\theta' = \theta - \alpha\,(t - y) \qquad \text{(B)}$$

There are three cases to consider:

i. If the network behaved correctly for the current set of data—that is, if the computed output y equals the desired output t—then the quantity $\alpha(t - y)$ has the value 0, so when we use formulas (A) and (B), the new weights and threshold value will equal the old ones. The algorithm makes no adjustments for behavior that is already correct.

ii. If the output y is 0 when the target output t is 1, then the quantity $\alpha(t - y)$ has the value α, a small positive value. Each weight corresponding to an input x_i that was active in this computation (that is, had the value 1) gets increased slightly by formula (A). This is because the output neuron didn't fire when we wanted it to, so we stimulate it with more weight coming into it. At the same time, we lower the threshold value by formula (B), again so as to stimulate the output neuron to fire.

iii. If the output y is 1 when the target output t is 0, then the quantity $\alpha(t - y)$ has the value $-\alpha$, a small negative value. Each weight corresponding to an input x_i that was active (that is, had the value 1) gets decreased slightly by formula (A). This is because the output neuron fired when we didn't want it to, so we dampen it with less weight coming into it. At the same time, we raise the threshold value by formula (B), again so as to discourage the output neuron from firing.

We will use the training algorithm to train an AND network. The training set will be the four pairs of binary values for the AND truth table shown earlier. (Here, the training set is the entire set of possible input values; in most cases, a neural network is trained on some input values for which the answers are known and then is used to solve other input cases for which the answers are unknown.) For starting values, we choose (arbitrarily) $w_1 = 0.6$, $w_2 = 0.1$, $\theta = 0.5$, and $\alpha = 0.2$. The value of α stays fixed and should be chosen to be relatively small; otherwise, the corrections are too big and the values don't have a chance to settle into a solution. The initial picture of the network is therefore the following:

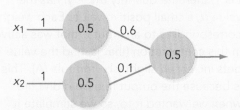

Note that with these choices we did not stumble on a solution because input values of $x_1 = 1$ and $x_2 = 0$ do not produce the correct result.

The table shows the first three training sessions. The current network behaves correctly for the

first two cases ($x_1 = 0$ and $x_2 = 0$; $x_1 = 0$ and $x_2 = 1$), so no changes are made. For the third case ($x_1 = 1$ and $x_2 = 0$), an adjustment takes place in the weights and in the threshold value.

After these changes, the new network configuration looks like this:

$$x_1 \xrightarrow{1} 0.7 \xrightarrow{0.4}$$
$$0.7$$
$$0.1$$
$$x_2 \xrightarrow{1} 0.7$$

Continue the table from this point, cycling through the four sets of input pairs until the network produces correct answers for all four cases.

3. Pick one of the technologies discussed in this chapter (neural networks, swarm intelligence, intelligent agents, expert systems, game-playing machines, robots, or drones) and write a report on how it has been applied to a real-world product or problem.

w_1	w_2	θ	x_1	x_2	y	t	$\alpha(t-y)$	w_1'	w_2'	θ'
0.6	0.1	0.5	0	0	0	0	0	0.6	0.1	0.5
0.6	0.1	0.5	0	1	0	0	0	0.6	0.1	0.5
0.6	0.1	0.5	1	0	1	0	−0.2	0.4	0.1	0.7

AFTER STUDYING THIS CHAPTER YOU WILL BE ABLE TO

- Describe the changes in movie animation techniques caused by computer generated imagery (CGI)

- List the steps in the graphics pipeline

- Explain how to create a computer model of a 3D object

- Understand how a transformation matrix can model the movement of an object

- Name three challenges involved in rendering a visual object

- Explain the purpose and function of a graphics processing unit (GPU)

- List and explain two techniques for achieving the real time graphics required for video game animation as opposed to movie animation

- Describe how large virtual communities work, and the particular challenges they face

16.1 Introduction

The first commercially marketed computer was the UNIVAC1, manufactured by Remington Rand. On March 31, 1951, the company delivered its first machine to the U.S. Census Bureau. Later systems went to the U.S. Army, the U.S. Air Force, the Atomic Energy Commission, U.S. Steel, General Electric, and CBS, which used it to predict the outcome of the 1952 presidential election. (Although UNIVAC's software correctly predicted Eisenhower's landslide victory, the results were not immediately reported to the viewing audience. The network did not trust the computer's output to be accurate.)

In 1952, a UNIVAC1 cost about $1,500,000, (about $13 million in today's dollars). It weighed 15 tons, contained 5,200 vacuum tubes, consumed 125,000 watts of electricity (generating an enormous amount of heat), and occupied floor space equal in size to a small apartment. These early machines were prohibitively expensive and required a massive financial investment in space, power, cooling, and support staff. Because of these costs, computers of the 1950s and early 1960s were only available to large organizations and only for what were deemed "important" purposes—classified military work, corporate research and development, or government policy analysis. The idea of using these systems for such "frivolous" pastimes as playing games, listening to music, chatting with friends, or watching videos would have been unimaginable.

Computer Graphics and Entertainment: Movies, Games, and Virtual Communities

AFTER STUDYING THIS CHAPTER, YOU WILL BE ABLE TO:

- Describe the changes in movie animation techniques caused by computer generated imagery (CGI)
- List the steps in the graphics pipeline
- Explain how to create a computer model of a 3D object
- Understand how a transformation matrix can model the movement of an object
- Name three challenges involved in rendering a visual object
- Explain the purpose and function of a graphics processing unit (GPU)
- List and explain two techniques for achieving the real-time graphics required for video game animation as opposed to movie animation
- Describe how large virtual communities work, and the particular challenges they face

16.1 Introduction

The first commercially marketed computer was the UNIVAC I, manufactured by Remington Rand. On March 31, 1951, the company delivered its first machine to the U.S. Census Bureau. Later systems went to the U.S. Army, the U.S. Air Force, the Atomic Energy Commission, U.S. Steel, General Electric, and CBS, which used it to predict the outcome of the 1952 presidential election. (Although UNIVAC's software correctly predicted Eisenhower's landslide victory, the results were not immediately reported to the viewing audience. The network did not trust the computer's output to be accurate!)

In 1952, a UNIVAC I cost about $1,500,000, (about $13 million in today's dollars). It weighed 15 tons, contained 5,200 vacuum tubes, consumed 125,000 watts of electricity (generating an enormous amount of heat), and occupied floor space equal in size to a small apartment. These early machines were prohibitively expensive and required a massive financial investment in space, power, cooling, and support staff. Because of these costs, computers of the 1950s and early 1960s were only available to large organizations and only for what were deemed "important" purposes—classified military work, corporate research and development, or government policy analysis. The idea of using these systems for such "frivolous" pastimes as playing games, listening to music, chatting with friends, or watching videos would have been unimaginable.

However, conditions changed dramatically in the late 1960s due to the development of transistors and integrated circuits, introduced in Chapter 4. Computers became more compact, more reliable, and much less costly. In 1965, Digital Equipment Corp. (DEC) rolled out the PDP-8, the world's first minicomputer, a term coined to describe a computer system that was smaller and less expensive than the unwieldy mainframes of the 1950s and early 1960s. A DEC PDP-8 minicomputer could be purchased for as little as $18,000 (about $120,000 in current dollars) and only took up as much space as two or three refrigerators.

Although still not cheap by today's standards, this lower price meant that computers were no longer accessible only to the military, government, and large corporations; instead, they were now within the financial reach of colleges, universities, and small to medium-sized businesses. Some of the first computer games were created in the 1960s and 1970s by college students experimenting to see what these new minicomputers were capable of doing. Games like Space Wars, Adventure, and Dungeons & Dragons were played on university computers, arcade machines, or custom-designed home consoles well before laptops, tablets, and smartphones arrived on the scene.

In 1972 Nolen Bushnell, an electrical engineering graduate of the University of Utah, started a company called Atari (named after a board position in the game of Go). Atari released its first product in 1975, an arcade game called Pong. It was wildly successful and quickly became the most popular computer game in the country with 40,000 units sold nationwide and hundreds of thousands of players eager to stuff coins into a slot just for the privilege of playing a primitive electronic version of Ping-Pong, as shown in Figure 16.1. It is amazing to see how far video game technology has progressed in the past 40 years!

In 1976 a home version of Pong allowed users to play on their televisions using a game console, complete with joysticks and on-screen scoring. It sold hundreds of thousands of units and became one of the most popular Christmas gifts of the late 1970s. Other games soon followed, and the decade

FIGURE 16.1

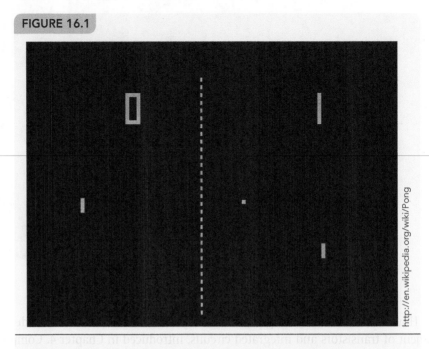

http://en.wikipedia.org/wiki/Pong

Pong—One of the first computer-based video games

of the late 1970s and early 1980s is termed the "golden period" of video arcade systems. By early 1982, Atari had $1.3 billion in annual sales and was the fastest-growing company in the United States.

Using computers for entertainment, once considered frivolous and a complete waste of valuable scientific resources, had by the early 1980s become an important, not to mention financially lucrative, industry, and that growth has continued unabated. Today, computer-based entertainment is a multibillion-dollar industry employing tens of thousands of talented designers, artists, computer scientists, and engineers, and many colleges offer degrees in computer game design. Gamers routinely download the latest and greatest video game releases as soon as they become available. Hollywood spends massive amounts of money and manpower producing computer-generated images that amaze and enthrall, all in the hope of reaping hundreds of millions or billions of dollars in income from movie tickets, Blueray/DVD sales, and online video streaming. Virtual worlds enroll millions of subscribers who spend hours wandering imaginary spaces, joining online virtual communities, and making virtual friends.

Using information technology to amuse, entertain, fascinate, and frighten is no longer viewed as a waste of time, least of all by the millions who watch, participate, and play. Instead, it is seen as an application that contributes significantly to the national economy and brings enjoyment to many people. Just as the Jeep and Hummer evolved from specialized military vehicles into passenger cars used for off-road fun and adventure, so too has the computer evolved from a research tool of the military, government, and universities into something available for our personal pleasure. By the start of the 21st century, computer-based entertainment had become an application that can stand alongside such traditionally "important" uses of computers as scientific modeling (Chapter 13), electronic commerce (Chapter 14), and robotics (Chapter 15).

16.2 Computer-Generated Imagery (CGI)

16.2.1 Introduction to CGI

On March 2, 1933, a sellout audience at Radio City Music Hall in New York City was treated to the premiere of the science-fiction movie *King Kong*. This was the first feature-length film (rather than cartoon) to have its central character, in this case a giant gorilla, generated using animation. Animation had been used before in feature films, but only in a few short scenes or to animate minor characters. Because the movie's premiere occurred years before the appearance of the first commercial computer, Kong's movements were created using a manual technique called stop-motion animation. The special effects staff built a small-scale clay mock-up of the creature, positioned it, and snapped a single photograph, called a frame. Then they made a tiny change in the position of the model to represent its location a fraction of a second later and shot another frame. This process of "move the model, shoot a frame" was repeated thousands of times and, when the frames were shown in sequence without interruption, Kong appeared to come alive on screen. (This is similar to the "flip-book" style of animation in which pages of a notebook are filled with drawings and riffled to produce the effect of motion.) Stop-motion special effects were used in many fantasy, adventure, and science-fiction movies of the 1940s through 1970s.

Although it is possible to produce reasonably good images using either hand-drawn frames or stop-motion animation (*King Kong* was voted one of the 100 best films of all time by the American Film Institute), both techniques have serious limitations. Hand-drawing frames can be a painstakingly slow process, requiring dozens or even hundreds of highly skilled artists. The most notable problem with stop-motion techniques is the difficulty of repositioning a clay model with a sufficient degree of accuracy so that the model's movements do not appear jerky and artificial. At 30 frames per second (the standard rate for video; film uses 24), one hour of stop-motion animation requires 108,000 separate images, each of which must be manually positioned and photographed. The effort required can make this a painfully slow and expensive way to create special effects.

However, until the early 1990s, there were really no other choices. As we will soon learn, using a computer to produce realistic visual images requires enormous amounts of computational speed and power, and the mainframes of earlier decades were generally not up to the task. In addition, the algorithms used to create realistic human and animal replicas were in their infancy and not well understood. There were some early attempts to produce computer-animated movies—for example, *Tron* (1982) and *The Last Starfighter* (1984)—but the quality of that early work was rather poor, and most movie directors opted to stay with either stop-motion or hand-drawn animation to produce their special effects.

Two groundbreaking movies of the early 1990s quickly changed Hollywood's mind: *Terminator 2: Judgment Day* (1991) used a computer to create the T-1000 Terminator character and the special effects used in action sequences. (The movie won the 1991 Oscar for Best Visual Effects.) *Jurassic Park* (1993) used computers to create and animate the movie's dinosaurs and paste them seamlessly into the background of the frames. (It also won an Oscar for its visual effects.) The quality of those early 1990s images was an order of magnitude improvement over what had been available just 8 to 10 years earlier. Both movies were huge financial as well as artistic successes, and they clearly demonstrated the rapidly improving capability of computer-generated imagery, usually referred to by its acronym CGI. By the mid-1990s, computer hardware could handle the massive computational demands required to create realistic three-dimensional images, and CGI software development had reached a point where its final product was as good as, if not better than, the manual output of human animators. By the beginning of the 21st century, CGI had become the method of choice for virtually all film and TV animation and special effects.

CGI has many advantages over manual techniques. It can produce extremely high-quality, lifelike images, called photorealistic animation, that are difficult to create using hand-drawn pictures or stop-motion models because of the high level of detail that is required. CGI can generate images that would be prohibitively expensive to produce manually, such as massive crowd scenes containing thousands of characters. Without CGI, directors would either have to hire thousands of extras, animate the scenes by hand, or produce thousands of miniature models, all of which would be quite costly and time-consuming. Computers can be used to produce scenes that would be dangerous if filmed using human subjects, such as car chases and explosions. Finally, CGI produces frames using only a single animator and a single tool—the computer—instead of a large team of animators, model builders, directors, camera crew, and lighting staff. This can also reduce costs and speed up the animation process.

Today, computer imaging is a multibillion-dollar industry, and the CGI budget for a wide-release feature film can easily exceed $40–$50 million. Furthermore, CGI techniques have moved well beyond the Hollywood sound stage and are now used in such fields as video gaming (discussed later in this chapter), computer software, scientific and medical imaging, television, advertising, flight simulation, and the production of still images for books and magazines.

Although most of us are well aware that computers generate many of the images we see in the theater or on TV, few of us know how this is done. In the following section, we'll describe some of the fundamental algorithms used to produce computer-generated images.

Computer Horsepower

Industrial Light & Magic (ILM) is the largest visual effects company in the world. It was founded by George Lucas in 1975 to produce the special effects for his science-fiction movie *Star Wars*. ILM went on to do the CGI work for *Jurassic Park*, *Star Trek*, *Pirates of the Caribbean*, *Mission Impossible*, *Avatar*, *Iron Man*, *Transformers*, the Harry Potter series, and dozens of other well-known and highly profitable films. The company, now owned by Disney, has won 15 Oscars for its outstanding visual effects work.

None of this would be possible, however, without an enormous amount of computing resources. At its San Francisco rendering center (called the "Death Star"), ILM has the computational power of 20,000 stand-alone computer systems and enough online storage to hold 10,000 trillion bytes of data. These systems are interconnected by a high-speed network capable of transmitting 12 trillion bits of information per second. This massive collection of equipment draws 2.4 million megawatts of power and is cooled by 32 air-conditioning units that require 25 tons of coolant to keep the building inhabitable—all of this computing power just to make sure that the intergalactic spaceships and alien creatures you see on the screen look totally realistic while you sit back and munch popcorn!

16.2.2 How It's Done: The Graphics Pipeline

The production of high-quality computer-generated images is an enormously complex subject. In this short chapter, we cannot possibly do justice to its many facets and details. Instead, we introduce and describe a few of the fundamental operations required to create and display computer-generated images. Our goal is to provide a basic understanding of CGI techniques and an appreciation for the powerful computers and sophisticated algorithms required to carry out this difficult task.

There is a sequence of operations, termed the graphics pipeline, which must be completed successfully to generate a realistic three-dimensional image. There is no agreement on exactly which steps should or should not be included, and the number of distinct items in a pipeline diagram can vary from three to eight, depending on the type of image being produced and whether certain operations are grouped together or listed separately. The following sections describe the three stages shown in the simplified graphics pipeline of Figure 16.2: object modeling, object motion, and rendering and

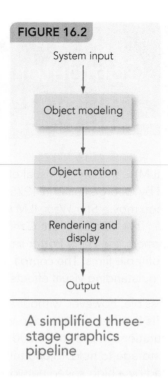

FIGURE 16.2

System input

Object modeling

Object motion

Rendering and
display

Output

A simplified three-
stage graphics
pipeline

display. (Exercise 1 at the end of the chapter asks you to find other examples
of a graphics pipeline diagram to determine which steps were omitted from
the simplified version shown in Figure 16.2.)

16.2.3 Object Modeling

The first step in generating a realistic three-dimensional image is object
modeling—the creation of a mathematical or computational model of a
three-dimensional object that can be stored in the computer's memory and
manipulated algorithmically. There are a number of different approaches to
object modeling. One popular technique is motion capture. In this method
an individual wears a tight-fitting *motion capture suit* that contains a number of visible markers, such as white dots or lights, as shown on the three
actors in Figure 16.3. The computer uses the location of these markers to
create a three-dimensional "stick figure" model of the individuals and stores
that model in memory, as shown on the left side of Figure 16.3. When the
actor moves his or her body, the computer tracks the new location of each
of the markers and moves the stick figure model in the identical fashion.

Another well-known and widely used object modeling algorithm, and the
one we will discuss in more detail, is wireframe modeling. In this technique,
the object's surface, but not its interior, is represented mathematically using
a set of simple nonoverlapping polygons, usually triangles or rectangles.

To create a scene containing a dolphin, we might start by inputting an image
of that object. There are a number of ways to provide this input—for example, an
artist could draw a picture of a dolphin by hand, or we could scan an existing

FIGURE 16.3

The Asahi Shimbun/Getty Images

Example of motion capture object modeling

photograph. Next, using special CGI software and an algorithm called tessellation, the image is subdivided into a set of plane figures that completely covers its surface. An example of this tessellation process is shown in Figure 16.4, using triangles. Figure 16.4 also explains the reason behind the name of this technique. The polygonal outline on the surface, called a *polygon mesh*, produces a model of a dolphin that looks as if it were built from many thin pieces of wire.

FIGURE 16.4

https://en.wikipedia.org/wiki/Polygon_mesh

Wireframe model of a dolphin (based on image in Wikipedia entry on polygon meshes)

Once the object's surface is tessellated, information about the individual polygons is stored in memory, usually in the form of a vertex list. This is a table giving the coordinates of each vertex on the object's surface and the identity of all other vertices to which this one is connected. In order to enter the proper (x, y, z) coordinates of each vertex, where z is the third axis, coming out of the plane, we need to know the *origin* of the coordinate system, that is, the (0, 0, 0) reference point. For simplicity, one of the vertices is usually specified as the origin. It does not matter which point is chosen, as long as the computer knows its identity.

As an example, the four triangles in Figure 16.5(a), which represent a pyramid coming out of the page, might produce the vertex list shown in Figure 16.5(b) using vertex v_1 as the origin point.

The simple four-triangle tessellation shown in Figure 16.5(a) produced the vertex list of Figure 16.5(b) containing about three dozen pieces of information. Realistic objects such as the dolphin of Figure 16.4 can result in enormous tables that consume massive amounts of computer time to generate and huge amounts of computer memory to store. Furthermore, our dolphin may be only one of hundreds of objects (for example, rocks, coral, algae, fish, water, sky) present in a single frame, all of which must be modeled and stored. You can now begin to understand the reasons why CGI places such huge processing and storage demands on a computer system.

FIGURE 16.5

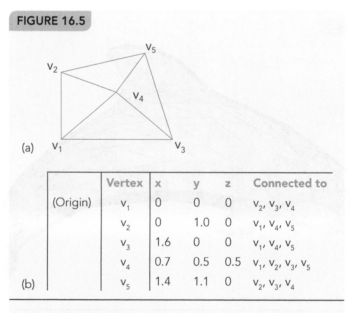

	Vertex	x	y	z	Connected to
(Origin)	v_1	0	0	0	v_2, v_3, v_4
	v_2	0	1.0	0	v_1, v_4, v_5
	v_3	1.6	0	0	v_1, v_4, v_5
	v_4	0.7	0.5	0.5	v_1, v_2, v_3, v_5
(b)	v_5	1.4	1.1	0	v_2, v_3, v_4

Simple tessellation and corresponding vertex list

16.2.4 Object Motion

After we have created and stored a model of our object in some convenient computational format, we can begin the next stage in the graphics pipeline of Figure 16.2—moving that object to its proper position in the next frame.

There are three types of rigid motion (motion that does not bend or deform an object): translation, rotation, and reflection. These three motions are illustrated in Figure 16.6.

Translation, shown in Figure 16.6(a), is the lateral (up/down, right/left, in/out) movement of every point in an object by the same amount and in the same direction. Rotation, Figure 16.6(b), is the circular movement of an object around a fixed point or, in 3D, around a fixed axis, much as a merry-go-round horse revolves around the ride's central mechanism. Finally, reflection, Figure 16.6(c), produces a mirror image of an object such that every point in the reflected image is the same distance from the mirror as in the original object, but on the opposite side of the mirror.

FIGURE 16.6

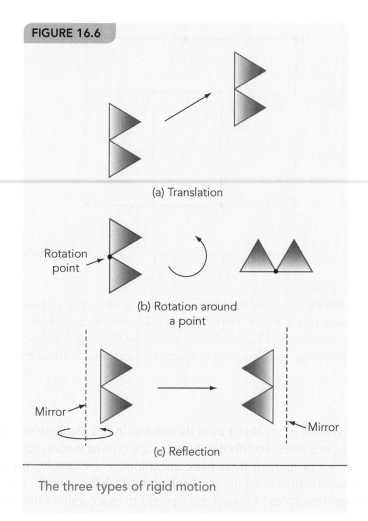

(a) Translation

(b) Rotation around a point

Rotation point

Mirror

Mirror

(c) Reflection

The three types of rigid motion

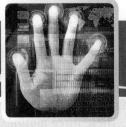

Practice Problem

The following is a polygonal mesh representation of a two-dimensional drawing of a house created using tessellation:

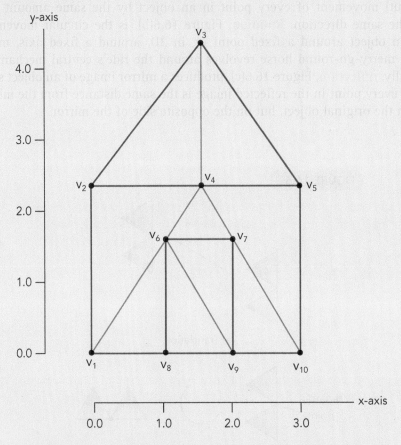

Using v_1 as the origin, show the vertex list generated by this wireframe model. (*Note*: Because this is a two-, rather than three-, dimensional model, the z entry in each column of Figure 16.5(b) would be 0.) How many distinct pieces of information are required to store the information about this model?

The movement of an object from its location in one frame to its new location in the next is often described not by a single type of motion but by a combination of two or more of these basic operations. For example, to model the motion of an airplane taking off and banking to the left, we might use translation to move the airplane forward and upward in space and rotation to model the turning operation. (*Note*: Some types of movement cannot be described using only these three operations. Motions that *deform* or *change* the shape of an object, such as scaling, squeezing, stretching, or ripping, are widely used in computer graphics, but they need additional operators not described here.)

To implement these three motions, we use a mathematical structure called a transformation matrix. When a vector containing the (x, y, z) coordinates of a single vertex point in the current frame is multiplied by this matrix, the result is a new vector containing the translated, rotated, or reflected (x′, y′, z′) coordinates of that one vertex point in the next frame. This same multiplication operation is then applied to every vertex in the vertex list, generating the entire set of new coordinates for the object in the next frame. Thus, in CGI the abstract concept of motion is defined in terms of matrix multiplication, an algorithmic operation easily programmed on a computer. However, even though it may be easy to implement, the potentially huge number of multiplications can make this a time-consuming task. Animating an object containing thousands of vertices, like the dolphin of Figure 16.4, can require billions of arithmetic operations. Again, we can begin to understand and appreciate the need for high-performance computers in the field of CGI.

Let's illustrate how this is done using translation, the straight-line movement of a single point. To move a single vertex point located at coordinates (x, y, z) to a new position at location (x + a, y + b, z + c), we multiply the current coordinates by the 4 × 4 *translation matrix* shown in Figure 16.7. (See Section 8.3.2 on page 410 for an explanation of matrix multiplication.) The results of this operation are the coordinates of this vertex point in the next frame after it has been moved by *a* units along the x-axis, *b* units along the y-axis, and *c* units along the z-axis.

After the operation of Figure 16.7 has been applied to every vertex in the vertex list, the entire object will appear to have moved laterally as a single unit. This behavior is diagrammed in Figure 16.8, in which the object of Figure 16.5(a) has been moved *a* units right in the x-direction and *b* units up in the y-direction. (Assume zero movement in the z-direction to make the picture easier to visualize.)

FIGURE 16.7

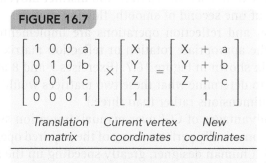

$$
\begin{bmatrix} 1 & 0 & 0 & a \\ 0 & 1 & 0 & b \\ 0 & 0 & 1 & c \\ 0 & 0 & 0 & 1 \end{bmatrix} \times \begin{bmatrix} X \\ Y \\ Z \\ 1 \end{bmatrix} = \begin{bmatrix} X + a \\ Y + b \\ Z + c \\ 1 \end{bmatrix}
$$

Translation   Current vertex   New
matrix   coordinates   coordinates

Using matrix multiplication to implement object translation

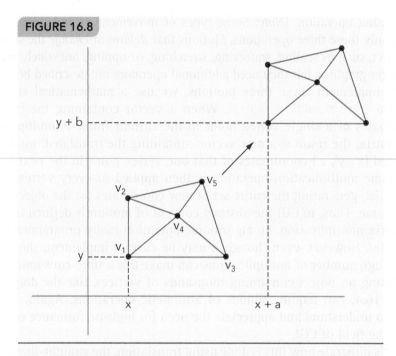

Example of a translation performed on the object shown in Figure 16.5(a)

What actually happened in Figure 16.8 is that the (x, y, z) coordinates of each of the five vertices in the vertex list of Figure 16.5(b)—that is, columns 2, 3, and 4—were multiplied by the 4 × 4 translation matrix in Figure 16.7, with c set to 0 because there is no movement in the z-direction. The newly generated (x', y', z') coordinates of each vertex point are copied back into columns 2, 3, and 4 of the vertex list, replacing the old coordinates. Now, when this object is displayed in the next frame, it will be in its proper location. If we repeat this entire operation 30 times, moving the object a tiny amount each time (i.e., using small values for a, b, and c), then when these 30 frames are shown in sequence, the result will be one second of animated motion. Our eyes will not see 30 separate and distinct movements like those in Figure 16.8, but one second of smooth, flowing motion.

Both rotation and reflection operations are implemented in a similar way, but using the appropriate rotation or reflection matrix in place of the translation matrix shown in Figure 16.7. (Exercises 7 and 8 at the end of the chapter ask you to determine what these two matrices would look like when working in two dimensions rather than three.)

One of the advantages of CGI over manual animation systems is that a computer can automatically perform many of the required operations without the assistance of a human designer, greatly speeding up the animation process. For example, assume the translation motion diagrammed in Figure 16.8 takes place over one second. At 30 frames per second, the standard rate for video, an animator would need to generate 30 distinct frames to obtain the desired effect. However, using a CGI technique called keyframing, a human animator only needs to produce the first frame, containing the starting location of the object; the last frame, containing the final location of the object; and the elapsed time, in this case one second. Using this information, a computer can automatically generate the 28 required intermediate frames, called *in-between frames* or, more simply, *tweeners*. The computer adds 1/29th of the distance between the object's location in the first and last frames to the coordinates of the object in the current frame to position it correctly for the next frame, because with N total frames, there are $N - 2$ in-between frames and $N - 1$ time intervals. The work of the animator has been reduced from creating 30 frames to creating two, the first and the last. This is a huge shift in workload from human being to computer.

In our discussions of motion, we have moved the entire object as a single entity in relation to a single origin point. For example, the polygon in Figure 16.8 moved up and to the right as an indivisible unit. However, sometimes we may want to move different parts of an object in relation to different points or axes, rather than one, in order to achieve a specific effect. For example, Figure 16.9 shows a figure-8 object with two axes of rotation, labeled A and B, with A lying outside the object and B lying at the center of the right circle. (*Note*: Assume the axes of rotation are parallel to the z-axis and are coming out of the page.)

If we perform a rotation operation around axis B on just the rightmost circle, that circle rotates like a wheel around its axle. If we do a second rotation on the entire figure-8 object, this time using axis A, the figure-8 flies around A like the Earth around the sun. We will have created two distinct types of motion—one part of the object spinning like a wheel, while both parts of the object are flying around in a circle. We have achieved this complex set of motions by using two different points of control. A point or axis used to control the motion of an object or part of an object is called a control point, also called an animation variable.

In an object like the dolphin of Figure 16.4, there may be dozens or hundreds of distinct control points that allow us to move the object's head, body, and tail independently. Similarly, if we are animating the image of a human face, we might want control points for the smiling and frowning movements of the mouth, a control point for the movement of the eyes, and

FIGURE 16.9

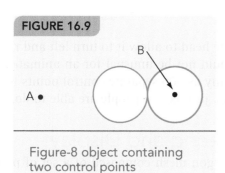

Figure-8 object containing two control points

Practice Problem

Assume that you want to animate the lateral motion of a triangle from its current location, in which:

vertex v_1 is at (0, 0, 0), vertex v_2 is at (1, 0, 0), and vertex v_3 is at (0.5, 1, 0) to a new location such that

vertex v_1 is at (4, 2, 0), vertex v_2 is at (5, 2, 0), and vertex v_3 is at (4.5, 3, 0)

This movement is shown in the following diagram:

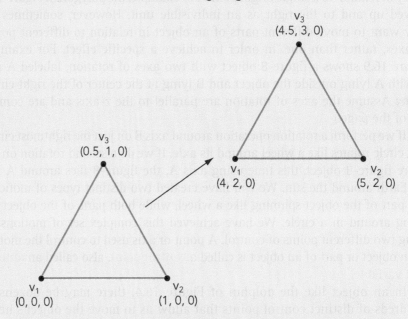

This motion will take two seconds to complete. Show the translation matrix that can be used to generate all the necessary in-between frames.

control points for the head to allow it to turn left and right as well as swivel up and down. It would not be unusual for an animated image of a human being to have as many as 500 separate control points to allow it to move in many different ways, just as real people are able to do.

16.2.5 Rendering and Display

We now have a polygon mesh composed of a set of plane figures, such as triangles, correctly positioned within the new frame after motion has taken place. The final step in the graphics pipeline of Figure 16.2 is rendering and displaying the final image. Rendering means taking an object stored as a mathematical model, such as the vertex list of Figure 16.5(b), and converting it into a fully formed, visually pleasing three-dimensional image.

Rendering is a highly complex set of operations that often consumes the great majority of computer time required to produce an image. (Rendering often requires so many separate computers that the overall complex is called a rendering farm. The Pixar rendering farm, for example, contains more than 2,000 individual computer systems.) Some of the issues that must be addressed during the rendering process are:

- *Lighting*—We specify the location and intensity of all light sources illuminating the image and determine the effect these light sources have on the final appearance.

- *Color shading*—We initially assign a single color or gray level to each vertex in the model and then blend and shade those colors across the face of the polygon. We also determine if there are any modifications to the intensity or appearance of that color due to the incidence of light falling on that plane.

- *Shadows*—We modify the color and brightness of each plane figure because of shadows cast on that plane by opaque objects.

- *Texture mapping*—In the first two stages of CGI, we assume that each plane is a homogeneous, detail-free surface. However, real surfaces like human skin or tree bark are far from homogeneous. Texture mapping allows us to add surface details (bumps, grain, indentations) to each of the plane figures.

- *Blur*—If an object is moving rapidly from one frame to the next, we might choose to blur the final image to represent that motion.

The operations just described (and many others not listed here) are carried out by CGI software running special-purpose rendering algorithms. Figure 16.10 shows a fully rendered color image generated from a polygon mesh representation of each object—glasses, pitcher, dice, ashtray, tiled walls, and table. This image clearly illustrates the many difficult issues that rendering software must deal with in producing a finished image—the color shading of the ashtray from bright green to almost black; the transparency of the glass objects, revealing objects located behind them; the opaqueness of the pitcher; shadows on the wall; reflection of light off the glass surfaces; and the complex texture on the bottom of the water glass.

Rendering a complex image like Figure 16.10 can be difficult and time consuming, especially when there are numerous objects and many light sources. It would not be unusual for a computer, or even a powerful multicomputer rendering farm, to spend hours rendering a single frame such as Figure 16.10.

There are many different algorithms for carrying out the rendering operations just described, such as *rasterization* and *radiosity*, but the most common algorithm, by far, is ray tracing. In this approach, the computer determines the total amount and direction of light falling on each plane surface in the model's vertex list. For example, in Figure 16.11 there are three

FIGURE 16.10

Example of a fully rendered frame

Source: Courtesy Gilles Tran

FIGURE 16.11

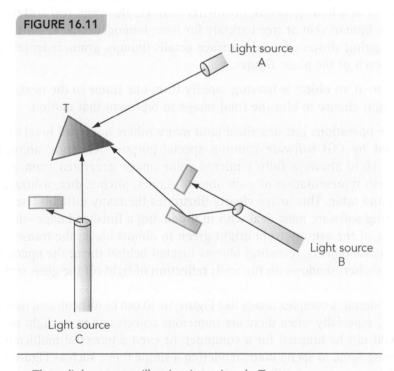

Three light sources illuminating triangle T

light sources illuminating triangle T, where T is a single triangle located on the object's surface. Light source A shines directly onto the surface of T. Light source B is blocked by an opaque object, so it does not contribute any direct light, although it does contribute some indirect lighting due to reflection off another surface. Light source C is partially, but not completely, blocked by an opaque object, so it contributes only a fraction of its potential light. The contributions of each light source are summed to determine the total amount and direction of light rays falling on the face of triangle T. This value, along with knowledge of the object's orientation in space, determines the proper intensity, color shading, and brightness of that face so that it can be rendered in a visually appropriate manner.

Tracing the individual rays of light falling on every face of a model is an extremely time-consuming operation, especially if there are numerous light sources and we are rendering a "busy" object, such as leaves on a tree or strands of hair on a human head. For these special surfaces, CGI often uses algorithms designed specifically to render this one special type of object.

The end product of rendering is a fully colored and textured three-dimensional image ready for display. The final step in the process is changing that three-dimensional image into a two-dimensional image for display on a two-dimensional screen that could be as big as a movie screen or as small as a smartphone display. This is a relatively simple step based on the position of each object in the frame, the location of the viewer, and some simple geometry. For example, Figure 16.12(a) contains three three-dimensional objects labeled A, B, and C, and a viewer whose position is indicated by the letter V. Knowing the three-dimensional coordinates of A, B, C, and V, we can determine that, from the perspective of point V, sphere B is totally obscured while pyramid C is partially obscured. This information can be used to produce a two-dimensional screen representation of what can be seen by a viewer from location V. This is shown in Figure 16.12(b).

16.2.6 The Future of CGI

High-quality CGI is one of the most computationally demanding applications of computers, and only in the last 20 years have processors become sufficiently powerful and memory units grown sufficiently large to carry out the operations described in this section in a reasonable amount of time. However, as we learned in Chapter 5, parallel and multicore computers are becoming far more common, and this increased level of parallelism has resulted in huge gains in speed, allowing for the production of far more detailed images at far less cost. For example, the Nvidia Geforce 1080Ti is a graphics processing unit that contains 3,584 independent processors with 8.2 teraflops of computational power, 11 gigabytes of image memory, and the capability to render approximately 340 billion pixels per second—all for a cost of about $700. In addition, computer scientists are discovering newer and better algorithms to handle such common CGI operations as modeling, animation, and rendering.

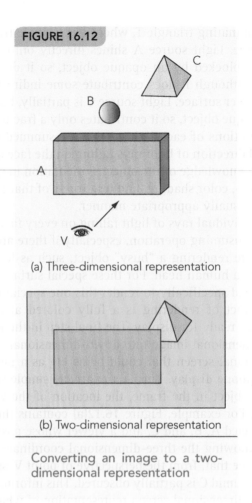

FIGURE 16.12

(a) Three-dimensional representation

(b) Two-dimensional representation

Converting an image to a two-dimensional representation

The future of CGI is bright, and it is quite likely that the next 40 years will see improvements in the quality of computer-generated imagery that may be as (or more) dramatic than the change from the primitive Pong game of Figure 16.1 to the amazing CGI images that we enjoy today at the local multiplex.

16.3 Video Gaming

The computer science issues involved in producing video games are much the same as those addressed by feature film CGI because game images displayed on a laptop, game console, tablet, or smartphone must still be modeled, animated, and rendered as described in the last section. However, there is one huge difference between CGI and video gaming that makes an enormous difference in how we approach and implement these two applications.

A movie is not an interactive environment. There is no change to the plot or action on the screen based on what the user is thinking or doing. If you watch a movie 10 times, you will see exactly the same images in exactly the same order 10 times. Therefore, movie animators can spend as much time as they want rendering each frame, even hours if necessary, because once each frame is completed, its content never changes and the order in which the frames are shown never changes—it is a finished film. Simply put, a movie is a static environment that is created once and shown as often as desired.

On the other hand, a video game is a highly dynamic environment. Using a joystick, wireless controller, finger taps, or body movements, a user controls the action on the screen and makes instant decisions about what happens next—Should I shoot that alien? Should I enter that door? How hard should I swing this golf club? The content of the next frame displayed on the screen depends on what the user does right now, so when you play a video game 10 times, 10 completely different sequences of events might take place. Therefore, we cannot render all the frames in advance because we don't know exactly how objects will move or behave and what should appear next. When the game is in progress, we must generate frames fast enough (typically, 24–30 frames per second) so that the action on the screen appears to happen at roughly the same rate as it would happen in the real world. For example, if I use my game controller to swing a virtual golf club, the screen image must immediately display the ball's proper flight based on the properties of the swing that I just made. If the processor cannot work that quickly, the action will be sluggish, and the game will be far less enjoyable to play.

The branch of computer graphics that studies methods for creating images at a rate matching that of the real world is called real-time graphics, and video gaming is an excellent example of a real-time application. This means that instead of having minutes or hours to render a frame, we have, at 30 frames per second, only 1/30th of a second to get the user's input, analyze what took place, generate a new frame representing the result of that action, and display the final image on the screen. That is a severe time constraint, and because of this limitation, the operative principle in producing video game images is:

If necessary, sacrifice image quality for speed of display.

One of the most common techniques for increasing imaging speed, termed the frame rate, is to use a GPU, an acronym for graphics processing unit. A GPU is an independent processing unit, similar to those described in Chapter 5 and diagrammed in Figure 5.24. (The Nvidia Geforce 1080Ti graphical processor mentioned previously is an excellent example of a modern high-performance GPU.) A GPU executes instructions in parallel with the CPU, the central processing unit, and carries out all of the graphics operations described in this chapter—modeling, motion, rendering, and display. If there is no GPU, these operations would have to be handled by the CPU in addition to its many other responsibilities—running user programs, updating disks, handling input/output, and managing network connections.

With a GPU, all imaging responsibilities are offloaded from the CPU to the GPU, and the two processors run in tandem, an excellent example of the type of parallelism first introduced in Section 5.4. Because a GPU does not have to do general-purpose computing, only image processing, its machine language instruction set can be optimized to perform the specific operations needed for CGI. These might include rendering and drawing triangles like those in the dolphin model of Figure 16.4 or searching two-dimensional matrices like the vertex list of Figure 16.5(b).

Typically, a GPU has its own dedicated random access memory, separate from primary memory, where it stores the image data. Together, the GPU along with this dedicated RAM, referred to as image memory or video memory, are located on a video card, sometimes referred to as a graphics card or a graphics board. This card is connected to the main CPU and primary memory through a plug-in expansion slot or via the system bus. This architecture is diagrammed in Figure 16.13. The configuration shown in Figure 16.13 allows the GPU to access image data (such as the vertex list, color information, location of light sources) from video memory without having to compete with, and be slowed down by, the CPU as it tries to access primary memory. Today, virtually every computer system and video game console contains a dedicated video card and GPU architecture similar to the one shown in Figure 16.13. In fact, high-end systems often contain not a

FIGURE 16.13

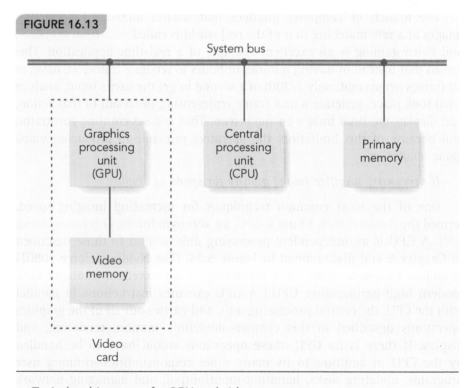

Typical architecture of a GPU and video memory

single video card but multiple cards, each one containing hundreds or even thousands of processors and dozens of gigabytes of video memory.

Another way to achieve speedup in real-time graphics is to avoid the use of algorithms that, although they produce high-quality images, simply take too much time. An excellent example of this is the ray-tracing algorithm introduced in Section 16.2.5 and diagrammed in Figure 16.11. Following millions (or billions) of light rays from their source to an object's surface and any subsequent reflections can produce truly lifelike images, such as the still life of Figure 16.10, but it can take minutes or hours to render a single frame. In a real-time environment, we don't have hours or minutes, only 1/30th of a second, to complete this task.

We can gain considerable speedup by rendering an entire plane (for example, a single triangle) using a uniform color, shade, and texture. As was mentioned in the previous section, many rendering algorithms initially assign a uniform color and texture to each triangle but then blend and mix adjacent colors to create a smooth and pleasing color transition. We can eliminate this step and instead use a single color and texture for the entire face; subtle color differences or brightness changes within a single plane would not be allowed. This reduces our workload significantly, but it comes at the cost of a less lifelike image.

Another technique to speed up rendering and display is culling. Rather than rendering every plane in the wireframe model and then determining which planes are visible from the user's perspective, as diagrammed in Figure 16.12, we could turn those two operations around. First determine which planes can be seen from the user's point of view, based on location and opaqueness, and then render only those objects visible in the next frame, omitting all operations on hidden surfaces.

Finally, video gaming often makes use of a technique called cut-ins. These are fully modeled and fully rendered objects stored in a video library in video memory. These already prepared objects can be dropped into a frame as is, producing a significant speedup in frame creation. These cut-ins often include images of the main game characters as well as standard background objects—cars, castles, weapons—that appear in many of the frames.

The end result of these optimizations (and many others not mentioned here) is the ability to accept user input, determine what action should be taken in response to this input, and render and display a frame representing the game state after that action has been completed. And all of this in only 1/30th of a second!

Even though real-time graphics is improving in quality and closing the gap with off-line CGI, the quality of a typical video game image still does not equal the level achieved by high-quality, feature-film CGI. However, as processors grow faster and as higher levels of parallelism become both technically and financially feasible, the quality of real-time video game images will certainly improve and perhaps begin to approach the level of the computer-generated imagery found in today's best feature films.

The Good, the Bad, and the Ugly

In the mid-19th century, a British literary genre called "penny dreadfuls" was extremely popular among English teenagers. These cheap magazines, costing a penny, contained lurid tales and drawings of horror, sex, and violence. Respectable Victorians detested these publications and fought to censor them, claiming they warped the minds of young, impressionable British lads. This was one of the earliest attempts at censoring a style of youth culture deemed inappropriate and degrading by adults of that era.

Similar attempts at censorship have been repeated numerous times against other popular pastimes such as comic books, rock and roll, R- and X-rated movies, body art, and rap music. Most recently, there has been a good deal of vocal opposition to modern video games.

There is no doubt that video games can contain controversial content—drug use, criminal behavior, sexual acts, violence, and strong language. In many cases, this extreme content forms the central theme of the game. For example, a widely played video game includes the simulated shooting of police officers and the rape and murder of prostitutes. Another game involves violent gang activity between competing ethnic groups. These games often use a "first person shooter" format, in which the player views the activity through the eyes of the main character, actually pointing the gun and shooting the victims.

This has led to public criticism of the entire video game industry from politicians, schools, parents, religious groups, and mental health organizations. To address these concerns, the Entertainment Software Rating Board (ESRB) adopted a voluntary rating system (E for everyone, T for teen, AO for adults only, etc.), but it is strongly opposed to any additional forms of censorship. The game industry argues that adults should be free to play these games if they so desire, and that there are few scientific studies linking the playing of violent video games to real-world crime or changes in the personality or behavior of their players.

This controversy will no doubt continue to grow, as governments around the world have passed, or are considering, legislation to regulate or restrict the production and sale of violent video games.

16.4 Multiplayer Games and Virtual Communities

Most video games involve a small number of players, typically one to four. However, the last 15 years have seen the development of a new game genre called massively multiplayer online games (MMOG). These games allow a large number of players, often thousands or even millions, to interact, form groups, and compete against one another within a simulated virtual world.

The world in which the action takes place is managed by special computers called game servers. Depending on the game complexity and the number of players, there may be one or two servers or many thousands. In an MMOG, the virtual world in which the game is played is *persistent*. This means the server software that creates the world is always running and always available, and it maintains the current state of every player, even after they have logged off the system. This is unlike games that can be turned off and on at will, but that lose state information when turned off and must be restarted from the beginning.

Users log on to the game server whenever they want, using client software running on their home computer, laptop, tablet, or smartphone. This client software may be either proprietary code purchased from the gaming company or a publicly available program such as a web browser. Thus, the architecture of an MMOG, shown in Figure 16.14, is virtually identical to the client/server network model introduced and diagrammed in Chapter 7, Figure 7.24.

The development of an MMOG incorporates a number of important computer science-related research topics that have been discussed earlier in the text. For example, the three-dimensional images displayed on the user's screen employ all the real-time graphics algorithms discussed in the previous section, but with the added complexity and tighter time constraints caused by delays across the network. In addition to rendering the game images, designers of MMOG must also address and solve the following technical problems:

- *Registration management*—There may be hundreds of thousands of existing users at various points in the game, as well as hundreds of new users joining or leaving every day. The responsibilities of the server software that manages this user base include ensuring that new users correctly join the community, saving the game state of existing users when they log off, and restoring that state when they log back on. This is similar to the "receptionist" responsibility of the operating system discussed in Section 6.4.1.

- *Client/server protocols*—In an MMOG, there are thousands or millions of users simultaneously accessing dozens or hundreds of game servers across multiple communication channels. The game designers must implement the network protocols that support this vast communications array. We discussed the topic of computer networks and protocols in Chapter 7.

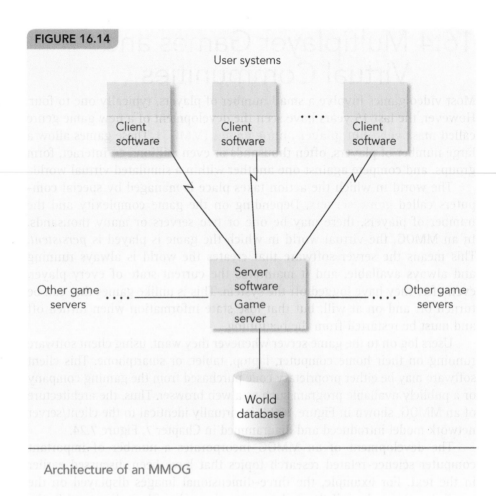

FIGURE 16.14

Architecture of an MMOG

- *Game security*—An MMOG must keep track of each user's activity to ensure that his or her actions do not incorrectly or inappropriately affect the actions of other players. Furthermore, the system must ensure that all users adhere to the rules of the game and do not attempt to carry out illegal operations. The topic of computer security was discussed in Chapter 8.

- *Database design*—The world database of Figure 16.14 can be a truly massive structure holding many terabytes of data. The game designers are responsible for implementing this database and making sure that it can be accessed quickly enough to provide real-time response to user actions. Databases were introduced and described in Section 14.3.

Because of these technical complexities, the cost of developing a sophisticated MMOG can run to millions of dollars and take hundreds or thousands of person-years to design and implement. Currently, the largest and most popular MMOG is *Happy Farm*, played primarily in China and Taiwan. It has 228 million registered users and approximately 20–25 million players logging on each day. Another popular MMOG is *World of Warcraft*, with

5–6 million subscribers playing each month. It has grossed over $10 billion since its release in 2004.

When we think of the word *game*, we usually assume an environment based on competition, scoring, winners, and losers. However, a recent development in MMOG design is the concept of a noncompetitive MMOG, sometimes called a metaverse, short for *metauniverse*. This is a simulated virtual world, much like what we have just described, but where the goal is not to destroy your opponent or get the highest score. Instead, the purpose of entering this collective shared environment is to explore the virtual world, interact with other people in the world (often called "residents"), form communities of residents with similar interests, and create new economic entities that have (virtual) value. Players behave in this metaverse in many of the same ways they do in the real world—communicating, working, building, and moving around. There is no winning or losing in a noncompetitive MMOG, just the enjoyment of experiencing a new environment and meeting new people—not unlike traveling (for real) to a foreign country.

The most widely used and well-known metaverse is *Second Life*, a virtual world created by Linden Labs in 2003. Many of the items in this virtual world (houses, cars, clothing) are user-generated objects constructed by individuals or groups using a CGI modeling tool that allows residents to customize their virtual environment. (This tool performs the operations listed in the graphics pipeline diagram of Figure 16.2.) According to many of its residents, it is the collaborative and creative activities, not competition, that make *Second Life* so popular.

Second Life uses the client/server model diagrammed in Figure 16.14. The client software that provides access to the virtual world is a free, downloadable program called Second Life Viewer. Currently, there are several thousand server computers and over 100 terabytes (10^{14}) of data in the *Second Life* world database. However, even with this vast amount of computing power, the popularity and growth of *Second Life* is beginning to strain the computational resources of Linden Labs, making it difficult to keep up with the growth of its virtual world, not unlike the problems encountered in rapidly growing real-world cities whose resources strain to keep up with an expanding population.

Currently, there are approximately 1.1 million active residents of *Second Life*, which (if it were a U.S. state) would make it larger than Delaware, South Dakota, Alaska, North Dakota, Vermont, Wyoming, or the District of Columbia. At any instant in time, there are approximately 50,000 people logged on to *Second Life*, wandering through this virtual world, chatting with members of virtual communities, and creating virtual economic wealth.

16.5 Conclusion

Not that long ago, almost all input to a computer was textual. Communication with the operating system was via cryptic textual commands that were hard to remember and difficult to understand. The primary applications of the 1960s, 1970s, and 1980s were also textual—email, word processing, databases, spreadsheets—and they often produced reams of incomprehensible textual output. The appearance of the first graphical user interfaces in the 1980s demonstrated the intellectual power of visualization. By the early 1990s, graphics had moved into the scientific domain via charts, diagrams, and images that made it easier to interpret the output of scientific programs. Businesses began to use graphics in the form of *computer-aided design* (CAD) tools that gave architects and manufacturers the power to create and edit designs online. Soon visualization had become an integral part of virtually every popular application.

But it is in the last 15–20 years that visualization has found one of its most compelling and exciting uses—the ability to amuse us, entertain us, and enhance our pleasure. The use of CGI in feature movies, TV, videos, and online gaming is growing to the point where nearly every imaginable environment and action can be created on a computer and displayed in a photorealistic fashion. The use of interactive real-time graphics takes us beyond passive viewing of virtual worlds to letting us play in them, function in them, and even "live" in them.

As graphics processing units and visualization algorithms grow faster and more sophisticated, and as massively parallel computing environments become cheaper and ever more common in laptops, tablets, and smartphones, the quality of computer-generated images will continue to improve, and the feeling of actually being inside a virtual world will grow more real. Perhaps the simulated-reality "holodeck" technology from the TV series *Star Trek*, usually thought of as a comic book fantasy, is no longer an unattainable goal.

The Computer Will See You Now

Computer imaging can be used to amaze, enthrall, and entertain. It can also be used to diagnose, treat, and heal—applications that most of us would agree are far more important.

Medical imaging is a rapidly growing area of computer and biological science research in which computers and graphics software are used to produce highly accurate two- and three-dimensional images of the interior of the human body without surgery or other invasive procedures. The instrumentation that generates the image data may be X-ray, MRI, PET scans, thermography, or ultrasound. However, in all cases, this raw data would be useless for diagnostic and treatment purposes if it could not be converted into

(Continued)

high-quality, lifelike images that can be examined and analyzed by health professionals. To do this, the initial data from these instruments becomes the input to a graphics pipeline similar to the one in Figure 16.2. This allows a computer to model, render, and display images in a photorealistic fashion. Today, medical imaging algorithms are helping physicians detect the early stages of breast cancer, perform delicate brain surgery, and track fetal development in the womb.

The algorithms that produce these highly precise medical visualizations are quite similar to, sometimes identical to, the algorithms originally developed to generate realistic images of alien invaders, prehistoric dinosaurs, and virtual worlds. This is an excellent demonstration of the importance of basic scientific research—you never know where that work may lead, or to which fields it may ultimately make fundamental contributions.

16.6 Summary of Level 5

At the beginning of Level 5, "Applications," we said that we would be able to cover only a small sampling of the many important applications of computers. After looking at the fields of simulation and modeling, electronic commerce, databases, data science, artificial intelligence, computer graphics, and online gaming, we hope you will seek to learn more about other application areas that might interest you but that were not covered here.

There is still one more level to our story of computer science. With all the capabilities that exist today and that will be developed tomorrow, what is the larger picture of computer technology within society? What are the ethical, legal, and social consequences of these capabilities? What should we welcome? What should we monitor or regulate? What should we fear? Is there anything we should prohibit? We have touched on some of these issues in talking about security, personal privacy, and violent video games. Level 6 raises such questions in more detail, though, of course, it provides no definitive answers. It does, however, suggest some tools to help us clarify thorny moral dilemmas or ethical decisions. Individuals, armed with adequate knowledge, must hammer out their own moral position on these complex social issues. This is one of the responsibilities that comes with our unprecedented opportunity to enjoy the benefits of computer technology.

EXERCISES

1. Locate sources describing the graphics pipeline of Figure 16.2 in greater detail. (A good place to start is the "Graphics Pipeline" entry at Wikipedia.org.) How many distinct steps are included in these versions of the pipeline? Which ones that are included were omitted in this chapter, and what operations do these missing steps perform? Write a report giving an overview of these more complete treatments of the sequence of steps involved in computer graphics.

2. Given the triangular model of a two-dimensional object shown here:

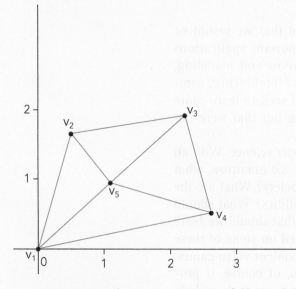

write a vertex list representation of this model. Because you are working in two dimensions rather than three, your vertex list will only have (x, y) coordinates rather than (x, y, z). Assume vertex v_1 is the origin.

3. a. Assume the matrix multiplication of Figure 16.7 requires a total of 28 arithmetic operations—floating-point additions and multiplications. If we want to move

(i.e., translate) a wireframe representation of an object containing 100,000 vertex points, and if that motion takes 10 seconds to complete, how many arithmetic operations in total does a computer need to perform to implement that movement?

b. If your GPU can execute 50 million floating-point operations per second, how long will it take the processor to complete this translation operation?

4. Assume a polygon mesh contains 250,000 vertices. If a single matrix multiplication requires 28 floating-point operations, how fast a GPU is needed (floating-point operations per second) to produce real-time graphics at the rate of 30 frames per second?

5. Here is the vertex list for a two-dimensional wireframe triangular model:

	Vertex	x	y	Connected to
(Origin)	v1	0	0	v2, v3, v4
	v2	0	1	v1, v4
	v3	1	0	v1, v4, v5
	v4	1	1	v1, v2, v3, v5
	v5	1.6	0.5	v3, v4

Draw the two-dimensional figure modeled by this vertex list.

6. We want to animate the movement of the object in Exercise 2 from its current location at (0, 0, 0), the coordinates of v_1, to the point (3, 5, 0). The motion lasts for a total of 2 seconds. Show the translation matrix that accomplishes this motion. That is, show the matrix that, when reapplied 30 times each second for a total of 2 seconds, will produce the desired ending position.

7. Assume you are working in two, rather than three, dimensions. Determine the four entries of the 2 × 2 *rotation matrix* that will take a vertex point located at position (x, y) and rotate it counterclockwise around the origin by an angle ø. The rotation is shown here: (*Hint*: You will need to use some trigonometric functions to accomplish this.)

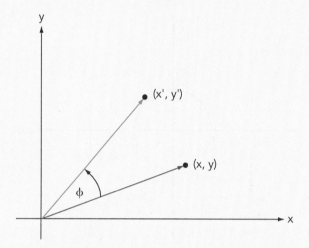

8. Again assume you are working in two, rather than three, dimensions. Determine the four entries of the 2 × 2 *reflection matrix* that takes a vertex point at position (x, y) and reflects it around the y-axis. That is, assume the mirror line in Figure 16.6(c) is the y-axis. This reflection operation is shown here:

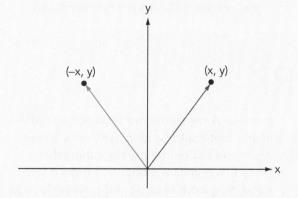

9. Shown below is an image of a human arm, from shoulder to hand. It has three control points labeled A, B, and C. Describe what type of motion might require the use of each of these three control points. Using these three control points, describe informally how you might animate the motion of an arm raising a glass held in the hand up to a figure's mouth.

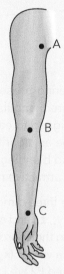

10. Would a flight simulator package used to teach pilots to fly an airplane be a real-time graphical environment? Explain your answer.

11. The diagram on the next page shows a single triangular face in the wireframe representation of an object. The three vertices of the triangle are labeled v_1, v_2, and v_3, and each has been assigned a color, either red, blue, or green.

The vertex color is stored as a three-tuple, with each entry an integer in the range 0 to 255, representing the contribution of the components red, green, and blue, respectively. (*Note*: This is identical to the RGB color model introduced in Chapter 4, page 171.) So, for example, the color red is represented by the three-tuple (255, 0, 0). Purple, an equal mix of red and blue, would be represented as (128, 0, 128).

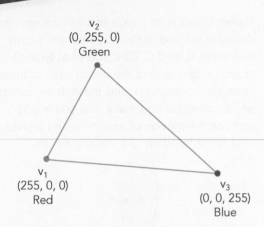

v_2
(0, 255, 0)
Green

v_1
(255, 0, 0)
Red

v_3
(0, 0, 255)
Blue

During the rendering phase, a computer must shade in the entire triangular face, according to the colors assigned to each of the three vertices. Describe an algorithm that would do color shading and blending of the triangular face in a visually attractive manner.

12. You are given the three-dimensional coordinates of a point P1 (x_1, y_1, z_1) and a point P2 (x_2, y_2, z_2). You are also given the coordinates of the location point of a viewer (x_v, y_v, z_v). You may assume that P1 and P2 are located on the same side of the viewer. Describe informally (you do not need to write out an algorithm) exactly how to determine if, from the point of view of the viewer, it is possible to see both points P1 and P2, or if one of these points is obstructed and not visible. In the latter case, describe how you can determine which is the occluded point.

13. The following diagram contains a circle of radius 1 with its center at the origin (0, 0). There is a mirror line parallel to the y-axis located at the point x = −2. For each of the following pairs of operations, describe the final result after each of the two pairs of motions has been completed, one at a time:

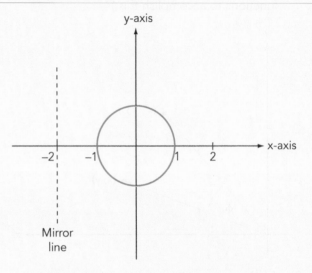

a. Translate the circle along the x-axis by +2 units.
   Reflect the circle around the mirror line.

b. Reflect the circle around the mirror line.
   Translate the circle along the x-axis by +2 units.

c. Reflect the circle around the mirror line.
   Reflect the circle around the mirror line.

CHALLENGE WORK

In Section 16.2.5, we described only the most basic aspects of the rendering process. It is a far more complex topic than the elementary material presented in that section. However, it is also the most critical and most difficult step in the overall imaging process. A wireframe model is not a finished image that could be displayed on a screen. It is the set of rendering algorithms that takes this primitive model and turns it into something both realistic and believable in its appearance.

Find sources of technical information on rendering and read about the steps involved in this visualization process. Specifically, read about some of these aspects of rendering that were not presented in this chapter:

- *Bump-mapping*—Creating small-scale bumps on the surface of an object
- *Fogging*—The dimming and dispersal of light as it passes through a partially obscure atmosphere
- *Refraction*—The bending of light associated with transparency

- *Indirect illumination*—Surfaces that are illuminated by light reflecting off other objects
- *Translucency*—The scattering of light as it passes through solid objects
- *Depth of field*—Objects that appear out of focus because they are too close to or too far from the object that is in focus

For one or more of these rendering topics, write a report that describes the algorithms used to address these issues.

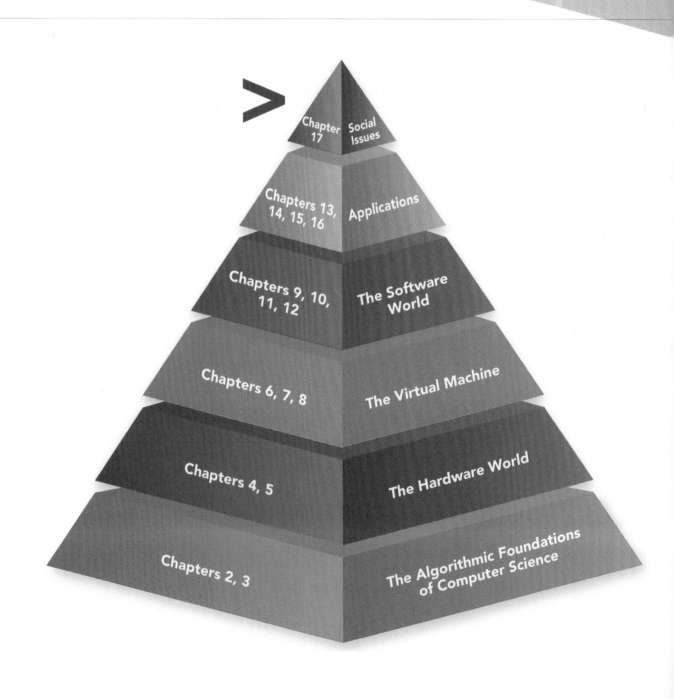

Chapter 17 — Social Issues

Chapters 13, 14, 15, 16 — Applications

Chapters 9, 10, 11, 12 — The Software World

Chapters 6, 7, 8 — The Virtual Machine

Chapters 4, 5 — The Hardware World

Chapters 2, 3 — The Algorithmic Foundations of Computer Science

We have now reached the highest and most abstract level in our discussion of computer science—the social, ethical, legal, and moral questions raised by the information-based technologies just presented. In this section, we are no longer interested solely in algorithms (Level 1), hardware (Level 2), virtual machines (Level 3), software (Level 4), or applications (Level 5). Instead, we investigate the impact, both good and bad, that these developments can have on business, government, society, and individuals. These concerns were not part of the original definition of computer science, and in the early days were often not included in the computer science curriculum but, instead, left to departments such as Philosophy, Religion, or Sociology to discuss and debate. However, as computing has become more pervasive, these social and ethical issues have become a critically important part of the study of computer science.

Making Decisions about Computers, Information, and Society

AFTER STUDYING THIS CHAPTER, YOU WILL BE ABLE TO:

- Use ethical reasoning to evaluate social issues related to computing
- Understand the issues involved in digitally sharing copywritten intellectual property, such as music, videos, photographs, books, and video game software
- Discuss trade-offs between the rights of personal privacy and governments' concerns with safety and security
- Provide arguments that support and oppose hackers who claim to be performing a social good
- Describe cyberbullying and why legal remedies are so difficult to apply
- Explain the potential dangers that have arisen from the enormous growth of social media
- Discuss how social media makes it easier to globally disseminate rumors and false information that can have a profound effect on governments worldwide

17.1 Introduction

Most of this book has focused on the *technical* issues of computing. For example, you have read about the mathematics of algorithmic efficiency (Chapter 3), the hardware implementation of computer systems (Chapters 4 and 5), computer networks (Chapter 7), and software development (Chapters 9 and 10). However, in this chapter, we focus on the *human* issues lurking behind these technical details. We can't provide a comprehensive list of such issues; such a list would be way too long, and it is growing daily. Instead, we introduce skills that will help you to think and reason carefully when making personal decisions about computing. This chapter also discusses important societal issues related to information technology and personal privacy and points you toward resources to help you explore these issues in greater detail. Making critical decisions about computing technology is unavoidable. Increasingly, our society is being driven by the access to and control of

information. As citizens of our communities, our country, and the world, we want our decisions to be well informed and well reasoned.

Whenever humans make decisions about things they value, there are conflicts and trade-offs. The field of ethics, the study of moral philosophy, has a long history of looking at how to identify and resolve such conflicts, and we will borrow from several classical theories of ethics. In this chapter, we present a number of case studies built around complex ethical issues related to computing and information. For each case study, we present the issues as well as arguments used to support and oppose certain positions. We then describe methods that allow us to understand and evaluate these arguments in terms of their ethical implications. Finally, we will investigate the enormous impact that social media is having on both our personal privacy and our access to information. When you finish this chapter, you should have an increased appreciation for the complexities of human/computer interactions as well as an enhanced set of skills for thinking and reasoning about these complex interactions.

17.2 Case Studies

17.2.1 Case 1: Is It Sharing or Stealing?

You are probably familiar with the concept of movie and music "piracy." You may have been bombarded with advertisements from the recording and movie industries warning of the negative repercussions of copying or sharing copyrighted material, such as music, videos, photographs, books, and video game software. In this section we introduce the basic concepts of ethical decision-making through a case study, the case of the first successful peer-to-peer file sharing system, Napster.

"Sharing" of music and movies was already commonplace prior to the popularity of the Internet, but it was fairly limited. At the time, music and movies were distributed on tapes, and it was not hard to physically duplicate a tape and give it to a friend. Although this type of sharing was illegal (and the recording and movie industries took some steps to prevent it), it wasn't a major threat to their businesses because the amount of labor involved in copying was high, and copies were usually only shared with a small number of close friends. True "piracy" involves the mass production of bootleg products for sale, not small-scale sharing between friends.

In the spring of 1999, two Northeastern University students, Shawn Fanning and Sean Parker, created a system intended to simplify the sharing of computer files with strangers. The users of the system were mostly other university students, who had ready access to fast Internet connections and who were interested in obtaining music files that other students were willing to share. Fanning and Parker called their system "Napster," and it became so popular that several universities noticed their campus networks slowing to a crawl because of student music downloads.

The Napster system is a wonderful example of how technical achievements in computing can have significant social effects. The Napster software set up what's called peer-to-peer file sharing. As diagrammed in Figure 17.1, Napster's software electronically "introduced" two users who are distant from

FIGURE 17.1

1. User B sends to the Napster central server a list of MP3 data files he/she is willing to share.

2. The Napster central server places this information into a database of MP3 song titles and their Internet (IP) locations.

3. User A connects to the Napster central server and queries it with the name of a song he/she wants to download.

4. The Napster central server searches its database and sends User A the names of all machines with this song and their Internet locations.

5. User A establishes a connection to User B (or any other machine with this song) and sends a download request message containing the song name.

6. User B sends the requested MP3 file to User A, who stores it on his/her machine and listens to it with an MP3 player.

Peer-to-peer file sharing system created by Napster

Napster and from each other. Once Napster helped these users find each other electronically, the file sharing took place between the users, *not* through Napster. This meant that although thousands and thousands of bootleg copies were being made, Napster itself wasn't making or distributing them. Napster simply helped connect individuals to enable one-to-one swaps. It was not clear if what Napster was doing was even illegal, let alone unethical.

In many ways Napster was acting like applications such as Angie's List or Home Advisor. These applications publish lists of companies who provide useful services such as plumbing or home remodeling. Users can digitally search these lists, select someone to provide the needed service, and contact that individual directly. The listing service itself only connects users to providers; it does not do any of the actual work.

On December 7, 1999, an organization of recording companies filed suit against Napster in U.S. district court on grounds of copyright infringement. During the highly publicized arguments that followed, the recording companies insisted that Napster was a conspiracy to encourage mass infringement of U.S. copyright law. By most accounts, the majority of music that Napster users "shared" was copyrighted, and most of the copyright holders objected to the copying of their music without royalty payments. The recording industry saw Parker, Fanning, and Napster as no different from the bootleggers who were mass-producing fake copies of CDs and movies.

Napster's supporters argued that the system was merely acting as a search engine, providing information on songs and their location, but not participating in the actual exchange of copyrighted information. They argued that Napster could not be held responsible for what peers (Users A and B) did with that information in the peer-to-peer file-sharing system depicted in Figure 17.1.

In addition, Napster contended that there were significant legal uses for the service. It pointed out that copyright law allows a person who has purchased a recording in one format to transfer it to a different format as long as it is for personal use and is not resold. Someone who legally owned a song on CD could use Napster to acquire a copy in MP3 format, something they are legally entitled to have. Furthermore, both peers in each swap were transferring the file without any payment to each other or to Napster, and therefore (according to Napster) the copying should be considered *fair use*, the legal doctrine that allows for brief excerpts of copywritten material to be copied or quoted under certain restricted circumstances.

Eventually, Napster lost the case and subsequent appeals, and it ceased operating as a file-sharing site in 2001. However, other peer-to-peer file-sharing systems sprang up on the web, and illegal music sharing (as well as movie, book, and video game software sharing) via the Internet continues, much to the chagrin of recording companies, publishers, game developers, and the movie industry. BitTorrent (the most popular peer-to-peer file sharing system) represents about 5% of all Internet traffic, while YouTube currently accounts for about 25% of all music streamed worldwide, far more than any other site.

This case leads to many ethical questions, but two are worth special attention:

1. Is it right to swap copyrighted music or book files, download and watch copyrighted videos, or use copyrighted photos without permission?

2. Is it right to provide a search engine whose only purpose is to allow users to search each other's databases of copyrighted music and book files, videos, and photos?

At its core, these are neither technical nor legal questions. The law tells you what you are allowed to do, while technology determines what you are able to do, but neither can tell you whether it is morally right or wrong to do it. In the best case we try to establish what is right, and then write the laws so as to encourage this type of right behavior. So how do we reason about what is right?

Asking Ethical Questions. A legal question, we take to a judge. A technical question, we take to a scientist or an engineer. But who can help us with an ethical question? In this section, we look to ethicists for guidance about getting an answer to an ethical question.

Earlier we defined ethics as the study of moral philosophy—how to decide if something is morally right or wrong. A fundamental question in ethics is what criteria to use when "measuring" the rightness or wrongness of a particular act. Over the centuries, ethicists have championed different criteria and developed schools of thought about how to label an act as good or bad, better or worse. One of the most influential schools is called consequentialism. As the name implies, a consequentialist focuses on the consequences, or outcomes, of an act to determine if the act is good or bad. If the consequences are on the whole good, then the act is good. If the consequences are mostly bad, then the act is bad. However, in focusing on the goodness of an act, we have to ask, "Good for whom?" For instance, in our music example the copying is certainly good for people who get free music. But, just as clearly, most music copyright holders are convinced that music copying without the payment of royalties is bad.

The most well-known consequentialists are the utilitarians. Utilitarians answer the question "Good for whom?" with a hearty, "Good for everyone!" Imagine a cosmic calculator that is capable of adding up human happiness. Utilitarianism holds that a moment before an act takes place, the cosmic calculator adds up all human happiness and puts a happiness number into the variable HAPPINESS_BEFORE. Then the act occurs. We wait awhile, long enough for the consequences of the act to become visible; then we use our cosmic calculator again and put a second happiness total into the variable HAPPINESS_AFTER. According to a utilitarian, the act in question is "good" if

HAPPINESS_AFTER > HAPPINESS_BEFORE

or "bad" if

HAPPINESS_AFTER < HAPPINESS_BEFORE.

(Just to satisfy the law of trichotomy, if HAPPINESS_AFTER = HAPPINESS_BEFORE, a careful utilitarian would declare the act to be ethically neutral.)

Of course, there is no cosmic calculator, and quantifying happiness is no easy task. Clearly, using the utilitarians' criterion requires subjective judgments. But making consequences count and ensuring that all people are taken into account when making an ethical judgment both seem like good ideas. So let's try out two short utilitarian arguments to explore whether mass copying of music files (as well as movies, books, photos, and videos) is morally right.

Utilitarian Argument #1: Copying Is OK. First, there are many more music listeners than there are music publishers. Music listeners are very pleased to get convenient, virtually free access to all this music. Furthermore, music publishers should be pleased to get so much free publicity for their product. When radio stations play music, it's free to listeners, and many listeners go out and buy the music that they've heard on the radio. The same thing happens to listeners who download music files. Many choose to buy legal copies, even though they do not need them, so that artists get paid, or they may choose to purchase additional music by the same artist. There

Death of a Dinosaur

The Virgin Megastores in New York City's Times Square and Union Square were the two largest music stores in the world, sprawling over 180,000 square feet of retail space and selling an estimated $55 million worth of recordings every year. Not only were they important economic engines for the entertainment industry, they were also popular gathering places for hard-core music lovers and emerging artists. Unfortunately, even megastores with massive sales volumes and huge financial backing are finding it difficult to compete with online music sites like iTunes and the ease of digital copying. "It's clear that the model of a large entertainment specialist working in a large retail space is not going to work in the future," said Simon Wright, the CEO of Virgin Entertainment Group, North America.

In February 2009, the Times Square store closed its doors for good, with the Union Square store following suit just four months later. In the words of a former Virgin employee, "The large retail music store is a dinosaur, and we all know what happened to them!"

is some market research that shows that downloading music files can even increase music sales. Although opponents of music file sharing point out that overall music sales revenue has fallen dramatically since 1999, this cannot be completely blamed on file sharing. During the CD era, people bought whole albums. Today music retailers like iTunes and Amazon encourage consumers to buy one song at a time, which has also hurt overall album sales.

Utilitarian Argument #2: Copying Is Not OK. Although some early research suggested that music file copying may have initially encouraged CD buying, later research has shown that overall retail music sales have declined rapidly—down over 50% since 2000. That's the real, long-term effect of widespread copying of copyrighted materials. If the people who publish music can't make a fair profit, then less and less music will be published. Eventually, both music listeners and music publishers (including the people who make the music) will lose. In addition, copyright protection is the law. This widespread criminal activity will result in a widespread disrespect for the law in general, and that is a very dangerous consequence.

We have used an ethicist's idea, a utilitarian argument, to try to clarify the music file copying question, but instead of getting a clear answer to our question, it seems we've only managed to make things more confusing. Both sides of this issue seem to have some reasonable points. How are we to decide between them?

Let's admit something up front: Deciding what is morally right and wrong is not always easy. There isn't an all-purpose "ethics algorithm" that is guaranteed to provide a definitive answer to every ethical question. Still, we do have to make decisions about these issues, and we want to make those decisions on reasonable grounds, not just on whims or gut instinct.

Ethicists depend on what is called a dialectic to try to make better ethical decisions. In a dialectic, we move back and forth between different viewpoints, criticizing each and trying to learn from each. In a debate, one side is trying to win by undermining the opposition and building up the arguments for its position. However, in a dialectic the ultimate goal is for both sides to "win" by moving closer to the truth from two different perspectives. It's perfectly OK for people engaged in a dialectic to change their minds; in fact, that's the point. By systematically reasoning about the issue, the back and forth of argument can bring all parties to a more well-reasoned and justified decision. There's never a guarantee that the two sides in a dialectic will arrive at identical positions (although that is possible). More often, the participants end the dialectic still disagreeing, but hopefully with a better understanding of the other side's viewpoints.

In the spirit of a dialectic, let's examine the strengths and weaknesses of the two previous utilitarian arguments on the issue of music file copying. Both arguments cite evidence about music sales to bolster their position: People for copying claim that it increases the sales of music; people against copying claim that it decreases overall music sales. This is an example of a difference in fact, not just a difference of opinion. If the effect of music file copying is, in fact, to increase music sales, then the "copying is OK" people have a strong argument; if the effect is instead to decrease sales, then the "copying is not OK" people have a strong argument. When the dialectic uncovers an empirical question at the heart of a disagreement, the smart move is to check the facts.

According to published statistics, by 2016 global revenues from the sale of recorded music were less than half what they were in 2000. Even with the introduction of legal alternatives like iTunes, Spotify, and Amazon Music, album sales have continued to decline. So it seems that, on this point, the file copying opponents have a stronger argument.

What about the happiness of the legions of listeners who get free music? The opponents of copying again make an argument about short-term and long-term effects of copying: In the short run, listeners might get tremendous benefits; but in the long run, there may be far less music available for copying because artists and publishers will have far less incentive to create and disseminate music. This seems to make a certain amount of economic sense.

A third point raised by opponents of music file copying is the issue of illegality. The claim is that widespread disregard of copyright protections will have as a consequence widespread disrespect of the law, leading to more illegal copying of movies, videos, books, game software, or photographs. This claim is harder to demonstrate empirically than the music sales claim, but file copying advocates don't often claim that breaking the law will have beneficial effects, and we don't see many legitimate claims for anarchy.

The dialectic so far seems to favor banning music file copying, but there are a few interesting counterarguments. For example, some musicians (particularly relatively unknown ones) are enthusiasts of free music sharing. These musicians have not yet been able to get recording contracts, so they use Internet file copying as a way to distribute and publicize their music as well as generate ticket sales for upcoming live performances. For them, copying has positive consequences for both listeners and music makers. Advocates of copying also point out that only a small percentage of the money spent on legally purchased music goes to the artists. The rest of the money goes to the people who market the music. Some artists (both famous and not) have decided to give away their music on the Internet and make their money via live concerts. They are content to accept reduced sales of their albums if it means more people listen to their music, and hence come to their concerts.

An ethical dialectic rarely has a clear stopping point. We can almost always make better and better arguments, and there are often good points remaining on both sides of an argument. For example, we haven't discussed the fact that some music copying takes place using university and corporate computers, equipment that isn't supposed to be used for these purposes. Another persuasive argument is that if the United States decides as a country that we are better off without copyrighted music, then the law should be changed. Until then, it seems unethical to encourage breaking the law that currently protects copyrighted music.

In response to these concerns, some distributors have come up with new ways to sell music online. Apple's iTunes music store has shown that consumers will opt for legal copying if the system is convenient and reasonably priced. (See the Special Interest Box titled "The Sound of Music.") Starting in 2011, online music storage services (such as Apple iTunesMatch, Amazon Music, and Google Play Music) started to appear. These services allow users to store their digital music in a "locker" in the cloud, and then listen to that music on any of their digital devices (smartphone, tablet, computer, or game console). Users can upload any music they want to the locker and the locker does not have a way to verify whether the music was legally acquired. Users pay a monthly or yearly fee for this service, and part of this fee is used to pay back music studios. Arguably, this allows the locker services (and through them, the music studios) to make at least some money from illegally acquired music. Another approach is the Creative Commons (CC) License, which is a copyright approach that allows intellectual property creators to have more control over copyright specifications, while encouraging legal sharing of music, videos, texts, and other intellectual property. Many artists release their works under a CC license, in return for donations through Patreon, Kickstarter, Indiegogo, or other crowdfunding sites.

Practice Problems

1. Review the music files you have listened to and movie files you have watched recently on your smartphone, tablet, or computer. What was the source from which you obtained these files? Do you know whether or not the files are legal to use? Or, if you have watched movies or listened to music on a site that allows user uploads (like YouTube, Twitch.tv, or SoundCloud), how do you know that the uploader didn't violate copyright? If you discover that a file was uploaded illegally, do you have any ethical obligation to stop using it?

2. Not every decision is an ethical one. For example, we usually don't think of choosing an ice cream flavor as being "good" or "bad." Write down 10 choices you have made in the past week. Then go back over the list and label each as ethical or not ethical. (*Note:* "Not ethical" is different from "unethical"; "not ethical" means there are no ethical issues involved.) After you've labeled all 10 choices, see if you can convince yourself to change your mind about one of the choices you labeled "not ethical."

3. To effectively build a utilitarian argument, we need to think of all the people who are affected by a decision. We call these people "stakeholders" in the decision. Choose one of the "ethical" choices you listed in Practice Problem 2. Now write down all the people or groups of people who are potentially affected, directly or indirectly, by your decision. Finally, list what each stakeholder may gain or lose from your decision.

The Sound of Music

Peer-to-peer music sharing became popular because it offered users virtually unlimited access to free music. Many computer scientists and ethicists thought that once people were accustomed to this, it would be virtually impossible to break them of the habit and charge for music. Steve Jobs and Apple Inc. did not believe this. Instead, they thought that if costs were reasonable and value-added services were provided (such as previewing, Billboard charts, audiobooks, and movie trailers), people would be willing to pay for legal access to copyrighted music. In 2003, Apple went public with the iTunes music store, a paid online music downloading service for its iPod MP3 player. The service started small with access limited to Mac OS X users and a few thousand songs on its playlist. However, it was an immediate success with more than 1 million downloads in the first week, and by 2016 it had reached nearly 30 billion downloads. It rapidly expanded to Windows machines as well as European and Asian users. Currently, the iTunes Music Store has the rights to hundreds of millions of songs and other audio and video materials. Amazon Prime uses a model where Prime users get free, legal access to millions of music tracks plus playlists and stations as part of their Prime membership. Obviously, those who did not think people would pay for online music after having free access were wrong. Perhaps the desire to act ethically is more deeply ingrained than we had thought.

17.2.2 Case 2: Legalized Snooping—Privacy vs. Security

Modern telecommunications networks have created significant problems for law enforcement. Over the past century, state and federal law enforcement officers have come to rely on the ability to set up "wiretaps," which allow them to intercept and record telephone conversations between suspected criminals. As phone technology has changed, however, it has become increasingly complicated to set up these wiretaps.

In the past, an intercept might have literally involved tapping a wire, using a piece of hardware similar to the Y-connector you might use to plug two sets of headphones into a single music player or smartphone. Such hardware could be installed at the local exchange (where the wire from your house connects to the phone company), and a recording device could be set up to record all calls.

Today, however, more than 50% of U.S. households have no landline-based phone, and that percentage is growing rapidly. Instead, people are turning to cellular phone and Internet phone technology (known as Voice over Internet Protocol, or VoIP) for their voice communications. This has created headaches for phone companies because it is no longer possible to tap a particular phone by simply hooking on to a particular wire in the local exchange. Cell phone calls can be made from anywhere, even from places where a person's phone company owns no cell towers. VoIP calls can be made from any place that the user can get an Internet connection, including the thousands of free wireless access points in cafes, libraries, and colleges. Phone companies now need complicated automated systems to follow a user from place to place, intercept his or her conversations, and forward them to law enforcement. Creating these lawful intercept (LI) systems can be both complex and expensive.

Furthermore, to make sure that every phone call could be tapped, it is necessary for Internet service providers (ISPs) to get involved. It is not hard for law enforcement to partner with phone companies, because there are only one or two major phone companies in each region of the country. With ISPs, however, there are sometimes dozens or even hundreds operating within a single city, and it is estimated that there are approximately 7,000 ISPs operating in the United States. It is also necessary for makers of VoIP software to get involved. In Chapter 8, you learned about cryptography and the use of encryption to protect communications on the Internet. If VoIP providers choose to implement cryptography on their systems, it would render wiretaps useless. Even though the police could listen in on the call, they would not be able to decrypt it, and it would sound like random pops and static.

By the mid-1990s, law enforcement officials saw these problems coming. They assumed (correctly) that smaller ISPs, VoIP software makers, and even some phone companies would not build LI systems unless required to. After all, building and operating an LI system costs a lot of money. As a result, many countries, the United States included, passed laws requiring everyone involved with telecommunications to cooperate with law enforcement and build LI capabilities into all of their systems.

Critics of LI worried that it would be a tempting target for computer hackers. Modern LI systems allow an authorized user to create a wiretap by filling in a few blanks in a computer program. It is no longer necessary to attach new hardware to create a wiretap. Because all phone calls now travel through computers as streams of data, that data can simply be copied and stored as it flows by. It is even possible to forward phone calls to another number, so every time a phone call is placed from a monitored number the police officer's phone rings, and he or she can pick up and listen in on the call in real time. For spies this functionality would be tremendously attractive. What if you could listen in on every call the president makes, or to all the phone calls of finance ministers or heads of major corporations?

This is exactly what happened to government and industry figures in Greece in 2004–2005. Persons unknown broke into the LI system for the major cellular phone vendor in Greece and installed illegal wiretaps on over 100 important Greek business leaders, civil servants, and politicians, including the prime minister. For nearly a year, hackers used the LI system to forward calls from tapped numbers to a series of "shadow phones," which allowed the hackers to listen in on conversations. This tapping was massive in scope and went undetected for almost a year. A more recent controversy over communications interception involved not hackers but the U.S. federal government itself, detailed in the Special Interest Box, "Hero or Traitor?"

Hero or Traitor?

In the summer of 2013, the exploits of American computer professional and former U.S. National Security Agency (NSA) contractor Edward Snowden came to light when he leaked classified information from the NSA to the international news media. Snowden disclosed thousands of classified documents that revealed the extent of the NSA's global surveillance programs, including monitoring of U.S. phone and email traffic and the phone conversations of over 35 world leaders. To some, Snowden was a hero, a "whistleblower" who showed how concerns for national security could be used to trample basic constitutional rights and invade personal privacy. To others, he was a traitor deserving imprisonment or worse. The U.S. Department of Justice charged him with violating the Espionage Act (punishable by up to 30 years in prison), and the State Department revoked his passport. Currently, Snowden lives in an undisclosed location in Russia and has received a Russian residency permit good until 2020. He has also applied for asylum to 21 countries, mostly in the European Union and South America.

Snowden's leaks have sparked numerous debates over mass surveillance, the proper balance between national security and personal privacy, and the constitutionality of the NSA's bulk data collection practices. The issues his case has raised will continue to be among the most controversial facing computer professionals and ordinary citizens alike in the years to come.

© Rena Schild/Shutterstock

In this case study, we will focus on the ethical implications of the decision to require all Internet and telecom companies to participate in the lawful intercept of voice communications. How does this decision impact personal privacy? How does it impact national security? We used utilitarian arguments to explore ethical questions about music file copying; but in this case study we will use a different kind of argument, argument by analogy, to explore questions about lawful intercept.

Analogies are commonplace, and that's one of the reasons they can be a useful way to think about ethical concerns. Most people are familiar and comfortable with the idea of explaining something unfamiliar by comparing it with something better known: "Rabbit tastes like chicken." However, when we apply analogies to ethics, we need to be more careful about the analogies we choose.

In any analogy between two "things," there will be both similarities and differences. For example, someone might say "swimming is like riding a bike—once you learn it, you never forget." Clearly, swimming is not *exactly* like riding a bike. (Just try swimming on a driveway or riding a bike in a lake.) The point of this analogy is clear: The person making the analogy thinks that the similarity (you don't forget it once it has been learned) is most important to the current conversation.

Analogies serve several purposes in ethical reasoning. When an analogy fits well, it helps us take advantage of decisions we have made in the past because if two situations are sufficiently similar we can apply the solution for the original problem to the new one. If the analogy does not fit well, this also provides useful information. If we can precisely identify the mismatch in the analogy, this often highlights some ethically significant aspect of the case.

In our analysis of lawful intercept, we consider two analogies that bear directly on privacy concerns raised by LI.

Analogy #1: Lawful Intercept Is Like Requiring Everyone to Record Their Face-to-Face Conversations. The first analogy focuses on Internet VoIP phone systems such as Skype, but most of our arguments apply equally well to cellular phone systems because they use similar technologies. Here's an expression of the analogy:

> If you and I decide to go for a walk in the woods and just talk, no one in his right mind believes that we should be forced by the government to carry microphones along to record our conversation so that they can listen to it. Before all this technology came in, every conversation was private. —Phil Zimmermann[1] in *Life on the Internet: Cyber Secrets* (PBS, 1996).

---

[1]Zimmerman played a critical role in enabling people to have access to high-quality cryptography. Until he designed and implemented PGP (Pretty Good Privacy) in 1991, most people did not have access to public-key cryptography software—a crucial building block of today's secure online shopping.

Using Analogy #1 to Analyze the Case. In this case, we can see some clear similarities between face-to-face verbal communication and Internet phone calls. They are similar in that people want to communicate directly with each other, and both types of communication are meant to include only the two individuals involved in the private discussion. In both types of communication, however, the actual audience may be larger than intended: In a voice conversation, people may be eavesdropping either by being physically close but unnoticed by the speakers, via a hidden microphone, or by a distant parabolic listening device. With VoIP, the conversation may be intercepted at any number of places along the electronic path between the sender and receiver.

In U.S. society, private conversations are, by default, free from government intrusion. This is not an absolute right—court orders can be obtained by law enforcement to use technology that invades private physical conversations. But these are the exceptions that prove the rule. Unless law enforcement officials can demonstrate probable cause, they are not permitted to take extraordinary measures to listen in on private physical conversations.

In both cases (VoIP and face-to-face conversations), there is a trade-off between privacy and security. In the case of face-to-face conversation, our society has decided not to record all conversations all the time, but to allow law enforcement officials to record certain conversations under the condition that they can demonstrate that they need to do so.

The analogy implies that requiring lawful intercept for all Internet-phone equipment would be the same as requiring everyone to record all of their private conversations, and to provide such recordings to the government as needed.

Problems with Analogy #1. The conclusion we reached just now may conflict with your intuition about the case. Notice that the argument we made applies to normal phone tapping as well as tapping VoIP. We know that most people accept the need for the occasional use of regular phone taps, so this seems to indicate a problem with the analogy. Our analogy must have left out some ethically significant factor.

This demonstrates another powerful use of analogy, which is to discover which parts of the case are most ethically relevant. Sometimes, when you make an analogy, the answer does not match your intuition. This could be because your intuition is wrong, but it could also be because the analogy simply does not fit. In this example, where is the mismatch?

There are many reasonable criticisms of analogy #1, but one big problem is that it has only three significant parties: The two parties in the private conversation plus the government. In the case of lawful intercept, there is a very significant fourth party, the telecommunications company. In the previous analogy, Zimmermann points out the absurdity of requiring individuals to record their own conversations and provide them to the government. But what if there was another party that was already well positioned to record any conversation? Could the government require that party to do so, and to hand over the recordings? This is exactly the case with Internet phone services. The Internet service provider is always in a position to record calls and provide them to the government. So the current analogy seems to fall down in that it is asking private citizens to perform the same task as a government-regulated telecommunications company. Perhaps we should look for an analogy that has this "middleman" feature built in.

Analogy #2: Lawful Intercept Is Like Suspicious Activity Reporting in Banking. There are two critical resources needed by criminals and terrorists that each require the help of a large corporation: means of communication and means of transferring and transporting money. With regard to the second need, U.S. banks are required to keep detailed records on all transactions and to notify the U.S. Department of the Treasury (through a Suspicious Activity Report, or SAR) whenever they detect unusual or suspicious transactions—for example, any deposit greater than $10,000. This careful recordkeeping and monitoring is expensive, but it allows law enforcement to find links between suspects and to discover and defeat criminal networks. In the same way, phone calls are an excellent source of information about the relationships between people—for example, intercepting phone calls between suspected terrorists is necessary to discover and prevent attacks.

Using Analogy #2 to Analyze the Case. This analogy seems to support the idea that telecommunication companies can be required to monitor phone usage and report certain data about suspicious activity. This would be consistent with the monitoring and reporting requirements placed on financial institutions. So, again, reasoning by analogy allows us to apply our solution to an old question (should banks be forced to report suspicious activity?) to a new one (should telecom companies be forced to report suspicious activity?).

What can we learn about lawful intercept from suspicious activity reporting? If you do a bit of research, you will discover that suspicious activity reporting differs in two very important ways from current lawful intercept systems. First, the suspicious activity report is initiated by the bank. The government does not get to continuously monitor what is going on in a bank. Instead, the bank is responsible for deciding what constitutes suspicious behavior and reporting it using the SAR form.

The SAR form is very simple, and this is the second major difference. It requires identifying information for those involved in the suspicious activity and a written description of the financial transaction. That is it. There is nothing in this comparable to completely recording a telephone call. The list of parties involved in the suspicious activity would be similar to listing the phone numbers or names of the people on the call. Listing the amount of the activity and the dates on which it took place would correspond to the times and dates on which phone calls took place, the lengths of the calls, and so on. But a financial transaction does not include the wealth of data that a phone call does, because a financial transaction is not a conversation.

So analogy #2 lends some support to the idea that we might require telecom companies to keep careful track of call records to monitor this information for suspicious patterns and to report suspicious activities to the government or law enforcement using a reporting form similar to the SAR. Like the previous analogy, it seems to contradict the idea that the government or law enforcement should be allowed direct or unsupervised access to the data. It does not seem to tell us, directly, whether or not the telecom companies should be recording and storing the actual contents of calls.

Making a Decision. In most cases, just having a convincing analogy is not enough to be sure we are making the right decision. Even if an analogy appears to fit, there is always a good chance that we are overlooking some morally significant factor in the case that would invalidate the analogy. Analogies are tremendously useful, however, in brainstorming. The analogies help us identify the most morally significant factors of a case, and they help us identify potential solutions based on previous solutions to similar problems. Nonetheless, it is always wise to double-check a solution using other methods.

In this case, we will use a utilitarian approach to check potential solutions identified by our analogies. So far, we have three possible solutions on the table:

- Option 1: Require all VoIP systems to implement lawful intercept (as in the current law).

- Option 2: Do not require VoIP systems to implement lawful intercept or do any other reporting. Law enforcement officials will have to use physical eavesdropping, after getting a warrant from a judge (as suggested by analogy #1).

- Option 3: Require VoIP providers to monitor and report suspicious activities, but do not build the ability to record conversations into the system (as suggested by analogy #2).

First, let's identify the interested parties, and how this decision might affect their happiness and well-being.

- *Those who make or operate VoIP systems*—Increased monitoring costs them money for building in the monitoring and for defending against privacy lawsuits.

- *Law enforcement officials and employees*—Increased monitoring saves them money because they do not have to do as much physical surveillance. This also allows them to catch more lawbreakers and do their jobs better.

- *Hackers*—Built-in lawful intercept provides them with greater opportunities for stealing (and selling) secrets, but increases their likelihood of being caught.

- *Nonhacker criminals*—Increased monitoring increases the likelihood that they will be caught or that their plots will be disrupted.

- *The public*—Increased monitoring means increased efficiency for law enforcement, saving tax money, and possibly increasing safety. It also, however, decreases privacy because it makes everyone's phone calls easier to tap, and possibly decreases safety by exposing the public to hacker attacks or to abuse by law enforcement officials.

For law enforcement officials, Option 1 (lawful intercept) is clearly the best. It gives them the most options and the most direct control over monitoring, at low cost compared with Option 2 (no monitoring). For VoIP providers, Option 2 (no monitoring) is clearly the best. Options 1 and 3 are probably about equally bad for them. Although Option 1 (lawful intercept) requires them to modify their systems significantly and opens them up to hackers, it requires much less manpower to operate than Option 3 (suspicious event reporting), because Option 3 would require humans to review cases, fill out forms, and interact with the police.

The stickiest part of this case, and the reason we will not be able to immediately come to a clear solution, is evaluating the effect on the public. Every option has pros and cons for the public. If we assume that the number of tax dollars going to law enforcement is held constant, then Option 2 (no monitoring) would result in a serious decrease in the effectiveness of the police. Option 1 (lawful intercept) might result in major abuses by hackers and rogue law enforcement officials. Option 3 (suspicious event reporting) might also seriously decrease police effectiveness because they might need the contents of the calls, not just a knowledge of the calls' existence, in order to prevent criminal schemes.

To reach a final decision on this case, we would need to make a prediction about how much harm hackers and rogue law enforcement officials might do if we choose Option 1, and weigh this against the loss of law enforcement capacity caused by Options 2 and 3. This is exactly what members of Congress went through when first drafting CALEA (the Communications Assistance for Law Enforcement Act, which created the lawful intercept requirement).

It may be a bit disappointing to spend so much time on a case without "solving" it, but the fact is that ethical decision making, done well, is very difficult. It takes a lot of time and careful work, just as any important problem does. In this section, however, we have learned about reasoning by analogy. This style of reasoning, by finding similar cases in the past and using them to reason about a new case, is fundamental to ethics and to law.

Practice Problems

1. An important skill in using analogies is noticing both similarities and differences. This skill can be practiced. Think of a book and a website that contain essentially the same information. How are they alike? How are they different? Make a list of similarities and differences, at least 10 of each. Don't ignore the obvious, but don't limit yourself to the obvious either.

2. Imagine that your public library decides to go completely digital. The library now has a policy to phase out physical books and replace them with ebooks, digital audiobooks, websites, and public access computers in the library. Using the list you made in Practice Problem 1, make a list of the people who would gain from this decision and a list of the people who would lose. Build a utilitarian argument either for or against the decision.

3. Some people think that the content of Internet sites should be regulated just as the content of radio and TV is, for example, with rules regarding obscenity and the amount of advertising. Other people think that the content of Internet sites, like private phone conversations, should not be regulated. Is the analogy between Internet sites and radio and TV broadcasts more appropriate, or is the analogy between Internet sites and telephone conversations more appropriate? Justify your position.

17.2.3 Case 3: Hackers—Public Enemies or Gadflies?

During the Middle Ages, a "hacker" was someone who made hoes. In the 17th century, a hacker was a "lusty laborer" who enthusiastically made chopping cuts using a hoe. But *hacker* has quite a different meaning today, far removed from its agricultural roots (see the Special Interest Box "The Metamorphosis of Hacking" in Chapter 8). Today, the term *hacker* describes someone who breaks into computer systems and launches Internet worms and viruses, or perpetrates other computer-related vandalism.

Not everyone sees hackers in this negative light, however. Some people view hackers as social gadflies, people who raise important, but irritating, questions about government or society. The Greek philosopher Plato used the word *gadfly* (Ancient Greek: μύωψ) to describe Socrates' fractious relationship with the political establishment of his day. While most people agree that purposeless vandalism or outright theft through hacking is wrong, some of the activities categorized as "hacking" may constitute a public service, and several computer hackers have written books and articles about the ethics of computer hacking. Some hackers are even hired by the owners of computer systems to test whether there are any weaknesses in their security software that could make it vulnerable to intrusion by unauthorized individuals.

In this section, we explore whether there is an ethical case to be made in support of computer hackers. To focus our discussion, we concentrate on a single type of hacking: gaining unauthorized access to someone else's computer system to obtain and publish secret information. This could be as simple as copying files from your company's private network and posting them on the web, or as elaborate as breaking into a government or military installation and circulating classified documents using an anonymization service to protect the hacker's identity.

These issues, which in the past were considered largely theoretical, have taken on particular urgency in recent years due to the founding of several organizations that specifically focus on information leaking as a form of hacktivism (hacking that is intended as a form of political activism). The two main groups discussed here are WikiLeaks and Anonymous.

WikiLeaks, which was launched in December 2006, is a site that specializes in protecting the identity of government and corporate whistle-blowers. Imagine that you discovered a document that proved your company's leadership was engaged in significant unethical behavior. Furthermore, imagine that you decide you need to blow the whistle on this behavior. How would you go about it? In the past, one common route was to share the incriminating documents with an investigative journalist. The journalist acts as a firewall between you and the authorities; most journalists hold to a code of ethics that says that they will not identify their sources, even if it is clear that the source has committed a crime. Journalists sometimes go to prison rather than reveal their sources. The problem with this approach today is that it is very hard to share an electronic document with a journalist without leaving traces that law enforcement (or corporate security) officers can follow. Most journalists don't have the necessary computer security skills to actually safeguard the anonymity of their sources. WikiLeaks' goal is to provide exactly this kind of technical expertise. It provides a secure electronic drop box, and tips on how to submit documents that will prevent the leaker from being traced. WikiLeaks then provides the submitted documents to journalists. In the past, it has partnered with *The New York Times*, *The Guardian* (in the United Kingdom), and *Der Spiegel* (in Germany), among others. WikiLeaks has been involved in several major leaks:

- In 2010, WikiLeaks began to provide leaked U.S. diplomatic cables to various newspapers. The *Daily Mail* (a U.K. newspaper) and others have attributed the 2011 revolution in Tunisia, at least in part, to allegations of Tunisian government corruption contained in the diplomatic cables.

- In 2012, WikiLeaks began to provide over 100 classified or restricted files from the U.S. Department of Defense on the rules and procedures with respect to military detainees.

- In 2016 WikiLeaks released over 8,000 confidential CIA documents related to the tools it uses to break into phones, communication apps, and other electronic devices.

Though not hackers themselves, WikiLeaks employs people with the technical skills required to provide defenses against government and corporate investigators. For example, in 2013, WikiLeaks provided documents for and traveled with Edward Snowden on his flight (both literal and political) from Hong Kong to Russia (see the Special Interest Box "Hero or Traitor?" earlier in this chapter).

The hacker group Anonymous is much harder to describe. Anonymous is a group of hacktivists that seem primarily interested in freedom of speech. Even this characterization, however, is in dispute. WikiLeaks is easy to describe because it has a known public spokesman (Julian Assange), a website, and an advisory board. Anonymous has no such official organizing body, or leader. In fact, its semiofficial logo is a suit with a question mark instead of a head, and members wear masks (all of them identical) when appearing in public. As a result, any hacker or activist can claim to be part of Anonymous, and there is no official spokesman to refute these claims. Among the best-known actions of Anonymous are:

- A 2010 attack in retribution for financial sanctions against WikiLeaks. Several companies, including PayPal and MasterCard, had blacklisted WikiLeaks, preventing donors from using those systems to donate to WikiLeaks.

- Attacks throughout the summer of 2011 that disrupted the government websites of Tunisia, Egypt, and Libya. These attacks were in retaliation for government censorship of the Internet and were meant to help support pro-democracy revolutions in those countries.

- A major sustained operation against ISIS following the 2015 Paris terrorist attacks.

Anonymous has also been accused of threatening the Westboro Baptist Church, a group known for protesting at the funerals of U.S. soldiers. Members of Anonymous have said that these charges are false, that they support all forms of free speech, even by people they disagree with. Due to the leaderless nature of Anonymous, however, facts on what Anonymous has, and has not, done are hard to obtain and confirm.

We will examine the ethics of this kind of hacktivism, first using the two techniques we have already introduced, analogy and utilitarian analysis. Then we will introduce a third analysis technique, deontological ethics. In our analogy, we will focus on the first step of the process, breaking into a computer system to steal information.

Analogy: Breaking into a Computer Is Like Breaking into Someone's House. Imagine that a burglar picks the lock on your back door, wanders around picking up valuables, and then escapes into the night undetected. When you find out you've been robbed, you feel outrage and fear.

If computer hacking is ethically linked to burglary, then we will have an instinctive revulsion toward both.

Clearly there are similarities between burglars and hackers; in both cases, the intruders are there without our permission and (at least in most cases) without us being aware of their presence. In most homes and with most computers, the owners take some precautions to discourage unwanted visitors, precautions that must be overcome by the intruder. There are laws against both forms of intrusion, although the laws against physical break-ins are clearer and easier to enforce.

There are also differences between the intrusions. A burglar is likely to take something from your house, and that removal will deprive you of something. A hacker may look at things, and even copy things from your computer, but the hacker is less likely to remove or destroy things from your system. A hacker takes your intellectual property and privacy, and that is different from taking physical objects.

When someone breaks into a house, there is a palpable threat of violence. If a burglar is detected during the act, things may turn nasty. This physical threat is not present in a computer break-in, although the information stolen may be personal and could lead to future physical threats. The physical degree of separation of a virtual break-in seems to be an ethically relevant distinction.

Utilitarian Argument: Costs and Benefits of Hacking. What is gained and lost when a computer is hacked? First, whoever owns the hacked computer loses some control over the information in that computer, and the hacker gains access to that information. Second, as a consequence of the break-in, there may be intentional or unintentional deletions or corruptions of data on the computer. These changes may be largely benign or may subsequently cause significant harm. Neither the hacker nor the person hacked can know with certainty the eventual consequences of these changes.

When computer system owners or system administrators discover that a system has been hacked, they often increase system security to reduce the probability of another successful intrusion. Some hackers claim that they provide a public service by alerting people to security holes in their systems. As long as the hacker doesn't hurt anything while "inside" the system, and especially if the hacker makes the intrusion obvious, then such hackers would argue that the consequence of the hacking is improved security against malicious hackers. An alternative consequential argument says that increased security wouldn't be necessary if hackers weren't such a threat.

This discussion illustrates two challenges when using a utilitarian argument in a dialectic about hacking:

1. It is sometimes hard to predict consequences with any accuracy.

2. There seems to be a distinction between "good hackers" (who are trying to act in the public interest) and "bad hackers" (who want to do damage or steal things for self-interested or pathological reasons).

These kinds of challenges arise in other discussions, and some people think they are difficult to overcome using a utilitarian argument. Let's try a totally different kind of ethical argument, a *deontological argument*, to try to meet these challenges in a different way.

Deontological Argument: Hacking with a Golden Heart. Utilitarian and other consequentialist arguments focus on the consequences of an act to determine if the act is ethical. Deontological arguments focus instead on the duties of the person acting and the way the act impinges on the rights of others.

The word deontology is from the Greek and means "the study of duty and obligation." Perhaps the most famous deontologist was the German philosopher Immanuel Kant (1724–1804). Kant wrestled eloquently about what duties we humans have to each other. He came up with "categorical imperatives" that characterized these duties. His second categorical imperative goes something like this:

Never treat a fellow human merely as a means to an end.

To boil that down to a bumper sticker slogan, we might say, "Every human being deserves respect." Notice that the categorical imperative is really about your mental attitude toward the other person: Do you see him or her as a person, or just as the means to an end? Kant's deontological approach encourages us to consider the intent behind the action, not just the results of the action.

Let's try out a deontological perspective on our question about hacking. Is the act of hacking into another person's computer system inherently unethical? If we take some hackers, such as WikiLeaks, at their word, their intent is not to harm the public. They characterize themselves as a foil against corporate and government abuse, and they characterize hacking as a form of investigative reporting. They also claim to want to help people discover security holes to protect against malevolent hackers.

Let's stipulate that hackers who break into other people's computers for personal gain are doing something unethical by any of the three arguments we've seen so far in this section (analogy, utilitarian, deontological). For the rest of this section, we concentrate on hackers who claim a benign if not benevolent intent to their computer break-ins.

First, we assume that "good hackers" are telling the truth when they claim to mean no harm to the public. In his influential history of hacking, *Hackers: Heroes of the Computer Revolution*, Steven Levy[2] describes six components of what he calls the "hacker ethic." Here we focus on two:

1. "All Information Should Be Free"—Information sharing is a powerful positive good because it is not possible to make good decisions if important information is hidden from the public. It is the ethical duty of hackers to facilitate access to information whenever possible.

---

[2]Levy, Steven. (2010). *Hackers: Heroes of the Computer Revolution.* http://shop.oreilly.com/product/0636920010227.do

2. "Mistrust Authority—Promote Decentralization"—The strict rules and hierarchical management structures that characterize government and corporate bureaucracies mostly serve to prevent people from getting things done, rather than solving problems. Each hacker should do what he or she thinks is in the public's best interest, and ignore the rules.

In claim 1, the idea of sharing information looks, at first glance, pretty good. But it seems a bit less noble when we remember that much of the information that hackers share isn't *their* information, it's someone else's! It's one thing to share open source computer code (like Linux or Apache OpenOffice) or the works of Shakespeare on the web. It's quite another thing to share material whose copyright is legally still in force (like Lady Gaga's latest hit) or to share classified information that might impact national security. Unless hackers consciously make these kinds of distinctions, and many hackers do not, then the duty to respect other people isn't being met. In the case of WikiLeaks' releases of government documents, WikiLeaks collaborated with major newspapers to help determine which cables were safe to release, and which needed redactions to protect innocent people from harm. Some groups that release leaked documents simply release all documents without doing any such filtering.

The second claim has a similar weakness. Hackers might argue that rules protecting electronic privacy are incorrect and thus can be violated. They might also argue that these rules exist because we expect electronic privacy, but it is that very expectation of privacy that is the problem, not their violation of that expectation. What's missing from the hackers' argument is why their ideas about information ("all information should be free and accessible") should take priority over the individual's view ("some of my personal information should be private"). Ethically, there's no problem with thinking and arguing that all information should be free, or to be suspicious of rules; there is a big problem, however, with acting on that belief in a way that treats people as a means to an end.

The preceding arguments won't convince most hackers, and you too might have some remaining questions about this issue. The sharing of information and resistance to authority are usually moral goods, and these values are part of the American identity. But the fact that these are ideals is not a slam-dunk ethical argument when applied to a specific act. Acts have both good and bad consequences, and utilitarians remind us that we have to weigh these consequences and think of them globally. Deontologists encourage us to remember that acts can be inherently good or bad outside the consequences, if they involve a right or duty, and to examine the intention behind an action. At the very least, the preceding brief analysis raises serious questions about the claims and behaviors of the hacker ethic.

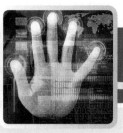

Practice Problems

1. There are times when you want someone to break into your house. For example, if your house is on fire, you probably won't object if firefighters use an ax on the front door. Can you think of other such situations? Try to make an argument based on an analogy between firefighters and hackers that supports the hacker ethic. Do you find this analogy convincing? Why or why not?

2. Sometimes we are invited to look into windows and to enter privately owned property. For example, stores spend money to make attractive windows to draw us in. What are some ethically significant differences between a store inviting us in and a computer being hacked? Focus on the issue of intent as you consider this question.

3. As mentioned earlier, some corporations and even government agencies have employed former hackers to improve security measures; the hackers test the security of the systems at the employing corporation or agency and report weaknesses, an invited form of hacking called *penetration testing*. Consider the analogy of an auto manufacturer hiring a former auto thief to test how easy it might be to break into a new car model. Is this a reasonable analogy? Does it support the hacker ethic?

4. Some Internet chat rooms allow and even encourage people to remain anonymous. As people type to each other in real time, the people chatting are identified by fictitious "handles." Is this a good idea? Think of two reasons why such Internet anonymity may be a good thing and two reasons why it may be a bad thing.

17.2.4 Case 4: Genetic Information and Medical Research

So far in this chapter, we've looked at three different cases using three different techniques: utilitarian analysis, deontological analysis, and reasoning by analogy. In this final case study, we propose a "paramedic method" for computer ethics that integrates these three techniques.

"Paramedic Ethics" for Technology. When you get sick, you often need medical help in a hurry. Paramedics aren't necessarily medical doctors, but they know quite a bit about how to help people, and they know who to ask when they aren't certain about a particularly puzzling case. We don't expect you to become a research ethicist by reading this chapter, but we hope you have started to gain some new skills: recognizing ethical questions regarding computing and reasoning carefully about answers to those questions. When you are faced with an ethical problem, there are several important questions you should ask yourself:

1. Who are the stakeholders in this situation?

2. What does each stakeholder have to gain or lose? (This is the utilitarian step.)

3. What duties and responsibilities in this situation are important to the stakeholders? (This is the deontological step.)

4. Can you think of an analogous situation that doesn't involve computing? If so, does that analogous situation clarify the situation that does involve computing? (This is reasoning by analogy.)

5. Either make a decision or revisit the above steps.

Before we illustrate how to apply these questions to a particular case, we need to announce a disclaimer. Unlike the formal algorithms studied earlier in this book, this "paramedic method" is not a step-by-step solution method, guaranteed to produce a result and then halt. Instead, it is an outline that can help guide you in your analysis and help you move toward a better understanding of the problem and toward a better ethical conclusion.

The Case Study. Many people believe that the Industrial Age is over and we are now living in the Information Age. In the last few years, human genetic information has taken center stage in scientific exploration. Computers are an integral part of this research and of the growing commerce connected to the human genome. Because this "new" information is contained in the cells of our bodies, the computerization of this information is simultaneously personal and mysterious. In our final case study, we explore a fictional case involving genetic information. We will use the paramedic method to examine this case from several different perspectives.

Imagine that you are at your family doctor for a routine checkup. The doctor asks you to participate in a research study of genetic diversity and disease by donating some skin cells for the study. The doctor informs you that your skin cells will be identified only by a randomly assigned number and your zip code. Should you donate your cells?[3]

---

[3]This case study is similar to the controversial case of Ms. Henrietta Lacks, an African-American woman whose cancer cells were taken after a biopsy without her consent or knowledge by doctors at Johns Hopkins Medical Center in Baltimore, MD. Ms. Lacks' cells have been invaluable in medical research right up to the present day, although her family did not learn of their existence until 1975 and were not granted any measure of control over their usage until 2013.

Step 1: Identify the Stakeholders. According to our paramedic method, the first question to ask is, "Who are the stakeholders?" Clearly the doctor and you are two stakeholders, but are these the only ones you should consider? Probably not. Unless the doctor is doing this study on his or her own (unlikely), there is someone else involved in this research. When you inquire, the doctor tells you that a pharmaceutical company is sponsoring the research and that it hopes to use the information gathered from around the country to identify genetic links to several diseases, some of them fatal. Now you've identified three more stakeholders: the pharmaceutical company (let's call it PHARM CO), skin cell donors all over the country, and people who have or will have these genetic diseases.

Step 2: What Is at Stake? Next, we should ask what each stakeholder might gain or lose from our decision. If we say yes and donate our skin cells, then we will undergo some sort of procedure and lose a few cells; our doctor will participate more fully in the study; PHARM CO will get a larger genetic database and may be able to develop new drugs; if the drugs are successful, then people with diseases may have new therapies. If, on the other hand, we say no, then our doctor, PHARM CO, and patients will have a slightly smaller chance of success with the research.

Enumerating these costs and benefits might lead to a few more questions. First, is the procedure for donating the cells dangerous? Your doctor assures you that the procedure is harmless and requires just a moment to scrape a tongue depressor lightly against your arm. You may also have questions about how your genetic information is going to be stored and processed. A logical way to store this information would be to assign a randomly generated number to each donor in the study, perhaps linked to information your doctor already has. We might envision something like the following table, which includes the use of your Social Security number (SSN):

Random Number	SSN	Name	Zip Code	Gender	Doctor
10568322	532 12 3456	Joe Smith	45321	M	Goodgene
952990981	532 11 9503	Sue Jones	55416	F	Goodgene
.					
.					
.					

The doctor has assured you that only the random number (from the first column) and the zip code (from the fourth column) will be associated with your genetic sample and the information derived from it. If we believe the doctor will in good faith send only that information to PHARM CO, can you be confident that your privacy is ensured? The answer is probably not. If a table such as the one just shown exists, then PHARM CO could potentially link the information it receives from your doctor back to you by gaining access to that table. At the very least, PHARM CO could find out the names and addresses of all the people who donated cells from a particular zip code, and if there were only one or two it would be easy for them to identify you. Furthermore, computerized files like the previous table have a habit of hanging around, in one form or another, for a long time unless they are explicitly and carefully deleted, including all backups and copies stored in the cloud. Unless your doctor has been scrupulous about data deletion, PHARM CO may indeed be able to track down your personal information if it becomes important for the company to do so.

In Chapter 7 you studied technical details about networks and communication over those networks. You know that information on the Internet can be intercepted at various points. Will your genetic information and/or the table described above be sent electronically to PHARM CO or anyone else? If so, will it be protected using one of the sophisticated encryption algorithms described in Chapter 8?

A final question involves finances and ownership of the final results. Presumably, PHARM CO plans to make a profit from the sale of any new drugs. Is anyone being paid for this research? If the government is not supporting this project, and if PHARM CO is paying for all the collection kits and the analysis, then the information collected and any new drugs developed will belong to PHARM CO.

Step 3: Identify Duties and Responsibilities. Your doctor has a primary responsibility to do his or her best to treat you and protect your privacy. You have a duty to pay your bills promptly and to follow instructions that the doctor prescribes. PHARM CO is responsible for developing safe and useful drugs, and in return its customers pay for those drugs. In this research effort, PHARM CO is hoping that doctors will enlist volunteer patient donors, and in return PHARM CO is promising doctors a small fee for each patient who volunteers. Both your doctor and PHARM CO have promised to protect donors' privacy and are obligated to make a good-faith effort to fulfill that promise.

Most of the responsibilities we've discussed so far are fairly straightforward and uncontroversial. There are other possible responsibilities that are less obvious and more controversial. We've already discussed the value of information in the earlier music file copying case. Analogous to the music in that case study, this example also involves valuable information. What if your genetic information includes an important clue to the treatment of cancer or some other fatal disease? If PHARM CO develops an effective drug based on your genetic information, it stands to make billions of dollars. Should you get a royalty on the information in your genes? (This was the argument put forth by lawyers in the case of the cells of Henrietta Lacks that led to the development of many important drugs.) Does PHARM CO have a duty to share your genetic information and the information from others, or does its initial funding of this research give it proprietary control of that information?

Your doctor told you that only a random number and a zip code would identify your donated skin cells. This coding procedure seems to afford you some confidentiality, and that's a good thing. But you might also want to know why the zip code is required at all. Is geographic location part of the research, or is the zip code important for subsequent marketing of drugs? Is this study being done all over the world, only in the United States, or only in select zip codes in the United States? If it turns out your genetic information is particularly valuable, can the doctor give you assurances that your privacy will not be invaded? As we've seen previously, maintaining strict confidentiality would require a sophisticated security protocol to make sure information could not be linked back to you and to protect information stored on computers and communicated over a network. Because both PHARM CO and your doctor want you to volunteer for this process, they have a duty to disclose these kinds of details before asking for your genetic information.

Another question is whether you have a duty to try to help cure disease in this case. If there is a chance for you to advance medicine by a simple donation process, is there an obligation for you to donate? In a situation like this, is altruism required?

Step 4: Think of Analogies. As we move through the paramedic method, the seemingly simple request for a few skin cells has taken on added depth and complexity. Ethical analysis often reveals a broader perspective than our first thoughts about a situation.

An important aspect of this case is the promise of confidentiality to donors. Another aspect of the case that emerged during the first steps is that two of the stakeholders are potentially gaining money, PHARM CO and the doctors. The other two stakeholders, you and patients who potentially will want the drugs developed, are not getting money now and may be paying later. To explore both the confidentiality and the financial aspects of donors and users of donations, we'll use an analogy to blood donations.

The Red Cross solicits blood donations. The Red Cross is concerned about the quality of the blood that it distributes. Therefore, when you make a donation, the blood is tested for certain diseases. If your donated blood turns out to be unusable, then your name is entered into a "deferred donor database" and you are prevented from giving blood. Clearly, the Red Cross cannot offer you complete confidentiality about your blood and any diseases it discovers in your donation. However, the Red Cross is sensitive to the issue of confidentiality. On the website *www.redcrossblood.org/donating-blood/donation-faqs*, the following appears on an FAQ (frequently asked questions) list:

> The Red Cross regards blood test results as private and confidential information. The Red Cross may contact you by letter or call to arrange a counseling appointment, but the Red Cross does not disclose information regarding positive blood test results to anyone but the donor, except as required by law. The Red Cross maintains a confidential list of people who may be at risk for spreading transfusion-transmitted diseases. When required by law, we report donor information, including test results, to health departments, military medical commands, and regulatory agencies. Donation information may also be used confidentially for medical studies.

The Red Cross is a nonprofit organization, but it incurs processing costs associated with collecting, testing, and distributing blood. To recover these processing costs, the Red Cross charges a reimbursement fee to hospitals that use the donated blood. The hospitals also incur operating costs, which appear on your hospital bill. One of the reasons that the Red Cross prefers volunteer donors is that it has been found that people who donate blood for altruistic reasons are the safest blood donors. Blood donation and skin cell donation (as proposed by your doctor) are similar in that the donors are volunteers, but the collectors and eventual users of the donated materials are paid. In both cases, it is something from donors' bodies that is being collected. And in both cases, the donors are asked to volunteer for altruistic reasons.

There are differences between the two situations. In the case of blood donation, the blood itself is the item of value, and both donor and collector are clear about what will happen with the blood. In the case of the skin cells, it is the genetic information in the cells that is of value, not the cells themselves. Also, PHARM CO is looking for something it might or might not find in your cells. If it finds valuable information, PHARM CO stands to make a profit; if it doesn't find valuable information, it might take a loss on the project. The Red Cross and hospitals presumably won't make large profits on your blood, although they do charge for its use.

Let's examine another analogy: companies that solicit money for a charity. In this case, a for-profit company solicits donations from volunteers. Again, confidentiality is an issue. On the one hand, we expect that a charity will keep records that we can use to confirm our donation if the government audits our tax returns; on the other hand, there are many reasons why we might not want our history of donations to become public information.

On the issue of finances, a for-profit solicitation company takes a certain percentage of donations to pay for its costs in soliciting and processing the donations and then passes on the rest of the money to the charity. This process becomes ethically objectionable when the percentage of money that goes to the solicitor becomes comparatively large. If the soliciting company pockets 80% of the donations it collects and passes along only 20% to the charity, donors feel cheated. If the soliciting organization keeps only 2% of the donations and passes along 98% to the charity, most people would not object.

The charity solicitation scenario is similar to the skin cell donation in that volunteers are asked to donate by someone who has a financial interest in that donation. In both situations, the donors are asked to make the donation for altruistic reasons. In both cases, the amount of money given to the person in the middle (the solicitor or the doctor) seems ethically relevant, as does the control and dissemination of personal information about donors. In all of the cases we've examined, this donor information is almost certainly in the form of computer files and therefore easy to store and distribute.

The scenarios are different in that the donation requested for charity is monetary, not physical. In the charity solicitation, only the solicitor is for-profit. In the skin cell donation, both the doctor and PHARM CO are for-profit entities, although the doctor is making just a little money and PHARM CO is both spending and hoping to make much larger sums.

Step 5: Make a Decision or Loop through the Method Again. We've moved through the first four steps of the paramedic method and now have developed a better understanding of the complexities of this situation. If you have to make a decision right away (the doctor is waiting!), you can do so with a more reasoned response than before. But perhaps you have the luxury of thinking it over some more ("Doc, let me get back to you about the skin cell donation, OK?"). You might want time to ask a few more questions of the doctor or PHARM CO. You also might want to think about such issues as privacy and security a bit more carefully. In cases where the decision is potentially more critical to you or someone important to you, you might want to seek professional help, perhaps a lawyer or accountant, in making your decision. If you have the time, you could revisit earlier steps in the paramedic method, but, at a minimum you have identified and thought about the key ethical issues involved in this important medical decision.

Professional Codes of Conduct

Many professional organizations in the fields of computing and engineering have established codes of ethical behavior to provide guidelines for their members. These codes outline standards of behavior and conduct that typically include general imperatives such as avoiding harm to others and being honest, as well as more specific professional responsibilities and duties such as respecting intellectual property and protecting client privacy. Here is a partial list:

1. The Association for Computing Machinery (ACM)
   Code of Ethics and Professional Conduct
   www.acm.org/about-acm/acm-code-of-ethics-and-professional-conduct

2. The Institute of Electrical and Electronics Engineers (IEEE)
   IEEE Code of Conduct
   m.ieee.org/about/corporate/governance

3. Computer Professionals for Social Responsibility (CPSR)
   Technology and Ethics
   cpsr.org/issues/ethics

Every computing professional should read over the appropriate code periodically, and keep it in mind as a regular part of his or her working life.

17.3 Personal Privacy and Social Media

In the previous section, we examined four issues that demonstrate the relationship between computing and ethics: illegal file sharing, surveillance, hacktivism, and medical privacy. We chose these topics not because they were necessarily the most important (although they certainly are important), but because they were useful in illustrating our four methods of reasoning about ethical cases: utilitarian analysis, reasoning by analogy, deontological analysis, and the paramedic method.

In this section, we look at ethical issues you might face in your everyday life. The concerns raised in the previous section were "big issues," big in the sense of having the potential to cause enormous economic and political damage to a vast number of people—the cracking of military or government databases, stealing intellectual property, and the theft of critical financial or medical information. However, there are ethical and legal issues regarding computing of a somewhat "smaller" nature—smaller in the sense of affecting as few as one or two individuals, but the "smallness" of the apparent harm is misleading. To a person whose privacy has been invaded or who has been subjected to public ridicule and shame, these are certainly not small problems, and the consequences can be devastating.

Bullying is a problem that has been around for a long time—being verbally tormented or physically abused is something that Greek and Roman citizens probably had to deal with thousands of years ago. However, the growth of the Internet and social media has allowed bullying and the violation of one's personal privacy to become much easier and far more virulent: Online taunting allows bullies to remain anonymous, gang up on victims in enormous numbers, harass victims in places they would normally be safe, such as the confines of their home, and have their hateful screeds live on in cyberspace long after they have moved on.

According to the Pew Foundation, about 93% of U.S. children and young adults regularly use the Internet and the web, with the great majority accessing it on a daily, even hourly, basis. Some of the most popular destinations are social media sites such as Facebook, YouTube, Snapchat, Twitter, Instagram, chat rooms, forums, and blogs. These applications are a fun and convenient way to exchange messages, share stories and photos, and keep in touch with friends and family; unfortunately, they are also a quick and easy way to spread personal information, malicious rumors, hate speech, outright lies, and disturbing images to a massive audience.

Cyberbullying is humiliating, taunting, threatening, or invading someone's privacy using the Internet, web, or other type of electronic technology. Cyberbullying can take many forms, from posting hurtful and insulting messages, to leaking sensitive and embarrassing personal data, to online threats of violence and physical assault. One popular form of cyberbullying is *impersonation*. A bully, masquerading as the intended victim, posts provocative images, racist, homophobic, or sexist comments, or knowingly false messages on a social network, chat room, or blog. The intent is to destroy the victim's reputation and invite retaliation from offended individuals and groups. The post will often include a home address and a cell phone number to make it easy for others to find and harass the targeted victim.

As in most high-tech fields, the enactment of state and federal statutes to deal with cyberbullying lags far behind the popularity and use of social media. Although 34 states have enacted laws against cyberbullying, these laws often apply only to minors and only to behaviors committed at school or on public property. Laws focusing on wider audiences, such as private communications between adults, have frequently been challenged and struck down in court for violating First Amendment rights of free speech, even speech that might be considered hurtful or embarrassing. In response, many cases have been prosecuted under other statutes, such as state or federal laws against fraud, bias, or making terroristic threats.

For example, in 2006, 13-year-old Megan Meier of St. Charles County, Missouri, who was being treated for depression, committed suicide after repeated harassment and persecution on the social networking site MySpace. The perpetrator was the 47-year-old mother of an ex-girlfriend posing online as a 16-year-old boy. The mother was not charged with cyberbullying but with fraud under the 1986 U.S. Computer Fraud and Abuse Act, a law written with a totally different concern in mind—the hacking of financial and governmental computer systems. The jury returned a not-guilty verdict, which led the state of Missouri to enact "Megan's Law," making it a felony to use the Internet or other electronic media to harass or frighten a child under the age of 17. In 2009, the first case testing the constitutionality of this new law was filed against a defendant for posting photos and personal information about a young girl in the Casual Encounters section of Craigslist, leading to numerous unwanted phone calls and emails of a sexual nature. In February 2011, a jury again returned a verdict of not guilty, saying the law as written was too vague in its definition of exactly what constitutes online harassment and the invasion of privacy.

In 2010, Tyler Clementi, an 18-year-old Rutgers University freshman, jumped to his death from the George Washington Bridge after a roommate used a hidden webcam to record his private sexual encounter with another man. The roommate then posted the video on the Internet, without Clementi's consent, even inviting Twitter followers to watch it online. In April 2011, a grand jury indicted the roommate on 15 counts, including the transmission of sexual images of another person without his knowledge and bias intimidation, a hate crime, but not cyberbullying because at the time there was no state law addressing this issue. In March 2012, the roommate was convicted on all 15 counts and was sentenced to 30 days in jail, 3 years' probation, 300 hours of community service, and a $10,000 fine. However, in September 2016 those convictions were overturned by an appeals court in New Jersey.

It will likely be many years and many court cases before there is widespread agreement on exactly how to craft a law to deal effectively with the many types of cyberbullying, from the relatively harmless online taunts of young children ("You are stupid," "You have big ears") to the truly frightening threats of disturbed adults and violent sexual predators. These laws need to carefully balance the public's right to a free and unfettered exchange of ideas and opinions, even controversial ones, with the individual's right to control the publication and dissemination of personal information. The difficulty of writing such legislation was highlighted by the judge in the Craigslist case who said that laws addressing cyberbullying and the online invasion of privacy are so new there was virtually no precedent to guide him with proper jury instructions.

Another problem exacerbated by the rapid growth of social networks and online communications is sexting, the transmission of sexually explicit messages or images, usually via smartphones or tablet computers, between consenting individuals. A recent poll from the Pew Research Center shows that more than 20% of young adults had recently sent either sexually explicit text messages or nude/seminude images of themselves to friends via a mobile phone.

Like bullying, the consensual circulation of sexually explicit material is not a new phenomenon, and sharing "pin-up" pictures has been around since the 1890s. However, the popularity of digital cameras and smartphones, as well as their ubiquitous use by teens, has greatly inflamed the problem. Unlike images from digital cameras and smartphones, older, film-based photographs generally had to be processed by a third party. If the photos contained questionable sexual content, the involvement of print shop personnel could lead to an embarrassing situation or, in extreme cases, arrest and prosecution. This tended to put a natural damper on the practice of circulating such photos, a damper that no longer exists. To make matters even worse, smartphones can record and transmit not just still images but videos, which can be far more explicit.

Compounding the problem is the ease with which images and videos can be distributed to a huge audience via popular websites, often without the knowledge or approval of the person being recorded, as was the situation with the streaming video in the Tyler Clementi case. Relationships that an individual thought would last forever can quickly turn ugly and spiteful, resulting in the public distribution of messages and photographs that were originally shared in strict privacy. Social networking sites like Facebook and Twitter are enormous in scale and highly persistent, so once documents or images have been posted, there is virtually no way to get them all back and no way to ever know how many people have viewed them. Years or decades later, long after that indiscretion has been forgotten, these photographs can resurface and damage a person's reputation and career. (An important maxim to remember whenever posting on social media is that "the Internet is forever.")

In June 2011, U.S. Representative Anthony Weiner (New York) was forced to resign in disgrace when a link to sexually explicit photographs he had placed on the web was accidently posted on his public Twitter account. Only a few months later, U.S. Representative Louis Magazzu (New Jersey), a Democrat, had to resign when nude photos he sent in private to a female "friend" ended up on a Republican activist's website. It turns out that the friend was really an employee of a political rival.

It is not simply one's reputation and employment that are at risk—there can be serious legal ramifications when one or both of the individuals involved in the image transmission are under 18. As with cyberbullying, state and federal laws have yet to determine how best to deal with the problem of sexting when the photographs are of minors, even if the transmission is consensual and private. In some states, this issue is dealt with under existing laws against the production and distribution of child pornography, an extremely serious felony that can lead to a long jail sentence and inclusion on the National Sex Offender Registry. For many, this seems like an overly harsh way to deal with the problem of individuals under age 18 who send sexually explicit images of themselves to a boyfriend or girlfriend without any intent to sell or distribute the photos. In 2009, the American Civil Liberties Union (ACLU) filed suit against a Pennsylvania district attorney who was threatening to file child pornography charges against a group of high school girls for posting risqué photos of themselves on a social networking site.

In response to this case, a number of states, including Connecticut, Ohio, Vermont, and New York, have reduced legal penalties for the *consensual* and *private* transmission of sexual images by individuals from age 13 to 17 from a felony to a misdemeanor. Many of these new laws also include mandatory educational and family counseling regarding the real and serious dangers associated with sexting, including encounters with sexual predators, and the humiliation and embarrassment caused by the unexpected distribution of these private photos, a situation that has resulted in numerous teen suicides.

Probably no court decision better exemplifies the complex legal trade-offs between the public nature of social networks and the individual's right to privacy than the 2009 California case *Moreno vs. Hanford Sentinel Inc.* A student at UC-Berkeley, returning during school break to her hometown of Coalinga, California, posted a story on MySpace ("Ode to Coalinga") containing extremely vitriolic and highly unflattering comments about her hometown and its residents. After six days, she deleted the article from her home page; but once an image or message has been posted in cyberspace, it is virtually impossible to control who is able to see it, how many people can copy it, and what can be done with it.

In this case, the offensive posting was viewed by the principal of Coalinga High School who forwarded it to the editor of the *Coalinga Record*, the local newspaper, which published it in full as a letter to the editor, including the author's full name. This led to death threats (a gunshot was fired into the family home), the closing of the father's business, and the family being forced to sell their home and move out of town in disgrace. The family sued the principal, the editor, and the newspaper's owners for invasion of privacy and emotional distress.

The California Court of Appeals ruled that the principal did not invade the young girl's privacy when he sent the article to the newspaper, and the newspaper did not violate her rights by publishing either the article or her full name, both of which had been available on MySpace. The court held that "[She] publicized her opinions about Coalinga by posting the Ode on myspace.com, a hugely popular Internet site. Her affirmative act made that article available to any person with a computer and thus opened it to the public eye. Under these circumstances, no reasonable person would have an expectation of privacy regarding the published material." What this decision is effectively saying is that any material posted to a popular social media website should, by definition, be considered public property, without legal protection against the invasion of privacy.

Many people argue that the best way to ensure personal privacy with regard to online information is simply to assume that any articles, facts, ideas, opinions, rants, photos, or videos you post on a social network might not remain private and, instead, go viral (become widely read and widely distributed via social media). Therefore, it is argued, if you don't want a large number of people to read something, *don't post it.*

However, this argument can sometimes lead to the phenomenon of *victim blaming.* Victim blaming is when the victim, rather than the perpetrator, of a crime or harassment is held responsible. It is not unusual for victims of rape to be extensively questioned about what they were wearing, whether or not they had been drinking, and their history of sexual relationships. While one might question a victim's life choices, this shouldn't excuse a crime against the victim. Finding a balance between these two perspectives is an ongoing debate.

In the Internet age, personal privacy is no longer as simple as putting a lock on your diary and hiding the key. When you say something or show something on a social media site, you are effectively sharing it with the world. At the same time, public sharing is not a justification for harassment and bullying.

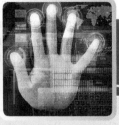

Practice Problems

1. Should cyberbullying be made illegal, or should it be something handled (more informally) by parents, teachers, and the social networking companies? Use a utilitarian analysis, deontological analysis, or argument by analogy to justify your position.

2. Think ahead to 15 years from now. You are Facebook friends (or whatever the equivalent will be in the future) with many of your coworkers. During a messy divorce proceeding, your coworker's ex-spouse posts old sexting messages, sent by the coworker, on Facebook, tagging them so that you and everyone else at work see the pictures. How should you react? What specific actions should you take, or not take, in response? What if you were the manager or owner of the business?

17.4 Fake News, Politics, and Social Media

The final topic we will address with regard to social media and the Internet is, in many regards, the polar opposite of the concerns discussed in Section 17.3—online privacy, sexting, and the unapproved distribution of personal information. In those areas, private communications were made public against the wishes of the author and accessed by individuals who should not be viewing these materials.

However, in the case of fake news, this is exactly what the author is trying to do—distribute (under the guise of objective news) misleading information, slanted opinions, or outright lies to as many people as possible in as short a time frame as possible. Fake news is not a new phenomenon and, in fact, has been around for hundreds of years, often under the perjorative term *yellow journalism*. However, in the past the ability to produce and distribute yellow journalism was generally limited to wealthy individuals who owned newspapers (such as Joseph Pulitzer and William Randolph Hearst) or had the personal wealth to pay the cost of printing and distributing leaflets, buy air time on radio or TV, or hire people to make thousands of telephone calls. However, the Internet and the web, along with the ubiquitous smartphones and tablets, have changed that situation dramatically. Now, with a single keystroke, an individual blogger can reach thousands of social network followers who may then choose to share that post with tens of thousands more. Suddenly, one person's voice has reached out to millions of readers. Because the Internet, many popular blogs, and social apps are unmoderated, that is, not monitored for inappropriate content or fact-checked for accuracy, they become a quick and easy way to distribute any idea we want, true or false, to a massive audience at virtually no cost. In a sense, everyone with a computer and a blog is now a "newspaper owner."

For a long time this ability to inexpensively reach mass audiences was used almost exclusively by mass-market advertisers who sprayed their irritating ads and pop-ups all over our email. The spammers soon followed, but most people quickly learned to ignore those desperate pleas from Nigerian princes who wanted to send us money if we would just provide our bank account number and password. However, as the political landscape has become more polarized and more combative, the idea of using social media to either gain a political advantage over one's opponents, or to generate advertising revenue from the millions of "clicks" of political supporters, is now a far more important usage for fake news and a far more dangerous threat to our democratic system.

While there are many types of fake news (including political humor and satire), some of the most malicious types are:

- *Imposter sites.* This is fake news that uses URLs designed to mimic the addresses of legitimate news sources (e.g., *TheNewYorkTimesNewspaperSite .com*) coupled with a screen layout that mimics the logos and fonts of the real site. The goal is to get readers to believe they are reading information from a well-known, well-respected news source. The content will most likely be totally false and unrelated to anything that would appear on the actual news site being copied.

- *Manipulated content.* This is when actual news stories or photographs are doctored to make them look like they are legitimate coverage of an actual event. Using apps like Photoshop, photographs can be manipulated for political gain, and real news stories can be edited to add or omit information that provides important facts and context for understanding the significance of what has happened.

- *Fabricated content.* This is what we generally think of when we hear the term fake news. This is information that is 100% fabricated and has no basis in reality. It emerges from the imagination of its creator who is only concerned with increasing advertising revenue or moving political opinions in a particular direction.

An amazing example of the power of fake news to foment a national political firestorm is the "Pizzagate" scandal of October 2016, during the height of the U.S. presidential election campaign. A white supremacist Twitter site claimed the New York City Police Department had discovered the existence of a child pornography ring run out of the Comet Ping Pong pizzeria near Washington, DC, that involved a number of high-level members of the Democratic party, including Hillary Clinton. The story, which was totally fabricated, was quickly reposted by a number of right-wing message boards, blogs, and fake news sites and then migrated to more mainstream websites such as Reddit and 4chan. In the following days and weeks the story went viral and was seen online by millions of viewers. It became so controversial that, on December 4, 2016, a man entered the Comet pizzeria with an AK-47, threatening to shoot anyone he encountered who was involved in pedophilia. (He was arrested, and no one was injured.) Eventually, the story was shown to be completely fictitious, fabricated to harm the campaign of Ms. Clinton, but by then the political and personal damage had been done.

It is difficult to prosecute the dispensers of fake news because of the free speech and free press guarantees contained in the First Amendment to the U.S. Constitution. Often, those who have been targeted file civil suits for defamation and slander, but even these civil suits can be difficult to win. The person must prove the printed statements were indeed false, actually harmed one's reputation rather than being merely offensive or insulting, and were made with fault—the person publishing the story knew the statements were false but willfully and recklessly disregarded that fact and published them anyway. This is a high legal bar to reach, often too high to justify the potentially huge cost of litigation. In addition, it can take a long time, often years, to bring a civil suit to trial, and in politics the damage done to a reputation usually happens within days or weeks, not years, as was the case with Pizzagate.

So, if the courts and Congress are not the solution, what can we as Internet and social media users do about this explosion of fake news? The best answer comes from one of our founding fathers, Thomas Jefferson:

An enlightened citizenry is indispensible for the proper functioning of a republic. Self-government is not possible unless the citizens are educated sufficiently to exercise oversight.

This idea can be applied to the functioning of our global communication systems, namely, that each person must educate herself or himself about how to be an intelligent consumer of online content and how to be a well-informed citizen and voter. We must learn to recognize and reject fake news that is presented as valid, objective information.

There are a number of legitimate websites that can help you to identify fake news websites, such as Snopes.com, PolitiFact.com, and FactCheck.org. Some of the techniques to help you spot fake news include:

- *Check the author.* Fake news stories often pump up the credibility and importance of the author of the story by making numerous false claims—for example, Pulitzer prizes won, prestigious university positions held. However, when these claims are fact-checked they turn out, like the story itself, to be fabricated.

- *Check the supporting links.* Fake news stories often include links to official-sounding websites to back up their assertions, for example, WhiteHouseDocumentCenter.com. However, when these links are followed it often turns out the supporting sites are just as phony as the site where the original story first appeared.

- *Look at who else is reporting the story.* In today's 24/7 news environment it would be virtually impossible for an important event to be covered by only one or a small number of blogs. Breaking news stories will (after the delay required to fact-check their authenticity) appear in all the major, responsible news outlets, including television, radio, newspapers, and large online news websites. If the story cannot be found there, it is almost certainly bogus.

- *Consider the apparent intent of the story.* Does the story appear to be heavily biased in favor of a particular point of view; does it contain overly emotional appeals for the "correctness" of that point of view?

So, although the Internet, the web, smartphones, and social media have made it faster and easier to disseminate information, it has become far more complex for people to become discerning and intelligent consumers of that information. It is now our personal responsibility to learn how to determine what is real and what is false, how not to be deceived by the biases and outright lies becoming all too common on the Internet, and not to pass fake news on to others. If we are not willing to accept that important responsibility, these amazing new technical achievements could become the seeds that sow both discord and chaos into our democratic process.

17.5 Conclusion

We don't want to end this chapter without warning you that we've only scratched the surface of some of the ethical and legal issues involving technology, privacy, and society. In the chapter exercises, we'll invite you to look at some of the many controversies in these developing areas of applied ethics. And although we've discussed how to apply utilitarian ideas, deontological ideas, and analogies to computer ethics, we haven't even mentioned Rawlsian negotiation, virtue ethics, or any other number of ethical techniques. We also haven't explicitly mentioned "science and technology studies," though many of the themes we've described are included in that emerging scholarly field.

You may think that the paramedic method is too involved for your decisions, and perhaps just trying to remember how to spell *deontological* gives you a headache. But we hope you'll at least remember that technical decisions involve human values, whether we recognize it or not. And when you have to decide if something having to do with technology is right or wrong, we hope you remember to think carefully about consequences and duties. Computers give us tremendous power. Let's hope we learn to use the power well. Happy computing!

17.6 Summary of Level 6

In this last and highest level of abstraction in our study of computer science, we looked at several case studies involving computer technology and saw how even seemingly straightforward situations, when examined closely, reveal multiple facets of ethical implications. But more than the particular cases involved, this level provided some tools for coping with ethical decision making.

Because of the increasing capabilities of computers and their increasingly pervasive presence in our private and public lives, the path ahead will be filled with instances in which the use of computers, information, and technology will have ethical consequences. As private citizens and as members of society, we cannot avoid making decisions on such issues, because even doing nothing is a decision that has ethical consequences. Finally, ethical decision making seems to be a purely human responsibility, not one that our computers can help us with directly, at least not yet.

EXERCISES

1. Here are some issues that you may have noticed in the news, each of which involves the intertwining of technology and human values:

    Personal privacy when surfing the web

    Software quality issues: How good is good enough?

    Licensing of software engineers

    The digital divide: The haves and have-nots of information

    U.S. Supreme Court ruling on virtual kiddie porn

    U.S. Supreme Court ruling on filters on public library Internet use

    U.S. Supreme Court ruling that children have the right to buy violent games

    Tracking terrorist and hate group websites

    Censoring information on the web about making bombs

    Loss of jobs due to technology

    Computer algorithms for determining the risks of subprime mortgages

    Virtual reality as recreation

    Computer simulations in the courtroom

    Email spam and legislation to stop it

    Online education and cheating

    Surveillance cameras in public areas

    Face recognition to scan for terrorists

    FBI databases of criminals

    Websites listing convicted sex offenders' addresses

    Stolen credit card numbers posted on the Internet

    Sales taxes on Internet sales

    Computing for the disabled

    Open source software versus commercial software

    Remixing pictures or videos found on the web to create art

    Term papers or problem solutions for sale on the Internet

    Internet-based plagiarism detection services

    States selling information compiled from drivers' licenses

    Database matching to find deadbeat parents

    Internet casino gambling

    Workplace monitoring using computers

    Legal rights for robots

    Smart bombs and other lethal robots/drones

    Artificial intelligence devices for medical diagnosis

    DNA evidence in death penalty cases

    The rise and fall of Anonymous, LulzSec, and WikiLeaks

    Edward Snowden's leaks of U.S. security documents

    Fake news as a political campaign tool

    a. *Practice creating analogies*—Pick three topics from the list shown here, or make up some topics of your own that involve technology and humans. For each topic, think of an analogous situation that does *not* involve computing. For example, if you picked "online education and cheating," an obvious analogy would be to consider face-to-face education and cheating. If you picked "personal privacy when surfing the web," an analogy might be "personal privacy when renting movies." When you've picked your three topics and your analogy for each, make a short list of how each analogy is like the topic and how the analogy is different from the topic.

    b. *Practice finding stakeholders*—Pick your favorite topic from among the three topics you chose in Exercise 1a. For that topic, make a new list of all the significant stakeholders in the topic. (*Hint*: Remember that a stakeholder can be an individual, a group of individuals, a corporation, perhaps the environment, or any other entities you think are important in your topic.) For each stakeholder, list what the stakeholder most values in this situation.

It might help you to frame a specific question or propose a particular action related to the topic. For example, if your topic is "online education and cheating," you might propose the action, "online education should be suspended until online cheating can be better controlled" or "online education should include automated cheating detection." This narrowing of the topic sometimes simplifies the task of imagining what people value with respect to this issue.

c. *Practice identifying costs and benefits*—For each stakeholder you identified in Exercise 1b, list the possible costs and benefits in the situation you chose. In many cases, these are *potential* costs and benefits, things that might or might not happen. Sometimes the words *vulnerability* and *opportunity* can be more accurate than *cost* and *benefit* because of uncertainties in the situation.

d. *Practice looking for duties and responsibilities*—In the previous two parts, you identified some stakeholders. Let's use the letter *N* to stand for the number of stakeholders you identified. Now, make a two-dimensional table that has $N \times N$ cells.

At the top of the table, label each column with one of your stakeholders. At the left of the table, copy the list of stakeholders, one for each row. If the stakeholders were {Fred, Ethel, Lucy}, then the table would look like this:

	Fred	Ethel	Lucy
Fred			Things that Fred owes Lucy
Ethel		Things that Ethel owes Ethel	
Lucy	Things that Lucy owes Fred		

Inside each cell, list any duties or responsibilities that the stakeholder on the left owes the stakeholder above. For example, three of the cells are marked in the sample table. Don't neglect the cells that describe duties people have to themselves.

2. *Pull it all together*—In Exercise 1, you looked at one topic in some detail. In this exercise, write a short paragraph about what you think is the right thing to do in the situation you selected. Justify your decision based on the analogy you developed, the costs and benefits you listed, and the duties in your table. After you've devised the best argument you can to show that you're right, write a short description of what you think is the best argument *against* your decision.

Answers to Practice Problems

Chapter 2
Section 2.2.2

1. | Step | Operation |
   | --- | --- |
   | 1 | Get values for x, y, and z |
   | 2 | Set the value of *average* to $(x + y + z)/3$ |
   | 3 | Print the value of *average* |
   | 4 | Stop |

2. | Step | Operation |
   | --- | --- |
   | 1 | Get a value for r, the radius of the circle |
   | 2 | Set the value of *circumference* to $2 \times \pi \times r$ |
   | 3 | Set the value of *area* to $\pi \times r^2$ |
   | 4 | Print the values of *circumference* and *area* |
   | 5 | Stop |

3. | Step | Operation |
   | --- | --- |
   | 1 | Get values for *amount*, the amount of electricity used, and for *cost*, the cost per kilowatt-hour |
   | 2 | Set the value of *subtotal* to *amount* $\times$ *cost* |
   | 3 | Set the value of *tax* to $0.08 \times$ *subtotal* |
   | 4 | Set the value of *total* to *subtotal* + *tax* |
   | 5 | Print the value of *total* |
   | 6 | Stop |

4. | Step | Operation |
   | --- | --- |
   | 1 | Get values for *balance*, the current credit card balance, for *purchases*, the total dollar amount of new purchases, and for *payment*, the total dollar amount of all payments |
   | 2 | Set the value of *unpaid* to *balance* + *purchases* − *payment* |
   | 3 | Set the value of *interest* to *unpaid* $\times$ 0.12 |
   | 4 | Set the value of *newbalance* to *unpaid* + *interest* |
   | 5 | Print the value of *newbalance* |
   | 6 | Stop |

5. | Step | Operation |
   | --- | --- |
   | 1 | Get values for *length* and *width* in feet |
   | 2 | Set the value of *length-in-yards* to *length*/3 |

3	Set the value of *width-in-yards* to *width*/3
4	Set the value of *area* to *length-in-yards* × *width-in-yards*
5	Set the value of *cost* to *area* × 23
6	Print the value of *cost*
7	Stop

6.

Step	Operation
1	Get values for *first*, *second*, and *third*
2	Set the value of *points earned* to (5 × *first*) + (3 × *second*) + (1 × *third*)
3	Print the value of *points earned*
4	Stop

Section 2.2.3

1.   If x ≥ 0 then

>   Set the value of *y* to 1

Else

>   Set the value of *y* to 2

2.   Get values for *x*, *y*, and *z*

If x > 0 then

>   Set the value of *average* to (*x* + *y* + *z*)/3
>
>   Print the value of *average*

Else

>   Print the message 'Bad Data'

Stop

3.   Get values for *balance*, *purchases*, *payment*

Set the value of *unpaid* to *balance* + *purchases* − *payment*

If *unpaid* < 100 then

>   Set the value of *interest* to *unpaid* × 0.08

Else

>   If *unpaid* ≤ 500 then
>
>>   Set the value of *interest* to *unpaid* × 0.12
>
>   Else
>
>>   Set the value of *interest* to *unpaid* × 0.16

Set the value of *newbalance* to *unpaid* + *interest*

Print the value of *newbalance*

Stop

4. Get a value for x

    While $x \neq 999$ do

        Set the value of a to x^2

        Set the value of b to sin(x)

        Set the value of c to $1/x$

        Print the values of a, b, and c

        Get a value for x

    End of the loop

    Stop

5. Get values for *length*, *width*, *price*

    Set the value of *length-in-yards* to *length*/3

    Set the value of *width-in-yards* to *width*/3

    Set the value of *area* to *length-in-yards* $\times$ *width-in-yards*

    Set the value of *cost* to *area* $\times$ *price*

    If *cost* $\leq$ 500 then

        Print the message 'You can afford this carpet'

    Else

        Print the message 'This carpet is too expensive'

    Stop

6. Add the following statement to the end of the solution, just before the Stop statement:

    (Assume that we have stored the cost of the carpet in the variable *cost*.)

    If (*cost* $\leq$ 250) then

        Print the message 'This is a particularly good deal.'

7. Get a value for x

    While ($x \neq 999$) do

        Set the value of a to x^2

        Print the value of a

        Set the value of b to sin(x)

        Print the value of b

        If $x = 0$ then

          Print the error message 'Cannot compute 1/x'

        Else

Set the value of c to 1/x

Print the value of c

Get a value for x

End of the loop

Stop

Section 2.3.1

1. Initial values

   $a = 2$ $b = 4$ $count = 0$ $product = 0$

   After pass 1

   $a = 2$ $b = 4$ $count = 1$ $product = 2$

   After pass 2

   $a = 2$ $b = 4$ $count = 2$ $product = 4$

   After pass 3

   $a = 2$ $b = 4$ $count = 3$ $product = 6$

   After pass 4

   $a = 2$ $b = 4$ $count = 4$ $product = 8$

2. Yes, the algorithm still works correctly. On Line 1, we input the two values $a = 0$, $b = 0$. On Line 2, the Boolean expression is true, so we set $product = 0$ and skip the entire else clause. The next line executed is "print the value of product" which outputs a 0, the correct answer to the problem 0×0.

3. case 1 ($a = -2$, $b = 4$):
   The value of *product* will be -8, which is correct.

   case 2 ($a = 2$, $b = -4$):
   The value of *product* will be 0 (the while loop does not execute at all), which is incorrect.

4. The original algorithm fails when $b < 0$ because *count* is never less than b. If $b < 0$, change the value of b to $-b$, but set the value of a variable called *bnegative* to YES to remember that b was negative. After the product is computed, the sign of *product* will be incorrect if b was negative, so change the sign. Here is a pseudocode version that works for all integer values of a and b:

   Get values for a and b

   Set the value of bnegative to NO

   If (either $a = 0$ or $b = 0$) then

   Set the value of product to 0

   Else

If $b < 0$ then

    Set the value of b to $-b$

    Set the value of *bnegative* to YES

Set the value of *count* to 0

Set the value of *product* to 0

While (*count* < *b*) do

    Set the value of *product* to (*product* + *a*)

    Set the value of *count* to (*count* + 1)

End of the loop

If (*bnegative* = YES) then

    Print the value of $-product$

Else

    Print the value of *product*

Stop

5. It is a highly inefficient algorithm because of the number of steps required to find the answer. For example, to add 234 + 567, we will have to repeat the addition of the value 234 to a running sum 567 separate times. When we do multiplication the "traditional" way that we learned in grade school, we have to carry out far fewer operations. (We will learn much more about how to evaluate the efficiency of algorithms in Chapter 3.)

6. Get values for *a* and *b*

If (either $a > 10,000$ or $b > 10,000$) then

    Print 'Please use a more efficient multiplication algorithm'

Else

    If (either $a = 0$ or $b = 0$) then

        Set the value of *product* to 0

    Else

        Set the value of *count* to 0

        Set the value of *product* to 0

        While (*count* < *b*) do

            Set the value of *product* to (*product* + *a*)

            Set the value of *count* to (*count* + 1)

        End of the loop

    Print the value of *product*

Stop

Section 2.3.3

1. We would need to change Line 1 so that the algorithm would input 1 million numbers and names rather than 10,000. We would need to change Line 3 so that the loop would repeat a maximum of 1 million times rather than a maximum of 10,000. Actually, that is not a lot of change given that the problem is 100 times bigger. We only needed to change two lines. In fact, if the phone book were 1 billion numbers in length, then we would only need to change the same two lines.

2. | Step | Operation |
    |------|-----------|
    | 1 | Get values for $NUMBER$, $T_1, \ldots, T_{10,000}$ and $N_1, \ldots, N_{10,000}$ |
    | 2 | Set the value of i to 1 and the value of $Found$ to NO |
    | 3 | Do |
    | 4 | If $NUMBER$ is equal to the ith number on the list, T_i, then |
    | 5 | Print the name of the corresponding person, N_i |
    | 6 | Set the value of $Found$ to YES |
    | | Else |
    | 7 | Add 1 to the value of i |
    | 8 | While ($Found$ = NO) and ($i \le 10{,}000$) |
    | 9 | If ($Found$ = NO) then |
    | 10 | Print the message 'Sorry, this number is not in the directory' |
    | 11 | Stop |

3. You must change the operation on Line 7 from a greater-than ($>$) to a less-than ($<$) sign. That line will now read as follows:

    If $A_i <$ *largest so far* then ...

    That is the only required change. However, to avoid confusion about what the algorithm is doing, you probably should also change the name of the variable *largest so far* to something like *smallest so far* on Lines 3, 7, 8, and 12. Otherwise, a casual reading of the algorithm might lead someone to think incorrectly that it is still an algorithm to find the largest value rather than the smallest.

4. If $n = 0$ (the list is empty), then there are no values for $A_1, A_2, \ldots, A_n$. In particular, setting the value of *largest so far* to A_1 gives a meaningless value to *largest so far*. The while loop will not execute at all because i has the value 2 and n has the value 0, so the condition $i \le n$ is false. The algorithm will print out nonsense values for *largest so far* and *location*.

    The algorithm can be fixed by putting a conditional statement after Line 1. If $n = 0$, then the algorithm should print a message that says the list is empty. The "else" case will be the rest of the current algorithm.

5. If $n = 1$, then *largest so far* is set to A_1, the only list element, and *location* is set to 1. Also i is set to 2, so the while loop will not execute because it is false that $i \leq n$ (i.e., it is false that $2 \leq 1$). The correct values of *largest so far* and *location* are printed.

6. Yes, it would still work correctly in one sense—it would find the largest numerical value in the list. However, if two numbers were equal, this change would cause the algorithm to find the last occurrence of that number rather than the first. So the value of *largest so far* would not change but the value of *location* might be different.

Section 2.3.4

1. a. NUMBER = (771) 921-5281

i	Operation	Found
1	Compare (771) 921-5281 to T_1, (648) 555-1285. No match.	No
2	Compare (771) 921-5281 to T_2, (247) 834-6543. No match.	No
3	Compare (771) 921-5281 to T_3, (771) 921-5281. Match.	Yes

Output = Adams

b. NUMBER = (488) 351-1673

i	Operation	Found
1	Compare (488) 351-1673 to T_1, (648) 555-1285. No match.	No
2	Compare (488) 351-1673 to T_2, (247) 834-6543. No match.	No
3	Compare (488) 351-1673 to T_3, (771) 921-5281. No match.	No
4	Compare (488) 351-1673 to T_4, (356) 327-8900. No match.	No

Output = 'Sorry, this number is not in the directory'

2. $n = 7$, $A_1 = 22$, $A_2 = 18$, $A_3 = 23$, $A_4 = 17$, $A_5 = 25$, $A_6 = 30$, $A_7 = 2$

Largest So Far	Location	i	Operation
22	1	2	Compare A_2 and *largest so far*. Is 18 > 22? No
22	1	3	Compare A_3 and *largest so far*. Is 23 > 22? Yes, so reset values
23	3	4	Compare A_4 and *largest so far*. Is 17 > 23? No
23	3	5	Compare A_5 and *largest so far*. Is 25 > 23? Yes, so reset values
25	5	6	Compare A_6 and *largest so far*. Is 30 > 25? Yes, so reset values
30	6	7	Compare A_7 and *largest so far*. Is 2 > 30? No

Output: Largest = 30. Location = 6.

3. Pattern = an $m = 2$. The pattern has 2 characters.
   Text = A man and a woman $n = 17$. The text has 17 characters.

k	i	Mismatch	Operation
1	1	No	Compare P_1, the "a", to T_1, the "A". No match.
		Yes	End of the check for a match at position 1 of the text.
2	1	No	Compare P_1, the "a", to T_2, the blank. No match.
		Yes	End of the check for a match at position 2 of the text.
3	1	No	Compare P_1, the "a", to T_3, the "m". No match.
		Yes	End of the check for a match at position 3 of the text.
4	1	No	Compare P_1, the "a", to T_4, the "a". Match.
4	2	No	Compare P_2, the "n", to T_5, the "n". Match.
4	3	No	i (3) is greater than m (2), so we exit the loop.

Output: There is a match at position 4

In a similar way, the program will produce the following two additional lines of output:

There is a match at position 7

There is a match at position 16

4. If $m > n$, then $n - m + 1 \leq 0$. Because the value of k is set to 1 right before the outer while loop, the condition $k \leq (n - m + 1)$ is false, the loop is not executed, and the algorithm terminates with no output.

5. If we had incorrectly initialized i to 0 rather than 1, then the algorithm would halt with a fatal error on Line 8. In that line, we reference the variable P_i. If i is 0, this would be P_0, but there is no such value, as the pattern begins with the element P_1. This shows how important it is to be very careful about not only the "big issues" but the little details as well. Even a very tiny initialization error can cause an entire algorithm to fail.

6. Yes, it will work correctly. The quantity $(n - m + 1)$ evaluates to 1. Since k is initialized to 1, the test $k \leq (n - m + 1)$ will initially evaluate to True and the loop will be executed. The text and the pattern will be matched beginning at position 1. Then when k is incremented to 2, the test will become false and we will exit the loop, as desired.

Chapter 3

Section 3.2

The numbers from 1 to n, where n is even, can be grouped into $n/2$ pairs of the form

$$1 + n = n + 1$$

$$2 + (n - 1) = n + 1$$

$$\ldots$$

$$n/2 + (n/2 + 1) = n + 1$$

giving a sum of $(n/2)(n + 1)$. This formula gives the correct sum for all cases shown, whether n is even or odd.

Section 3.3.2

N	Best Case	Worst Case	Average Case
10	1	10	5
50	1	50	25
100	1	100	50
1,000	1	1,000	500
10,000	1	10,000	5,000
100,000	1	100,000	50,000

Section 3.3.3

1. a. 4, 8, 2, 6
      4, 6, 2, 8
      4, 2, 6, 8
      2, 4, 6, 8

   b. 12, 3, 6, 8, 2, 5, 7
      7, 3, 6, 8, 2, 5, 12
      7, 3, 6, 5, 2, 8, 12
      2, 3, 6, 5, 7, 8, 12
      2, 3, 5, 6, 7, 8, 12

   c. D, B, G, F, A, C, E, H
      D, B, E, F, A, C, G, H
      D, B, E, C, A, F, G, H
      D, B, A, C, E, F, G, H
      C, B, A, D, E, F, G, H
      A, B, C, D, E, F, G, H

   d. The list is already in sorted order. Although the selection sort algo-
      rithm will go through all of its operations, the largest element will
      always be at the back of the unsorted section and will be exchanged
      with itself, resulting in no change.

2. This question can be answered using the formulas from Section 3.3.3:

   Number of comparisons $= \dfrac{1}{2} n^2 - \dfrac{1}{2} n$ Number of exchanges $= n$

   a. Comparisons: 6   Exchanges: 4
   b. Comparisons: 21   Exchanges: 7
   c. Comparisons: 28   Exchanges: 8
   d. Comparisons: 10   Exchanges: 5

Section 3.3.4

The basic shape of the curve as n gets large is still n^2 because as n gets large,
the n^2 term dominates the other two terms.

Section 3.4.1

1. *legit* = 3

2	4	1	1

2.

2	0	4	1

2	4	1

3. *legit* = 3

2	1	4	1

4. For example,

1	2	0	0

Section 3.4.2

1. 5656170224, 7719215281, 6485551285

2. 5656170224, 7719215281, 8796562127

3. If the data file is sorted numerically by SSN, then the binary search algorithm can be used. The worst case is 29 (2^{28} = 268,435,456 and 2^{29} = 536,870,912). If the data file is sorted alphabetically by the individual's last name, then as far as searching for a SSN is concerned, the file is unsorted. The sequential search algorithm must be used, with a worst case of 453,700,000.

Section 3.4.3

Pattern = AAAB; Text = AAAAAAAAA; m = 4; n = 9; $m \times n$ = 36; the exact number of comparisons is 4×6 = 24.

Section 3.5

1. 38 paths

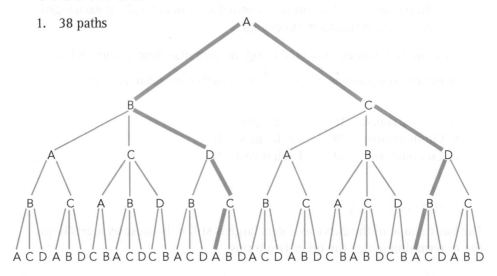

2.

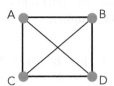

3. Algorithms of $\Theta(n^2)$ are polynomial algorithms because n is raised to a constant power. An algorithm of $\Theta(2^n)$ is an exponential algorithm. It is the nonconstant exponent that makes this value grow so quickly, as opposed to polynomial algorithms. An algorithm of $\Theta(n^n)$ would still be considered an exponential algorithm because its exponent is n. In fact, such an algorithm grows even faster than one of order 2^n because of the nonconstant base.

Chapter 4
Section 4.2.1

1. a. $10101000 = (1 \times 2^3) + (1 \times 2^5) + (1 \times 2^7)$
    $$= 8 + 32 + 128$$
    $$= 168 \text{ as an unsigned integer value}$$

    b. $10101000 = (1 \times 2^3) + (1 \times 2^5)$
    $$= 8 + 32$$
    $$= 40$$

    This is the value of the magnitude portion of the number. The left-most bit represents the sign bit. In this example, it is a 1, which is a negative sign.

    $$= -40 \text{ as a signed integer value}$$

2. To answer this question, you must represent the decimal value as a sum of powers of 2 and then convert that representation to binary.

    $99 = 64 + 32 + 2 + 1$
    $$= 2^6 + 2^5 + 2^1 + 2^0$$
    $$= 1100011$$

    However, this is only 7 bits and we need 8, so we must add one leading 0 to fill out the answer.

    $$= 01100011$$

3. The 10 bits would be represented as 9 bits for the magnitude and the leftmost bit for the sign. To represent the magnitude, we must rewrite 300 as the sum of powers of 2, as we did in the previous question.

    $300 = 256 + 32 + 8 + 4$
    $$= 2^8 + 2^5 + 2^3 + 2^2$$
    $$= 100101100 \text{ in 9 bits}$$

To make it a negative value, we must add a 1 bit (the negative sign) to the leftmost position of the number.

$-300 = 1100101100$
$254 = 128 + 64 + 32 + 16 + 8 + 4 + 2$
$ = 2^7 + 2^6 + 2^5 + 2^4 + 2^3 + 2^2 + 2^1$
$ = 011111110$ to 9 bits of accuracy for the magnitude

To make it a +254, we must add a 0 (the + sign) to the leftmost position of the number.

$+254 = 0011111110$

4. Because the leftmost digit is a 1, the number is negative. The magnitude is represented by the remaining 7 digits, 0010111, which is $1 + 2 + 4 + 16 = 23$. Thus, the number is -23.

5. Writing the numbers 0000 through 1111 around a circle, the positive values count up from 0000 and the negative numbers count down from 1111.
   a. $+6$ is 0110
   b. -3 is 1101

6.
   ```
    1110      ← carry digit
    01110
   +01011
   ───────
    11001
   ```

7. a. To see what this value would look like in ASCII, we first look up the characters "X", "+", and "Y" in the ASCII conversion table to see what their internal representation is in decimal.

   "X" = 88
   "+" = 43
   "Y" = 89

   We then convert these decimal values to unsigned 8-bit binary values.

   "X" = 88 = 01011000
   "+" = 43 = 00101011
   "Y" = 89 = 01011001

   The internal representation of the three-character string 'X+Y' is formed by putting together all three of the preceding values, producing the following 24-bit string:

   010110000010101101011001

   which is how a computer stores 'X + Y' using ASCII encoding.

   b. From the Unicode tables,

   "X" = 0058
   "+" = 002B
   "Y" = 0059

where these representations are in hexidecimal (base 16) form. In base 16, digits run from 0–F rather than 0–9 as in the decimal system. Translating these representations into decimal, we get

$$\text{“X”} = 0 \times 16^3 + 0 \times 16^2 + 5 \times 16^1 + 8 \times 16^0$$
$$= 80 + 8$$
$$= 88$$

$$\text{“+”} = 0 \times 16^3 + 0 \times 16^2 + 2 \times 16^1 + 11 \times 16^0$$
$$= 32 + 11$$
$$= 43$$

$$\text{“Y”} = 0 \times 16^3 + 0 \times 16^2 + 5 \times 16^1 + 9 \times 16^0$$
$$= 80 + 9$$
$$= 89$$

These are the same decimal values as under ASCII encoding (Unicode for common characters agrees with ASCII encoding) but will be written in 16-bit binary form, with extra spaces for readability.

“X” = 88 = 0000 0000 0101 1000
“+” = 43 = 0000 0000 0010 1011
“Y” = 89 = 0000 0000 0101 1001

Putting these together produces the following 48-bit string for 'X+ Y':

0000 0000 0101 1000 0000 0000 0010 1011 0000 0000 0101 1001

8. a. $+ 0.25 = 0.01$ in binary
$$= 0.1 \times 2^{-1} \text{ in scientific notation}$$

so the mantissa is $+ 0.1$ and the exponent is -1.

$$= 0 \underbrace{100000000}_{\text{mantissa}} \qquad \underbrace{1\ 00001}_{\text{exponent}}$$

b. $-32\ 1/16 = -100000.0001$
$$= -0.1000000001 \times 2^6$$
$$= 1 \underbrace{100000000}_{\text{mantissa}} \qquad \underbrace{0\ 00110}_{\text{exponent}}$$

Note that the last 1 in the mantissa was not stored because there was not enough room. The loss of accuracy that results from limiting the number of digits available is called a *truncation error*.

9. 1111   ← carry digits
   00001
+01111
  10000

Here $15 + 1 = -16$

10. You are adding the two values $+7$ and $+14$, which should produce the value $+21$. But when you add the two values together, you get 10101, which is a negative value because the leftmost digit is a 1. In fact, it is the value -5. What happened is that we got an *arithmetic overflow*. The value $+21$ is too big to represent in sign/magnitude with only five digits.

Section 4.2.2

1. 44,100 samples/second $\times$ 16 bits/sample $\times$ 3 minutes $\times$ 60 sec/minute = 127 million bits

   Compressed at a ratio of 4:1, this becomes about 32 million bits.

2. 66,000 samples/sec $\times$ 24 bits/sample $\times$ 180 seconds = 285,120,000 bits

3. 2,100,000 pixels $\times$ 24 bits/pixel = 50,400,000 bits or 6,300,000 bytes

4. To reduce 6,300,000 bytes to 1,000,000 bytes requires a compression ratio of almost 7:1.

   To reduce 6,300,000 bytes to 256,000 bytes requires a compression ratio of almost 25:1.

5. Compression ratio = original size / compressed size = 9.6 / 3 = 3.2

6. The fixed-length 4-bit representation of ALOHA requires 5 $\times$ 4 = 20 bits. Using the variable-length code requires the following:

A	L	O	H	A
00	1111111	0111	010	00

   which is a total of 18 bits. The compression ratio is 20 / 18 = 1.11.

7. The number of bits required per song is:

   44,100 samples/sec $\times$ 16 bits/sample $\times$ 180 sec/song $\times$ 0.1 (compression) = 12,700,800 bits/song = 1,587,600 bytes/song (at 8 bits/byte)

   If there are 16 GB available on your smartphone for music storage, then the total number of songs that can be stored is approximately:

   16×10^9 / 1.587×10^6 = 10,080 songs

Section 4.3.1

1. a. $(x = 1)$ AND $(y = 3)$
      True AND False
      False   The final answer is False.
   b. $(x < y)$ OR $(x > 1)$
      True OR False
      True   The final answer is True.
   c. NOT $[(x = 1)$ AND $(y = 2)]$
      NOT [True AND True]
      NOT [True]
      False   The final answer is False.

2.

A	B	C	((NOT A) AND B) OR C
F	F	F	F
F	F	T	T
F	T	F	T
F	T	T	T
T	F	F	F
T	F	T	T
T	T	F	F
T	T	T	T

3. $(x = 5)$ AND $(y = 11)$ OR $([x + y] = z)$
   True AND False OR True

   We now must make an assumption about which of the two logical operations to do first, the AND or the OR. If we assume the AND goes first, then we get

   False OR True
   True

   If we assume that the OR goes first, then the expression would be evaluated as follows:

   True AND True
   True

   In this case, the answer is the same, but we arrive at the answer in different ways.

4. $(x \geq 0)$ AND $(x \leq 100)$ AND $(y \geq 0)$ AND $(y \leq 100)$ AND $(NOT(x = y))$

5. NOT$[(score \geq 200)$ AND $(score \leq 800)]$

6. The expression $(A$ OR $B)$ OR $(NOT\ A)$ is true for all values of A and B and, therefore, is never false. A Boolean expression that is always true is called a *tautology.*

7. $(year = 4)$ AND $((major = $ Chemistry$)$ OR $(major = $ Physics$))$

Section 4.4.2

1. The four separate cases are

   $\bar{a} \cdot \bar{b} \cdot \bar{c}$ $\bar{a} \cdot b \cdot \bar{c}$ $\bar{a} \cdot b \cdot c$ $a \cdot b \cdot \bar{c}$

   Combining them by using the OR operator produces the following Boolean expression:

   $\bar{a} \cdot \bar{b} \cdot \bar{c} + \bar{a} \cdot b \cdot \bar{c} + \bar{a} \cdot b \cdot c + a \cdot b \cdot \bar{c}$

When this Boolean expression is represented as a Boolean diagram, it appears as follows:

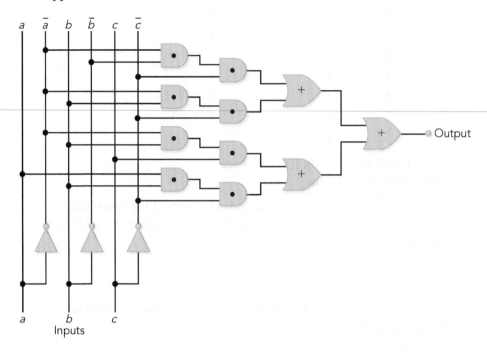

2. The Boolean expressions for the two cases are

$\bar{a}{\cdot}b$
$a{\cdot}\bar{b}$

Combining these two by using the OR operator produces

$\bar{a}{\cdot}b + a{\cdot}\bar{b}$

Pictorially, the corresponding circuit diagram is

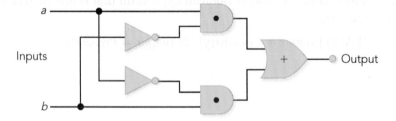

3. The Boolean expression for this is

$\bar{a}{\cdot}\bar{b}{\cdot}\bar{c} + a{\cdot}b{\cdot}c$

Pictorially, the corresponding circuit diagram is

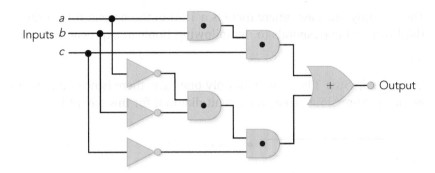

4. If we use the circuit construction algorithm described in this chapter, we produce the circuit: $\bar{a}\cdot\bar{b} + \bar{a}\cdot b$. When this expression is implemented as a logic circuit, it takes two NOT gates, two AND gates, and one OR gate for a total of five gates. However, looking carefully at the truth table, we see that the output is a 1 whenever a is a 0, and the output is a 0 whenever a is a 1. The output is not affected by the value of b. Thus, an equivalent circuit is $\bar{a}$, which takes only 1 gate—an improvement of 80%. This is a good example of how much optimization can improve a preliminary design, and how important it can be to the efficiency of a computer system.

5. Since the truth table for C has 4 distinct inputs, there would be $2^4 = 16$ rows, representing the 16 possible inputs, 0000 to 1111. There are 4 input columns (for a, b, c, d) and 3 output columns (for *output-1*, *output-2*, and *output-3*), for a total of 7 columns. Thus the dimensions of the truth table for circuit C would be 16×7.

Section 4.4.3

1. Each 1-CE circuit contains two NOT gates, two AND gates, and one OR gate. This will require $(2 \times 1) + (2 \times 3) + (1 \times 3) = 2 + 6 + 3 = 11$ transistors. The 32-bit compare-for-equality circuit of Figure 4.28 has the following components:

   32 1-CE circuits $= 32 \times 11 = 352$ transistors
   31 AND gates $= 31 \times 3 = 93$ transistors
   Total $= 352 + 93 = 445$ transistors

2. Bit-compare $a > b$, where both a and b are 1 bit in length.

   The truth table for this circuit would be as follows:

a	b	Output	
0	0	0	
0	1	0	
1	0	1	(because a is greater than b)
1	1	0	

There is only one case where there is a 1 bit in the output. It is in the third row and corresponds to the following Boolean expression:

$a \cdot \bar{b}$

We can skip Step 3 because with only one case, there is no combining of Boolean expressions. Thus, the circuit diagram for this circuit is

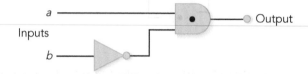

3. The truth table is already given, and again there is only one case with a 1 bit in the output. This occurs in the first row and corresponds to the Boolean expression

$\bar{a} \cdot \bar{b}$

Given this single subexpression, we can proceed immediately to draw the circuit diagram:

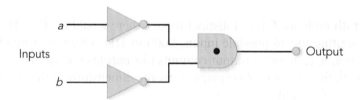

4. The truth table is already given. There are two cases with a 1 bit in the output, occurring in rows 1 and 4. The corresponding subexpressions are:

Case 1: $\bar{a} \cdot \bar{b}$

Case 2: $a \cdot b$

The final Boolean expression is $\bar{a} \cdot \bar{b} + a \cdot b$ and the circuit diagram is

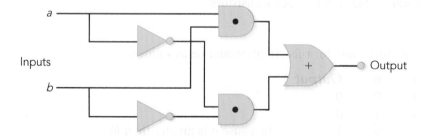

Chapter 5

Section 5.2.1

1. If the memory unit is a two-dimensional grid 1,024 (2^{10}) by 1,024 (2^{10}), then it contains a total of 1,048,576 (2^{20}) memory cells. We need a total of 20 bits to represent all the possible memory addresses, which range from 0 to $2^{20} - 1$.

2. Because there are $2^{10} = 1,024$ row lines and $2^{10} = 1,024$ column lines, we would need to send 10 (of the 20) bits in the MAR to the row decoder and 10 bits to the column decoder.

3. The instructions that are fetched from memory are usually much larger than 8 bits in size, often 16 or 32 bits. If the MDR were only 8 bits, then to fetch a 16-bit instruction we would have to go back to memory twice. If the instruction were 32 bits, then we would have to go back to memory four separate times. This would greatly slow down the fetch phase of the instruction cycle. The MDR should be at least as large as the largest instruction that we fetch.

4. Average access time = $(0.80 \times 10) + 0.20 \times (10 + 25) = 15$ nsec

5. Average access time = $(0.90 \times 10) + 0.10 \times (10 + 25) = 9 + 3.5 = 12.5$ nsec

6. With a cache hit rate of 92%, the average access time is

    $(0.92 \times 10) + 0.08 \times (10 + 25) = 12.0$ nsec

7. Each byte contains 8 bits, so 8 bytes contain 64 bits. Using two's complement representation, the largest positive value would be:

    $+2^{63} - 1 = +9,223,372,036,854,775,807$

    while the largest negative value would be:

    $-2^{63} = -9,223,372,036,854,775,808$

8. For example: If we think that human memory consists of "cells" in which information is stored and from which it can be retrieved, then human memory does not seem to have the property of a uniform time to access every cell. "Short-term memories" seem to be more quickly accessible than long-term memories.

Section 5.2.2

1. The total number of characters (ch) is

    2 surfaces/disk $\times$ 50 tracks/surface $\times$ 20 sectors/track $\times$ 1024 ch/sector, which is 2,048,000 characters on a single disk.

2. The seek time depends on the number of tracks over which the read head must move. This could range from 0, if the arm does not need to move,

to a worst case of the arm having to move from the far inside track to the far outside track, a total of 49 tracks. The average, as stated in the problem, is a move across 20 tracks. The best-case rotational delay is 0, whereas the worst case is one complete revolution. The rotational speed is 2,400 rev/min = 40 rev/sec = 25 msec/rev. On the average, we will wait about one-half of a revolution. Finally, the transfer time is the same in all cases, the time it takes for one sector (1/20 of a track) to rotate under the read/write head, which is 1/20 rev × 25 msec/rev = 1.25 msec. Putting all this together in a table produces the following values for the time (in msec) required for each task:

	Best Case	Average Case	Worst Case
Seek time	0.0	20 × 0.4 = 8.0	49 × 0.4 = 19.6
Latency	0.0	0.5 × 25 = 12.5	1 × 25 = 25.0
Transfer	1.25	1.25	1.25
Total	1.25	21.75	45.85

3. The new rotational speed is 7,200 rev/min = 120 rev/sec = 8.33 msec/rev. The seek time is unaffected by the rotational speed. The new average latency time is 0.5 rev × 8.33 msec/rev = 4.17 msec. The new transfer time is 1/20 rev × 8.33 msec/rev = 0.42 msec. The total average case time = 12.59 msec.

4. average seek time = 20 tracks × 0.2 msec/track = 4 msec
   average latency = 0.5 rev × 8.33 msec/rev = 4.17 msec
   transfer time = 1/20 rev × 8.33 msec = 0.42 msec

   So the average access time = 4 + 4.17 + 0.42 = 8.59 msec.

5. If many pieces of the file are on the same track, then no movement of the read head arm is required and seek time is 0.

6.

	Best Case	Average Case	Worst Case
Seek time	0.0	0.0	0.0
Latency	0.0	0.5 × 25 = 12.5	1 × 25 = 25.0
Transfer	1.25	1.25	1.25
Total	1.25	13.75	26.25

Section 5.2.4

Assuming that variables a, b, c, and d are stored in memory locations 100, 101, 102, and 103, respectively:

1.

Memory Location	Op Code	Address Field	Comment
50	LOAD	101	Register R now contains the value of b
51	ADD	102	R now contains the sum $b + c$
52	ADD	103	R now contains the sum $b + c + d$
53	STORE	100	And we store that sum into a

There are many other possible solutions to the previous and the following problems, depending on which instructions you choose to use. The previous solution uses the one-address format. The two- and three-address formats would lead to different sequences.

2.

Memory Location	Op Code	Address Field	Comment
50	LOAD	101	Register R contains the value of b
51	MULTIPLY	103	R now contains the product $b \times d$
52	STORE	101	b now has the value $b \times d$
53	LOAD	102	R contains the value of c
54	DIVIDE	103	R now contains the quotient c/d
55	STORE	103	d now has the value c/d
56	LOAD	101	Load the product $b \times d$ back into R
57	SUBTRACT	103	R now contains $(b \times d) - (c/d)$
58	STORE	100	Store the result into a

3.

Memory Location	Op Code	Address Field	Comment
50	LOAD	100	Register R now contains the value of a
51	SUBTRACT	104	R now contains the value $a - 1$
52	STORE	100	Store the result into a

4.

Memory Location	Op Code	Address Field	Comment
50	COMPARE	100, 101	Compare a and b and set condition codes
51	JUMPNEQ	54	If they are not equal, go to address 54
52	LOAD	103	Otherwise load R with the value of d
53	STORE	102	And store it into c
54			The next instruction begins here

5.

Memory Location	Op Code	Address Field	Comment
50	COMPARE	100, 101	Compare a and b and set condition codes
51	JUMPGT	55	Jump to address 55 if $a > b$
52	LOAD	103	Load R with the value of d
53	STORE	102	And store it into c
54	JUMP	58	Jump to address 58
55	LOAD	103	Load R with the value of d
56	ADD	103	R now contains $2d$
57	STORE	102	And store that result into c
58			The next instruction begins here

6.

Memory Location	Op Code	Address Field	Comment
50	LOAD	103	R contains the value d
51	STORE	100	And store it into a
52	COMPARE	100, 102	Compare a and c, set condition codes
53	JUMPGT	58	Jump to address 58 if $a > c$
54	LOAD	100	R now contains the (current) value of a
55	ADD	101	R now contains the value $a + b$
56	STORE	100	And store that sum into a
57	JUMP	52	Jump back to test loop condition again
58			The next instruction begins here

Chapter 6
Section 6.3.1

1. Initial values $R = 20$ memory location 80 = 43
    memory location 81 = 97

	Operation	Final Contents of Register R	Final Contents of Mem Loc 80	Final Contents of Mem Loc 81
a.	LOAD 80	43	43	97
b.	STORE 81	20	43	20
c.	COMPARE 80	20 (and the GT indicator goes ON)	43	97
d.	ADD 81	117	43	97
e.	IN 80	20	Whatever value is entered by the user	97
f.	OUT 81	20	43	97

2. Initial value   memory location 50 = 4

	Operation	Final Contents of Register R
a.	LOAD 50	4
b.	LOAD 4	A copy of the contents of memory cell 4.
c.	LOAD L	Because L is equivalent to 50, this operation is equivalent to LOAD 50, which is the same as part (a).
d.	LOAD L+1	A copy of the contents of memory cell 51. This operation means LOAD $(L + 1)$, which is equivalent to LOAD 51. LOAD $L + 1$ does arithmetic on addresses, not contents.

3. The HALT operation tells the CPU to stop program execution. If the program is organized as in Figure 6.6, then without the HALT instruction the CPU will fetch the data value stored in the next memory location after the last instruction and attempt to execute it. The .END pseudo-op tells the assembler to stop the translation process. The assembler is a piece of software that is acting on the source code, loaded into memory, as its "data"; without the .END pseudo-op, the assembler will try to translate whatever might be stored in memory after the last legitimate source code statement.

4. The first instruction will cause the memory location labeled L to be loaded into register R. Because L contains the data value +1, this will go into R, overwriting whatever was there previously. After completing one instruction, a processor will go on to the next one unless told to do otherwise—that is the essence of the Fetch/Decode/Execute cycle. Thus, the processor will next try to execute the "instruction" +1. As we explained in the text, this will be incorrectly interpreted as the op code 0 and address field of 1, which is a LOAD 1. Thus, the value +1 in register R will be overwritten with the contents of memory location 1.

5. a. The SUBTRACT op code is 0101. The binary representation for the unsigned integer 20 using 12 bits is 000000010100. Putting this together results in:

        0101000000010100

    b. The LOAD op code is 0000. The binary representation for the unsigned integer 31 using 12 bits is 000000011111. Putting this together results in:

        0000000000011111

    c. The HALT op code is 1111. HALT does not require an address but something has to be put into those 12 bits. Typically, an assembler will set all the bits to 0, although it does not really matter. Assuming we put zeroes into the address field we will end up with:

        1111000000000000

Section 6.3.2

1. a.   INCREMENT X

                        .

                        .

                        .

        X: .DATA   0
        Another way to do the same thing is
                LOAD   X
                ADD   ONE

```
             STORE       X
               .
               .
               .
ONE:         .DATA       1
X:           .DATA       0
```

However, the first way is much more efficient. It takes two fewer instructions and one fewer DATA pseudo-op.

b.
```
             LOAD        X
             ADD         FIFTY
             STORE       X
               .
               .
               .
FIFTY:       .DATA       50
X:           .DATA       0
```

c.
```
             LOAD        Y        --Load the value of Y into register R
             ADD         Z        --R now holds the sum (Y + Z)
             SUBTRACT    TWO      --R now holds (Y + Z − 2)
             STORE       X        --Store the result in X
               .
               .
               .
X:           .DATA       0
Y:           .DATA       0
Z:           .DATA       0
TWO:         .DATA       2
```

d.
```
             LOAD        FIFTY    --R holds the constant 50
             COMPARE     X
             JUMPGT      THEN     --if X > 50 go to label THEN
             IN          X        --input a new value
             JUMP        DONE     --and jump to done because we are
                                  --all finished
THEN:        OUT         X
DONE:                             --the next statement goes here
               .
               .
               .
X:           .DATA       0
FIFTY:       .DATA       50
```

e.

	LOAD	ZERO	--Put 0 in R
	STORE	SUM	--Initialize *SUM* to 0
	STORE	I	--Initialize loop counter to 0
LOOP:	LOAD	FIFTY	--Put 50 in R
	COMPARE	I	
	JUMPEQ	DONE	--*I* equals 50, exit loop
	LOAD	SUM	--Put *SUM* in R
	ADD	I	--R now holds (*SUM* + *I*)
	STORE	SUM	--Store result in *SUM*
	INCREMENT	I	--Add 1 to *I*
	JUMP	LOOP	--end of loop body
DONE:			--the next statement goes here

.
.
.

I:	.DATA	0	
SUM:	.DATA	0	
ZERO:	.DATA	0	
FIFTY:	.DATA	50	

2.

	.BEGIN		
	IN	NUMBER	--get first number
LOOP:	LOAD	ZERO	
	COMPARE	NUMBER	--see whether number < 0
	JUMPLT	DONE	--the number is negative so --go to DONE
	INCREMENT	COUNT	--it is nonnegative so --increment count
	IN	NUMBER	--get next number
	JUMP	LOOP	--and repeat the loop
DONE:	OUT	COUNT	--print out the final count
	HALT		
COUNT:	.DATA	0	--count of number of --nonnegative values
ZERO:	.DATA	0	--the constant 0 used for --comparison
NUMBER:	.DATA	0	--place to store the input --value
	.END		

3.

	.BEGIN		
	IN	NUMBER	--get first number
LOOP:	LOAD	ZERO	
	COMPARE	NUMBER	--see whether number < 0
	JUMPLT	DONE	--the number is negative so --go to DONE
	INCREMENT	COUNT	--number is nonnegative so --increment count
	LOAD	HUNDRED	
	COMPARE	COUNT	
	JUMPEQ	DONE	--count = 100 so go to DONE
	IN	NUMBER	--count < 100 so get next --number
	JUMP	LOOP	--and repeat the loop
DONE:	OUT	COUNT	--count is either 100 or a --legitimate count of the less --than 100 nonnegative --numbers read, so print --count in either case
	HALT		
COUNT:	.DATA	0	--count of number of --nonnegative values
ZERO:	.DATA	0	--the constant 0 used for --comparison
NUMBER:	.DATA	0	--place to store the input --value
HUNDRED:	.DATA	100	--the constant 100
	.END		

4. The most important thing was that you were looking at a program that contained English words and familiar mathematical terminology. That made it much easier to understand what was going on and where the modifications were to be made. Also, the use of labels allowed you to make changes in the program without having to make changes to binary memory addresses.

Section 6.3.3

1.

	.BEGIN		
	CLEAR	NEGCOUNT	--Step 1. Not really necessary --because --negcount is already set to 0

```
                LOAD      ONE            --Step 2. Set i to 1. Also not
                                         --really
                STORE     I              --necessary because i is
                                         --initialized to 1
LOOP:           LOAD      FIFTY          --Step 3. Check whether i > 50
                                         --and if so
                                         --terminate the loop
                COMPARE   I
                JUMPGT    ENDLOOP
                IN        N              --Step 4. Read a value
                LOAD      ZERO           --Step 5. Increment
                                         --negcount if
                COMPARE   N              --N is less than zero
                JUMPGE    SKIP
                INCREMENT NEGCOUNT
SKIP:           INCREMENT I              --Step 6. Count one more
                                         --loop iteration
                JUMP      LOOP           --Step 7. and start the loop
                                         --over
ENDLOOP:        OUT       NEGCOUNT       --Step 8. Produce the final
                                         --answer
                HALT                     --Step 9. and halt
NEGCOUNT: .DATA           0
I:        .DATA           1
N:        .DATA           0
ONE:      .DATA           1
FIFTY:    .DATA           50
ZERO:     .DATA           0
          .END
```

2. a. COMPARE = 0111   Y = decimal 10 = 0000 0000 1010
      instruction = 0111 0000 0000 1010

   b. JUMPNEQ = 1100   DONE = decimal 7 = 0000 0000 0111
      instruction = 1100 0000 0000 0111

   c. DECREMENT = 0110   LOOP = decimal 0 = 0000 0000 0000
      instruction = 0110 0000 0000 0000

3. LOOP is the address of an instruction (IN X), but decrement is treating this instruction as though it were a piece of data and subtracting 1 from it. Thus, what this instruction is doing is "computing" (IN X) – 1, which is meaningless. However, the computer will be very happy to carry out this meaningless operation.

4. The address values that you come up with will depend entirely on your solution. The symbol table for the program in Practice Problem 1 would look like the following example. (*Note*: The solution assumes that each instruction occupies one memory location.)

Symbol	Address
LOOP	3
SKIP	11
ENDLOOP	13
NEGCOUNT	15
I	16
N	17
ONE	18
FIFTY	19
ZERO	20

5. No, it is not illegal, just highly misleading. You can label a piece of data with any name you want, but you should pick something that is helpful to the people who have to read and modify the program at some future time. By labeling the constant +1 with the symbolic name TWO, you will confuse and mislead the people looking at your code.

Section 6.4.1

1. If there is one chance in four that a program is blocked waiting for input/output, then there is a $(1/4) \times (1/4) = 1$ chance in 16 that both of the two programs in memory are simultaneously blocked waiting for I/O. Therefore, the processor will be busy 15/16, or about 94%, of the time. This is the processor utilization. If we increase the number of programs in memory to four, then the probability that all four of these programs are blocked at the same time waiting for I/O is $(1/4) \times (1/4) \times (1/4) \times (1/4) = 1$ chance in 256. Now the utilization of the processor is 255/256, or about 99.6%. We can see clearly now why it is helpful to have more programs in memory. It increases the likelihood that at least one program will always be ready to run.

2. Passwords are not secure because people often write them down on a piece of paper put in plain sight for all to see. Furthermore, when choosing passwords people will often pick something that can be easily guessed, like their child's name or birthday. You can reduce the risk of using passwords by requiring passwords to (1) be at least 8–10 characters in length, (2) include at least one special character like /$*&, and (3) not be something found in a dictionary. You can also use *personal information* rather than a memorized password. Personal information is a fact that you would know without having to write it down, but which an acquaintance or coworker would likely not know—maybe the name of your first pet or your maternal grandfather's first name.

Chapter 7
Section 7.2.1

1. The figure shows the representation of a binary signal using frequency modulation of a carrier wave.

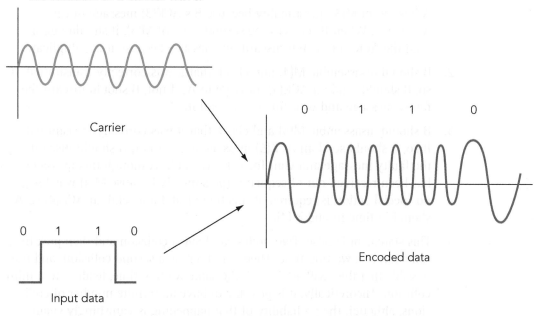

2. The number of bits in the image is 1,200 × 780 × 8 = 7,488,000. To transmit this in 1 second requires a transmission speed of 7,488,000 bps, or nearly 7.5 Mbps.

3. The number of bits in the image is 1,200 × 780 × 8 = 7,488,000.
   7.488 million bits / 1 billion bits/sec = 0.007488 seconds or 7.48 milliseconds

Section 7.2.2

1. Because the message is to be broadcast, there is no need to include a destination address. Each node reads the message.

2. Node A sends the message on LAN1, where every node receives it, but only bridge B1 keeps it. All other nodes discard it because it is not addressed to them. Bridge B1 removes the message from LAN1 and rebroadcasts it on LAN2. Every node on LAN2 receives the message, but again, only bridge B2 keeps it. All others discard it. Bridge B2 knows that node B is located on LAN3, so it rebroadcasts the message on LAN3, where node B receives it, recognizes its own address, and removes the message from the network. The message has arrived at its intended destination.

3. The main security concern is that in an Ethernet-like bus topology every node receives a copy of every message sent. A node is supposed to look at the address field of the message to see if it is the desired recipient

and, if not, discard that message. However, a malicious node could keep, read, and record every message on the network, even those that are not intended for it.

Section 7.3.2

1. A has resent M(3), presumably because B's ACK(3) message never reached A. When B receives the second copy of M(3), it should again send the ACK(3) to A but discard the message because it is a duplicate.

2. B should disassemble M(4) and check that it was correctly transmitted. If so, B should send an ACK(4) message to A; if not, B should discard the faulty message and wait for A to resend it.

3. B should disassemble M(5) and check that it was correctly transmitted. If so, B should send an ACK(5) message to A; if not, B should discard the faulty message and wait for A to resend it. Although this message has been received out of sequence (presumably because M(4) was lost), no special action is required at this time; B did not send an ACK(4) so A should in time resend M(4).

4. This statement is false. Two nodes can have a collision and then pick the same random waiting time. There will then be a second collision, and it is possible that they will again pick the same waiting time, leading to a third collision. Theoretically, it is possible to have an infinite number of collisions, although the probability of that happening is vanishingly small.

5. Collisions can occur in a ring topology because all nodes share the ring and a node may want to send a message at the same time that a message from another node is passing by. In a star topology, collisions are avoided because each node has a direct line (via the hub node) to any other node.

6. Sending a 100-character message, 800 bits, across a 100 million bit per second (100 Mpbs) Ethernet takes about 8×10^{-6} seconds, or 8 µsec. The likelihood that one of the other 19 users on the system would transmit during that tiny window of time is quite small, so the probability of a collision would be small.

Section 7.3.3

1. There are four distinct paths from node A to node D, and their total weights are

ABCD	Weight $= 16$
ABFD	Weight $= 14$
AEFBCD	Weight $= 25$
AEFD	Weight $= 15$

   So the shortest path is ABFD, found by computing the weight of every possible path and then picking the smallest. This is essentially a "brute force" approach to the problem.

2. This approach would not work with larger graphs such as one with 26 nodes and 50 links. The number of possible paths would grow much too large for us to enumerate and evaluate them all in a reasonable amount of time. We must use a more clever algorithm.

3. If the link connecting node F to node D fails, then the paths ABFD and AEFD will not work and their weights become "infinite." Of the two paths remaining, path ABCD with weight 16 now becomes the shortest path. No one link in the network will disconnect nodes A and D. We can see that clearly by noting that the two paths ABCD and AEFD do not share any links in common. Therefore, if a link along one of these paths fails, we can use the other path.

4. Yes, the shortest path would change. The shortest path from A to E would now be the route AEFD with a cost of $4 + 2 + 7 = 13$ units. It had been ABFD with a cost of $3 + 4 + 7 = 14$ units.

5. If node B failed, no other nodes in the network would be brought down, although their communication delays might increase. Nodes A, C, D, E, F could all send and receive messages from the other active nodes.

Chapter 8
Section 8.2.1

1. **Step 1:** chjbup5 → 3 8 10 2 21 16 5

   Step 2: $3 + 8 + 10 + 2 + 21 + 16 + 5 = 65$

   Step 3: 65 / 7 leaves a remainder of 2 ($65 = 9 \times 7$ with 2 left over)

   Steps 4 and 5: are identical to the example.

2. ed

3. No; from Problem 2, the encrypted form of Judy's password "judy" is *ed*, but "mike" hashes to *fc*. The encrypted versions do not match.

4. The file is not legitimate. Using the hash function described, the final step is to change each digit back to a letter. The maximum digit is 9, which would correspond to *i*, so no letters beyond *i* can appear in an encrypted password.

Section 8.3.2

1. STB NX YMJ MTZW

2. Because there are 26 letters in the alphabet, a shift of $s = 26$ encrypts each character as itself, so you should not trust the messenger.

3. a. Step 1. Apply the S mapping to $(M\ Q)$ to get $(13\ 17)$.

Step 2. Multiply result times M: $(13\ 17) \times \begin{bmatrix} 3 & 5 \\ 2 & 3 \end{bmatrix}$

$$= (13 \times 3 + 17 \times 2 \quad 13 \times 5 + 17 \times 3) = (73\ 116) \rightarrow (21\ 12)$$

Step 3. Apply S' to $(21\ 12)$ to get $(U\ L)$.

b. Step 1. Apply the S mapping to $(U\ L)$ to get $(21\ 12)$.

Step 2. Multiply result by M': $(21\ 12) \times \begin{bmatrix} 23 & 5 \\ 2 & 23 \end{bmatrix}$

$$= (21 \times 23 + 12 \times 2 \quad 21 \times 5 + 12 \times 23) = (507\ 381) \rightarrow (13\ 17)$$

Step 3. Apply S' to $(13\ 17)$ to get $(M\ Q)$

Section 8.3.3

In the example, where $n = 21$ and $e = 5$, then $d = 5$ as well. To decode, compute

$$C^d = 17^5 = 1419857 = 67612 \times 21 + 5 \rightarrow 5$$

Therefore the original numeric message was 5.

Chapter 10
Section 10.2.2

1. ITIME .LE. 7

2.
```
     IF (X .LT. 3) THEN
           A = 2
     ELSE
           A = 1
           B = 3
     ENDIF
30  ...
```

3. Because X has the value 2 and $2 < 3$, control transfers to statement 10, which sets the value of A to 2. The next statement transfers control to statement 30, at which point A has the value 2 and B still has the value 1 because statement 20 was never executed. Therefore the new value of A is $2 + 1 = 3$.

Section 10.2.3

1. In Ada:
```
    outputNumber := inputNumber;
    sumOfValues := sumOfValues + inputNumber;
```

In C++, C#, or Java:
```
outputNumber = inputNumber;
sumOf Values = sumOfValues + inputNumber;
```

In Python:
```
outputNumber = inputNumber
sumOfValues = sumOfValues + inputNumber
```

Section 10.2.4

1. *Rate* refers to the contents of the memory cell called *Rate*; *&Rate* refers to the address of that cell.

2. 10

3. 500; 29

Section 10.2.5

The program prints the numbers from 1 through 10 on a single line with a blank space between them.

Section 10.2.6

```
The answer is7
```

Section 10.2.7

The Python version is answer c,
```
print("Hello World")
```

Section 10.2.8

The name entered in the text box will be displayed in the label.

Section 10.3.3

1. It results in the names of all vendors from Chicago.

2. These are the *times* that try **men's souls**

Section 10.4.1

1. a. (2 3 4)
    b. 5

2.  ```
    (define (threeplus x)
    (+ 3 x))
    ```
    ```

Section 10.4.2

1. before(jefferson, kennedy).
   false

2. president(X, lewisandclark).
   X = jefferson

3. precedes(jefferson, X).
   X = lincoln
   X = fdr
   X = kennedy
   X = nixon

Section 10.4.3

1. One processor could compute A + B while another computes C + D. A third processor could then take the two quantities A + B and C + D and compute their sum. Parallel processing uses a total of two time slots: one to simultaneously do the two additions A + B and C + D, then one to do the addition (A + B) + (C + D). Sequential processing would require a total of three time slots: (A + B), then (A + B) + C, then ((A + B) + C) + D.

2. One solution would be to have the input/output processor set a timer for the maximum possible response time from each of the search processors and if that time is exceeded, it reports that NUMBER was not found. This is not foolproof, because it could simply be that the communications link between the input/output processor and the one processor that found NUMBER is broken, so it was unable to report back the corresponding NAME. A better solution would be to have each search processor report back to the input/output processor when it cannot find NUMBER; when the input/output processor has received that message from all 1,000 search processors, it would then report that NUMBER was not found.

Chapter 11
Section 11.2.1

1. a.

Token	Classification
x	1
=	3
x	1
+	4
1	2
;	6

b.

Token	Classification
if	8
(	10
a	1
+	4
b42	1
==	7
0	2
)	11
a	1
=	3
zz	1
-	5
12	2
;	6

2. a. This would most likely be classified as three tokens: the name abc, the minus sign '-', and the name def. The reason is that a minus sign is rarely allowed to be part of a variable name.

   b. This would likely be classified as a single token with the name abc_def. In many programming languages, the underscore character is allowed to be part of a name to allow the different parts of the variable to stand out, for example, the names inches_per_yard or cost_per_square_meter.

   c. This would definitely be classified as two separate tokens, abc and def, because a space is always used to end one token and to identify the start of the next one.

3. A scanner is not involved in the determination of the legality or illegality of a programming language statement; that is done in the next two steps. A scanner is only concerned with finding and classifying tokens. So it would simply return the following six tokens:

Name	Classification
X	1
=	3
;	6
(	10
14	2
hello	1

4. The symbol "else", which was chosen as a variable name, will not be assigned symbol category 1 as we would expect. Instead, it will be assigned to category 9, the reserved word "else". In the next phase of translation, when the compiler analyzes the syntactic structure of this

statement, it will not be able to understand what the user meant and will produce an error message. This is why in most programming languages you are not allowed to use reserved words (such as while, do, if, else) as names of variables.

Section 11.2.2 (Set 1)

1. <Boolean operator> ::= AND | OR | NOT

2. <identifier> ::= <first><second>
    <first> ::= i | j
    <second> ::= <letter> | <digit> | Λ
    <letter> ::= A | B | C | D | ... | Z
    <digit> ::= 0 | 1 | 2 | ... | 9
    <identifier> is the goal symbol

3. <expression> ::= (<var> <op> <var>)
    <var> ::= x | y | z
    <op> ::= < | == | >

4.

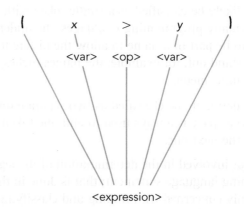

5. You eventually reach the point in the parse where you have the following sequence:

    (<var> <op>)

    which does not match the right-hand side of any rule, and the parse fails.

6. The first rule of Practice Problem 3 could be changed to

   <expression> ::= (<var> <op> <var>) | <var> <op> <var>

7. The symbol Λ and the blank are NOT interchangeable. Blank is a character, just like A or 5 or *. However, the symbol Λ means the absence of any character, including a blank space.

Section 11.2.2 (Set 2)

1.

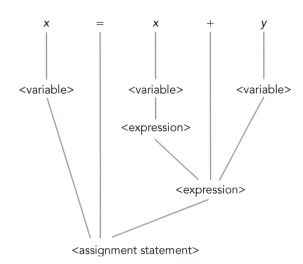

2.

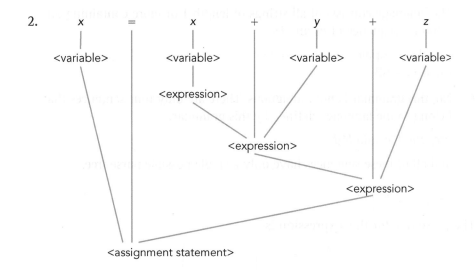

3.

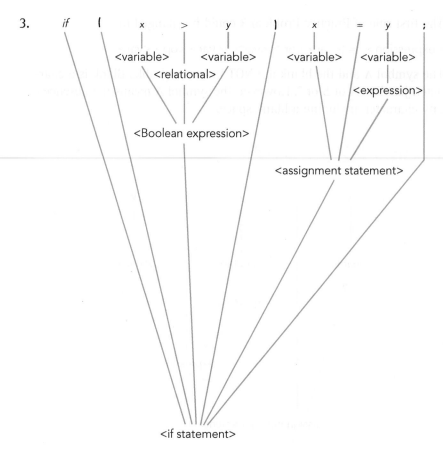

4. The language consists of all strings of length 1 or more containing an arbitrary sequence of *a*s and *b*s.

5. <goal> ::= <pair> | <pair> <goal>
<pair> ::= AB

6. No, this grammar is not ambiguous. There are only four sentences that belong to the language defined by this grammar:

a*c, *a*d*, *b*c*, and *b*d*

and all of these sentences have only a single possible parse tree.

Section 11.2.3

The parse tree for this expression is

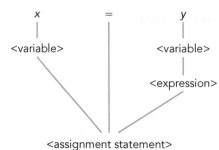

During the construction of this parse tree, you will build four semantic records: two for <variable>, one for <expression>, and one for <assignment statement>.

The code generated is

```
        LOAD      Y
        STORE     TEMP
        LOAD      TEMP
        STORE     X
          .
          .
          .
X:        .DATA     0
Y:        .DATA     0
TEMP:     .DATA     0
```

Chapter 12
Section 12.2

1.

Rate in mph	Time in hours	Distance in miles
58	0.5	29
61	0.5	30.5
57	0.5	28.5
62	0.5	31
	Total	119

2. Piloting a boat, performing an operation, fighting a fire

3. Soil conditions, water supply, types of industrial waste. It could illustrate long-term effects of various waste-disposal policies. If it were inaccurate, policies based on the model might be pursued that would result in environmental damage.

Section 12.3.2

1. $b\ 1\ 1\ 1\ b$
    ↑
    3

2. a. $b\ 1\ 0\ 1\ b$
    ↑
    2

   b. $b\ 1\ 1\ 1\ b$
    ↑
    2

    c. $b\,1\,1\,1\,b$
        ↑
        2

    d. $b\,0\,1\,1\,b$
        ↑
        1

3. $b\,0\,1\,0\,b$

4. $b\,0\,0\,0\,b$

Section 12.5.1

1. It is not equivalent. There is no transition from State 1 for an input symbol of 0, and no transition from State 2 for an input symbol of 1.

2. The machine would halt immediately because there are no instructions for what to do when looking at a blank cell.

Section 12.5.2

1. a. $b\,1\,1\,0\,1\,0\,b$

Section 12.5.4

1. $b\,1\,1\,1\,1\,b\,1\,1\,1\,1\,1\,b$ becomes
   $b\,b\,b\,1\,1\,1\,1\,1\,1\,1\,1\,b$

2. a. $(1,1,1,1,R)$
   $(1,0,0,1,R)$
   $(1,b,1,2,R)$

   b. The machine for part (a) also solves the general problem.

Section 12.7

1. To prove that something is not true, assume that it is true and arrive at a contradiction. The assumption must then be wrong.

Chapter 13
Section 13.2.3

1. Without this instruction, server S_i is serving a newly arrived customer but is still marked as idle; the next newly arrived customer could try to go to that server.

2. Without this instruction, server S_i has finished serving a customer and there are no customers waiting in line, but the next newly arrived customer will not try to be served by S_i.

3. It most likely would make the conclusions less valid and much less usable. The idea of every customer taking the same amount of time is unrealistic. Therefore, making this assumption would cause our model to be a very poor abstraction of the real system. If your assumptions are wrong, then there is a far greater likelihood that your conclusions will be wrong as well. (We called this "garbage in, garbage out" in the text.)

4. There are many other possibilities, but here are a few:

   a. The possibility of mechanical breakdowns. The model could be designed to include the occasional breakdown of a critical component (e.g., the French fryer) to study how the system responds to these types of unexpected events.

   b. Rather than say no customer ever takes more than 5 minutes to be served, the model could be designed to allow for an occasional massive order—someone purchasing 100 hamburgers—to see what happens to our waiting times when this unusual event occurs.

   c. Some servers could be used only for special orders, rather than have all servers be identical.

Chapter 14
Section 14.2.4

1. For example:

   www.webmd.com
   https://en.wikipedia.org/wiki/Portal:Environment
   https://www.fantasysp.com
   www.petersons.com
   https://www.dawnbreaker.com/portals/altenergy

2. As an alternative, students could be asked to compare two such sites.

Section 14.3.3

1. 149   12.35

2.
```
SELECT LastName, FirstName, MonthlyCost
FROM Employees, InsurancePlans, InsurancePolicies
WHERE LastName = "Takasano"
AND ID = EmployeeID
AND InsurancePolicies.PlanType =
   InsurancePlans.PlanType;
```

3.
```
SELECT EmployeeID
FROM InsurancePolicies
WHERE PlanType = "B2";
```

4. Referential integrity. Removing this tuple leaves the InsurancePolicies table with tuples that have EmployeeID foreign key values no longer existing as a primary key value in the Employees table.

Section 14.4.1

The decision tree after adding the new tuple would be

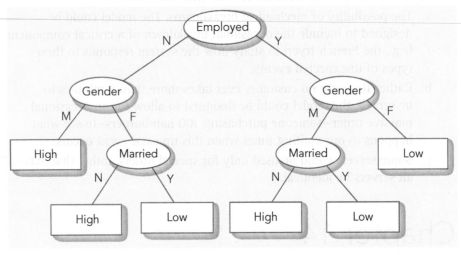

Chapter 15
Section 15.3

1. For example, a hamburger is a kind of sandwich. As such, it comes between two pieces of bread, but it is hot. It must contain ground meat, but it may also have various condiments, such as mustard, ketchup, and a pickle.

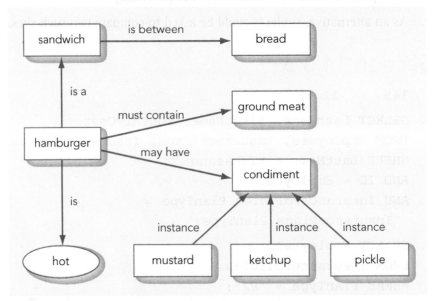

2. a. $(\forall x)(\text{hamburger}(x) \to \text{sandwich}(x))$
   b. $(\forall x)(\text{grilledCheese}(x) \to \text{sandwich}(x))$
   c. $(\forall x)(\text{sandwich}(x) \to \text{onBread}(x))$
   d. $(\forall x)(\text{grilledCheese}(x) \to \text{vegetarian}(x))$

Section 15.4

1. No. N1 and N4 fire, but N2 and N3 do not, so N5 does not.

2. It will never fire. The maximum incoming signal that node N5 can receive is $2 + 2 = 4$, which is not enough to make it fire if its threshold value is 5.

Section 15.5.4

1. Frank is tall. Knowing that Frank is tall does not necessarily mean that he is bald.

2. No conclusion can be inferred. Frank might or might not be tall.

3. No conclusion can be inferred. Frank might or might not be tall.

4. Frank is not tall (because if he were, he would be bald).

Chapter 16

Section 16.2.3

(*Note:* In the following answer, the z column has been omitted because it will contain all zeros.)

Vertex	X	y	Connected To
V_1	0	0	$V_2\ V_6\ V_8$ (Origin)
V_2	0	2.4	$V_1\ V_3\ V_4$
V_3	1.5	4.5	$V_2\ V_4\ V_5$
V_4	1.5	2.4	$V_2\ V_3\ V_5\ V_6\ V_7$
V_5	3	2.4	$V_3\ V_4\ V_{10}$
V_6	1	1.7	$V_1\ V_4\ V_7\ V_8\ V_9$
V_7	2	1.7	$V_4\ V_6\ V_9\ V_{10}$
V_8	1	0	$V_1\ V_6\ V_9$
V_9	2	0	$V_6\ V_7\ V_8\ V_{10}$
V_{10}	3	0	$V_5\ V_7\ V_9$

A total of 67 pieces of information are stored in this table.

Section 16.2.4

Because the motion takes place over a period of 2 seconds, we need to produce a total of 60 frames, given that 30 frames/second is the standard frame rate for video. These 60 frames represent 59 time intervals. So in each of the 58 in-between frames, we must move the triangle 1/59th of the total distance from its position in the first frame to its position in the last frame. This information allows us to compute the translation matrix.

Total x-distance moved = 4 units
a = 1/59 × 4 = 0.067796

Total y-distance moved = 2 units
b = 1/59 × 2 = 0.033898

Total z-distance moved = 0 units
c = 1/59 × 0 = 0

Now, using the model shown in Figure 16.6, we can say that the translation matrix required to perform the desired motion is as follows:

1	0	0	0.067796
0	1	0	0.033898
0	0	0	0
0	0	0	1

Index

A

AAC (Advanced Audio Coding), 169
ABC system, 25–26, 29
abstraction, 80–81
access control list, 312, 401
accessibility of ecommerce websites, 681
accuracy of computational models, 642–644
acknowledgment messages (ACKs), 361
ACLU (American Civil Liberties Union), 825
ACM (Association for Computing Machinery), 5, 821
ACO (Ant Colony Optimization), 733
ACPA (Anti-Cybersquatting Consumer Protection Act), 677
Ada
    converging-pointers algorithm, 444–446
    development, 492–493
    favorite number program, 441
    feature analysis, 456–461
ADA (Americans with Disabilities Act), 681
addition circuits, 202–208
address(es), 227
    IP, 363, 676
    network, number, 364
    symbolic, assembly language, 290–291
address fields, machine language instructions, 250
address space, 228
adequacy of knowledge representation schemes, 721
Adleman, Len, 417, 618
Advance Research Projects Agency (ARPA), 382
Advanced Audio Coding (AAC), 169
Advanced Encryption Standard (AES), 417
Advanced Step in Innovative Mobility (ASIMO), 747
Adventure, 759
advertising, ecommerce, 676
AES (Advanced Encryption Standard), 417
agile software development, 474–475
Agnew, Spiro, 29
AI. *See* artificial intelligence (AI)
Aiken, Howard, 25
Al-Khowarizmi, Muhammad ibn Musa, 10

algorithm(s), 6, 12–18, 42–91
    analysis of, 97
    approximation, 136
    ARQ, 360–361
    attributes, 92–97
    back propagation, 728
    binary search, 123–130
    binary-to-decimal, 155
    brute force, 135
    bubble sort, 141
    circuit construction, 195–200
    computational tasks, 715
    computing agents. *See* computing agents; Turing machine
    correctness of algorithms, 92–93
    data cleanup, 115–123, 444–454
    deadlock recovery, 316
    decimal-to-binary, 156
    definition, 6, 12–17
    designing and developing, 6–11
    Dijkstra's shortest path algorithm, 365
    efficiency, 97–114
    examples of problem solving using, 60–83
    exponential, 134
    favorite number, 440–443
    find largest, 70–75
    Hamiltonian circuits, 132–136
    importance, 17
    intractable problems, 135–136
    limitations, 716–717
    mergesort, 142
    model, 602–604
    operations used to construct, 7
    parallel, 271
    parsing, look-ahead, 561
    pattern matching, 77–84, 130–131
    polynomially bounded, 132
    problems unsolvable by, 620
    pseudocode, 44–48
    representing, 44–60
    Rijndael, 417
    search, decision trees, 730–731